AF722458

TOILING FOR OIL

Often referred to as the 'Oil Century', the Twentieth Century marked the rise of petroleum as a pivotal force in global economics and politics. While many studies have explored the political relations between oil corporations and the Iranian state, this innovative book builds an intricate picture of the social history of petroleum in Iran, after its discovery there in 1908. Through expert interviews and on-the-ground reports, Touraj Atabaki shows the seismic impact of oil: from the building of roads to an influx of migrant labour. Offering insights into the lives and challenges of oil workers alongside analysis of wider geopolitical conflicts, *Toiling for Oil* traverses two world wars, industrialisation and modernisation, attempts at nationalisation in the 1950s and the political crises of the late 1970s. An essential read for anyone interested in Iran's unique position in the global economic landscape as oil continues to shape our world.

TOURAJ ATABAKI is Senior Researcher at the International Institute of Social History and Professor Emeritus and holder of the chair of the Social History of the Middle East and Central Asia at the Leiden University. He is a past President of the Association for Iranian Studies and European Society for Central Asian Studies. Previous publications include *Azerbaijan: Ethnicity and the Struggle for Power in Iran* (2000), and as an editor, *Men of Order: Authoritarian Modernization under Atatürk and Reza Shah* (2004), *The State and the Subaltern: Modernisation, Society and the State in Turkey and Iran* (2007), *Iran in the 20th Century: Historiography and Political Culture* (2009), and *Working for Oil: Comparative Social History of Labour in the Global Oil Industry* (2018).

TOILING FOR OIL

A Social History of Petroleum in Iran

TOURAJ ATABAKI

International Institute of Social History

CAMBRIDGE
UNIVERSITY PRESS

CAMBRIDGE
UNIVERSITY PRESS

Shaftesbury Road, Cambridge CB2 8EA, United Kingdom

One Liberty Plaza, 20th Floor, New York, NY 10006, USA

477 Williamstown Road, Port Melbourne, VIC 3207, Australia

314–321, 3rd Floor, Plot 3, Splendor Forum, Jasola District Centre, New Delhi – 110025, India

103 Penang Road, #05–06/07, Visioncrest Commercial, Singapore 238467

Cambridge University Press is part of Cambridge University Press & Assessment, a department of the University of Cambridge.

We share the University's mission to contribute to society through the pursuit of education, learning and research at the highest international levels of excellence.

The research for this book was conducted within the framework of the Global Labour History research program at the **International Institute of Social History**.

www.cambridge.org
Information on this title: www.cambridge.org/9781108845878

DOI: 10.1017/9781108991186

© Touraj Atabaki 2025

This publication is in copyright. Subject to statutory exception and to the provisions of relevant collective licensing agreements, no reproduction of any part may take place without the written permission of Cambridge University Press & Assessment.

When citing this work, please include a reference to the DOI 10.1017/9781108991186

First published 2025

A catalogue record for this publication is available from the British Library

Library of Congress Cataloging-in-Publication Data
Names: Atabaki, Touraj, author.
Title: Toiling for oil : a social history of petroleum in Iran / Touraj Atabaki, International Institute of Social History.
Description: Cambridge, United Kingdom ; New York, NY, USA : Cambridge University Press, 2025. | Includes bibliographical references and index.
Identifiers: LCCN 2024024365 | ISBN 9781108845878 (hardback) | ISBN 9781108991186 (ebook)
Subjects: LCSH: Oil industry workers – Iran. | Petroleum workers – Iran. | Oil industries – Iran. | Petroleum industry and trade – Iran.
Classification: LCC HD8039.O52 I738 2025 | DDC 331.7/62233820955–dc23/eng/20241008
LC record available at https://lccn.loc.gov/2024024365

ISBN 978-1-108-84587-8 Hardback
ISBN 978-1-108-99399-9 Paperback

Cambridge University Press & Assessment has no responsibility for the persistence or accuracy of URLs for external or third-party internet websites referred to in this publication and does not guarantee that any content on such websites is, or will remain, accurate or appropriate.

To Sharareh, Atossa, and Armin – my cherished ones, enduring from the past, through the now, into the forever

CONTENTS

FIGURES

MAPS

TABLES

NOTE ON TRANSLITERATION

In transliterating Persian words, the present work adheres to the guidelines set forth by the journal *Iranian Studies*. Hence a modern Persian pronunciation approach has been uniformly applied across the text, with two exceptions. Firstly, for geographical names, effort has been made to utilise their widely established anglicised forms. Secondly, for personal names, I use a doubled 's' to render phonetically common Persianised Arabic names such as Hassan or Hossain; however, the preference of individuals for specific spellings has been respected. For instance, the variation between 'Manuchehr' and 'Manouchehr' illustrates this principle: while the former aligns with the standardised transliteration rules, the latter reflects the personal choice of the individual concerned when applicable. I do not use diacritical marks to distinguish between the Persian long and short vowels.

PREFACE AND ACKNOWLEDGMENTS

In the wake of the Iranian Revolution of 1979, there was a marked surge in academic interest towards a comprehensive reassessment of Iran's historical discourse, spanning both its proximate and distant antecedents. The intricate nature of the Iranian Revolution and its ensuing ramifications, juxtaposed with the newfound accessibility of a plethora of the Twentieth Century documents and materials – liberated from the confines of archival obscurity through the advent of the digital era – led to a renewed scrutiny of historical narratives, their authentication, and the broadening of historiographical comprehension. This critical revaluation was driven by a quest to address historical inquiries that have been unconvincingly determined by the teleological constraints of certain historiographical perspectives, regardless of whether they are Marxist or non-Marxist orientations. The endeavour to reconceptualise historical accounts necessitated transcending traditional grand narratives, encompassing both overarching and nuanced historical examinations. This initiative was directed towards unveiling the foundational social structures and the side-lined entities that have critically influenced the principal dynamics of Iran's historical trajectory over an extended period.

A predominant characteristic of former grand narratives was their unilateral dependence on an elitist construct for the reinterpretation of historical events. Such narratives, by principally assigning historical agency to elite factions – including but not limited to clerics, secular intellectuals, colonial or national economic and political bodies, as well as key events or epochs – effectively marginalised the autonomous engagement and agency of non-elite collectives. Moreover, these interpretations, by adopting essentialist methodology, inevitably lead to dehistoricising sociocultural transformations.

Indeed, the valour of social history, inclusive of 'history from below' and 'the history of everyday life', resides in its prowess to proffer a richer and more nuanced tableau, thus affording a more holistic portrayal of the populace and societal fabric. Without negating the import of alternative historiographical methodologies, social historiography is committed to acknowledging the spectrum of agents pivotal in societal evolutions. However, the articulation of social history has perennially emerged as a domain of political contention for historians and social scientists possessing a profound historical acumen.

The recognition of non-elite agency, its temporal and contextual manifestation, invites rigorous scrutiny. Is it the structured embodiment of non-elite, delineated within specific temporal frameworks and targeted objectives, that is under consideration? Or does the social historian's narrative transcend these confines to duly recognise the significant role of historical agency? These queries, among others, have occupied a central place in the extensive contemplation and discourse at the International Institute of Social History, focusing on global labour history. Marcel van der Linden's specific contribution, through his incisive critique of the structuralist approach to labour history, has been central to the shift from the traditional 'old labour history' paradigm, characterised by its focus on institutional and organised labour movements, to a more inclusive and diverse historiographical paradigm. This new paradigm broadens the scope to include unorganised labour, informal sectors, and non-Western perspectives, thereby enriching the understanding of labour history in a global context.

In this book, I have traversed this path. My exploration of the social history of the petroleum in Iran transcends the traditional analysis focused on labour and employee unions or the narrow scope of trade unionist-political activism. Rather, I have sought to understand the emergence and identity shaping of the labour force not merely through their confrontations with state but also through the prism of their extensive lived experiences – including their workspaces, residential environments, educational and healthcare provisions, and leisure pursuits. Concurrently, I have afforded a considerate yet critical observation of other political and social transformations within Khuzestan, across Iran, throughout the region, and globally. Indeed, my prolonged engagement with the International Institute of Social History has been an invaluable privilege and blessing for which I am grateful.

Throughout the extensive duration of my affiliation with the International Institute of Social History, I have initiated and completed a myriad of research projects, encompassing topics related to Iran and extending to other nations within Western and Central Asia. It is with great satisfaction that I note the publication of the results from all these scholarly endeavours. Among these, the study focusing on the social history of labour within the Iranian petroleum sector emerges as particularly noteworthy – a comprehensive investigation that unfolded over more than ten years. This ambitious project originated fifteen years ago through a collaborative effort with my colleagues. We embarked on a comprehensive study focused on labour relations within the sector producing local commodities for the global market: *Working for the World: Asians Producing Commodities for Far-Flung Markets*. Assigned various commodities – sugar, coffee, and indigo – my research was dedicated to oil. The process of formulating the research proposal, predicated on the accessibility of resources necessary for documenting a hundred years of social history of labour in the Iranian oil industry, spanned two years. Following this, the challenge of acquiring funding for this extensive research was met with eventual success, notably with support from the Dutch Research Council. The subsequent phase involved the assembly of the research team, comprising four members: three doctoral students, each delving into distinct segments of this century-spanning history, and myself, with my focus being the interval from the discovery of oil until the 1979 revolution. For me, the epoch post-revolution remains too proximate in time to be considered historical.

My doctoral students, Kaveh Ehsani, Peyman Jafari, and Maral Jefroudi, have successfully concluded their research endeavours. Additionally, it behoves me to mention another researcher, Robabeh Motaghedi. Although I was not her primary advisor, I had the privilege of partly supervising her research from a distance. Their achievements fill me with pride. Their scholarly work has been recognised not solely by my own evaluation but has also garnered considerable praise from all members of the doctoral thesis review committees at Leiden University, distinguishing itself as exemplary academic research.

In regard to my own research, I made a conscientious decision to delay its publication until after these scholars had defended their doctoral theses and their findings were officially disseminated. This decision was predicated on a commitment to preserving the integrity of their data and analyses, ensuring they remained untarnished by any direct citations or attributions. The role these individuals have assumed, now adorned in academic regalia, in nurturing a culture of inquiry, research, and scholarly critique during their doctoral pursuits at the International Institute of Social History, will perpetually resonate with me.

For my scholarly inquiry, I ventured far and wide, yet the longing to visit Iran persistently accompanied me. My status as a political refugee precluded any travel to Iran. Thus, I was compelled to rely on indirect methods such as questionnaires, telephone interviews, letters, and friends who, upon their return from Iran, brought with them a wealth of books for my research. Despite these constraints, the exploration and examination of archives abroad offered a semblance of solace. My academic travels spanned from Delhi and Mumbai to Baku, Tashkent, Yerevan, Tbilisi, and Moscow. In the United Kingdom, the BP archives at the University of Warwick, the National Archives in London, and the India Office represented unparalleled repositories of knowledge. Moreover, my research was significantly enhanced through engagement with the National Archives and Library of Congress in Washington, D.C., as well as the Foundation for Iranian Studies, which boasts an exceptional collection of oral histories. It is pertinent to acknowledge my profound gratitude towards the personnel of these archives, who generously supported my inquiries. The instances of denial in response to my requests for access to documents were exceptionally rare. Nevertheless, it is imperative to underscore the unparalleled contribution of Ms Golnaz Golzarian, whose steadfast support and facilitation of access to remarkable publications stand as a testament to her exceptional dedication.

In addition to the engagement with my students at Leiden University, my research benefitted significantly from consultations with colleagues at the International Institute of Social History. Paramount among these individuals is my esteemed friend, Marcel van der Linden, whose insight and support have been indispensable. Furthermore, the contributions of Jan Lucassen, Willem van Schendel, and Jan Breman merit acknowledgement; their guidance and expertise have been invaluable to my work.

Beyond the confines of the International Institute of Social History, it was primarily my long-standing friends from Khuzestan, as well as newly acquainted individuals – most of whom hail from Khuzestan or possess expertise in the oil industry – who offered their indispensable support and assistance. My interviews with workers, engineers, and managers within the Oil Company led me to traverse the province of Khuzestan, visiting notable locations such as Abadan, Ahvaz, Aghajari, and Dezful, among others. My appreciation for their willingness to engage in dialogue is immeasurable. Through earnest and repeated conversations, individuals such as Nasim, Nasser, and Mashallah Khaksar, Yadollah Khosrowshahi, and Mohammad Safavi, graciously provided me with profound insights into the quotidian experiences, work conditions, and living circumstances within the oil sector of Abadan, other Khuzestan cities, and Tehran. Regular discussions with Manouchehr Mohandes and Qader Zahtab-Fard enriched my understanding of numerous facets of the oil industry's industrial milieu.

Moreover, Ebrahim Golestan, Rahmat Jazani, Hassan Kamshad, ʿEsmat Yazdanpanah-Daʾi, and Farideh G. (who requested anonymity until her passing) shared their written and oral recollections, offering a narrative of the Tudeh Party's activities preceding the coup d'état of August 1953 and the immediate years that followed, particularly among the workforce and employees of the oil industry. Alinaghi Alikhani elucidated the initial years following the establishment of the Consortium, the trials of workers' buy-back endeavours, and the National Iranian Oil Company's efforts to ameliorate workers' living conditions.

Parviz Mina, having graciously accepted my invitation for multiple discussions, imparted insights into the nationalisation period and international oil relations, including interactions within OPEC and beyond. Masoud Akhbari and his spouse, Willie Nijman-Akhbari, recounted their mixed experiences throughout the 1960s and 1970s in Khuzestan, with Willie addressing the discrimination emblematic of the Anglo-Iranian Oil Company's early decades. Lastly, Mehrzad Boroujerdi shared observations on the months preceding the revolution and the utilisation of violence by revolutionary Islamists to mobilise workers.

Furthermore, I wish to express my profound appreciation for the friends whose support has not only enriched this work but also contributed substantially to its quality and substance. Their engagement and encouragement have been indispensable, helping to shape the narrative and insights that define this project. Among these cherished contributors, Ali Banuzazi and Ali Gheissari warrant special acknowledgement for their thorough review of the manuscript and the provision of insightful suggestions. Their efforts have been instrumental in elevating the calibre of this text, and for this, my gratitude is immeasurable.

Moreover, the encouragement and assistance of numerous friends have been critical to my research pursuits, including Ervand Abrahamian, Gholam-Reza Afkhami, Reza Allamehzadeh, Ahmad Ashraf, Asef Bayat, Ali Ansari, Masoud Behnoud, Gregory Brew, Matin Biglari, Rasmus Christian Elling, Mazdak Daneshvar, Hassan Hakimian, Farhad Keshvari, Abdolali Lahsaeizadeh, Mohammad Maljoo, Ali Mirza'i, Ali Moazami, Nasser Mohajer, Hossein Pourbagheri, Ali Rafi, Siavush Randjbar-Daemi, Solmaz Rustamova Tohidi, Kian Tajbakhsh, Stefan Tetzlaff, and Katayoon Khalilpour. Their contributions, both directly and indirectly, have been instrumental in the fruition of this work, for which I am immensely grateful.

I would like to express my gratitude to the anonymous reviewers of my manuscript for their insightful and constructive feedback. Furthermore, I extend my sincere appreciation to the editorial team at Cambridge University Press: Maria Marsh, Natasha Burton, and Rosanna Barraclough. I also wish to thank Subathra Manogaran and her team from Lumina Datamatics, who did the final touch before forwarding the manuscript for print.

Embarking upon a reflective journey that encapsulates a decade of rigorous research in the field of oil studies, it becomes imperative to extend my sincerest and most profound gratitude towards my family. Their enduring patience and support have been the bedrock upon which this scholarly endeavour has been built. Foremost in this circle of invaluable support is my spouse, Sharareh, alongside our cherished children, Atossa and Armin. The profound impact of Sharareh's contributions, marked by her willingness to adeptly manage a considerable share of our familial responsibilities, is beyond what can be adequately appreciated. Without her unwavering dedication, the realisation, completion, and eventual publication of this work might well have lingered as a distant dream.

To Sharareh, Atossa, and Armin, I am bound by an immense debt of gratitude – a sentiment that mere words struggle to encapsulate fully. Their steadfast support and sacrifices have not only underpinned my academic journey but have also been the cornerstone of my ability to pursue and achieve scholarly aspirations. Dedicating this book to them is a tribute!

CHRONOLOGY

1901, May	William Knox D'Arcy, a British businessman, was granted a concession by Mozaffar al-Din Shah of Persia, authorising him to explore, extract, process, commercialise, transport, and sell petroleum and its derivatives across the vast territories of the Persian Empire, with the exception of five northern provinces adjacent to Russian Empire. The concession ultimately led to the establishment of the Anglo-Persian Oil Company (APOC).
1906, August	The Iranian Constitutional Movement, buoyed by the dual wings of liberty and progress, and challenging despotic politics and a religion burdened by rigid sharia, took flight in the mid nineteenth century. It culminated in 1906 with the Constitutional Revolution, forcing the Qajar Shah to sign the decree of constitutionalism.
1906, October	The First Parliament officially convened.
1907, August	The Supplementary Fundamental Laws were ratified, enhancing the initial constitution with more detailed laws, including executive limitations and the rights of citizens. This came after pressure from further civic unrest and demands for a more defined legal structure.
1907, August	Britain and Russia resolved their colonial disputes in Persia (Iran) by delineating their respective spheres of influence.
1908, May	Oil is discovered in Masjed-Soleyman in southwestern Iran, marking the birth of the Middle East's petroleum industry.
1908, June	Mohammad Ali Shah, the new king, with the support of Russian troops, bombed the Parliament building, effectively staging a coup d'état against the constitutionalists. This resulted in the temporary

	suppression of the revolution, known as Minor Tyranny.
1908, July–September	Widespread resistance against Mohammad Ali Shah's arbitrary rule, including uprisings in Tabriz, Rasht, and Isfahan.
1909, April	APOC is officially incorporated. The company is formed to exploit the new oil discovery and manage the production and sale of oil in Iran. D'Arcy and Burmah Oil Company of Glasgow, Scotland, were the initial investors.
1909–1912	Construction was underway for the pipeline that would transport oil from the fields in Masjed-Soleyman to the refinery site in Abadan. The refinery itself was also under construction during this period. To manage and execute these vast engineering and construction projects, APOC employed a large workforce. Skilled labour, particularly from India, and the local, primarily non-skilled, Iranian labour.
1909, July	Constitutionalists regained control from Mohammad Ali Shah, who was subsequently deposed and exiled. His son, Ahmad Shah Qajar, ascended to the throne under a regency until he reached maturity.
1909, September	The Second Parliament reconvened and began to function more effectively as a parliamentary body.
1911, April–June	Russian forces invaded northern Iran, ostensibly to protect Russian interests but also to suppress the constitutional movement, leading to increased foreign intervention in Iranian affairs.
1911, December	The Second Parliament was dissolved, specifically following the Russian ultimatum and subsequent military actions to enforce their demands.
1912, May	The Abadan Oil Refinery, whose foundation was laid in 1909, became operational. This marked a significant development in the global oil industry, establishing Abadan as one of the key centres of oil refining in the early the Twentieth Century.
1914, June	Amid the strategic imperatives of the First World War and the growing importance of oil for naval power, the British government decided to secure its oil supply by investing in APOC, acquiring a majority share of 51 per cent. This not only ensured a steady oil supply for Britain's navy but also gave the British government significant control over Iran's oil resources.

1914, July	Austria-Hungary declared war on Serbia, marking the beginning of the First World War. Subsequently, the Ottoman Empire joined the conflict on the side of the Central Powers, which also included Germany and Austria-Hungary.
1914, November	A primarily Indian infantry military contingent landed in southern Iran, with the strategic objective of securing the oilfields and the Abadan Refinery.
1914, November	The Ottoman Empire engaged the British Navy in the Shatt al-Arab (later Arvandrud) region, marking a significant early conflict in the First World War.
1915, January	The Ottomans and Germans launched a significant infiltration campaign in southern Iran. They deployed numerous agents to the region with explicit missions to incite popular rebellions against the Allied forces and to conduct sabotage operations targeting British installations and interests.
1915, February	German agents set ablaze to the pipeline transporting oil from the Masjed-Soleyman oilfields to the Abadan Refinery, disrupting operations for four months.
1915, June	The Ottoman and German agents launched a concerted assault against the APOC facilities at Salkh on Qeshm Island. This surprise attack was orchestrated by local tribes, operating with the covert assistance of operatives from the Ottoman Special Branch, *Teşkilat-i Mahsusa*.
1917, October	The APOC integrated a contingent of 300 members from the Indian Labour Corps into their operations in Abadan.
1918, November	The First World War ended in Europe, but the British military presence in Iran continued until 1921. Following the Russian February Revolution of 1917, Russian troops withdrew from Iran. However, the Red Army landed in northern Iran in 1920.
1919–1922	Labour unionism and activism persisted in Iran, marked by well-documented workers' strikes in major Iranian cities advocating for shorter working hours and wage increases.
1920, December	Approximately 3,000 Indian workers employed at the Abadan Oil Refinery staged a strike, demanding higher wages, shorter working hours, and improved sanitary conditions. The striking workers' demands were partly met by APOC.

1921, February	Reza Khan, an officer in the Persian Cossack Brigade, and Seyyed Zia al-Din Tabataba'i, a journalist and politician, launched a coup d'état. Following his gradual consolidation of power and subsequent ascension to the Peacock Throne as Reza Shah Pahlavi, his twenty years reign from 1921 to 1941 was marked by the meticulous implementation of authoritarian reforms that resonated with the aspirations of his enlightened supporters.
1922, March	The second strike by Indian workers, which was later joined by their Iranian counterparts, demanded an increase in wages. In response, APOC dismissed all Iranian participants and repatriated approximately 2,000 Indian workers using two ships.
1924, December	Reza Khan, then serving as Prime Minister and Minister of War, personally led a military expedition to Khuzestan. The expedition resulted in the dissolution of local autonomy under Sheikh Khazʿal in Khuzestan, a figure widely recognised as a longstanding British protégé in the Persian Gulf.
1929, May	On First of May in 1929, coinciding with International Labour Day, a significant strike took place in Abadan Refinery. Among the demands of approximately 9,000 striking workers – out of a total workforce of 28,000 – were a 15 per cent wage increase, official recognition of the workers' union, acknowledgement of the International Labour Day as a legitimate holiday, and a reduction in working hours: from ten to seven hours during summer and to eight hours in winter.
1932, December	The Iranian government cancelled the D'Arcy oil concession.
1933, May	A new Agreement signed. Under the terms of the new Agreement, the APOC was mandated to exclusively employ Iranian nationals for all unskilled positions. Furthermore, when it came to hiring for clerical and technical roles, the agreement specified a preference for Iranian nationals, provided they possessed the requisite skills and experience.
1935, May	The APOC renamed as Anglo-Iranian Oil Company (AIOC). This change reflected the new national name of Iran, which was adopted by the country from its former name of Persia.
1939, September	The Abadan Institute of Technology was inaugurated.

1941, August	Two years after it began in Europe, the Second World War reached Iran with the occupation by British and Soviet military forces.
1941–1945	The occupying forces agreed to prohibit labour activities in certain key industries in Iran, including oil and railways.
1941, September	Tudeh Party of Iran was established.
1942–1944	Two labour unions were founded: the Trade Union of Iranian Workers, an independent union, and the Tudeh Party-affiliated Central Council of Unified Trade Unions of Iran.
1943, February	The Iranian government approached the Standard Vacuum Oil Company to explore potential cooperation for exploiting oil in south-east Iran.
1943, November–December	The Tehran Conference of Allied leaders agreed that all forces should withdraw Iran within six months after the end of the Second World War.
1944, September	Sergei Kavtaradze, a Soviet official and representative, visited Tehran on a mission to obtain an oil concession for the oilfields in northern Iran.
1944, December	Proposed by Mohammad Mosaddeq, the Iranian Parliament passed a law barring the government from granting any oil concessions to foreign companies.
1945, September	The Second World War ended, and the Allied forces committed to withdrawing from Iranian soil within six months.
1946, April	The Qavam–Sadchikov Agreement on northern Iran oil was signed in Moscow between Iran and the Soviet Union.
1946, July	A sixty-hour general strike united all Iranian and Indian employees of the Oil Company, including workers and clerks, who rallied for tangible demands such as wage increases, Friday pay, improved housing, and better medical services. The strike, which resulted in 47 fatalities and 173 injuries, was considered the bloodiest workers' strike in the Middle East up to that time.
1947, October	The Iranian Parliament cancelled the Qavam–Sadchikov Agreement. While barring the government from granting any concessions to foreign countries in the future, the Iranian Parliament called on the government to reclaim Iran's oil rights in the southern region of the country.

1948, August	The proposal to nationalise Iranian oil, made by 'Abbas Eskandari, was presented to Parliament.
1949, February	Following an unsuccessful assassination attempt on the Shah, the Tudeh Party and its affiliated labour unions were banned.
1951, March	Both the Iranian Parliament and the Senate ratified the bill for oil nationalisation.
1951, March–April	The strike by oil workers in Bandar Maʿshur, initially sparked by a reduction in the 'outstation' allowance, quickly spread to the oil fields and refinery, as well as to the Abadan Institute of Technology and the Abadan Artisan School. Described as 'thugs and mobs', crowds filled the streets of Abadan. The unrest resulted in nine fatalities and eleven injuries, affecting both Iranian and British individuals.
1951, April	The National Iranian Oil Company (NIOC) was established.
1951, June	The Provisional Board of Directors for the Nationalisation of Oil arrived in Abadan and raised the Iranian flag over the offices of the AIOC in both Abadan and Khorramshahr. Foreign employees of the AIOC resigned en masse.
1951, July	The Abadan Refinery ceased operations.
1951, September	The Provisional Board of Directors for the Nationalisation of Oil issued a call to all British employees who had refrained from joining the NIOC but were still residing within Iranian territory. They were given an ultimatum to either return to work or face the cancellation of their residence permits by 4 October.
1951, October	All British employees and their families remaining in Iran departed from Iranian territory.
1951, November	Representatives from the United States and Britain in Tehran, in a joint statement, declared that their chief goal is to prevent Iran from falling into the communist camp.
1952, January	Mosaddeq called on the United States to support Iran to prevent the emergence of a communist revolution.
1952, June	Mosaddeq declared in his speech the International Court of Justice at The Hague, defending the nationalisation of Iranian oil.
1952, July	Mosaddeq was resigned from the prime ministership, and Qavam al-Saltaneh was appointed by the

	Parliament as the new Prime Minister. Following the widespread mass uprising, the Parliament reinstalled Mosaddeq as Prime Minister once again.
1952, July	The International Court of Justice at The Hague ruled in favour of Iran, declaring that it did not have jurisdiction to deal with the oil crisis in Iran.
1953, April	Mass demonstrations occurred in major Iranian cities, including Abadan and Tehran, in support of Mosaddeq.
1953, 3–10 August	At the initiative of Mosaddeq, a referendum was held in Iran calling for the dissolution of the Parliament.
1953, 15 August	An hour after midnight, Colonel Nasiri, the commander of the guard, delivered the Shah's Farman dismissing Mosaddeq from the premiership.
1953, 16 August	In a public statement, Mosaddeq announced the neutralisation of a coup d'état plot. The Shah and queen left Iran. A mass demonstration was organised in Tehran, during which the slogan 'Democratic Republic' was chanted.
1953, 17 August	Statues of the Shah were pulled down, and there were demonstrations and clashes in Tehran.
1953, 18 August	Mosaddeq and his entourage gathered at his house to discuss determining the country's definitive regime. They agreed to refer the matter to a public vote, recognise the resignation of the king, and form the Sultanate Council.
1953, 19 August	Demonstrations in favour of the Shah and against Mosaddeq's government occurred across Tehran starting in the morning. By noon, mobs had attacked and taken control of the municipality, telegraph office, and some government buildings. In the afternoon, the radio station fell into the hands of coup d'état plotters, who announced the fall of Mosaddeq's government. By day's end, Mosaddeq's house was looted and set on fire by rioters. At dusk, the coup d'état successfully concluded in Tehran.
1953, 19 August	News of the coup d'état in Tehran was transmitted to Abadan via radio. Throughout much of the day, the city remained relatively calm, showing no signs of agitation. However, as evening approached, a palpable sense of disorder began to take hold, leading to a series of demonstrations throughout the city.
1953, 21 August	The Shah and queen returned to Iran.

1953, September	In the days and weeks that ensued, while the shadow of the coup d'état continued to cast a long pall over Khuzestan, the everyday routines of life and work remained largely undisturbed. There were occasional detentions of individuals with known affiliations to Tudeh Party or its affiliated labour union.
1953, October	AIOC renamed British Petroleum (BP).
1953, November	Mosaddeq's trial started.
1954, August	The discovery of the Military Organisation of the Tudeh Party led to a pronounced escalation in the severity of the situation across the country. Extensive detentions were reported in Khuzestan.
1954, September	The formal establishment of a Consortium holding company known as Iranian Oil Participants Ltd. (IOP) was announced.
1955–1961	The Consortium persisted in adhering to a predefined criterion for workforce reduction. A compensation plan was devised, offering the equivalent of two months' salary for each year of service in the oil industry.
1958, February	Oil workers in Khark launched a three-day strike in protest of poor working conditions.
1958, June	The oil workers in Aghajari and Masjed-Soleyman initiated a strike for better pay.
1959	The Consortium planed for establishing a resettlement community in Ahvaz, where houses were to be constructed by the company and offered to retiring workers from Abadan. Additionally, a home-ownership scheme was initiated in Ahwaz, envisioning the construction of over 500 houses to be sold to active employees with low down payments and a twenty-year amortisation period.
1960, January	The Organisation of Petroleum Exporting Countries (OPEC) was established.
1963, January	A referendum was held to ascertain public support for the Shah's initial reform plan, known as the White Revolution.
1960s–1970s	As part of the development plannings, the government initiates major development projects funded by oil revenues, including land reforms and social welfare programs. This period sees rapid urbanisation, with significant migration from rural areas to cities with oil-related industries.

1973, July	The 1954 Consortium Agreement was terminated.
1974, May	Oil workers went on strike for housing allowances and additional annual bonuses.
1977, June	Amid the economic crisis that followed a decade of prosperity, the initial stage of the protest featured a gathering where cries for freedom were prominently heard.
1978, May	Abadan Oil College initiated a strike in solidarity with the students' strike in Tehran.
1978, August	Cinema Rex in Abadan was set ablaze by followers of Ayatollah Khomeini in an effort to radicalise the workers and employees in the oil industry to join the revolution. Official reports stated a death toll of 377.
1978, 1 October	Oil workers from several departments in the refinery staged a strike, demanding a salary increase and housing allowances.
1978, 16 October	Oil workers from certain departments of the refinery launched a new strike in solidarity with the fortieth day since the tragic incident at Zhaleh Square in Tehran. Meanwhile, the refinery's military guards entered the premises and detained some of the protesters.
1978, 18 October	Workers from additional departments of the refinery joined the strike, demanding the release of their co-workers.
1978, 21 October	Workers at the Tehran Oil Depot embarked on a strike that lasted several hours, primarily to press for their welfare demands.
1978, 22 October	Another wave of strikes hit the refinery; this time accompanied by additional political demands.
1978, 23 December	Despite the prevailing calls for strikes, two senior managers of the Iran Oil Service Company in Ahvaz, Paul E. Grimm, and Malek Boroujerdi, continued working and were assassinated by Islamist militants.
1978, December	As the strikes continued to spread, oil exports came to a complete halt, posing a significant challenge for the populace in obtaining necessary fuel. Lengthy queues at petrol stations, where people waited for meagre fuel allocations, grew longer with each passing day.
1978, 28 December	The Revolutionary Council, established by Ayatollah Khomeini, formed the Domestic Fuel Supply Board appointed Mehdi Bazargan as its chairperson.

1979, January	Representatives of the Domestic Fuel Supply Board visited Abadan, conveying Ayatollah Khomeini's message to the oil workers to halt their strike and return to work to meet domestic needs. The strike ended.
1979, 10–11 February	With the popular uprising, the government of Chapour Bakhtiar collapsed.

Introduction

Writing the Sociohistorical Chronicle of Iranian Oil

The discovery of oil in Iran in 1908, at the dawn of the Twentieth Century, often referred to as the 'Century of Oil', marked the inception of a significant transformation in the history of Iran. This transformation was accompanied by the subsequent establishment of an extensive oil refinery, shipping infrastructure, and industrial settlements in the southwestern regions of Iran. As the nineteenth century transitioned into the Twentieth Century, the dominance of heavy oil gradually replaced coal as the primary energy source in Western economies.

Simultaneously, the demand for Iranian oil witnessed a remarkable upsurge during the First World War, leading to a substantial expansion in the workforce and related labour engagements within the oil sector. This influx of labourers into the burgeoning oil communities laid the foundation for a burgeoning societal stratum. This stratum was characterised by a discernible class consciousness, which intersected with elements of the pre-existing communal and tribal identities of its constituents.

While the colossal scale and significance of petroleum, along with its undeniable economic and strategic ramifications, are beyond dispute, the intricate complexities intrinsic to its extraction and processing, contingent upon the diligent labour and expertise of both men and women operating within the multifaceted sectors of this industry, have often been overshadowed and underestimated by scholars.

The oil industry in Iran evolved within a complex web of interrelated formative relationships that underwent substantial transformations throughout the Twentieth Century. Labour relations in Iran, particularly within this critical industrial sector, were shaped by a succession of evolving dynamics involving the national state and a significant colonial entity (Anglo-Persian Oil Company, 1908–35; Anglo-Iranian Oil Company, 1935–54; British Petroleum, 1954-present), the national state and a Consortium of multinational corporations (1954–73), the national state and the local and national labour force employed in the industry, as well as the intricate interactions between the Oil Company and its workforce. Consequently, these relationships had a multifaceted impact on both the formation of labour and the dynamics of labour relations at various historical junctures. Undeniably, the everyday lives of the workers profoundly influenced their collective and individual aspirations and activities.

The historiography of Iran's oil industry has largely been framed by political narratives, predominantly analysed through the lens of Eurocentric structural-functionalist theories of modernity. These narratives have typically provided a top-down perspective, focusing primarily on state-society relations. This study, however, endeavours to offer an alternative history of oil in Iran a social history meticulously woven from the intricate tapestry of Iran's oil industry. It is a study that delves into the reciprocal influence of modernisation and social change within the Iranian context, but from a grassroots perspective, emphasising the experiences and contributions of individuals at the heart of this transformative industry.

Examining the Subsequent Influence of Oil in Iran

The fall of the Safavid Empire (1501–1722) in Iran, coinciding with the dawning era of global industrialisation and integration spanning from 1750 to 1900, represented a critical juncture in Iran's historical trajectory. This period marked the inception of the Industrial Revolution, a transformative epoch characterised by significant global changes. The dissolution of the Safavid Empire had profound implications, triggering a resurgence of tribal politics, and engendering a schism in the evolution of capitalism within Iran.

This political fragmentation and economic decline endured for nearly a century, casting a long shadow over Iran's development. It was not until the threshold of the nineteenth century, with the establishment of the Qajar Empire (1796–1925), that Iran embarked on a path towards reclaiming the territorial and political coherence reminiscent of the Safavid era. However, this newly constituted empire quickly found its territorial integrity under constant threat in an era when emerging colonial powers aggressively sought to expand their territorial dominions. In this challenging geopolitical landscape, the frontiers of the Qajar Empire proved to be inherently vulnerable, given the relentless territorial ambitions of the colonial powers. For Iran, the treaties of 1813 and 1828, which resulted from protracted military conflicts with the Tsarist Empire, marked a pivotal juncture in its history. These treaties not only entailed the complete relinquishment of its territorial holdings in the Caucasus but also initiated a gradual yet profound transformation in its political and socio-economic landscape.

As the Twentieth Century dawned, Iran found itself ensnared in a semi-colonial status, subject to the interests and machinations of two dominant powers: Britain and Tsarist Russia. These powers regarded Iran as their own sphere of influence, where they wielded considerable political and economic control. In response to this semi-colonial subjugation, the Twentieth Century in Iran unfolded as an era characterised by a series of revolutions.

The Constitutional Revolution (1905–1909) brought about profound transformations in the socio-economic and sociocultural fabric of the nation. Its primary objective was the restructuring of the political landscape, the abolition of the monarchical regime, the establishment of the rule of law, and the imposition of accountability in the exercise of both political and economic power. During this period, a foundational principle emerged, asserting the equality of all citizens before the law, although it should be noted that this equality initially extended only to male citizens. Additionally, the Constitutional Revolution aimed to modernise Iranian society by fostering the industrialisation of the nation's economy. However, the path of the Constitutional Revolution was fraught with formidable challenges. Initially, the absence of a strong central state hindered its progress. Subsequently, it encountered resistance and coercion from Tsarist Russia. The outbreak of the First World War further complicated matters, casting additional obstacles in its path.

The discovery of petroleum reserves in the southern region of Iran in the year 1908 coincided with the unfolding of the Constitutional Revolution, marking a pivotal juncture in history that significantly elevated the geopolitical importance of the nation. As the outbreak of the First World War abruptly terminated what Karl Polányi aptly referred to as the European 'hundred years' peace', a transformation of paramount consequence unfolded on the global stage.[1] This transformation was characterised by a momentous shift from coal to oil as the primary energy source across various domains, including technology, military applications, and industrial sectors. This paradigmatic shift carried profound implications for the strategic relevance of Iran and the Persian Gulf region, distinguished by its possession of the world's most extensive oil reserves.

Oil, in this context, emerged as a remarkable and strategically significant commodity, shaped not merely by geological processes but also by intricate social and economic factors. On a global scale, oil capitalism emerged as the pre-eminent economic system, supplanting the financial capitalism that had predominated during the preceding nineteenth century. This ascendancy of oil capitalism endured throughout the entirety of the Twentieth Century exerting a pervasive and enduring influence on global affairs.

The pivotal role played by Iranian oil during the First World War profoundly reshaped the trajectory of the nation throughout the Twentieth Century. The annals of Iranian history bear witness to the confluence of geopolitical events and the enduring significance of this invaluable resource. Indeed, two notable coups d'état in 1921 and 1953, as well as the seismic reverberations of the second revolution in 1979, are all intrinsically linked, either directly or indirectly, to the omnipresent spectre of oil.

Contours of Social History

The composition and dissemination of social history have consistently engendered profound political contention across various global contexts. It is evident that historians and scholars grounded in historical inquiry have increasingly recognised and engaged with three key concerns. The initial concern emanates from the imperative to craft social histories that counteract prevailing paradigms of political historiography. The endeavour to write social histories serves as an antidote to the narratives centred around towering figures, ruling lineages, or fervent nationalist uprisings. To exemplify, the emergence of nationalist historiography, which gained momentum during the latter part of the nineteenth century in Europe and gradually assumed prominence within Iran, stands as a relatable illustration.

Within this framework, political celebrities were depicted as genuine national icons, epitomising the collective consciousness of the entirety of society. These nationalist historiographic accounts recounted the saga of the political elite and their undisputed involvement in the nationalist enterprise. Within the context of modern Iran, the composition of nationalist histories was purposefully underpinned by a reclamation of identity and a rediscovery of the privileged agents designated, according to such narratives, with the preservation of the homeland's integrity.[2]

The second concern has prompted the imperative to scrutinise the interplay between politics and society across all strata – a task that conventional political history often neglects to comprehensively address. Consequently, social history, or more appropriately termed societal history, provides the essential arena wherein the documentation of the past through the lens of these complex interactions becomes acceptable.

The third concern implicitly recognises that contemporary politics exercise a significant influence over the outlines of historiography. Within a world characterised by the dominance of nation state constructs, the delineation of a nation's collective identity emerges as a politically driven endeavour fostered by political historiographical discourse. This undertaking endeavours to bridge the disparities existing between a nation's factual or ideational historical narrative and its current political actuality. Consequently, nation states necessitate the services of historians to validate their established political hierarchy and power configuration. As a result, the past, whether remote or proximate, is subject to reinterpretation by historians through the lens of present-day political pragmatism.

The exploration of nation state historiography brings a pair of essential inquiries. Might social history find applicability within the confines of the nation state? Moreover, surpassing the former query in urgency, can social history, particularly in its contemporary sociocultural manifestations, armed with broader discursive frameworks than those traditionally proffered by canonical social historians, engage with investigations extending beyond the boundaries of the nation state? The response to the initial query emerges rather conspicuously, as a considerable number of social historians operate within the established boundaries of the nation state. However, their distinctiveness lies in their endeavour to excavate national histories from the perspective of the marginalised or less dominant segments of society. Noteworthy instances encompass those social historians who undertake the task of documenting the metamorphosis of subjects into citizens through the complex tapestry of nation state formation. As posited by Ranajit Guha, the emergence of a nation transpires not solely as an outcome of elite exertions, but equally as a consequence of the struggles waged by the subaltern groups.

However, the latter question is of great importance. Can the field of social history, especially in its contemporary sociocultural iterations, equipped with broader and more inclusive discursive frameworks than those traditionally offered by conventional social historians, cope with research that transcends the boundaries of the nation state?[3]

Addressing the latter query, it is imperative for historians to acknowledge the omnipresence of numerous social dynamics that transcend national boundaries. Among these are the transnational circulation of people, the spreading of political ideals and aspirations, and the proliferation of popular cultures.[4] Furthermore, social historiography that extends beyond the limitations of the nation state can actively forge connections with a plethora of social science disciplines, encompassing fields such as development studies, tribal studies, women's studies, and various sub-disciplines within history, including but not limited to labour history, agricultural history, business history, and family history. It turns out that reconstructing everyday life in a given context can actually enhance social historiography by giving it an essential layer of depth and insight.

Within the boundary of these argument, I consider social history as a historical study that focuses on the lives, experiences, and activities of ordinary people rather than just political elites and major events. For me, social history aims to understand the social, cultural, economic, and everyday aspects of a society. The 'agency' in this study refers to the capacity of individuals or groups to make choices and take actions that shape their own lives and society. Here my reference to 'Subaltern agency' refers to the actions and perspectives of marginalised and less powerful groups, often hidden from traditional historical narratives.[5]

By addressing these challenges and working towards a more comprehensive and rigorous approach, the social historiography of oil in Iran can be advanced. This would involve understanding not just political events, but also societal structures, cultural practices, and the lives of ordinary people during 1908–79.

The Role of Oil in Shaping Iranian Society

As the nineteenth century drew to a close, one of the paramount challenges confronting British enterprises on a global scale was the quest for the discovery and mastery of dependable and secure reservoirs of oil. Imperial Russia's possession of the Baku oilfield, the world's second-largest known oil deposit at that time, following the United States oilfields, granted Russia a dominant position in the burgeoning and burgeoning energy market. British competitors were resolute in their determination to alter this state of affairs by embarking on a mission to uncover and exploit fresh oilfields across the globe.

In May 1901, the British determination reached a successful culmination when William K. D'Arcy secured an exclusive concession. This agreement granted him comprehensive rights to explore, extract, process, commercialise, transport, and sell oil and all its derivatives throughout the extensive territories of the Persian Empire. Seven years later, in the early hours of a spring day, on the 26 May 1908, after months of rigorous exploration and excavation in the southwestern region of Iran, one of the wells situated in the foothills of the Zagros Mountains, not far from the remnants of a Parthian temple known as Takht-e Soleyman, ultimately struck oil.

It is noteworthy that the discovery of oil in southern Iran occurred concomitantly with a period known in the Iranian constitutional movement as 'Minor Tyranny'. This era was marked by the Iranian Parliament being subjected to bombardment by Russian forces under the directive of Qajar King, Mohammad-Ali Shah, which transpired in the aftermath of the Constitutional Revolution in Iran. However, it is intriguing to observe that the historical records within the oil archives do not make any reference to this synchronicity. This omission can be attributed to the British perspective, which owing to its supremacy in the region, regarded Southern Iran as a separate colonial entity, substantially disconnected from the wider political dynamics unfolding across the nation.

Following the successful discovery of oil deposits, the Anglo-Persian Oil Company (APOC) faced an immediate and formidable challenge: the transportation of oil from the wellhead to the global market, either in its crude or refined state. In pursuit of maximising profitability, the company made the strategic decision to conduct oil refining operations within Iran. The geographical advantage of proximity to the Persian Gulf granted APOC convenient access to the international market. Along the Persian Gulf's coastline, Abadan Island, situated in the north-western corner and adjacent to the waterway of Arvandrud, provided excellent anchorages for shipping tankers. It emerged as an ideal location for the construction of a refinery.

The commencement of construction on the Abadan Refinery was initiated in October 1909. Merely three months later, in January 1910, an ambitious project was launched, entailing the construction of approximately 220 kilometres

Map I.1 Iran in the Twentieth Century

of pipelines to facilitate the transportation of oil from the fields of Masjed-Soleyman to Abadan.

This endeavour marked the onset of an extensive construction effort that ushered in a new chapter in Iran's labour history. Roads, pipelines, an oil

Figure I.1 Laying pipeline to transport oil from Masjed-Soleyman to Abadan, 1910

refinery, shipping docks, and entire company towns were established, signifying a monumental transformation in the industrial landscape of the region.

With its complete monopoly over oil mining, production, and marketing, the APOC embarked on an extensive labour recruitment campaign within the region. The bulk of its workforce was sourced from the tribal-pastoralist and village-based labouring communities. This new labour force was subjected to advanced industrial labour discipline, ultimately giving rise to the initial clusters of the working class within the Persian/Iranian oil industry.

From the very outset of the oil discovery, it became evident that a project of such magnitude would necessitate a skilled labour force, a resource that Iran lacked at that time. The initial group of Indian migrant workers who became part of the Iranian oil industry were directly transferred from the Yangon Refinery, facilitated through the coordination of the Burmah Oil Company. In Iran, these workers hailing from Burma were collectively referred to as 'Ranguny', a distinction from other Indian migrants.

With the establishment of the Abadan Refinery in 1909, the population of Indian migrant workers saw a steady increase. The recruitment of labourers from India continued and even intensified notably during the First World War. By the conclusion of the war, the expanded contingent of Indian migrant workers engaged in the Iranian oil industry hailed from various regions across India.

The conclusion of the First World War marked the end of what had been somewhat ironically termed the 'long peace of the nineteenth century'. The war signalled the breakdown of an international system that had been constructed around high finance and marked the culmination of the industrialisation of warfare, following a period of escalating capitalist competition and transformative technological advancements. Just before the war erupted, a global transition took place in industry, armies, and naval forces as they shifted from using coal to oil fuels, resulting in an exponential surge in the demand for petroleum products. The extraction and refining of substantial and cost-effective supplies of petroleum were fundamental prerequisites for this global shift, and the Iranian oil industry, managed by the APOC emerged as the principal supplier of this new energy source in the Persian Gulf. The Iranian oil thus became not only an economically vital resource for British interests worldwide but also a strategically significant military asset.

The aftermath of the war was equally momentous. Eric Hobsbawm aptly labels the period encompassing the First World War and its aftermath as 'the age of catastrophe',[6] attributing its destructiveness to its resemblance to unrestrained competitive capitalism, driven by the relentless pursuit of limitless accumulation, acquisition, and global expansion. The war engulfed the general public as conscripts, workers, and cannon fodder, ultimately forcing them to bear the costs of the carnage. Paradoxically, however, the sheer scale of the war brought about an expansion of the public sphere and unintentionally paved the way for greater political participation by the working classes and ordinary citizens.

This pivotal shift in political dynamics coincided with global structural changes in corporate capitalism, compelling the state and large corporations such as APOC to reassess labour and labour relations from an entirely new perspective. In this reconfigured landscape, industrial workers were no longer viewed solely as anonymous producers of surplus value but increasingly as 'human capital' and, ultimately, as political citizens whose votes and political actions could influence laws and policies.

As the First World War came to an end, Iran remained entangled in the aftermath of the Constitutional Revolution. The post-war political climate in Iran was characterised by surges of anti-colonial nationalism, reformist movements, and radical regional developments. In the aftermath of the First World War, a new political paradigm emerged in Iran, with a central focus on diminishing provincial and tribal autonomy. In 1921, Reza Khan, a commander of a local army unit, orchestrated a coup d'état, and four years later, he ascended to power as the new king, establishing the Pahlavi dynasty. Reza Shah's rule was characterised by an authoritarian monarchy built upon a centralised governance model. Employing an approach often described as authoritarian modernisation, he embarked on an ambitious modernisation agenda, marked by the rapid urbanisation and industrialisation of the nation.

While facing pressure from the Iranian government, the APOC was obligated to enhance the working and living conditions of oil labourers. Nevertheless, the government prevented labour from acting independently as a participant in the modernisation process. These policies gave rise to a tripartite dynamic, outlining the intricate interplay between the state, labour, and the Oil Company. Concurrently, as the king's modernisation initiatives gained momentum, the role of oil underwent a transformation, shifting from being primarily an export commodity to becoming a fundamental resource designated for supporting state-sponsored economic development.

Nonetheless, it would be an oversimplification to confine Reza Shah and his statesmen's perspective on oil solely to its revenue generation for economic change. As we will explore further in this study, the labour and daily lives of oil industry workers were integral components of the economic development program of that era, even though they did not always receive the priority they deserved in practice. For instance, when Reza Shah visited the southern Iran oil industry in 1924, prior to ascending to the throne, he expressed profound disappointment upon discovering that not a single Iranian expert was employed at the Abadan Refinery.

Following Reza Shah's rise to power, his new government promoted territorial-state nationalism as a means to exalt the authoritarian modernisation program and the fresh state-building initiative. State-sponsored nationalism had a significant impact on the oil industry, as it exerted pressure on the APOC to enhance working and living conditions within the sector and expedite Iranianisation by training Iranian workers and replacing Indians with Iranians.

The new agreement reached in 1933 between the Iranian government and APOC, which effectively annulled the D'Arcy concession of 1901, placed a strong emphasis on the earlier demand that APOC should recruit artisans, technicians, and commercial staff from among the Iranian populace. According to the Iranian press, the cancellation of the D'Arcy concession was viewed as an act of 'political emancipation' and a 'new chapter in Iranian honour'. This development not only returned the 'national wealth' to the country but also marked the end of a protracted era of favouritism towards Indian employees.

The influx of this new workforce into the burgeoning oil industry resulted in rapid industrialisation and significant demographic shifts. The emergence of oil towns brought about substantial changes in almost every aspect of social relations, social organisation, and government administrative structures, both at the local and national levels.

Abadan, characterised as a tripartite city, was spatially segmented according to the residency of British, Indian, and Iranian communities. This division was founded on the principles of social stratification imposed by British colonialism. A highly stratified ethnic hierarchy prevailed, a hierarchy that British employees of APOC brought with them from their home countries and from

India. The city was divided into three main ethnic groups, with Europeans at the top, Indians in the middle, and native Iranians at the bottom. This ethnic segregation was consistently maintained, even as new neighbourhoods were added to the city due to the expansion of the oil industry, the extension of the refinery, and changes in employment policies.

Crossing these rigid ethnic boundaries was possible on certain occasions, such as when higher-ranking Indians (and later, Iranians) were invited to attend official ceremonies, gatherings, or worship services with the European community. However, mixing across ethnic borders was generally discouraged, and segregation was promoted as the preferred practice.

With the onset of the Second World War, Iran's government adopted a policy of neutrality, which was respected for two years by both the British and the Soviets. However, as the German Eastern Front began to crumble, the British and Soviet forces invaded Iran on 25 August 1941. While the official pretext for the invasion was accusing Reza Shah of having pro-German sympathies, it is evident that both the British and the Soviet Union had long-standing desires to gain unrestricted access to Iran's oil resources, located in the north and south of the country. The invasion of Iran provided a strategic opportunity for both powers to pursue these longstanding ambitions.

The occupation of Iran by Great Britain and the Soviet Union in 1941 disrupted the course of authoritarian modernisation in Iran and had a profound impact on Reza Shah's centralised authority, eventually leading to his abdication in favour of his son, Mohammad-Reza Shah Pahlavi. Indeed, this transitional period created a more conducive environment for the expansion of political open space and the emergence of social movements that contributed to the strengthening of civil society in Iran. One significant aspect of this development was the rapid formation of political parties and trade unions throughout the country. The labour movement, in particular, gained prominence, primarily within Iran's major industries during that era.

Within the context of the oil industry the organised labour movement for better working and living conditions, launched significant initiatives, including strikes, sit-ins, and public demonstrations. This increasing political awareness, combined with heightened labour activism, the emergence of trade unions, and growing class consciousness, played a pivotal role in the eventual nationalisation of the oil industry in 1951.

The necessity to ramp up oil production to meet the wartime needs of the Allied forces collided with the shortage of available labour within the oil industry. In addition to the workers directly employed by the AIOC, there were also individuals who were assigned specific tasks on a casual or seasonal basis by the company. These casual workers, or as they were called, the non-contract workers, were not considered part of the AIOC's regular labour force and were not included in the company's official statistics. Nonetheless, due to the scarcity of available labour, the AIOC had no choice but to return to its previous practice of recruiting migrant workers, primarily from India, to fill both skilled and unskilled positions within the industry. This migration of Indian workers played a significant role in addressing the workforce shortages faced by the AIOC during this period.

During the Second World War, the labouring poor in Iran experienced intolerable living conditions due to widespread famine, inflation, and the ever-increasing cost of living. The non-contract workers, along with the majority of the salaried registered workers and waged contractor workers, were still living in tents, huts, or in a shantytown known as *Kaghazabad* (Paper Town). These dwellings lacked basic amenities such as running water and electricity.

In a report submitted to the Iranian government by the AIOC, the company admitted that despite the sharp increase in the number of employees in the oil industry during the war, no measures had been taken to provide decent housing for the workers. Additionally, during the war, Iranians faced the threats of diseases and epidemics. The oil industry, which operated two hospitals in Abadan with a total of 350 beds and one in Masjed-Soleyman with 86 beds, had to contend with new diseases such as typhus, along with longstanding and more enduring ones such as trachoma, malaria, tuberculosis, and the plague.

For about thirty years since the initial discovery of oil in 1908, the absence of a unified platform to represent the interests of labour allowed the AIOC to address issues related to workers' living and working conditions on an individual rather than a collective basis. This approach extended to matters such as labour recruitment, wages, education, healthcare, housing, and welfare. The Oil Company had the freedom to terminate workers without notice, and there was no recourse for workers to appeal against unfair dismissals. Despite several signs indicating the emergence of a nascent labour movement during this period, the AIOC's labour policies exhibited little to no inclination to adapt or change accordingly.

The working and living conditions of the Oil Company's employees during this period laid the foundation for a series of significant labour protests in the 1940s and early 1950s. Some of these protests, as elaborated in detail in this volume, escalated into the bloodiest labour uprisings not only in Iran but also across the entire region. These protests were a direct result of the harsh working conditions, lack of collective bargaining power, and the general dissatisfaction among labourers, culminating in violent confrontations with severe consequences.

The declaration of the nationalisation of the Iranian oil industry on 20 March 1951, was not solely the product of determined efforts by certain political elites, as commonly emphasised in the historiography of Iranian oil nationalisation. Equally important was the sustained pressure from below, primarily driven by oil workers.

Figure I.2 Demonstration in support of oil nationalisation, Tehran, 1951

With the departure of all European and a majority of Indian employees of the AIOC in October 1951, the culmination of oil nationalisation marked the end of forty-five years of British dominance within the Iranian oil industry. This transition underscored the significant role played by both political leaders and grassroots movements, particularly oil workers, in shaping the course of this historic development. However, the initial euphoria surrounding this nationalisation was short-lived, as the 1950s witnessed one of the most challenging periods of economic decline and political repression in the country's history. The coup d'état of 1953 and the subsequent denationalisation of the oil industry's management in 1954 emerged as major factors contributing to this era of repression and stagnation.

One of the immediate outcomes of the August 1953 coup d'état was the widespread repression that extended into all corners of the political sphere in Iran. The return of autocratic rule marked the end of twelve years of practising participatory politics. The overthrow of Mosaddeq's government not only ushered in a new political era in Iran but also marked a transformative juncture in which other international oil corporations, notably those from the United States, entered the Iranian oil industry. The coup d'état of 1953 wrought a transformative shift in Iran's political landscape, yielding profound implications for the nation's destiny in the decades that followed.

In the aftermath of the Second World War, the global landscape experienced a profound transformation characterised by the onset of the Cold War, a restructuring of political alliances, and a focused endeavour aimed at economic and social reconstruction, predominantly through the establishment of the developmental states. In the bipolar context of the Cold War, the United States delivered a stark message to its allies in the Global South: initiate comprehensive top-down reforms or risk being overthrown by bottom-up grassroots revolutions that could end their governance!

In August 1961, the Shah conducted a rally in Tehran during which he unveiled his intentions to introduce a comprehensive set of economic reforms. After nearly two years of meticulously assessing various reform options, the Shah officially announced an outline of an authoritarian development plan on 26 January 1963. This proposal was subsequently presented to the public through a referendum. At the heart of these reforms lay a series of extensive socio-economic initiatives, later to become known as the White Revolution.

At the core of the White Revolution lay the central tenet of land reform, aimed at changing prevailing pre-capitalist social relations in rural areas, thereby facilitating a rapid surge in capitalist economic growth. Additionally, the objective was to bypass the pre-industrial stages of societal development, propelling a primarily agrarian-based society into a capitalist one, fully prepared to engage in the global economic arena. Central to this transformative endeavour was the industrialisation of the economy, serving as a fundamental pillar in this process.

This developmental strategy yielded several significant results, most notably an increase in female participation across various professions. There was a rise in the number of female workers, extensive literacy programs were implemented, opportunities for higher education expanded, healthcare services improved, and communication networks were enhanced, among other advancements. These initiatives profoundly influenced population mobility. During this period, a significant phenomenon occurred: the workforce migrated from rural to urban areas. This shift led to a decrease in the agricultural labour force and a corresponding rise in the urban industrial workers.

The rural-to-urban migration led to a substantial influx of hundreds of thousands of villagers into the cities, primarily settling in the suburbs of major urban centres. However, many of these migrants encountered significant challenges in their daily lives, including traditional-modern and rural-urban cultural disconnection, along with a series of material hardships such as a lack of access to essential amenities such as water and electricity in their residential areas. It soon became evident that this concentrated population had the potential to drive significant political change.

In the post-war era, particularly during the 1960s, the United Nations identified it as a time of widespread economic and political reforms on a global scale. Notably, there was a significant linguistic shift during this period: what were once referred to as 'underdeveloped countries' were now considered part of the 'developing world'. This reclassification symbolised their potential to overcome longstanding economic stagnation and poverty. However, it is important to acknowledge that the distribution of economic development during this time was not uniform across these nations.

Indeed, Iran's oil revenue played a significant role in facilitating the implementation of development projects. With an estimated increase of 13.6 per cent, oil served as a crucial component in the country's economic reconstruction. The fiscal impact of oil revenues had a dual effect on the Iranian economy: firstly, it provided a substantial source of income for the government to supplement its budgetary expenditures, and secondly, these oil revenues were directed towards various development projects.

In the 1960s and 1970s, oil revenues made a significant contribution to the welfare and living standards of oil industry employees. The economic development during the 1960s brought about a substantial transformation in the lives of oil workers. Their monthly income comprised various components, including basic wages, overtime payments, location-based allowances, housing subsidies, travel allowances, child allowances, and New Year bonuses. The benefits of high income were not exclusive to oil workers; they also had access to affordable and high-quality products offered by the Consumptive Cooperative Organisation of the Oil Industry.

The impact of oil revenues transcended the realms of education, housing, and healthcare, significantly permeating into the domain of leisure for oil workers. However, this impact was not uniform and varied considerably across different regions and social groups. This variation becomes particularly apparent upon analysing the spatial differentiation in the leisure activities of these workers. It is evident that the primary setting for leisure activities among oil workers lay beyond the boundaries of their workplace. Their leisure time was predominantly spent within the private confines of their homes, as well as in public and semi-public spaces, illustrating a diverse range of environments for relaxation and recreation outside of their professional duties.

In conjunction with the economic advancements facilitated by the developmental state, there existed a notable disparity between economic and political progress. Iran of 1960s and 1970s witnessed considerable economic growth and substantial socio-economic transformations. However, this era was markedly devoid of corresponding political evolution. The landscape lacked robust representation of political and trade unions, as well as independent and non-governmental entities. The prevailing political climate continued to be characterised by exclusivity and coercive tactics, reminiscent of earlier times. This was in stark contrast to the dynamic shifts occurring within social classes, which anticipated greater synchronicity between economic and political developments. Nonetheless, the political sphere remained marred by the repressive aftermath of the 1953 coup d'état, hindering the alignment of economic and political progress.

In the 1940s, the labour movement, aimed at achieving improved living and working conditions, was markedly confrontational, particularly in its challenge to the state. During this period, aligning the demands of labour unions for better living and working conditions with the agendas of political parties was viewed as a hallmark of progress. Advocating for independent labour unions was perceived as an alignment with reactionary forces. However, from the mid-1950s onwards, and leading up to the months preceding the 1979 revolution, the labour movement predominantly adhered to the principles of trade unionism and adopted a more conciliatory rather than confrontational stance.

Interestingly, there were reports indicating that during the strike and protest, workers displayed photographs of the Shah and placards featuring quotes from the Shah, underscoring the role of workers in the White Revolution. Additionally, there was a narrative suggesting that during their meetings, the workers used large posters of the Shah as shields to safeguard themselves from potential attacks by the police and security services. This tactic meant that any would-be assailants would only be able to enter the meeting venue by forcibly tearing down the pictures.

The two decades spanning the 1960s and early 1970s witnessed rapid and substantial socio-economic growth in Iran, facilitated by the rentier developmental state. Concurrently, the nation grappled with an underdeveloped political system. This juxtaposition would later foreshadow the crises that unfolded in the mid-1970s. The uneven distribution of wealth, social services, and opportunities, stemming from this rapid yet unequal growth, inevitably led to the widening of sociopolitical disparities. According to a report prepared by the International Labour Organisation in 1972, Iran was among the countries with the most unequal income distribution. In that year, the average income for the working population in the country stood at 1248 rials. In urban areas, this figure was 1569 rials, while in rural areas, it was 660 rials. Additionally, government civil workers enjoyed an income 2.2 times higher than government-employed workers and 3.4 times higher than workers in the private sector during the same year.

The massive rural-to-urban migration led to the unchecked proliferation of informal squatter settlements, serving as another manifestation of the disproportionate population growth. Over a span of fifteen years, Iran's population swelled from 23 million individuals in 1960 to 34 million individuals in 1974. Cities experienced a twofold increase in population, surging from 8 million to 16 million, while rural areas witnessed a more modest increase from 15 million to 18 million individuals.

The most substantial growth occurred in Tehran, where the population skyrocketed from 2.7 million people to 4.5 million within a single decade, from 1966 to 1976. Due to the rapid influx of migrants, Tehran was unable to serve as an ideal destination for newcomers or adequately meet the needs of its existing residents. By the mid-1970s, squatter settlements had reached their zenith, encompassing urban inhabitants within the bounds of the urban economy but remaining largely excluded from it. The proliferation of urban squatter settlements underscored the considerable influence wielded by this demographic trend, arguably even surpassing that of the working class. Consequently, political forces could not afford to disregard the dynamics of this mobile population.

The fifteen years period that commenced with the initiation of the White Revolution in 1962, laying the foundation for new developmental advancements and rapid economic growth until 1976, concluded with an aggravated economic crisis in 1977. Unlike conventional models of revolution, the Iranian Revolution was the product of more than a decade of swift economic expansion followed by a brief phase of economic recession or downturn.[7]

Nonetheless, it would be overly simplistic to attribute the revolution solely to the prominent role of the economic crisis, while overlooking other contributing factors. One such factor was the political impasse resulting from the neglect of political development in parallel with economic progress. Within the framework of authoritarian modernisation, political agency remained confined to the Shah and his political elite. There was no recourse for the populace to hold anyone accountable for the pervasive misconduct of coercive institutions and economic mismanagement. Political parties, unions, and other independent institutions were virtually non-existent. Repression of dissent, corruption, inequality, and misallocation of financial resources compelled either protest or passive acceptance of authoritarian modernisation. The government's inability to address economic disparities and maintain economic stability fuelled discontent.

At the international level, the Iranian Revolution was also shaped by broader geopolitical factors, including the dynamics of the Cold War, Iran's relationship with the United States, and regional power struggles. The significant support provided by the United States to the Iranian government during the Cold War and Western intervention in Iran's internal affairs had such a substantial impact that any significant shift in American policies quickly reverberated within Iran, affecting its political stability or instability. This intricate relationship with the West fuelled anti-government sentiments and gave rise to demands for independence and freedom.

The belated participation of oil industry workers in the sweeping protests that ultimately led to the 1978–79 revolution can be attributed to their relatively comfortable economic circumstances. This prosperity initially made them less inclined, much like their counterparts in larger industries, to engage in the early stages of the protests. However, as the revolutionary tide surged and harnessed the twin forces of coercion against non-participants and the compelling appeal of religious convictions, even those initially hesitant found themselves drawn into the fold. This was the story for those who did not share an affinity with political Islam or the Islamic Revolution but, in the face of the prevailing circumstances, felt compelled to become participants.

A Note on Methodology

The methodology employed in this study, which endeavours to present a social history of oil, is inherently complex and interdisciplinary in nature. To address the multifaceted dimensions of this topic, a carefully considered approach was adopted. The methodology encompassed a diverse range of research methods, including archival research, oral history interviews, content analysis of documents and media, as well as quantitative data analysis, among others. This comprehensive approach was essential to capture the rich tapestry of the social history of oil.

Primary and secondary data, essential to this study, were gathered through extensive research activities that spanned across various geographical locations, including Delhi, Mumbai, Tehran, Moscow, London, and Washington. These efforts included visits to archives, such as the BP archive, British National Archives, U.S. National Archives, Indian National Archives, Iran National Archives, and the Archive of Indian Office, which contain a wealth of invaluable historical documents related to the oil industry. While these archives were invaluable sources, a cautious approach was taken to avoid over-reliance on them. Rigorous cross-referencing and verification of sources were undertaken to ensure the reliability of the information.

The theoretical framework guiding this study drew upon concepts from social history, labour history, and the history of everyday life. Additionally, insights from a range of disciplines within the social sciences and humanities were incorporated, enriching the analytical perspective.

Historical periodisation serves as a pivotal determinant of the historiographic methodology employed by scholars in the compilation of history. This concept underscores the inherent differentiation in the approach to periodisation across various historical disciplines. Specifically, the criteria for periodising political history diverge markedly from those applied to social history. While political historians prioritise political events as the primary markers for defining historical epochs, social historians emphasise transformations in work and societal life as the critical determinants. Consequently, a political event might hold negligible significance in the periodisation schema of social history if it fails to effect a tangible change in the daily lives of individuals.

The structure of this book is reflective of a nuanced understanding of periodisation, acknowledging the aforementioned disciplinary distinctions. In a marked departure, this narrative adopts a bottom-up approach, diverging from the traditional top-down historiographical narratives prevalent in the studies of the oil industry in Iran, which are characterised by their detailed chronologies of events. This methodological shift underscores a commitment to foregrounding the lived experiences and societal transformations over the enumeration of political events, thereby offering a more inclusive portrayal of historical periods. Thus, the book embraces a perspective that prioritises the broader social fabric and work-related transformations over mere chronological event listing, aligning with the methodological preferences of social history. Therefore, a chronological list has not been provided here.

Throughout the course of this research and writing endeavour, my commitment to maintaining a balanced and objective approach remained steadfast. In doing so, I was reminded of the sagacious counsel of the distinguished Persian historian Abolfazl Beyhaqi, who, over a millennium ago, emphasised the importance of avoiding bias and vindictiveness when presenting historical account of a recently deceased vizier:

> Although I disliked him – by no means. Since my age has reached sixty-five, and I follow him, I should go forth and not say anything in my narrative that I am writing, which leads to bigotry and arrogance, and the readers of this ballad will say: 'Shame on this old man!' Rather, I say it so that the readers will agree with me and not be sarcastic'.[8]

1

Oil Discovery and the Formation of a New Iranian Society

On 26 May 1908, in the nascent hours of a spring day, a pivotal moment in the history of Iranian energy unfolded. After enduring months of exploration and excavation in the southwestern regions of Iran, a discovery was made at one of the wells nestled in the foothills of the Zagros Mountains: oil was struck. This seminal event catalysed a substantial construction endeavour, heralding a novel epoch in Iran's labour history. Infrastructure such as roads, pipelines, an oil refinery, shipping docks, and entire company towns were constructed in swift succession.

The Anglo-Persian/Iranian Oil Company, wielding an unchallenged monopoly over oil mining, production, and marketing, embarked on an extensive labour recruitment campaign within the region. The primary source of this burgeoning workforce was the tribal-pastoralist communities and the village-based labouring poor. These new workers were introduced to a regime of advanced industrial labour discipline, a transition that was instrumental in cultivating the initial segments of the working class within the Iranian oil industry.[1]

As recruitment for the rapidly expanding oil industry progressed, it precipitated swift industrialisation and significant demographic shifts. The oil towns became influential agents of change, reshaping social relations, societal organisation, and governmental administrative frameworks at both the local and national levels.

Nevertheless, the recruitment process for the oil industry proved more challenging than the company had initially envisioned. In a region characterised by minimal human needs, which were easily and inexpensively met, convincing young men to relinquish their traditional lifestyles for an industrial setting with its radically altered work patterns and novel labour discipline was far from straightforward. It is noteworthy that during this early phase, women were conspicuously absent from the workforce.

At the dawn of the Twentieth Century, securing and controlling significant and reliable oil reserves represented a primary challenge for British enterprises globally. The Baku oilfield, held by Imperial Russia, was then the world's second largest known oil deposit, surpassed only by those in the United States. This possession granted Russia considerable influence over the burgeoning energy market.[2] British rivals, eager to alter this dynamic, were actively engaged in identifying and developing new oilfields internationally.

In May 1901, William K. D'Arcy, an Australian entrepreneur backed by the British embassy in Tehran, successfully obtained an exclusive concession. This concession authorised him to 'search for, obtain, exploit, develop, render suitable for trade, carry away and sell natural gas, petroleum, asphalt and ozocerite throughout the whole extent of the Persian Empire, with the exception of the five Northern provinces for no less than sixty years'.[3]

The exclusion of the northern provinces from the agreement was clearly a strategic move designed to maintain amicable relations with Iran's northern neighbour, Tsarist Russia. A year following the acquisition of this substantial concession, the Oil Company commenced operations in the western part of Iran. Nevertheless, the modest oil revenues generated in this region fell short of anticipated financial returns. This shortfall prompted D'Arcy's representative, now known as the First Exploitation Company, to relocate to the southern province of Khuzestan.

After witnessing a substantial surge in oil revenues and navigating through a series of intricate financial transactions in London, the Anglo-Persian Oil Company (APOC) was established on 14 April 1909. With a capital base of 2,000,000 British Pounds sterling, APOC monopolised the extraction, production, and distribution of Iranian oil, enjoying the full spectrum of rights afforded by the D'Arcy concession. Furthermore, to garner favour and support from local Bakhtiari tribal leaders, APOC also established the Bakhtiari Oil Company, investing 300,000 pounds sterling into this provincial venture.

Following its successful discovery of oil reserves, APOC faced the significant challenge of transporting oil from the wellhead to the market, either as crude or refined product. To enhance profitability, APOC opted to refine the oil within Iran itself, taking advantage of the Persian Gulf's proximity for easy access to international markets. The Abadan Island, located in the north-western corner of the Persian Gulf near the Arvandrud waterway, presented ideal conditions for anchoring shipping tankers and was thus selected as the site for constructing a refinery. Construction of the Abadan Refinery commenced in October 1909. Subsequently, in January 1910, an ambitious project was initiated to build approximately 220 kilometres of pipeline, which would transport oil from the Masjed-Soleyman fields to Abadan.

Labour Recruitment and Settlement

Prior to striking oil in Masjed-Soleyman, and while the surveying mission was still under way, the fieldwork employees included no more than a 'dozen drillers, a few blacksmiths and mechanics, an accountant, a transport overseer, a doctor, an assistant and a number of local muleteers'.[4] The needs of the mission, including a labour supply, were met largely through negotiations with

Bakhtiari tribal chiefs. A 1907 report compiled by engineer H. E. Bradshaw, who was in charge of the road works, refers to the workers sent by Samsam al-Saltaneh (a Bakhtiari khan) to build the road to Masjed-Soleyman.[5] Similarly, Arnold Wilson recalls his days acting as the British political officer in the region, when he often contacted the 'small tribal chiefs from whom to draw labour, pack animals and even supplies of straw, barley, wood for fuel and other local supplies' for the Oil Company.[6] In another agreement, reached in 1908 between Sheikh Khazʿal, a local Arab tribe chief from Mohammareh (Khorramshahr) and P. Z. Cox, political resident in the Persian Gulf, the Oil Company offered the Sheikh 'a guarantee that no tribesmen be engaged without [the Sheikh's] permission'.[7] However, it turned out that in all the negotiations to recruit labour, the need for manpower guarding the Oil Company's activities, its machinery, and its personnel was the most troublesome.

Conducting production in a region where the Iranian central government could not assert its unmitigated authority, and that was a tricky business. The company quickly realised that in order to proceed, it needed the blessing of the chiefs of the local tribal, particularly the Bakhtiari, whose cooperation was essential to guard the company against possible attacks by the pastoral nomads and peasants accusing the Oil Company of seizing their pastoral land. The consecration of the tribal chiefs was also vital for supplying the workface the company needed.[8]

In the early Twentieth Century, the Bakhtiari tribes, who were the predominant tribal group in southwest Iran, had a social hierarchy based on five distinct class positions. This structure was influenced by factors such as economic status, the size of livestock herds, and the control of pastoral lands. The hierarchy included:

1. *Ilkhan*: The chief of the confederation of Bakhtiari tribes, alongside his deputy, the *ilbeg*. This position represented the apex of power within the tribal confederation.
2. *Khan*: The leader of each individual tribe. The *Khan* played a pivotal role in tribal governance and was a key figure in the sociopolitical landscape of the tribe.
3. *Kalantar*: The head of the *tayefeh*, or clan/subtribe. The *kalantar* managed the affairs of their respective clan, holding significant influence within their community.
4. *Kadkhoda*: The leader of the *tireh*, or branch/sub-*tayefeh*. This role involved overseeing the smaller subdivisions within the tribe and managing their day-to-day operations.
5. *ʿAmaleh*: The lowest rank within the tribal structure, which included roles such as *tofangchi* (gunmen), *chubaki* (stick-holders), *tubreh-kesh* (bag-holders), and *dast-pati* (empty-handed). Individuals in this class typically had little to no livestock ownership and were responsible for various logistical tasks and protective duties within the tribe.[9]

This hierarchical system reflects the intricate social organisation of the Bakhtiari tribes, illustrating the distribution of power and responsibilities based on class distinctions.

Within the Bakhtiari tribes' hierarchy, the *ilkhan*/*ilbeg* held hereditary positions, though they were recognised and accredited by the central government. Similarly, the role of the *khan*, and occasionally that of the *kalantar*, was inherited. By contrast, the *kadkhoda* was selected based on their reputation for trustworthiness within the tribe.

The lowest class, the *ʿamaleh*, typically owned no herds or only small flocks of sheep or goats. The term *ʿamaleh* (singular, with the plural being *ʿamalehjat*) referred to nomadic individuals responsible for the tribe's logistical needs. Known as *ʿamal konandeh*, they dealt with practical matters within the tribe. Their primary duties included protecting the clan from external threats and organising raids, predominantly targeting the settled populations of nearby villages. The *tofangchi* and *chubaki* formed the cavalry, while the *toubreh-kesh* or *dast-pati* were responsible for collecting the spoils from these raids. Interestingly, it was this *ʿamaleh* class that first integrated into the burgeoning oil industry. They took up roles at the wellheads and served as guards, safeguarding the company's assets. This transition marked a significant shift in their traditional roles within the tribal structure.

On the brink of initiating operations at Masjed-Soleyman in November 1905, the British Consul-General of Isfahan reached an agreement with Sardar As ʿad, the primary representative for the Bakhtiari chiefs (comprising *ilkhans* and *ilbegs*). Under this agreement, the Bakhtiari chiefs were to receive an annual payment of 2,000 pounds sterling in exchange for providing regiments of guards from their tribes and for ensuring the security of the company's property against theft within Bakhtiari territories.[10]

Subsequently, a regiment of eighty Bakhtiari men was established to secure the drilling sites from three strategic positions. The guards, who were to be compensated by the Bakhtiari khan, were promised an annual wage ranging between 50 and 100 Tumans (the Iranian currency), in addition to provisions for their horses.[11] However, it became apparent that these guards, all drawn from the *ʿamaleh* stratum of the tribe, did not receive 'no penny in hard cash' payment and had to resort to 'other means' to sustain themselves.[12] It was not until March 1909 that a new agreement was reached with the Bakhtiari chiefs, wherein the guards began receiving their salaries directly from the head guards, with an allowance of 600 pounds sterling. This amount was deducted from the accumulated arrears, which by then had totalled 2,500 pounds sterling.[13]

When oil was finally struck at *Meydan-e Naftun* in Masjed-Soleyman, a relatively underpopulated area, the recruitment of a large workforce emerged as a formidable challenge for the Oil Company. Arnold Wilson noted the diverse origins of the labour force: 'Much labour is being imported from India, and much from other parts of Persia; some from the Gulf ports and some from Turkey (Ottoman Empire).'[14]

Initially, the Indian workers formed the backbone of the semi-skilled labour force. They, along with Iranian workers, were primarily engaged in road construction, transportation, and unskilled drilling tasks. However, specialised tasks such as masonry, carpentry, and painting were predominantly carried out by skilled workers from Isfahan. Over the subsequent year, the ethnic makeup of the workforce began to shift, increasingly favouring a predominantly Iranian composition. This change reflected the evolving dynamics of labour recruitment and employment in the burgeoning oil industry of the region.

By the close of 1909, concurrent with the expansion of drilling activities, the completion of the transport pipeline, and the commencement of construction of the Abadan Refinery, the nascent oil industry saw a rapid increase in its workforce. Within just a year, the number of Iranian workers employed in various segments of the industry had grown significantly. Specifically, the field operations had 457 Iranian workers, while the pipeline project and the Abadan Refinery employed 770 and 590 Iranian workers, respectively. This marked a substantial growth in employment, reflecting the industry's expanding scale and the increasing involvement of local labour in its operations.

The workforce composition in the initial phase of recruitment for the oil industry was influenced by the terms set forth in the 1901 oil concession agreement. Article 12 of this Agreement stipulated, 'the workmen employed in the service of the company shall be subject to His Imperial Majesty the Shah, except the technical staff, such as the managers, engineers, borers and foremen'.[15] This clause allowed APOC considerable flexibility in hiring skilled and semi-skilled labour from outside Iran, a policy they implemented by primarily recruiting from India.

For unskilled labour, APOC predominantly turned to the local population in the vicinity of the oil fields. The Bakhtiari peasants and pastoral nomads residing in these areas became a significant source of the workforce. However, there were exceptions to this local recruitment strategy. For instance, some correspondence from Sadiq al-Saltaneh, the Iranian government's oil commissar, to the Iranian Chargé d'Affaires in London, mentioned APOC's employment of some Ottoman coolies from the Basra region and lower Mesopotamia.[16]

In reaction to Sadiq al-Saltaneh's objections to this practice, Arnold Wilson, who was then the British consul in Mohammareh (Khorramshahr), emphasised the necessity to

> … obtain foreign labour for other than technical work. The Arabs of Mohammareh were, he said, agriculturalists who derived an ample sustenance from their lands with the expenditure of a relativity small amount of labour. As a rule, they are probably more prosperous and less hard working than any other in Persia. They are under no necessity to work hard and prefer not to do so.[17]

Sadiq al-Saltaneh's protest and Arnold Wilson's subsequent response primarily concerned the recruitment practices of the APOC in the Southwest, particularly along the Persian Gulf shoreline, which was predominantly inhabited by the Iranian Arab community. However, in the northern part of the province, closer to the oilfields of Masjed-Soleyman, the composition of the workforce was different. Here, the majority of the unskilled labour force was comprised of Iranian workers, drawn both from the Bakhtiari pastoralists and the local sedentary agricultural communities.

This distinction highlights the regional variations in labour recruitment strategies employed by APOC. In the south, near the Persian Gulf, there was a more diverse recruitment approach, including workers from various ethnic backgrounds, while in the north, closer to the oilfields, the company relied heavily on the local Bakhtiari populations, both nomadic and settled, for unskilled labour. This approach was likely influenced by the geographical proximity of these communities to the oilfields and their availability for unskilled labour roles.

Recruiting *ʿamaleh* from the Bakhtiari pastoralists presented a significant challenge for APOC due to the clash between the nomadic lifestyle of the pastoralists and the employment needs of the company. The Bakhtiari pastoralists engaged in biannual seasonal migrations, a practice integral to their way of life but incompatible with the consistent labour demands of APOC.

During the late spring, the Bakhtiaris would leave the hot desert plains in the South, moving with their flocks and herds towards the northern highlands and the snow-covered Zagros mountains. This region, known as their *yeylaq* or summer quarter, offered fresh pastures for their livestock. Conversely, in late autumn, as the grass withered in the cold of the elevated Zagros plateau, they would descend to the lowlands. Here, in their *qeshlaq* or winter quarter, the plains provided abundant food for their sheep and goats.

Additionally, the *qeshlaq* period was a crucial time for economic activities. It was during these months that the Bakhtiaris engaged in trading, selling surplus livestock, and purchasing necessities in market towns such as Dezful, Shushtar, Ramhormoz, and Isfahan. This seasonal rhythm of migration and trade was deeply embedded in their culture and posed a logistical dilemma for APOC, which required a stable and non-migratory workforce for its operations.

The Bakhtiari pastoralists adhered to a deeply ingrained routine of biannual migration, a practice central to their way of life. They generally resided in tents, particularly during their seasonal movements or while in their *yaylaq*, the summer quarters in the cooler highlands. With the arrival of *qeshlaq*, the winter period, they typically settled in more permanent structures made of sandstone or sun-baked mud, located in villages to the north of Masjed-Soleyman. These villages were conveniently situated near their winter pastures, which lay in proximity to the oilfields.

An eyewitness account sheds light on their modest way of living:

> The inhabitants of that part of Persia in which the work was to be done were, for the most part, pastoral nomads, consisting mainly of the famous Bakhtiari tribes. The Bakhtiari follow the grass … they live in tents or in rude shelters … their wants are few and the hardships of such a life is to them scarcely irksome. Of money they have little need and such exchange as they require is done largely by barter. It was from this nomadic human material that the company had to enlist the labour it required.[18]

The practice of seasonal migration among the Bakhtiari tribe was not a uniform obligation for all its members. In certain situations, such as during periods of drought or when the conditions in either the *yaylaq* (summer quarters) or *qeshlaq* (winter quarters) were unfavourable, members of the tribe, typically from the *ʿamalehjat* class, had the option to approach the khan to request permission to remain behind. Such requests were generally approved.

It was from these *ʿamalehjat*, those who stayed back from seasonal migrations, that the APOC initially recruited its early unskilled labour force. These workers were employed in various capacities, starting as assistants in basic rig-building and drilling operations, and extending to roles in road construction, transport, pipeline laying, and the construction of the Abadan oil refinery.

However, given that the Oil Company operated throughout the year, a significant challenge emerged: how to retain this recruited labour for extended periods, particularly for more than six months at a time, which exceeded the typical duration of a seasonal migration. This issue was particularly pertinent as the traditional lifestyle of the Bakhtiari involved returning to their migratory practices, necessitating a re-evaluation of employment strategies to ensure a stable and consistent workforce for the company's ongoing operations.

> … few men to come for six months and then return, the nomad to his flocks, the townsman to his city. This was partly due to the climate: a few, if any, nomad had ever remained in the sultry foothills during the summer months. They went with the flocks to the highlands in quest of grass at the first breath of the hot summer winds, and there remained till the autumn.[19]

In addition to the challenge of securing a stable supply of permanent employees, instilling a culture of labour discipline, orderliness, and punctuality presented significant difficulties for both the employer and the workers. Adapting to the structured environment and expectations of regular employment was a considerable shift for the tribesmen, who were accustomed to a more flexible, nomadic lifestyle. 'It was not sufficient to attract the tribesmen to service with the company by the prospect of regular pay and additional comfort that pay could bring; measures had to be taken to keep them when enrolled.'[20]

This necessitated a dual approach: on one hand, offering incentives that made the prospect of working for the company appealing, and on the other, creating a work environment and support system that helped these new employees adapt to the unfamiliar demands of their roles. This adaptation process was crucial for the long-term success of the company's operations, ensuring not only that workers were recruited but also that they remained productive and engaged over time.

Arrival of Indian Migrant Workers

The historical trajectory of the Persian Gulf, a region characterised by its intricate spatial networks, commercial connections, and exchange of ideas, underwent a significant transformation with the advent of British colonialism. By the mid nineteenth century, the British had effectively transformed the Persian Gulf into what was often referred to as a British Lake, signifying their dominant influence in the region.

During the initial phases of the expansion of British hegemony, Indian subjects of the British Empire arrived in Iran primarily as soldiers, emblematic of the military presence that underpinned British control. However, with the discovery of oil in southern Iran in 1908, there was a notable shift in the composition of the Indian presence in the region. Skilled and semi-skilled Indian workers began to arrive in increasing numbers, eventually surpassing the number of Indian soldiers. This transition marked a significant change in the nature of Indian involvement in Iran, shifting from a primarily military role to one centred on the burgeoning oil industry and the technical expertise it required.

The discovery of oil in Iran necessitated an immense construction effort to extract, process, and transport this resource to global markets. This endeavour involved building access roads, pipelines, an oil refinery, and shipping docks. However, a significant challenge that the oil industry faced was the scarcity of skilled and semi-skilled labour within Iran. The unique and large-scale nature of this project required a substantial recruitment campaign extending from Mesopotamia to South Asia.

While local tribal-pastoralists and villagers could provide the unskilled labour needed, the demand for skilled and semi-skilled workers led to recruitment efforts reaching as far as India and Burma. This recruitment of Indian workers by the oil industry continued for over four decades, illustrating the vital role they played in the development and sustainability of the industry.

These Indian migrant workers not only contributed significantly to the workforce but also formed distinct social and residential communities in the major oil towns of Iran. They represented a notable and influential segment of the labour force in the Iranian oil industry well into the mid Twentieth Century. Their presence and participation underscored the international dimension of labour and skill transfer that was essential to the success and growth of the oil industry in Iran.

The historiography of Indian migration beyond the borders of British colonial rule offers valuable insights into the broader narrative of labour history in India. Pioneering research on trans-oceanic Indian indentured labour migration, focusing on the movement of Indian workers to Africa and the Americas, has been extensively documented. Notable contributions in this field come from scholars such as Gillion, Lal, Emmer, Carter, and Mohapatra, whose classic works have significantly shaped our understanding of these migration patterns and experiences.[21]

Further, researchers such as Singha and Tetzlaff have delved into the study of Indian indentured labour in Mesopotamia and the northern regions of the Persian Gulf. Seccombe and Lawless, on the other hand, have focused on the migration of Indian labour to the Arabian Peninsula, situated at the southern end of the Persian Gulf.

Despite these extensive studies, the specific experiences of Indian workers who migrated to West Asia, the Persian Gulf, and Persia/Iran during the era of British colonial rule have been relatively underexplored.[22] This gap in historical research leaves a rich area for further investigation, offering the potential to deepen our understanding of the complexities and nuances of Indian labour migration and its impact on both the regions they migrated to and the broader context of labour movements during the colonial period.

In December 1907, a significant event marked the early interactions between Indian labour and the Iranian oil industry: twenty Indian cavalrymen arrived at the port of Mohammareh (Khorramshahr), a gateway to the Persian Gulf. Their primary objective, as defined by the British Consul in Mohammareh, was to provide security for the exploratory activities of the Burmah Oil Company, which was conducting oil exploration in the southern part of Khuzestan, a province in Iran.[23]

The discovery of oil at Masjed-Soleyman in Southwest Persia/Iran just five months later underscored the strategic importance of this region in the burgeoning oil industry. The deployment of Indian cavalrymen for protective duties in these early stages foreshadowed a long era of employment for Indian skilled and semi-skilled workers, as well as clerical staff, in the Iranian oil industry.

This period of Indian employment in the Iranian oil sector extended for several decades, coming to an end in 1951. This cessation coincided with the nationalisation of the oil industry in Iran, a pivotal event that resulted in significant changes in the industry's structure and management. Following nationalisation, the Anglo-Iranian Oil Company (AIOC)[24] underwent a transformation, becoming part of an international Consortium. This shift marked the end of an era of Indian labour in the Iranian oil industry, reflecting the broader geopolitical and economic changes that were reshaping the region during the mid-twentieth century.

The initial group of Indian migrant workers who became part of the Iranian oil industry were primarily recruited in two ways. Some were hired through intermediary agencies based in India, while others were directly transferred from the Yangon Refinery. This transfer was facilitated through the coordination of the Burmah Oil Company, which held a significant stake in the D'Arcy concession.[25]

The Burmah Oil Company's involvement in both the Yangon Refinery and the Iranian oil industry created a unique channel for the movement of skilled labour. The company's established presence and operations in these regions allowed for a relatively seamless transfer of workers from one area of operation to another. This approach was particularly effective in ensuring that the Iranian oil industry had access to a pool of experienced and skilled workers right from its inception, significantly contributing to its early development and success. The recruitment through intermediary agencies in India further diversified the skills and expertise available in the Iranian oil industry, making it a hub of multinational labour and talent in its early years.

In its formative years, the primary focus of the Oil Company was on establishing the essential infrastructure necessary for the supply of oil to the market. Consequently, setting up training facilities for local labour was not a priority during this phase. To address the pressing need for skilled and semi-skilled labour, APOC's recruitment and employment strategy heavily relied on bringing in a large number of migrant workers. The majority of these workers were from India, and they were employed in a variety of roles, ranging from clerical positions to skilled and semi-skilled manual professions.[26]

As I will elaborate in this book, this initial approach to labour recruitment and employment underwent significant changes as the industry expanded. The employment of labour in the oil industry became increasingly influenced by political dynamics. This included the tripartite interactions among APOC, the Government of India, and the Iranian government, which played a crucial role at the top echelons of decision-making. Equally impactful were the efforts from the grassroots level, where labour activism began to emerge, focusing on improving conditions for workers.

This evolution in labour policy within the oil industry reflects the complex interplay between economic needs, political agendas, and social movements. It underscores how the industry's growth, and its increasing prominence not only altered its operational strategies but also reshaped its interactions with various stakeholders, both within and outside Iran.

Shaw Wallace & Co. Ltd, a British Indian trading company, played a pivotal role as the intermediary agent in recruiting labour for Iran, with Strick, Scott & Co. serving as its representative in the region. The establishment of the APOC significantly increased the workload of Shaw Wallace's Mumbai office. This office was responsible for coordinating a wide range of tasks, including shipping various types of equipment to the Persian Gulf, where Mohammareh (Khorramshahr) served as the central base office. Additionally, Shaw Wallace was involved in the recruitment of clerical staff as well as household domestics and servants for office operations.[27]

Shaw Wallace maintained a close working relationship with both the Burmah Oil Company and APOC. This collaboration in labour recruitment continued until 1926, after which APOC took over the recruitment process directly through its office in Bombay. Shaw Wallace's role as the sole agent for these oil companies in India encompassed a variety of services, extending beyond just labour recruitment.

An interesting figure in this context is Charles Greenway, who initially worked in the oil department of Shaw Wallace as an agent for the Burmah Oil Company in India. His career path led him to join the Iranian oil industry in 1910 as managing director, and he later served as the chairman of APOC from 1914 to 1927.[28] Greenway's movement between these entities highlights the interconnectedness of British commercial interests in the Indian and Iranian oil sectors during this period. His career trajectory is indicative of the close ties and shared personnel among companies involved in the burgeoning oil industry across these regions.

The recruitment of migrant workers from Burma to the Iranian oil industry predominantly involved Indians who were employed by the Burmah Oil Company. Their extensive experience in the Burma oilfields and the Yangon Refinery rendered them a highly valuable labour source. Shaw Wallace & Co. facilitated their transfer to Persia using a free-contract system, arranging for their passage from Burma.

Figure 1.1 Local labourers, supervised by an Indian foreman (on the left side of the image), constructing the Gach-Qaraguli (Gachsaran) road, 1909

A significant portion of these workers were Chittagonian Sunni Muslims who had initially entered the Burmese oil industry in the 1890s.[29] In the administrative records of the APOC and the British colonial archives, there was no specific categorisation based on the social, territorial, ethnic, or religious backgrounds of Indian migrant workers, a practice that was also applied to Iranian workers. As a result, all migrant workers from India in the Persian oil industry were generically classified as 'Indians'.

However, by examining and correlating data from various sources – including national archives of India, Iran, and Britain, APOC, and British Petroleum Company archives, and records from the Indian migrant worker community in Iran – it is possible to identify some distinct groups within this broad classification. For instance, workers originating from Burma were specifically referred to as 'Ranguny' (from Yangon), distinguishing them from other Indian migrants.

In the city of Abadan, the presence of a distinct Ranguny community is evidenced by the existence of their own mosque, separate from those used by other Indian Sunni and Shiite Muslims. Known as the 'Ranguny Mosque', this institution reflects the significant Burmese influence within the local population. Such nuances in the composition of the migrant worker community highlight the diverse and complex nature of labour migration in the context of the Persian oil industry.

Shaw Wallace's recruitment efforts for the Iranian oil industry extended beyond sourcing Indian migrant workers from Burma. They also actively recruited both skilled and semi-skilled workers from urban centres like Mumbai and Karachi, utilising subsidiary offices or subcontractors. Firms such as I.A. Ashton & Sons and Bullock Brothers specialised in hiring various categories of workers, including fitters, oil and diesel engine drivers, marine signalmen, marine ratters, boilermakers, and pipe fitters.[30]

To attract potential candidates, recruiters frequently advertised in Mumbai newspapers, particularly for clerical positions. Additionally, intermediaries like I.A. Ashton employed other methods, such as posting notices, posters, and wallpapers in regions like the Punjab.[31]

Candidates interested in these positions were required to undergo a qualification examination as part of the recruitment process. For those recruited in Punjab, interviews were conducted in Lahore, while Mumbai recruits were interviewed at Mazagaon Dock in Mumbai. Upon successful selection, these candidates would join the ranks of employees departing for Iran.

The intermediary companies involved in this process typically charged each new recruit a fee amounting to 25 per cent of their first month's pay. Workers who had previously been employed by the Oil Company in Iran and returned to India within two years were subject to an admission fee of ten rupees.[32]

This recruitment model was also applied to those hired for household and domestic services, such as butlers, cooks, domestic servants, hospital ward orderlies, and sweepers. These positions were primarily filled through recruitment by Osborn & Co., a firm affiliated with the Parsee enterprise based in Mumbai.[33] Such a comprehensive and structured approach to recruitment played a crucial role in assembling a diverse and skilled workforce for the burgeoning Persian oil industry.

The establishment of the Abadan Refinery in 1909 marked a significant milestone in the Iranian oil industry, leading to a steady increase in the number of Indian migrant workers. By 1913, this workforce comprised approximately 1,000 clerical and manual employees. However, the onset of the First World War in 1914 brought about two major developments that significantly impacted the recruitment of labour from India for the oil industry.

Firstly, the British Admiralty made a strategic decision to convert its marine steam engines – encompassing industrial, army, and naval units – from coal to oil fuels. This transition, which had begun in 1912, rapidly elevated oil to a position of critical economic importance for British interests globally. As a result, the oil industry experienced a substantial boom within a few years.[34]

Secondly, in a move that further underscored the strategic value of oil, the British government increased its shareholding in the APOC to 51 per cent, thus becoming the company's majority owner.[35] This change in ownership was accompanied by the signing of a preferential contract in 1914. Under this agreement, the British Admiralty was entitled to purchase Iranian oil from APOC at a fixed price for the next thirty years, exclusively for use by the Royal Navy.[36]

These two developments transformed oil into a strategic military commodity within the British Empire, highlighting its critical role not only in economic terms but also in terms of national security and military operations. The increasing importance of oil and the British government's direct involvement in APOC substantially influenced the dynamics of labour recruitment and the overall expansion of the oil industry.

As demonstrated in Table 1.1, the increasing number of Indian migrant workers in the Iranian oil industry over the years clearly indicates a growing

Table 1.1 *Anglo-Persian Oil Company staff and labour in Iran, 1910*

Sections	Iranians	Europeans	Indians	Other	Total
Field	457	17	66	1	541
Ahvaz	67	3	1	12	83
Abadan	590	8	218	70	886
Pipeline	770	26	49	188	950
Total	1,884	54	334	105	2,460

Source: British Petroleum (BP) Archive, University of Warwick, Britain ARC 141294, January 1938. Laurence Lockhart, Unpublished. Record of the Anglo-Iranian Oil Company, Volume I: 1901–1918.

reliance on and the importance of this labour force. In 1910, there were 157 Indian migrant workers, constituting approximately 9 per cent of the total workforce, which then stood at 1,706. This proportion and absolute number saw a considerable rise over the following years, reaching a peak in 1925. By that time, the number of Indian workers had escalated to 4,890, making up about 16 per cent of the total workforce, which had expanded to 28,905.

Regulatory Landscape for Creating Oil Workers

As the Iranian oil industry developed, the *ʿamaleh* recruits began to adapt to the new industrial lifestyle, leading to the emergence of a distinct workforce segment known as the *sarkar*, derived from the term *sar-kargar* (headworkers). The role of the *sarkars* was notably different from that of the foremen, a position initially reserved exclusively for European skilled workers in the early operations of the Oil Company.

One of the key responsibilities of the *sarkar* was to recruit labour for the company. In the initial stages of oil excavation, it was the Bakhtiari khan who primarily negotiated with the Oil Company to provide labour. However, this dynamic evolved with the introduction of *sarkars*, who not only supervised the performance of newly recruited labour but also took an active role in the recruitment process. They were incentivised with bonuses for each new recruit they successfully hired.

In the formative years of the oil industry in Iran, the role of the *sarkar* as an intermediary was twofold. They were responsible for conscripting men for the burgeoning workforce and ensuring their commitment and loyalty to their new roles. Effectively, the *sarkar* functioned both as a recruiter and a foreman, playing a crucial role in the expansion and stabilisation of the industry's workforce. This shift highlights the evolving labour dynamics within the industry, as it transitioned from traditional tribal labour arrangements to more structured industrial employment practices.

The recruitment practices involving the Bakhtiari khan and the *sarkar* were pivotal until a significant shift occurred with the establishment of the Abadan Refinery.[37] As the APOC expanded its operations, particularly with the building of the Abadan Refinery, there was a strategic decision to consolidate and extend its activities.

The establishment of the Abadan Refinery not only represented a significant advancement in APOC's technical and industrial capabilities but also signalled a shift in the nature of labour relations and employment practices within the company. As APOC grew, the company increasingly moved towards more direct and structured methods of labour recruitment and management, aligning with the broader industrial and organisational needs of its expanding operations. Such an expansive range of activities

> ... was not confined to the oil business but included authorisation to act as merchants, bankers, traders; commission, commercial and general agents; ship-owners, carriers, and dealers in all kinds of commodities. The right was given to establish, acquire and expand branches, trading stations, factories, stores, depots, docks, and ships, and to takeover or enter into partnership with any business or persons running businesses of a similar nature.[38]

The establishment of a new Labour Office at the Abadan Refinery represented a strategic shift in the approach to workforce management by the APOC. One of the primary objectives of this office was to transition from seasonal employment to more stable, permanent job positions. This change was significant in creating a consistent and reliable workforce, essential for the sustained operations of the expanding industry.

To achieve this goal, the Labour Office employed a novel strategy that leveraged the concept of ancestral bonding in organised, networked migration. By encouraging the employment of workers' descendants, the office initiated in 'an elementary apprenticeship in use of lathes and simple machine tools'.[39]

Over time, this employment policy profoundly reshaped social relations among oil workers. By encouraging successive generations to work in the oil industry, it cultivated a sense of continuity and loyalty to the industry. This policy's impact extended beyond the confines of the workplace, influencing the broader public space of the Iranian oil towns. It contributed to the development of a new culture, one that was closely intertwined with the oil industry and its operations.

The emphasis on training and employing workers' descendants also facilitated the development of a skilled local workforce, reducing reliance on migrant labour and contributing to the socio-economic development of the region. This strategy reflected a more holistic approach to labour management, considering not only the immediate operational needs of the refinery but also the long-term sustainability of the workforce and the community's welfare.

With the expansion of drilling operations and the construction of access roads and pipelines to bring the oil to the Persian Gulf, 'gradually a community began to settle on the spot and [the] problem[s] of health and housing came to the fore; carpenters from Isfahan and ironworkers from Dezful and Shushtar, finding employment regular, commenced to settle'.[40]

The Labour Office launched its activities in major cities in the southern part of Iran, to recruit a workforce – both from tribal Bakhtiari pastoralists and village-based cultivators, as well as from a non-Bakhtiari workforce, drawn from other cities: 'The great majority of the elaborate machinery both at Abadan and at Masjed-Soleyman and Ahvaz [was] worked by these men, as well as by tribesmen, for truth to tell, the nomad has shown a greater willingness and aptitude to take to machinery than has the townsman.'[41]

The influx of people to Masjed-Soleyman, drawn by employment opportunities in the oil industry or to provide services to its workers, significantly contributed to the expansion and development of this nascent city. From a modest oilfield employing 523 individuals in 1910,[42] Masjed-Soleyman evolved into a bustling company town with a population of around 17,000 by 1920.[43] This growth reflected the transformative impact of the oil industry on the region's demographic and urban landscape.

The Oil Company provided varied housing accommodations for its diverse workforce. European staff were housed in brick bungalows, reflecting a higher standard of living and comfort. Indian employees, on the other hand, were accommodated in large communal barracks, which, while not as comfortable as the bungalows, still offered a form of organised housing.

Contrastingly, the Iranian recruits initially faced less favourable living conditions. They were left to reside in makeshift shelters constructed from sticks or bamboo, tied loosely together, with roofs made of palm leaves. These rudimentary structures highlighted the disparities in living conditions among the different groups of employees within the company.

It was only during the interwar period that APOC initiated its first housing project for Iranian workers.[44] This move towards providing better living conditions for the Iranian employees indicated a gradual recognition of the need to improve the welfare of all workers, regardless of their national or ethnic backgrounds. The development of housing for Iranian workers marked a significant step in the company's efforts to address the disparities in living standards and to foster a more inclusive and equitable environment for its diverse workforce.

APOC employed several strategies to attract and retain workers in Masjed-Soleyman, recognising that monetary compensation alone was not sufficient to ensure the loyalty and long-term service of its employees. One key initiative was the provision of free basic medical care for labourers and their families. This benefit was particularly significant, as it offered a form of security and well-being that went beyond mere wages, addressing a crucial aspect of the workers' lives.

In addition to healthcare, APOC also focused on improving the overall living experience for its workforce. The establishment of a local market or bazaar within the vicinity of the work areas was another strategic move. This market provided the workers with a place to spend their earnings on a variety of goods such as food, clothing, utensils, tobacco, and ornaments. The availability of these items for purchase played an important role in making the job more attractive.

> It has been indicated that the prospect of regular pay, in the first instance, attracted the nomadic tribesmen to service with the Company. The wages, of themselves, could do little, however, to keep the men in service unless opportunities were provided of purchasing with the wages those commodities and comforts not obtainable in nomadic life. It was not enough to give money; ways of spending the money had also to be provided.[45]

The establishment of the first market in Masjed-Soleyman was a significant development for the burgeoning oil community. Migrants from Shushtar, a nearby city, played a pivotal role as the leading vendors in this bazaar. Their entrepreneurial spirit and initiative in setting up stalls and shops provided essential services and goods to the oilfield workers and their families. Additionally, these Shushtar migrants were among the first to establish a permanent community near the oilfields, forming a neighbourhood known as *Kalgeh* on the outskirts of the first oil well.[46]

As the oil industry in Masjed-Soleyman continued to grow, attracting more labourers, new districts emerged. Areas like *Sarkureh* and *Malkarim* were developed by the newly recruited workers, with shelters typically roofed with palm leaves. These districts were initially organised along Bakhtiari tribal lines, reflecting the social and cultural associations of the workers.[47]

However, as the oil industry expanded and drew in migrants from other parts of the country, the initial tribal-based divisions in these settlements began to blur. This influx of new workers from diverse backgrounds led to the formation of a more heterogeneous community with various identities and cultures. The evolving demographic composition of Masjed-Soleyman reflected the transformative impact of the oil industry, not only in terms of economic development but also in fostering a melting pot of different cultures and social backgrounds. This demographic shift contributed to the creation of a unique cultural landscape in the oil town, shaping its social fabric and community dynamics.

Governing the Workforce

In the foundational years of Iran's oil industry, recruiters played a dual role: they not only hired new workers but also ensured their ongoing productivity. This period saw the establishment of specific labour discipline practices to manage and maintain an effective workforce.

To address the issue of workers abruptly leaving their jobs after just a few days,[48] the Oil Company implemented specific regulations regarding wage payments. Initially, workers were paid daily, and in Indian rupees instead of Iranian Rials. To encourage longer-term commitment, the company shifted to a fortnightly payment schedule.

This change in the payment method was the company's initial strategy to promote job continuity. However, this new payment rule had potential long-term implications. It risked drawing workers into indebtedness to local bazaar moneylenders. Such indebtedness, while unintended, could inadvertently bind workers to their jobs longer as they worked to pay off debts, thereby securing a more stable workforce for the company.

In the early years of the APOC, there were instances where less favourable methods were used to enforce labour discipline, despite the absence of direct references to fines or physical punishments in the company's official work regulations charter. Evidence of such practices can be found in the company's archives.

A confidential report dated 24 July 1911, details an incident involving a British foreman named Melvie, who physically assaulted an Iranian worker for allegedly not working 'properly'. This incident was notable not just for the act itself but for the worker's reaction, which was unexpected at the time. The worker's response was surprising to the management, as it was uncommon for a local worker to confront a European in such a manner. The report also reflects an acknowledgment of the workers' usual submissiveness to fines and even physical discipline, with complaints being rare.[49]

Following this incident, another case surfaced involving a European engineer and manager, Mr. Ritchie. He issued a warning stating that 'a fine of 50 qerans (Iran's currency. In 1932 the rial replaced qeran) would be imposed on any offender, and which would be doubled, for any subsequent offense in the matter of assault'.[50]

These incidents highlight some of the challenges and complexities of labour management in the early the Twentieth Century, particularly in a context where cultural and power dynamics between European managers and local workers were starkly contrasting. Such practices, while indicative of the times, would later lead to increased awareness and eventual reforms in labour relations and workers' rights.

Figure 1.2 Payday, Masjed-Soleyman, 1910

In the initial phase of the Oil Company's operations, labour discipline was enforced through long working days and modern time measurement. The early narratives from the Iranian workforce indicate a lack of a standardised workday. Iranian workers, along with their Indian and Ottoman counterparts (often referred to as 'Turks'), were expected to work seven days a week, from sunrise to sunset. This demanding schedule was reflective of the intensive labour demands during the early development of the oil industry.

However, as the industry evolved and particularly on the eve of the First World War, a new workday regime was introduced. The revised schedule entailed a six-day workweek, with the length of the workday varying between nine to twelve hours depending on the season. During winter, work hours were set from six in the morning to six in the evening, while in the summer, the workday would start at six in the morning and conclude at three in the afternoon.

Initially, the Oil Company designated Sunday as the weekly day off, diverging from the local custom of observing Friday as a day of rest. This decision likely reflected the influence of European managerial practices. However, in subsequent years, the company adjusted its policy to better align with local cultural norms. The day off was changed to start at noon on Thursday, extending through Friday. This shift not only acknowledged the cultural and religious practices of the local workforce but also represented a broader adaptation of the company to its operational context in Iran.

The clock and measured time brought about by the oil industry in Iran significantly impacted the national culture, particularly in terms of time consciousness and work discipline. In a society traditionally divided into an upper class of literati and a predominantly peasant population, the concept of time was generally perceived in terms of days and months, rather than minutes or hours. The clock, as a tool for measuring and structuring time, had not yet become a central aspect of daily life for the majority.[51]

Within the oil industry, to accommodate the demands of production, the workday was divided into two shifts, each consisting of a twelve-hour period.[52] However, given the relative unfamiliarity with watches and clocks among the workers, a different method was needed to instil a sense of time discipline in the workplace.

The solution was the use of a horn or claxon, typically mounted atop towers within the oilfield. This horn, known in the industry as the *feydus* (derived from 'fagottist', meaning bassoon player), played a crucial role in regulating the workday. It was sounded twice daily, at six o'clock in the morning to signal the start of the workday, and again at six o'clock in the evening to mark its end. On Thursdays, when the workday was shorter, the horn was sounded at noon. This practice of using audible signals to mark the start and end of work shifts was an innovative way to introduce time discipline to a workforce largely unaccustomed to strict timekeeping. It represented a practical adaptation of the Oil Company to the local cultural context, ensuring the smooth functioning of operations while respecting the existing temporal norms of the society.

In 1929, the workers of the Abadan Refinery launched a strike to improve their working conditions and pay. Among the demands of some nine thousand striking workers – out of an oilfield workforce numbering fifteen thousand – was the reduction of the working day from ten hours to seven hours in the summer, and eight hours in the winter.[53] Since the police crushed the strike, this call for a shorter working day had no effect.[54]

From ʿ*Amaleh* to *Kargar*: Representation and Recognition

The transition of the ʿ*amaleh* from their traditional pastoral or village-based livelihoods to roles within the burgeoning oil industry represents a multifaceted metamorphosis, encompassing not only a shift in labour dynamics but also a potential reconfiguration of their social status. This process warrants a nuanced interpretation: it signifies a progression from a primarily agrarian existence to an industrial labour role, effectively transcending their erstwhile occupational identity. Concurrently, this shift raises questions about the extent to which this new social status, as industrial workers or *kargar*, was a tangible elevation in their societal standing or merely an aspirational construct. The real versus perceived change in status invites an examination of the dichotomy between the material realities of their new working and living conditions and the imagined betterment of their societal position. This juxtaposition of the ʿ*amaleh*'s anticipated integration into a modernised, industrial milieu against the backdrop of their actual experiences in this new realm underscores the complex interplay between structural economic transformation and individual social mobility.

In the realm of labour historiography, both in global Northern and Southern societies, there is a prevalent interpretation of working-class formation and representation as being intrinsically linked to structural economic changes and the advent of capitalist development. Iran's experience aligns with this perspective. Within Iranian labour historiography, a predominant narrative, often espoused by teleological Marxists, postulates that the emergence and proliferation of capitalist relationships in Western Europe, as evidenced by the massive growth of heavy industries and widespread commodity production, spurred European powers to broaden their influence. This expansion was driven not only by the quest to open new markets but also by the urgent need to secure raw materials for their burgeoning industries.

This shift heralded a new global division of labour. From the mid-nineteenth century, Iran became enmeshed in this global capitalist web. By the century's close, coinciding with the introduction and integration of capitalist modes of development into Iran and its entry into the world markets, a distinct working class began to crystallise within the country. However, the maturation and consolidation of a collective working-class consciousness in Iran were primarily achieved through the unionist and political movements organised by Iranian workers in the early the Twentieth Century. By this period, the establishment of the Iranian working class was, in essence, a fait accompli.

This interpretation underscores the significant impact of global economic shifts and the pervasive spread of capitalism on the formation of a working class in various societies, with Iran serving as a case study in how these larger forces catalysed profound social and labour transformations within its borders.[55]

The traditional structuralist and objectivist approach to defining the worker and working class, as articulated by Zachary Lockman, especially when coupled with a restrictive view of what constitutes genuine activism, can be contested for its limitations. In his examination of the working-class formation in Egypt, Lockman identifies a similar paradigm prevalent in Egyptian labour historiography, a pattern that he also acknowledges in his earlier work. He now posits that this perspective warrants critical reassessment.

Lockman's critique suggests that such an approach might oversimplify the complexities of working-class formation by focusing predominantly on macroeconomic structures and capitalist dynamics, potentially overlooking the nuanced, lived experiences of workers and the diverse forms of their activism. This perspective can inadvertently marginalise the variegated and often grassroots nature of labour activism, which may not always align with conventional or mainstream understandings of worker movements.

By advocating for a re-evaluation of this paradigm, Lockman underscores the need for a more inclusive and multifaceted understanding of labour history. This approach should integrate a broader spectrum of worker experiences and recognised wider range of activist expressions as legitimate and integral to the understanding of working-class formation and dynamics. Such a 'conventional structuralist, objectivist definition of the worker and working class', as Zachary Lockman puts it, combined with a 'narrow sense of what should be classified as authentic activism', can be challenged as inadequate.[56]

In his study of the formation of the working class in Egypt, Lockman traces out the same kind of paradigm in Egyptian labour historiography, including in his own previous work, which he now believes should be criticised:

> Working-class formation (in fact, all class formation) is as much a discursive as a material process. In Egypt, as elsewhere, the working class as an entity and 'worker' as a form of subjectivity can be usefully conceptualised as product, as effect, not only of certain material practices (for example, wage employment in large enterprises as the result of capitalist development), but also of a particular discourse that, by providing categories of worker and class identity, gives people a (never unambiguous) language with which to organised their experience, to make one of several different and possibly conflicting kinds of sense of the world and their own places and possibilities within it. These categories are moreover, the (always provincial) outcome of conflicts in which, by promoting certain

> representations of self, society, and the world, various forces seek to organise some group around some pole of identity in order to realise some particular sociopolitical project.[57]

In examining the formation of the working class within the Iranian oil industry, which encompasses both discursive and material dimensions, the present study aligns with Zachary Lockman's critical stance on the traditional structuralist and objectivist definitions of workers and the working class. My approach goes beyond merely challenging the notion that the emergence of a working class is a straightforward consequence of structural economic changes and capitalist development. Instead, it delves into a more profound exploration of the self-perception and collective social identity that emerged among working people in Iran following their integration into a new labour discipline.

My inquiry seeks to understand whether these workers, through their experiences and adaptations to the industrial work environment, came to see themselves as a distinct group, bound together by more than just their shared labour conditions. The study ventures into the intricate dynamics of group solidarity within the working class, probing whether there has been the emergence of an iconic vision of unity that transcends mere class consciousness. This exploration seeks to unravel the depths of collective awareness that encompass not just shared economic interests or occupational affiliations, but a broader, more complex tapestry of communal experiences and identities.[58]

In this context, 'iconic vision of group solidarity' refers to a potent, unifying image or concept that resonates deeply with the group, symbolising their shared experiences, struggles, aspirations, and values. It's about understanding how these workers, bound by common circumstances, might also share a collective psyche that reflects their social, cultural, and political realities.

This approach to studying the working class shifts the focus from traditional economic and structural analyses to a more holistic understanding of what binds individuals together in solidarity. It acknowledges that while economic conditions and labour roles are crucial in shaping class consciousness, there are other significant elements – such as shared cultural practices, social struggles, communal narratives, and political aspirations – that contribute to the formation of a collective identity.

This perspective considers the cultural contestations and everyday life experiences that contribute to forging a collective identity. It acknowledges that workers' self-perception and group cohesion might be influenced by a myriad of factors, including shared struggles, common aspirations, and the cultural milieu within which they operate.

Borrowing Raymond Williams' phraseology, we are dealing with the fashioning of a kind of practical consciousness, of what is 'actually being lived', as distinct from that which is 'thought to be lived'.[59] Along with an examination of such self-perceptions of belonging to a class, it is, of course, just as important to understand how the social representation of working people was recognised, defined, and marked out by their employer, the Oil Company, and by society at large.

Such recognition and representation of a new social existence created a new language, a new vocabulary. Moreover, the newly adapted and adopted vocabularies used by the worker and the employer often differed from each other. In my study, the petitions signed by protesting workers are worth examining for evidence of the new vocabulary of the workers.[60] As regards the vocabulary of the employer, correspondence between the different departments of the Iranian government and with APOC reveals much about how the working people in the oil industry were actually regarded by both the Oil Company and the Iranian government.

In an early correspondence between the oil commissioner of the Iranian government and the Iranian Chargé d'Affaires in London concerning labour recruitment in the oil industry, the terminology used to describe unskilled labour, including Ottoman subjects, encompassed both the terms *ʿamaleh* and 'coolie'. Notably, in this same document, the term *kargar* was reserved specifically for the non-Asian workforce, which included British, Australian, Portuguese, and some Ottoman subjects.[61]

Over the ensuing years, the nomenclature used by both the employer and government agencies to refer to the unskilled workforce within the oil industry predominantly remained *ʿamaleh*, with occasional references to *coolie* or *tandil*.[62] This linguistic practice persisted until the late 1920s, reflecting the distinct categorisations and perceptions of the workforce based on skill level and ethnic or national background. Such terminology not only illustrates the hierarchical structure of the workforce but also sheds light on the broader sociopolitical context in which these labour categories were embedded.

In the nascent stages of the oil industry, the self-perception of the working people was primarily that of *raʿiyat* (subject) or *bandeh-e haqir va jan-nesar-e homayuni* (the slightest and most obedient servant of his majesty, the King), rather than identifying themselves through labour-specific terms like *ʿamaleh* or *kargar*. This perspective is evident in the absence of self-referential use of *ʿamaleh* or kargar in any petitions from the workers prior to the First World War. During this period, it was predominantly the employer and the government that utilised the term *ʿamaleh* to categorised certain segments within the unskilled workforce.

However, a noticeable shift occurs in the post-First World War era. Some petitions from this period begin to adopt the term kargar to describe the workforce. An illustrative example of this change in self-identification is found in a 1924 petition to the national Parliament. In this document, the workforce, while detailing their 'extremely miserable and beyond any human endurance' working and living conditions in Abadan, refers to themselves using the following terms:

> Abadan is a city where the majority of its residents are poor and wretched. Facing unemployment in their hometown, these residents accepted the offer of the Oil Company to work in the very harsh and hot climate of Khuzestan, with all infections around for the period of nine months a year, receiving a salary of thirty rupees per month. However, every month, the company deducts some amount from their salaries. According to the company, paying the full salary stops the workers (*kargaran*) from staying at work during summer when the weather is hot. Therefore, the company needs to stay in debt to all workers.[63]

In reaction to the 1924 petition, wherein the workforce articulated their dire working and living conditions in Abadan, the head of the national Parliament took a significant step. He urged the Ministry of Foreign Affairs to employ every available measure to ensure that the workers of APOC received the fullest support from the Iranian government.[64]

By the conclusion of the First World War, approximately a decade after the initial discovery of oil in Khuzestan, the Iranian oil industry had undergone significant transformations. With extensive oil extraction underway and an oil refinery established, the industry had cultivated its own dedicated workforce, which had largely transitioned from seasonal to permanent employment. This shift had profound implications for the identity and consciousness of the workers.

The ancestral, religious, tribal, and regional identities of these workers persisted, yet their shared working and living conditions in the oil industry began to meld new class and territorial identities. This evolution was evident in the changing language used by the employees, the employer, and the state. The term *kargar* (worker) emerged as a new linguistic icon, supplanting the traditional tribal status denoted by *ʿamaleh*. Moreover, a new territorial distinction became apparent, with terms like *Masjed-Soleymani* or *Abadani* (denoting residents of Masjed-Soleyman or Abadan) starting to overshadow tribal or regional affiliations such as *Bakhtiari* or *Shushtari*.

These linguistic shifts reflected a broader change in the self-perception and societal categorisation of these individuals. The workers in the Iranian oil industry were not only forging a new class identity but were also redefining their connection to place and community, moving beyond traditional tribal and regional associations. This transition marked the gradual emergence of a distinct working class within the Iranian oil industry, a class increasingly defined by its role in the industrial landscape rather than by tribal or regional origins.

2

Oil and Labour in the First World War

The cessation of the First World War marked the end of what has been somewhat paradoxically termed the 'long peace of the nineteenth century'. This conflict heralded the collapse of an international order predominantly underpinned by high finance and represented the zenith of militarisation driven by industrial progress, set against a backdrop of escalating capitalist rivalry and technological innovation. On the cusp of the war, a pivotal global transition occurred with the shift in industry, military, and naval resources from coal to oil, engendering an unprecedented surge in the demand for petroleum products. The successful extraction and processing of substantial and economically viable petroleum reserves constituted a fundamental prerequisite for this worldwide transformation. Central to this development was the Iranian oil industry, managed by the Anglo-Persian Oil Company (APOC), with the British government as its principal shareholder since 1911. Iranian oil thus emerged as a resource of critical economic and strategic military value, profoundly influencing British global interests.

During the war, the oil industry witnessed an exponential escalation in the demand for petroleum products. This surge necessitated the expansion of the industry and prioritised the allocation and maintenance of the workforce responsible for producing petroleum in its various forms, particularly within the Iranian oil sector. However, the APOC faced numerous significant challenges during this period.

As the war progressed, Iran's strategic importance, underscored by its vast oil reserves and the proximity of its oil fields and refinery to the Mesopotamian warfront, elevated it to a critical area of interest for the warring factions. Consequently, Iran transitioned from being just one of the many battlegrounds to a central hub of military operations, and in many respects, an enduring combat zone. This shift had profound implications for the operations and security of the Iranian oil industry during the war.

The proximity of the Iranian oil fields to the warfront resulted in severe repercussions for the oil industry. As the industry sought to increase production, a significant segment of the workforce, particularly skilled labourers, became apprehensive about working in such close proximity to the conflict. This led to a considerable number of these workers ceasing their employment in the oil industry. Concurrently, there was a notable scarcity of local unskilled labour, further complicating the situation for the industry.

In response to this labour shortage, the APOC implemented a wartime labour policy focused on the recruitment of migrant labour, primarily from India. This policy shift led to a growing dependence of the Oil Company on migrant labour, extending beyond local, regional, and national boundaries. The strategy involved reinterpreting and negotiating the terms of the Indian Migration Act to facilitate the influx of workers during the war. Additionally, the Oil Company enforced mandatory related labour practices under the King's Regulations, which effectively restricted labourers from leaving the company's employment. These operational challenges were further compounded by external factors such as periods of famine and several epidemics, which adversely impacted the daily lives of labourers in the oil industry.

The indispensable involvement of the working class, inclusive of those employed in the oil industry, during the First World War played a pivotal role in facilitating the rise of Fordism, a novel politico-economic system. Post-war, this system was predominantly defined by its focus on mass industrial production and consumption, supported by systematic labour management and an increase in labour activism. While the war engaged the general population in various roles – as soldiers, workers, and essentially as the human cost of the conflict – and imposed upon them the burden of this devastation, it also, quite paradoxically, led to an expansion of the public sphere. This expansion, albeit unintended, laid the groundwork for enhanced political involvement by the working class and the general populace, marking a significant shift in the landscape of political participation and representation in the aftermath of the war.

Ironically, the extensive nature of the war, which initially seemed to subjugate these classes, ultimately facilitated an unplanned enlargement of social and political spaces. This expansion provided the working classes with new avenues to assert their presence in the political arena more assertively. They did so through a combination of strategies including participating in electoral politics, engaging in trade unionism, and undertaking radical actions. These developments marked a significant shift in the dynamics of political participation and representation in the post-war period.

This chapter provides a comprehensive analysis the Oil Company's evolving labour policy, contextualised within the broader framework of significant global geopolitical transformations during the First World War. Additionally, this exploration will encompass an examination of the living and working conditions of oil workers during the wartime. We will also scrutinise the methods of negotiation and forms of resistance employed by these workers in the years immediately preceding the armistice, offering a comprehensive understanding of their experiences and strategies during this tumultuous period.

A War That Changed the World

In the aftermath of the First World War, characterised by its catastrophic practices, the world was fundamentally transformed. The war's impact was felt across various regions including Eastern and Western Asia, Europe, and North Africa, each emerging profoundly altered from the conflict. In Britain, a major imperial power with significant presence in Asia, the transformations were the result of multiple intertwined factors: firstly, the war itself, marking the first occurrence of total warfare that engaged entire populations and utilised new, technically advanced means of destruction; secondly, the escalating crisis of capitalism, particularly post-1890s, which heralded a shift to a new regime of economic accumulation; and thirdly, the more gradual yet profound effects of what has been termed as the second industrial revolution. This convergence of factors reshaped Britain and the world in profound and lasting ways.

The First World War represented the apex of warfare's industrialisation, a process driven by increasing capitalist competition and technological advancement. During this era, major European powers engaged in direct combat on the continent only sporadically, while they were frequently involved in colonial skirmishes and wars.

By the close of the nineteenth century, industrial technology had profoundly altered the nature of warfare. Innovations such as railroads, steamships, and the telegraph not only made total warfare feasible but also implicated entire populations in the conflict. These technological advancements facilitated the coordinated mass movement of troops, a stark contrast to the long marches and limited transport capabilities of sailing ships that had characterised earlier conflicts. Consequently, warfare shifted from isolated skirmishes and battles to the formation of extended fronts, fundamentally changing the landscape and tactics of military engagements.

In 1914, the British Navy, successfully championed the conversion of all British naval boilers from coal to oil. The switch to oil presented numerous advantages over coal. Oil was more efficient in terms of weight per thermal unit and easier to transport. It offered twice the thermal energy of coal by volume and could be fed automatically into engines through pipes, eliminating the need for manual stoking. This automation not only saved labour but also freed up considerable space within battleships, allowing for expanded operational range and reduced crew requirements.

Furthermore, internal combustion engines, which were compatible with oil, presented a smaller, more economical alternative to steam power, especially during periods of off-peak use due to their ability to be easily turned on or off. Another significant advantage of oil over coal was its cleaner burn, producing less smoke, which was particularly beneficial in naval warfare where stealth and the element of surprise were critical. This transition to oil-powered engines marked a pivotal moment in naval technology, influencing the design and strategy of future naval fleets.

The strategic challenge posed by oil in the context of the First World War was its uneven geographic distribution. Most of the major powers involved in the war, with the notable exceptions of the United States and Russia, were reliant on oil imports. For Britain, this reliance presented a particular problem as oil was considerably more expensive than coal, costing four to twelve times more. This was especially significant given Britain's abundant coal reserves and status as a major coal exporter.

However, the situation for Britain changed with the timely discovery of oil in the southern Iranian province of Khuzestan in 1908. This discovery significantly alleviated Britain's strategic concerns regarding oil supply. Britain's prior investment in acquiring shares in the company exploiting Iranian oil further facilitated this transition. This development was crucial in enabling Britain's eventual shift from coal to oil, smoothing the path for its navy's conversion to oil-fired boilers and securing a more stable and strategic energy source for future military and industrial use.

The uneven geographic distribution of oil presented a strategic dilemma, particularly evident during the First World War. Apart from the United States and Russia, the principal nations involved in the conflict were reliant on oil imports. For Britain, this reliance was particularly pronounced due to the substantial cost disparity between oil and coal, with oil being four to twelve times more expensive. This discrepancy was accentuated by Britain's abundant coal reserves and its status as a major coal exporter. However, the timely discovery of oil in the southern province of Khuzestan, Iran, in 1908 significantly mitigated this challenge for Britain. The country's prior acquisition of stakes in the corporation exploiting Iranian oil further facilitated this transition, paving the way for a more seamless conversion to oil reliance.

Iran in the First World War

The conventional European chronology of the First World War, spanning from 1914 to 1918, does not align with the experience of Iran, where the implications of the war extended beyond these dates within its national borders. This divergence can be traced back to the aftermath of the Constitutional Revolution (1905–1909) in Iran. In 1911, Russian military forces occupied Iran's northern provinces, presenting an ultimatum to the Iranian government to protect Russian interests in the region. This ultimatum culminated in the dissolution of Iran's Second Parliament.

The conclusion of the war in Iran also lagged behind the Armistice in Europe by three years. It was not until 1921 that the last British troops withdrew from southern Iran and the Russian Red Army vacated the northern regions of the country. This extended period of foreign military presence and the delayed resolution of conflict in Iran highlights the unique and prolonged impact of the First World War on the nation.

The onset of the First World War intersected with a pivotal moment in Iranian history. Following the Constitutional Revolution, Iran was at a juncture where its people were ready to reshape their constitutional framework and establish a government that was independent, accountable, and effective. However, the global conflict involving the major powers significantly impacted Iranian society, economy, and political institutions. This external strife exacerbated existing political factionalism within Iran and severely impeded the nation's efforts to reform and stabilise its government. The war's intrusion into Iran's domestic affairs thus played a crucial role in shaping the country's political trajectory during this critical period of modern state-building.

The conflict, which initially began as a European war, extended to Iran following the Ottoman Empire's alliance with the Central Powers, thereby positioning Iran as a direct neighbour to combatants from both factions. This alliance resulted in Russia and Britain confronting the Ottoman Empire, which had aligned itself with Germany. For Iran, the escalation of war in Europe and among its imperial neighbours translated into increased external pressure to choose a side in a conflict that held no intrinsic national interest for the country. This situation placed Iran in a precarious position, caught between the opposing forces of major global powers, and compounded the nation's struggle to maintain its sovereignty and neutrality amid the growing international turmoil.

In November 1914, the eastern front of the war intensified when British forces advanced towards Mesopotamia, making a strategic landing in Basra. This move by the British was not solely aimed at securing a route to Baghdad, which served as a conduit to the Russian army stationed in northern Iran and as a defensive line against incursions by the Central Powers in Central and South Asia. A critical and increasingly prominent motive for the British was to ensure the uninterrupted flow of oil from Iran, which had become a vital element of their geopolitical and military strategy.

The strategic significance of this region was underscored by the proximity of Khuzestan's oil fields and the Abadan Refinery, located just sixty kilometres from Basra. The Arvandrud was the only geographical barrier separating Khuzestan from Ottoman-controlled Mesopotamia. This geographical closeness made the region particularly vital for the British, both in terms of securing a crucial energy resource and in maintaining a strategic foothold in a region increasingly embroiled in the complexities of the First World War.[1]

Upon the outbreak of the First World War, the Iranian government swiftly responded by officially declaring the country's strict neutrality through a royal decree issued on 1 November 1914.[2] However, the practicality and efficacy of this declaration of neutrality were called into question, considering the existing occupation of a substantial portion of Iran's northern territory by Russian troops.

In an attempt to address this situation, Iran's Prime Minister, Mirza Hassan Ashtiani (Mostowfi al-Mamalek), approached the Russian authorities with a request for the withdrawal of their forces from Azerbaijan. He argued that the Russian presence provided the Ottoman Empire with a pretext to invade Iran. The response from the Russian ambassador in Tehran was notably terse and sceptical. He acknowledged the Iranian viewpoint but raised a critical concern: what assurances could Iran provide that, in the event of a Russian withdrawal, Turkish forces would not seize the opportunity to occupy the vacated territories?[3]

This diplomatic exchange highlighted the complex geopolitical situation in which Iran found itself. The country's desire to maintain neutrality was hampered by the strategic interests of the warring powers in the region, leaving Iran in a precarious position amid the escalating global conflict.

In the face of an incapacitated central government unable to withstand the pressures exerted by Russian and British influences, certain factions within Iran began to view an alliance with Germany as the most viable strategy for safeguarding the nation's sovereignty and territorial integrity. The situation was compounded by the geopolitical interests of Iran's powerful neighbouring empires: Russia, the Ottoman Empire, and Britain, the latter of which bordered Iran through its Indian dominion. These neighbouring powers had vested interests in Iran, leading them to frequently intervene in Iranian affairs.

In contrast, Germany, despite being a formidable power, was geographically distant from Iran. This distance led some Iranians to perceive Germany as a less immediate threat to their national interests. Consequently, for those seeking a counterbalance to the influence of the neighbouring empires, Germany appeared to be a potentially beneficial ally. This perception was shaped by the complex geopolitical landscape of the time, where aligning with a distant power seemed a strategic choice to preserve Iran's independence in the midst of the global conflict.

Upon the convening of the Third Iranian Parliament in December 1914, a notable faction within the legislative body was aligned with pro-German sentiments. Out of a total of 136 deputies, thirty were members of the pro-German Democrat Party.[4] This alignment did not go unnoticed by Britain, which regarded the activities of the pro-German Democrats with suspicion and unease. Similarly, the Russians, wary of the growing German influence in Iran, responded by bolstering their military presence within the country.

The escalating tensions led to a dramatic turn of events when Russian troops advanced towards the Iranian capital. They stationed themselves in Qazvin, a city located approximately 160 kilometres northwest of Tehran, effectively posing a direct threat to occupy the capital itself. This military manoeuvre by the Russians underscored the intense geopolitical pressures Iran faced, caught in the crossfire of competing interests among the major powers of the time. The situation highlighted the delicate balance Iran had to maintain in its quest for sovereignty and political stability amid the broader context of the First World War.

Faced with escalating external threats, the cabinet of Mostowfi al-Mamalek, along with the support of the majority of Democrat deputies, prominent journalists, and influential politicians, seriously contemplated relocating Iran's capital from Tehran to Isfahan. This coalition, motivated by the desire to preserve the legitimate government of Iran, embarked on what can be termed a 'long march' towards Isfahan.

However, this endeavour did not culminate in reaching Isfahan as planned. Instead, the group ultimately established their base in Kermanshah. Here, they formed what they called the *Dowlat-e Movaqat-e Melli* (the Provisional National Government).[5] This government garnered official recognition from the Central Powers as the sole legitimate authority of Iran, marking a significant moment in Iran's political history during the First World War.

Despite this recognition, the Provisional National Government was unable to withstand the intensifying pressures exerted by Britain and Russia. In 1916, the situation reached a critical point when Russian forces captured Kermanshah, leading to the collapse of the Provisional National Government.[6] This event marked the end of an ambitious attempt to maintain Iranian sovereignty and governance amid the overwhelming influences of the major powers involved in the global conflict.

After successfully defeating the Ottoman army in southern Mesopotamia, the British forces managed to secure the strategically vital oilfields located in Khuzestan. This victory allowed them to establish a significant foothold in the territories previously under Ottoman control. From this position, British forces incrementally extended their influence over the rest of Mesopotamia and into the Arabian Peninsula, gradually eroding Ottoman dominance in these regions.[7]

A pivotal moment in this campaign was the initiation of the Arab Revolt against the Ottoman Empire in 1916, led by T.E. Lawrence, more famously known as Lawrence of Arabia. This revolt, which began in earnest in 1916, was a significant factor in the subsequent British victories, including the capture of key cities such as Baghdad, Kirkuk, Mosul, and ultimately Jerusalem in 1917. These successive defeats significantly altered the dynamics of the war in the Middle East, including Iran.

However, it was the Russian Revolution in February 1917 that arguably had an even more profound impact on the situation in Iran. The revolution brought about substantial changes in Russian foreign policy and military engagements, which in turn had significant implications for the geopolitical landscape of the region, including the ongoing conflict and power struggles in Iran.

In the wake of the Russian February 1917 Revolution, October of the same year witnessed the ascendance of the Bolsheviks, who seized control of the remnants of the erstwhile Tsarist empire. This geopolitical shift was closely followed by the onset of the final phase of conflict in Iran a year later. The Armistice of Mudros, marking a pivotal cessation of hostilities, was signed on 30 October 1918. Concurrently, in Istanbul, the Committee of Union and Progress's cabinet relinquished power, leading Ahmed Izzet Pasha to form a new government and order the repatriation of Ottoman troops.

However, the withdrawal of foreign military forces from Iran – initially the Russians, followed by the Ottomans – did not fortify the Iranian government. Instead, the nation grappled with profound economic despair: a populace mired in poverty, a virtually bankrupt economy, and depleted state coffers. This fragility soon became apparent as the government faced escalating challenges from centrifugal forces. Regional protest movements began to question the prevailing order, particularly in the northern provinces of Azerbaijan, Gilan, and Khorasan. Here, reformist and revolutionary figures harboured aspirations of instigating change within their locales, with the hope that such reforms would gradually permeate the rest of the country.

Notably, the regional campaigns led by Kuchek Khan Jangali in Gilan, Sheikh Mohammad Khiabani in Azerbaijan, and Colonel Mohammad-Taqi Khan Pesian in Khorasan, while not separatist in nature, sought to establish stable and accountable political frameworks. Their aim was to address local grievances regarding the inequitable distribution of power between the central government and regional authorities across Iran.[8] Simultaneously, other local insurgencies emerged in the southern and western parts of the country. These, unlike the northern campaigns, were not primarily reformist but aimed at undermining the central government's authority in favour of local magnates.

During this tumultuous period, the political turmoil in Iran was paralleled by dire social and economic conditions, particularly for the labouring poor. The First World War exacerbated their plight, bringing widespread misery characterised by hunger, famine, drought, and the perils of armed violence. Inflation soared, and unemployment surged, compelling many to flee their homes in search of safety, either within Iran or across its borders.

Tens of thousands of Iranian migrants, who had found employment in factories, oilfields, mines, and construction sites in the Caucasus, at the southern edge of the collapsed Tsarist empire, faced a grim reality upon their return post the 1917 Russian Revolution. They swelled the ranks of the unemployed, further straining the country's fragile economy.[9]

Nature, too, was unyielding. Successive seasonal droughts in 1917–18 caused widespread famine, exacerbating the already critical situation. The occupying armies, prioritising their needs, requisitioned and confiscated food supplies to sustain their troops, thereby intensifying the famine.[10] A stark example occurred in November 1915 in the south-eastern province of Sistan, where the entire granary was sold to British troops, causing the price of wheat to skyrocket: 'the price of one *kharvar* (100 kilos) of wheat was raised to 20 tomans, if there is any to be found'.[11]

In the north-eastern province of Khorasan, the presence of Russian troops further aggravated the crisis. Their strategy of blockading roads and restricting grain transfers, permitting only those allocations intended for their own consumption, significantly exacerbated the food scarcity.[12] Moreover, the commandeering of pack animals, mules, and camels for transportation purposes in both the oil industry in Khuzestan and for the use of British and Russian military forces, severely disrupted Iran's transport infrastructure.[13]

This disruption had far-reaching effects on the nation's logistical capabilities, impeding the efficient distribution of food and other vital supplies throughout Iran. The situation was so dire that, in many areas of the country during the war, the cost associated with transporting grain was often higher than the expense incurred in its cultivation. This imbalance in costs further compounded the hardships faced by the Iranian populace, making the procurement and distribution of essential commodities a challenging and costly endeavour.

As if the existing challenges were not daunting enough, a series of severe droughts commencing in 1916 further devastated Iran's agricultural output. By early February 1918, a widespread famine had engulfed the nation, triggering panic and chaos in major cities as desperate crowds resorted to looting bakeries and food stores. This desperation led to violent confrontations, such as in the western city of Kermanshah, where clashes between the starving populace and police resulted in casualties.

In Tehran, the crisis was exacerbated by unscrupulous practices such as hoarding and short-selling by bakers.[14] The labouring poor, already reeling under the pressure of scarce resources, were further incensed by the adulteration of bread and the exorbitant prices charged by some bakers. This outrage culminated in a significant protest in 1919, led by printing-house workers who had recently unionised. They staged demonstrations in Tehran, targeting bakeries and granaries, demanding that the government intervene to increase food rations, standardised bread prices, and regulate the quality, supply, and sale of foodstuffs.

However, in this turbulent post-war era, neither the national government nor foreign powers were adequately equipped or positioned to effectively address these human crises. The aftermath of the war, coupled with the ravages of famine and contagious diseases, continued to wreak havoc across the country for many years, underscoring the profound and lasting impacts of these compounded calamities.

In addition to the tragic toll of starvation, Iran was further beleaguered by deadly epidemics during this period.[15] The colossal food crisis, compounded by the incessant movement of a vast number of soldiers, refugees, and destitute individuals in search of work and sustenance, created a fertile ground for pandemics and contagious diseases. Cholera, plague, and typhus rapidly swept across the country, leading to a staggering daily death toll.

Beginning in 1915, cholera outbreaks were reported in Azerbaijan,[16] and by the following year, the disease had not only engulfed all northern provinces but had also spread to the south. Typhoid fever was rampant in various parts of the country, causing so many deaths that, according to an eyewitness, 'the high mortality in Tehran was not due to famine, but rather because of typhoid and typhus'.[17]

As the war in Europe was drawing to a close, the Spanish Influenza pandemic also made its way to Iran. Reports from foreign diplomatic missions in the capital detailed widespread devastation across the country, with particularly horrific conditions in Hamadan. A British officer, stationed in northwest Iran and the south Caucasus, provided an eyewitness account of the severe famine and disease in Hamadan.[18] He reported that 30 per cent of the city's 50,000 inhabitants were on the brink of starvation, leading to numerous deaths. Additionally, there were even reports of cannibalism, highlighting the extreme desperation and dire circumstances faced by the population.[19]

In the collective historical memory of Iran, the First World War is etched as a time of profound devastation and suffering. This period is recalled not primarily for the fatalities resulting from combat, although these were undoubtedly numerous, but rather for the immense toll exacted by famines and epidemics. These crises claimed a vastly greater number of victims, overshadowing the direct impacts of military engagements. The war, in the Iranian context, is thus predominantly associated with the indirect but devastating consequences of widespread hunger and rampant disease, which left indelible marks on the nation's psyche and history.

Securing Labour and Resources in Wartime

On the eve of the First World War, the global shift from coal to oil as the primary fuel for technological, military, and industrial applications elevated oil to a strategically crucial commodity, a status it retained for decades thereafter. In response to this rapid transition, the British government, holding a majority stake of 51 per cent in the APOC, endorsed a substantial expansion of the oil industry under its indirect control.[20]

Following the completion of the initial construction phase, which included pipelines transporting oil from Masjed-Soleyman to Abadan and the establishment of a refinery, Abadan became a critical supplier for the British Royal Navy, providing up to two-thirds of its fuel needs. Additionally, nearly 200,000 tons of refined petroleum products were supplied to British forces in Mesopotamia.[21] The military requirements for fuel during the war were immense, especially considering that, at its peak, the British war machine stationed almost 450,000 troops in Mesopotamia alone,[22] predominantly recruited from India.[23]

This war effort, increasingly reliant on mechanisation, generated an enormous demand for the output of the Abadan Refinery. The military deployed around 6,400 motorised vehicles and 45 airplanes, all powered by internal combustion engines. Beyond petroleum products, the British war effort also heavily utilised the regional manpower, employing nearly 900,000 people during the course of the war.[24]

On 1 November 1914, a primarily Indian infantry military contingent landed in the south of Iran, with the strategic objective of securing the oilfields and the Abadan Refinery.[25] This deployment was supplemented by the British warship Odin, which patrolled the Shatt al-Arab. This move was a pre-emptive strategy to safeguard these vital assets against potential attacks by Ottoman and German forces. Intelligence reports indicated the presence of approximately 30,000 Ottoman troops in Basra, heightening the perceived threat.[26]

Christopher Sykes noted that the Germans, allegedly with the assistance of their secret agent in Iran, Niedermayer, had formulated a plan to ignite the Abadan Refinery. This plan also included sinking the German cargo steamer Ekbatana and other vessels south of Abadan, with the intent to obstruct British access up the river, thereby hindering any rescue efforts for their European employees at the refinery.[27]

The British fears were partially realised on 6 November 1914, when the Ottoman army's coastal batteries launched an attack on the British Navy sloop Espiegle. The Espiegle had been navigating the Shatt al-Arab (later Arvandrud) since September 1914. Subsequently, the Ottomans attempted, albeit unsuccessfully, to block the river above Khorramshahr, by sinking the Ekbatana and three smaller ships.[28]

Following this offensive, there were sporadic skirmishes over the ensuing days, which ultimately culminated in the retreat of the Ottoman forces. This series of events underscored the strategic importance of the region's oil resources and the lengths to which nations were prepared to go to control them during the heightened tensions of the First World War.[29]

Following the Ottoman retreat and the British capture of Basra on 22 November 1914, the British forces made further advances towards Amara and along the Tigris. Basra evolved into a stronghold for the British in Mesopotamia, effectively preventing the Ottomans from launching any direct offensives against the oil industry in southern Iran. However, for the APOC, the threat of Ottoman and German intrusions and acts of sabotage remained a significant concern.

The Ottoman military campaigns in northern Mesopotamia necessitated APOC to implement precautionary measures. In January 1915, the company made the strategic decision to relocate all its European employees from Ahvaz and Abadan to Mohammareh (Khorramshahr), a move aimed at ensuring their safety amid the escalating conflict.

On the brink of the war, the workforce in the Iranian oil industry comprised 4,277 individuals. This number included 64 Europeans, 2,744 Iranians, and 1,074 Indians. The diverse composition of the workforce underscored the

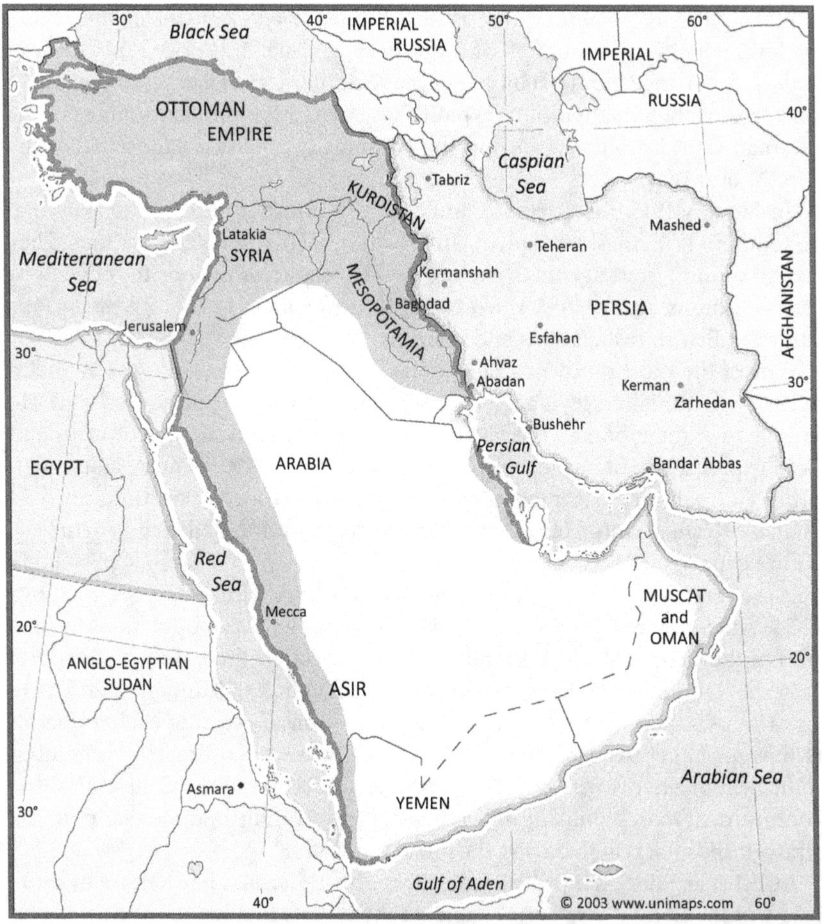

Map 2.1 Iran and Mesopotamia, 1915

international scope of the industry and the varied nationalities drawn into the region's strategic significance, particularly in the context of the oil sector during the turbulent times of the First World War.[30]

The Ottoman defeat in Basra, although significant, paled in comparison to the losses they sustained on the northern front. This setback in the north prompted the German–Turkish alliance to refocus their efforts on the southern front. However, instead of engaging in direct military confrontations, they adopted a different strategy. They aimed to incite popular uprisings within the region from the grassroots level and simultaneously sought to negotiate deals with tribal chiefs from a position of authority.

This dual approach – stirring unrest among the local population while negotiating with tribal leaders – indicated a tactical shift in their operations. It was a move designed to undermine British influence and control in the region by leveraging local discontent and the sway of tribal authority. This strategy reflected a nuanced understanding of the sociopolitical dynamics of the region and represented an attempt to exploit these dynamics to the advantage of the German–Turkish alliance during the complex geopolitical landscape of the First World War.

In January 1915, the Germans launched a significant infiltration campaign in southern Iran, marking a pivotal moment in their strategic operations. They deployed numerous agents to the region with explicit missions to incite popular rebellions against the Allied forces and to conduct sabotage operations targeting British installations and interests.[31]

One of the most renowned figures in this espionage network was Wilhelm Wassmuss, initially serving as the German Acting Consul at Bushehr. He later earned the moniker 'the Lawrence of Persia' due to his adventurous and bold exploits, which garnered considerable attention. Wassmuss, along with other German and Ottoman agents, operated in strategic locations such as Isfahan, Kermanshah, Hamadan, Najaf, Karbala, and the oil-rich province of Khuzestan.

The overarching goal of these agents was to secure a Jihad decree from both Shiite and Sunni religious leaders and to mobilise the local populations in support of the Central Powers. In line with this objective, there were also reports that the Ottomans had dispatched approximately 2,000 infantry and cavalry troops, along with artillery, with the intention of crossing Mohammareh (Khorramshahr) to reach Basra.[32] This multi-pronged approach, combining military movements with covert operations, underscored the Central Powers' commitment to destabilising Allied control and gaining an upper hand in this strategically vital region during the First World War.

In February 1915, the protracted efforts of the German and Ottoman campaign to incite local Arab tribes against the APOC finally bore fruit.[33] These tribes launched an assault on the oil infrastructure, specifically targeting pipelines and certain installations north of Ahvaz.

During this attack, the tribes caused significant damage; they sabotaged pipelines, causing oil spills which they then set ablaze. Additionally, they severed telephone lines, disrupting communication between Abadan and the oilfields, and raided the Oil Company's stores.[34] This act of sabotage had a lasting impact, with the disruption persisting until June of the same year. As a result, the output of the Abadan Refinery plummeted dramatically, from 23,500 tons to just 5,600 tons.

The situation at the oil fields was dire. 'At the field, large quantities of oil had to be burned, since all available storage was soon filled, and the producing wells could not be completely shut off'.[35] Moreover, the wells that were actively producing oil could not be entirely shut off, exacerbating the problem. This series of events underscored the vulnerability of the oil infrastructure in Iran during World War I and the strategic importance such installations held in the broader context of the war.

The February 1915 sabotage incident emerged as the sole significant, direct assault on the oil infrastructures in Khuzestan throughout the war period. In the subsequent months and years, an absence of any major incidents was noted, leading to the effective preservation of security for oil installations in the region.[36] This outcome can be predominantly attributed to the safeguarding measures enacted by the Bakhtiari Khans, who played a crucial role in ensuring the 'securing the Oil Company's employees and properties within the limits of their jurisdiction'.[37]

The Bakhtiari Khans explicitly expressed their dedication to defending British interests in the southern region.[38] This encompassed not only the oil-fields but also the refinery and the intricate network of transportation. Their commitment extended to collaboration with Sheikh Khazʿal the British most trustee Arab tribe chief in the south.[39]

In a proactive response to a request from the APOC, Nasir Khan Sardar Jang, the chieftain of the Bakhtiari tribe, issued a stern directive to the leaders of the Bavi and Bani-Torof tribes. He commanded an immediate evacuation from the Bakhtiari territories. Confronted with this ultimatum, the Bavi and Bani-Torof tribes acknowledged the supremacy of their adversaries, the Arab Kaʿbian tribe, led by Sheikh Khazʿal, who was backed by the British.

As a consequence of these developments, the Bavi and Bani-Torof tribes withdrew their allegiance from the Ottoman and German forces. They adopted a new role, undertaking the responsibility of guarding the Oil Company's pipelines and other infrastructural assets in the region. This shift in alliance played a pivotal role in maintaining the security and operational integrity of the oil installations during a tumultuous period.[40]

Following the accord with the Bakhtiari Khans and the subsequent pacification of the Arab tribes, there was a prevailing sentiment that the strategic interests of the British in the south, along with the safety of their employees, were no longer under threat. However, this initial optimism soon proved to be overly sanguine, failing to fully account for the complexities of local politics in the region.

Within the Bakhtiari leadership, a notable rift was evident between the established older chiefs and the emergent younger generation. The latter seized every opportunity to challenge the authority of their seniors, a tension that was exacerbated by the ongoing war and the competition among great powers for influence in the region. This tumultuous backdrop provided the younger Bakhtiari leaders with a platform to elevate their standing within the tribal hierarchy.

Moreover, the failure to completely disrupt the oil operations in Khuzestan led German and Ottoman agents to extend their focus beyond the region's borders, closely monitoring the activities of the Oil Company. This shift in strategy reflected the evolving nature of external interventions and the ongoing instability in the broader geopolitical landscape.

After the initial discovery of oil in southern Iran at Masjed-Soleyman, the APOC planned to broaden its exploration efforts to the western and southern regions of Iran. However, the limited availability and extraction challenges of the oil reserves in the west redirected the British focus back to the southern territories.[41]

A team comprising British and Burmese geologists arrived in Iran for this purpose. Their initial investigations centred around Ahvaz and Haftgel, areas noted for their abundant boiling springs of white oil. Subsequently, guided by recommendations from the British Navy, the exploration extended to the south-eastern coast of Iran. This area spanned the coastline of Makran, stretching from Baluchestan to Bushehr and included Qeshm Island.

The geologists' exploration in these regions, coupled with APOC's incrementally increasing excavation activities, particularly in Qeshm, led to a significant conclusion. It was projected that Qeshm would soon emerge as another major oilfield, comparable to the Naftun field in Masjed-Soleyman. These unfolding developments, notably significant in the realm of energy resources, naturally attracted the attention of German and Ottoman agents. These agents closely monitored APOC's activities in the region, driven by both interest and concern over the potential implications of these oil discoveries.

Upon evaluating the British influence in the region and considering their limited success in inciting the Arab tribes of southwestern Iran against the British, the Germans and Ottomans resolved to withdraw from Khuzestan. They shifted their strategic focus to other areas. Consequently, apart from the western front in Kordestan, the primary area of German and Ottoman activities during the war was located west of a line drawn between Isfahan and Bandar Abbas. This region encompassed key locations such as Shiraz, Bushehr, Tangestan, and Dashtestan.

In these areas, the Germans and Ottomans employed a strategy that leveraged existing tribal rivalries and sought the support of local Muslim *ʿulama* (religious scholars) to advocate for *Jihad* against the British and Russian forces. This approach effectively opened a new front in the south-east of Iran, serving the political and military objectives of their sponsors.

The Germans resumed their roles as political and military advisors to the tribal leaders in these regions. Meanwhile, operatives of the *Teşkilat-i Mahsusa* (Special Branch), the Ottoman secret service, were active in disseminating decrees from Najaf and Karbala, as well as local Muslim ʿulama's Jihadi Fatwas, among the southern Iranian populace. This strategy was aimed at galvanising the local population against foreign influences and bolstering the position of the Central Powers in this strategically important area.[42]

In response to a thorough examination of the subversive actions undertaken by their adversaries, the British dispatched military forces to Bushehr in August 1915.[43] This strategic move to occupy Bushehr was a significant step in countering the activities of the enemy in the region.

Following the occupation, the British initiated a pivotal military development in the spring of 1916 with the formation of a special proxy military unit named the South Persia Rifles (SPR). This unit was composed predominantly of locally recruited troops, and its primary mandate was to quell tribal uprisings and suppress any form of local resistance that posed a threat to British interests in the area.[44]

The establishment of the SPR was facilitated and supported by several local tribal chiefs who were aligned with British interests. However, the Iranian government expressed strong opposition to this move. The creation of the SPR, particularly the manner in which it was executed, was perceived by the Iranian authorities as a blatant infringement on their territorial sovereignty. This action by the British not only highlighted the geopolitical tensions in the region but also underscored the complexities involved in navigating the intricate balance of local power dynamics and international interests.[45]

In June 1915, a concerted assault was launched against the APOC facilities at Salkh on Qeshm Island.[46] This surprise attack was orchestrated by local tribes, operating with the covert assistance of operatives from the Ottoman Special Branch, *Teşkilat-i Mahsusa*. The immediate aftermath of this camisado, a sudden and unexpected military assault, resulted in the cessation of APOC's operations on the island.

This springtime attack on the British-controlled enterprise in Qeshm heralded a more severe challenge for Britain in the region. In the early summer of the same year, the British military forces stationed in Bushehr found themselves encircled and besieged by local tribal factions.[47] In response to this escalating hostility, the British authorities imposed Martial Law and proceeded to assert complete control over the port of Bushehr.

An intriguing historical account by Mehdi-Qoli Khan Hedayat, who served as the Iranian government's representative in Bushehr at the time, reveals a notable act by the British troops during this period of occupation. They reportedly produced a postal stamp bearing the inscription 'Bushehr under British Occupation'.[48] This symbolic gesture underscored the extent of British control and the heightened tensions between the occupying forces and the local population, reflecting the complex interplay of local resistance and foreign military presence in the region.

The establishment of the British military presence in Bushehr significantly exacerbated tensions, sparking widespread discontent among the local population. This unrest manifested in public demonstrations directed not only against the British but also against their wartime ally, the Russians. The protests rapidly spread to various regions, including Isfahan, Ramhormoz, and Bushehr. In this charged atmosphere, local *ʿulama* seized the opportunity to incite the populace, calling for a *Jihad* against the Allied troops. The intensity of the local opposition was further demonstrated by several incidents where offices of the Oil Company were targeted and set ablaze.[49]

In response to these escalating tensions, the British regional command, rather than seeking avenues for compromise, opted for a more confrontational approach. A key element of this strategy was the formation of the SPR, a military unit tasked with quelling local insurgencies. In particular, the unit played a significant role in suppressing notable uprisings, such as the Tangestani revolt in August 1915.

While the British authorities engaged in these forceful measures, they simultaneously attempted to mitigate the situation by cultivating relationships with local tribal chiefs. The aim was to pacify these influential figures, if not entirely align them with British interests. This dual strategy of suppression and diplomatic engagement underscored the complex and often contradictory nature of British efforts to maintain control and stability in a region marked by deep-seated resistance and geopolitical significance.

Wartime Labour: Local and Cross-Border Migration

Amid the operational security challenges, the Oil Company grappled with a significant issue during the war: the persistent scarcity of both skilled and unskilled labour. With the wartime expansion of the Iranian oil industry, the dynamics of labour recruitment underwent a logistical transformation.

In the nascent phase following the discovery of oil in 1908, APOC's primary focus was on laying the foundational infrastructure. This phase included constructing roads, laying pipelines, and building refineries, crucial for establishing a robust oil extraction and production base. As APOC held an unchallenged monopoly over the entire spectrum of oil operations – from extraction to production and marketing – the company embarked on an extensive labour recruitment campaign to support its expanding operations.

As oil production intensified, the Abadan Refinery experienced a considerable expansion, driven by the rising demand for petroleum products. Concurrently, the issue of labour scarcity became increasingly pronounced. This labour shortage presented a significant challenge for APOC, as the company strived to keep pace with the burgeoning needs of the oil industry amid the complexities of a rapidly expanding operational scale.

Two primary factors contributed to this shortage of labour. Firstly, the high wages offered by the British Army proved to be a strong incentive, drawing away a substantial number of skilled and unskilled employees from the oil industry. These individuals opted to join the army as casual labourers, attracted by the better financial prospects.

Secondly, the geographical proximity of the oilfields and the refinery to the warfront added to the labour challenges. The ongoing conflict and its associated risks led to a significant exodus of workers from the oil industry, further exacerbating the shortage.[50]

In light of these circumstances, APOC had to prioritise not only the recruitment and retention of labour but also initiate negotiations with the British

Army regarding its manpower recruitment policies. Addressing these labour issues was crucial for APOC to maintain its operational efficiency and meet the growing demands of the wartime oil industry.

The labour shortage at the Oil Company reached such a critical point that the company found it necessary to appeal to the British military for intervention. APOC requested the issuance of an order prohibiting army and naval units from employing individuals who had previously worked in the oil industry. Additionally, APOC advocated for the establishment of a Labour Corps specifically dedicated to supporting and serving the oil industry's needs.

In response to these requests, the Admiralty took decisive action. On 6 August 1915, it issued an order declaring the Abadan Refinery to be classified as a 'munitions factory'. According to this order, which was grounded in the King's Regulations, employees working at the refinery were prohibited from leaving the service of the company. This move was a significant intervention, illustrating the strategic importance of the oil industry during the war and the lengths to which the British government was willing to go to ensure its smooth operation.[51]

With the expansion of the Iranian oil industry during the First World War, securing a consistent and adequate labour supply became a critical concern. This urgency transformed the management of the workforce into a top priority for the APOC, drawing significant attention and intervention from high-level authorities, including the British Raj.

In an effort to address this pressing need, APOC reached out to the Government of India, 'to issue instructions through the Mumbai Government to all concerned to facilitate recruitment and dispatch' of labourers for the Persian oil industry, an industry run by a company in which 'the majority of shares are held by the British Government which has full power of control and of British Indian subjects, being under the British jurisdictions'.[52]

APOC identified a major hindrance in sourcing labour from India for its operations in Persia: a legislative obstacle rooted in the Indian Emigrations Act of 1883. This act-imposed restrictions on labour migration, limiting it to specific destinations that, notably, did not include Persia. This legal constraint presented a significant challenge for APOC in meeting its labour requirements in the Persian oil industry, necessitating governmental intervention and potential amendments to existing legislation to facilitate the migration of Indian workers to Iran (Table 2.1).[53]

In March 1915, in response to the escalating labour needs of the Iranian oil industry, the Board of the APOC put forward a proposal to the Government of India. This proposal addressed the restrictive measures stipulated by the Indian Emigrations Act of 1883, which significantly hampered APOC's ability to recruit the necessary skilled labour for its operations in Iran:

Table 2.1 *Employment in the APOC, 1914–21*

Year	Iranians	Indians	Europeans	Others	Total
1914	2,744	1,074	64	395	4,277
1915	2,203	979	80	187	3,449
1916	2,335	1,366	120	104	3,925
1917	n.d.	n.d.	n.d.	n.d.	n.d.
1918	n.d.	n.d.	n.d.	n.d.	n.d.
1919	3,979	2,641	117	47	6,784
1920	8,447	3,616	244	35	12,342
1921	9,009	4,709	271	51	14,040

Sources: R. W. Ferrier, *The History of the British Petroleum, The Developing Years 1901–32* (London: Cambridge University Press, 1982).

> Owing to the non-existence of such [skilled] labour in Persia, and the impossibility of training Persians in sufficient number for their requirements, the Company is compelled to indent largely on Indian for skilled labourers of many kinds, such as riveters, engine drivers, assembling machine men, iron and brass moulders, solders, core makers and others. At the present time, the number of Indian employees in Abadan and the oil fields is about 1,020. It is found nevertheless that it is very difficult to induce men of these classes to leave Mumbai, Yangon, Karachi, or the other ports where they are recruited and to accept employment in Persia. ... Government of India's Emigration Act, which are unduly magnified in their imagination, and consequently act as a serious deterrent to their taking the service offered.[54]

To reinforce its case, the APOC emphasised its unique position as a predominantly British-owned company. Highlighting that the British government held a significant shareholding in APOC, the company underscored its status, which afforded it 'full power of control and of British Indian subjects being under the jurisdiction of His Majesty's Consul'. This delineation was crucial in establishing the strategic significance of APOC's operations, not only in economic terms but also in the broader context of British imperial interests.

Leveraging this position, APOC petitioned the Government of India to modify its emigration policies to align with those implemented in other British territories, specifically citing Ceylon (present-day Sri Lanka) and the Straits Settlements as benchmarks. The company proposed that the emigration rule applied to these regions should be extended to Persia as well. This adjustment would facilitate the recruitment of skilled labour from India to support APOC's expanding operations in the Persian oil industry.

APOC's argument was anchored in the idea that the administrative authority of the Government of India should be expanded to include new territories, such as Iran. This expansion would not only address the immediate labour needs of APOC but also reflect the evolving dynamics of the British Empire's economic and strategic interests in the region. The proposal highlighted the interconnected nature of colonial governance, economic enterprise, and global labour mobility during this period:

> ... under the provisions of the Persian Coast and Islands Order of 1907, British Indian subject in the Persian littoral are entirely under the jurisdiction of the Consul-General and Political Resident and his subordinate officers. British Indian law is in force and under the provision of the Order, the Indian Code of Criminal and Civil Procedure have effect '*as if the Persian Coast and Islands were a neighbourhood in the province of Mumbai*'. In these circumstances the position of Indian emigrants in the Gulf approximates to their position in Ceylon and the Straits Settlements, which are expressly exempted from the operation of the Government of India's Emigration Act, and the object of this letter is to enquire whether a similar exemption cannot be accorded to the areas occupied by the Company's Work at Abadan, Mohammareh and the Oilfields.[55]

The Persian Coast and Islands Order of 1907, mentioned in the Anglo-Persian Oil Company's petition, was a critical component of the Anglo-Russian Convention of 1907, signed in St. Petersburg. This convention was a significant diplomatic agreement, aimed at stabilising international relations in response to the geopolitical shifts that occurred after the Russo-Japanese War and the Russian Revolution of 1905.

One of the key developments leading up to the convention was the mutual recognition by Russia and Britain of Persia's territorial sovereignty since 1903. However, an exception was made for the Persian Gulf, which was predominantly viewed as a 'British lake', indicating Britain's substantial influence and control over the region.

Despite formally acknowledging Iran as a sovereign state, the 1907 Convention effectively undermined this sovereignty in practical terms. The heart of the convention was its initial section, which delineated Russian and British territorial spheres of influence in northern and southern Persia, respectively. This division of Iran into spheres of influence effectively reduced its status as a fully sovereign nation, as it placed significant portions of its territory under the indirect control of these two imperial powers.[56]

In April 1915, the Department of Commerce and Industry of the Government of India reacted to APOC's petition in the following terms:

> The Government of India are very reluctant to extend the exemption to other countries. The conditions mentioned above do not apply to the Persian Gulf. Emigration of artisans to the Persian Gulf is of very recent date and living very expensive. It is possible that an account of these reasons

> that artisans are unwilling to proceed to the Persian Gulf even on the high Burma rates and not because of the restriction imposed by the Government of India's Emigration Act. The artisan class is not so ignorant as the ordinary coolie class and are not likely to be frightened by requirements of the Act, which are not of harassing nature.[57]

The Government of India, in its response to APOC, did not entirely dismiss the possibility of further negotiations. In the same memorandum, it was noted that the government would consider the feasibility of granting an exemption to APOC's request, with the condition that if 'His Majesty's Government would consent to be a party to the agreement', then it would consider the desirability of an exemption, provided that 'the Governments of Mumbai, Punjab – where the emigrant proceed mostly from there – United Province, Bengal, and Bihar and Orissa [were] consulted'.[58]

The protracted debate between the APOC and the Government of India over the legal status of Iran as a destination for Indian labour migrants eventually reached a resolution in February 1918. At that juncture, the Government of India acquiesced to a temporary suspension of the Government of India's Emigration Act's restrictions for territories under APOC's jurisdiction. This decision came as the government increasingly recognised the strategic importance of a steady oil supply, especially in the context of the ongoing war. Consequently, it expanded its cooperation with APOC to ensure that oil production was not impeded by a lack of labour.[59]

Throughout this period, APOC persistently underscored the critical need for a continuous supply of labour from India. The company was acutely aware that any disruption or diminution in this labour pipeline could pose significant operational risks. This concern was particularly heightened when Indian workers, lured by the prospect of higher wages, left their positions with the Oil Company to join the British military. Reflecting on this situation, a manager from the company commented:

> A large number of Sikh fitters are pressing to get leave to return to their country, and a number of them have worked here at least a year. We cannot very well force them to remain as they are not under agreement, and their chief grievance is one of money.
>
> I have no doubt that some of the men wish to go to India than return for work in Basra, and by this way evades the Force Routine Order of 4th April. Others again will, no doubt, apply in India to Shaw Wallace and Co. for work either at the Gunboats or the I.O. Barges, as they will thus get much higher wages than we can offer. Regarding the fitters who wish to go to their country, I have had a talk with the Head Fitter Mastery, and he tells me that some of his men here are writing to their friends in Lahore, Amritsar etc., telling them not to apply for work in this Company owing to the troubles caused by the war, dearness of living, and coercive methods that they say we use in order to retain their services.[60]

APOC's concerns about the loss of its workforce to military recruitment were taken seriously by the British Army. In response to these concerns, the Army issued a 'special order was issued to effect that no labour *ex* Abadan to be employed by any Military or Naval unit'.[61]

During the war, the APOC faced significant challenges not only due to the exodus of skilled workers from the Iranian oil industry but also due to a critical shortage of unskilled labour. Several factors contributed to this complex situation. One of the primary issues was the prevalent anti-British sentiment among local tribes in Iran. This tribal strife, fuelled by opposition to British presence and influence, had a direct impact on the labour force availability for APOC. Additionally, the region experienced severe famines and epidemics, which led to widespread dislocation of the population. Especially in the early stages of the war, these calamities caused major disruptions in the local labour market, as many individuals were forced to move or were incapacitated.[62]

Another significant factor was the proximity of APOC's oilfields and refineries to the warfront. This proximity heightened the risks for local unskilled labourers, leading many to abandon their jobs with the Oil Company in search of safer environments or more stable employment elsewhere. This migration away from the conflict zones further exacerbated the labour shortage faced by APOC, complicating its operations during a critical period of the war.

As British forces made advancements in Mesopotamia and engaged actively on the Baghdad front, a new labour market emerged, offering more favourable working conditions. This development attracted a diverse workforce, including both local skilled and unskilled workers, as well as migrant workers from other regions, notably from India:

> We have, all along, been having the greatest difficulty in retaining coolies at Abadan, [and]. ... I regret to say that matters have got very much worse during the last fortnight, and we are now nearly a thousand Coolies under strength. ... Last payday (six days ago) some 200 men cleared off and this morning Abadan have rung up to say that a similar number went yesterday. ... I suppose it is the fall of Baghdad, which it so some extent responsible for this sudden extra demand for Coolies by the [British] government.[63]

The decision by the APOC to include *coolies* in their recruitment strategy marked a significant shift in their labour policy during the war. This change led to the invitation of the Indian Labour Corps to join APOC's workforce in Persia, reflecting an expansion in the company's approach to sourcing labour.[64]

By October 1917, APOC had successfully integrated a contingent of 300 members from the Indian Labour Corps into their operations in Abadan. Building on this initial success, the company approached the Government of

India with a request to significantly increase this number. APOC petitioned for the expansion of the Indian Labour Corps in Abadan to a total of 800 men, indicating the company's growing reliance on this source of labour to meet its operational needs in the face of ongoing labour shortages: 'We understand that Persian coolies are available and will accept some with very many thanks but if it were possible for our existing Indian Corps to be increased, we imagine it would save having two separate organisations'.[65]

Despite the challenges posed by worker desertions and the constraints of the Government of India's Emigration Act, the recruitment of migrant labour from India to the Iranian oil industry not only continued during the war but also saw a significant increase. By the time the war ended, the workforce in the Iranian oil industry had become quite diverse, with migrants sourced from various regions across India, each group bringing specific skills and fulfilling different roles.

Chittagonian workers, hailing from the region around Chittagong (present-day Bangladesh), were primarily engaged in harbour engineering and naval transport, leveraging their maritime and engineering skills. Punjabi Sikhs, known for their robustness and technical aptitude, were predominantly employed as drivers, technicians, and security agents, contributing to the operational and safety aspects of the oil industry.

Migrants from the Madras Presidency, which was known for its educational institutions, often occupied clerical and administrative functions, bringing their organisational and office management skills to the fore. The Gazars from Punjab, traditionally involved in service occupations, were employed as *dhobi* (washermen), providing essential maintenance services. Additionally, Goans, who were part of the extensive Portuguese colonial influence in India, were often employed as cooks and servants, utilising their culinary skills and experience in household management.

This diverse composition of the workforce reflected the varied requirements of the oil industry and demonstrated how the sector drew upon a wide spectrum of skills and services from different parts of India, each group contributing uniquely to the functioning of the industry in Iran.[66]

The contention between the APOC and the Government of India regarding the legality of Persia as a destination for Indian labour migrants lingered until February 1918. It was only then that the Government of India consented to a temporary suspension of the Government of India's Emigration Act restrictions for territories under the purview of APOC. This decision was a pivotal moment in the relationship between the two entities.

By February 1918, the Government of India had come to fully appreciate the strategic significance of uninterrupted oil supplies during wartime. Recognising the vital role of the oil industry in the war effort, the government altered its stance to support APOC more effectively. This change in policy was primarily aimed at ensuring that oil production was not adversely affected by a lack of labour.[67]

Despite these hurdles, APOC persisted in its efforts to recruit migrant workers from India. The company's insistence on maintaining a steady influx of Indian labour underscored the vital importance of these workers in sustaining its operations, especially in the context of the expanding oil industry during the war. APOC's commitment to overcoming the challenges of labour scarcity and regulatory constraints highlighted the strategic value they placed on the Indian workforce in meeting the demands of their operations in Iran.

Oil Workers' Everyday Life in Wartime

During the war, the living conditions for workers in the oil industry saw little improvement. Before the discovery of oil, Abadan was primarily an agrarian island with a sparse population, predominantly comprising the *Maniuhi* and *Nassar* Arab tribes settled across several villages. Masjed-Soleyman, on the other hand, emerged as a newly established Oil Company town, developed around the oilfields which were located along the migratory routes and spring pastures of the Bakhtiari nomads.

The discovery and subsequent development of the oil industry in Masjed-Soleyman triggered a wave of migration to the city. People were drawn either by employment opportunities in the oil sector or by the prospect of providing services to its burgeoning employee population. This influx transformed Masjed-Soleyman from a small oilfield town with just 523 employees in 1910[68] to a substantial company town, hosting a population of around 17,000 by 1920.[69]

Similarly, the population of Abadan witnessed a remarkable increase. In 1917, the town reported a population of 5,000, including APOC's employees, local residents, shopkeepers, and petty traders who had recently migrated to cater to the needs of the oil workers.[70] The end of the war saw a continued influx of people into Abadan, either in search of employment in the oil industry or to provide services to those employed in the sector. This migration led to extraordinary growth in Abadan. By the mid-1920s, the population of Abadan Island had soared to between 50,000 and 60,000.[71] In the early 1930s, the town of Abadan alone had a population of 30,000–40,000, about half of whom – approximately 17,370 men – were employed at the oil refinery.[72]

This rapid growth, driven by the oil industry, significantly altered the demographic and social landscape of both Masjed-Soleyman and Abadan, turning them from modest settlements into bustling urban centres within a relatively short period.

During the war, the living arrangements provided by the APOC for its employees were distinctly stratified along class and ethnic lines. This segregation was evident in the three different types of accommodations allocated to various groups of workers.

The European staff of APOC, who typically held higher-ranking positions within the company, were afforded the most comfortable living conditions.

They resided in exclusive, furnished brick bungalows, complete with gardens. These bungalows represented a significant level of comfort and privacy, reflecting the privileged status of the European employees within the company's hierarchy.

In contrast, the Indian employees, who often occupied intermediate roles in the company, were provided with semi-furnished accommodations. They lived in large, communal barracks. While these barracks were a step down from the individual bungalows of their European counterparts, they still offered a degree of furnishing and communal living facilities.

The Iranian unskilled workers, who formed the lower tier of APOC's workforce, had the most basic accommodations. They lived in makeshift shelters constructed from sticks or bamboo, loosely lashed together, and topped with roofs made from palm leaves. These rudimentary shelters underscored the stark disparities in living conditions among different employee groups within the company.

It was not until after the war, in the 1920s, that APOC began to reassess and reform its approach to employee welfare, recruitment, and urban planning. This shift in the company's social policy led to a more serious consideration of housing and living conditions for all its employees, indicating a move towards improving the overall welfare and quality of life of its workforce, regardless of their class or ethnicity.

Figure 2.1 An APOC official admissions ceremony for high-ranking Indian employees, Abadan, 1925

The oil towns of Masjed-Soleyman and Abadan in the era of British colonial influence were characterised by a distinct tripartite urban structure, reflecting the deeply entrenched social stratifications of the time. This spatial division within the cities mirrored the hierarchical ethnic segregation that was a hallmark of British colonialism.

At the apex of this hierarchy were the Europeans, primarily APOC's British employees, who brought with them the ethnic stratification principles prevalent in Britain and India. Occupying the middle tier were the Indian workers, serving in various capacities within the company. At the bottom of this hierarchy were the native Iranians, who largely comprised the unskilled labour force.

This ethnic division was not only a social construct but was also manifested in the physical layout of the towns. Different residential areas were designated for each ethnic group, a practice that was meticulously maintained and reinforced even as the towns expanded. New neighbourhoods, developed in response to the growth of the oil industry and changes in employment policies, adhered to the same principles of ethnic segregation.[73]

Although there were instances where higher-ranking Indian (and later, Iranian) employees were permitted to cross these rigid ethnic boundaries for official ceremonies, congregations, or worship services with the European community, such interactions were the exception rather than the norm. Social mixing across these ethnic divides was generally discouraged, with segregation being promoted as the preferable arrangement.

This system of segregation remained firmly in place for many years, only being dismantled in 1951 with the nationalisation of Iranian oil. The nationalisation marked a significant shift in the social and political landscape of the region, leading to the eventual breakdown of these long-standing ethnic barriers.

3

Oil and Authoritarian Modernisation During Interwar Period

At the conclusion of the First World War, Iran found itself mired in the complexities and turmoil resulting from the post-Constitutional Revolution era. Further compounded by its role as a battleground for major world powers. Since the early nineteenth century, both Russia and Britain had exerted significant influence in Iran, effectively making it a chessboard for their strategic interests. However, the landscape altered dramatically following the Russian Revolution of 1917, which temporarily diminished Russian presence in the region. This shift left Britain as the predominant international force in Iran. Capitalising on this, Britain sought to strengthen its grip by imposing the bilateral Anglo-Persian Treaty of 1919, aiming to bring Iran under semi-colonial control. However, it was the widespread resentment towards this treaty that galvanised ordinary Iranians, sparking resistance not only against British influence but also against Iran's longstanding political establishment.[1]

The intellectual elite of the country found themselves polarised between two distinct ideological camps. The first group was influenced by notions of social egalitarianism, liberalism, and a romantic form of territorial nationalism. In contrast, the second faction was primarily focused on the concept of a modern, centralised, and authoritative state – one not necessarily despotic, but robust enough to ensure the nation's sovereignty. This latter group, deeply concerned by the fates that befell the Austro-Hungarian, Ottoman, and Tsarist empires, believed that the survival of their nation hinged on finding a strong, orderly leader. They perceived such a figure as essential to effectively piece together the country's fragmented jigsaw, thereby maintaining national unity.

As a result, when Seyyed Zia al-Din Tabataba'i, a young journalist, in collaboration with Reza Khan, a Cossack officer, advanced towards Tehran in 1921 to proclaim their initiated coup d'état – the second in Iranian history – they strategically aligned their action with the prevailing public discontent against the Anglo-Persian Treaty of 1919. Capitalising on this sentiment, the annulment of the treaty became their inaugural act, symbolising their alignment with the nationalistic fervour and the desire for sovereignty that was widespread among the populace at that time. This move was a calculated effort to garner support and legitimacy for their newly established rule.[2]

After the coup d'état, the fortunes of its initiators diverged significantly. Seyyed Zia's prominence was short-lived, lasting no more than three months before he was compelled to go into exile. In contrast, Reza Khan not only retained his position of power but was also destined to be etched in Iranian history as a pivotal figure in the country's modernisation. His enduring influence and strategic actions marked him as a central architect in the transformation of Iran, shaping the nation's trajectory in significant ways.

Following his gradual consolidation of power and subsequent ascension to the Peacock Throne as Reza Shah Pahlavi, his twenty years reign from 1921 to 1941 was marked by the meticulous implementation of reforms that resonated with the aspirations of his enlightened supporters. His approach to authoritarian modernisation fundamentally altered the traditional social and political fabric of Iran.

Key reforms during his tenure included the establishment of new institutions. These encompassed a national standing army, underpinned by universal male conscription and extensive reserve units, reflecting a significant military modernisation. The education sector saw transformative changes with the introduction of a secular curriculum and a nationwide literacy program emphasising Persian, thereby reducing linguistic disparities. A secularised judicial system was instituted, marking a significant shift from religious to secular law. In the financial realm, a national monetary system was established, further centralising economic control.

Moreover, his centralisation policy involved rigorous measures such as the forced relocation and settlement of tens of thousands of nomads. This was part of a broader strategy to achieve greater national uniformity, often at the cost of significant social disruption and upheaval. These measures reflect a deliberate and systematic effort to reshape Iran into a more unified, centralised, and modern state under his leadership.

In the period following the First World War, Iran witnessed the rise of a new political order, characterised by the creation of coercive institutions designed to forge a modern, centralised state. A primary objective of this new state structure was to reduce provincial and tribal autonomy across the country, thereby increasing the interdependencies among the provinces. This shift towards centralising government power was accompanied by the implementation of extensive political and economic reforms. These reforms significantly hastened the processes of urbanisation and industrialisation, marking a transformative phase in Iran's socio-economic landscape. The country was thus steered away from its traditional, decentralised past towards a more unified, modern state structure, reflecting a deliberate effort to reshape Iran's political and economic dynamics in the post-war era.

The state-driven industrialisation process in Iran, particularly in 1930s, not only expedited urbanisation but also significantly altered the country's class structure. At the end of the First World War, out of Iran's total population of

11.5 million, about 2.5 million resided in urban areas. By the eve of the Second World War, despite the national population growing to 14.5 million, the urban population had disproportionately increased to 3.2 million.[3]

This demographic shift was largely attributed to the economic policies implemented throughout the 1920s and 1930s, coupled with the burgeoning oil industry in the south, especially in Khuzestan. The expansion of the oil industry not only enhanced the country's manufacturing capacity but also played a pivotal role in reshaping its economic landscape. Additionally, significant urban investments made by the government spurred labour migration from rural and tribal areas to cities. This movement was driven by the growing opportunities in urban centres, reflecting the broader economic and social transformations occurring in Iran during this period.

The trajectory of industrialisation in Iran during the interwar period can be segmented into two distinct phases: 1919–31 and 1931–41. In the initial phase, the government played a facilitative role in promoting private investment through the introduction of new legislations. These laws were designed to create a conducive environment for private capital to thrive and contribute to the country's industrial growth.

However, the second phase, spanning from 1931 to 1941, saw a significant shift in governmental policy, partly influenced by the global impact of the Great Depression. The government implemented a series of protective measures that effectively curtailed the role of private capital in the economy. Concurrently, the state became more actively involved in both the investment in and management of economic enterprises. This transition towards a more state-centric approach was marked by a greater emphasis on centralisation.

As a direct consequence of this shift, the processes of urbanisation and industrialisation gained momentum. The period saw the establishment of numerous modern industrial plants, which in turn led to a substantial increase in the industrial labour force (Table 3.1). This phase thus represents a critical juncture in Iran's economic history, where state intervention and centralisation played a pivotal role in accelerating industrial and urban development.

In the early 1920s, Iran's industrial landscape was relatively modest, with only a handful of industrial plants employing over a hundred workers. Outside of the burgeoning oil industry in the south, these enterprises were predominantly situated in the northern provinces. Notable among them were an arsenal in Tehran, a sugar refinery on the outskirts of Tehran, two textile mills in Tabriz, and a match factory in Khoy.

Over the subsequent two decades, there was a remarkable growth in industrial investment, which was reflected in the country's annual budget. The average annual increase in industrial investment was about 25 per cent.[4]

Table 3.1 *Growth of the labour force in selected large modern industries (per sector)*

Industries	Early 1920s	Early 1930s	Late 1930s
Oil	7,000–8,000	17,000	31,000
Spinning and textile	<1,500	1,800	25,700
Leather tannery	Not available	Not available	>5,000
Electricity plants	100	200	600
Construction/Road	3,300	Not available	60,000
Mining	200	Not available	3,000
Railways	–	–	14.500
Car transport	–	12,000	20,000
Carpet	Not available	Not available	250,000

Sources: British National Archive, F.O. 371/9027. Ahmad Mahrad, *Iran am Vorabend des II. Weltkrieges. Eine Materialsammlung deutscher, britischer und sowjetischer Geheimberichte* (Osnabrück: Selbstverlag, 1978). Willem Floor, *Industrialisation in Iran 1900–1941, Working Paper at the Centre for the Middle Eastern and Islamic Studies* (Durham: University of Durham, 1984).

This significant infusion of capital into the industrial sector led to a substantial increase in the number of modern industrial plants, totalling 346 by the late 1930s.[5]

Following the oil industry, the most substantial employment sector was the established cotton and wool spinning and textile production industries. These industries became the second-largest employer, with approximately 25,700 workers. This growth is illustrative of the broader trend of industrial expansion in Iran during this period. A notable aspect of this expansion was the diversification of industries and the increase in the industrial labour force, which outlines the growth of the labour force in selected large modern industries. This table would provide a clearer picture of the specific trends and changes in employment within these key industrial sectors.

In the subsequent sections of this study, I will delve into an analysis of how the social and political transformations during the interwar period in Iran impacted the living conditions of the burgeoning working class. This examination will focus on understanding the extent to which these changes enhanced the agency of the working populace in influencing the social and political evolution of the country. The analysis aims to shed light on the dynamic interactions between industrial growth, urbanisation, and the emergence of a more prominent working class, and how these elements collectively contributed to shaping the broader sociopolitical landscape of Iran during this critical historical juncture.

Rising Tide: Radicalisation of the Labour Movement

The severe economic crisis that struck Iran in the aftermath of the First World War led to extensive protests in numerous major cities across the country. These protests, catalysed by the pervasive influence of global news covering the movements of the labouring poor and the subaltern in the post-war period, were instrumental in the formation of Iran's first trade unions.

Founded in 1919, the Union of Printing Workers was Iran's first labour union. Initially comprising approximately 180 members, the union promptly initiated a fourteen-day strike, advocating for several key reforms: the reduction of the workday to eight hours, regulation of overtime compensation, prohibition of arbitrary dismissals, and the provision of medical care along with compensation for illnesses and injuries sustained in industrial accidents.[6] This strike escalated into a nationwide movement, attracting workers from various sectors, including bakeries, who subsequently established the Union of Bakery Workers. As a result, Tehran, with its population of 400,000, became home to two labour unions. The initial successes of these unions inspired workers from other sectors to pursue improved working conditions and establish their own unions. By 1921, the number of unions in Tehran had grown to ten, as detailed in Table 3.2, However, it remains debatable whether some of these entities were traditional guilds rather than modern unions.

Later that year, in an effort to assert their influence in the national political sphere and articulate their demands, the founders of the Tehran-based unions collaborated to establish the *Showra-ye Markazi-ye Koll-e Kargaran-e Tehran* (Central Council of All Labour Unions of Tehran – CCLUT). This initiative marked the first significant step towards the creation of a nationwide labour union, a milestone achieved the following year.

Labour activism extended beyond the capital, with workers in various Iranian cities, particularly those in the north, influenced by the Russian Revolution, establishing their own unions. In Rasht, a city of 250,000 inhabitants and a labour force of 15,000, unions were formed by printers and shoemakers, collectively amassing 3,000 members. In the Caspian city of Anzali, the Union of Fishermen boasted a membership of 3,000, while the Union of Dockworkers reported having 200 members.[7] In Tabriz, with a population of 300,000 and a labour force of 30,000, the city's labour activists founded the *Hezb-e Kargaran* (Workers' Party), a union with a distinctive policy: 'membership was restricted to those who did not derive their livelihood from the exploitation of others'.[8] The Workers' Party in Tabriz succeeded in attracting 3,000 members.[9]

The year 1922 commenced with a direct confrontation between the government and labour unions. In January 1922, when postal and telegraph workers initiated a strike for wage increases, the government swiftly responded by issuing a decree that barred civil servants from joining unions. In response to this decree and in pursuit of restitution, Tehran's schoolteachers also launched a

Table 3.2 *Membership of labour unions in Tehran, 1921 and 1923*

	Membership	
Unions	1921	1923
Bakery workers	3,000	3,720
Tailors	2,000	2,000
Shoemakers	1,800	1,800
Postal workers	90	120
Telegraph workers	180	564
Confectionary workers	300	400
Printers	180	200
Embroidery workers	150	150
Shop apprentices	350	80
Trading house clerk	250	–
Teachers	–	400
Municipal workers	–	500
Cigarette makers	–	2,500
Pharmaceutical workers	–	130
Total	8,300	12,564

Sources: Seyyed Mohammad Dehgan, 'Report to the International Red Labour Union (Profintern)', in *The Historical Documents: The Workers, Social Democrats, and the Communist Movement in Iran (1903–1963).* Cosroe Chaqueri (ed.), Volume 6 (Florence: Mazdak, 1976), Volume 6, 105.

strike. These public sector strikes brought the unions into direct conflict with the government, infusing their actions with a political dimension. Facing severe economic difficulties, the government was resistant to negotiating salary increases. However, when the employees of the Parliament's printing office went on strike for higher pay, their demands were reluctantly met, including the provision of ten days of paid vacation per year.

In 1922, following a collaborative effort between the unions of Tehran and those from other provinces, Iran's first nationwide labour union was established. This new labour federation was named *Showra-ye Markazi-ye Ettahadiyeh-ha-ye Herfeh'i-ye Kargaran-e Iran* (The Central Council of Professional Labour Unions of Iran – CCPLUI). Seyyed Mohammad Dehgan, a journalist who had translated *The Communist Manifesto* into Persian,[10] was elected as the secretary of this nascent labour federation. In the same year, the CCPLUI became affiliated with the Moscow-based *Red International of Labour Unions (Profintern)*, and Dehgan represented the organisation at its Fourth Congress held in Moscow. During his address, he announced that the CCPLUI, boasting a membership of 20,000, had successfully organised approximately 20 per cent of Iran's industrial labour force.[11]

Labour unionism and activism persisted throughout 1922, marked by well documented workers' strikes advocating for shorter working hours and wage increases. Notably, the dockworkers' strike in Anzali and the railway workers' strike in Tabriz are significant events from this period that warrant mention.

By mid-1923, the crackdown on labour unions intensified, leading to the arrest and temporary imprisonment of numerous labour activists. Consequently, union leaders were compelled to adopt semi-clandestine operations. These actions, however, were merely preliminary measures in the government's broader anti-union campaign. In 1925, following Reza Pahlavi's ascension to the throne, the government launched a comprehensive campaign that outlawed all union activities nationwide. This left Iranian labour activists with no choice but to operate covertly.

Modernisation: Authoritarian vs Participatory Trends

The establishment of political parties in Iran can be traced back to the period preceding the Constitutional Revolution. The emergence of the first bona fide political parties in Iran was a significant development during the second parliamentary term, spanning from November 1909 to December 1911. This period marked a pivotal transition in the nation's political landscape, characterised by the establishment of officially recognised and genuinely representative political factions. These parties represented various factions within Iran's nascent mass politics. Prominent among them in the Second Parliament was the *Hezb-e Demokrat-e Iran* (Democrat Party of Iran). The Democrat Party of Iran demonstrated a strong commitment to civil rights, as reflected in their program's list of demands. These demands emphasised equality for all individuals under the state and its constitution, without discrimination based on race, religion, or ethnicity. The party also advocated for the protection of individuals from any form of assault (notably, gender was not specified), as well as the freedoms of speech, press, assembly, and the right to strike. Additionally, the program asserted the rights to residence and travel, underscoring a broad spectrum of civil liberties.[12]

Embracing a steadfast commitment to the rule of law, individual rights, and autonomy, the Iranian social democrats broadened their vision of equality to encompass all Iranian citizens. This inclusive approach was also reflected in the criteria for joining the party. 'As stipulated in the party's bylaws, a candidate wishing to join a party cell must agree to the party's program and bylaws. Additionally, the application of the candidate must be endorsed by two existing party members. Candidates are expected to have an unblemished reputation and should not be identified as scroungers or clerics'.[13]

Moreover, the Democrat Party's daily newspaper, *Iran-e Now* (New Iran), which was published in Tehran from 1909 to 1911, consistently championed the notion of citizenship and individual rights within the broader framework of constitutionalism.[14] Under the chief editorship of Mohammad-Amin Rasulzadeh, *Iran-e Now* achieved significant influence and popularity. With a circulation ranging between 2,000 and 3,000 copies, it was the most widely read periodical of its time in Iran, serving as a key platform for disseminating the party's ideals and perspectives.[15]

In its coverage of labour activism across the globe, *Iran-e Now* endeavoured to educate its readers about the history and accomplishments of the international labour movement. The newspaper highlighted the evolution of workers' strategies in Europe, initially characterised by direct action against the instruments of capitalism, such as machine breaking. The paper noted, 'At first in Europe, workers in the struggle against capitalism did such things [break the machines]. Later on, however, they realised that they could not halt the progress of history in this manner. Subsequently, they discovered a more direct and innovative method of resistance – the formation of workers' unions (*ettehad-e 'amaleh*), The workers' union adopted a pragmatic approach, stating, 'Let the machines reduce the number of workers; in response, we will decrease the working hours instead'. This narrative underscored the shift from initial reactive measures to more structured and strategic forms of labour organisation.[16]

The political upheavals in Russia profoundly influenced social democratic and labour movements around the world. While many of these movements continued to champion the practice of basic civil rights, the aspiration to establish a more egalitarian society introduced new facets to the discussions on civil liberties and political democracy. In Iran, one of the political parties that progressed towards formulating a more explicit definition of liberty was the *Ferqeh-ye Sosiyalist-e Iran* (Socialist Party of Iran).[17] The party's program encapsulated a range of progressive articles, including: the equality of all Iranians, both male and female, irrespective of religious affiliation, race, or ethnicity before the law; freedom of conscience, speech, press, assembly, and the right to strike; the liberty of women; and the abolition of capital punishment. These tenets signified a significant shift towards broader and more inclusive concepts of individual rights and freedoms within the political discourse of Iran.[18]

The program of the Socialist Party of Iran marked a distinct departure from those of earlier social democratic parties, particularly in its explicit articulation of civil rights, with a notable emphasis on gender equality. This program expanded the boundaries of individual rights and freedoms, extending beyond the political sphere and enriching the discourse on civil and individual liberties. The influence of this movement became even more pronounced with the publication of *Haqiqat* (The Truth), through which the labour movement directly engaged in the expansive discourse of civil society in post-Constitutional

Revolution Iran. This intervention signified a critical juncture, intertwining labour activism with broader societal and political debates, thereby deepening the impact of the labour movement on the nation's ongoing transformation.

Building on its organisational success, the CCPLUI initiated the publication of *Haqiqat*, a nationwide newspaper. The inaugural issue of *Haqiqat* was released on 30 December 1921, with Seyyed Mohammad Dehgan serving as its chief editor. Several months later, *Haqiqat* positioned itself as the official mouthpiece of the newly formed labour confederation, the CCPLUI. The newspaper, characterised by its unequivocally socialist stance, prominently featured the slogan *Ranjbaran-e Ru-ye Zamin Ettehad*! (Toilers of the World Unite!) at the top of its front page and declared its mission as the 'supporter of workers and labour unions'.[19]

Sultanzadeh, a prominent theorist of the Communist Party of Iran and an active representative of the Comintern, commented on the Iranian press in one of his articles. He described *Haqiqat*, which had a circulation of between 2,000 and 2,500, as the 'true adherent of Iranian workers' and peasants' class struggle'. However, it is noteworthy that Sultanzadeh never asserted any formal affiliation between *Haqiqat*.

In its inaugural editorial, *Haqiqat* outlined its mission, aiming to introduce a new actor onto Iran's political landscape. The editorial emphasised the significance of the concept of *kar* (Work), asserting that it should stand alongside *sarmayeh* (Capital) and *servat* (Wealth) in the country's political discourse. *Haqiqat* issued a call to action to *kargaran* (workers) and *ranjbaran* (toilers), urging them to collaborate with other social forces in educating the populace and advocating for social justice in both politics and public life. This stance reflected the publication's commitment to elevating the role and recognition of labour within the broader societal context, highlighting the newspaper's role as a champion of workers' rights and a proponent of sociopolitical change. 'We don't take bread from anyone. We serve all Iranians, even those who consider us as their enemy. We want happiness and prosperity for all!'[20]

In subsequent editions, *Haqiqat* diligently pursued its mission to enlighten the labouring poor about civil rights, both in individual and collective contexts. The newspaper emphasised various civil liberties, including equal access to education, the right to work, the right to join professional organisations or labour unions, the right to strike, and crucially, gender equality. These civil rights were consistently highlighted and advocated for within the pages of *Haqiqat*, demonstrating the publication's dedication to informing and empowering its readership on these fundamental issues. 'Every individual is held accountable for their actions, devoid of any preferential treatment. This principle of equality extends across all strata of society, encompassing farmers, workers, writers, teachers, soldiers, ministers, and Parliament deputies alike. Each is equal before the law, and all are entitled to the fundamental right of leading a dignified life'.[21]

In an editorial under the title of *Hefz-e azadi, vazifeh-ye mellat ast* (Guarding liberty is the duty of the nation). *Haqiqat* called for freedom of expression, press, assembly, and association: 'It is imperative not merely to restore the constitutional code and ensure the liberty of parliamentary elections, but equally vital is the establishment of provincial assemblies and city councils. In these esteemed forums, representatives elected by the people shall convene to deliberate and make informed decisions regarding the welfare and prosperity of the citizenry'.[22]

Moreover, in addressing civil liberties, including matters of religious practice, *Haqiqat* urged the religious establishment to refrain from meddling in the private lives of individuals. This stance highlighted the newspaper's advocacy for the separation of religious authority from the personal affairs of citizens, emphasising the importance of individual autonomy and freedom in matters of faith and personal conduct: 'Each individual bears responsibility for their actions. It is incumbent upon the government to refrain from intruding into the private lives of its citizens. Let people be accountable to their own beliefs and deities as they see fit, free from governmental oversight or intervention'.[23]

It is important to recognise that the earliest expression of anti-clerical sentiment during the Iranian Constitutional Revolution came from *Sur-e Esrafil*, a periodical with social democratic leanings. *Sur-e Esrafil* notably appealed to the Iranian clergy, urging them to cease their involvement in the daily lives of Iranians and to allow the people to determine their own future independently. This call represented a significant moment in the history of Iranian social and political thought, marking a clear stance for individual autonomy and a move towards secularism in public life. The message conveyed to 'both spiritual and worldly leaders' was clear and concise: 'Our message to both the temporal and the eternal realms is clear: The time has passed for ideals to be imposed upon us through force, stringent logic, or the fervent zeal of preaching. Rather, we seek the freedom to discern and comprehend our own ideals, guided by the light of our personal autonomy'.[24]

This statement reflects a profound shift towards self-determination and individual freedom in discerning one's beliefs and ideals, moving away from imposed doctrines or ideologies.

Haqiqat articulated its stance on the role of religion in the nation, aligning it closely with its political perspective. The publication regarded Iranian clerics as mere 'puppets in the hands of reactionaries', categorising them into two distinct groups. The first group was labelled as *din-forush* (religion dealers), comprising individuals who, aside from their clerical status, lacked any other *kasb va sanʿat mashruʿ* (legitimate profession). The second group consisted of affluent clerics who led lives of aristocratic luxury. This critique underscored *Haqiqat*'s view of the religious establishment as being out of touch with the common people and entangled in reactionary politics.

> The clerics of the first category are driven by monetary incentives, aligning themselves with those who offer the highest remuneration. They are swayed by material comforts, ready to sit at any table that promises a more sumptuous feast and to extol the virtues of whoever provides them with greater benefits. The second group comprises aristocratic mullahs who caution the populace against any form of change or progress within the country. The establishment of law and justice poses a threat to their very existence, as it challenges the foundations of their privileged status and influence.[25]

Haqiqat drew parallels between the position of Iranian clerics and their counterparts in France and the Ottoman Empire, particularly in how they aligned themselves with the ancien régime and Ottoman despotism. The newspaper critically remarked on the stance of Ottoman clerics: 'In the Ottoman Empire, they often proclaimed, *shariʿat isteriz – shariʿat mikhahim* (we need sharia) and were complicit in the execution of tens of thousands of innocent Muslims'. Such actions by the Ottoman clerics, according to *Haqiqat*, left the populace with no choice but to overthrow these clerics and liberate themselves from these *mikrob-ha-ye muzi* (insidious germs).[26] This perspective underscored *Haqiqat*'s criticism of religious figures who used their authority to support oppressive regimes, thereby betraying the fundamental principles of justice and morality.

Haqiqat maintained its anti-clerical stance throughout its publication, albeit with noticeable variations in approach and tone. For instance, in an editorial titled 'Ramadan finished' published at the end of the Muslim fasting month of Ramadan, *Haqiqat* sharply criticised the mullahs for exploiting the sanctity of this holy month. The newspaper accused them of using Ramadan as a platform for preaching against groups and forces within the country that were striving for *azadi va ʿedalat* (freedom and justice). This criticism reflected *Haqiqat*'s ongoing concern that religious figures were manipulating religious practices and occasions to hinder progressive movements and suppress calls for societal reforms:

> Our stance is clear: discussing the faith of individuals falls beyond our policy. We firmly believe that religion is a matter of personal conviction, an integral part of the private lives of our citizens. Consequently, we urge the government to refrain from intervening in this domain. It is not within the government's purview to prohibit public eating or to restrict access to music. (…) We welcome the conclusion of the holy month, for it removes any pretext the *mullahs* might use to assail the advocates of freedom in our country under the guise of opposing religious impiety.[27]

Haqiqat frequently criticised the government for its lack of sincerity in implementing its professed policy of change and reform. The newspaper pointed out that while the government claimed to advocate for radical change towards establishing a modern state, it simultaneously appeased conservative clerics.

Haqiqat suggested that these conservative clerics believed any shift in the state-society dynamics in Iran would threaten their dominance. Concurrently, official secular political tendencies focused on introducing top-down modernisation, establishing a modern, centralised, and authoritarian state.

This focus was driven partly by concerns over the fates that had befallen the Austro-Hungarian, Ottoman, and Russian Empires. Proponents of this approach sought a figure of authority who could maintain national sovereignty and unity while implementing extensive social and political reforms. However, *Haqiqat* did not align itself with this camp. Instead, it rejected the notion of authoritarian modernisation. *Haqiqat* argued that:

> Within the liberal press of the capital, two distinct schools of thought have emerged regarding the necessity of revolution or reform. One faction advocates for the emergence of a strong, authoritative figure who can spearhead change and reform in Iran. In contrast, another group champions the idea of reform emanating from within society itself. To our esteemed readers, it is clear that our allegiance lies with this latter camp. We believe in the power of societal-driven reform, grounded in the collective will and actions of the populace, rather than in the imposition of change by a singular authoritative figure.[28]

With this introduction, *Haqiqat* proposed practical steps for the public to actively contribute to the advancement of modernity and internalised the process of modernisation. The newspaper advocated for the active participation of the people in legislative processes and their engagement through parliamentary, provincial, and city councils. These platforms, according to *Haqiqat*, provided opportunities for the public to have their representatives, engage in debates, offer criticism, and ultimately arrive at social and political consensus.

Furthermore, *Haqiqat* emphasised the importance of civil institutions in shaping political culture. These institutions brought together individuals from various professional backgrounds, enabling them to share their experiences and collectively shape the future. The newspaper acknowledged that those who did not believe in the power of the people would not align with these ideas.

As the voice of the labour union, *Haqiqat* primarily addressed Iranian workers and the labouring poor, endorsing their rights, and emphasising their vibrant presence in public politics. The publication's advocacy for the active participation of workers and the labouring class underscored its commitment to advancing social justice and empowering those at the grassroots level.

On the occasion of International Labour Day, 1 May 1922, Haqiqat published a lengthy editorial in which it articulated its stance not only towards the government but also outlined its short and long-term policies regarding the labour movement.[29] The editorial began with a brief review of the history of International Labour Day.

Haqiqat then called upon the government to lift Martial Law and officially recognised Labour Day as a public holiday. This demand was in alignment with the global significance of International Labour Day, which is dedicated to workers' rights and labour movements.

> Our proposal, presented by those who oppose despotism and the rule of tribal lords and chieftains, is straightforward. Designating the First of May as a public holiday should not be misconstrued as a sanction of disorder within the country, nor should it be viewed as a symbol of revolution. Rather, this day is a platform for the working people to assert their rights. It serves as a reminder to the government that its primary role is to serve the people, and not the other way around. This day symbolizes the collective voice of the workforce, underscoring their contributions and affirming their entitlement to recognition and respect.[30]

On International Labour Day, *Haqiqat* expressed its aspiration to witness the eventual realisation of socialism in the country. However, the newspaper acknowledged the practical limitations of the current situation in Iran. It admitted that 'today Iran is not ready for the abolition of private ownership' primarily because there was insufficient accumulated capital in the country that could be allocated to the public. *Haqiqat* emphasised the need to first generate wealth within Iran before pursuing more extensive socialist measures. It clarified that this perspective did not contradict the fundamental principle of socialism.[31]

This nuanced stance recognised the economic realities of the time while still advocating for a socialist vision in the long run. *Haqiqat* aimed to balance its ideals with pragmatic considerations, acknowledging the importance of building wealth and resources before implementing broader socialist policies.

Haqiqat believed that the journey towards wealth generation in the country was contingent upon the promotion of modernity and the practice of modernisation. The newspaper envisioned a society in which a 'strong and centralised national state' would lead efforts to modernised various aspects, including administration, education, ethics, and even attire and cuisine. According to *Haqiqat* workers should be actively engaged in the work process throughout their working day, as any deviation from work during working hours was considered a sin. It was only after working hours that workers could gather and engage in political discussions.[32]

The editorial for the Labour Day concluded with the following words, emphasising the importance of diligence and unity among workers: 'Long live the Constitutional Code! Long live justice and equality! Long live a civilised and modern Iran, embracing progress and innovation. Long live a youthful Iran, vibrant with energy and potential. Long live the First of May, a symbol of solidarity with the rights of oppressed people worldwide! Long live freedom!'[33]

As the labour movement in Iran was still in its early stages of development, the consolidation of political power in the country aimed at establishing authoritarian rule progressively limited the space for free and permissible political activities. Ultimately, after its 106th issue in November 1922, the Iranian government suspended the publication of *Haqiqat*. This closure marked a continuation of earlier efforts by the government to hinder the activities of labour unions. Such efforts persisted to varying degrees throughout the remaining years of the interwar period.

The suspension of *Haqiqat* was indicative of the challenges faced by labour unions and progressive movements during this era, as they navigated a political landscape characterised by authoritarianism and restrictions on free expression. Despite these obstacles, the labour movement and its ideals continued to play a significant role in shaping Iran's political and social landscape during this period.

Petroleum, Labour, and Statecraft in Interwar Iran

While the archives of the Anglo-Persian Oil Company (APOC) do not document significant labour unrest or large-scale protests in the oil industry during its nascent phase, the company's activities were not devoid of challenges. There were numerous instances of conflict and altercations between European foremen, often characterised by abusive behaviour, and the aggrieved labour force. These incidents underscored the underlying tensions and difficulties prevalent in the industry.

In the formative years of the oil sector, disputes and disagreements between employees and foremen were typically resolved through intermediation by the foremen, with casual workers showing little inclination towards collective self-organisation or class-based representation. However, this dynamic started to shift following the conclusion of the First World War.

In December 1920, approximately 3,000 Indian workers employed at the Abadan Refinery staged a strike with a list of demands that included:

1. An increase of 80 per cent in wages.
2. A reduction in daily working hours.
3. Additional pay for overtime work.
4. Improvement of sanitary conditions.
5. An end to vilification and mistreatment of workers by staff members.

Notably, these Indian workers were soon joined by their Iranian co-workers, which pressured the refinery authorities to concede to some of the workers' demands. This development was a matter of concern for the directors of the APOC, as they feared the radicalisation of their skilled Indian workers and the spread of 'subversive ideas' among unskilled Iranians.

Additionally, Ronald Ferrier, a historian of British Petroleum, noted that the 1920 strike was influenced by the 'bitter resentment in India following the Amritsar massacre riot of April 1919. He also mentioned the involvement of Indian 'semi-organised' political agitators in provoking the strike'.[34]

Figure 3.1 The Punjabi Gazars employed as *Dhobi* (Washermen), Abadan, 1921

Recent historians have pointed to the Amritsar massacre as a possible cause of the 1920 Indian workers' strike in Abadan.[35] However, it's important to note that there is doubt surrounding the direct association between the two events, given the significant time gap of more than a year and a half between them. Such an interpretation may overlook the dire living conditions and low wages that workers in the oil industry were facing during that period or may stem from a colonial perspective on historical events.

The workers' call for an 80 per cent increase in salary highlights the inadequate compensation received by both Indian and Iranian employees. Petitions filed by Iranian workers to the Tehran government consistently referenced concerns such as insufficient wages, poor facilities, unhygienic living conditions, and the absence of disability compensation. These grievances underscore the economic and workplace conditions that were significant factors in igniting labour activism within the oil industry.[36]

Despite APOC's efforts at reconciliation ultimately acknowledging the strikers' call for higher wages, this response failed to address several other critical issues raised in workers' petitions. These unresolved demands included better accommodation for married workers, improved medical services, enhanced leisure amenities, fair exchange rates, and the issue concerning the sale of discharge certificates of Indian workers. Given this partial resolution, it was predictable that workers' discontent would resurface. Indeed, this re-emergence of dissatisfaction occurred some two years later.

In March 1922, another strike of Indian workers broke out, which was soon joined by Iranian workers The strike's call was for increase on wages. However, this strike was short-lived due to the company's prompt and stringent response. APOC dismissed all Iranian participants in the strike and repatriated approximately 2,000 Indian workers using two ships. Despite assertions from APOC management attributing the strike to the orchestration by 'Iranian communists', there is no substantiating evidence for such claims. In reality, it would take several more years before Iranian communists could significantly penetrate APOC's operations in Khuzestan.[37]

George Thomson, an APOC employee, characterised the 1922 strike as a 'well-organised' movement led by 'skilled artisans, involving about 2,000 Indians'. However, Thomson did not delve into the underlying causes of this strike. In contrast, an 'eyewitness account' by an Indian APOC employee named Mudliar detailed the substandard working and living conditions faced by Indians at APOC. This account echoed an earlier statement by Dr Ghore, published in the Mumbai Chronicle under, the title 'Indian Workers in Persia, Miserable Condition'. According to Dr Ghore's statement:

> The Anglo-Persian Oil Company alone employed 95 percent Indians. There is no restriction in the number of hours worked every day. Neither coal nor ice was supplied to workers until agitation was stared. Workers die of sunstroke in summer and pneumonia in winter as little is done to look to their wants and comforts. I request Indian labour to take up the cause of their comrades in Persia particularly those employed by the Anglo-Persian Oil Company, whose Agents are the Shaw Wallace & Co., Mumbai.[38]

Following Dr Ghore statement, Mudliar narrates his personal experience of working for APOC, where 'Large numbers of workers, both skilled and unskilled, are brought in rapidly via steamers and trains, with negligible care for their well-being during transit, resulting in considerable suffering. Upon reaching Mohammareh (Khorramshahr), these workers, despite being second-class passengers, are transported to the oilfields on the open decks of steamers, enduring the harsh cold and chilling weather of the severe Persian winter'.

Regarding their accommodation, Mudliar notes, 'on arrival at such a bleak location, suitable lodging is often not provided. In cases where accommodation is offered, it lacks basic facilities like latrines and cookhouses'. He also highlights the erratic and extended working hours, mentioning: 'There is no fixed schedule for working hours, which can sometimes extend to 10 to 12 hours a day under all weather conditions'. Mudliar describes the working environment as 'humiliating' and 'unbearable', corroborating Dr Ghore's mention of 'men dying from sunstroke and pneumonia', affirming these as accurate observations.[39]

Table 3.3 *Employment in the Anglo-Persian/AIOC, 1910–40*

Year	Iranian	Indian	European	Other	Total
1910	1,362	158	40	146	1,706
1915	2,203	979	80	187	3,449
1920	8,447	3,616	244	35	12,342
1925	15,820	4,890	994	7,201	28,905
1930	20,095	2,411	1,191	7,549	31,246
1935	25,240	954	1,035	119	27,348
1940	26,484	1,158	1,056	15	28,713

Sources: R. W. Ferrier, *The History of the British Petroleum, The Developing Years 1901–1932* (London: Cambridge University Press, 1982); J.H. Bamberg, *The History of the British Petroleum, The Anglo-Iranian Years, 1928–1954* (London: Cambridge University Press, 1994).

Mudliar's testimony also includes a detailed description of the extremely poor living conditions faced by Indian workers: 'The living accommodation provided is inadequate and large number of people are huddled tighter in small room, incompletely furnished, by way of furniture and lights, nothing to say of cook houses and latrines, thus making life extremely hard'.[40] In addition to the 'unbearable' working and living conditions, Mudliar highlights the escalating costs of essential commodities and the overall high cost of living as significant challenges. He notes that prices were consistently high and 'increasing daily', rendering it 'impossible' for Indian workers to 'command even the necessaries of life' in Persia, let alone 'to support their dependents in India'.[41]

The quelling of the 1922 labour protest by the British authorities and APOC, while effectively halting the immediate momentum of labour activism, nonetheless served to intensify and accumulate the demands of the labour force within the oil industry. Concurrently, on the Iranian governmental front, the significant social and political developments previously mentioned set the stage for the establishment and consolidation of Reza Shah's authoritarian rule.

The Iranian government's inclination towards capitalist Western nations, particularly its cooperation with the British, combined with the suppression of communist organisations and labour unions, prompted the Comintern (Communist International) to revise its stance. Initially offering unequivocal support to Reza Shah, the Comintern shifted to a more cautious, yet non-aggressive approach. This policy adjustment was largely influenced by the interests of the Soviet Union.

The 1927 trade treaty between Iran and the Soviet Union played a pivotal role in this change. While the treaty convinced Moscow of the possibility of coexistence with Iran, fostering a neighbourly, albeit not always amicable, relationship, it did not deter the Comintern from re-evaluating its policy towards Iran. This reassessment reflected the complex interplay of geopolitical interests and ideological alignments in the region.

In the early months of 1927, Yusof Eftekhari, an alumnus of the Moscow-based University of the Toilers of the East (KUTV), found himself unexpectedly reassigned from Dushanbe, Tajikistan, to undertake a new mission in Iran. Originally deployed to Tajikistan for the purpose of disseminating communist propaganda, Eftekhari had harboured a preference for returning to Iran, a desire that had been previously thwarted by the Comintern. In a significant shift in directive, the Comintern now reversed its earlier decision, tasking him with the reorganization of Iran's dispersed labour unions and the mobilization of oil industry workers. Heeding this call, Eftekhari proceeded to Khuzestan. There, in collaboration with Rahim Hamdad – a fellow activist also designated by the Comintern from Moscow – and Ali Omid, they spearheaded unionization efforts amongst the oil workers and established a clandestine network within the labour union at the Abadan Refinery.

In 1929, following two years of covert organising among the workers of the Abadan Refinery, a significant strike took place in Abadan on First of May, coinciding with International Labour Day. Among the demands of approximately 9,000 striking workers – out of a total workforce of 28,000 – were a 15 per cent wage increase, official recognition of the workers' union, acknowledgement of the International Labour Day as a legitimate holiday, and a reduction in working hours: from ten to seven hours during summer and to eight hours in winter.[42]

However, the description of the strike's demands as reported by APOC to its headquarters in London differed. APOC's report characterised the demands as a call for a six-hour working day, a minimum wage of forty-five rials per month for labourers, representation of labour in management, and complete equality between Indian and Iranian employees.[43] This discrepancy between the workers' stated demands and the company's report underscores the differing perspectives and possibly the company's interpretation or portrayal of the workers' grievances.

In their initial response to the strike, APOC authorities labelled it a 'Bolshevik plot', purporting that its true intent was to incite unrest in Khuzestan.[44] The management at APOC speculated that the demands being 'formulated to cloak real Bolshevik activity and not likely to materialise'.[45] The strike persisted for three days before it was quelled. The resolution came about through a combination of 'strong action by the [provincial] government of Abadan together with immediate reinforcement of Masjed-Soleyman garrison'.[46] Additionally, in a move reflecting the seriousness with which the British authorities viewed the situation, the British consul in Khorramshahr requested the warship 'Cyclamen to move down the Shatt al-Arab to point within easy reach of Abadan',[47] indicating a readiness to intervene if necessary. This militaristic and governmental intervention highlights the perceived threat of the strike and the lengths to which the authorities were willing to go to suppress labour unrest.

Following the widespread detention of strikers at the Abadan Refinery and the ensuing expulsion of 103 activists from the city, Yusof Eftekhari found himself arrested and detained in Tehran. It was here, within the prison walls, that he encountered other Iranian communists. During this period, the harrowing details of the Soviet Great Terror, spanning from 1935 to 1939, permeated Tehran's detention facilities, igniting intense debates among the incarcerated communists. Despite a predominant endorsement of the Stalinist purges among his peers, Eftekhari persistently expressed his dissent. His opposition might have been perceived as sympathetic to Trotskyism by other prisoners, even though he did not formally identify his anti-Stalinist views with Trotskyism.[48]

In the aftermath of the labour movement's suppression at the Abadan Refinery, management attempted to downplay the significance of the upheaval.[49] Despite these efforts, the 1929 strike resonated far beyond its initial confines, signalling a broader impact across various sectors. The unrest not only permeated other parts of the oil industry, notably the Masjed-Soleyman oilfield, but also extended its influence on different industries within the region. A report sent from Abadan to APOC's London office on 28 May 1929 noted that approximately 300 workers of the Ulen Company, involved in railway construction near Ahvaz, had also demanded higher wages. In a recurring pattern of response, and now acting upon the advice of APOC, the Ulen Company approached the Governor General of Ahvaz to facilitate the arrest of the strikes' 'ringleaders'.[50]

This move, mirroring the approach taken in Abadan, indicates a consistent strategy by industry authorities and governmental officials to quell labour unrest through law enforcement and suppression of key activists, rather than through negotiation or addressing the underlying grievances of the workers.

It's noteworthy that, just across the Iranian border in the Soviet Union, the Comintern was closely monitoring the developments of the Abadan strike. The reaction in Moscow to the news of the strike was one of considerable enthusiasm. This keen interest underlines the geopolitical significance of labour movements in the oil-rich regions and their potential alignment with broader communist objectives.

A telling instance of this heightened interest is detailed in a telegram sent by APOC to its London office. According to this communication, a Soviet cargo ship, the *Michael Frunze*, arrived at Khorramshahr – located near the Abadan Refinery – on 2 May and remained anchored there for eight days. The telegram alleged that this vessel not only delivered general cargo but also offloaded cases containing propaganda pamphlets, and as suspected by APOC, potentially arms and ammunition.[51]

The situation intensified when another Soviet cargo ship, named *The Communist*, anchored at Khorramshahr on 15 May. The arrival of this second ship caused considerable alarm for APOC. The presence of these Soviet ships in close proximity to the strike's epicentre, especially at a time of such labour unrest, was perceived as a direct challenge and a source of significant concern for both APOC and the British authorities, reflecting the intricate interplay of industrial, political, and international dynamics at play in the region. The APOC which was voiced in the following words:

> Certain Customs officials are pro-Soviet which renders it impossible to keep cargoes under surveillance. We have requested Government to remove these officials. The Governor of Abadan has confiscated 540 shot guns besides number of revolvers at Abadan. While confident our counter propaganda will prove effective and improvement situation maintained, we cannot emphasise too strongly the unsettled atmosphere which persisted by reasons of Soviet propaganda and that if lead given by sudden acts of sabotage and/or incendiarism perpetrated by even a few Soviet Agents labour would break out again [sic].[52]

It is important to recognise that the claims made by APOC regarding the alleged activities of the Soviet cargo ships – the landing of propaganda materials, arms, and ammunition – were not corroborated by evidence from other sources. Investigations into documents housed in the Soviet-Comintern archives, as well as various Iranian archives and eyewitness accounts, do not support these assertions made by APOC.

This lack of corroboration from independent and diverse sources raises questions about the accuracy and motives behind APOC's allegations. It suggests that these claims might have been influenced by the prevailing geopolitical tensions and the company's own interests in portraying the labour unrest in a certain light, potentially as a means to justify their response to the strike or to garner support from British authorities. The discrepancy between APOC's claims and the findings from other archival and eyewitness sources highlights the complexity and the contested nature of historical narratives, especially in the context of labour movements and international politics.

In response to the labour strike in Abadan, the Executive Committee of the Comintern in Moscow made a strategic decision to send an envoy directly to the scene for an in-depth, first-hand report. The individual selected for this mission was Sultanzadeh, who discreetly travelled to Abadan under the guise of a merchant, utilising a passport issued by the Kingdom of Serbs, Croats, and Slovenes.[53] This choice of cover highlights the need for caution and secrecy, given the tense political climate and the potential risks involved in such a mission.

Additionally, the Comintern established a special commission with the specific mandate to closely monitor the strike in Abadan, analyse its outcomes, and explore ways to support it. This move underscores the significance the Comintern placed on the strike, viewing it as a potentially pivotal event in the broader context of labour movements and communist activities in the region. The establishment of this commission reflects the Comintern's commitment to supporting labour activism and its strategic interest in the developments within the oil industry, particularly in areas of geopolitical importance such as Abadan.[54]

Upon his arrival in Abadan, guided by the Comintern's directives, Sultanzadeh took up residence in the home of an Armenian photographer, who also ran a studio within the city's vibrant heart. This strategic placement, however, unravelled swiftly as the eyes of British intelligence, operating within the pulse of Khuzestan, penetrated his veil of anonymity. His arrest followed, revealing the depth of British knowledge about his true identity, his integral role within the Comintern, and his specific mission to reassess the aftermath of the pivotal May 1929 strike.

During a tense interrogation, the British authorities laid bare their comprehensive understanding of his clandestine activities. Yet, in a move that veered from the expected path of extradition to Iranian custody, they chose a route of calculated leniency. They decided to release him, but with a stern warning for the Comintern: to cease sending agents to Khuzestan and to stop interfering with the British oil industry. With this message, Sultanzadeh was sent back to Moscow, marking a subtle yet impactful moment in the shadowy dance of espionage and international politics.[55]

The influence of the Abadan Refinery strike resonated well beyond the provincial boundaries, illustrating the growing momentum of labour activism in Iran. Two years after the Abadan strike, in May 1931, a more organised and specifically articulated labour movement emerged in Isfahan, a city renowned as the hub of Iran's textile industry and often referred to as the 'Iranian Manchester'. Workers at the Vatan state-owned textile factory in Isfahan initiated a strike, demanding significant improvements in their working and living conditions.

This strike was characterised by an almost complete participation of the workforce, which notably included even children as young as eight years old. The solidarity among workers was such that those in the weaving department who initially intended to continue working were persuaded to join the strike.[56]

As the workers marched towards the city centre, they clearly articulated their demands. These included a transition from piecework to a fixed monthly salary system, the establishment of an eight-hour workday with adequate compensation not falling below five qeran, paid half-day leisure time per week, and a stipulation that the maximum working day, including any overtime, should not exceed ten hours (implying a maximum of two hours of overtime per day).

This strike in Isfahan's textile sector, following closely on the heels of the Abadan strike, indicates a broader and deepening awareness among Iranian workers about their rights and the importance of collective action. It also signifies the spreading of labour activism from one industry to another, potentially influenced by the successes and strategies of previous movements. The Isfahan strike, while initially met with police resistance and the arrest of several strike leaders, demonstrated the resilience and determination of the workers. After a brief return to work following the police action, the workers ceased their activities once again after completing an eight-hour shift, steadfastly refusing to abandon their demands despite further police harassment.

The persistence of the workers eventually led to more substantial negotiations involving government representatives, the director of the factory, and the workers' representatives. These negotiations proved to be a turning point. The government, recognising the determination and solidarity of the workers, decided to concede to many of their demands.

A significant outcome of these negotiations was the revision of the working day regulations. The agreement stipulated a reduction of the workday from 12 to 9 hours, and an extension of the lunch break from half an hour to one hour. This concession by the government marked a notable victory for the workers, reflecting the effectiveness of their collective action and negotiation strategies. It also underscored a growing recognition of workers' rights and the importance of labour conditions, setting a precedent that could influence future labour movements in Iran and possibly in other regions.

Throughout the 1930s, the successful efforts of the Isfahan textile workers in securing improved working day regulations stood as a significant milestone. This achievement served as a benchmark for other Iranian workers aiming to establish fixed working hours. Furthermore, it had a profound impact on governmental policies, influencing the introduction of new legislation aimed at regulating the associations of employers and employees.

The Isfahan strike's legacy extended beyond the immediate sector, setting a precedent in the broader labour movement across Iran. It demonstrated the potential power of organised labour and collective bargaining, inspiring workers in various industries to advocate for their rights and seek improvements in their working conditions. Moreover, this event played a crucial role in shaping labour laws and regulations in Iran. The government's response to the strike, which involved negotiating with workers and ultimately conceding to their demands, indicated a shift in the official approach to labour issues.

The textile strike in Isfahan during the interwar period marked the culmination of a series of labour strikes in Iran. The subsequent decline in labour activism in the late 1930s was not solely a consequence of the repressive political measures implemented by the new regime. A significant factor contributing to this decline was the state-sponsored economic reforms, which were primarily focused on industrialising the country's economy. This shift led to a growing demand for skilled and semi-skilled workers, changing the dynamics of the labour market.

During this period, the Iranian Parliament passed several decrees aimed at improving the conditions for workers and government employees, reflecting a gradual yet significant shift in labour policies. These legislative measures included:

- The Factory Act of 1936: This act mandated the organisation of various training projects and emphasised the improvement of working conditions, housing, health, and nutrition for factory workers. This comprehensive approach indicated a recognition of the multifaceted needs of the industrial workforce.
- The 1937 Act on the Employment of Prisoners: This legislation pertained to the use of prisoner labour in industrial and agricultural sectors. It was part of a broader effort to integrate different segments of the population into the burgeoning industrial economy.
- The 1939 Act on the Working Conditions of Medical Personnel: This act specifically addressed the employment conditions of medical staff in government service, highlighting the government's attention to different professional sectors.

These acts collectively marked a progressive development in labour legislation in Iran. They signified an increasing governmental inclination towards regulating labour relations, improving working conditions, and acknowledging the rights and welfare of workers across various sectors. This legislative trend not only responded to the changing economic landscape but also reflected the influence of the earlier labour movements, which had highlighted the need for such reforms.

The legislative reforms introduced by the Iranian Parliament in the 1930s, aimed at improving labour conditions, included several significant acts. However, these reforms faced varied responses from different sectors and companies. These acts, collectively, represented an attempt by the Iranian government to modernised and regulate labour practices across various sectors.

The mixed reception to these legislative efforts, especially the rejection by APOC, underscores the complexities involved in reforming labour laws in an environment where foreign interests and internal policies often clashed. Despite these challenges, the introduction of such legislation marked a significant step towards acknowledging and addressing the needs of the Iranian workforce.

Convergence of Labour Activism and Iranian Nationalism

The interplay between nationalism and labour movements during the era of colonial dominion in Asia and Africa has been examined in a limited number of significant scholarly works.[57] This period saw an escalation in large-scale labour migrations, becoming a prominent characteristic of imperial societal structures. Concurrently, as anti-colonial nationalist fervour intensified, there emerged a growing trend of animosity towards migrant labourers. This was notably evident among labour activists and movements that were influenced by nationalist ideologies. Frequently, transnational migrant labourers were viewed as unwelcome intruders, present solely due to the indulgence of colonial patronage, either to undermine the indigenous populace or to facilitate their further exploitation.

In particular, the oil towns of Iran, established as hubs for migrants, encapsulated this phenomenon. These towns provided accommodation for extensive contingents of labourers migrating from various regions within Iran, as well as for colonial subjects originating from the Indian subcontinent. Within the APOC, a distinct classification system was employed: all Iranian workers, regardless of their regional origins, were uniformly labelled as 'Persians' and typically relegated to a third-class status. Conversely, migrant workers from the Indian subcontinent were categorised as second-class employees and treated in accordance with this designation.

In the context of the Iranian oil industry, the social stratification imposed by British colonial governance played a pivotal role in fostering nationalist sentiments. This effect was observed not only among the Indian migrant workers but also within the ranks of the 'native' Iranian populace.[58]

While the archives of the APOC do not document significant labour unrest or widespread protests in the nascent stages of the oil industry, it is evident that the company's operations were not devoid of challenges. There were frequent instances of tension and confrontations between European foremen, often accused of abusive conduct, and dissatisfied workers. In the formative years of the oil industry, these disputes were typically resolved through the intervention of Iranian foremen, and casual workers did not exhibit a tendency towards collective self-organisation or class-based activism.

This dynamic underwent a notable shift following the conclusion of the First World War. As mentioned earlier, a pivotal moment occurred in December 1920 and again in 1922 when Indian workers at the Abadan Refinery initiated a strike, which was promptly joined by their Iranian counterparts. However, a more significant transformation was observed in 1929. During this year, approximately 9,000 workers, predominantly Iranian, at the Abadan Refinery engaged in a substantial strike. One of their principal demands highlighted the need for absolute parity in treatment between Indian and Iranian employees.[59]

Intriguingly, the Indian workers abstained from participating in this 1929 strike. Moreover, protected by the company's security personnel, a contingent of workers from Yangon attempted, albeit unsuccessfully, to breach the picket line and proceed to the refinery, an act known as 'scabbing'.[60] This incident underscores the complex interplay of ethnic and national dynamics within the labour force and the evolving nature of labour relations in the context of colonial industrial enterprises.

While the Oil Company attributed the May 1929 strike to a 'Bolshevik plot', alleging an intention to 'foment intense labour trouble' in the oil industry and 'ultimately ablaze in the southern Persian',[61] the national press presented a contrasting narrative. These media outlets accused the Oil Company of minimising the genuine reasons behind the labour discontent. They suggested that the APOC's explanation was an oversimplification, possibly intended to deflect attention from more deep-rooted issues within the company's operational and employment practices:

> The strike among the workers of the Oil Company can be attributed to two primary factors. Firstly, there has been a perceptible shift in the mindset of workers across various sectors. Contemporary labourers are increasingly prioritizing their personal comfort, aspiring for less strenuous work and higher wages. This shift is partly driven by the natural increase in both individual and social expenses. Workers are becoming more conscious of their needs and rights in the workplace, reflecting a broader societal change in attitudes towards labour and compensation.
>
> Secondly, and crucially, the discontent stems from the discriminatory treatment meted out by company officials towards Iranian workers. While it is acknowledged that these workers may not possess formal education, they are still endowed with human sensibility and natural intelligence. They have observed a preferential bias where the company seemingly favours Indian and Iraqi workers, treating them more favourably in terms of working conditions and remuneration. This perceived inequity has been a significant source of grievance.
>
> The suggestion is that if the Company were to rectify its approach, treating Iranian workers equitably and ensuring parity with their Indian and Iraqi counterparts in terms of pay and conditions, it would likely result in a harmonious work environment. The workers themselves assert that with fair and equal treatment, they would not be inclined to cause disruptions and would remain indifferent to any external influences, such as Bolshevik propaganda. This situation underscores the importance of equitable treatment in maintaining industrial peace and worker satisfaction.[62]

From the early years of the Anglo-Persian Oil Company's operations, the issue of inequality between Indian and Persian workers was a recurring theme. This disparity was frequently highlighted in the petitions submitted by Iranian workers to various authorities, including the national Parliament, as well as local and national officials. These petitions often cited the discriminatory policies implemented by APOC, which manifested in distinct segregation between Indian and Iranian employees across several aspects of their working and living conditions.

The areas where this discrimination was most evident included wages, housing accommodations, the availability and quality of drinking water, sanitation facilities, medical care, and leisure amenities. The Iranian workers felt that their

Indian counterparts received preferential treatment in these critical aspects, which significantly impacted their quality of life and work environment.[63] These grievances underscored a systemic issue within the company's operational policies, reflecting broader colonial practices of ethnic and national segregation. 'Why should be there differences between Indians and Iranian, while they are both workers? The Indian hospital located in the neighbourhood called *company* is well equipped, while the Iranian hospital in the dirty and malodourous neighbourhood of *Sheikh* is nothing [and] lacks all essential equipment'.[64]

Following Reza Khan's ascent to power in the 1920s, who subsequently became Reza Shah in 1925, his regime advanced a form of territorial-state nationalism. This movement aimed to exalt the authoritarian modernisation efforts and the nascent state-building endeavour. Reports from the APOC officials indicate that during his 1924 visit to the oil sector in southern Persia, in his capacity as Prime Minister, Reza Khan was markedly disheartened upon observing that not a single Iranian was employed at the Abadan Refinery.[65]

The effort to increase Iranian employment within the oil industry, commonly termed as the 'Iranianisation' of the oil industry, was concurrent with national attempts to establish a centralised modern state in the aftermath of the First World War. This period was marked by a brief military campaign led by Reza Khan, who held dual roles as prime minister and commander-in-chief, between 1924 and 1925. The campaign resulted in the dissolution of local autonomy under Sheikh Khazʿal in Khuzestan, a figure widely recognised as a long-standing British protégé in the Persian Gulf. His subsequent arrest and transfer to Tehran were pivotal in bolstering Iranian territorial nationalism. This shift played a crucial role in paving the way for Reza Khan's ascension and coronation as Reza Shah Pahlavi, thereby inaugurating the Pahlavi royal dynasty.

A significant consequence of state-sponsored Iranian nationalism on the oil industry was the exertion of pressure on the APOC to enhance working and living conditions, and to expedite the Iranianisation process. This involved training indigenous workers and substituting Indian employees with Iranians. During a subsequent visit to Khuzestan in 1928, Reza Shah opted not to tour the oil facilities despite APOC's invitation. As reported by *Shafaq-e Sorkh* (Red Twilight), a national newspaper, it was 'popular dislike' that influenced the King's decision to forgo the visit:

> The Oil Company does not conduct its operations with fairness towards the people, prioritizing only its own interests. The officials of the company do not perceive themselves merely as representatives of a commercial entity; rather, they intrude into all aspects of affairs, even maintaining a political office. This office essentially functions as the embassy of a powerful nation within a weaker country. Broadly speaking, the stance of the Oil Company prior to the establishment of the Pahlavi dynasty bore a striking resemblance to the approach of the East India Company in India

> two centuries prior. It is for this reason, among hundreds of other minor grievances, that the people of Khuzestan harbour aversion towards the Oil Company. As a result, public opinion was not supportive of their King appearing as a guest of the Company.[66]

The widespread anti-colonial sentiment among Iranian workers towards the APOC manifested in a heightened confrontational attitude towards Indian employees. In reaction to this hostility, Indian workers sought greater protection from APOC, increasingly distanced themselves from the local community, and began to align more closely with the European staff within the oil industry than with the Iranian community. This division was exemplified on 11 March 1928, when rumours circulated about APOC's alleged plan to 'fire 10,000 Iranians, while thousands of Indian and Iraqis are still working for the Oil Company', This rumour led to the Indian working community in Abadan facing harassment. The next day, a gathering of Iranian workers convened in front of the Oil Company's Labour Office in Abadan, culminating in the stoning of the Office.[67]

The 1929 strike serves as the most striking illustration of the dominant nationalist sentiments of the time. As previously mentioned, one of the primary demands of the strikers was the establishment of complete equality between Indian and Iranian employees. In Tehran, the capital, the press openly supported the strike. Accusations were levelled against APOC for engaging in ethnic discrimination, and there were widespread grievances about the dominance of its Indian employees over Iranians.

During this period, a nocturnal leaflet (*shabnameh*) was distributed, addressing 'Our Crowned father, Government and Court Officials'. In this hand out, the Iranian worker was exalted as the 'glorious and noble son of Darius', lamenting their subjugation under the British, and more specifically, under their Indian clerks and intermediaries. The leaflet portrayed the Iranian workers as sacrificing 'everything for the interest of the Anglo-Persian Oil Company'.[68] Such propaganda, as noted by historian James Bamberg, was significant, acting as a 'ritual prophylactic incantation' against harmful foreign influence.[69]

From D'Arcy to New Deal: Labour Recruitment Change

In the interwar period, Iran was experiencing a phase of authoritarian modernisation, underpinned by a developmental state framework. In the wake of the Constitutional Revolution and the First World War, Iran emerged with a renewed nation state identity, carving out its place on the international stage. The post-war period saw the decline of the Qajar monarchy and the emergence of the Pahlavi monarchy, which was determined to maintain power while spearheading authoritarian development, regardless of the costs.

Approximately eighteen years had elapsed since the coup d'état of 22 February 1921, which elevated Reza Shah to the pinnacle of Iranian politics, and about fourteen years since the constituent assembly had voted to transition the monarchy from the Qajar to the Pahlavi dynasty. During this period, Iran had entered a new era, undergoing transformative changes similar to those experienced in both distant and neighbouring countries in the interwar period.

Over a span of ten years, particularly in its latter half, the industrialisation of Iran emerged as a focal point in the nation's development policies. The government's role in transforming the economic landscape rendered Iran during Reza Shah's reign a unique case among Middle Eastern and Near Eastern countries. Within a five years' timeframe, the government's intensified efforts towards establishing major industries led to a remarkable 250 per cent increase in the workforce within these sectors. During this period, the proportion of investments in industry escalated to over 20 per cent of the nation's total budget.[70] This sustainable development of assets was facilitated by revenue generated from oil sales, which saw a significant price increase in the aftermath of the First World War.

Despite the less-than-favourable terms regarding Iran's share in oil revenues, the country's income from oil nonetheless exhibited a notable increase, albeit with some fluctuations, from 754,830 to 4,783,073 pounds sterling.[71] This rise in revenue was not a consequence of the Oil Company's benevolence, but rather a result of the substantial expansion of the oil fields and the subsequent increase in oil exports. The commencement of operations at the Haftgel oil field in 1927, Naft-e Sefid in 1935, Aghajari in 1937–38, and Lali in 1938, led to a significant increase in oil production, which escalated from 9,333,344 tons in 1925 to 19,610,000 tons in 1938.[72]

The Iranian government, acutely aware of the surge in oil production and the consequent increase in profits for the Oil Company, began to express its dissatisfaction with the existing arrangement starting from 1928. Motivated by a desire for rapid economic development, the government's discontent was a response to the growing realisation of the disparity in benefits accruing from the oil industry. Throughout the entirety of Reza Shah's reign, protracted negotiations, and disputes over the ownership of Iranian oil reserves, the equitable distribution of financial dividends, and the debts owed to Iran by the Oil Company cast a persistent pall over the Anglo-Iranian relationship. These negotiations, which commenced in 1928, persisted until the eventual abrogation of the D'Arcy Concession. Even after the signing of a new agreement, discussions continued until August 1941, when the Allied forces entered Iranian territory.

During the early 1930s, as the global financial crisis intensified, there was a noticeable decline in the market demand for oil. This downturn led to a significant reduction in oil-related income. Consequently, to mitigate expenses, the oil industry implemented substantial cutbacks in its labour force.[73]

The ripple effects of the global financial crisis precipitated an economic downturn in Iran, leading to escalating unemployment across various sectors. This situation, coupled with the Iranian government's pressing need for funds to sustain developmental projects and military expenditures, exacerbated the already challenging economic, social, and welfare conditions in the oil-rich regions. The unfavourable circumstances of labourers in the oil industry, especially the rising unemployment in this sector, further convinced Reza Shah of the urgency to terminate the D'Arcy Concession and expedite the negotiation of a new agreement.

The British government, which held a 51 per cent stake in the APOC, was also discontented with the D'Arcy Concession. According to the terms of this concession, Iran was entitled to 16 per cent of the net profits of the company. This share was calculated not only from the company's operations utilising Iranian resources but also from its global activities, spanning regions from Burma to Iraq to Trinidad. The British government's dissatisfaction was further heightened by Iran's threat to unilaterally annul the concession. This threat was particularly concerning to Britain, which had anticipated that Iran, under its new ruler, would be a compliant ally rather than a confrontational adversary. Such a predicament posed a significant challenge to the British Empire, known for its claim that the sun never set over its dominions.

The groundwork for the Oil Agreement of 1933 was laid during the protracted negotiations that commenced in 1928, led by Teymourtash and Cadman. As the discussions evolved over the subsequent years, other notable figures such as Davar, Taqizadeh, and Foroughi also became instrumental in the negotiation process.[74] The British government's grievances regarding the conduct of the Iranian government were escalated to the economic commission of the League of Nations. This international involvement ultimately culminated in the signing of a new agreement.

The Iranian government's revocation of the D'Arcy Concession, while leading to financial losses for Britain, also presented a more profound challenge for the British Empire. This act not only was a bitter pill for Britain to swallow but also raised questions about its hegemony. It held the potential to establish a precedent that could influence other nations under British rule at the time. Reginald Hoare, the British Minister in Iran, strongly advocated for a naval response to confront Iran's actions. He took a significant step by introducing to the House of Commons the proposal from the British government and the Foreign Ministry, which advocated for the use of military force as a response to what they termed the 'illegitimate' demands of the Iranian government.[75]

The 1907 agreement between Britain and Tsarist Russia, which effectively partitioned Iran into spheres of influence for the two powers, was cited as a justification for the proposed military intervention. However, it's important to note that opinions regarding British policy towards Iran at that time were not uniform. A faction of British statesmen argued against military confrontation, advocating instead for a resolution through diplomatic negotiations. Among these advocates was Cadman, the Chairman of the APOC, who stood as a prominent figure in favour of seeking a negotiated settlement to the dispute.[76]

Nearly five years after the commencement of the initial round of negotiations between Teymourtash and Cadman, a new agreement between Iran and the APOC was finally signed in 1933. This period saw numerous subsequent discussions, where key aspects such as the duration of the agreement, the percentage of profits to be allocated to Iran, and the Iranianisation of the labour force in the oil industry were thoroughly debated. However, it took an additional five years to iron out the specifics and execute the substantive elements of the agreement.

Despite the eventual signing of a new agreement between Iran and the Oil Company, the relationship between the two entities remained strained, with little trust persisting. This atmosphere of mutual distrust and unresolved tensions showed no signs of improvement prior to the occupation of Iran by Allied forces in August 1941.

Following the signing of the agreement, a celebratory atmosphere enveloped the Iranian government, which proclaimed that it had rescued the nation from the grips of colonisation. In a symbolic gesture reflecting this sentiment, Gholam-Ali Bayandor, the commander-in-chief of the Iranian navy, ordered the removal of the British flag from Ba Saeido port on Qeshm Island, replacing it with the Iranian flag. This act provoked a strong protest from the British government, leading to a prolonged period of tension.[77]

In retaliation, the British Navy detained the head of the Qeshm customs office under the guise of conducting an investigation in areas of the island that the British admiralty claimed as part of its jurisdiction. This move intensified the situation. Concurrently, the Iranian press lauded Bayandor's action and condemned British actions, affirming Qeshm as an integral part of Iran and denying any special rights of Britain over the island. This incident exemplified the deep-seated tensions and conflicting national interests that characterised Anglo-Iranian relations during this period.[78]

Contrastingly, The Times of London featured an article titled 'Nationalism and the Shah'. This piece not only detailed the escalating confrontations between Iran and the APOC but also delved into the emergence of a nationalistic discourse among Iranians. According to the article's author, this surge in nationalism was attributed to the 'dictatorial' regime of the Shah. The article provided an analysis of how the Shah's authoritarian rule had fostered a sense of nationalism, shaping the political and social landscape of Iran during this tumultuous period.[79]

Despite efforts by the APOC, and even Cadman's personal approach to Reza Shah, to alleviate the mounting tensions between Iran and Britain, these efforts were ultimately ineffective. In fact, the tensions were further exacerbated by

Table 3.4 *The Iranian oil share between the years 1937 and 1941 (in Pound Sterling)*

Year	Iranian share
1937	3,545,313
1938	3,307,478
1939	2,770,814
1940	2,786,104
1941	2,025,364

Source: British Petroleum (BP) Archive, University of Warwick, Britain, ARC 4308.

Iran's insistent demands for increasing its share (Table 3.4) and the prompt implementation of the provisions of the 1933 agreement.[80]

Additionally, the Iranian government's restrictions on British naval operations in the Persian Gulf further strained relations. Beyond the oil dispute, two other significant geographical issues contributed to the conflict between the two countries. The first concerned Bahrain, whose sovereignty Iran sought to reclaim, challenging the longstanding control exerted by Britain. The second issue revolved around the rights to navigate the Shatt al-Arab waterway, which became a point of contention between the two countries.

Amid these various issues and challenges, disputes concerning Iran's share of oil revenue and the enforcement of other stipulations of the new agreement persisted. Despite any criticism that might be levelled against Iran's economic policymaking during this period, such as the analogy of Iran's uneven development to a chronic ailment, it was widely recognised that Iran had legitimate grounds to claim its fair share of oil revenues. Iran's demands for improved working and welfare conditions for the oil industry's labour force, as specified in the new agreement, were also seen as justifiable.[81]

In 1937, a notable incident occurred when there was a decrease in Iran's share of oil revenue compared to the previous year, prompting a formal protest from the Iranian government. This action underscored Iran's firm stance on ensuring compliance with the terms of the agreement and protecting its economic interests.

In his insistence on preserving Iran's share of oil based on the 1937 benchmark,[82] Reza Shah conveyed a cautionary message to Cadman, emphasising that Iran's oil production should not diminish below its 1937 levels.[83] This caution evolved into an explicit threat: the Iranian government warned the Oil Company that any decrease in Iranian revenue would prompt Iran to reconsider its restraint from selling oil to alternate markets. Such a move would essentially equate to abrogating the existing oil agreement. In a dialogue with the British Foreign Minister, Mohammad-Ali Moqaddam, Iran's Minister in Britain, articulated Iran's policy regarding its oil sales share as follows:

> The representative of the Oil Company in Tehran has intimated an impending decline in oil revenue. In response, we unequivocally declare our refusal to accept any diminution in our oil income below the 1937 figures. Indeed, we anticipate an augmentation of revenue to fund military acquisitions, railway development, and other infrastructural enhancements. The strategic significance of Iran's geographical location should not be understated, as it indirectly accrues benefits to your nation as well. Had this not been the case, we might have remained as passive as we were during previous episodes of comparable reductions in oil revenue...[84]

Iranianisation of Labour

The contention over Iran's share of oil revenue represented merely one aspect of the multifaceted dispute between Iran and the APOC. As previously noted, in the months preceding the November 1918 armistice, the Government of India provisionally suspended the enforcement of its Emigration Act in Persia, thereby liberalising migration flows. This suspension, however, was fleeting. By 1920, the Government of India had reversed its stance, reimposing restrictions on labour migration to the Iranian oil fields. Subsequently, in 1922, the erstwhile Government of India's Emigration Act underwent a significant modification through an amendment. This amendment was primarily aimed at abolishing the indentured labour system, a practice that had become widespread during the wartime period. As explored earlier, a key factor driving this shift in labour policy was the progressive intensification of protests by Indian migrant workers.

In the wake of the 1922 amendment to the Government of India's Emigration Act, a significant change was instituted in the recruitment policies of the APOC. The maximum duration of employment contracts for migrant labour, previously set at three years, was truncated to one year. This reduction in the contract term was a strategic move by both the Government of India and APOC, intended to enhance their leverage in addressing labour unrest. However, this policy revision was not without its challenges. Given APOC's reliance on both skilled and unskilled Indian migrant labour, the company soon faced the dual predicament of labour shortages and escalating labour costs:

> The withdrawal of this concession is extremely detrimental to the interests of the Company who have been obliged to rely on India not only for unskilled but for skilled labour as none is obtainable in Persia. You will readily realise how very seriously the limitation of the agreement affects the Company seeing that Indians very often do not reach the oilfields until

> 6 or 8 weeks after the agreement comes into operation and should a similar period elapse before they reach India on the return journey, the Company gets only 8 or 9 months' work for 12 months' pay, accordingly not only are labour costs very much increased but there are more frequent changes in the personnel which it is to be avoided as far as possible.[85]

The introduction of a new Emigration Act in 1922 marked a significant shift in the employment policies of the APOC. With the cessation of wartime policies and the prohibition of the indentured labour system, APOC was compelled to directly engage in workforce recruitment. Consequently, the company established its own labour recruitment office in Mumbai, aiming to harness the local Indian labour market for its operations in Iran.

In a pivotal move in November 1925, APOC directed Shaw Wallace & Co. to cease its labour recruitment activities for the Iranian oil industry in India, effective from January 1926. APOC attributed this decision to an anticipated 'lowered requirement for Indian labour', citing a strategic shift towards employing locally trained Iranian workers. However, this redirection in policy was not solely driven by the desire to reduce reliance on Indian labour.[86] There were additional underlying reasons for this significant policy transformation.

The labour strikes during 1920–22, culminating in the large-scale repatriation of Indian workers, significantly expedited the Iranianisation process of the workforce in the oil industry.[87] This shift was concurrent with the burgeoning of Iranian territorial-state nationalism, a phenomenon catalysed by the Iranian Constitutional Revolution and the formation of a new political society in the post-First World War era.

In the early post-war period, Iranian society witnessed the establishment of new institutions, including political parties, guilds, labour unions, cultural associations, and private schools. These entities were instrumental in the drive towards creating a modern, centralised state. Their emergence reflected a broader societal aspiration for progress and reform, encapsulating the collective effort to build a cohesive national framework. These institutions not only facilitated the development of a robust civil society but also played a critical role in shaping the political and cultural contours of the nascent Iranian state.

In response to the burgeoning movement for Iranianisation of labour, the Iranian Ministry of Finance, in 1927, urged its counterpart, the Ministry of Endowment and Education, to advance the education and training of Iranians for technical roles in the oil industry. This initiative included the proposal to establish technical institutes in the southern province of Khuzestan, a key region for oil production.

> The Ministry of Finance's request was informed by a report from the Oil Company, which indicated that there were 4,598 non-Iranians employed in the company at the time. While the Oil Company retained the right to hire non-Iranian labour for technical positions as per the 1901 concession

> agreement, the Ministry emphasised the importance of taking all necessary steps to transition these roles to Iranian nationals. This strategic move is part of a broader effort to bolster national self-sufficiency in the oil industry and align with the Iranianisation policy, reflecting a significant shift towards greater national control and expertise in this critical sector.[88]

By the late 1920s, the APOC had normalised the practice of training Iranian labour within its workshops, marking a significant shift in its workforce development strategies. This training, akin to contemporary 'on-the-job training', involved Iranian workers being mentored by Indian engineers, functioning in a capacity similar to apprentices.

During these training sessions, Iranian workers were instructed in a variety of technical and skilled trades. The curriculum covered a broad spectrum of vocations, including 'fitters, turners, moulders, blacksmiths, carpenters, armature winders, general repair electricians, boiler makers, welders (both electric and acetylene), and instrument makers'.[89] This approach not only facilitated skill transfer but also played a crucial role in the gradual Iranianisation of the workforce within the oil industry, aligning with the broader national objective of enhancing local expertise and self-reliance in this pivotal economic sector.

In a pivotal move in 1933, the Iranian government abrogated the D'Arcy concession, which had been a cornerstone of Iran's oil industry since 1901. Subsequently, a new agreement was offered to APOC, one that presented terms more favourable to Iran. This 1933 agreement between the Iranian government and APOC reinforced the earlier stipulation that APOC should prioritised the recruitment of Iranians as artisans, technicians, and commercial staff.

The cancellation of the D'Arcy concession was hailed by the Iranian press as a significant act of 'political emancipation' and lauded as a 'new page in Iranian honour'. This perspective reflected a broader sentiment that the new agreement represented not just the reclaiming of 'national wealth' but also marked 'the end of a protracted period of preferential treatment towards Indian employees in the oil industry'.[90]

Under the terms of the new 1933 agreement, the APOC was mandated to exclusively employ Iranian nationals for all unskilled positions. Furthermore, when it came to hiring for clerical and technical roles, the agreement specified a preference for Iranian nationals, provided they possessed the requisite skills and experience. This directive was a significant stride towards the Iranianisation of the workforce in the oil industry.[91]

Article 16 of this agreement was meticulously crafted to align with Iran's employment objectives. The wording of this article reflected a deliberate effort to ensure that the employment practices of APOC were in harmony with the Iranian government's push for greater national participation and control in the oil industry:

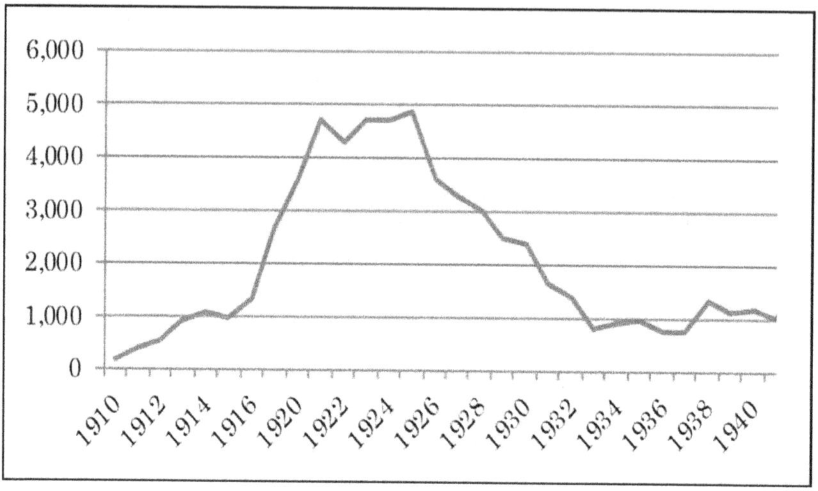

Figure 3.2 Indian employment in the Anglo-Persian/AIOC, 1910–40[92]

> … the company shall recruit its artisans as well as its technical and commercial staff from among Persian nationals to the extent that it shall find in Persia persons who possess the requisite skill and experience. It is likewise understood that the unskilled staff shall be composed exclusively of Persian nationals.
>
> The parties declare themselves in agreement to study and prepare a general plan of yearly and progressive reduction of the non-Persian employment with a view to replacing them in the shortest possible time and progressively by Persian nationals.[93]

In an effort to promote a larger Iranian workforce, the Oil Company was encouraged to broaden the reach of its job advertising. This approach involved not only placing advertisements in the local Iranian press but also in national newspapers and at employment offices. Such a strategy was aimed at ensuring that information about job opportunities in the oil industry was widely accessible to potential Iranian applicants across the country.[94]

As part of this initiative, the Oil Company took a more grassroots approach by calling upon its existing employees to spread the word. Employees were encouraged to inform their friends and relatives throughout Iran about the available job vacancies in the oil industry. This tactic was not just about widening the recruitment net; it also served to leverage personal networks and community ties to attract a diverse and extensive pool of applicants from all over Iran.[95]

The significant decrease in the number of Indian migrant workers in the oil industry from the mid-1920s and throughout the 1930s[96] (Figure 3.2) can be attributed to a confluence of factors. These include the implementation of new employment policies, sustained political pressure from the Iranian government, and a rise in labour activism, initially among Indian migrant workers but subsequently encompassing Iranian labour as well. The initial protests and demands for better conditions by Indian migrant workers raised awareness about labour rights and set a precedent for Iranian workers to follow. As Iranian labourers became more involved in activism, it furthered the momentum for employing a predominantly Iranian workforce.

The convergence of these developments – policy shifts, governmental intervention, and labour movements – collectively contributed to the substantial decline in the reliance on Indian migrant labour in Iran's oil industry during this period. This transformation was not just an economic or industrial shift, but also a reflection of broader sociopolitical changes within Iran, particularly in terms of national self-determination and labour rights.

The substantial increase in oil production and refining from 1920 to 1939, as outlined in the 1933 agreement, can be directly attributed to the growth in the number of both skilled and unskilled Iranian labourers in the oil industry. This period saw a remarkable expansion in the workforce, with total employment in the industry escalating from 12,342 employees in 1920 to 51,060 by the onset of the Second World War in 1939.

At the beginning of this period, Iranian labourers constituted 8,447 individuals, accounting for 68.5 per cent of the total workforce. By 1939, this number had surged to 47,678, representing an overwhelming 93.3 per cent of the industry's employees.[97] This shift underscores the successful implementation of the Iranianisation policy, which significantly increased the participation of Iranian nationals in the oil industry.

An important milestone during this era was in 1935 when the Oil Company began hiring female staff for administrative roles for the first time. This marked a significant step in diversifying the workforce and promoting gender inclusivity within the industry. The inclusion of women in administrative positions not only reflected the changing dynamics of the labour market but also mirrored broader societal shifts towards gender equality in professional spheres.[98]

One of the significant demands of the Iranian government, in line with the 1933 agreement, was the improvement of welfare and living standards for workers in the oil industry. In response to this demand, in 1934, the Oil Company was compelled to implement a plan to construct adequate housing for both skilled and highly skilled labourers, irrespective of their marital status.

However, the efforts undertaken by the Oil Company in this regard fell short of the Iranian government's expectations. While steps were indeed taken to improve the living conditions of the workers, the scale of these initiatives was not commensurate with the dramatic increase in the workforce.[99] The housing plan did not sufficiently expand to accommodate the growing number of workers in the industry.

This discrepancy highlighted a gap between the government's vision for worker welfare and the reality of the implementations by the Oil Company. The government had envisaged a more comprehensive and extensive improvement in living standards, aligning with the substantial growth in the number of oil industry workers. The insufficient scale of the housing and welfare projects, therefore, became a point of contention, reflecting the ongoing challenges in fully realising the goals set forth in the 1933 agreement for the betterment of the workers' conditions.

As the Second World War commenced, the living conditions of the majority of Iranian labourers employed in the refineries and oil fields were starkly inadequate. These workers resided not in modest homes but in what could only be described as dilapidated huts situated in the shantytowns of cities. These makeshift dwellings, often constructed from bamboo, were far from being suitable or safe living spaces.

The severity of their living conditions was further underscored by the fact that some labourers did not even have the basic shelter of a roof over their heads. Instead, their only cover was the open sky of Khuzestan.[100] This situation was a far cry from the improved housing and living standards that the Iranian government had envisioned and demanded for its workers in the oil industry.

Regarding the training of both skilled and unskilled Iranian labourers, who were to replace the predominantly non-Iranian workforce, the Oil Company had made a significant commitment. This commitment involved the establishment of educational institutions, including primary schools, technical high schools, and a technical college. By offering tailored education and training, the Oil Company aimed to ensure that Iranian labourers could effectively fill technical and skilled roles previously held by non-Iranians, thereby promoting national self-sufficiency in the industry.

In parallel, the Iranian government also played a crucial role in this endeavour. It committed to contributing as many staff as possible for the primary and technical high schools. This cooperation between the Oil Company and the Iranian government in the field of education and training was a strategic move towards developing a homegrown pool of talent.

The establishment of the Abadan Institute of Technology (AIT) in September 1939 marked a significant milestone in the educational and professional development initiatives within Iran's oil industry. Reza Fallah, an alumnus of the University of Birmingham, was appointed as the inaugural head of this institute.

The curriculum at the AIT was diverse and forward-thinking. It included courses in electrical engineering and mechanical engineering, reflecting the technical demands of the oil industry.

The founding of the AIT represented a crucial step in fulfilling the Oil Company's commitments to training and education as outlined in the agreements with the Iranian government. Notably, this initiative was one of the few actions by the APOC that received unequivocal approval from Reza Shah during his final visit to Khuzestan in the spring of 1940.[101]

Abadan: A Tripartite City

In Janet Abu-Lughod's influential research on colonial urbanisation in Morocco, she describes Rabat as a 'dual city', characterised by a stark segregation between the urban spaces occupied by the coloniser and those inhabited by the colonised. This dualistic urban structure is a common feature in many colonial cities, reflecting the distinct and often rigidly divided socio-spatial realities of the colonisers and the indigenous populations.[102]

However, in the context of colonial urbanisation, the concept of intermediary urban spaces is integral to understanding the complex social dynamics of colonial cities. These intermediary spaces, often overlooked in historical narratives, function as buffer zones between the colonial settlers and the colonised indigenous population. These zones are distinct from the clearly demarcated areas predominantly inhabited by the colonisers or the colonised.

Understanding these intermediary spaces is important for a comprehensive analysis of colonial urbanisation. They reveal the complexities and nuances of colonial rule, showing that beyond the apparent binary of coloniser and colonised, there were layers of social interaction and negotiation that shaped the colonial experience. This perspective offers a more detailed and intricate view of the colonial urban fabric, highlighting the diversity of experiences and the multiplicity of roles played by different groups within colonial societies.

For instance, in the context of Calcutta, British colonists strategically fostered a segment of the indigenous elite.[103] This elite group functioned as intermediaries, bridging the gap between the colonisers and the colonised. They were pivotal in facilitating communication, negotiation, and the administration of colonial policies. This cultivation of an intermediary elite not only served the interests of the colonial rulers by creating a layer of local administration but also altered the social and urban landscape, leading to complex dynamics of power, collaboration, and resistance in the colonial city.

When the cornerstone of the refinery was laid in 1910, the island of Abadan (historically spelled as ʿAbbadan) was sparsely populated, primarily by the Nassar Arabs. The local leader at that time was Sheikh Khazʿal, residing in the nearby town of Mohammareh (Khorramshahr). The establishment of the refinery marked the beginning of a dramatic transformation for Abadan, particularly in terms of population growth and urban development.

The influx of people to Abadan, drawn by employment opportunities in the burgeoning oil industry or to provide services to the industry's employees, surged unexpectedly, especially in the aftermath of the First World War. This period coincided with a global increase in the reliance on fuel oil, which further amplified the growth of Abadan as a hub for oil production and refining.

By 1930, Abadan had evolved from a modest village under the leadership of a local Sheikh to a large company town. It boasted a population of approximately 30,000–40,000 inhabitants.[104] Notably, about half of this population, approximately 17,370 men, were employed at the oil refinery.[105] This remarkable growth highlighted the rapid urbanisation and industrialisation of Abadan, driven primarily by the development of the oil industry and the consequent economic opportunities it presented.

Initially, the APOC provided temporary housing exclusively to its British and European staff, reflecting the prevalent colonial attitudes and policies of the time. This preferential treatment in housing was a common feature in many colonial enterprises, where European employees often enjoyed better living conditions compared to their local counterparts.

In August 1912, coinciding with the completion phase of the refinery that allowed for a trial run, APOC further developed its housing provisions for European employees.[106] They were accommodated in brick villas and bungalows, which were notably enhanced with surrounding gardens. This residential area was located at the north-western side of the refinery, an area known as Braim. Notably, this was also the area where Sheikh Khazʿal, had one of his residence.

The construction of these brick villas and bungalows for European employees in close proximity to Sheikh Khazʿal's residence is indicative of the socio-spatial dynamics of the time. It reflects the hierarchical structure that APOC implemented in Abadan, where European staff were given preferential treatment in terms of living conditions. This practice was not only a manifestation of colonial policies but also played a role in establishing a physical and social divide between the foreign and local employees within the company town. Such spatial arrangements were common in colonial settings, where segregation often extended to residential areas, reinforcing the social hierarchies of the colonial system.

In contrast to the preferential housing provided to British and European staff, a distinct neighbourhood was established for Indian clerks and artisans on the opposite side of the refinery, southeast and north of the old village. The refinery itself served as a kind of 'buffer zone' between this new neighbourhood and the more privileged area of Braim.

In its early years, this neighbourhood was known as Coolie Lane. The name of the area underwent several changes, reflecting the shifting demographics of the workforce. It was later renamed Sikh Lane, recognising the majority Sikh population of Indian workers at the refinery during that period. Eventually, the area came to be known as Indian Lane.

The housing provided to Indian employees in Coolie/Sikh/Indian Lane was markedly different from that of their European counterparts. The living quarters consisted of long and round barracks, arranged in parallel lines. These barracks were further divided into several units by wall partitions. Each unit was designed to accommodate multiple employees or, in exceptional cases where the company permitted, a family.

In the early stages of the development of Abadan's oil industry, the living arrangements for Iranian recruits were quite basic. Many resided in sun-baked mud houses located in the old village, particularly around the Sheikh-bazar, or in makeshift shelters in the old town. These shelters were typically constructed from loosely lashed sticks or bamboo and roofed with palm leaves, reflecting the traditional building methods of the region.[107]

However, as time progressed, there was a shift in the residential patterns of Iranian workers. They began moving, often on their own initiative, to areas such as Ahmadabad, Bahmanshir, and Kofeysheh. This migration was indicative of a desire among Iranian workers for better living conditions and perhaps a greater sense of community.

In the early 1920s, the APOC introduced two new neighbourhoods in Abadan: The Bovardeh area and the Indian Quarter (*Kuarter-e Hendi-ha*). Bovardeh was specifically constructed to house Iranian clerks and skilled workers. This development marked a shift in APOC's housing policy, as it began to provide more structured and formalised housing solutions for its Iranian employees.

The Indian Quarter, on the other hand, was designed to accommodate Indian semi-skilled workers and security agents. This neighbourhood featured row houses and a public toilet, which was a novel addition to Iranian architecture at the time. The Indian Quarter was also notable for its religious inclusivity, featuring both Sunni and Shi'ite mosques, as well as a home-based Hindu temple, catering to the diverse religious needs of its residents.[108]

The old Indian Lane, which had housed Indian clerks and artisans, was well-maintained and continued to be used. The existence of these distinct neighbourhoods, each catering to different segments of the refinery's workforce, is reflective of the socio-economic stratification and ethnic divisions that were typical in colonial and company-run towns (Map 3.1). These residential developments in Abadan illustrate how housing policies and urban planning were intricately linked with the broader social dynamics and labour policies of the time.

Abadan, as a tripartite city, exemplified the spatial division and social stratification principles characteristic of British colonialism. The city's layout and residential zoning reflected a deeply ingrained ethnic hierarchy, a legacy of the attitudes and practices that APOC's British employees had internalised from their experiences in both Britain and colonial India.

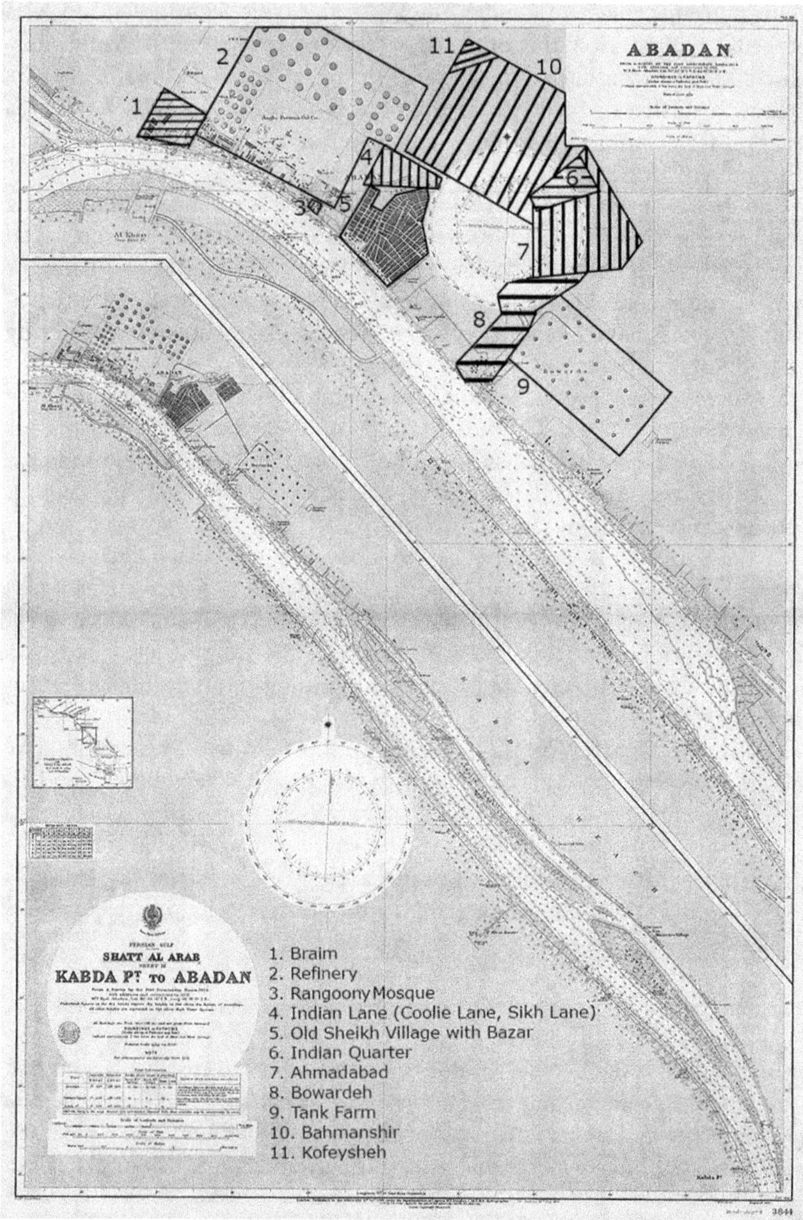

Map 3.1 Abadan in 1926: the new suburbs built in 1920s and 1930s

This hierarchy placed Europeans at the apex, Indians in an intermediary position, and native Iranians at the lower end of the social spectrum. Such an ethnic partition was not just a social construct but was tangibly manifested in the physical layout of the city. The residential areas were segregated, with Europeans, Indians, and Iranians each living in distinct neighbourhoods that corresponded to their perceived status in the colonial hierarchy.[109]

This segregation had profound implications not just for the living conditions of the various ethnic groups but also for their interactions and social dynamics. The tripartite division of Abadan serves as a stark reminder of the lasting impact of colonial policies and practices on urban planning and social structures in the regions under their influence.

The rigid ethnic partition in Abadan was occasionally traversed, particularly during official events where higher-ranking Indians, and later Iranians, were invited to participate in ceremonies, congregations, or worship services alongside the European community.[110] These instances, however, were exceptions rather than the norm and did not signify a broader integration across ethnic lines. In fact, interaction across ethnic boundaries was generally discouraged, with segregation often advocated as the preferable arrangement. This policy of segregation was not only socially enforced but also institutionalised within the organisational structure of the APOC.

An illustrative example of this segregation is found in a 1926 memorandum from the APOC archives, signed by an APOC executive named Armstrong in Abadan.[111] This document reveals the extent of the segregationist attitudes prevailing at the time. When Indian clerks at APOC approached Armstrong for permission to use the library, his response was marked by reluctance. He expressed concern that allowing Indian clerks access to the library might lead to European employees avoiding it. As a solution, rather than integrating the library, he suggested that the Indian clerks establish their own library, using old and used books from the European library.[112]

Ethnic segregation in colonial cultures often led to a cascade of discriminatory practices, as seen in the case of Abadan under the APOC. This segregation was not limited to living quarters but extended to various aspects of community life, including access to education, health care, and recreational facilities.

In Abadan, the practice of ethnic segregation was evident in the establishment of separate community libraries for different ethnic groups. Indian employees, who were barred from using facilities designated for Europeans, were encouraged to set up their own library. In turn, 'native' Iranians were also excluded from the Indian Library by Indian officials and were similarly encouraged to establish their own separate library. This segregation of educational resources based on ethnicity was a clear manifestation of the prevailing colonial mindset that prioritised and perpetuated ethnic hierarchies.

The division also extended to health care and sports facilities. Europeans had exclusive access to hospitals and sports clubs, which were typically of a higher quality standard compared to those available to Indian and Iranian employees.[113] This segregation not only reflected the ethnic and social hierarchy but also had tangible impacts on the quality of life and well-being of the workers based on their ethnic background.

APOC's justification for such segregationist policies and actions was likely rooted in the prevailing colonial attitudes of the time. These policies were often rationalised on the grounds of cultural differences, administrative convenience, or even purportedly for the benefit of the segregated groups: 'Under European guidance, Persians were learning to separate themselves from fellow Indian workers. Separate Persian clubs would serve the dual purpose of stilling complaints in Tehran and keeping labour divided in Khuzestan'.[114]

4

The Second World War: The Great Powers' Rivalry for Oil

'The empire belongs to the one who owns the oil'.

Henri Bérenger, French Commissioner General for Gasoline and Combustibles, 1919.

On 28 June 1919, when delegates from the victorious governments of the Great War and those of the defeated Central Powers convened at the Palace of Versailles, located on the outskirts of Paris, to ratify a peace treaty aimed at concluding the most catastrophic conflict in the annals of human history, there was a prevailing sense of optimism that this marked the commencement of an enduring era of tranquillity. Little did they foresee that merely two decades later, the global stage would be marred by yet another world war, one surpassing the preceding in terms of both fatalities and devastation.

At the commencement of the Great War, petroleum emerged as a substitute for coal across both military and civilian sectors. Throughout the course of the war, the pivotal significance of oil became increasingly evident, not only to the imperialistic global powers but also to local proprietors of oil resources. In the Asian theatre, the British Empire had exerted control over Burma's oil reserves since the nineteenth century, and in the early decades of the Twentieth Century, it commenced efforts to extend its dominion to Iran's oil resources as well. With the discovery of oil reserves in British-administered Iraq in 1928, the British Empire perceived itself as the unchallenged hegemon in Asia. It envisioned that by leveraging the abundant oil wealth of this continent, it could maintain its pre-eminence over this region without encountering competition from either established or emerging contenders for several decades. However, the eruption of hostilities on 1st September 1939, shattered any illusions Britain may have harboured regarding its enduring dominance. The British Empire was abruptly compelled to confront the reality of new threats to its interests in both East and West Asia. In the East, the Japanese Empire posed a menace to the Burma oil fields and the Yangon Refinery, while in the West, Germany coveted the oil resources in Iran and Iraq.[1]

Within the historiography of contemporary Iran, the examination of events pertaining to the Second World War predominantly commences in August

1941 with the occupation of Iran by the Allies. Curiously, notwithstanding the fact that the preceding two years witnessed the unfolding of a global conflict that significantly impacted not only Europe but also various other regions, including Iran, this period remains conspicuously underrepresented in Iranian historiographical discourse. While the major stakeholders in the war readily recognised the strategic significance of this timeframe, Iranian historiography tends to neglect these two years. Apart from political memoirs, available sources pertaining to Iran's history from the outbreak of war in Europe until it encroached upon Iran's borders predominantly consist of, although not exclusively, curated collections of documents sourced from Iranian archives and translated memoirs authored by British representatives stationed in Iran.[2]

Several months prior to the military occupation of Iran, a journal based in Mumbai conducted an analysis of Iran's stance regarding the war. In its assessment, the journal highlighted the German efforts to gain access to the oil fields in Khuzestan and the Abadan Refinery. Notably, the journal asserted that the number of Germans in Iran exceeded 25,000.[3] However, it is evident that both of these estimates were markedly inaccurate. Concurrently, the headquarters of the British Army Intelligence estimated the German population in Iran to be approximately 4,000, a figure that also proved to be unreliable.

Upon the outbreak of the war, the *Ettelaʿat* newspaper provided a more precise estimate of the foreign residents in Iran.[4] Subsequent research conducted by scholars with access to the archives of British, Soviet, and American sources, including Elwell Sutton, confirmed the accuracy of the newspaper's estimate. According to their findings, when the Allies arrived in Iran, they encountered no more than 650 Germans residing in the country.[5]

It is not surprising that Sir Reader Bullard, in his memoirs as the British Minister in Iran, might have exaggerated the number of Germans residing in Iran. However, it is regrettable that some contemporary Iranian historiographers still adhere to the erroneous figures cited by prominent diplomats such as Abdolreza Houshang Mahdavi. These sources posit that the primary rationale behind the Allied occupation of Iran was the apprehension over a substantial German presence in the country, assumed to be engaged in subversive activities and espionage against British and Soviet interests.[6]

The validity of the argument suggesting that Britain and the Soviet Union were genuinely concerned about the presence of German citizens in Iran remains a topic of debate. To what extent these arguments are persuasive is contingent on various factors. It is essential to consider that in the confidential correspondence of British politicians, discussions regarding the geopolitics of Iran are frequently intertwined with references to Reza Shah's intransigence and the imperative of deploying military forces to safeguard Iranian oil fields. This suggests that the protection of oil interests in Iran played a pivotal role in the Allied decision-making process. While concerns about German activities in Iran may have been a factor, the significance of securing Iranian oil reserves and the strategic imperative for both the British and Soviet governments cannot be understated. Therefore, the motivations behind the occupation of Iran encompass a complex interplay of geopolitical, economic, and strategic factors, extending beyond the mere presence of Germans in the country.[7]

On the inaugural morning of 1st September 1939, as the formidable warplanes of Germany rained devastation upon the city of Warsaw, marking the incipience of the world's most colossal cataclysm, a remarkable disjunction manifested itself in the distant land of Iran. Here, the newspapers boldly proclaimed, amid the tumultuous symphony of global conflict, an event of seemingly incongruous nature: the 'Glorious Sporting Festival of Boy Scouts in Manzarieh', a serene resort nestled to the north of Tehran. The festivities unfolded beneath the august gaze of His Majesty, the Crown Prince, casting a poignant juxtaposition between a world embroiled in the throes of war and the seemingly idyllic innocence of youthful camaraderie.[8]

In stark contradistinction to the pervasive alarm that gripped other nations ensnared in the maw of warfare, this spectacle in Manzariyeh offered a vivid portrayal of the prevailing tranquillity that cocooned the capital, a capital enmeshed in the intricate web of Reza Shah's resolute and authoritarian modernisation agenda. While tumultuous tidings of war reverberated across the globe, it was not until a day had elapsed that the Iranian press was graced with a report, bearing witness to the oration delivered by Adolf Hitler within the hallowed precincts of the German Parliament. Within this oration, Hitler delineated the imperative of war, accompanied by his sanguine affirmations that Germany's triumph would prove both expeditious and enduring.[9] Subsequently, the Iran's Foreign Ministry pronounced a decree, decreeing that 'all news be channelled through its august offices, from whence it would be judiciously curated and disseminated to the press, contingent upon its deemed propriety'.[10]

While the advent of the war ushered in a profound shock, it is conceivable that this perturbation was confined to a select few among the Iranian populace. For the vast majority, Europe existed as an exceedingly remote and disconcerting realm, a place of such remoteness that scarcely anyone could have harboured the notion that the conflagration consuming that distant continent might one day cast its ominous shadow upon the very soil of Iran. With the commencement of the war in Europe, the Iranian government's tug of war with the Anglo-Persian Oil Company (APOC) and the British government took a new turn. As mentioned earlier, the signing of the 1933 Agreement and its consequences soured the relationship between Iran and Britain. In the second half of the 1930s, and particularly during the two turbulent years following the outbreak of the war in Europe and its arrival on Iranian soil, Reza Shah's attempts to enhance the country's military supremacy was one of the causes of dispute between Iran and Britain. One of the major concerns of the government was how to ensure the country's combat readiness in the event of the war reaching the Iranian frontiers. One of the Iranian government's main strategies was to rely on military cooperation with Britain and to fortify the Iranian army with British military hardware.

Furthermore, following the Iranian government's efforts to avoid dependence on importing oil from the Soviet Union, which provided fuel to the northern parts of Iran, the refinery in Kermanshah came into operation in 1935. As a result, Iran was able to sever the financial umbilical cord which had tied it to the Soviet Union and this, in turn, reduced Iran's political dependency on the Soviet Union.[11] Now with the ongoing fighting and the invasion by the Soviet forces of the Balkan countries one after another, the first cracks in the borders on the other side of Iran began to be visible.[12] The Iranian government, worried about the northern and western borders of the country, was hopeful that it could come to an agreement with Britain regarding military cooperation and that Britain would provide credit to Iran for the purchase of weapons.[13]

Although the British government initially showed a positive response to Iran's request and on 16 February 1940 a military cooperation agreement between the two countries was signed, Britain did not take any practical steps towards actually providing credit and handing over the arms that Iran had requested. Probably the reason Britain avoided implementing the agreement was its concern about the possible reaction of the Soviet Union government, which at that time was backing Germany and had not yet joined the Allies. We know that Articles Five and Six of the Russo-Persian Treaty of Friendship of 1921 authorised the Soviets, in the event of the presence on Iranian soil of forces hostile to the Soviet Union, to have the right to send its own forces to Iran. Nevertheless, the Iranian government, concerned about the expansion of war, was impatiently waiting for a positive response from the British government. In February 1940 Colonel Sadeq Sheibani, based in Switzerland and the head of the commission for arms purchases for the Imperial Army of Iran in Europe, reached out to the British Foreign Ministry, and demanded that Britain honour its commitments to Iran. The reaction of the British Foreign Ministry to the request of Colonel Sheibani was full of ambiguity, in particular where it stated: 'acceptance and execution of those commitments will depend on the situation'.[14] But, the reply of the Iranian Foreign Ministry did not lack clarity. Mozaffar Aʿlam, the Iranian Foreign Minister, wrote in a telegraph to his Minister in Britain:

> Their reply is shocking and not what was expected. What we needed was their assistance to help meet our urgent needs, not this kind of reply which is clearly a tactic to delay or evade having to act. It is quite obvious from this kind of reply that there is a hidden political agenda behind it. It is becoming clear that the British government has still not fully appreciated the advantages and importance of our present situation, as it should have done. It does not want to comprehend, particularly given the present state of global affairs, just how vital and beneficial for the British themselves is

> Iran's policy of neutrality, which must, in fact, be further strengthened by the supply of military and industrial necessities. Moreover, they do not understand, following the exchange of the collaboration agreement, how much damage their delay and refusal to help will cause to Britain's reputation among Iranian political circles and the rest of the world. It is essential that you make these points clear in an effective way to the officials who deal with these matters. Furthermore, you must add that we did not want to have to resort to asking others to provide what we needed. If we had done that, our requests would have been met with open arms and fulfilled. Negotiations will also be conducted with the British Minister from here.[15]

In June 1940, Reza Shah, disheartened by the fact that the British had not met their obligations outlined in the agreement of February 1940, ordered its cancellation; a unilateral step that Britain, of course, did not favour.[16] Once again, with its unilateral cancellation of yet another agreement with the British government, Iran not only challenged the British government but also caused the APOC, deep concern about its future. This was, of course, a valid concern. Reza Shah's insistence on securing Iran's share of the oil revenue based on the 1937 level and the opposition to this by the Oil Company which argued that the reduction in the export of oil would not enable the share of Iran to be fixed, once again led the Iranian government to seriously consider the cancellation of the oil agreement of 1933.[17]

On 2 July 1940, Reza-Qoli Amir-Khosravi, the Iranian Finance Minister, gave a warning to the APOC that the cancellation of the 1933 agreement was on the agenda of the Iranian government and that if the Oil Company did not comply with Iran's requests, a bill to cancel the agreement would be introduced to Parliament.[18]

While the company endeavoured to downplay the ramifications of its substantial layoffs, the concerns raised by the Iranian government could not be ignored. Consequently, in a move towards reconciliation, the Oil Company accepted that instead of paying more than the 1937 rate, offering an annual fixed payment of four million pounds, regardless of the volume of oil extracted from Iranian soil. This commitment on the part of the Oil Company remained in force throughout the period spanning 1940–43.[19]

Ahmad Matin Daftari, prime minister of Iran (October 1939–June 1940) mentions in his memoirs that when the representative of the APOC was handing over the cheque for four million pounds to the deputy of the Iranian finance minister, following his removal from office, he said: 'We will never forget this blackmailing by Reza Shah'.[20] According to James Bamberg, the historian of the British Petroleum Company, it is from this date that the countdown towards the ending of Reza Shah's reign began; a reign that the British Government was happy to refer to, in a 'linguistic turn', as a dictatorship.[21]

There were clear discrepancies between the inflexibility of Reza Shah and the conservative policies of Britain on the one hand and, on the other hand, the insistence of the Shah that they should receive an increase rather than a decrease of the oil share and that global economic fluctuations should not be taken into account. These discrepancies caused significant frustration among the British statesmen on all sides of the political spectrum. Gradually, a group of British statesmen concluded that the sole guarantee for the stability of trouble-free oil production was the removal from power of Reza Shah. However, there was also a group of statesmen who disagreed with this suggestion. This is illustrated in correspondence between the British Minister in Iran, Sir Reader Bullard, and the British Foreign Office dated 24 May 1940. In this correspondence, Sir Reader Bullard insists on the neutrality of Iran and the fact that this neutrality must not be violated from the British side or even by the Soviets or the Germans. Britain must only act to occupy the oil fields of the south of Iran and nothing more.

On the contrary, another faction of British statesmen emerged, exclusively dedicated to the occupation of Iran and the ousting of Reza Shah. Eventually, they realised their objectives, paving the way for the deployment of battalions, primarily composed of soldiers from the British Imperial Army stationed in India, to Iran. Sir Reader Bullard, at a later juncture, aligned himself with this faction that sought the removal of Reza Shah from power. Several months prior to the occupation of Iran, he penned a confidential letter in which he expressed: 'The Shah is the object of almost universal execration and we also as his supposed supporters... Movement for the removal of the Shah and even of his dynasty would be popular....'[22]

Subsequently, a concerted effort was made to manipulate historical narratives. As part of this propaganda campaign, a pamphlet titled 'Iran and Britain' was promptly published in India by the British press attaché stationed in Iran. Within this pamphlet, the era of Reza Shah's rule was characterised as a dark chapter in Iran's long history.[23]

The Onset of the Second World War in Iran

On 25 August 1941, a synchronised military offensive was launched by British and Soviet forces against Iran, ostensibly predicated upon Reza Shah's purported alignment with pro-German sentiments. This military campaign unfolded despite Iran's steadfast commitment to an official policy of neutrality. The British contingent, comprising a substantial complement of Indian Riflemen, executed an incursion into the Khuzestan region, concomitantly with Soviet forces seizing control of the northern Iranian provinces spanning from Azerbaijan to Khorasan.

It is noteworthy that, for a duration of two years, both the British and the Soviets had duly honoured Iran's avowal of neutrality. However, a momentous shift in their approach toward Iran ensued with the initiation of German hostilities on the Eastern front. This policy pivot was primarily catalysed by the imperativeness of reinforcing the beleaguered defences of the Soviet Union, teetering on the verge of collapse. Amid the array of potential routes available for transporting vital supplies to the Soviet Union, including passages from San Francisco to Murmansk or Arkhangelsk, the Persian Gulf Caucasus route emerged as the preeminent choice, marked by its practicality and expediency.

In the aftermath of the invasion of Iran, a Tripartite Treaty of Alliance was executed in January 1942, involving Britain, the Soviet Union, and Iran. Article Five of this treaty stipulated that 'the Allied armed forces shall be withdrawn from Iranian territory no later than six months after all hostilities between the Allied powers and Germany and her associates have been suspended by the conclusion of an armistice or armistices or on conclusion of peace between them, whichever date is earlier'.[24]

Subsequently, with the capitulation of the Third Reich on 7 May 1945 and the surrender of Japan on 2nd September of the same year, the Allies had a grace period of six months, extending until the prescribed deadline of 2 March 1946. However, it is noteworthy that while the United States and Britain withdrew their troops from Iran before the specified time limit elapsed,[25] the withdrawal of Soviet military forces from Iranian territory was not completed until 9th May of that same year. This withdrawal followed strenuous negotiations with the Iranian government during the tumultuous period known as the 'Crisis of Azerbaijan'.[26]

The Iranian Oil Amid the Second World War

Urban Iranians monitored the onset of the European war diligently via the nation's primary newspapers. Geographically distant from the conflict, they harboured a prevailing belief in the Iranian government's official stance of neutrality, trusting that it would shield them from the adversities of the global conflict. Consequently, life persevered with relative normalcy, particularly among the majority of Iranians. However, in the southern province of Khuzestan, a discordant political and social milieu diverged from the relative tranquillity prevalent further north in the capital city.

In the initial years of the war, the Anglo-Iranian Oil Company (AIOC) grappled with a significant setback resulting from Axis attacks. Notably, the AIOC suffered a considerable blow, with a staggering 46 per cent of its oil-laden vessels, responsible for the perilous journey around the African continent via the Cape of Good Hope en route to Western Europe, falling victim to the demands of the conflict. The previously convenient route to Western Europe, which involved traversing the Suez Canal and the Mediterranean Sea, had been forcibly closed by the British Admiralty in August 1939, just prior to the British declaration of war.[27]

These losses in oil tankers, coupled with the protracted African maritime journey now necessitated, engendered a tangible diminution in the production and export of Iranian oil. This decline not only had repercussions on the Iranian government's oil revenue but also compelled the AIOC to undertake a significant downsizing, reducing its workforce by a substantial 44 per cent, from an August 1939 figure of 51,060 employees to a mere 28,713 by August 1941, thereby precipitating widespread redundancy within the province.

The occupation of Iran by the Allied Forces marked a pivotal juncture in the annals of the AIOC. For both the British and, subsequently, the United States, the newly established Iranian Transnational Railway, bridging the oil-rich southern province of Khuzestan to the northern expanse abutting the Caspian Sea, emerged as a secure conduit for furnishing the Soviet warfronts with indispensable oil reserves and logistical resources. Throughout the duration of the war, the Abadan Refinery played a pivotal role by contributing an impressive quantity of up to one million tons of oil to sustain the Soviet Army.[28]

In a milieu where the war machinery of both Allied camps hinged profoundly on the steadfastness and continuity of their oil supply, the Japanese invasion of the Dutch East Indies and Burma in 1942 imposed a significant constraint. This development effectively severed the Allied Forces' access to East Asian oil, rendering the revenue generated from Iranian oil resources in West Asia all the more indispensable for their strategic interests.[29] Consequently, the production and export of Iranian oil, which had experienced a substantial reduction during the initial two years of the conflict, gradually recuperated by the third year and, indeed, witnessed an expansion in subsequent years, as shown in Figure 4.1.[30]

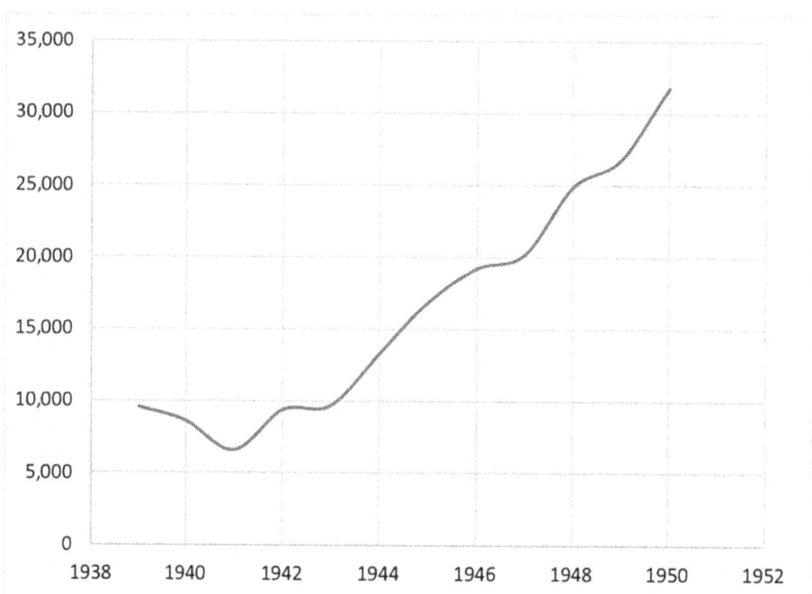

Figure 4.1 The crude oil production of the AIOC, 1939–50 – in thousands of tons[31]

L.P. Elwell Sutton, who served on the staff of the labour administration of the AIOC in Abadan during the period 1935–38 and later from 1943 to 1947 as Press Attaché and Head of Broadcasting at the British mission in Tehran, recalls the beginning of the Second World War and the occupation of Iran as being a relief for the Oil Company:

> For eight years [prior to the occupation] British management and staff had been irked by the painful necessity of considering Persian susceptibilities, of paying lip service to the national revival dimly observed in the rest of the country. Many fundamental changes had taken place. Persian numerals now shared pride of place with English on the backs of cars and the gates of bungalows. First and second-class staff had become senior and junior grade (third class remained third class – after all it sounded different in Persian, and anyway they knew no English). The letters 'B.P.' on the petrol pumps, it turned out, stood not for British Petroleum, as everyone thought, but for *Benzin-e Pars* – the petrol of Persia.[32]

The occupation provoked major changes in Iranian labour employment. By 1942, some quarter of a million Iranians, mostly agricultural labour, gained employment with the Allied Occupation Forces and opted for the country's major cities as their permanent residence.[33] One of the early economic agreements reached by the Allies was to refrain from adopting any wage increases during their occupation. In 1939 the average minimum wage package, which included the provision of flour, meat and oil as well as housing, was eleven rials, while in the south of the country the Oil Company set the minimum wage of local unskilled labour at five or six rials a day.[34] This was the minimum wage endorsed by the then Anglo Persian Oil Company, following the strike of 1929.[35] During the period 1936–41, although the total cost of living index increased by 2.5 per cent, the Oil Company maintained the 1929 endorsed minimum wage.[36]

The immediate economic outcome of the Allied occupation in Iran was high inflation. By 1944, the index of the cost of living reached as high as ten times that of the year preceding the outbreak of war. The immediate economic hardship caused considerable employment problems for the Oil Company. The wages paid by the British and particularly the U.S. armies in their affiliated service sectors led many workers in the oil industry to quit their jobs in the AIOC and join these sectors for better pay. To stop the outflow of workers, the AIOC had no option but to increase salaries. The minimum wage was first raised to eleven rials and then to sixteen.[37] However, to avoid additional increases in wages, the AIOC signed a pact with the British and the U.S. armies agreeing not to raise the minimum wages in Khuzestan.[38]

On the eve of the Allied occupation, the Iranian oil industry, boasting an employment roster of nearly 30,000 workers, stood as the preeminent labour-intensive sector within Iran. Over the subsequent years, as a consequence of heightened production at the Abadan Refinery, partly attributed to the Second

Table 4.1 *Employment in the Anglo-Persian/AIOC, 1940–50*

Year	Iranian	Indian	British	Other	Total
1940	26,484	1,158	1,056	15	28,713
1941	28,035	1,005	918	9	29,967
1942	41,081	1,716	1,261	234	44,292
1943	44,944	2,102	1,442	279	48,767
1944	60,073	2,493	1,710	476	64,752
1945	60,366	2,498	2,357	240	65,461
1946	60,807	2,557	1,869	169	65,402
1947	67,190	2,461	2,134	89	71,874
1948	76,994	2,126	2,472	81	81,673
1949	78,162	1,977	2,698	82	82,912
1950	72,681	1,744	2,725	34	77,184

Sources: James Bamberg, *The History of the British Petroleum Company, The Anglo-Iranian Years, 1928–1954*, Volume 2 (London: Cambridge University Press, 1994).

World War Soviet Aid Programme, which saw output levels rise from 7 million tons in 1941 to a substantial 16.5 million tons in 1945, the oil industry underwent a remarkable expansion. This expansion manifested in the significant increase in the workforce, with the number of employees soaring to approximately 65,000 by the year 1946.

However, it is worth noting that during the 1930s, subsequent to the ratification of a new agreement in 1933, the Oil Company had been mandated to vigorously pursue the Iranianisation of labour within the oil industry. Nevertheless, the rapid growth of the oil industry during the Second World War era, coupled with the scarcity of local skilled labour, prompted the AIOC to turn its attention once again towards Indian migrant workers as a potential source of manpower (Table 4.1).

Throughout the duration of the war, the AIOC implemented modifications to its labour recruitment procedures. In the post-First World War era, owing to pressure exerted by the Iranian government, the Oil Company was compelled to advertise job vacancies in both local and national newspapers.[39] However, during the Second World War, a departure from this practice ensued.

Instead of relying on national newspapers, the Oil Company adopted an alternative approach. Every week, during the mornings of Saturday, Sunday, and Monday, the Company would make its workforce selections from the throngs of labourers congregated outside the AIOC's Labour Offices in Abadan, Tehran, and Isfahan. Following rigorous medical examinations, the selected labourers would commence their employment at the minimum wage level, subject to an indeterminate probationary period that could extend for several months.

It is important to note that during this probationary phase, labourers were bereft of access to essential benefits, including healthcare and other welfare provisions such as food rationing, educational opportunities, or housing, where available.

As per a report compiled by the International Labour Office, apart from the workforce directly employed by the AIOC, there existed another category of labourers whom the Oil Company engaged on a casual or seasonal basis. These casual labourers were not categorised as part of the AIOC's regular labour force, and their numbers were not incorporated into the official statistics maintained by the Oil Company.

The casual labourers functioned as contract workers and were typically assigned to various tasks, including riveting, tank cleaning, painting, handling sulphur, and participating in activities related to the oilfield pipe track, road construction, and maintenance work. In the year 1945, alongside the 29,704 wage earners directly employed by the Oil Company at the Abadan Refinery, there were an additional 6,953 contract workers, contributing to a notable 23 per cent increase in the overall workforce.[40]

Similarly, within the context of the oilfield, during the same period, there were 8,613 contract workers in addition to the 5,190 workers formally included on the Company's payroll. These contract workers constituted a significant majority, comprising 60 per cent of the total workforce in the oilfield.

The contract workers, a substantial portion of whom hailed from the Khuzestani Arab ethnic group, were never afforded the same level of job security as those directly employed by the AIOC. The contractors overseeing these workers consistently paid them wages below the legally mandated minimum wage and sidestepped statutory regulations pertaining to the remuneration of weekly rest days, overtime rates, paid holidays, and other entitlements.[41]

Moreover, in addition to receiving subpar wages, contract workers were denied access to the services provided by the Oil Company, including the ability to purchase subsidised goods from Company stores. Consequently, the income of contract workers amounted to merely half the purchasing power of their counterparts employed directly by the Oil Company.[42]

The heightened recruitment of skilled Indian labourers led to the Indian community becoming the most prominent migrant population in the southern province. This community comprised not only workers and clerks employed in the oil industry but also a significant, albeit unspecified, number of Indian military personnel from the British Army. These Indian soldiers were strategically stationed by the British Command in Khuzestan to protect vital oil installations and bolster security in major oil cities. Regrettably, this circumstance gradually gave rise to tensions in relations between the Iranian and Indian communities.

A noteworthy episode illustrating the escalating tension unfolded in 1942, famously known as the 'Bahmanshir incident'. In this regrettable event, three Indian soldiers availed themselves of the services of a prostitute in the Abadan bordello, referred to as 'Dub', but controversially refused to compensate her for her services. Furthermore, six Indian employees of the Oil Company engaged in excessive consumption of '*araq*', a locally brewed spirit, and mistreated local boys and girls as they passed by. These occurrences ignited profound ethnic tensions within the city, ultimately culminating in violent clashes between the Indian and Iranian communities, resulting in casualties and significant property damage.[43]

It is important to note that while events such as the Bahmanshir incident were undoubtedly influenced by sectarian, ethnic, and cultural factors, these sectarian aspects did not eclipse the underlying class solidarity shared by Iranian and Indian workers. A compelling instance of this class interaction materialised during the 1946 strike within the Iranian oil industry. This labour strike erupted among the workers of the Abadan Oil Refinery on 14 July 1946, quickly spreading throughout the Khuzestan Province, and enveloping the entire oil industry. Over its sixty-hour duration, the general strike mobilised approximately 70,000 Iranian and Indian manual and clerical workers, eclipsing any previous labour walkout in Iranian history in terms of scale and magnitude. However, this historic strike, marked by its unprecedented labour solidarity, was tragically marred by the loss of some 47 lives and 170 casualties, ultimately making it the bloodiest labour protest ever recorded in the history of the Middle East's labour movements.

Oil Workers' Living Conditions

During the wartime period, the Iranian populace faced widespread famine, skyrocketing inflation, and an ever-increasing cost of living, which rendered the living conditions of the labouring poor exceedingly unbearable. The consumption of domestically produced foodstuffs by the Allied Forces, if not the primary cause, was undoubtedly a contributing factor to this dire famine.[44] For instance, between 1941 and 1946, there was a dramatic reduction in the availability of livestock across the country. At one point, the Ahvaz Field Butchery alone saw the daily slaughter of up to 1,000 sheep and goats.[45] In the northern regions of the country, the export of rice to the Soviet Union or for the consumption of the Red Army in 1942 caused significant grievances among the impoverished populations in Gilan and Mazandaran provinces.[46]

Consequently, major urban centres in the country became hotbeds of daily protests, sometimes escalating into violent clashes. One of the most serious incidents occurred in Tehran in December 1942 when a bread riot erupted, resulting in 20 fatalities and 700 injuries.[47] In Kazerun, located in the south, during the same period, enraged crowds looted the city's grain depot and bakeries.[48] Reports from the oil-rich province of Khuzestan also depicted popular unrest in cities such as Ahvaz and Abadan, primarily in response to the exorbitant cost of living.[49]

While the AIOC had an agreement with the Allied Occupation Forces not to increase wages,[50] the situation in the south, characterised by a scarcity of essential commodities and constantly surging commodity prices that imperilled the continuity of work and the flow of oil, prompted the AIOC to introduce a novel rationing scheme. This initiative aimed to provide staple products such as wheat, rice, ghee, sugar, and tea to its employees. By establishing subsidised food stores in workers' residential areas, the Company sought to address a pivotal issue afflicting its workforce and mitigate the potential for further unrest.

Regrettably, the cooperative initiatives implemented by the AIOC proved to be of limited efficacy in mitigating the hardships faced by the labouring poor employed by the Oil Company. While the national minimum wage stood at thirty rials, the oil industry maintained a minimum wage of sixteen rials, supplemented by free rations of flour, sugar, and tea, valued at approximately eight rials per day at Company prices.[51]

However, in mid-May 1946, in the wake of the mass demonstration by oil workers on the International Labour Day and a series of sporadic strikes across various departments of the refinery and the oil field, the AIOC responded by raising the minimum daily wage to thirty-five rials. This adjustment, however, eliminated the provision of free rations while retaining the availability of the same rations at controlled prices (Table 4.2).

The substantial increase in the minimum wage, amounting to nearly 120 per cent, although indicative of the inadequacy of the previous minimum wage, remained insufficient, especially when considering that the cost of living had surged by more than 900 per cent during the war.[52]

Table 4.2 *Ration commodities sold at the Company's stores, 1946*

Commodities	Weekly ration	Subsidised price Rls.	Market price Rls.	Monthly ration*	Subsidised price Rls.	Market price Rls.
Wheat	5 kilos	20	30			
Tea	335 grams	5	13			
Sugar	335 grams	10	19.50			
Rice				5 kilos	35	45
Cigarettes				250	75	75
Dried milk				450 grams	10	–
Ghee				2 kilos	120	184

Source: National Archive of Iran, DocNo. 240-1424, 1946. For families: each adult member 8.5 and each child member 4.5 kg wheat plus 220 grams tea.

Workers under the age of eighteen, excluding those under fourteen who were predominantly apprentices and trainees, were among those who received the minimum wage. Likewise, women labourers, albeit employed in limited numbers, were typically assigned roles in medical services, laundry, and sanitation rather than in direct industrial work, and they too received the minimum wage. Despite these wage adjustments, there were still notable omissions, including the absence of Friday pay (compensation for a paid day of rest) and disability compensation within the industry. These deficiencies, however, were addressed in the aftermath of the 1946 strike.[53]

In addition to grappling with high inflation and low wages, workers in the oil industry also contended with a severe shortage of suitable housing, further exacerbating the precariousness of their lives. Life in labour districts such as Bahmanshir in Abadan was described as 'too disgraceful to waste words, paper, and ink on describing its pitiful condemned condition'.[54]

According to Ivor Jones, the General Manager of the AIOC, the Company's housing policy stipulated that no housing should be provided for unskilled labour, constituting 36.5 per cent of the total labour force in Abadan, which numbered 31,259 employees.[55] Jones himself acknowledged that 'housing conditions in the town [Abadan] were deplorable'. He recounted a distressing case where he witnessed 'sixty people – men, women, and children – living in a room measuring 12 by 6 yards (approximately 11 by 5.5 meters) with a mud floor, a leaking roof, only one door, and no sanitary facilities or access to water, all for a monthly rent of 500 rials'.[56]

Eyewitness accounts from the era shed light on the deplorable living conditions endured by workers, even three decades after the discovery and substantial extraction of the much-celebrated black gold for the international market. In 1945, despite the AIOC employing over 60,000 individuals in the refinery and oilfields, there were only 5,500 houses designated for married workers and 2,900 rooms allocated for unmarried workers.[57]

Manuchehr Farmanfarmaian, who served as the minister of finance at the time, recalled his visit to Abadan in 1945, painting a grim picture of the workers' living conditions. He noted that 'the workers lived in a shantytown called *Kaghazabad*, or Paper Town, without running water or electricity, and devoid of basic amenities such as iceboxes or fans'. During the winter, the earth would flood, forming a flat, muddy lake. The town's streets were knee-deep in mud, necessitating the use of canoes for transportation. After the rains subsided, swarms of small-winged flies would emerge from stagnant waters, filling the air and accumulating in black piles around cooking pots and clogging refinery fans with a sticky residue.[58]

Farmanfarmaian's eyewitness account finds corroboration in a report prepared by the British Parliamentary Mission, which visited the Iranian oil industry in 1946. According to the report, while there were 'splendidly built modern houses with air-conditioning and iceboxes' in Abadan, there were also

Figure 4.2 Mud Huts in the shantytown of Kaghazabad, Abadan, 1948

'makeshift shacks, some constructed using empty paper cement bags as roofs' (Figure 4.2). The report also highlighted cases such as an Oil Company worker who had waited for thirty-eight years for a 'decent house' and families of up to twelve people crammed into two rooms. Perhaps the most damning observation made by members of the mission was the sight of '200 elderly men living under distressing conditions' in an old bakery.[59]

During the Second World War, in addition to the looming threat of famine and food shortages, Iranians also had to contend with the dangers posed by diseases and epidemics. In 1942, typhus was introduced to the northern provinces of Iran by Polish soldiers and civilian evacuees arriving from the Soviet Union.[60] The disease swiftly spread throughout the country, eventually reaching the southern province of Khuzestan. Within the oil industry, which boasted two hospitals – one in Abadan with 350 beds and another in Masjed-Soleyman with 86 beds – the healthcare system faced the challenge of combatting this new disease, alongside the already prevailing endemic illnesses such as trachoma, malaria, tuberculosis, and the plague.

The scarcity of medical doctors during the war exacerbated the situation, leading to situations where 'as many as 150 to 400 Sick employees were attended to by a single Oil Company medical officer in an 8-hour shift'. This circumstance deterred labourers from seeking medical care at hospitals.[61] The Company's dental service was equally inadequate, with '2 or 3 dentists serving around 40,000laborers and staff, excluding families'.[62] The exorbitant fees charged by independent doctors in the town, along with the 'astronomical' cost of medications, left the Company's employees in a state of desperation.[63]

An 'internal and confidential' report documented a particularly distressing example, which is described in the following terms:

> Consider a man after twenty-five years' service contracting tuberculosis. He is paid his gratuity, which is only sufficient to keep him for a very short time, and in addition he immediately falls into the hands of local doctors who give the man hopes of a cure through treatment, thus draining his entire gratuity. It is a pitiful sight to see these people, especially when they have a large family to look after their income discontinued, and their Company house withdrawn. One can understand why they dislike going to hospital. ... The release of such employees into the town without any attention and income can only cause a future major social catastrophe in Abadan.[64]

Despite the organisational division of the Company's healthcare system into two branches – one for treatment and the other for preventive medicine – and the assurance of non-discrimination based on the employment status of the Company's workers, there were ongoing grievances about the subpar treatment and services provided by the clinics to workers. An illustrative instance occurred during the visit of the British Parliamentary Mission, when workers' representatives led an independent expedition in Abadan, distinct from the AIOC's prearranged excursion. Their objective was to reveal and expose the deplorable and degrading conditions endured by Iranian workers.

The mission was directed to Abadan Hospital, where they heard complaints of 'overcrowded conditions and poor food'. On one occasion, the mission members were presented with samples of bread provided to English workers, which they compared with the bread given to Iranians. The mission affirmed that 'the latter certainly seemed to be of very poor quality'. These observations underscored the disparities in treatment and provisions between English and Iranian workers.[65]

Oil Workers' Activism during the War

During the reign of Reza Shah (1924–41), an initial attempt was made to regulate industrial relations through the introduction of a labour law. However, any efforts to establish or promote labour associations faced severe repression. Following the deposition of the reigning monarch, the caretaker government under Foroughi assumed power with the primary objective of temporarily ensuring political stability and territorial integrity. This was crucial to maintaining the Allied support route to the Soviet Union. One of the measures implemented by the Foroughi cabinet was the issuance of a general amnesty decree for all political prisoners. A substantial number of these political detainees were affiliated with the outlawed Communist Party of Iran or other communist networks, as well as labour union activists. Notably among the latter group were Yusof Eftekhari, Ali Omid, and Rahim Hamdad, who, as discussed earlier in Chapter 3, played pivotal roles in leading the 1929 strike within the oil industry.

Following his release from prison in 1941, Eftekhari made the deliberate choice of not aligning himself with the newly established Tudeh Party or its associated labour union. Instead, in collaboration with his former comrades, he opted to establish an independent labour union known as *Ettehadieh-ye Kargaran-e Iran* (Trade Union of Iranian Workers – TUI), with its official newspaper being *Giti*. Concurrently, in 1942, the Tudeh Party initiated the formation of its own affiliated labour union, the *Showra-ye Markazi-ye Ettehadieh-ha-ye Kargari-ye Iran* (Central Council of Trade Unions of Iran – CCTU), which, a year later, underwent a name change following its merger with certain minor unions. The new name became *Showra-ye Motaheddeh-ye Markazi-ye Kargaran va Zahmatkeshan-e Iran* (Central Council of Unified Trade Unions of Iran – CCFTU), and it published *Zafar* as its official newspaper.

The leadership of the CCFTU maintained close affiliations with the Tudeh Party. Out of the fourteen prominent members elected to the leadership positions during the inaugural congress, all were active cadres of the Tudeh Party. Among them, four held membership in the Central Committee of the party, and an additional four later assumed leadership roles within the party. Three of these individuals had previously been associated with the early Communist Party of Iran. Impressively, ten of them had endured prolonged periods of incarceration during the reign of Reza Shah, attesting to their dedication to their political beliefs, while nine had a history of active involvement in labour union activities.[66]

During the wartime period, the CCFTU grappled with a significant concern: how to continue its activities without disrupting the Allied support for the Soviet fronts. It is noteworthy that during the war, nearly two-thirds of Iran's economy had some form of association with Allied operations within the country. Any potential disruption of these associations could be perceived as an act of sabotage.[67] The oil sector, particularly the supply of oil to the Soviet Union, was considered sacrosanct by the CCFTU, and labour agitation in this domain was strictly prohibited. Consequently, the CCFTU refrained from engaging in open agitation among labourers in the oil and transportation industries, particularly among rail workers during the wartime period. Instead, the CCFTU opted to initiate its activities in the central and northern provinces of the country.

Conversely, the independent TUI (Trade Union of Iranian Workers) was less apprehensive about jeopardising its relations with the Allies, particularly the Soviet Union, during the war. The TUI expanded its network throughout the country and established headquarters in Abadan, Ahvaz, and the western province of Kermanshah, where the Oil Company maintained a small installation and refinery. Furthermore, the TUI organised two consecutive strikes among the workers of the Iranian National Railroad and the Kermanshah Oil Installation in 1943. These workers were collectively demanding a pay raise.

It is worth noting that the Tudeh Party, its affiliated union, CCFTU, and even the Soviet Union's labour syndicate strongly condemned these actions. In an article published in *Trud*, the central publication of the All-Soviet Trade Unions, the TUI was labelled as the 'fascist fifth column', and Yusof Eftekhari was denounced as a 'dangerous provocateur'.[68]

As the Allies achieved successive victories against the Axis powers, particularly on the Eastern fronts, and with the Soviet Union's decisive triumph in the Battle of Stalingrad in February 1943, a noticeable change occurred in Soviet policy towards Iran. This shift was accompanied by a simultaneous alteration in the political stance and policies of both the Tudeh Party and the CCFTU both on the national and international fronts.

According to a report compiled by the British diplomatic mission in Iran, while the Tudeh Party initially maintained a more cooperative policy towards the Allies during the early stages of the war in Iran, there was a significant and stark transformation in the stances of both the Tudeh Party and the CCFTU following the Soviet victories in early 1943. At this juncture, their attitude was described as increasingly leaning towards a pro-Russian perspective, and it was suggested that they were poised to undertake substantial efforts to extend their influence southward, particularly with the aim of establishing a network among the workers in the oil industry.[69]

Approximately thirty years after the initial discovery of oil in 1908, a conspicuous absence of a centralised platform for labour arbitration empowered the APOC/AIOC to address labour-related concerns, such as living conditions, working conditions, labour recruitment, wages, education, healthcare, housing, and welfare, on an individual rather than a collective basis. This approach also extended to matters of employment termination, as the company retained the prerogative to terminate workers without prior notice or recourse for unjust dismissal.[70] Despite numerous signs indicating the emergence of a burgeoning labour movement during this era, the Oil Company's labour policies exhibited limited indications of adapting to these changing dynamics.

The evacuation of southern Iran by the Allies occurred on 10 March 1946, coinciding with the conclusion of the Soviet Aid Programme. As previously mentioned, this program, spanning five years, tacitly required all active institutions and organisations, including the Oil Company, the government, labour unions, and political parties, to adopt a policy that effectively suppressed labour disturbances in the country's vital sectors, particularly the oil industry. This implementation of an obstructive policy unfolded against the backdrop of worsening working and living conditions for Iranian labourers and aligned with the Allied imperative to prevent any disruption in the supply chain to the Soviet Eastern front during the Second World War.

With the war's end, the CCFTU and the Tudeh Party seized the opportunity to establish the covert network they had cultivated and nurtured during the wartime period. This effort was likened to 'releasing a horse in a paddock', and it manifested in the streets of Abadan, Aghajari, and Masjed-Soleyman.[71] In most cities within Khuzestan, the Tudeh Party and the CCFTU, or as it was known in the province, the *Showra-ye Mottahedeh-ye Kargaran va Zahmatkeshan-e Khuzestan* (Council of Unified Trade Unions of Khuzestan), shared offices and cooperated closely in coordinating their public activities. Additionally, the CCFTU's recruitment policy within the oil industry was comprehensive, targeting not only Iranian workers but also actively enrolling non-Iranian labourers, including those from India.[72]

After approximately five years of clandestine activities in the southern province of Khuzestan, the Labour Day of May 1946 marked the first occasion for the communist Tudeh Party and its affiliated labour union, the CCFTU, to assert their strength within the oil industry of the province. The International Labour Day commemoration was followed by a series of strikes that gradually engulfed the entire industry, eventually culminating in a violent and tragic climax on 14 July 1946.

To gain a deeper understanding of the extent of involvement by the oil workers and the levels of violence exerted by both the military and the protestors during the brief but intense general strike, and to comprehend the subsequent repressive policies adopted against the labour movement in the oil industry, it is pertinent to address several key questions:

- Who were the primary actors and entities that played pivotal roles in this strike?
- What were the circumstances and historical context that led to their involvement?
- Can one attribute the outbreak of this strike and the bloody clashes that transpired on the evening of 14 July to a deliberate plan instigated by certain key players, or were these events the result of unforeseeable and coincidental circumstances?

Exploring these questions will provide valuable insights into the complex dynamics, motivations, and outcomes surrounding this significant labour strike in the Iranian oil industry's history.

The International Labour Day demonstration of 1946 in Abadan caught the AIOC off guard. Earlier, in response to a request from the Iranian Prime Minister, the Oil Company had agreed to recognise the First of May as a public holiday. This marked the International Labour Day celebration publicly observed by oil workers in seventeen years. The last openly celebrated International Labour Day by oil workers occurred in 1929, and it had concluded with the mass arrest and expulsion of workers, as discussed earlier, now, after nearly two decades, the workers had returned to the streets.

In Abadan, the CCFTU and the Tudeh Party jointly organised a series of lively and spirited processions, leading to the closure of government offices and shops.

The rally commenced in the impoverished neighbourhood of Zolmabad on the outskirts of the old city, coinciding with the formal inauguration of the Workers' Club headquarters of the CCFTU in Abadan on the same day. Approximately 80,000 demonstrators paraded through the old town, endeavouring to transform the processions into an undeniable symbol of the CCFTU and the Tudeh Party's influence and power.

The march exuded a festive atmosphere with national anthems blaring, and workers chanting slogans in various languages, including Persian, Arabic, Hindi, Armenian, and Assyrian. A labour art exhibition was also held during the march, which was organised and supervised by the labour organ's administrative officers, identifiable by their white armbands.[73] Towards the conclusion of the rally, several speakers delivered anti-British speeches, criticising the Oil Company's operations in Iran. Notably, one woman, named Maryam, addressing the crowd went further, alleging that the Oil Company's directors spent more on dog food than on workers' wages. She implored the marchers to seize control of the 'black jewel', referring to oil production, with their own hands.[74] This remarkable achievement of peaceful mass mobilisation did not escape the astute observations of the local British consul, who documented the event in detail.[75]

Following the International Labour Day procession, a strike occurred on 5 May at the Distillation Plant, which was an act of solidarity with another strike that had taken place earlier in the Locomotive Section of the Abadan Refinery's workshop. The initial strike involved approximately fifty workers protesting against the violence perpetrated by one of the British foremen. In the subsequent strike at the Distillation Plant, around 350 workers joined in solidarity with their colleagues, advocating for several demands:

- Reinstatement of the locomotive shop strikers.
- Full payment for the days during which the strike occurred.
- Removal of the British foreman in the locomotive shop.
- Establishment of an arbitration committee to investigate labour conditions and complaints.

This committee was proposed to comprise two members from the management and two members from the CCFTU.

The Oil Company consented to the first two points but declined to comply with the third demand. Regarding the arbitration committee, the Company initially agreed to its formation, but once the strike concluded, the Company failed to honour this commitment.[76]

Following the strike in Abadan, it was Aghajari's turn to become involved in the next sequence of labour unrest.[77] Aghajari's oilfield held significant importance, as it produced 21 per cent of Iran's total crude oil in 1946, making it one of the largest fields with substantial production potential. By 1950, Aghajari's oilfield had increased its production to nearly 50 per cent of Iranian crude oil output.[78] The workforce in Aghajari had grown significantly, 'proportionately much more than that of any other Company area', without a corresponding increase in essential services such as housing and water facilities.[79] The absence of basic labour amenities, a fact acknowledged by the British Legation in Tehran, coupled with long working hours – 44.5 hours per week in winter and 45 hours in summer – aggravated the discontent among workers in Khuzestan more than in any other region.[80]

An account from a British Parliamentary Mission that visited the area following the strike sheds light on the dire conditions: 'Here were Persian laborers living in squalid conditions under tents, etc., and without a doubt, this was the worst place we visited in terms of social amenities'.[81]

On 10 May, approximately 10,000 workers and staff in the Aghajari oilfield, which even included the domestic servants of British personnel, initiated a strike. The strikers articulated several demands, including:

- A wage increase.
- Provision of drinking water and ice.
- Extra compensation due to the harsh working conditions.
- The availability of midwives and other medical facilities.[82]

While the CCFTU extensively covered the news of the Aghajari strike in its daily newspaper, *Zafar*, and offered wholehearted support for the strike, it acknowledged that the strikers were not members of the CCFTU. This was primarily because the Aghajari oilfield was relatively new compared to Abadan or Ahvaz, and the CCFTU had not had the opportunity to unionise the oil workers or establish an office there.[83]

The initial response from the AIOC management closely mirrored the company's historical approach, characterised by the rejection of workers' demands and categorising them as political actions, hence deeming them illegal. The AIOC called upon local military forces to intervene and suppress the labour unrest, seeking to restore order. This request received a favourable response from the provincial military command.[84]

Furthermore, the Oil Company issued a threat to completely withhold food and water supplies from the strikers, explicitly stating that it intended to make the 'workmen' starve if they did not return to work.[85] To some extent, this threat was realised in the subsequent days, intensifying the challenges faced by the striking workers.[86]

The strike in Aghajari coincided with a visit from an Iranian government commission to the southern region. This commission was led by the newly appointed Minister of Finance, Morteza-Qoli Bayat (Saham al-Soltan), and the head of the Concession Department, Hossein Pirnia (Mo'tamen al-Molk). In a report generated following their visit, the commission raised significant questions regarding the Company's claim that its wartime challenges had prevented it from fulfilling its obligations to provide essential labour amenities.

Furthermore, the commission's acknowledgement that the deplorable living conditions of the workers were a primary catalyst for the Aghajari strike directly undermined the Oil Company's assertion that the strike had been instigated by the CCFTU and was therefore coloured by potentially questionable political objectives. This recognition by the government commission suggested that the strike was driven by legitimate concerns and grievances related to labour conditions and not solely a political manoeuvre orchestrated by the CCFTU.[87]

The situation in Aghajari continued to deteriorate, and there were indications that the CCFTU was struggling to maintain strict 'official union discipline' among the strikers.[88] In a coordinated effort, the British Consul in Ahvaz, along with the Oil Company's security officer and Governor-General International Labour Day-Naqi Mesbah-Fatemi, compiled a list of 'principal ringleaders' to be apprehended. However, the Iranian government initially declined to arrest the 'three musketeers'.

Amid escalating tensions, the Iranian authorities opted to send a delegation to Aghajari. On 18 May, the eleventh day of the strike, the government published a new Labour Law and called for its implementation across the country.[89] Simultaneously, a government commission was sent to Aghajari to investigate labour conditions and engage in negotiations to end the strike. The four-member commission represented both the government and the CCFTU, reflecting the evolving political landscape in Tehran. This period of political manoeuvring ultimately led to Prime Minister Qavam reshuffling his cabinet and appointing three prominent Tudeh Party leaders in August 1946, marking a significant development in Iranian politics.

During the latter half of May, the commission engaged in a series of meetings with the striking workers and the local management of the Oil Company in Aghajari. During these discussions, the striking workers conveyed a warning to the Company: if all of their demands were not met within three days, they would call for a general strike, urging all workers in the oil industry to join them. It is important to note that this threat, which included the possibility of a general strike, was primarily articulated by the CCFTU's representative within the commission, rather than reflecting the immediate demands of the strikers. Interestingly, when the issue of a general strike was raised, the government's representatives on the commission opted for abstention, not actively endorsing the threat.

Lacking the broader support of the Iranian government in these negotiations, the AIOC representative within the commission had little choice but to make concessions and agree to certain demands put forth by the striking workers. These concessions included a substantial 118 per cent increase in the minimum wage, raising it from 16 rials to 35 rials per day. Additionally, the Company agreed to abolish the practice of deducting a portion of workers' pay in lieu of rations such as bread, tea, and sugar. This effectively increased the minimum wage by 50 per cent. Moreover, the workers were offered the opportunity to purchase staple commodities, including the aforementioned items, as well as cheese, ghee, beans, and peas, from the Company's stores at cost price.[90]

Regarding the issues of strike pay, Friday pay (a paid day of rest), and annual vacation pay, which had not been included in the initial demands of the strikers but were part of the government's new Labour Law, the local management of the Oil Company in Aghajari deferred the decision to the Company's headquarters in Abadan.[91] The commission then proceeded to Abadan, where they met with the AIOC's general management. The general management agreed to the commission's request for full strike pay. The matter of Friday and annual vacation pay was left for future negotiations. With their demands largely met and their objectives achieved, the Aghajari oil workers ended their fifteen-day strike on 25 May, feeling confident and satisfied with the significant progress they had made.

The conclusion of the strike in Aghajari was met with overwhelming approval and positive reactions from the CCFTU, the Tudeh Party, and the liberal press in Iran. CCFTU's *Zafar* publication extended congratulations to the Iranian populace, characterising the Aghajari workers' victory as a historic achievement. They further declared it a significant setback for the Oil Company. Additionally, *Shahbaz*, a newspaper affiliated with the Tudeh Party, expressed satisfaction with the 'successful termination of the strike'. They added that 'the criminal authorities of the Oil Company were forced to yield in the face of the unwavering will of the working class'.[92]

These responses underscored the sense of triumph and achievement felt by labour organisations and progressive elements in Iran following the resolution of the Aghajari strike. In the weeks following the resolution of the Aghajari strike, what was described by one of the Oil Company's managers as the 'Aghajari fever' rapidly spread throughout Khuzestan and beyond. In Tehran, approximately 1,500 workers at the Oil Depot initiated a one-day strike. Their demands were reminiscent of those in Aghajari, including wage increases from 20 rials to 35 rials per day and recognition of their affiliation with the CCFTU by the Oil Company. The Oil Company promptly accepted these demands.

News of other smaller-scale strikes in various departments of the oil industry began to reach the AIOC General Management. Additionally, there were reports of workers displaying 'insolent and aggressive' behaviour as part of a deliberate *kam-kari* (go-slow) strategy, which involved intentionally reducing their working speed and production output across all sections and departments.[93]

The CCFTU continued its negotiations with the Oil Company and presented a list of further demands, which included Friday pay, the appointment of worker representatives in the workshops to settle labour disputes, annual wage increases, and improved transportation facilities for workers. However, in this instance, the Oil Company displayed less willingness to meet these demands, particularly regarding the issue of Friday pay, despite having committed to this promise in previous negotiations.

The month of June and early July 1946 stood out as different from previous years, marked by a sense of anticipation and uncertainty. Numerous rumours circulated during this period, hinting at the expectation of significant events. These rumours were widely discussed in the Tehran press, revealing a mixture of anxiety and confidence among workers in the oil industry and within the country's political sphere.

The CCFTU was actively working to assert its influence over workers in various regions and departments of the oil industry, seeking to unionise them under its organisation. At the same time, workers were hopeful that the Oil Company would soon embrace the new Labour Law and fully implement its provisions, particularly regarding Friday pay, a commitment the Company had made after the resolution of the Aghajari strike.

The atmosphere became increasingly tense and volatile with reports of the arbitrary arrest of CCFTU activists in different parts of Khuzestan and the return of Governor-General Mesbah-Fatemi to Tehran. Mesbah-Fatemi had been summoned to the capital due to his assertive handling of the Aghajari strike in May.[94]

Further apprehensions emerged when rumours circulated in Abadan suggesting that certain Arab sheikhs and labour contractors, reportedly encouraged by certain Company officials with previous ties to the British Army, were promoting a campaign for the autonomy of Khuzestan. This campaign was likened to the autonomy movement unfolding in Azerbaijan at that time, adding to the overall uncertainty and tension in the region.[95]

These rumours were not without substance. In late May 1946, several Arab sheikhs visited the British Consulate in Khorramshahr and sought financial support and advice on establishing an 'Arab Union'. which would 'bind them together and form a counterpoise to the Tudeh Party whose malignant activities they regarded with no little anxiety'.[96] In reaction, the British Consul reminded them that he was 'not in a position to advise them' and 'they must follow their own star' with 'moderation [which is] particularly necessary at this juncture'.[97]

However, as the political landscape evolved, the British Consul decided to align himself with the sheikhs' appeal. There were other instances that illustrated the sheikhs' aspirations more clearly. According to a memorandum from the Khorramshahr Police to the Abadan Police, on June 24, around 7,000 Arabs in Khorramshahr staged a demonstration, carrying banners in Arabic and calling for greater autonomy for the Arab province of Khuzestan.[98] Additionally, reports indicated that Sheikh ʿAbdullah, an Arab Sheikh from Khuzestan, had appealed to the Arab League (then known as the League of Arab States) for support in Khuzestan's secession from Iran and its recognition as a new state.[99]

In Abadan, leaflets were distributed announcing the establishment of the Arab Union's headquarters in the city on July 15th, which corresponded to the 15th of Sha'ban in the Islamic calendar, the birthdate of the Twelfth Imam in Shi'ite Islam. These rumours deeply concerned both the CCFTU and the Tudeh Party, especially because there were Oil Company officials within the AIOC who supported the efforts of the Arab sheikhs. Notably, Colonel Underwood, a former member of the British Military Attaché who had been employed by the Oil Company in 1945 as the Chief Security Officer, and his assistant, Major Jeacock, the Company's Field Security Officer, were among the most dedicated supporters of the sheikhs. Both men had a close working relationship with Governor-General Mesbah-Fatemi.[100]

The attempt by certain Arab sheikhs in Abadan to establish a political party to counter the activities of the CCFTU and Tudeh Party in the province had the potential to escalate into a violent confrontation, potentially leading to direct military intervention.[101] Since its inception in 1941, the Tudeh Party had been secretly involved in establishing operational networks in Khuzestan, occasionally witnessing the apprehension and expulsion of its activists from the province. The decision to adopt a clandestine approach was rooted in the agreement between the British and the Soviet Union during their occupation of Iran, which explicitly prohibited labour union activities that could disrupt the Soviet war effort. This restriction primarily applied to sectors critical to the war effort, such as the oil and transportation industries.[102]

The victory of the International Labour Day 1946 provided an opportunity for the Tudeh Party to extend its influence by establishing a network of labour clubs throughout the entire province. Workers and individuals increasingly began reporting their complaints directly to the Tudeh Party, which, in turn, wrote strongly worded complaints to local authorities, including the police and the Governorate.[103]

The growing labour protests across the country, particularly in the oil industry, posed a new challenge for the Tudeh Party: how to assert its authority over these protests and leverage them to extract additional concessions from the government.[104] Based on the Iranian government's stance during the Aghajari strike and subsequent labour protests, the Tudeh Party believed it had the government's support, at least in Khuzestan. However, political developments in other parts of the country were causing the Tudeh Party to revaluate its confidence. To extract significant concessions from the government, including the possibility of joining the cabinet, the Tudeh Party recognised the need for a major, yet controlled, display of political strength. Calling a general strike was seen as one such option, provided that its conclusion could be ensured.

The AIOC's actions following the Aghajari strike were a subject of debate and careful consideration. While the strike was partially settled with reference to the new Iranian Labour Law, the Company did not commit itself to implementing and enforcing all the articles of this law, particularly the provision for Friday pay. The Company's ambiguous stance toward the labour movement compelled the British government to send a Parliamentary Mission to Khuzestan. This mission included two Labour MPs, both associated with the British Trade Union Congress (TUC), and a Conservative MP who had previously worked for the British-owned Imperial Bank of Iran.

Although the members of the mission did not reach a consensus, three key points from their report can be highlighted:

- The Company should focus solely on labour-related issues, such as wages, the length of the working day, and labour conditions, and should distance itself from matters outside the workplace, including housing, food, public health, education, etc.
- The Company was advised to launch a robust pro-British propaganda campaign in Iran.
- The labour movement should be handled by trained personnel with a deep understanding of collective bargaining.[105]

Among these recommendations, the last two were considered more feasible. Consequently, a Public Relations Office was established in Abadan and London. Furthermore, Ernest Bevin, the Foreign Secretary in the new Labour government, urged the Oil Company to hire Frederick Leggett as the Company's labour officer.

While the British labour government took a more cautious and measured approach to political developments in Iran and the labour movement within the oil industry, the Company's management adopted a more uncompromising and confrontational stance, seeking a final solution to labour unrest in the industry. Ivor Jones, in a letter to Edward Elkington, the influential Deputy Director of the AIOC in Iran, went so far as to suggest that 'it is probably not an exaggeration to say that at least 75 per cent of our labour are willingly or otherwise members of the [Tudeh] Party and that a number of our junior staff are also actively associated with it'.[106]. Edward Elkington also asserted that the Tudeh Party had the capability to bring the entire operation of the Company to a standstill at any moment.[107]

Local civilian and military representatives of the Iranian government, who cooperated regularly with the Company's management, believed that the only solution to deal with restive and dissatisfied labour was the complete termination of Tudeh Party and CCFTU activities in the region. However, achieving this goal would likely require imposing Martial Law and bringing the entire province under military rule, an option that Governor-General Mesbah-Fatemi had raised on several occasions.

During the early stages of labour unrest, Indian workers actively participated in labour protests both in the oilfields and the refinery. What concerned the Oil Company was the solidarity that some Indian workers displayed with the CCFTU. According to a report from the Consul for Indian Affairs at the British Embassy in Tehran, an Indian worker named Mohammad Ahmad

Farooqi, with a 'very pronounced communistic tendencies, managed to secure the leadership of the Indian artisans, who number about 1400 to 1500 and appealed [to] Tudeh [Party] leaders to help the Indians'. The report continues by arguing that 'this contact between the Indian community and the Tudeh and Mohammad Ahmad Farooqi's leadership was the beginning of the trouble amongst the Indian workers'.[108]

On 5 July, approximately one thousand Indian workers marched to the British Consulate in Khorramshahr, sat in front of the Consulate, and demanded to meet the British Consul to convey their grievances. During their meeting with the Consul, the Indian workers confirmed that they had come from various parts of the province. Leaders among the Indian workers, such as Kabul Singh and Shamsher Khan, called for the removal of the Indian Assistant Labour Officer, Asghar-Ali, Welfare Officer, Alaf Shah, and his Quarter Master, Mohammad-Ismaʿil.

On the following day, the protestors presented their grievances in a petition signed by 1135 Indian workers, delivering it to the British Consulate through a committee of seventeen men. The petition highlighted issues such as the Labour Officer's arbitrary power to lay off workers without providing compensation for their return travel costs to Mumbai, as required by the Company's own rules. They also raised concerns about poor accommodation and the lack of sports facilities provided by the Welfare Officer. The petitioners demanded the immediate removal of both the Assistant Labour Officer and the Welfare Officer.

In a meeting with the British Consul, the Labour Officer rejected the complaints of the protesters and accused them of engaging in subversive activities. According to an intelligence report by the British Consul in Khorramshahr, the Labour Officer revealed the emerging solidarity between Indian and Iranian workers in the preceding years. The Labour Officer explained that 'the Indian artisans came in contact with some prominent members of the Tudeh Party [CCFTU], especially Hossein Moradi, Jahangir, Safa, and Torabi, when they visited the artisans club frequently and addressed the Indian artisans several times in their club. On one occasion he [Asghar-Ali] was also present and Torabi, a prominent Iranian Tudeh Party [CCFTU labour activist] told the artisans in a forceful speech that the Tudeh is willing to help the Indians who were their brothers, and that they must unite and should get rid of their Labour and Welfare Officers and that these officers should be selected from amongst the members of the labour class'.[109]

In early June 1946, the solidarity between Indian and Iranian workers had grown to such an extent that on June 16, during one of the CCFTU's meetings in the South Ahmadabad neighbourhood of Abadan, a group of 200 Indian workers marched from their quarters and attended the meeting, chanting pro-CCFTU slogans.[110] By this time, 700 Indian workers had joined the CCFTU.[111] The Deputy General Manager of the Oil Company, along with the Consul for

Indian Affairs at the British Embassy in Tehran, compiled a list of 41 Indian labour activists and 'revolutionary speakers', with 10 of them having communist leanings. All of the workers named in this list were nominally Muslim, except for two Sikhs.

On 5 July, faced with growing frustration among workers, the CCFTU provincial office once again presented its demands to the Oil Company and set 13 July as the final deadline for meeting its demands. While the Company's representatives committed themselves to the deadline, the instruction from the Company's Tehran office was more evasive and postponed further negotiations in Tehran and with the Iranian government.[112]

Meanwhile, despite the CCFTU headquarters in Tehran dispatching a telegram to the local union instructing them to refrain from any radical actions, on 10 July, the Aghajari workers, once again and without deliberation with the CCFTU, launched another strike.[113] On the same day, the Council of Ministers in Tehran authorised the Governor-General of Khuzestan to declare Martial Law in the province at his own discretion. The Governor-General declared Martial Law in Aghajari, and the military commander arrested two local union leaders in Gachsaran and the CCFTU provincial leader, Ali Omid, in Ahvaz. Reacting to the news of the Aghajari strike, the AIOC management appealed to the CCFTU provincial leader Najafi to fly to Aghajari to persuade the workers to resume their work by promising the release of the arrested activists through the intervention of the government in Tehran; an appeal which proved successful.[114]

As the CCFTU was losing its influence over the workers, the Tudeh Party leadership in Tehran was still cautious about taking an overtly combative stance against the Oil Company and the Iranian government. One option they considered was to manage the workers' frustrations and engage in a game of cat and mouse with the Oil Company while attempting to secure a place in Prime Minister Qavam's cabinet. However, with Aghajari under Martial Law, Tudeh Party local activists under arrest, and reports of planned armed Arab activists coming to Abadan, the CCFTU and Tudeh Party felt they had no choice but to call for a general strike across the oil industry.

They hoped that a general strike would not only help them regain control over the workers and maintain their influence in the labour movement but also increase their political bargaining power in negotiations with the Iranian government.[115] The situation had escalated to a point where a show of strength through a general strike seemed to be the only viable option for them.

Chronicle of a Bloody Strike Foretold

The general strike that began on Sunday, 14 July 1946, involved workers from all areas of the oil industry in Khuzestan, including the Abadan Refinery, oilfields in Ahvaz, Aghajari, Masjed-Soleyman, Gachsaran, Naft-e Sefid, and Haftgel. It also included both Iranian and Indian refinery and field workers, clerical and manual workers, firemen, drivers, dockworkers, and even domestic servants and cooks employed in British households.[116]

In Abadan, the strike started with workers forming picket lines at various locations, including the Main Time Office of the Abadan Refinery, the Jetty, and the Post Office. As the morning progressed, more picket lines were established, and the workers' presence extended not only to the oil industry but also throughout the city. Martial Law was declared in the province by Governor-General Mesbah-Fatemi, who was in Ahvaz at the time, and he ordered the establishment of picket lines in Abadan. A curfew was imposed from 10:00 PM to 4:00 AM.

Despite these measures, the strike continued in an orderly fashion, with no reported incidents. Workers operating essential services continued their tasks and went on shifts and the CCFTU members posted as guards throughout Abadan took control of the urban transport, 'preventing damage to Company property and looting by provocateurs'.

In the afternoon, the British Consul in Khorramshahr met the civil Governor of Abadan, Vosouq, and when the Consul expressed his trepidation over the events underway in the city, the Governor somewhat ambiguously assured him that there was no need to be concerned, since 'there is a certain ongoing arrangement'. The Consul later confessed that he realised that 'some deep game was being played'. Later in the day, he was informed that 'there was a meeting between some Arab sheikhs and the Governor and following this meeting when the sheikhs were leaving the Governorate House, the voice of the Governor could be heard shouting on Arab sheikhs if they had their mandate!'[117]

The minutes of the meeting between the Governor of Abadan and the Arab sheikhs were not officially recorded. However, following the meeting, the Arab sheikhs decided to change their plans. Instead of inaugurating the Arab Union's headquarters on 15 July, the birthdate of the Twelfth Imam as originally intended, they hastily called on their supporters to gather in front of the headquarters on the same day for its ceremonial opening. Notably, their new call did not reference the Twelfth Imam's birthday.

Rumours began circulating from the Governorate House that the 'Tudeh mob were marching to the Arab Union headquarters and a number of Arabs already had been killed.'[118] In response to these developments, in the late afternoon, approximately two hundred Iraqi Arabs were transported from across the border to provide assistance to government troops. Colonel Underwood played a significant role in coordinating these efforts, setting up his office next to the office of Colonel Ahmad Fateh, the Military Governor of Abadan, to oversee the activities of the Arab operatives. This marked a critical turning point in the events unfolding in Abadan.[119]

As preparations were being made for the CCFTU-Tudeh evening rally in Ahmadabad, rumours started to circulate that the Arab unionists were planning an attack against Tudeh and CCFTU activists. Upon hearing these rumours, some young Tudeh activists decided to head to the Arab Union headquarters. When they arrived, they encountered a crowd of approximately 200 Union members in the street. The crowd did not allow the Tudeh members to pass, leading to a confrontation and a gunshot from an unidentified source.[120]

It took some time for news of the shooting to reach the crowd at the CCFTU-Tudeh rally, which began at 19:30. The rally featured several 'inflammatory' speeches by workers and Tudeh activists, and the atmosphere was charged with the energy of the thousands in attendance. When at 20.30 the news of the shooting of two Tudeh members reached the rally, it was just the spark needed to set the rally ablaze. According to the Company's intelligence report, at this stage, a man by the name of Ali Pahlevan, a city wrestler, foreman and taxi driver, who was known in Abadan as a Tudeh partisan, incited the crowd by declaring:

> Brothers! You should not be afraid of these Arabs even if they are armed with guns. Attack them bravely, they will be successful no doubt in killing two or three persons from us, but in the end, they will be killed by the mob there and then. If we let these traitors live, they will not allow our movement to develop and progress.[121]

The crowd heeded Pahlevan's call and proceeded towards the Arab Union headquarters. According to certain accounts, apart from the Union's supporters, the Governor of Abadan had gathered hundreds of unemployed workers, who had been conspicuously present at the intersections of major streets in Abadan since the conclusion of the conflict.[122] By the time the CCFTU-Tudeh assembly reached the Arab Union building, clashes had erupted between Union guards, armed with firearms, and the CCFTU-Tudeh supporters, who were armed with clubs and knives.[123] Enjoying numerical superiority over the Union guards, the crowd of CCFTU-Tudeh supporters, along with the previously assembled unemployed workers, took control of all documents housed within the Union building before incinerating them. Among the casualties in the incident were Sheikh Haddad, an Arab labour contractor who happened to be within the building, his assistant, and several others, including a Persian merchant and landowner named Seyyed Mohammad Qodsi. Subsequently, the crowd proceeded to the residences of Hossein Ghazi, a prominent Persian merchant from Isfahan, and killed him. The houses of all these contractors, including Yusof Kuwaiti, a Persian Jewish contractor who was coincidentally away on a business trip, were looted by the crowd. The violence escalated to other areas of Abadan, and the rioting persisted until midnight. At this point, government troops intervened, and the Military Governor of Abadan issued orders to open fire on the crowds. In the following days, the casualty count from the events of 14 July increased to 47 fatalities and 173 individuals injured. According to the CCFTU, among the total casualties, Arabs constituted 10 per cent, while non-Arabs accounted for the remaining 90 per cent.[124] No records indicate Indian worker casualties.

In the early hours of 15th July, with the arrival of 100 troops dispatched as reinforcements to Abadan, the military took control of the Tudeh Party and CCFTU headquarters, commencing a search for activists affiliated with both organisations. Colonel Ahmad Fateh, summoned several CCFTU leaders, including Najafi, under the pretext of initiating negotiations. The union leaders, unaware of the impending arrest, complied with the summons, only to be promptly apprehended by Colonel Fateh. Subsequently, a military court was hastily convened to prosecute them.

On the morning of 15 July, Abadan awoke to a sense of dread, haunted by the memories of the previous night's violent clashes that had left a deep scar on the city. News of the night-time military reinforcements and the mass arrests of workers and Tudeh activists had spread through word of mouth, casting a sombre shadow over the populace. Despite the grim atmosphere, the strike persisted in all of the AIOC's departments across the province, and picket lines remained as they had on the previous day.

The national radio broadcasted reports of an extraordinary state commission, formed under the authority of the prime minister, which was en route to Abadan with the mission of resolving the crisis. By 5:00 PM, the commission, led by Prince Muzaffar Firouz, the prime minister's personal deputy, had arrived in Abadan. Among its members were Aramesh, the Minister of Commerce and Industry, his deputy Saqafi, and two prominent leaders from the CCFTU and Tudeh Party, Radmanesh and Jowdat.

Meeting at the Governor House, the commission swiftly took action, ordering an immediate halt to all gunfire and securing the release of the five leaders of the Tudeh Party and the CCFTU who had been detained since the early hours of the previous night. The commission conducted a series of meetings with all stakeholders involved, including the CCFTU, the Tudeh Party, the Oil Company, and local government representatives, continuing their deliberations throughout the night into the early hours of the following day.

On July 16th, Firuz travelled to Khorramshahr, where he summoned the Arab sheikhs and cautioned them against any confrontation with the Oil Company workers. Returning to Abadan, he addressed a gathering of 30,000 workers, assuring them that the government was committed to resolving their grievances and emphasising that the Company was prepared to meet the workers' demands.

On 16 July, work resumed in Abadan around noon, following the announcement made by the commission, which declared that a settlement had been reached between the striking workers and the Oil Company. According to the statement, the workers' demands for a minimum wage of 35 rials per day and Friday pay were settled retroactively to the date on which the Labour Law was enacted, which was 18 May. However, the Oil Company refused to concede on the issue of payment for the three-day strike period and the removal of two Oil Company security officers, namely Colonel Underwood and Major Jeacock.

Regarding other matters such as improving transportation facilities, housing, and better medical services, the Company made some promises without providing specific details. At 2:00 PM on 16 July, the striking workers returned to their duties.[125]

The Day After

The sixty-hour general strike in July 1946 brought together all Iranian and Indian employees of the Oil Company, including workers and clerks, in support of tangible demands such as wage increases, Friday pay, improved housing, and better medical services. The Oil Company's partial compliance with these demands represented a form of social capital for the Iranian labour movement and for Iranian society as a whole. The society, not accustomed to methods of exerting pressure and bringing about change from below, was empowered by this movement.

After enduring twenty-five years of authoritarian modernisation that systematically suppressed the agency of the labour movement and other subaltern voices, this newfound empowerment and sense of agency were most notable among ordinary workers rather than within the labour union, the CCFTU. This newfound sense of empowerment and the ability to effect change would become a driving force, in the years that followed, behind the movement for the nationalisation of the oil industry.

The sixty-hour general strike also fostered alignment between the workers of the oil industry and the labour union, a development that held significant political leverage. This alignment was strategically utilised by the CCFTU to facilitate the entry of the Tudeh Party into the government. The concluding remarks made by Najafi, the head of the Abadan office of the CCFTU on 16 July, following Firuz's return to Tehran, exemplified the position of the Tudeh Party and the CCFTU regarding the labour movement in the southern region.

In a meeting of the Tudeh Party and CCFTU activists in Abadan, Najafi informed the workers that the entire matter had been referred to the Iranian government for arbitration by the CCFTU, and as a result, no further strikes would be called in the foreseeable future. He also pointed out that Firuz's visit to Abadan and his seemingly pro-worker stance during negotiations with the Oil Company were promising indicators. Najafi's optimism was not universally shared by the majority of strikers at the meeting. However, his perspective seemed to be validated when, nearly a month later, on 1st August, three members of the Tudeh Party were invited to join Qavam's cabinet.

The sixty-hour general strike presented a significant challenge for the Oil Company, revealing a conflict between the company's entrenched old management and the newly elected reformist Labour government in the United

Kingdom. The majority of AIOC's management consisted of colonial-era bureaucrats, many of whom had experience in the Burmese oil industry or had served as military officers in the British Raj. These individuals enjoyed political patronage from the Conservative Party in the British Parliament and perceived the growing assertiveness of labour movements worldwide through the lens of the emerging Cold War.

The Cold War was already reshaping international relations globally in the aftermath of World War II, creating new geopolitical dynamics. For instance, a report by William Cuthbert, a Conservative MP and member of the British Parliamentary Mission visiting Khuzestan in June 1946, characterised Iranians 'not strong enough nor morally sound enough ever to form a really democratic government and rule their own country'. Cuthbert's recommendation to the British government was 'to re-establish spheres of influence in Persia, similar to the arrangement in 1907, with a Russian sphere in the North and a British sphere in the South'. He also suggested that 'the future of Persia should be discussed with Russia'.[126] This perspective of retaining colonial-era influences and divisions clashed with the evolving global political landscape and the aspirations of Iranians for greater self-determination.

The proposal of Cuthbert was shared by Sir Orme Sargent, a veteran diplomat who had represented Britain at the Versailles Conference of 1919, and in 1946 held the post of permanent undersecretary at the Foreign Office. According to the record of a meeting with some high-ranking members of the Foreign Office and the Ministry of Fuel and Power convened by Sargent on 17 June 1946, the question of the maintenance of British oil supplies from Iran was discussed. Several options were considered:

- Encouraging the local separation in South-West Persia (Khuzestan) and promoting a region similar to Azerbaijan under British influence.
- Reducing the Persian government's royalties in case of a strike.
- Attempting to weaken the Tudeh Party by winning over those members who were not committed communists and were open to reform but not aligned with Moscow's directives.
- Considering the use of force as an option, with a clear message to the Persians that it would be used if necessary to maintain order or resist any Persian attempt to nationalise the AIOC.
- Providing additional amenities such as housing and cinemas if that was genuinely what the local population desired.[127]

These options reflected a range of strategies, from geopolitical manoeuvres to addressing social and economic issues, as Britain sought to maintain its interests in Iran amid changing political dynamics and labour unrest.

Two days later, in a letter addressed to Ernest Bevin, the Secretary of the Foreign Office in the new Labour government, Sir Orme Sargent expanded on his secessionist proposal. He suggested that 'measures might have to be devised for stirring up tribesmen in opposition to the Tudeh Party and in favour of local autonomy'. This proposal indicated a willingness to support and manipulate tribal factions in order to counter the influence of the Tudeh Party and promote the idea of regional self-governance, aligning with the broader strategy of securing British interests in Iran.[128]

In light of the convenient and unexamined use of the 'communist provocation' narrative, many British Foreign Office agents and Oil Company employees consistently downplayed or obscured the linkages between poverty, the absence of basic welfare provisions, and the grievances expressed by workers who took to the streets in the southwestern region of Iran. For Colonel Underwood, the Oil Company's Security Officer, the strike was simply a 'political plot engineered by the pro-Russian Tudeh Party and other elements' that had infiltrated the labour ranks. Due to this simplistic worldview, his proposed solution was to eradicate the issue of labour unrest once and for all. In his own words, 'a friendly atmosphere between the Company and its labour cannot be expected, unless the present Tudeh leaders are removed for good, dead or alive'.[129] Colonel Underwood had taken it upon himself to pursue this mission in the days leading up to the violent events of 14 July, attempting to stoke ethnic conflict in Abadan and incite elements of the Arab community against the striking workers. The subsequent declaration of Martial Law, which remained in place for years, led to the widespread arrest of Tudeh Party and CCFTU activists, an outcome that had not been anticipated by Underwood.[130] According to Elwell Sutton, in the weeks preceding the general strike, 'it was common talk amongst the supporters of the left that Britain was encouraging separatist movements amongst Arabs'. Following the strike, both the British government and the AIOC were accused of 'deliberately fomented the strike and clash between Persians and Arabs to provide an incentive for British intervention'. While not definitively supporting these claims, Elwell Sutton suggests that 'without going as far as that, it certainly does appear that Company officials had been indiscreet in encouraging 'Arab' activities in the area'.[131]

Simultaneously, following the decisive victory of the Labour Party in the British parliamentary elections of July 1945, pressure mounted on the AIOC to implement some reforms regarding its overall policy in Iran. As reports flowed in from the AIOC and various branches of the British political establishment, detailing political developments within Iran, particularly the recent labour unrest in Khuzestan,[132] the new Labour government grew increasingly alarmed by the AIOC's pursuit of an independent political agenda concerning the Iranian oil industry. This agenda diverged from the British government's overarching policy toward Iran. Responding to Sargent's 'Persian Situation' report, Ernest Bevin summarised the government's concerns in the following manner:

> Your paper leaves out the account of the history of this business and the action of the Anglo-Iranian Oil Company in their dealing with labour in the past. The first point I would like to make is that there was a law in Persia which prohibited workpeople from joining a trade union, and that law, I understand, was carried at the request of the oil companies, for, be it remembered, it was only at the outbreak of this last war that the oil companies in England were willing to recognise a union for their transport people and that had to be forced through the Control Board. This background of anti-trade union organisation by the companies has inevitably brought the present situation to a head.
>
> . . .
>
> It is quite clear from your paper that you have not studied the Tudeh Party's programme and I called attention the other day to moderation of the programme in most of its items, which in any ordinary industry would be adopted. I recognise therefore that there is a fertile field here for reform, and it is no more fertile than in England some years ago when the mass of general labour organised itself. In my view, the way to tackle this problem is vigorous application by the Company of their social programme and greater consultation with their workpeople, and the building up within the undertaking itself of human relationships with the actual men, not on a feudal basis but with the appreciation that all over the world the sense of equality is rapidly developing.
>
> . . .
>
> You speak of stopping the royalties in the case of a strike. Would it not be better to work out some different method of sharing with Persian Government instead merely paying royalties? They will be able to point to us and say we are nationalising our resources, why should we deny the same to them.
>
> . . .
>
> A propaganda campaign might at once be started in Persia on anti-Communist lines, emphasising the need for reform, but supporting Persian nationalism and Persian independence and opposing political parties which take their inspiration and their money from foreign sources.[133]

Ernest Bevin's conciliatory and reformist stance was a reflection of the broad political mandate of Clement Attlee's Labour government, which held power from 1945 to 1951. This government implemented a range of radical economic and political policies, both domestically and internationally, during its time in office. While the Labour government's approach to the Iranian oil industry shifted significantly when the question of nationalisation arose in the late 1940s, it nonetheless initiated the gradual dismantling of some of the more problematic aspects of the British Empire. Additionally, it oversaw the nationalisation of major industries and the establishment of a comprehensive welfare system often described as 'cradle to grave'.

The internal struggle within the British political establishment regarding policies for the working class after the Second World War was intensified during a new phase in the global labour movement. This period was marked by the significant influence of workers' willingness to strike, spanning continents from Africa to Europe, Asia, and the Americas. These strikes occurred in both non-colonial and colonial contexts, including hybrid situations like that of Iran, where a form of colonialism was practised indirectly while maintaining formal recognition of Iranian sovereignty.

Within the British colonial sphere, the pressing question revolved around whether colonial administrators could predict, control, and manage the escalating political and social discontent that had intensified during the two World Wars and the two decades in between. In the aftermath of the Second World War, the British Empire faced a dire need for rapid recovery from mounting economic challenges, including a substantial debt owed to the United States. It was believed that one of the most viable solutions to address these financial difficulties was to secure a more robust position for hard currency in the global market, achieved through the sale of resources such as oil from overseas colonies or the export of domestically produced goods. British Empire administrators were not willing to tolerate any potential disruptions to their envisioned plans aimed at ensuring the Empire's continued dominance in the long term, particularly when it came to labour movements demanding improved working conditions and living standards.

During the war, when dealing with striking workers and the potential threat they posed to colonial rule, the use of coercive and divisive tactics was a common approach. However, in the post-war period, as the labour movement continued to grow and escalate, there was a recognised need for new and complementary measures both within the colonial territories and back in the United Kingdom.

The impetus for reform largely came from the colonial periphery. As noted by historian Frederick Cooper, 'Great Britain's colonial labour policy was to a large extent pulled along from the periphery, as local officials had to come to grips with the challenges posed by workers.'[134] Ernest Bevin, for example, emphasised that 'we must be careful that our plans for the development of our Colonial Dependencies cannot in anyway be represented as springing solely from our selfish interests. It is above all important that in their presentation there is no possible suggestion of exploitation of the colonial population.'[135]

These principles were evident in Bevin's correspondence with the AIOC and the immediate reactions to the July strike. However, in the months and years that followed, the politics of the Cold War, which quickly emerged after the Second World War, would largely overshadow and, in many cases, undermine the earlier promises of development.

The labour movement that unfolded in the Iranian oil industry from May to July 1946 was a significant historical event, marking the largest industrial strike in Iranian history up to that point. Its culmination in the sixty-hour general strike and the violent events in Abadan had far-reaching consequences for all the parties involved, both in the short term and in the years to come. While the workers' protest was initially driven by the labour unions and the Tudeh Party, the general strike provided an opportunity for the Tudeh Party to gain influence and ultimately secure positions within the Qavam cabinet through its alignment with the labour movement. However, the Oil Company's mishandling of the protests escalated the strike into a major crisis, which was met with the imposition of Martial Law and the subsequent arrest and exile of prominent labour activists. The primary objective was to dismantle and destroy the entire labour union and workers' network in the province.

The close integration of the Tudeh Party and the CCFTU in the oil industry made it nearly impossible to distinguish between their activities, leaving the labour movement vulnerable. The CCFTU, effectively operating as an extension of the Tudeh Party, became subject to the party's changing fortunes, leading to its eventual decline and demise.

In summary, the 1946 labour movement in the Iranian oil industry had significant and lasting effects, including political shifts, violence, and the weakening of the labour union's influence due to its close ties with the Tudeh Party.

The Oil Company seized the opportunity presented by the violence of that fateful day to finally eliminate organised labour and suppress the political activism of the Tudeh Party in Khuzestan. The outbreak of violence provided the pretext for the imposition of Martial Law in Abadan. Although the leadership of the CCFTU and the Tudeh Party had anticipated the potential dire consequences of a direct confrontation with the AIOC, they felt compelled to navigate the rapidly approaching crisis. As a result, they attempted to shape and exploit the strike opportunistically for their political gain, aligning it with their own political agenda and priorities.

The Oil Company employed a combination of violence and conciliatory measures during the strike. While accepting most of the oil workers' demands and pledging improvements in housing and healthcare in the years ahead, the company achieved its short-term goal of dismantling the organisational foundation of the CCFTU and the Tudeh Party's influence, as Martial Law would remain in effect for several years.

Despite the appearance of defeat in the immediate aftermath, the workers would eventually reap the benefits of their struggle and set a precedent that would prove challenging to reverse. Moreover, the tranquillity and complacency of the Oil Company would be disrupted on an unprecedented scale in the following years by the historic movement for oil nationalisation, which would once again thrust the AIOC, the Iranian government, and Iranian oil workers onto the international stage.

5

Poised to Leap: Towards Oil Nationalisation

The five years period following the July strike of 1946 was marked by turbulence and significant developments in the movement advocating for the nationalisation of the Iranian oil industry. This period ultimately culminated in the successful nationalisation of the industry in March 1951. The political landscape in Iran during this time can be divided into two distinct periods, each with its own defining events and outcomes.

The first period commenced with the downfall of the Autonomous Government of Azerbaijan on 12 December 1946. It encompassed events such as the failed assassination attempt on the Shah on 4 February 1949, which led to the government's decision to outlaw the Tudeh Party's network and the Central Council of Unified Trade Unions of Iran (CCFTU)[1] across the country. This period concluded with the campaign for the sixteenth parliament, which took place in late 1949.

The second period began with the campaign for the sixteenth parliament in October 1949 and included the pivotal moment of the nationalisation of Iranian oil, which was ratified on 20 March 1951, by both Iranian parliamentary bodies. This period concluded six months later, on 4 October 1951, with the departure of the last British AIOC employee from Iran.

The nationalisation of the Iranian oil industry in 1951 has been extensively studied by historians, economists, and political scientists. While there may be some variations in interpretation, there is a broad consensus among these studies that the nationalisation was primarily driven by a concerted effort from the political elite. When references are made to the involvement of actors from below, it is often limited to organised crowds supporting the elite's political agendas.[2] In the following pages, we will examine this interpretation and assess the significance of both organised and non-organised pressures from below in the context of the nationalisation of Iranian oil.

On 12 December 1946, the Iranian government deployed troops to the province of Azerbaijan, effectively bringing an end to the one-year rule of the Soviet-backed Autonomous Government of Azerbaijan. This event had significant political repercussions not only in Azerbaijan but also throughout the entire country. The fall of the Autonomous Government and the subsequent flight of many of its leaders and activists to the Soviet Union led to a period of political turmoil in Iran. In this chaotic political environment, the ruling government of the Qavam Democrat Party saw an opportunity to suppress and silence its opponents, particularly the Tudeh Party and its affiliated labour union, the CCFTU. The offices of the Tudeh Party and the CCFTU were ransacked in Tehran and other major Iranian cities, and their activists were subjected to assaults and arrests by local police or gendarmerie forces.

The Azerbaijan crisis triggered a significant internal crisis within the Tudeh Party. Some members of the party strongly disagreed with certain party policies, leading to a faction of dissidents who referred to themselves as party reformists. Khalil Maleki emerged as a prominent figure leading this dissenting faction. Maleki, a mid-level leader in the party, had been involved in communist activities during the reign of Reza Shah, which had resulted in his imprisonment for three years prior to the Shah's abdication.[3]

Khalil Maleki and his supporters criticised the leadership of the Tudeh Party for various reasons, one of which was the party's policy of offering unconditional support to the Soviet Union on issues such as the oil concession or the Azerbaijan revolt.[4] It's important to note that a more nuanced understanding of Maleki's criticism can be achieved by considering that he expressed his disagreement with the party approximately 18 months before Yugoslavian communist leader Josip Broz challenged Soviet hegemony within the international communist movement and departed from the Cominform.

The first manifesto authored by Khalil Maleki and his fellow dissidents was published in January 1948. This manifesto criticised the executive leadership of the Tudeh Party, accusing it of practicing a defeatist policy in various aspects, including labour, ethnicity, and politics. The dissidents called for reforms within the party leadership and advocated for a more radical approach in their political activities.[5]

In response to this dissent within the Tudeh Party, both the party itself and the Soviet Union's propaganda apparatus condemned the division and labelled those advocating for it as traitors, conspirators, or even as agents of the British government infiltrating the Iranian labour movement. Such accusations were regularly broadcasted, even though outlets like the Moscow Radio Persian Service.[6]

In the years following this split in the Tudeh Party, the supporters of the rift managed to survive by establishing a socialist political platform as an alternative to Tudeh communism. However, their presence in the organised labour movement remained limited and was mainly confined to the capital, Tehran.[7]

The split within the Tudeh Party was not the sole challenge the party encountered after the fall of the Autonomous Government of Azerbaijan. In the summer of 1946, shortly after the violent strike in Abadan, the first Ministry of Labour in Iran was established under the name of the Ministry of Labour and Propaganda. It became apparent that one of the primary objectives of this newly created ministry was to initiate a campaign to establish a new 'independent' labour union as an alternative to the CCFTU.

In Tehran, the government imposed a ban on all outdoor meetings and activities, including a general labour strike and demonstration organised by the CCFTU. Reports from other cities suggested a widespread crackdown on CCFTU and Tudeh Party activists and leadership, leading to arrests and imprisonment on charges of supporting the 'secessionist' revolt in Azerbaijan.

The government-sponsored labour union, the Union of the Syndicates of Iranian Workers (*Ettehadieh-e Sandika-ha-ye Kargaran-e Iran – ESKI*), was established in September 1946. While the Ministry of Labour and Propaganda claimed that ESKI's creation aimed to provide Iranian workers with a non-political trade union alternative to the CCFTU, the first Minister of Labour, Habib Nafici, admitted that 'the danger of Tudeh was too great… to have waited for a non-communist union to develop from grass roots'.[8] According to a labour report from the American Embassy in Iran, ESKI's actions aligned with the political agendas of the government and the Court and had been adapted to serve the interests of the United States in Iran. The report noted, 'the basis of ESKI's existence is political opposition to Tudeh. ESKI is opposed to international and domestic Communism, and, on the positive side, is pro-Court, to a lesser degree pro-army'.[9]

ESKI was not the sole anti-Communist union formed during this time. Concurrently, the Central Union of Workers and Peasants of Iran (*Ettehadieh-ye Markazi-ye Kargaran va Keshavarzan-e Iran – EMKA*) was established independently of the Ministry of Labour and Propaganda. Nevertheless, neither of these unions succeeded in becoming a viable alternative to the Tudeh union. According to Ladjevardi, in 1947, the British Embassy in Tehran encouraged the Ministry of Labour and Propaganda to consolidate all anti-Tudeh unions into a single federation, following the model of the British Trade Union Congress (TUC). The outcome of this merger was the Iranian TUC (*Kongereh-ye Ettehadieh-ha-ye Kargaran-e Iran – ITUC*).[10] However, in the early 1950s, the ITUC adopted a more anti-Mosaddeq stance and aligned with the opponents of the nationalisation of the oil industry.[11] Throughout their existence, neither ESKI nor EMKA nor the resulting ITUC managed to gain significant support among oil workers.

With the assistance of the Ministry of Labour and Propaganda, ESKI initiated an extensive nationwide anti-Tudeh and CCFTU propaganda campaign, levelling accusations of 'illegal' activities against both the Tudeh Party and its affiliated labour union. In particular, the CCFTU officials in Khuzestan were alleged to have misappropriated union funds. According to a report sent to Tehran by the CCFTU Khuzestan inspector, union officials in Abadan were accused of diverting around two million Rials of financial aid, which had been collected from CCFTU members, Tudeh Party supporters, and others in Khuzestan for the families of those who were killed or injured during the 1946 strike. This diversion not only infuriated the workers but also eroded their trust in both the union and the party.[12]

Concurrently with the government's endeavours to establish a comprehensive labour union in Iran, a policy shift emerged in Khuzestan under the new Ministry of Labour and Propaganda. This shift aimed to dismantle the existing CCFTU network within the oil industry. In the wake of the tumultuous strike in July 1946, Khuzestan had fallen under Martial Law, resulting in the closure of all Tudeh Party and CCFTU offices. The authorities detained and subsequently deported key CCFTU figures from the Khuzestan province, including notable founding members Ali Omid and Mehdi Hashem Najafi.[13]

The process of reconstituting the Tudeh Party and its affiliated workers' union in Khuzestan proved to be a protracted and intricate endeavour, considering the extensive disruption caused by these events. By 1948, Abolfazl Farrahi, a member of the Advisory Commission of the Central Committee of the Tudeh Party who resided and worked as a schoolteacher in Khorramshahr, assumed the crucial role of reorganising the Tudeh Party and its associated labour union. ʿEsmat Yazdanpanah-Daʾi, a young member of the Tudeh Party Youth Organisation in Abadan at the time, alluded in her diary to Bahmanshir as the Abadan neighbourhood wherein the most expansive subterranean network of the Tudeh Party was covertly situated.[14]

Simultaneously, the immediate and rushed response from the Oil Company's management to the strike materialised in the formation of a Supreme Labour Council located in Abadan. This council consisted of three worker representatives, three Oil Company deputies, and ten government officials, encompassing both military and civilian personnel. Its primary mandate was to deliberate upon the working and living conditions of the oil workers.

One of the key outcomes of the Supreme Labour Council's deliberations was the decision to broaden its scope to encompass all workshop floors. Here, it was proposed to establish factory councils comprising workers, Oil Company members, and government officials, with regular meetings involving one representative from each of these three constituent groups. This initiative, initially spearheaded by the Oil Company, would subsequently be adopted, and coordinated by the government labour office in Khuzestan. Further details regarding this development will be explored in subsequent sections of this chapter.

On the government's front, the establishment of a new labour union for oil workers was viewed as a clear alternative to the Tudeh-affiliated union. In February 1947, the Oil Company appointed Mostafa Fateh, a seasoned senior employee of the company who headed the Oil Company's Distribution Department, to the role of AIOC Assistant General Manager in Abadan. His primary responsibility was to address the welfare concerns of the Iranian employees of the Oil Company.

Upon assuming his new role, Mostafa Fateh approached some well-respected local activists associated with the CCFTU who had distanced themselves from the union following the 1946 strike. He proposed the idea of inviting Yusof Eftekhari, a prominent labour unionist, to Abadan to help establish a new labour union. Eftekhari, along with ten labour activists, including some former CCFTU members, arrived in Abadan in January 1947. They collectively founded a new organisation called the Unions of Oil Workers, which was affiliated with ESKI. On 21January 1947, they published a Founding Declaration, in which the Unions of Oil Workers stated:

> Our organisation had actually come into existence solely with the aim of being an industrial union of workmen, not to be involved in political affairs and to only use its power to organise the workmen and protect their rights. Unfortunately, we had been deceived, and they used us as a tool for foreign policy, collected a considerable amount of money from us and sent it to Tehran and now that we want to claim the money back, we are given a negative response.
>
> The name of our Union will in future be 'The Unions of Oil Workers', which is completely independent and unattached to any other union or *Shura*.
>
> The Unions of Oil Workers has no connection with any political party and its actions will be exclusively to safeguard the interests and rights of the workers within the limit of the Iranian rules and regulations.
>
> The management of our Union is comprised of those who are either workmen themselves or have experience in the Iranian oil industry and are thus well informed about the affairs of the workmen's lives and needs and will not use the workmen's support for political interests.[15]

While Yusof Eftekhari had the support of the Iranian government and the endorsement of the AIOC, it was challenging to gauge the level of confidence among the oil workers, given the recent memory of the bloody confrontation in July and the subsequent political repression. The following dialogue between Eftekhari and one of the former members of the CCFTU, which occurred during one of the inauguration meetings of the new union and was reported by an informant within the AIOC, highlights the workers' mistrust in any organised activities within such a repressive environment. Speaking to a gathering of 200 oil workers in Abadan on 20 February 1947, Yusof Eftekhari urged the workers to join the new union using the following words:

> Eftekhari: 'Comrades, the rules and regulations of the new Union of Oil Workers which will be enforced in future, will be according to the Labour Law for the welfare of the workers not like the Tudeh Party which has raised the good cause of the workers. Had the Tudeh leasers worked tactfully, they would have obtained every concession such as wage increases, good housing, schools, education of children, health, etc. These things can still be achieved easily. If you all become members of our new union and work united with us, we will try our utmost to get you your rights from the Company in a constitutional manner'.

> One worker: 'We have no confidence in this new union. As to the previous union leaders, they have been sent to prison and we are afraid that if we become members of this new union, the government will put us too into jail or exile us as before'.[16]

The Unions of Oil Workers faced not only the workers' mistrust but also another challenge from the Khuzestan Labour Department. In March 1947, Shapour Bakhtiar, a young Iranian lawyer, was appointed as the Director of the Khuzestan Department of Labour. Bakhtiar held a PhD degree in Law from the Sorbonne University and had actively participated in the French Resistance during Second World War. After the war, he returned to Iran and was initially appointed as the Director of the Isfahan Labour Department.

In March 1946, Isfahan, known as the 'Iranian Manchester' due to its textile industry, experienced significant labour unrest. The unrest was rooted in labour demands for various improvements, including a wage increase, an eight-hour workday, Fridays off with pay, and the prohibition of worker dismissals without the consent of the labour union. However, with the involvement of certain government agents, what had initially been a peaceful labour protest escalated into a violent confrontation between supporters and opponents of the Tudeh Party.

Bakhtiar's success in resolving the labour unrest in Isfahan and securing workers' demands marked the first of many achievements during his extensive career in public service.[17]

The recollection of the violent Abadan strike that had occurred eight months prior undoubtedly played a significant role in the selection of Bakhtiar as the Director of the Khuzestan Labour Department. There existed a hopeful expectation that he would replicate the same accomplishments in his new role as he had previously demonstrated in Isfahan. Moreover, Bakhtiar's ethno-cultural affiliation may not have been inconsequential in his appointment. Shapour Bakhtiar, owing to his association with the Bakhtiari tribe, managed to establish a notable presence within the ranks of the oil workers, a considerable portion of whom shared his Bakhtiari tribal heritage.

The designation of Bakhtiar coincided with the visit of Ahmad Aramesh, the Minister of Commerce and Industry, to Abadan. In the early spring of 1947, during his negotiations with the Anglo-Iranian Oil Company (AIOC) concerning the welfare status of the Iranian employees of the Oil Company, he successfully persuaded the Company to augment the minimum wage by 14 per cent, raising it from 35 to 40 rials. Furthermore, the Company committed to establishing workers' cooperatives and reducing the disparity between high-grade and low-grade employees.[18]

Ahmad Aramesh's notably productive visit to Abadan served to enhance Bakhtiar's newfound role. A report crafted by the British Consulate in Isfahan assessed Bakhtiar as 'an energetic and well-meaning official, [who] may find the atmosphere of Abadan more congenial than that of Isfahan, [where] the mill-owners closed their ranks against his efforts of labour reform'.[19]

Upon his arrival in Abadan, Bakhtiar, in a report directed to the Minister of Labour and Propaganda, Ahmad Aramesh, along with his deputy, Habibollah Nafisi, referenced the deplorable living and working conditions of the workers. He consented to assume his new position on the condition that his superiors would intercede with the AIOC to institute reforms favourable to the oil labour force. These reforms encompassed the establishment of labour councils within the oil industry, salary increments, the construction of housing for workers residing in Kaghazabad, and the provision of daily free potable water and ice in the workers' residential areas. The formation of these labour councils evidently served as an alternative to the CCFTU, an organisation affiliated with the Tudeh Party, which had faced prohibitions on its activities throughout the province following the tumultuous strike of July 1946.[20]

Reassured by both the minister and the AIOC's public relations officer, Bakhtiar commenced his mission in Khuzestan, beginning with Masjed-Soleyman Haftgel and Lali, where he established the Labour Council. This initiative primarily aimed to unite Bakhtiari employees of the Oil Company in the field areas.[21] Notably, this move posed a direct challenge to the parallel effort led by Yusof Eftekhari to organise oil workers. Initially, according to the British Consulate in Khorramshahr, the General Management of the Oil Company placed confidence in Mustafa Fateh's support for Eftekhari and even endorsed Fateh's call for Bakhtiar to remain in Abadan and back the new Union led by Eftekhari.[22]

However, Bakhtiar had his own strategy for organising oil workers through non-political councils. The clash between Bakhtiar on one side and the partnership of Mostafa Fateh and Yusof Eftekhari on the other appeared to be inevitable. For Bakhtiar, following his success in Isfahan, the organisation of oil workers within non-political councils, particularly against the backdrop of the lingering memory of the previous year's violent strike, held the promise of becoming a career-defining achievement. Conversely, Fateh perceived Eftekhari's scheme as a 'matter of personal prestige'.[23]

The Labour Day of 1947 transpired without any official celebration. The prime minister had prohibited processions on International Labour Day in all regions where military governates had been established.[24]

By the summer of 1947, Bakhtiar had drafted a constitution for his envisioned Workers' Councils, alternately referred to as the Central Council of Khuzestan Workers' Unions.[25] This newly established constitution designated the association as a 'legal union which was certainly not attached to any political party or policy' with its sole mission being 'the improvement of the workers' social situation and raising the standard of education and living'.

In an English translation of a 'Proclamation' signed by 'Dr. Shapur Bakhtiar, General Technical Adviser and Director of Labour and Propaganda Department, Khuzestan', we encounter the following:

> The Work's Councils and Unions will, from the law point of view, be the only organisation officially recognised and all the organisations outside the Work's Councils and Union will not be officially recognised by the government and no notice will be taken of them. It goes without saying that these organisations, should, by the hands of the workers and to the benefit of the worker, remain under the banner of the law and protection of the government. Abadan workers will judge in action that the Khuzestan Labour Department has had no intention other than persuading the workers to form a fundamental organisation by the hands of the Iranians and for the benefit of the workers and I myself who have with such grave responsibility undertaken the guardianship of this department, hope to make the sense of freedom and the purpose of patriotism clear in practice.[26]

The 'Proclamation' had a profound impact on Eftekhari, leading to increased 'disillusionment and frustration' on his part. By the end of August 1947, despite his Union of Oil Workers having only 2,800 members, he convened an emergency meeting of the union to elect a new Executive Committee and then departed for Tehran. While in Tehran, he dispatched a telegram to the newly elected Executive Committee members, expressing his regret that 'pressure of other work will keep him away indefinitely from Abadan and wishing the union every success'.

For numerous oil workers and external observers, including the British Consulate in Khorramshahr, Yusof Eftekhari's telegram was regarded as the definitive blow that sealed the fate of the Union of Oil Workers.[27]

The departure of Eftekhari and the subsequent dissolution of the Union of Oil Labour left the labour activism landscape within the oil industry with only two prominent players: Bakhtiar's nascent Workers' Councils and the clandestine cells of the illicit CCFTU. However, the presence of Bakhtiar's Workers' Councils, boasting approximately 3,000 members, would soon prove to be short-lived as well.[28]

Upon the commencement of the campaign for the sixteenth parliamentary election, Bakhtiar put forth his candidacy for the province of Khuzestan. His popularity among the Bakhtiari workers in Abadan and Masjed-Soleyman was unquestionable and demonstrated that solidarity based on kinship ties continued to hold significance, sometimes even superseding other forms of solidarity, including class-based unity.[29] His electoral rival in the campaign was Abdolhossein Raj, the Director of the AIOC Health Department, who enjoyed the support of the Oil Company.

Bakhtiar's influence in Khuzestan began to wane as his supporters launched their campaign for the sixteenth parliament. What initially started as a low-key election effort gradually evolved into organised rallies, with some even seeking refuge in the Telegraph Houses. At one juncture, Bakhtiar's supporters issued threats to instigate strikes across Khuzestan, particularly within the oil industry, if Bakhtiar's candidacy for the parliamentary election was not approved.[30]

Reports from Tehran indicated that, in certain instances, the rallies of Bakhtiar's supporters culminated in violent clashes with covert CCFTU activists. It's worth noting that the majority of Bakhtiar's backers were affiliated with the Bakhtiari tribes, which fostered a newfound sense of identity and solidarity among them. Following the tumultuous strike of July 1946, this marked the first instance of ethnic and tribal divisions within the Khuzestan oil industry's workforce, reminiscent of the ethnic tensions that had previously pitted the majority of Arab contract laborers against the majority of non-Arab workers in the aftermath of the bloody July 1946 incident. These events underscored the existence of different forms of solidarity among the workers, transcending mere class-based affiliations.

In light of the escalating tensions and concerns arising from these developments, the Khuzestan local authorities urged the government in Tehran to intervene and take measures to restrict Bakhtiar's election campaign in the region.[31] Tehran responded affirmatively to this request, prompting Bakhtiar to be summoned and instructed to leave Khuzestan immediately. According to Bakhtiar, on the day of his departure from Khuzestan, which occurred on 9 October 1949, approximately '6000 workers came to the Abadan Airport to offer him [Bakhtiar] their wholehearted support'.[32]

Bakhtiar's departure from Abadan in 1949 effectively left the Tudeh union as the solitary oil workers' union, albeit it remained clandestine and illegal. The intensifying crackdown on the Tudeh Party and its associated union compelled both entities to shift their operations underground. Meetings, typically comprising 20–30 members, were clandestinely convened, often under the shroud of darkness, within private residences. These gatherings occurred both in residential areas outside the purview of the Oil Company, such as Farahabad or Ahmadabad, as well as within the labour quarters of Bahmanshir.

While Abolfazl Farrahi had indeed accomplished noteworthy strides in the revitalisation of the Tudeh and CCFTU networks during his leadership tenure within the Tudeh Party in Khuzestan, the Central Committee of the Party in Tehran recognised the imperative to broaden the scope of Tudeh and CCFTU activities within the oil industry. This decision was spurred by the growing momentum behind the call for oil nationalisation that was gaining prominence across Iran.

In 1950, Rahmat Jazani and Manuchehr Behzadi,[33] prominent members of the Tudeh Party, were sent to Khuzestan. Jazani assumed the role of the executive of the Tudeh Party Provincial Khuzestan Committee, while Behzadi took charge of the Abadan local branch of the CCFTU. They held these positions until 1953 when Akbar Shahabi and Houshang Garman succeeded Rahmat Jazani and Manuchehr Behzadi, respectively.[34]

Their presence in Khuzestan coincided with the nationalisation of the oil industry. Thanks to Jazani's efficient management, the Tudeh Party managed to expand its network in Khuzestan and beyond, extending its reach to cities such as Ahvaz, Aghajari, Bandar, and Haftgel in the late 1940s. During an interview with the author, Jazani revealed that following the July 1946 strike, the activities of the Tudeh Party and CCFTU in Khuzestan had declined. Moreover, after the government illegalised the Tudeh Party and CCFTU activities nationwide in February 1949, the number of CCFTU members in the oil industry saw a significant drop.

A confidential report drafted by an undercover agent of the British Council in Khorramshahr noted that in the remaining CCFTU cells, each recruited worker was instructed to enlist five trustworthy followers, who were then tasked with enrolling five members each, operating under the 'cell' principle.[35] However, according to Rahmat Jazani, expanding the underground CCFTU cells proved exceedingly challenging. This was not only due to the stringent measures imposed by the ongoing Martial Law in the province but also because of the growing popularity of Mohammad Mosaddeq and the Iranian National Front, which advocated for the nationalisation of the Iranian oil industry.

Rahmat Jazani recalled that the Tudeh Party and CCFTU had called for the 'nationalisation of the Iranian southern oil industry' rather than the 'nationalisation of oil throughout Iran'. This stance aligned with their support for the Soviet Union's approach to the Iranian government. The acceptance of an oil concession in the northern provinces had prompted many CCFTU activists to exit the union. Jazani elaborated, 'We couldn't even distribute Tudeh Party and CCFTU publications originating from Tehran among our members. "We had to destroy all periodicals advocating for the nationalisation of the Iranian southern oil industry" to prevent dissent among our members and sympathizers'.[36]

In contrast to the political activity surrounding oil nationalisation in Tehran and other major cities across Iran, the politics of oil nationalisation had a relatively subdued impact on the streets of the major cities in Khuzestan. There were no reported demonstrations or picketing in Abadan, other oil cities, or districts in the south during the three years period from 1947 to 1950. Khuzestan experienced a relatively tranquil phase during this time.

It wasn't until early 1951, following the Iranian Parliament's ratification of the oil nationalisation bill, that the labour movement in the oil industry was reignited in Khuzestan after nearly four years of relative quietude.

Abadan's Social Fabric: An Insight into Daily Living

What a hellish heat! This is how the Abadan of early Spring 1951 was described by the *Ettelaʿat-e Haftegi*'s visiting correspondent:

> In this hellish heat, there exist laborers who toil within the refinery's furnaces, facing the immense and searing machinery. The fumes emitted from the oil fill their nostrils, and Abadan's scorching sun beats down upon their iron helmets. Among the many challenges faced by Abadan

> residents is the noxious odour emanating from the refinery, permeating the entire city. Its stench is more pervasive and offensive than any noxious fumes. In Abadan, life is dictated by the weather. This blistering and draining climate not only affects working hours but also subjects workers to it during strikes, protests, and rallies.[37]

The doubling of oil production between 1941 and 1946, which subsequently tripled by 1950, significantly contributed to the expansion of the labour force within the oil industry. This surge elevated the workforce from approximately 29,000–65,500 and 77,200, as detailed in Chapter 4. However, despite this substantial increase in oil production, there was no observable enhancement in the quality of life for the workers and the labouring poor in the oil industry.

During the war, a widespread narrative prevailed among Iranians, emphasising the pivotal role of Khuzestan's oil in facilitating the military advancement of the Allied powers and underscoring Iran's geostrategic significance as the Allies' 'Bridge of Victory'.[38] Moreover, the news reports originating from the southern region of the country frequently highlighted the intricate military infrastructure supervised by United States and British personnel, which continually required a labour force and offered wages exceeding those found elsewhere in the nation. This portrayal of the circumstances in the south prompted a significant influx of unemployed laborers from various regions of Iran to migrate southward in pursuit of employment opportunities

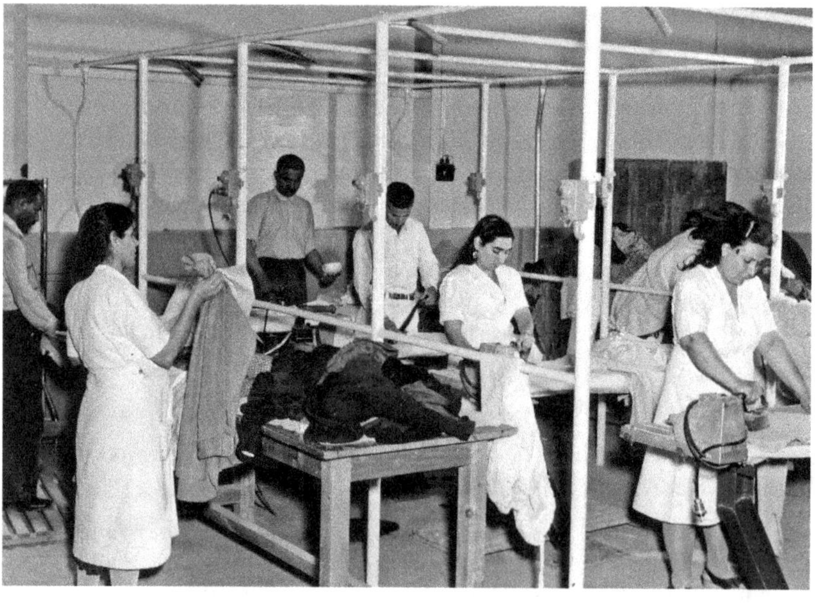

Figure 5.1 Laundry facility, Abadan Refinery, 1947

In tandem with these optimistic portrayals of the south, there was a conspicuous absence of narratives shedding light on the everyday lives of laborers in Khuzestan. The first published first-hand account during this period emerged through Vala, the editor of *Tehran-Mosavvar*, a conservative weekly periodical based in Tehran. In his Travel Notes, Vala candidly admitted that prior to his visit to Abadan, he had held the expectation that the 'AIOC, with its annual income of three million pounds, would offer the most comfortable living and working conditions for its employees – a condition that might arouse envy among laborers outside the oil industry'. However, his shock was palpable upon landing in Abadan and witnessing the stark reality of the working and living conditions endured by the employees of the oil industry.[39]

Vala categorised AIOC employees into two distinct groups: Iranians and non-Iranians. He noted that the working and living conditions of the Iranian employees, when compared to their British, Indian, Palestinian, and other counterparts hailing from the colonial territories of the British Empire, were remarkably dire. In addition to enduring dreadful working and living conditions within an inhospitable climate, what Vala found even more unacceptable was the prevailing dominance of non-Iranian employees over their Iranian counterparts.[40]

During his visit to Abadan, Vala encountered three distinct classes of Iranian employees within the AIOC:

1. Unskilled laborers, commonly referred to as 'coolies', who lacked formal work contracts.
2. Skilled workers who possessed employment contracts.
3. High-level Iranian employees, primarily individuals holding university degrees, occupying more elevated positions within the company.

The destitute labouring coolies endured daily wages ranging from 4 to 30 rials for a gruelling sixteen-hour workday. As casual laborers without formal contracts, these coolies lacked shelter and were often forced to sleep outdoors along the streets. Their diet primarily consisted of dates and bread. The appalling conditions faced by the coolies deeply moved a compassionate observer who generously donated his own clothing to help cover their exposed skin.

Furthermore, lacking access to health insurance, there were distressing instances where coolies failed to emerge from the oil installations after a day of work. Tragically, their fellow workers would later report that these individuals had passed away while on duty.[41]

The second group in Vala's narrative comprised Iranian laborers employed within the Abadan oil installations, and unlike the coolies, they did possess formal work contracts. Their work schedule consisted of alternating twelve-hour day and night shifts every week, which mandated them to work a continuous twenty-four-hour shift four times each month. While some of these workers resided in the densely populated urban areas of the city, it was common for many of them to live on the city's outskirts, often under bamboo shelters.

The third group identified by Vala was composed of high-level Iranian employees, totalling approximately 2,000 individuals according to his estimation. These Iranian high-level employees worked three eight-hour shifts in a twenty-four-hour period, with shifts alternating each week. This schedule contrasted significantly with the six-hour working day observed by their non-Iranian high-level counterparts.[42]

Vala's travel account brought into sharp focus the unmistakable disparity in the treatment of Iranian and non-Iranian employees, underscoring the discrimination faced by Iranian employees at all levels. He described the treatment of Iranian workers, especially the unskilled laborers, by Indian foremen as 'cruel' and 'beyond imagination'. This treatment stood in stark contrast to the agreements between the Iranian government and the Oil Company.[43]

Vala further elaborated that discrimination was not limited solely to unskilled Iranian laborers. Even Iranian high-level staff holding university degrees were subject to systematic segregation, as they were denied opportunities to hold high-level technical positions, which were exclusively reserved for British nationals.[44]

This discriminatory hierarchy was notably pronounced in the Abadan neigbourhood, where the city exhibited a stark division between neighbourhoods inhabited by AIOC official employees and the 'other' neighbourhoods. Furthermore, within each neighbourhood, stringent hierarchical directives were clearly in place, underscoring the pervasive nature of the discrimination.

The island of Abadan, often described by visitors as resembling a shoelace, is bordered to the north by the Karun River, to the east by the Bahmanshir River, to the south by the Persian Gulf, and to the west by the Arvandrud. At its centre lies the city of Abadan, encompassing a total area of seventy-six square kilometres in 1950. This city was primarily dominated by the oil refinery and various other institutions affiliated with the Oil Company.[45]

The city of Abadan was distinctly divided into two separate neighbourhoods (*Mahalleh*): the 'company' neighbourhoods referred to as '*sherkati*' in Persian, and the 'non-company' neighbourhoods known as '*shahr*' (city). The company districts were established concurrently with the founding and expansion of the Abadan Refinery during the 1910s and 1920s. These new districts were developed based on a novel model of social engineering, similar to the approach employed in Oil Company towns worldwide.[46]

In this new model, urban planning was meticulously organised with a focus on segregation and hierarchy, mirroring the practices of British overseas industries. The design of the new neighbourhood and its housing took into account two key criteria: ethnicity and employment ranks within the Company's organisational structure.

According to an account provided by an Iranian visitor, the company neighbourhoods were described as 'perhaps without exaggeration one of the most beautiful cities in Iran in terms of houses and facilities, where nearly

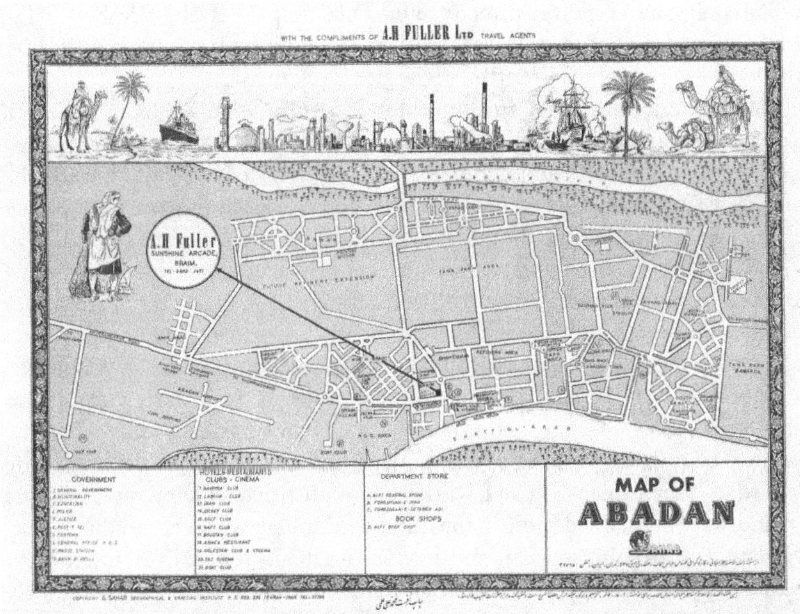

Map 5.1 Abadan and its districts in 1950–60

twelve thousand houses have been built. One-story residences were equipped with a variety of amenities, surrounded by trees, grass, and flowers, with no dust to be seen on any of the streets within the area'.[47]

In Abadan, situated at the northern edge of the city, on the route to the airport and Khorramshahr, lay the most prosperous neighbourhood affiliated with the Oil Company. Known as Braim, this area featured spacious villas and bungalows surrounded by elegant gardens and adorned with English hedges. From the early days of the Oil Company's presence in Abadan, Braim had been exclusively reserved for high-ranking European staff. By the late 1930s, Braim began to admit a few Iranian high-ranking employees. Like other neighbourhoods controlled by the Oil Company, Braim adhered to a strict hierarchical structure. One section was designated for senior oil executives and employees, while the other accommodated engineers and married staff members. Engineers and unmarried employees resided in the R.A. Camp and Sunshine. Sunshine consisted of a series of adjacent rooms intended for single British staff members. For the families of Braim residents, a social facility was available, featuring a spacious restaurant, library, lounge, billiards room, a large indoor area utilised for roulette on casino nights, and an open-air cinema.[48]

Security and protection for the Braim neighbourhood fell under the jurisdiction of the Oil Company's police force, which operated independently from the

Iranian police and reported directly to the Oil Company itself. Members of the Oil Company's police force were identifiable by their cream-colored uniforms, which closely resembled the attire of the British Army.[49]

The southern boundary of Braim extended to the Abadan Refinery, which occupied an area of approximately thirteen square kilometres. Positioned between the Arvandrud and Bahmanshir River, as noted by Kaveh Ehsani, the refinery assumed the role of a colossal metallic barrier in the heart of Abadan Island, effectively dividing the city into its northern and southern sectors.[50]

To the south of the refinery, the quarters primarily housed lower-ranking administrative officers and workers. Immediately adjacent to the refinery was the Sikh-Lane neighbourhood, which extended westward to the Arvandrud and eastward to the Oil Company Hospital. As discussed in Chapter 4, this neighbourhood derived its name from its original residents. In its early years, it was referred to as Coolie-Lane, and it later became known as Sikh-Lane when the majority of Indians working at the refinery were Sikhs. Eventually, the name evolved to Indian-Lane. The Sikh workers had constructed their temple near the Arvandrud.[51] With the decline in the number of Indian workers and their eventual departure, Iranian workers and foremen gradually settled in Sikh-Lane.

East of Sikh-Lane lay the Kofaysheh neighbourhood, which was originally associated with a 'coffee shop', leading to its subsequent name change to Kofaysheh. To the north of Kofaysheh was the Company workers' neighbourhood of Bahar, an expansive neighbourhood subdivided into twelve sections, each associated with a specific bus station. Adjacent to Bahar were the labour districts of Farahabad and Bahmanshir, characterised by terraced houses featuring high walls and small courtyards, built in close proximity to one another.

In 1950, these three districts were home to approximately one-sixth of the Company's 30,000 workers in Abadan.[52] According to an ILO report, this equated to 5,298 individuals or roughly 16.6 per cent of the total 31,875 Company wage earners.[53]

The old town of Abadan was situated to the south of Sikh-Lane, and it housed government offices and a bazaar. This area was adjacent to the residential zones occupied by non-Company employees, characterised by the dirtiest and oldest streets and alleys:

> In these older neighbourhoods, the streets resembled barracks, with sludge and garbage accumulating over time, akin to ancient swamps, emitting a nauseating odour that affected passers-by. Despite the Oil Company's purification of 80,000 gallons of water daily, the residents' homes lacked plumbing. There were communal taps at intersections that people relied on, as well as water stored in old tin barrels. Garbage was a common sight along the streets, and anyone entering an alley would be swarmed by millions of flies. Trachoma and baldness were prevalent among the residents, and the city lacked adequate health and hygiene measures. Although two municipal clinics had recently been established, they were insufficient to serve the needs of the city's 200,000 ordinary residents.[54]

Bovardeh, a newly developed neighbourhood located to the east of the old city, was designed in the 1940s with the aim of bridging ethnic divides in Abadan by housing both Iranians and non-Iranians. Initially, the primary residents of Bovardeh consisted mainly of Britons, along with some British-educated Indians and Iranian middle-grade employees.

To the northeast of the old city was the non-Company neighbourhood of Ahmadabad, an older neighbourhood of Abadan situated outside of the land owned by the Oil Company. Ahmadabad was home to approximately 60 per cent of the Company's employees. The Arab community in Abadan primarily resided in the city centre of the old city or in Ahmadabad.[55] In the 1940s, the Arab population in Abadan numbered 43,000 individuals, divided among nine different tribes. The primary sources of income for the Arab community included date cultivation and sales, as well as fishing.

At the outskirts of Ahmadabad resided the migrant unskilled laborers, often not native to the region, who were employed by the Oil Company. They were commonly referred to as 'contract labour'. Their living conditions were characterised by a collection of cardboard huts, giving rise to the neighbourhood's name, Kaghazabad or Kaparabad. Additionally, non-contract laborers also resided in the southern area known as Tanurabad, named after the ovens (*tanur*) that had existed in the past. These ovens were originally built in the ground for baking purposes but had since been repurposed as makeshift homes for workers. Families would cover the pits with mats to create living spaces for themselves.[56]

The Bovardeh neighbourhood occupied the southernmost area of Abadan. It was divided into Bovardeh North and South, both of which served as residential quarters for lower-grade staff of the Oil Company. In addition to Iranians, a contingent of low-ranking British or Indian employees also resided in these neighbourhoods. North Bovardeh was home to the Technical School, which later evolved into the Faculty of Petroleum, while the renowned Taj Cinema was situated in South Bovardeh.

The Oil Company took responsibility for the maintenance and upkeep of houses in the Company districts. Hassan Kamshad, who worked in the General Housing Office of the AIOC, recalls that, in general, due to the segregated hierarchical structure, the neighbourhoods inhabited by higher-grade employees and workers tended to have the most well-equipped housing. For instance, villas and bungalows in Barim were equipped with amenities such as air conditioning and water coolers. In Bovardeh, where lower-grade staff resided, houses were fitted with ceiling fans. However, despite the extreme summer heat in Abadan, workers' houses were not equipped with any cooling devices.[57]

Each of the residential quarters belonging to the Oil Company was equipped with its own set of facilities, ranging from medical and welfare centres to supermarkets, recreation areas, and sports facilities. Among the twelve clinics operated by the Oil Company in 1950, four were located within the refinery compound, and the remaining eight were situated in the residential districts.[58]

In addition to the local clinics, an International Labour Organisation (ILO) report, following their delegation's visit to the Iranian oil industry in Khuzestan in 1950, mentioned that Abadan had the Company's main hospital with 450 beds, of which 313 beds were designated for Company workers.[59] However, the Iranian government disputed this figure in their response to the ILO account. According to the government's response, out of the 407 beds in the Company's hospital in Abadan, the workers were allocated 256 beds.[60] Masjed-Soleyman and Aghajari were the other oil towns that had Company hospitals, while in the other oilfields, the Company maintained small detention wards.

It's worth noting that none of these figures account for temporary workers, commonly referred to as contract workers. Contract workers were not entitled to any of the welfare or health facilities provided by the Company for its graded employees. After working hours, they and their families were denied access to Company hospitals or clinics. According to the ILO report:

> A worker employed by a contractor has no claim to be admitted to the only hospital in Abadan (which is a Company hospital) and even if he is received there, he does not have the privilege which is granted to Company workers in case of non-industrial accident or sickness, of being treated free. The contract labourer, moreover, is not entitled to make purchases in the Company shops, which means that for him the statutory minimum wage has hardly more than half the purchasing power of that of a Company worker.[61]

Figure 5.2 Bovardeh superstore, 1948

One of the most popular and highly valued recreational amenities in Abadan was the swimming pools. However, the quality and features of these services varied from Braim to Bovardeh and to Bahmanshir. Each neighbourhood's facilities were exclusively reserved for its own residents, and residents from other neighbourhoods were not granted access. To use the sports amenities, swimming pools, and even the stores in a particular neighbourhood, a special card was necessary, and these cards were issued only to the residents of that specific neighbourhood.

Siamak Lotfollahi recalls a childhood incident when his father, a member of the Bovardeh Tennis Team, was invited to play a match with the Braim Tennis Team and took him along. At the gate of the Braim neighbourhood, the Oil Company police initially denied him entry because he didn't have a pass himself. It was only after his father made a scene and threatened not to participate in the match that the gate officer allowed Siamak to enter the neighbourhood with his father.

In another recollection, Siamak Lotfollahi mentions the Gymkana Club in the Braim neighbourhood, a private club exclusively for bosses and high-ranking Oil Company employees. At the Gymkana Club, he saw dogs chained to the club entrance gate. There were two signs in English at the entrance: one saying, 'No Dogs Allowed' and the other saying 'No Iranian Entry'. Except for a few high-ranking Iranian employees, the only Iranians allowed to enter the Gymkana Club were waiters and waitresses (mostly Bakhtiari and Iranian Arabs) who had received training and could speak enough English. These wait-staff members wore white shirts and bow ties.[62]

The Gymkana Club, the oldest 'gentlemen's' leisure club in Abadan, was established during the interwar period in Braim, exclusively for the Oil Company's European high-ranking staff. Its name was derived from a British colonial term for sports clubs in the Indian Raj. In the 1940s, only a few high-ranking Iranian executives were allowed entrance to the Gymkana Club.[63]

For Iranian staff, the Oil Company provided three clubs in Abadan: Golestan Club in Braim for high-ranking staff, the Bovardeh Club in Bovardeh for medium-ranking Iranian staff, and the Iran Club for low-ranking Iranian staff in Sikh-Lane. The Indian's Club was exclusively for Indian employees, while in Bahmanshir, the workers had their own Bahmanshir Club. Abadan also had a Sailor's Club in South Bovardeh, catering to foreign sailors who would spend their free time there when their ships were anchored at the docks of Abadan. This club offered various leisure and entertainment facilities, including indoor and open-air cinemas that screened films in their original languages for sailors.[64]

The AIOC employees had their own cinemas, which were segregated between Iranian and non-Iranian staff and workers. The Bahmanshir Cinema was for the workers, while the Taj Cinema in south Bovardeh, considered the best cinema in Abadan, was for the Iranian staff. The European and Iranian high-ranking staff had their own cinemas in Braim. To enter these cinemas, individuals had to show their passes, and they were only allowed into cinemas corresponding to the category assigned on their pass.

Najaf Daryabandari, who was an AIOC employee at the time, mentions in his memoirs a small hall in Braim where all movies were screened before being shown in AIOC cinemas. These screenings were supervised by a team of AIOC public relations officials. Daryabandari's duty was to write film reviews for Oil Company periodicals in case of public screenings.[65]

The daily transport of the Oil Company's workers and staff was also segregated and varied in quality. The staff transport mainly consisted of British-made Bedford buses, which, according to Mostafa Fateh, were initially free and primarily for British and a few high-ranking Iranian staff before 1946.[66] However, after the 1946 strike, the Oil Company began allowing non-high-ranking Iranian staff and their families to use these buses by purchasing tickets.

The workers had their own means of transportation, which included open-topped trailers towed by cars. These trailers were also used for school transport in the working-class neighbourhoods.[67]

Siamak Lotfollahi, who grew up in a working class family in Abadan and later became a low-grade staff member, recalls his childhood in Abadan and acknowledges that despite the hierarchical order based on class and ethnic segregation, the living conditions and facilities provided to Oil Company workers and employees were far superior to those of non-oil workers and employees.

For example, in the 1940s, the monthly salaries of contract workers employed by the Oil Company were approximately two to three times higher than the salaries of non-Company workers and employees. In addition to the disparity in salaries, the Oil Company's employees enjoyed various benefits, including company-provided housing with access to water and electricity, free medical care, and other amenities.

Each neighbourhood of the Oil Company, varying in size and population, had a medical clinic known as a 'dispensary'. These clinics offered outpatient treatment, vaccinations, wound dressings, and injections. In addition to these clinics, the Oil Company maintained a well-equipped hospital located between Sikh-Lane and Bahmanshir, serving all Oil Company employees and their families. Initially, the hospital was staffed with British general practitioners and surgeons, but later, Indian, and Iranian doctors also joined the medical team.

Aside from providing free medical services, the Oil Company's healthcare system regularly offered preventive care measures to combat the spread of infectious diseases. For example, school students received annual vaccinations against smallpox and were screened for trachoma, with treatment provided as needed. Thanks to these attentive care practices and free medical services, infectious diseases, particularly trachoma, alopecia, malaria, and smallpox, became less prevalent in the Oil Company neighbourhoods.[68]

In addition to these welfare services, it is crucial to highlight the significant environmental pollution resulting from advanced industry and the lack of adequate supervision over these industrial activities. Nasim Khaksar, a writer from Abadan who belonged to the Oil Company's working class, recollects his childhood experiences in the 1940s when the city's oil and non-oil neighbourhoods were separated by channels, locally known as 'haffar'. These channels served as conduits for the refinery's industrial and non-industrial wastewater, as well as waste disposal from the neighbourhoods. Unfortunately, the haffars emitted a foul odour and were a source of numerous diseases in the city.[69]

However, the negative aspects of Abadan extended beyond the foul odour of the haffars. Abadan was also characterised by high levels of crime and corruption, akin to many port cities around the world. According to a survey conducted by a columnist in the late 1940s, there were approximately 'about 250 opium smoking houses in Abadan, all operating with the knowledge of the local police, plus several hundred brothels… [making] prostitution very popular, and the best source of income for local officials'.[70] This environment led to stories about British or Indian employees of the AIOC visiting these brothels and being involved in scandalous activities. One such incident, known as the 'Bahmanshir Riot' of 1942, has been extensively studied by Elling and refers to an episode in which 'locals' attacked three Indians with stones after they had visited a 'certain prostitute' in Ahmadabad and apparently left 'without paying for the service rendered'.[71]

Nasim Khaksar, in one of his novels, *Qafas-e Tuti-ye Jahan Khanom* (Mrs. Jahan's Parrot's Cage), vividly describes incidents where British or Indian employees of the Oil Company, in their quest for brothels, accidentally entered local homes in the old city:

> The hot news of every-night fights of the youth around the Shatt bank with the Britons who had mistakenly entered the surrounding houses whilst searching for a brothel occupied everyone's minds. Asadullah Khan, as well as visiting the workers and conducting his usual work, tried hard to organise gangs to prevent the assault of the Britons. The colonel, on the other hand, with his MPs and dogs was trying to disperse the youth of the Shatt bank in order to protect the Britons, who, intoxicated, were mistakenly knocking on the door of people's house in the middle of the night.[72]

The trade of the young prostitutes was common in the city.[73] A correspondent of *Asiya-ye Javan* testified about his visit to one of the traders, a wealthy woman of thirty from Isfahan, who was living in Bahmanshir neighbourhood:

> Despite the fact that the sale and purchase of slaves has been banned for many years and explicit laws have been enacted for this purpose, this practice is still common in Abadan and the sale and purchase of women in Abadan is a common practice which everyone is aware of.

> I went to see an Isfahani woman in Bahmanshir neighbourhood. This lady is buying and selling young girls in Abadan. Every year, she brings twenty to thirty beautiful, young girls between the ages of 12 and 18 from Isfahan or from the Bakhtiari regions to Abadan. These girls are generally homeless. The price of each girl, depending on their beauty, is from 500 to 1000 Tomans. I myself witnessed a fake deal with my own eyes. My young guide, who introduced himself as a buyer, when he saw the identity card of the girl he had chosen and realised she was fourteen years old, said that as she was underage it was not possible to be formally married in Abadan. The lady told him not to worry since Sheikh Soleyman and Sheikh Abdullah could both arrange a formal marriage.[74]

Abadan's strategic location near international land and sea routes turned it into a haven for drug dealers and smugglers. Smuggling activities involving goods from the southern ports of the Persian Gulf and Iraq were rampant in Abadan. In one-year alone, approximately 12,000 boxes of smuggled tea were distributed throughout Iran via Abadan. Nasim Khaksar, in his novel, vividly portrays the complicity of some shopkeepers with the smugglers. During a street chase, as a smuggler attempted to evade the pursuing police, the city's streets would reverberate with police sirens. In response, 'shopkeepers would throw wooden boxes of rotten fruit, which they had prepared in advance, in front of the police cars'. This act was a form of solidarity with the smugglers, attempting to obstruct the police's pursuit.[75]

Human trafficking was another prevalent issue in Abadan. Iranian pilgrims, looking to reach the holy shrines in Iraq, often resorted to illegal border crossings facilitated by human traffickers. These pilgrims would pay approximately 500 rials to the traffickers for their services.[76]

Additionally, Iraqi Jews seeking to escape from Iraq to Iran faced exorbitant costs, typically ranging from 20,000 to 50,000 rials per person. After converting their assets into cash, these individuals would make their way to Khorramshahr or Abadan, from where they continued their journey to Tehran. During this journey, they would bribe both Iraqi and Iranian border guards to facilitate their passage.[77]

The proximity of Abadan to the Iraqi border facilitated border trafficking, making it relatively easy for various individuals, including small-scale traders, unemployed laborers, and even thieves from both Iraq and Iran, to cross the border without detection by border guards. There were stories circulating about local Iranian thieves having contracts with Iraqi thieves. Under these agreements, stolen property would be transported to Iraqi territory and then sent on to Basra and Kuwait. This illicit trade across the border added to the complex dynamics of the city.[78]

Indeed, Abadan was a city of two worlds, with the Oil Company's presence and its meticulously regulated spaces on one side, and the unruly and independent community on the other. The residents of this second Abadan, although connected in various ways to the Oil Company, had their own distinct world that came to life after the working day concluded and carried on until the next morning. Within this alternate world, various networks – whether based on religion, ethnicity, or even criminal activities – intermingled, forming an informal space that was shaped and influenced by both coercive and non-coercive government institutions.

On the contrary, the Oil Company maintained strict control over its own spaces, governing them directly and leaving little room for the indigenous public to assert itself. As Kaveh Ehsani eloquently points out, the public spaces within the AIOC Abadan could not be considered 'genuinely public' since 'they were owned and tightly controlled by the Company'.[79]

The coexistence of these two contrasting spaces in Abadan, one belonging to the Oil Company and the other representing the local, was a complex dynamic. The Oil Company had, to a certain extent, allowed the autonomy of the local community to avoid causing problems for the company. This arrangement was beneficial for the Oil Company as it absolved them of some responsibilities and accountability for life on the island.

However, this peaceful coexistence was not without its challenges. The population of Abadan was growing, and both the workplace and the urban environment were becoming increasingly politicised. These developments raised concerns for the Oil Company and forced them to address the growing problems. The previous decades of operation in Abadan could not continue indefinitely without change.

The changing circumstances and the need for a new approach in Abadan likely led to shifts in the relationship between the Oil Company and the local community, as well as changes in the way the company operated and interacted with the city and its residents.

The extensive prevalence of discrimination and poverty eventually culminated in a meticulously prepared report authored by Donald McNeil, who served as the AIOC Manager for Industrial Relations based in London. Encapsulated in his confidentially circulated essay titled 'The Lesson of 1946', McNeil directly confronted the persistent issue of housing in Abadan through the following discourse:

> The vast majority of our labour force are still living in scandalous accommodation in urine-tainted squalor – in little *manzels* (houses), built against the hillside as in Janaki village and a dozen other places in fields, or houses of empty paper cement bag construction as in *Kaghazabad* in Abadan, without sanitation or no ventilation at all.
>
> Overcrowding is rampant and up to ten persons sleep on the damp floor of ten-foot room, huddled together to keep warm in the winter or to keep out of the sun in the summer afternoon. These are the conditions under which many of our workers live in what is misleadingly called private accommodation, and unfortunately, some of these living in old style non-standard Company accommodation have very similar conditions.[80]

In a report submitted to the Iranian government in 1946, the AIOC acknowledged a glaring oversight: despite the substantial surge in the oil industry's workforce during the war, no measures had been undertaken to provide suitable housing for the workers. This deficiency was particularly pronounced in Abadan, where the population had ballooned to 120,000 in 1946, with a staggering 85 per cent being employees and their families associated with the Company. Shockingly, there were merely 5,600 Company houses in Abadan, encompassing the exclusive bungalows and furnished residences reserved for white-collar employees and clerks situated in the Braim and Bovardeh neighbourhoods. The majority of salaried registered workers and contract laborers still endured the dire conditions of residing in tents and huts. These makeshift homes were located in virtually inhospitable areas like Abolhassani, characterised by marshlands teeming with mosquitoes, or the densely populated and stifling municipal districts of Abadan, where local landlords ruthlessly exploited workers without repercussions.[81] It wasn't until the 1946 strike that the AIOC initiated a new housing initiative to construct habitable dwellings for its married employees in the emerging districts of Bahar and Farhabad. Additionally, accommodations featuring four-bed rooms were established for single workers in Ahmadabad.[82]

Everyday Life Amid Propaganda Wars

The significantly negative and contentious depiction of the AIOC as the primary catalyst behind the violent 1946 strike, along with the gradual proliferation of anti-British and anti-Soviet sentiments within the domain of Iranian popular nationalism, instigated a proactive response from the Oil Company's leadership. This response aimed to initiate a comprehensive strategy dedicated to fostering a more favourable public perception of the company and its associated social policies.[83] Mostafa Fateh's observations underscore the unexpected nature of the 1946 general strike, which caught the Company's management off guard. They had not envisioned that Iranian employees of the Company could rapidly organise themselves with such cohesion in a relatively brief timeframe.[84] Consequently, this marked the first instance in which the Company recognised that the scope of discontent extended beyond its own workforce. Rather, it encompassed the broader Iranian public, and to some extent, it had implications for the international perception of the Company. As a result, there emerged an immediate necessity for the Company to undergo a transformation in both its actions and its public image. While Khalil Kazeruni retained responsibility for overseeing the Company's Public Relations Office, which managed the Company's internal and external communications, a separate department was conceived to exert influence over public opinion concerning the Company among its employees, Iranians, and the global community.

In the summer of 1946, concurrently with the appointment of an industrial relations specialist to operate in Abadan, the AIOC established an innovative Information Department, which was referred to as *Edareh-ye Ettelaʿat* in Persian. This department comprised two branches, one situated in Abadan and the other in Tehran. Its primary objective was to overhaul the public perception of the AIOC and to instil a renewed sense of confidence in the company's management of the oil industry over the preceding four decades. This strategic initiative was a direct response to the pervasive grievances articulated by the Iranian public against the AIOC. Subsequently, the department underwent a name change, transitioning to the Publishing Department, primarily due to the unfavourable associations linked to the Persian translation of 'information' among a significant portion of Iranians.

The directorship of the Tehran office of the Information Department was entrusted to Laurence Lockhart, a long-serving employee of the AIOC who had dedicated many years to the Oil Company. His primary task was to compose the company's history for internal circulation, intended as a management guide. Lockhart's compiled volumes detailing the AIOC's operations in Iran subsequently served as the foundational and principal source material for the two volumes of the British official history of Petroleum, published in 1982.[85]

Heading the Abadan office was Geoffrey Keating, a renowned official photographer during the Second World War, associated with both the British Ministry of Information and the British Army Department of Film and Photography.[86]

In one of the advertisements sponsored by the Oil Company's Information Department, which appeared in one of the Iranian national newspapers, we find the following statement:

> The AIOC hereby announces that the wages of regular Company workers will increase from 35 Rials to 40 Rials and will be paid for 6 working days. Similarly, the wages of other Company workers will be adjusted proportionately to these increments and the new minimum wage, which stands at 40 Rials per day as per the minimum wage law. This minimum wage is determined by the Ministry of Labour in accordance with the cost of living. The Company has devised a comprehensive plan encompassing housing, club facilities, cinema, and healthcare services for its workers. Moreover, there are plans to construct residences equipped with 2-3-4 bathrooms and gardens. Each month, 250 houses will be made available for worker accommodation, leading to the construction of 12,000 houses for workers over the course of four years. In addition to housing, the Company also intends to establish libraries, cinemas, swimming pools, and recreational centres for its workers. Several cooperatives will be established to benefit the workers, and each workshop will feature a spacious restaurant offering food services to employees.[87]

In April 1947, nearly a year after the strike, the Information Department organised a week-long visit to Abadan, Masjed-Soleyman, and Aghajari for a group of fifteen journalists representing various national and provincial newspapers. The purpose of the visit was to provide these journalists with an opportunity to inspect the oil facilities and gain insights into the living and working conditions of laborers in the area. The visiting journalists represented a diverse spectrum of Iranian political affiliations, ranging from chief editors of Tudeh Party publications like *Mardom* and *Rahbar* to conservative newspapers like *Dad* and *Emruz va Farda*, as well as liberal outlets such as *Ettelaʿat*, *Mard-e Emruz*, *Seda-ye Iran*, *Iran-e Now*, and *Tehran Mosavvar*.

Upon their return, the journalists published eyewitness accounts of their visit in their respective periodicals. These accounts provided a range of perspectives, including descriptions of the advanced technology of the oil installations and the generous hospitality extended to the visitors. However, some journalists also offered detailed descriptions of the living conditions endured by the unskilled laborers, particularly those working in the oil industry.

For journalists from newspapers like the liberal *Ettelaʿat* or the communist *Mardom*, what proved particularly puzzling were the stark disparities not only between technological advancement and laborers' living and working conditions but also the striking contrast between the living and working conditions of high-ranking employees and low-level workers. Khalil Maleki from the Tudeh Party's *Mardom* articulated this stark juxtaposition:

> During the trip to Abadan, I witnessed beautiful scenes juxtaposed with terrifying ones. In Khuzestan, heaven and hell exist in parallel; Heaven for some, Hell for the majority. Nowhere in the world can there be such ugliness and beauty in such close proximity; on the one hand, the sprawling modern industry of the Twentieth Century with European-style mansions and guesthouses and the beauties of the Orient, on the other hand, the primitive life of the Middle Ages with all its misery in major industrial centres.[88]

Mohammad Mortazavi, the publisher of the weekly satirical publication *Piruzi*, which was a nationalist periodical associated with the Liberty Party, echoed Khalil Maleki's observations: 'Two extremely contrasting aspects of life lying side by side! Pomp and beauty in the widest sense of the words prevailing on one side and misery and destitution ruling on the other side, at close range.'[89] Not only nationalist and communist journalists, but also Abulqasem Payandeh, the publisher of the conservative weekly Saba, expressed his outrage at the contradictions he witnessed:

> Next to the glorious Abadan with its very advanced industry, there is another Abadan: poor Abadan, devoid of all necessities of life. In the suburbs of the city, in the slum neighbourhood of Kaghazabad, people live in holes covered with palm leaves or paper, which look more like sheepfolds, ragged, dirty, and miserable creatures whose living conditions are of prehistoric cave dwellers.[90]

Hossein Za'imi of the periodical *Kasra* also joined the chorus of critics regarding the labour living conditions and stated: 'The AIOC section of Abadan, with its beautiful and neat buildings and decent living conditions for the inhabitants, cannot be compared with the other section of the town, which is quite unsuitable for human habitation'.[91]

According to a prearranged schedule, the delegation was supposed to visit specific parts of Abadan and Masjed-Soleyman designated by the Oil Company. However, some members of the mission decided not to limit themselves to the official program and explored other parts of Abadan and Masjed-Soleyman. Khali Maleki was one of these members and he documented his observations as follows:

> We managed to visit the workers' neighbourhood of Kaghazabad, located on the outskirts of the Ahmadabad neighbourhood. This visit was not part of the official program we were supposed to follow. Kaghazabad was an area densely packed with paper huts, epitomizing poverty, misery, and sorrow. In one of these huts, measuring approximately one and a half meters in size, I saw about eight people, including women and children, squeezed inside. The residents of this hut informed me that extreme weather conditions penetrate through the ceiling and floor of this shelter, subjecting them to cold in winter and heat in summer. During rainy weather, they are surrounded by water and mud from all directions.
>
> ...
>
> Following this heart-wrenching scene, we proceeded to another part of the city and visited the Company's pigsties. Each pair of pigs had two rooms with two troughs, along with proper hygiene facilities. The meat from these pigs was consumed by high-ranking officials and their esteemed Muslim guests... One of our companions remarked, 'Mr. Maleki, observe that these individuals take better care of their pigs than they do of the Iranian workers.'[92]

The eyewitness accounts provided by Maleki received further validation from Mohammad Mortazavi, the publisher of *Piruzi*:

> Kaghazabad comprises a handful of small huts constructed from mats, wood, paper, and cardboard. The floor is merely covered with a piece of mat. These huts serve as homes for families, each consisting of no less than 5 or 6 members, who struggle through their wretched lives. They lack basic necessities, and various diseases are rampant among them.[93]

As described by Abolqasem Payandeh in the weekly *Saba*, life in Kaghazabad was nothing short of miserable, with alleys resembling mire and sludge, and the air filled with the stench of human waste. The sight of half-naked and distressed children amid heaps of garbage was all too common. Swarms of flies darkened the alleys, making it difficult to discern the few items for sale, such as fish and dates.

The delegation's visit to the oil field of Masjed-Soleyman revealed further distressing scenes. Khalil Maleki and some members of the group decided to deviate from the scheduled program and explore the neighbourhood where the laborers lived. What they encountered left a lasting impact:

> One must personally witness the dire conditions in this neighbourhood to truly comprehend its misery. I couldn't help but think that being incarcerated in Qasr Prison would be far preferable to residing in this wretched working-class community. Workers cautiously approached us and, with a palpable sense of fear, shared some of the appalling living conditions they endured. When I inquired if similar neighbourhoods existed in Masjed-Soleyman, one worker hesitated before asking if any place could still be considered fit for human habitation. He then gestured toward a nearby hill, urging us to explore the living conditions of the workers there, which he claimed were even more deplorable than those of animals.[94]

While in Abadan and Masjed-Soleyman, the AIOC representative provided the delegation with information about workers' insurance and social welfare programs. However, during their visit, the delegation encountered numerous workers who voiced concerns about their health and well-being. These workers shared accounts of injuries that had left them disabled and expressed grievances regarding the Oil Company's alleged negligence in addressing these issues.

Among the various accounts of disability, perhaps the most distressing was the story of a frail elderly man who had lost two fingers, was completely blind in one eye, had issues with the other eye, and could only walk with the assistance of his young son. This elderly man handed a petition to the members of the delegation and implored them to help him pursue his grievance. In his petition, he detailed his seventeen years of employment with the Oil Company, which had ended eight years prior due to a tragic incident. He had been dismissed from his job following a protest that led to his brutal assault by a British engineer. During the assault, he had been beaten with an iron bar, resulting in a severe head injury and the permanent loss of one eye. He was summarily terminated from employment, and his efforts to seek compensation or disability benefits from the Oil Company had been in vain.[95]

Regarding the conditions of work, housing, and wages, Ebrahim Golestan, who was one of the visitors, upon his return, provided a comprehensive report on the conditions of education and living for the students at the Oil Company Technical School as well as the work and lives of the workers in several issues of the publication *Mardom* – the Tudeh Party's journal. In their conversation with Golestan, the students spoke about their educational restrictions, the constant threat of expulsion hanging over them, and the harsh and unsanitary conditions of their dormitories.[96] In his narrative about the workers' daily life and labour, Golestan mentions that workers endure seven to eight hours of work beside machinery in the refinery that reaches temperatures of up to 600 degrees, with wages so low that they are perpetually in debt and compelled to accept the hellish work conditions. According to the British manager of the Aghajari oil fields, there are 731 homeless workers, with 273 living in tents in the desert. The acceptance of such disastrous working and living conditions is what the oil company expects from its workers, and any opposition to improving these conditions results in nothing but dismissal. In conversations with Golestan, the workers named individuals who had been dismissed solely for protesting against the lack of basic safety in the workplace or for receiving wages below the agreed-upon average.[97]

It is noteworthy that at the final dinner organized by the Anglo-Iranian Oil Company at the Iran Club in Abadan, which marked the conclusion of the journalists' visit, Ebrahim Golestan engaged in conversation with Clifford Tucker. Bamber describes Tucker as a person with 'a sympathetic view of trade union rights' who 'as senior industrial relations officer in Abadan, and in the following year, strengthened its industrial relations management by forming a separate department to deal with labour issues.'[98] In the margins of Clifford Tucker's remarks on the less-than-illustrious history of labour relations within the oil company, he admits that 'the efforts of the unions established by Bakhtiar and Youssef Eftekhari have completely failed.'[99]

To counteract the negative propaganda campaign portraying the ill-treatment of the Oil Company's employees, Geoffrey Keating considered it a primary task for the Information Department to reshape the interpretation and imagery associated with the Company, both among its employees, Iranians, and the wider world.[100] One of the initial initiatives undertaken by the Information Department's Abadan office was to invite young Iranians with backgrounds in the Arts and Humanities to create periodicals in both Persian and English languages. They also encouraged the production of documentary films that showcased the AIOC's history and contemporary operations. These films were screened in the oil towns and oilfields for the Company's employees.

Furthermore, the Information Department published news and documentary photography, both for internal Company use and external dissemination. They designed propaganda posters, established local and regional radio stations in Khuzestan, organised public lectures about the AIOC's past and present in Khuzestan and across Iran, and hosted exhibitions in cultural and educational centres within Khuzestan and nationally. The department actively countered any activities aimed at propagating negative images of the Oil Company in Iran and globally.[101] With its headquarters in Braim, the Information Department maintained an extensive network throughout Khuzestan.[102]

Among the periodicals associated with the history of APOC and later AIOC press publications published in English, *Naft* and the *Daily News Bulletin* were prominent. The Information Department enlisted several Iranian individuals to contribute to its efforts, including Hamid Notqi, Ebrahim Golestan, ʿAli Javaher-Kalam, Mahmud Fakhr-Daʿi, Abolqasem Halat, Mohammad-Ali

Movahhed, ʿAli-Asghar Nikzad, and Houshang Pezeshknia. According to Ismaʿil Raʾin, the Information Department employed a total of twenty-four individuals.[103]

Hamid Notqi, later recognised as the father of modern public relations in Iran, assumed the role of the head of the Persian Section within the Information Department. Following the establishment of the Information Department, its Persian Section initiated the publication of a daily news bulletin in Persian, *Khabar-ha-ye Ruz* (Daily News) which was issued daily except for Fridays. Additionally, they introduced an illustrated weekly periodical, *Akhbar-e Hafteh* (Weekly News), with a circulation of 5,000.[104]

While *Khabar-ha-ye Ruz* essentially served as the Persian translation of the English Daily News Bulletin, *Akhbar-e Hafteh* was an illustrated weekly periodical. In addition to covering the history of the oil industry in Iran and beyond, it featured a diverse range of content. This included articles on Persian and world literature, discussions of social life issues such as culinary instructions for preparing both local and international dishes, insights into handicrafts, and various entertaining quizzes and competitions.[105]

Another publication by the Information Department in Persian was the sport bulletin, *Nameh-ye Varzeshi-ye Kargaran-e Sherkat-e Sahami-ye Naft-e Englis va Iran* (Sport Bulletin of Workers of the AIOC). This bulletin not only covered world and national sports news but also provided extensive coverage of the sporting activities of the oil industry workers. Additionally, it reported on workers' promotions and the allocation of newly constructed houses to them. The bulletin featured poetry, serialised stories, and news related to the entertainment and leisure pursuits of the workers and their families.

The AIOC's efforts to establish its own daily and weekly publications in Persian, with the intention of portraying a positive image of its operations in Iran, initially seemed to achieve positive outcomes. According to an observer, it was common for educated Iranian workers and employees in Abadan to regularly read these periodicals:

> Perhaps everyone purchases and reads three or four different newspapers daily, listens to radio news, and stays updated on Iranian and world news. It was on this basis that last year the Oil Company published the daily newspaper and the weekly magazine, which are now the most widely circulated publications in the city, with a copy available in every employee's home.[106]

Nonetheless, the extensive propaganda campaign initiated by the Oil Company to reshape its image after the 1946 strike, with the goal of presenting the Company's historical narrative in a favourable light, raised concerns among certain Iranians. Central to the Oil Company's campaign was its purported continuous commitment to enhancing the lives and living conditions of its employees.

During Iran's post-Second World War period, the issue of oil took centre stage, becoming increasingly politicised and overshadowing its economic aspects. What began as discussions about revising the 1933 Agreement eventually escalated into the total nationalisation of Iran's oil industry. Amid the push for oil nationalisation, the dire and impoverished working and living conditions of oil industry workers, particularly contract workers, were not less important than the financial aspects of the oil industry.

In response to the extensive propaganda campaign launched by the AIOC, which aimed to showcase the favourable working and living conditions of its employees, and recognising that the company had not fulfilled its duties adequately, not only as an employer but also in fulfilling its contractual obligations to the Iranian government in various matters related to its employees,[107] in November 1948, the Iranian government requested the ILO to send a fact-finding mission to investigate the conditions in the Khuzestan oil industry. However, it took two years for this ILO mission to be realised, as the issue of oil became a prominent and pressing concern in Iranian political circles during that time.

The ILO mission took place over a period of twenty days, from 11 to 31 January 1950. During this time, the delegation not only visited the Abadan Refinery but also conducted inspections of the oilfields in Masjed-Soleyman, Aghajari, and Ahvaz. The delegation consisted of three senior ILO officials representing the ILO Industrial Committee and Condition of Work Section.

The report of the ILO mission was published in Geneva in the same year, 1950.[108] This eighty-seven-page report, however, did not receive a warm reception from the Iranian government, and its contents were not what they had anticipated. The Iranian government had expected the mission 'to carry out with the greatest impartiality an investigation on conditions of labour in the Petroleum Industry of Iran and to make a factual as well as faithful report of their findings to the International Labour Organisation'.[109] Nevertheless, the ILO report, according to the Iranian government, was nothing but biased and 'remarkable for its masterly wavering and indecision; each problem hardly touched upon is followed by series of explanations and excuses for its cause'.[110]

Additionally, the Iranian government raised concerns about the credibility of the members of the mission. It pointed out that 'the head of the mission, John Price, was of British nationality, P.P. Fano had Italian origins, and Mohammad-'Ali Jamalzadeh, the only Iranian member of the mission, played a limited role as an interpreter'. The government questioned why the mission members were not selected from among individuals from countries not directly involved, given the ILO's vast pool of staff from various nationalities. They also highlighted meetings between the ILO delegation and high-ranking British officials, including Sir Frederic Lagget, the AIOC's chief industrial adviser, during their mission, raising suspicions about potential bias.[111]

The Iranian government's assessment of the ILO report highlighted several shortcomings, including concerns related to contract workers. These contract laborers comprised 16,400 individuals, which was 25 per cent of the total workforce employed by the Oil Company, numbering 48,300 in 1949. In the ILO report, these contract laborers were described as individuals 'assigned work which generally falls outside its normal activities or does not justify the employment of a regular labour force. Thus, inside the refinery contract labour is employed in navvy work, building, riveting and tank cleaning, painting, and handling sulphur. Outside the refinery and in the oilfields, it is engaged in pipe track and road construction, building and maintenance work'.[112]

However, the Iranian government disagreed with this characterisation, asserting that 'the Company employed contract labour simply to shrink from its obligations under the terms of the concession as well as vis-à-vis the labour law. Practically all jobs enumerated by the mission [in the] report as the type of work assigned to contract labour, are works of permanent nature and there is no excuse whatsoever for the employment of contract labour'.[113]

The ILO report was critical of the contractors who, according to the report, paid their workers less than the legal minimum wage and disregarded statutory regulations related to payment of weekly rest days, overtime rates, and holidays with pay. Furthermore, the report acknowledged that contract workers were excluded from all the schemes operated by the AIOC for the benefit of its regular employees.

For instance, 'a worker employed by a contractor has no claim to be admitted to the only hospital in Abadan (which is a Company hospital) and even if he is received there, he does not have the privilege which is granted to the Company workers in case of non-industrial accident or sickness – of being treated free. The contract labourer, moreover, is not entitled to make purchases in the Company shops, which means that for him the statutory minimum wage has hardly more than half the purchase power that it has for a Company worker'.[114]

The ILO report criticised the Iranian government for not effectively enforcing labour laws for contract workers, effectively leaving them without protection. However, the report did not delve into the reasons behind the Oil Company's refusal to upgrade contract laborers to workers with signed contracts who would be covered by the Company's labour regulations.

Housing was another point of contention between the ILO report and the Iranian government's reaction. According to the ILO report, since the establishment of the AIOC some forty years ago, 'the small village of a few hundred fishermen and date growers' had developed into one of the largest cities in Iran with a population of 173,000 in 1949, consisting of 133,000 Oil Company employees and their dependents, and 40,000 labouring poor primarily employed by contractors, craftsmen, petty traders, and their families.[115]

The ILO mission visited both rich and poor districts of Abadan. According to the ILO report, in the rich part of Abadan, which the report refers to as 'the

Company area', there are modern European housing estates with trees, parks, and open spaces. In contrast, the report describes the poor area where laborers 'live in mud houses or huts made of all sorts of materials, or in the 360 tents which the Company put up in 1949 as an emergency measure to accommodate homeless workers'.[116] However, the report did not mention that these tents were not provided to their residents free of charge but for twelve rials per month.[117]

The issue of scarce labour accommodation continued in the ILO report with the following statement:

> The great majority of the oil workers live in the older overcrowded sections of the municipal districts, where more often than not the entire family or three or four bachelors occupy a single room. Rents are very high, and an attempt made by the government to fix a celling, to rent in relation to statutory minimum wage has utterly failed.[118]

The ILO mission also visited the oilfield areas. In these areas, according to the ILO report, approximately 62.5 per cent of the salaried staff had accommodation, whereas only about 36 per cent of the workers had accommodation. Within this percentage, artisans accounted for 48.22 per cent, skilled workers for 49.19 per cent, and unskilled workers for 10.53 per cent.

The origins of the scarcity of housing and the spatial segregation in the oil towns and fields, according to the ILO mission, were not solely due to the absence of long-term labour welfare policies by the Oil Company during its forty years existence. Instead, it was exacerbated by the increase in oil production during the Second World War, which led to a significant influx of labour migration to the southern oil industry. According to the ILO mission, the housing problem began when 'following the tremendous expansion of the refinery, the number of Company employees doubled, and the population of the town increased in about the same proportion'.[119]

Furthermore, while the report acknowledges the new housing policies of the Oil Company, such as constructing new senior staff family houses with 'four or five bedrooms, two bathrooms, toilets, servant's room, store, and courtyards', as well as junior staff family houses with 'three rooms, one bathroom with toilet, kitchen, and courtyard', and bachelor salaried personnel's 'bed-sitting-room with individual or communal bathroom and toilet facilities', mostly built during or after the war, it raised concerns about the housing provided for the workers:

> The problem of providing houses for the oil workers is a gigantic one, especially in Abadan, because of the large number to be housed, the fact that there have been periods of extremely rapid increase in the population, the almost complete absence of building materials and housing components, and the shortage of qualified building labour. These factors increase the difficulty of providing houses in sufficient numbers and render the cost

> of building extremely high. The provision of homes for such a large population would be a major problem even in a well-organised country where there were no shortages and where all the resources of municipal and private enterprise could be mobilised. It must be recognised therefore that the Company has had a colossal task to face in coping with this situation.[120]

From the Iranian government's perspective, the references in the ILO report appeared to be justifications for the Oil Company's unfair treatment of its workers. In response to the ILO report, the Iranian government pamphlet raised a challenge, questioning why the workers' neighbourhoods were deprived of the water they needed, despite the availability of water in the region. While acknowledging a shortage of construction materials like bricks and cement, it emphasised that there was certainly no scarcity of water.

> In Abadan town, where five sixths of the Company's direct labour as well as all its contract labour lives, and for whose standard of health and hygiene the Company was obligated to have responsibility, in order to fulfil part of that responsibility, the Company had, as early as 1936, undertaken to provide the town with an adequate supply of water and electricity. In these municipal areas to which the mission has referred in their report, congested and over-populated as they are, the Company provided a supply of water based on a grid of water points, each some 300-yard distance from the next.
>
> By way of comparison, it is interesting to quote the following figure: Ahmadabad a labour neighbourhood with a population of 40,000 has two water distribution tanks with total capacity of 120,000 gallons. Braim area, inhabited mainly by British staff, at the same time, with a total population of 8,000 (including servants) has no less than five distribution tanks with a total of 144,000 gallons.[121]

The Iranian government's anti-propaganda campaign against the Oil Company and the ILO, which it believed had not shown impartiality in composing its report, extended to the use of photographs depicting workers' residential areas in Iran's oil industry. In the ILO report, there were photos of buildings under construction that were allegedly intended for artisans and workers. However, the Iranian government pamphlet rejected the accuracy of this claim. It described the photos in the ILO report as not being intended for workers and artisans but rather for senior staff. The pamphlet also included photos of poor labour districts, depicting scenes of life in huts with roofs made of cardboard and bamboo branches (Figure 5.3).

Both the AIOC and the ILO viewed the widespread disparity in welfare development in the oil towns and fields as a direct result of the efficient organisation of the Oil Company and the ineffective policies of the Iranian government over the years. The residential districts of the oil towns and fields were divided into two categories: the old or traditional neighbourhoods under the

Figure 5.3 Propaganda and counterpropaganda about housing in the oil industry, Abadan and Aghajari, 1948–49

Iranian government's jurisdiction, and the new districts constructed by the Oil Company, which were often characterised as the poorer neighbourhoods and the newly prosperous ones.

In this context, the level of welfare in the prosperous districts was compared to the poverty in the poorer neighbourhoods. This comparison invariably highlighted the success of the prosperous areas as being attributed to the discovery of oil and the efficient management of the Oil Company. Abolfazl Lesani's observations on this analogy reflect the political climate that prevailed throughout Iran in the late 1940s:

> From this serene and idyllic vantage point [in Braim], this captivating and peaceful *Golestan*, where an aura of tranquillity and serenity permeates every aspect, one can discern the root of all class distinctions, the very origin of ethnicity and religious divisions. It is here that social corruption takes its inception and the seeds of the struggles within the impoverished slums of Abadan are sown.
>
> When the Oil Company showcases these slums to visitors, they argue that without the extraction, refining, and sale of this black gold, Iranians would be left with no alternative but to dwell in such dire conditions. However, the lingering question that remains unanswered is why the vast and fertile lands of Khuzestan, situated along the banks of the Shatt al-Arab and the Karun River, were allowed to deteriorate to such a deplorable state.[122]

Abadan in Fire and Blood

The Nowruz celebration in Iran in 1951 took on a distinctive character. On the evening of 20 March 1951, which marked the onset of the Iranian New Year, a significant event occurred: the Iranian upper house, known as the Senate, formally approved the nationalisation legislation concerning Iranian oil. This legislation had received prior endorsement from the Iranian Parliament five days earlier. It is noteworthy that both houses unequivocally supported this bill. Originally proposed by Mosaddeq and presented to a specialised parliamentary committee, the Oil Commission, on 8 March 1951, the bill called upon both legislative bodies to acknowledge the following:

> In the pursuit of the Iranian nation's prosperity and with a view to contributing to global peace, the undersigned propose the complete nationalisation of the Iranian oil industry in every region of the country, without exception. Consequently, all aspects of exploration, extraction, and management shall be vested in the hands of the Iranian government.

The nationalisation of the Iranian oil industry represented the culmination of an exhaustive and intricate five years period of political negotiations cantered around the oil sector. This process had its origins in December 1944 when Mohammad Mosaddeq introduced a bill to the Iranian Fourteenth Parliament. This bill sought to prohibit the Iranian government from granting oil concessions to foreign countries or enterprises. Five years later, following approval from both Parliament and Senate, ratified by Shah, this bill was formally enacted into law on 30 April 1951.

During the initial half of this five years' timeframe, the movement to nationalise the Iranian oil industry successfully rallied the support and leadership of the Iranian middle class, workers, and labouring poor. However, in the latter half of this period, the responsibility for addressing the oil issue shifted predominantly to the political elites and disbanded groups. Lobbying efforts took place discreetly, with minimal evidence of public support for this demand on the streets until one week after the joint announcement by the two parliamentary bodies in April 1931, declaring the nationalisation of the oil industry.

The elation following the Senate's endorsement of the bill on the New Year's Eve, however, proved to be short-lived. On March 21, 1951, the last day of the Iranian solar year 1329, the AIOC made a decision that the company's official history later referred to as an outcome of an 'imperfect understanding of the situation'.[123] The decision entailed reducing the 'outstation' allowances that had been provided to workers since the 1946 strike, compensating them for the challenging living conditions in severely deprived areas.

The rationale behind this reduction, as stated by the Company, was that there had been significant improvements in the services and amenities available to the workers compared to previous conditions, more than offsetting the need for these allowances. Although the Company claimed to have notified the workers of these impending cuts months in advance, the British Embassy in Tehran viewed the AIOC's decision, made without regard for changing circumstances, as a 'highly risky move'.[124]

The initial group affected by the withdrawal of these allowances were the oil workers in Bandar Maʿshur. The reduction in allowances varied, ranging from 20 to 40 per cent of their base wage, depending on whether they resided in non-Company or Company accommodation and the amenities provided by various AIOC departments. The Oil Company had previously provided the following benefits to workers in this area:

- Those who resided in tents, categorised as third- and fourth-degree workers, received 30 per cent of their salaries.
- Workers living within a three-kilometre radius from their workplace and residing in private houses or rented accommodations received 40 per cent of their salary.
- Those residing in Company housing were entitled to 20 per cent of their salary as an allowance.

Consequently, after the allowance withdrawal, a worker earning forty rials per day found themselves receiving only twenty-four rials, while those previously earning twenty rials were now compensated with sixteen rials.[125]

It is challenging to accept that the actions taken by the Oil Company were solely the result of an imperfect understanding of the critical situation at that time. For a company with a long history in Iran, even if it had not previously recognised the Iranian New Year in its working schedule, it should have been apparent that for Iranian employees, the New Year represented an occasion for receiving the *Nowruzaneh* bonus, not a reduction in income. This act by the Oil Company could possibly be interpreted as a subversive move aimed at undermining the passage of the nationalisation bill by both the Parliament and the Senate. It was a gesture to convey that the Oil Company not only refused to accept the bill but was also willing to obstruct the Iranian government's independent resolution by any means possible.

Nonetheless, the Oil Company later justified its actions by claiming that the decision to withdraw the allowance was based on the perceived improvement of conditions in the deprived regions, which rendered the allowance unnecessary.[126]

The workers' protest against the reduction in allowances commenced in Bandar Maʿshur, a relatively new oil port located in the Persian Gulf. According to a report filed by the local Gendarmerie, at 10 o'clock on 21 March 1951, approximately 1,500 oil workers gathered in front of the Oil Company Labour Office. They vehemently demanded the reimbursement of the portion of their salaries that had been deducted the previous day.

It's worth noting that the local Gendarmerie report acknowledged the extremely poor living conditions of the workers, who resided in tents without access to basic amenities such as baths, toilets, or washing facilities. Despite these conditions, the report urged the striking workers to return to work, invoking Martial Law. Simultaneously, the report called upon the Oil Company to reconsider its decision until improvements in the workers' living conditions were implemented.[127]

The local Gendarmerie's call for a return to work went unanswered by the AIOC's local Labour Office, and as a result, the strike extended to Aghajari and Naft-e Sefid, where similar allowances had been revoked. By the morning of 24 March, the number of striking workers in these three regions had grown to 6,000.

On 26 March, recognising the potentially volatile situation, the Iranian government, in response to an urgent plea from the British Ambassador and Ernest Northcroft, the AIOC's Chief representative in Tehran, declared Martial Law in several key areas, including Bandar Maʿshur, Aghajari, Abadan, Gachsaran, Haftgel, and Masjed-Soleyman. This Martial Law decree imposed a strict curfew to regulate the movement of people at night and was set to last for a period of two months.

Five days later, on 1st April, the cabinet appointed a three-member Conciliation Commission with the task of negotiating with the Oil Company to seek the restoration of the allowances. However, despite these preventive measures, the strike continued to spread rapidly to other oil regions, encompassing Abadan, Lali, and Masjed-Soleyman. In these regions, the striking workers were not solely focused on reinstating the allowances; they were also demanding that their local grievances be addressed. For instance, their demands included improvements in working and living conditions, and in the case of Masjed-Soleyman, where 3,500 workers had walked out, and Lali, where 600 workers were on strike, they were seeking a wage increase of approximately 80 per cent.[128]

On 24 March, 375 students, referred to at the time as the Technical Trainees of the Abadan Institute of Technology (AIT), joined the strike. Their primary demand was a reduction in the examination pass marks, which were set at 50 per cent as mandated by the Iranian Ministry of Education, to a more lenient 30 per cent. Subsequently, they added additional demands to their list, which included advocating for a bus service to be provided to AIT.[129]

In a show of solidarity with both the striking workers and the AIT students, the apprentices of the Abadan Artisan School, known as the Artisan Trainees, also decided to participate in the strike.[130]

In the subsequent days, despite the imposition of Martial Law, the students of the AIT continued to organise daily demonstrations on the AIT grounds. In the evenings, they convened meetings, often joined by apprentices from the Artisan School, at the latter's dormitory, commonly referred to as the Hostel.

As time passed, several locations emerged as focal points for the strikers, encompassing not only workers but also students and apprentices. These key gathering places included the AIT grounds, the Hostel, the vicinity of the refinery, the Iran Club (Bashgah-e Iran), and the Taj Cinema.[131]

According to a report from the British Embassy in Tehran, during its visit to the oil industry, the three-man Conciliation Commission met with 'delegations representing various groups of strikers and made a call for all workers to end the strike and return to work'. Simultaneously, the Commission strongly encouraged the Oil Company to meet the demands for strike pay and to reinstate the hard-living allowances. Additionally, they urged the reopening of the Company Food Store, which had been closed since the onset of the strike.[132]

The report indicates that the Oil Company responded affirmatively to these suggestions, agreeing to reinstate the allowances by 6 May. By that time, a committee comprising representatives from the Iranian government, the Oil Company, and the workers would assess the provided amenities and agree upon the rate of reduction:

a. Allowance should be restored in the 'new' area by 6 May, by which time a joint panel of government, employer and labour representatives should have examined the existing scale of amenities and reached an agreement upon the rate of reduction. At the same time, the Commission publicly declared its acceptance that the principles of adjusting the allowance to meet improved conditions was fair and just.
b. Immediate discussions should be started through the proper channels regarding all other demands.
c. Loans of wages through the illegal strike action should be off set against leave due, so that men and their families should suffer no immediate loss of money in respect of the period of the strike.[133]

Furthermore, 'the Company offered to regard the days spent on strike as part of the workers' annual leave'.[134]

The initial oil workers' strikes, which began with the withdrawal of allowances in Bandar Maʿshur, were primarily reactive and non-political during the first two weeks. As the strikes spread from city to city and field to field, they encompassed a wider range of demands, diversifying the strikers' objectives.[135]

In contrast, the government, acting as a mediator, aimed to encourage both parties involved – the workers and the Oil Company – to temporarily cease their actions. The goal was to create an environment conducive to negotiations and the peaceful resolution of the dispute. However, as time passed, the workers' demands gradually took on a more political dimension, and there were indications of the Tudeh Party's involvement in the strike. This became evident when two Tudeh activists, Mostafa Lankarani and Ghafari, were arrested but managed to escape while en route to Ahvaz.[136]

Additionally, a newly formed entity, the Association of Fighting Against the Colonial Oil Companies in Iran (*Jamʿiyat-e Melli-ye Mobarezeh ba Sherkat-ha-ye Esteʿmari-ye Naft dar Iran*), which was one of the legal fronts of the Tudeh Party, accused the ruling cabinet through the following words:

> Let the world know how the Iranian cabinet in collaboration with the Iranian army is defending the interests of the Oil Company and endeavouring to break down our just resistance; resistance which is coloured with the blood of our women and children. It is an endeavour to sustain the interest and influence of British colonialism. Let the world know how the honourable workers of Iran are even willing to sacrifice the blood of their beloved women and children for the final defeat of British imperialism and the Oil Company, which is nothing more than a brazen agent, supporting the interest of British colonialism.[137]

Just when it appeared that the situation was stabilising, the Oil Company made an unexpected announcement regarding its intention to deduct pay for the duration of the strike. This decision left even the British diplomatic staff in Tehran astonished.[138] As a result, a fresh wave of protests erupted among the workers in the oilfields and the refinery, as well as among the AIT students and

Figure 5.4 The machine shop in the Abadan Refinery, 1950

the Abadan Artisan School apprentices. This time, the protests took on a more militant and violent character.

On the early morning of 12 April, a new strike commenced in Bandar Maʿshur, triggered by the Oil Company's recent announcement regarding pay deductions. The Bandar Maʿshur military governate attempted to persuade the strikers to return to work by distributing leaflets both on the ground and from the air. However, disregarding these calls, the workers took to the streets once more, this time in even greater numbers, with some even accompanied by their wives and children.[139]

By 11 o'clock, the military governor had ordered his troops to open fire on the workers and their families who were marching towards the headquarters of the military governate in the port. According to a petition signed by the strikers, five women and three men lost their lives, and many more sustained injuries.[140] According to Elwell Sutton, two women were killed, and twenty men were injured. An eyewitness account also corroborated the deaths of two women and numerous injuries.[141]

In the subsequent days, prior to the arrival of another conciliation delegation from Tehran, the fear of a confrontation with the Martial Law enforcement troops compelled the workers in Bandar Maʿshur and their families to relocate to the desert areas surrounding the port for safety.[142]

In contrast to the situation in Maʿshur, the strike in Aghajari did not result in any violent incidents, and the workers chose to engage in a sit down strike. Around 1500 workers who had joined the strike[143] sent a telegram to Tehran, conveying the following message: 'Government representatives threatened our representatives and then brought them to the rally site under guard and forced them to call the workers to leave the strike. Furthermore, they stated that if the workers did not break the strike and three people gathered, they have orders to machinegun the protestors. In this way, they aim to compel the workers to return to work without them receiving their legal rights…' This telegram highlighted the tactics employed by government representatives to pressure the workers into ending the strike and returning to their duties, even at the expense of their legal entitlements…'[144]

Subsequent to the events in Aghajari, the second wave of the strike rapidly spread to other oil fields and towns, extending from Masjed-Soleyman to Abadan. In Abadan, five years after the bloody strike of 1946, the town once more became a battleground for a highly confrontational clash between the workers and the Martial Law enforcement troops.

On the morning of 11 April, workers at the Abadan Refinery initiated a strike, this time demanding an 85 per cent increase in wages, an extension of annual leave from 10 to 20 days, and several other benefits. On the same day, the apprentices, who had previously returned to their classrooms, resumed their strike due to the Oil Company's announcement that it would not be paying wages for the strike days.

In response, the military governate took a harsh stance. They closed the gates of the Hostel, detained the striking apprentices on the campus, and denied them access to food and water. Some refinery workers, in a telegram sent to Tehran, described the situation in the following words:

> On 11 April, Marital Law enforcement officers cordoned off the Hostel grounds and beat a number of apprentices. On the same day, the workers protested in front of the military governate's office for the release of their envoys. The reaction of the military governate was conciliatory and three of the detained deputies were released. The Hostel is still under military occupation and apprentices have decided not to leave the Hostel and to go on strike from April 14 in protest at the military's violent conduct.[145]

A mass gathering persisted at the Hostel, with attendees gathered around the body of Asghar Mortezi'i, one of the apprentices who had been shot on the preceding day. Meanwhile, at the refinery, a well-coordinated picketing operation was established. On that day, only 3,000 individuals crossed the picket line and reported for work. Consequently, the refinery's production output dwindled to 4,500,000 gallons per day.[146]

Amid the turmoil, two military command vehicles traversed the city with loudspeakers, appealing to the populace to remain calm. Meanwhile, on the streets in the vicinity of the refinery, young cyclists played a crucial role in updating the striking workers with the latest news and developments. 'Esmat Yazdanpanah-Dai'i chronicled in her diary that these cyclists even ventured into residential neighbourhoods to keep the families of the workers informed about the ongoing strike.[147]

In addition to these activities, there were reports of British staff members from the Oil Company receiving telephone threats. This prompted the military governor to dispatch troop detachments to Braim and Bovardeh neighbourhoods to safeguard the non-Iranian staff members of the Company. Besides the British staff, the Company's Indian employees also expressed concerns about their safety, although there were no reported hazards targeting this group of employees.[148]

The siege of the campus lasted for less than twenty-four hours, and on the morning of 12 April, Martial Law enforcement troops launched an operation at the Hostel. During this operation, they arrested some of the apprentices and forcibly removed the remaining occupants from the Hostel.[149]

This day, which began with the Martial Law enforcement troops' raid on the Hostel, subsequently unfolded into one of the bloodiest days in the history of the Oil Company. Some British residents residing in Abadan referred to it as 'Black Thursday'.[150]

The presence of striking workers both within and outside the Hostel, coupled with the impassioned and radical slogans being chanted by the angry apprentices directed at Iranian officials, left little room for any alternative to a violent confrontation. The Martial Law enforcement forces were determined to quell the protests swiftly.

Efforts were made by the troops to disperse the crowds, and in the process, they resorted to opening fire. This tragic turn of events resulted in nine fatalities and eleven injuries. By this point, the city's centre had transformed into a battlefield, with shops closing their doors, and residents hurriedly retreating to their homes for safety.

The streets around the Iran Club and the Taj Cinema became filled with anger and animosity directed towards foreign nationals. The crowds, described as 'thugs and mobs' by the reporter of *Asiya-ye* Javan, engaged in violent acts, including the raiding of cars on the streets. They forcibly pulled non-Iranians out of these vehicles and attacked them with sticks and stones.[151] Tragically, three British employees of the AIOC, one of whom was an Italian sailor working for the AIOC, were beaten to death, and eight other British nationals, including women and children, sustained injuries and had to be hospitalised.[152] The enraged crowds also targeted the Company's Taj Cinema, looting it and detaining a number of staff and spectators, including twenty-five British individuals.[153]

The British Consulate in Khorramshahr, in its assessment of the violent outbreak, stated that there was 'no evidence that the rioting on 12 April was in any way premeditated. It may have been precipitated by the actions of the Martial Law enforcement troops, who, following the instructions they received, resorted to more drastic measures than before'.[154]

As night fell over Abadan, the city took on the appearance of a 'fortified garrison, with nests of machine guns and tanks surrounding the British homes at Braim, though there were still insufficient forces to patrol Bovardeh'.[155]

In the ensuing days, Abadan began to resemble a deserted ghost town. Shops and bazaars remained shuttered, and traffic in the city came to a complete halt. Heavy machine guns were positioned on the rooftops of several government buildings by Martial Law enforcement troops, further contributing to the war-torn appearance of the town. People were rarely seen venturing out onto the streets.[156]

The emergency evacuation of all British employees and their families to Basra was a topic of discussion between the British Consul in Khorramshahr and the AIOC General Manager, Eric Drake.[157] According to Nasim Khaksar, his father, and many others he knew who had the opportunity, relocated their families to nearby cities in order to ensure their safety. There was a widespread fear of potential British retaliation.[158]

The news of the violent clashes in Abadan and the British government's threat to deploy troops to Khuzestan in support of British citizens deeply concerned the Iranian government in Tehran due to the precarious situation in Khuzestan. This concern on the part of the Iranian government was not unfounded.

In London, the British Foreign Secretary, Herbert Morrison, a member of the Labour Party, made a declaration during a parliamentary debate on the situation in the Iranian oil industry. He stated that the British government reserved the right to 'act as we see fit to protect British lives and property, and we hold the Persian government responsible for all injuries and losses that may be sustained by British nationals and interests'.[159] This interventionist ultimatum by the British government became a reality when news of the British navy's repositioning in the Persian Gulf reached Tehran: 'A third frigate, *Wren*, had arrived in Persian Gulf, and the cruiser *Euryalus* was reported to be on her way from the Mediterranean to join *Gambia*.'[160] The escalating, volatile, and violent situation in Abadan on 12 April deeply alarmed the government in Tehran. In response, Mosaddeq made the strategic decision to deploy some of its most seasoned and eminent generals and high-ranking officers to Khuzestan. On the morning of Friday, 13 April, General Shahbakhti, General Bagha'i, and Brigadier General Kamal, accompanied by fifteen high-ranking officers from the ground forces, embarked on their journey to Abadan. General Shahbakhti possessed prior familiarity with Khuzestan, dating back to the era of Reza Shah.[161]

Upon their arrival in Abadan, General Shahbakhti appointed Brigadier General Kamal as the new military governor of the city. Subsequently, a new military commission was established, tasked with initiating dialogues with representatives from the striking workers, AIT students, Artisan School apprentices, and a representative from the Oil Company. This military commission later proceeded to Bandar Maʿshur with a similar mission, engaging with representatives from both the workers and the Oil Company in that location.[162]

The Commission urged the Oil Company to halt the withdrawal of allowances and engage in negotiations with the workers concerning their various demands, including compensation for the days of the strike. While responding to this call, the Company's management exhibited reluctance and opted to use the term 'absence from work' instead of acknowledging it as 'strike pay'. Nonetheless, on 27 April, they publicly declared that 'following discussions with the three-man commission, the Company, recognizing that intimidation was the primary reason for employees not reporting for duty, had agreed to provide full wages to workers in Khuzestan for the days they were absent'.[163]

The arrival, presence, and interventions of General Shahbakhti and his accompanying entourage were met with tremendous enthusiasm in Abadan. Nasim Khaksar vividly remembers how residents gathered along the roadsides, waving, and cheering as Shahbakhti's car passed by.[164] Additionally, a rumour circulated within the city that one week prior to the strike's conclusion, General Shahbakhti had summoned the heads of the Oil Company who were proficient in Persian to Ahvaz via phone. During this communication, Shahbakhti had provided them with an update on the situation in Abadan, stating:

> In my meeting with British officials of the Oil Company, I conveyed that I arrived in Khuzestan with full authority and was prepared to take any necessary actions. I emphasized that I would not obstruct the workers' rallies and demonstrations in any manner and was committed to safeguarding the rights of the striking workers. However, I also made it unequivocally clear that I would not tolerate harm to come to a single British or Iranian individual, nor would I permit any disruption of peace and security in the city or the region. I issued a stern warning, urging them to address the workers' grievances within a 48-hour timeframe; otherwise, I would personally take control of the refinery and initiate its operations. The British officials, witnessing the general's resolute stance on that day, became increasingly concerned, and within a mere 24 hours, they conceded to all of the striking workers' demands.
>
> Following this ultimatum, British officials, having observed the unwavering determination of the general, grew apprehensive, and within 24 hours, they acceded to all of the striking workers' demands.[165]

It must be acknowledged that confirming the accuracy of this narrative is challenging. Nevertheless, the narrative itself serves to illustrate not only the expectations that the general populace and workers held regarding the Iranian government and its authority during that period but also reflects the perception of the Oil Company's ineffectiveness from the perspective of the people.

On 12 April, the company issued a statement reporting that a significant portion of the Abadan oil installations had become the focal point of protests. According to the statement, workers had refused to continue their work, resulting in a reduction in daily oil output from eighteen million gallons to ten million gallons. Additionally, the statement highlighted that during these demonstrations, workers were heard chanting slogans such as 'throw the pirates into the sea!'[166]

Interestingly, these alleged worker slogans, as quoted in the company's statement, bore a striking resemblance to the motto of the Tudeh Party during that era. This slogan could be found in the party's publications and heard during solidarity demonstrations by workers in Khuzestan and various Iranian cities like Tehran and Isfahan.

In the following days, the Company responded by expelling around fifty-seven apprentices, alleging that they had incited unrest.[167] However, there were no reports of regular workers being terminated. In reaction to the company's announcement, the majority of workers exhibited renewed confidence and resumed their duties, leading to an increase in refinery output to fifteen million gallons per day.[168] The remaining 10 per cent who persisted with the strike and continued to advocate political slogans were primarily individuals who aligned themselves more closely with the Tudeh Party.

As recounted by Rahmat Jazani, who was the head of the Tudeh Party's Khuzestan Provincial Committee at that time, the Tudeh Party's endeavours

Figure 5.5 'Confer liberty upon the workers of Khuzestan to expel maritime plunders into the sea'. Anti-British demonstration, April 1951

to prolong the strike were aimed at establishing a more substantial presence in Iran's daily political landscape.[169] However, these efforts ultimately did not achieve their intended success. Nevertheless, as described by an eyewitness, a lingering spark remained in the wake of the strike: Today, the strike in Khuzestan is nearly concluded, yet the embers that it has ignited here, in Tehran, and throughout the country are concealed beneath the ashes. If these ashes do not cool down, it won't be long before we witness more days of violence.[170]

Nevertheless, an atmosphere of apprehension cast a pall over the city until Sunday, 15 April, when substantial demonstrations unfolded in front of the refinery, drawing the participation of approximately 20,000 individuals. The workers were vociferously demanding the immediate nationalisation of the oil industry.

Should you require further refinements or assistance with any additional text, please feel free to let me know.

On 1st May 1951, International Labour Day transpired quietly within the Iranian oil industry, devoid of any celebratory signs in Khuzestan. Martial Law prevailed throughout the region, and the wounds stemming from the casualties of the preceding days remained too raw to entice workers into any form of celebration. It was in Tehran and Isfahan that workers congregated in the streets for the International Labour Day demonstrations, demonstrating their solidarity with their compatriots in Khuzestan.

When examining the organisation of the strike and its outcomes, the various assessments available offer a vivid portrayal of the xenophobic political

Figure 5.6 Demonstration in support of the oil workers, Tehran, May 1951

climate in Iran, substantially reshaped by the movement advocating for the nationalisation of the oil industry. During the weeks that followed, different entities, such as political parties like the Tudeh Party and the National Front, the Oil Company's management, and the Iranian government, each evaluated the strike through their distinct perspectives.

Initially, a widespread and serious rumour circulated that the Company had orchestrated the strike itself. According to the Khorramshahr Consular report, 'the popular theory is held amongst Iranians that the Company deliberately provoked the strike for the following reasons: to ensure the imposition of Martial Law for the two months, during the discussions in Tehran when local trouble might be expected; to provide an excuse for sending British Forces to the neighbourhood; to force agitators into the open in order to be able to identify and arrest them'.[171] These rumours about the Company's involvement in instigating the strike even reached certain official circles in Tehran.

Ernest Northcroft, the AIOC representative in Tehran, recounted his meetings with Iranian officials, stating that one of the Prime Minister's assistants conveyed that 'the cabinet was very perturbed by reports from Khuzestan that the Company had encouraged the strikes for ulterior purposes'. Even in his meeting with the Shah, Northcroft recalled that the Shah shared 'a very popular story that the Company had instigated the strike'. Eric Drake, the General Manager of the AIOC, vehemently denied these allegations, dismissing them as 'ridiculous'.[172]

In the subsequent days, the Iranian press continued to make references to Britain's involvement in the violent events of April 12, and accusations were levelled against the Oil Company, suggesting that it had orchestrated that fateful day:

> The bloody incident that unfolded in Abadan on the past Thursday, 12 April, resulting in the martyrdom of several impoverished workers, was not in any way connected to the honourable Iranian workers. Rather, it was exclusively orchestrated by the Oil Company with the intention of imposing Martial Law in Khuzestan, all as part of its sinister future agenda. The Oil Company vehemently opposes the nationalisation of the oil industry because British dominance relies heavily on Middle Eastern oil, particularly Iranian oil. It is essential to recall the words of Morrison, the British Foreign Secretary, who declared that the British government could not remain passive or apathetic regarding its interests in the Middle East. Both the British government and the Oil Company employ various stratagems to deceive Iran and obstruct it from realizing its fundamental objectives.
>
> One must ponder why, on the very day of the incident, certain English individuals, who had never ventured into areas where Iranians congregated and held themselves in a self-aggrandizing manner, suddenly found themselves in the vicinity of the Iran Club neighbourhood, where the strikers had gathered. This is one of the reasons why it is believed that the Oil Company itself played a more significant role in this tragic event than anyone else.[173]

The Tudeh Party and the CCFTU interpreted the strike that occurred in March and April of 1951 as a significant indication of the oil workers' reengagement with the broader 'anti-imperialist movement' that was gaining momentum throughout the country.[174] However, the party's attempts to organise workers' walkout came rather belatedly. Rahmat Jazani recalled how the Tudeh Party's leadership was caught off guard by the news emerging from Bandar Maʿshur. The party found itself incapable of directing the workers' protests in the refinery and oilfields. According to Jazani, it was only in the final days of the strike that the party was able to arrive on the scene in a somewhat organised manner. During this time, the party managed to prevent further British employees from being harmed by irate demonstrators.[175]

The testimony of Rahmat Jazani in later years was corroborated by accounts from the British Consulate in Khuzestan during the same days of the strike. These accounts, compiled by undercover agents of the Consulate, suggest that 'it is probably correct to say that Tudeh played little or no part in the early stages of the strikes. That they eventually made the most of developments, and turned them to their own account, is not to be doubted, but the impression has been gained that Tudeh were not yet ready for a showdown and that the strike went off at 'half cock'... Had it taken place a few weeks later, it is probable that it would have found Tudeh in a better state of organisation and results might have been more serious'.[176]

As for the interpretation of the strike by Mosaddeq's National Front supporters, it closely aligned with the prevalent conspiracy theories. *Bakhtar-e Emruz*, a prominent publication affiliated with Mosaddeq, posited the notion that 'the provocations orchestrated by the Company and the radical incitement ultimately achieved their objectives. In contrast to the fervent Iranian desire for oil nationalisation, Abadan bore witness to a tragic denouement'.[177]

In stark contrast, the Tudeh Party later asserted its triumph in garnering the support of the oil workers during the strike. Nevertheless, Rahmat Jazani held a divergent perspective. He contended that the ranks of Tudeh Party adherents and activists had markedly dwindled compared to the 1946 strike. According to Jazani, a significant number of the party's supporters had realigned themselves with the National Front, thereby explaining the party's inability to successfully orchestrate the envisaged strike'.[178]

During the concluding days of the strike, various stakeholders, including the Iranian government, the Oil Company, and the oil workers, undertook measures to address the potential repercussions of the unfolding events. The Iranian government, deeply concerned about the prospect of ethnic tensions resurfacing in the region, reminiscent of the 1946 unrest, and apprehensive that 'the British might be engaging in what they perceived as a form of espionage..., involving local tribes as part of preparations for a possible invasion', initiated contact with Arab Sheikhs and Bakhtiari Khans. They conveyed a stern warning, cautioning them against any collaboration with British agents operating in the vicinity.

On 26 April, during an address delivered at a gathering of local Sheikhs in Khorramshahr, General Shahbakhti made a resolute statement. He asserted that 'the strike had been orchestrated by external actors, driven by the objective of disrupting the ongoing nationalisation of the oil industry'. He further emphasised that 'should a situation reminiscent of the one that unfolded in Azerbaijan in 1945–1946 arise in Khuzestan, he would be adequately prepared to manage it, as he could rely on the support of the tribal communities'.[179]

Bittersweet Farewell: End of Britain's Oil Era

With the British Navy significantly augmenting its presence and operations in the Persian Gulf, a sense of unease gripped some British employees of the Company.[180] They harboured concerns that the unfolding events in Khuzestan and Abadan could lead to irrevocable and potentially perilous consequences. Consequently, following the initial days of the strike, a number of these British employees decided to relocate their families away from Abadan. According to the weeklies *Tarraqi* and *Kushesh*, as early as 26 March British residents in Abadan began escorting their families to Basra.[181]

In the subsequent days, the evacuation of women and children accelerated, under the supervision of the Company, with more than 120 individuals departing each day. Additionally, apart from the British families, a contingent of fourteen American technicians employed at the refinery also chose to depart for the United States.[182]

While in Tehran, a complex and multifaceted arbitration process was underway, involving various stakeholders. Concurrently, in the capital city, the Iranian cabinet, now led by Prime Minister Mosaddeq, initiated practical measures to set the nationalisation of the oil industry in motion. Following the establishment of the National Iranian Oil Company (NIOC) in April, which replaced AIOC, a Provisional Board of Directors for the Nationalisation of Oil was formed. The Board arrived in Abadan on 10 June. Eric Drake, who served as the General Manager of the AIOC, facilitated the Board's accommodation as guests of the Company and orchestrated a tour of the refinery for the Board members.

According to correspondence from *Ettelaʿat-e Haftegi*, the events that transpired during this tour constituted the 'most fascinating and memorable account' of the Provisional Board of Directors' inaugural day in Abadan:

> On Friday, the 15 June, representatives of the Provisional Board received an invitation from Drake to visit the Abadan Refinery and various other oil installations in the area. When Drake arrived to guide the representatives, Makki, the head of the Provisional Board, greeted him with a smile and remarked:
>
> 'Indeed, we are eager to tour the refinery, but we would appreciate the opportunity to visit the workers' residences first.'
>
> Drake smiled in response and, with no alternative, acquiesced to their request. The Provisional Board proposed to visit Tanurabad, a modest labourer's neighbourhood situated in the southern part of Abadan.
>
> However, in a rather peculiar turn of events, Drake insisted that Tanurabad was not the dwelling place of AIOC workers but rather the residential area for the general populace of Abadan. He went on to explain that the Company had constructed new, splendid houses for the workers along the banks of the Shatt River.
>
> Makki furrowed his brow and turned to a man standing in front of one of the thatched huts, inquiring:
>
> 'Where do you work?'
>
> The man replied, 'I am a refinery worker.'
>
> Makki pressed further, asking, 'How many years have you been employed there?'
>
> The worker proudly responded, 'Seventeen years, here is my employment card for your reference.'
>
> Makki examined the card and then handed it to Drake. He continued his inquiry, asking the worker:
>
> 'Are there any other oil workers residing here besides yourself?'
>
> The worker chuckled and replied, 'Certainly, sir. All the inhabitants in this area are oil workers, with ten or twelve years of service for the Company.'[183]

Mosaddeq's national broadcast on 20 June 1951, heralding the termination of the Anglo-Iranian Oil Company's fifty years dominion, stands as a momentous and pivotal milestone in the annals of the Company's history. The following measures and directives were put into effect:

- Any executive orders and decisions made by officials of the AIOC necessitated the countersignature of a member from the Provincial Board of Directors of the NIOC.
- The administration of the Kermanshah Refinery and the Naft-e Shah oilfield was to be transferred to Iranian control.
- Iranians were to assume responsibility for all other departments within the Company, encompassing administrative and sales offices in Tehran.
- All signboards and posters affiliated with the AIOC were to be rebranded as those of the NIOC.
- The revenue generated from oil sales was mandated to be deposited in the National Bank of Iran, specifically into the account designated for the NIOC.
- The closure of the AIOC Information Office was decreed.

On Wednesday, 20 June 1951, as per Mosaddeq's directives, marked the day when the entire technical and administrative apparatus of the Company was scheduled to be transferred to the NIOC. Furthermore, all revenues generated from the sale of oil in the domestic market of Iran were to be exclusively deposited into the account of the Iranian government. This momentous occasion also entailed the removal of AIOC signage, to be replaced with the new name of the NIOC.

The standoff between the Provisional Board of Directors and the management of the AIOC progressively escalated, assuming a more antagonistic nature. AIOC personnel received instructions to regard themselves as employees of the NIOC while retaining their existing salaries, allowances, and employment benefits. According to Bamberg, 'The Board contended that Drake, like the rest of the Company's staff and workforce, was now an employee of the Iranian government and that any refusal to cooperate with the government representatives was illegal'.[184]

In addition to this, the Provincial Board insisted that Eric Drake, who served as the General Manager of the dissolved Company, must surrender various critical documents and information. These demands encompassed the provision of 'the organisation charts of the industry, a statement of the oil export sales proceeds since 20 March and 75 per cent of all money received in Iran or London on account of oil sale after that date'.[185]

The animosity between the actions of the Provincial Board and the management, led by Eric Drake, persisted for a period of two weeks. Eventually, on 20 June, adhering to the deadline established by Mosaddeq, the Provisional Board of Directors made the decision to raise the Iranian flag above the offices of the AIOC in Abadan and Khorramshahr. This act was met with strong protest from Eric Drake.

As recounted by Norman Kemp, a freelance correspondent for the News Chronicle stationed in Abadan, Hossein Makki delivered an address to a gathering of around 3,000 workers at the refinery. In his speech, he 'advised the people to work calmly with the British oilmen' This guidance was offered at a significant juncture when the Iranian flag was being raised atop the refinery office, signifying a transition in authority and control.[186]

On that very day, Eric Drake received a warning that he had two choices: either accept employment with the NIOC or formally announce his resignation.[187] Eric Drake's response to this ultimatum was not favourable, and a week later, on 26 June, he departed from Iran for Basra.

The response of the Provincial Board to Eric Drake's departure was one of anger, and as a form of retaliation, they adamantly refused to recognise the appointment of Alick Mason as Drake's successor. Just one day after Drake's exit, the remaining non-Iranian employees of the Company, primarily British with some Indian, Dutch, Swedish, and Belgian nationals, collectively submitted their resignations.

While certain heads of various departments opted to remain physically present in their offices, they refused to carry out any work. In response, the Provincial Board issued a directive to station police personnel outside these offices, preventing the employees from gaining access to their workspaces. In a specific instance involving Derek's office in Khorramshahr, where Alick Mason had temporarily taken over in Derek's absence, Mason was prohibited from entering the office on the morning of 28 June. Instead, he was instructed to surrender the office key to Matin Daftari, one of the three Provincial Board members.[188]

On 26 June, Mosaddeq conveyed a message to the employees and foreign workers of the oil industry, urging them to extend their support to the NIOC. This appeal was accompanied by an assurance that their existing employment contracts with the AIOC would continue to be honoured, and their salaries, benefits, and pensions would remain unaltered.

However, the response to Mosaddeq's message was lukewarm from the majority of the Oil Company's employees. Only a small group of Indian workers displayed a willingness to entertain the idea, while the rest remained hesitant or unresponsive.

The resignations of non-Iranian employees did not necessarily entail an immediate departure from Iran. On 26th of August, approximately 350 British oil workers from various locations in Khuzestan congregated in Abadan to make preparations for a potential prompt departure from Iran, if circumstances demanded it.[189] They remained in a waiting status in Abadan for an additional month.

However, on 25 of September, the Provincial Board, acting under the directives of the Iranian government, issued a call to all British employees who had refrained from joining the NIOC but were still residing within Iranian territory. They were given an ultimatum to either return to work or face the cancellation of their residence permits by 4 October. This move reflected the Iranian government's stance on the matter.[190]

The British government's confrontational reaction to the warning issued by the Iranian government on 25 September 1951, had a profound impact on the political atmosphere within Iran. Britain insisted that the Iranian government withdraw the proposals it had presented to British Oil Company employees or bear the responsibility for the potential repercussions of those demands. In response to this international tension, on 27 September 1951, Mohammad Mosaddeq convened a parliamentary session with the objective of securing a vote of confidence in his favour. This move was emblematic of the escalating political turmoil surrounding the nationalisation of Iran's oil industry.

Nonetheless, when the Parliament proved unable to convene due to a lack of quorum, Mosaddeq left the parliamentary building and proceeded to address a sizable gathering that had assembled in Baharestan Square, situated in front of the Parliament. During his address, he delivered a message that would come to symbolise his distinctive style of governance: 'The Parliament is wherever the representatives of the people are, and you are the true representatives of the people!' This statement underscored his profound connection with the Iranian public and his firm belief in their role as the genuine representatives of the nation.

The resonance of Mosaddeq's statement reverberated through the oilfields, igniting a surge of nationalist fervour. Iranian troops were swiftly dispatched to the refinery, assuming responsibility for its protection. In the oilfields, Iranian flags were proudly raised above the oil facilities, while photographs of Mosaddeq adorned the exteriors of shops. Everywhere on the streets of the oil towns, slogans advocating the nationalisation of the oil industry were prominently displayed. 'Cyclists wrapped red, white and green paper streamers around the bicycle frames, and covered saddles with cloth in Persian colours'.[191] Norman Kemp vividly recollects the massive demonstration in Abadan: Persians from Abadan joined with hundreds from Khorramshahr in a mass parade around the British Consulate, and an excited procession to the telegraph office, where they sent a telegram to Mosaddeq affirming their support for his nationalisation policy.[192]

On 3 October, the British Royal Navy vessel Mauritius dropped anchor in the Arvandrud, accompanied by another Royal Navy destroyer, Armada, positioned downstream. Fighter planes were put on standby at Iraqi air bases as well. In response to the escalating diplomatic tensions, the Iranian government revoked the residence permits of foreign workers who were not actively employed. Within a span of forty-eight hours, all British employees and their families who were still residing in Iran boarded the Mauritius and departed for Basra, further intensifying the strain between Iran and Britain.[193]

According to Norman Kemp, who was present in Abadan on the Evacuation Day, there were 'only 290 Europeans in the oil city built to house 5,000; with them were 350 Indians and Pakistanis, whom the Company were returning to

Figure 5.7 AIOC British employees waiting at the Gymkana to board the HMS Mauritius, Abadan, October 1951. Persian text: 'The British departure: The end of half a century of colonialism'

their countries'.[194] Additionally, there were 350 Indians and Pakistanis, whom the Company was repatriating to their respective countries. However, some Indian employees of the AIOC petitioned the Iranian Parliament, requesting permission to stay. The Parliament responded favourably to their appeal.[195]

Although the exact number of Indian workers who chose to remain in Iran is unknown, it is evident that there were a significant number of them, primarily Muslims who, following the partition of India, identified themselves as Pakistanis. Even today, senior citizens of Abadan recall the presence of Indian workers' families in the daily life of their city, highlighting the lasting impact of this community on the region (Figure 5.8).

'Departure meant heartbreak, solitude's bleak companion', as recounted by Norman Kemp, eloquently captures the emotional resonance of the mass exodus from Abadan in October 1951. To Iranians who had long embraced the presence of Britons and other non-Iranians in their town, this departure held a unique and poignant significance. The sudden absence of these enduring figures left behind a profound sense of loss and a haunting emptiness, akin to the silence that follows a once-familiar song.

Figure 5.8 Provisional Board of Directors for the Nationalisation of Oil with the Indian workers' representatives, Abadan, 1951

Indeed, over the preceding five years, the call for the departure of non-Iranians from the oil industry had served as a rallying cry for some political activists in Company towns and throughout the nation. However, when the departure finally materialised, it triggered not only a sense of jubilation but also a profound sense of bewilderment among the Iranian population. The abrupt absence of long-standing residents and colleagues left a void that many found difficult to comprehend, as the presence of non-Iranians had been an integral part of their daily lives for generations.

> Thursday, 11 Mehr 1330 (4 October 1951). I awoke slightly earlier than usual today. Last night, we had arranged to meet with fellow comrades earlier in the morning and continue our discussions on our way to high school. The news had reached us yesterday that the last British citizen had departed from Abadan. From April until now, our rallying cry had been 'the British must go.' Now, they have left, much swifter and more directly than we had anticipated.
>
> Now, what comes next? What are we to say now? The organisation has not provided any guidance on what steps should follow. Our fellow comrades have not received any information either. We find ourselves uncertain about how to proceed, especially regarding the Mosaddeq supporters at our high school who are understandably jubilant.
>
> Mehri remarked that both the party [Tudeh], and the organisation [Youth Organisation of the Tudeh Party] were falling behind. Are we truly lagging in our efforts?[196]

On 4 and 5 October 1951, as the British staff completed their withdrawal from Iran, Nasser Najmi, who held the position of head of the Publishing Department at the National Oil Company, dispatched his reporters to the Port with the specific task of covering the evacuation. *Akhbar-e Ruz* published a special issue in large quantities, featuring photographs of the British departure from Iran.

This publication was met with tremendous enthusiasm by the people of Abadan. It was in such high demand that individuals were observed eagerly grabbing copies from one another's hands. Despite efforts to increase its circulation, the special issue was completely sold out within just an hour. The residents of Abadan were seen reading the related report aloud to each other, and their indescribable joy over this historic event was palpable and contagious.[197]

6

Sovereignty's Interlude: Iran's Oil in 1951–1954

September 1950, if not the hottest month of that year in Abadan, was unquestionably as sweltering as July or August. The streets' asphalt seemed to melt like tar, and water in cast iron or iron pipes reached a boiling point. The wind generated by rotating fans felt akin to the scorching heat emanating from a bakery oven.

Between ten o'clock in the morning and four or five in the afternoon, the streets of Abadan were eerily deserted, with only those compelled by necessity venturing outdoors. The closure of the refinery, which occurred on 31 July 1951, a month before the final departure of British personnel from the oil industry in Khuzestan, intensified the midday silence that enveloped the city manyfold.

Out of the 24,000 employees originally associated with the Abadan Refinery, only four thousand remained employed during that period, primarily in the Power Plant and Ice Factory. The remaining 20,000 were not actively engaged in work and were instead on the government payroll. However, it's worth noting that this number did not encompass contract workers.

According to correspondence documented in the *Ettelaʿat* newspaper, the local office frequently received copies of petitions sent to the Chairman of the Board of Directors of the National Iranian Oil Company from contract workers, urging the provision of employment or unemployment allowances. One such petition read as follows:

> Addressed to the Chairman of the Board of Directors of the National Iranian Oil Company,
>
> I, a humble worker named Hossein Deilaman, labouring in Refinery No. 30, earn a daily wage of 43 Rials. I bear the responsibility of providing for my wife, my mother, and two children. How can I manage this burden? I am aware that the Iranian government is expected to provide this financial support out of its own resources. But I wonder, from where does this funding originate.
>
> Resident of the Hasirabad neighbourhood in Abadan.[1]

Regarding the non-contract workers, a substantial group of them followed a routine each day. They would leave their homes early in the morning, as they did when they were still employed, and gather in front of the main gate of the refinery. There, they would discuss the news they had heard the previous night on Radio Tehran, read newspapers, and subsequently return to their homes around ten o'clock.

According to local correspondence reported in *Ettelaʿat*, these workers displayed remarkable serenity and composure. Their community, consisting of several thousand individuals, remained so quiet and composed that not even the faintest disturbance could be discerned. Their sentiment was clear: they believed it was essential to maintain calm and patience until the situation in the oil industry was resolved.[2]

The three-and-a-half year's gap between the announcement of the nationalisation of Iranian oil and the implementation of the Agreement between Iran and the Consortium of Oil Companies (March 1951–October 1954) marked a profoundly significant period in the history of Twentieth Century Iran. Its impact extended far beyond those years, leaving a lasting imprint on the remainder of the Twentieth Century and even into the subsequent century.

The most pivotal event during this period was the 1953 coup d'état, a momentous event that brought about a dramatic transformation in the dynamics between the state and society in Iran. This coup d'état had far-reaching consequences, reshaping the course of Iranian history, and influencing its trajectory for decades to come.

Political Turmoil Period: March 1951–October 1954

In Iranian Twentieth Century historiography, the narrative of the nationalisation of the oil industry is intricately interwoven with the life and leadership of Mohammad Mosaddeq on one hand, and with Iran's positioning within the context of the Cold War on the other. This historical account is marked by a prominent focus on anti-colonial and anti-imperialist actions and discourse that emerged in the wake of the Second World War. This emphasis on global south struggles against colonialism and imperialism has often overshadowed the development of social historiography within Iran, leaving little room for it to offer its own perspectives on the past.

Indeed, the Cold War duality emerged as a central and defining theme for Iran. It had its origins in the crisis that unfolded in Azerbaijan in 1945–46 and subsequently gained momentum through the nationalisation of Iran's oil industry in March 1951. This period of heightened tension and political manoeuvring ultimately culminated in the momentous coup d'état of August 1953. These pivotal events not only left an indelible mark on Iran's domestic political landscape but also positioned the country as a significant player within the broader global dynamics of the Cold War. This interconnectedness between Iran's internal affairs and its role in the global Cold War stage underscored the complexity and significance of this historical period for the nation.

This chapter, however, does not aim to provide an exhaustive review of Mohammad Mosaddeq's government or the policies of the major powers of that era, namely Britain, the United States, and the Soviet Union, in relation to Iran and Mosaddeq's administration. Instead, it focuses on the concise yet eventful three years period from the departure of the last British employees and their associates from Iran in October 1951 to the entry of the Oil Consortium into the Iranian oil industry in October 1954.

During this relatively brief but significant period, Iran experienced a series of transformative events that had a lasting impact, potentially altering the course of the nation in the late Twentieth Century. These events included the July 1952 uprising, the August 1953 coup d'état, Iran's engagement with the United Nations, protests against Britain's stance on the nationalisation of the Iranian oil industry, and the favourable vote of the Hague Court of Justice in Iran's favour. While these episodes have been extensively examined in other studies, this chapter seeks to provide a focused perspective on this critical period in Iran's history.[3]

This chapter, and indeed the broader scope of this study, will centre on a key aspect often overlooked in previous research: the everyday lives of the employees within the oil industry and the communities in close proximity to it.[4] The period under examination spans from the departure of British employees from Khuzestan to the transfer of oil industry management to an international petroleum Consortium holding company known as Iranian Oil Participants Ltd.

Central to this study are questions pertaining to the intricate dynamics that evolved between the workforce and the management of the oil industry during this transformative period. Additionally, the study delves into crucial issues such as housing conditions, healthcare, wage structures, workplace safety measures, and the training and employment of labourers. Equally significant is the exploration of how labour activism, both within the industry and throughout the country, was shaped during this time. These aspects collectively shed light on the comprehensive societal and labour dynamics that were at play during this pivotal period in Iran's history.[5]

Post-Colonial Dawn: Oil after British Exit

As the British and British-controlled non-Iranian employees made preparations to leave Abadan and Khorramshahr, the residences of these foreign employees and engineers were subjected to looting. Items such as bedding, cutlery, crockery, and dining sets were pilfered during these incidents. The theft of both company property and the personal possessions of non-Iranian employees, occurring both before and after their departure from Iran, became a frequent occurrence.

Reports further indicate instances of looting, including the theft of electric fans belonging to British employees during their departure, the pilfering of oil well drilling equipment that was smuggled to Bandar Maʿshur, and even the unlawful siphoning of a significant amount of gasoline from the pipeline stretching from Masjed-Soleyman to Abadan, which was then transported overseas.[6] Shortly after the British experts left, the British Consulate in cities like Shiraz and others was closed, prompting the local townspeople and tradespeople to celebrate this development with illumination and rejoicing.[7]

Expressing concerns about the potential unforeseen consequences of nationalising the oil industry, the government took several measures in August 1951. It established a Petroleum Commission and urged all ministries to collaborate fully with it, with the commission's primary responsibility being to ensure the safety and continuity of the oil industry. Prime Minister Mosaddeq issued a statement outlining a series of measures that needed to be taken, including:

- Sending a minister to the province of Khuzestan each week to address its needs and boost the morale and hope of its people.
- Facilitating the return of unemployed workers in Khuzestan, especially Abadan, to their home provinces to reduce unemployment.
- Launching a propaganda campaign, including a daily program dedicated to Khuzestan on Radio Tehran, and sending a pious preacher to Abadan to uplift the spirits of its residents.
- Maintaining Martial Law to protect the lives and property of foreigners.
- Providing support to the provincial Bank of Agriculture to encourage unemployment reduction and promote agricultural activities, especially in Abadan.
- Ensuring the availability of water for agriculture to motivate unemployed workers to engage in farming.
- Initiating a campaign through the Ministry of Health to meet the health and medicinal needs of the people in Abadan and other cities in Khuzestan.[8]

In the subsequent months, the security situation in Khuzestan province deteriorated significantly, posing substantial challenges to the uninterrupted operation of the oil industry. Despite the ongoing issue of post-war unemployment, the decrease in oil extraction and refining operations led to the dismissal of a considerable number of contract workers. Additionally, the departure of non-Iranian employees left many service sector workers without any employment prospects.

Local and national newspapers regularly reported on raids occurring in homes and shops in Khuzestan. Esmaʿil Raʾin, a future popular historian, visited Abadan in 1951 and provided a comprehensive account of the widespread underground criminal activities in the city. He noted that a significant number of individuals residing in the city lacked proper birth certificates, and this number was increasing daily. Furthermore, due to the city's proximity to the Iraqi border, many unemployed traders, and even Iraqi thieves, could move in and out of the city without the police being aware of their presence. It was even reported that local thieves would make agreements with their Iraqi counterparts to transport stolen goods into Iraq or Kuwait territories.[9]

During the 1950s, Abadan was home to approximately 250 opium dens, all of which operated with the knowledge of local law enforcement. The city also had hundreds of brothels scattered throughout various districts, and these establishments allowed smoking. Both opium dens and brothels represented significant sources of income for the corrupt law enforcement.

Esmaʿil Raʾin described the challenging law enforcement situation in Abadan during this period. The city had a population of 300,000 but was served by just 5 police stations with a total of 250 local policemen. This limited number of officers made it difficult to effectively combat pickpockets and thieves, often leaving the policemen with no choice but to either yield to criminal activity or turn a blind eye to it. Moreover, in a city where even a simple bunch of radishes could cost as much as four rials, police officers found it hard to make ends meet with a monthly salary of only 1,000 rials, which often led them to accept bribes.[10]

In another report, it is noted that individuals are openly and audaciously pilfering bicycles from cyclists on the streets, and even daring to snatch wristwatches before hastily making their escape. Recently, there has been an influx of unemployed individuals observed in Abadan, with groups arriving from Azerbaijan. The scarcity of employment opportunities has led to a proliferation of beggars occupying the streets, with destitute individuals encountered at every corner.[11] Additionally, a petition was dispatched from Aghajari to the Prime Minister's Office, expressing deep-seated concerns regarding the city's security, even during daylight hours.[12]

In addition to the pressing security concerns, the living conditions of labourers in the province were deteriorating rapidly, particularly in terms of escalating food prices. The cost of sustenance for the populace was incomparable to even the wartime and post-war years; it had reached a considerably more dire state. During the war, potatoes were retailed at four rials per kilo, while bread was priced at five rials. However, in the early 1950s, potatoes were being sold at an exorbitant twelve rials per kilo, with bread following suit at the same steep price point. The press speculated that the primary reason for this sharp increase in food prices was their exportation. Reports suggested that, despite the removal of the British influence, local traders were still engaging in the sale of provincial products to them. It was further reported that ten to twelve ships, laden with smuggled foodstuffs, were making daily journeys to Kuwait. However, it remained unclear why customs officials were turning a blind eye to these activities.

Bakhtar-e Emruz, a pro-government periodical, expressed profound concern over this issue, emphasising that unless a prompt and effective solution was devised for this critical problem, the province faced an imminent crisis of existence. The people of Khuzestan were at risk of plunging into a state of profound desperation and abject poverty, inevitably resorting to begging in order to eke out a living.[13]

The discontent among the population in Khuzestan regarding the exorbitant prices and the scarcity of essential food items eventually prompted them to take to the streets. A significant number of Khorramshahr residents gathered at the telegraph office and conveyed a message to the government in which they voiced their grievances regarding the food shortage in both Abadan and Khorramshahr. They laid blame on colonialists, agitators, and malcontents for the situation. They alleged that a substantial amount of food was leaving the borders with the complicity of customs officers and being smuggled to Iraq and Kuwait. With the price of food continuing to surge each day, the people found themselves in a dire predicament. It was believed that this famine was deliberately engineered to incite unrest in the Khuzestan region, necessitating urgent and independent action by the national government to find a solution.[14]

Two weeks later, reports of the closure of the city's bakeries circulated, but the governor of Khuzestan shifted the blame onto former agents of the Oil Company for spreading rumours. An Indian butcher, accused of disseminating false information, was apprehended, and swiftly ordered to leave the country.[15]

In the midst of the scorching expanse of the Lali region, rich with coveted oil reserves, the Oil Company imposed stringent restrictions on the distribution of drinkable water. The meagre quantities provided during the turbulent conditions were heated to such an extent that they became unsuitable for consumption. As per the Company's guidelines, workers were allocated a modest amount of ice. Unfortunately, due to severe financial constraints, even this limited supply of ice was discontinued after a certain period.[16]

Not only were the working conditions within the Iranian oil industry substandard, but the spectre of layoffs also cast a shadow over the workers. Government correspondence attributed these terminations to the reduction or cessation of production, coupled with a shortage of funds to cover the workers' salaries. Parviz Mina contends that the substantial decline in Iranian oil output resulted from the AIOC's boycott of Iranian oil sales, supported by U.S. Oil Companies with the intention of weakening Iran.[17] This situation exposed the limited knowledge of Mosaddeq and his oil advisors concerning the extent and intricacies of international oil operations. Parviz Mina identifies Mehdi Bazargan, Kazem Hasibi, and Seyyed ʿAli Shaygan as the three principal oil advisors to Mosaddeq: They were deficient in their understanding of the colossal influence held by the eight major international oil companies that dominated the entire oil market and its distribution. Consequently, Iran found itself incapable of matching the levels of oil production and exportation it had previously achieved under the AIOC.[18]

As per Parviz Mina, in early 1951, Iran's total oil production averaged 660,000 barrels per day, whereas global crude oil production reached 10.9 million barrels per day. However, the major oil corporations significantly increased production levels in Iraq, Saudi Arabia, Kuwait, and the United States, effectively raising the total global production to thirteen million barrels by 1952, nearly three times the amount produced in Iran. By doing so, they could impose an embargo on Iranian oil while still satisfying global demand.[19]

Furthermore, when the British employees withdrew in October 1951, the Iranian government held high hopes of being able to recruit technicians from other countries to manage the industry and expedite the training of their own citizens to assume these roles. Regrettably, this optimism proved to be misplaced.

Unfortunately, Iran's predicament deteriorated as several countries, including the United States, Sweden, Belgium, the Netherlands, Pakistan, and Germany, declined to provide their technicians to work in Iran's nationalised industry.[20] Consequently, Iran's total oil exports plummeted to a mere 118,000 tons during 1952 and the first half of 1953. This was a stark contrast to the total oil exports in 1950, which was the last full year of AIOC's operations in Iran and amounted to thirty-one million tons.

To provide context, Iran's total oil sales during this period were equivalent to the output of just a single day under the AIOC. This starkly illustrates the significant ramifications of the embargo and the challenges Iran encountered in sustaining oil production and exports without the assistance of foreign experts.[21]

The decrease in oil production presented numerous challenges for Mosaddeq's government. One significant issue pertained to the budget: the Iranian treasury was no longer receiving the AIOC's oil royalties and indirect contributions, including income taxes from Company employees and customs duties on non-exempt imported goods. To offset this loss of revenue, the government resorted to a series of measures, which included issuing public bonds, raising income taxes on urban wage earners, increasing customs duties on non-essential imports, and raising prices on government-controlled monopolies such as sugar, tobacco, opium, and tea.[22]

While Mosaddeq held hope that these measures would enhance the national treasury's financial stability and showcase to the world that Iran could, at least in the short term, endure without its oil industry, they proved ineffective in ameliorating the living conditions of thousands of oil workers or mitigating the extent of unemployment in oil-producing regions.

Initially, unemployment primarily impacted many domestic workers who had previously found employment with non-Iranian personnel. Subsequently, workshops that were not directly linked to the Oil Company but had been rendering services to it, such as ice production workshops, were compelled to cease their operations due to reduced activity. Consequently, their workers joined the ranks of the unemployed labour force, seeking assistance from the government.

Furthermore, there were workers who had been terminated for various reasons, whether political or non-political, during the AIOC's administration, and they were now seeking reemployment. In response to petitions submitted by these groups of workers, the NIOC explained that rehiring was not feasible due to the refinery's closure and the absence of necessary funds.

A similar response was issued concerning contract workers, indicating that the NIOC could not accommodate them as permanent employees and advising them to either return to their previous places of residence or explore alternative employment opportunities.[23]

In a significant study, Maral Jefroudi utilises data gleaned from the archives of the International Labour Organisation, British Petroleum, and the British National Archive to illustrate that between 1949 and 1953, the number of foreign staff and workers experienced a sharp decline, plummeting from 3,095 and 1,163 in 1949 to zero by 1953. Concurrently, the number of Iranian staff increased from 4,343 to 6,764. However, the count of Iranian workers, including contract workers, decreased from 62,369 to 52,748 during the same period. It is noteworthy that this decrease in the worker count was primarily attributed to a reduction in contract workers, whose numbers dwindled from 15,000 in 1949 to 4,000 in 1953.[24]

In addition to employment and unemployment, the housing and health conditions of workers and other employees within the oil industry emerged as two other critical issues that drew the genuine concern of the management of this nationalised industry. It is worth remembering that the strike in March 1951, triggered by the discontinuation of corporate housing assistance, led oil workers to legitimately call for improved housing conditions, with the anticipation that the nationalised industry's management would undertake appropriate measures to address this demand.

In an interview with the representative of the NIOC in Haftgel and Naft-e Sefid, a reporter from *Bakhtar-e Emruz* inquired about any improvements made in the living and working conditions of oil workers in the region since the nationalisation of the oil industry. In response, the NIOC representative highlighted several initiatives, including:

- Allocating seventy new houses in Neft-e Sefd for workers previously residing in tents.
- Providing land and house building materials to workers interested in constructing their homes.
- Establishing a new power plant and supplying electricity to over a hundred houses that previously lacked lighting.
- Installing a new water pump to provide drinking water sourced from the Zard River in Ramhormoz.
- Organising literacy classes for elderly oil workers and establishing primary and secondary schools for their children.
- Promoting recreational activities during workers' free time by encouraging vegetable cultivation in newly established gardens.
- Constructing a swimming pool at the Workers Niru Club.[25]

These initiatives demonstrate the commitment to improving the living and working conditions of oil industry employees following its nationalisation.

Following the departure of foreign employees from Khuzestan, the health-care network experienced a significant disruption. Up until 1950, the oil-rich regions boasted 10 specialists, 7 dentists, and 130 nurses. Furthermore, 4 hospitals with a combined capacity of 853 beds and 35 clinics had been established in the area. However, following the nationalisation of the oil industry, British doctors and nurses employed in these medical facilities declined to provide medical services to patients. Their refusal was attributed to their non-recognition of non-British management of the Oil Company. This refusal, coupled with acts of vandalism, equipment damage, and the removal of medical equipment from these centres, posed serious challenges to hospitals throughout Khuzestan.[26]

Following the departure of sixteen female nurses and twenty-six British medical staff on 3 October1951, Prime Minister Mosaddeq took immediate action. He appointed Nematolahi, a professor from Tehran University Medical School, to oversee the hospitals in the oil-rich regions of Khuzestan. Additionally, the Temporary Board of Directors of the National Oil Company dispatched medical doctors from Tehran to the hospitals in Khuzestan and strongly encouraged the doctors and medical staff of the Oil Company to remain in their positions.[27]

An article in the newspaper *Ettelaʿat* highlighted the health and nutrition challenges faced by workers in the oil-rich areas. The report indicated that the health condition of workers in these regions was generally poor. Many of them lacked fuel for cooking, forcing them to resort to using black oil, which posed several issues. Black oil, when burned, emits a foul odour, and it produces black soot, which can contaminate food. Unfortunately, due to inhaling the polluted air and consuming food contaminated with soot, these workers often fell ill, experiencing severe chest pains and frequent bouts of constipation.[28]

As per a report in the newspaper *Ettelaʿat*, the health conditions of workers residing in oil-rich areas were notably unfavourable. The report highlighted a significant issue: many workers lacked access to quality cooking fuel, leading them to resort to using black oil. Unfortunately, the combustion of black oil and the release of soot into the air had detrimental effects. Not only was it harmful to breathe the polluted air, but the soot settling on their food also contaminated it. Consequently, these workers often suffered from health issues, including severe chest pain and constipation, resulting from inhaling polluted air and consuming contaminated food.[29]

Additionally, the report emphasised that a significant portion of the workers faced a shortage of quality cooking fuel, resulting in their reliance on black oil as a substitute. The combustion of this oil, coupled with the release of soot into the air, had detrimental effects on both respiratory health and food safety. The deposition of soot particles onto their food items led to food contamination, heightening the risk of illnesses among the workers. As a consequence of their exposure to polluted air and consumption of contaminated food, these workers often suffered from health issues, including severe chest pain and constipation.[30]

Workers who resided in tents were often deprived of the opportunity to consume warm meals. Their usual diet was typically limited to yogurt and dates, and when yogurt was scarce, bread and dates became the norm. Furthermore, these workers faced a lack of adequate lighting at night and frequently inhabited remote desert regions, which posed a significant challenge in terms of accessing clean water. As a consequence of the absence of running water or proper plumbing facilities in these locations, workers had to either transport water from distant sources or utilise stagnant and unclean water sources such as fetid marshes. This precarious situation underscores the dire conditions endured by workers living in tents.[31]

In conclusion, following the departure of foreign nationals from Khuzestan, the healthcare sector was severely impacted by a shortage of medical professionals, particularly doctors and nurses. Attracting medical practitioners to the region, amid widespread staff shortages nationwide, posed a significant challenge for the National Oil Company. The revolutionary fervour that swept the country during the oil nationalisation campaign hindered the development of effective contingency plans, resulting in a lack of foresight in addressing the issue.[32] Additionally, health insurance issues acted as an impediment, further exacerbating the difficulties faced by the workers. With an insufficient number of medical personnel, patients were compelled to seek care in the private healthcare sector, where workers' health insurance was not accepted. This unfortunate situation underscores the inherent challenges in providing adequate medical care to workers in Khuzestan.

> A petition, signed by a significant number of Abadan Refinery workers, has come to the attention of the newspaper. The petition highlights various shortcomings within the social insurance law, particularly regarding healthcare and hospitalisation. Given the challenging circumstances prevailing in Khuzestan, the workers express their dissatisfaction with the existing law and advocate for a comprehensive reform that better serves the underprivileged class. It is worth noting that the workers of Abadan Refinery played a pivotal role in supporting the foundations of the current government during the most challenging phases of the national movement. Therefore, the petition serves as a compelling reminder of the importance of addressing the needs and grievances of the working-class population, who have made significant contributions to the nation's progress.[33]

Labour Perseverance: Efforts and Aspirations

The labour movement during the period following the nationalisation of the oil industry was a complex and multifaceted phenomenon influenced by a range of political, economic, and social factors. While the nationalisation of the oil industry conferred greater control over resources to the state, it also had the potential to create new tensions and conflicts between workers and the state. These conflicts, in particular, were grounded in the rising expectations of workers regarding state performance.

Furthermore, the post-oil nationalisation period likely witnessed substantial shifts in labour relations and power dynamics, with workers advocating for enhanced rights and protections in light of escalating political instability. The state's response to these demands might have been apathetic, potentially resulting in some neglect of workers' well-being and concerns.

When examined through the perspective of the organised and unorganised labour movements within the oil industry, the three years period encompassing the full management by the National Iranian Oil Company over Iran's entire oil industry from 1951 to 1954 can be divided into two distinct phases: the period preceding the August coup d'état of 1953 and the period following until the arrival of the Oil Consortium in 1954.

During the initial phase, the government of Mosaddeq was deeply involved in negotiations aimed at resolving the issues stemming from the nationalisation of Iran's oil industry. Consequently, it did not prioritise the working conditions and livelihood of oil labourers as it should have. Instead, Mosaddeq hoped that the workers would understand the pressing nature of the situation and remain cooperative. In his assessment of Mosaddeq's labour policies, which inevitably encompassed oil labourers, Habib Ladjevardi astutely observes that during this period, various domestic matters, including labour organisation policies, were given secondary importance due to the primary focus on resolving the international dispute related to the nationalisation of the oil industry. Ladjevardi notes, 'Prime Minister Mosaddeq paid no particular attention to workers as a group; nor did he have any especial interest in the formation of labour organisations or political parties. To him labour was just another segment of the Iranian population which supported him. He demonstrated neither support for nor opposition to trade unions.'[34] According to the American embassy, Mosaddeq had 'plainly' stated to a visiting delegation of the International Confederation of Free Trade Unions in November 1952 that he had 'no use for organised labour nor did he intend (nor think it useful) to enlist its support for the government'.[35]

When analysing the first period from the perspective of the labour movement, two distinct trends become evident. Firstly, there was a faction within the labour movement that, while supporting Mosaddegh's government and its nationalisation of the oil industry, continued to advocate for improved working and living conditions. This movement grew increasingly persistent as the government remained in power. Within the oil industry, this inclination was primarily represented by the supporters of the National Front.

In contrast to this inclination, another trend was observable, primarily among organised workers in Khuzestan affiliated with Tudeh Party. This faction aimed to undermine Mosaddegh's government by accusing him of supporting the U.S. oil proposal and political agenda for resolving the oil crisis. As a result, they directed all their efforts towards weakening the government's position.

The Tudeh Party's stance on the nationalisation of the oil industry in Iran was marked by a notable ambiguity. This indecision stemmed from a lack of clear directive from the Soviet Union regarding its position on both the nationalisation process and Prime Minister Mohammad Mosaddeq's pivotal role in it. On one side, the Soviet Union perceived Mosaddeq's opposition to British interests as part of a broader anti-colonial struggle, aligning with the global movement against traditional colonial powers like Britain.[36] Conversely, within the inner circles of Kremlin policymakers, there was a faction that interpreted the nationalization efforts as playing into the strategic interests of the United States. This perspective posited that the move was a calculated attempt by the U.S. to displace Britain's influence, viewing it through the lens of the burgeoning Cold War dynamics. According to this school of thought, the nationalization of Iran's oil industry was merely a manoeuvre engineered by the United States to secure its own hegemonic position in the Cold War geopolitical landscape.[37]

Following the violent Nowruz strike of 1951, Khuzestan was once again placed under military rule. After suppressing the strike, the military administration initiated a concerted effort to dismantle the networks of the Tudeh Party and the CCFTU in Khuzestan, utilising all available means at its disposal. This encompassed a series of arrests, imprisonments, and deportations from Khuzestan that persisted throughout Mosaddeq's tenure. However, with the coup d'état of August 1953, this campaign expanded significantly, and we will delve further into these developments in the following pages.[38]

During this period, the phenomenon of workers' protests can be attributed to two distinct reasons. Firstly, protests were instigated by workers who had previously been employed in specific service sectors either directly managed by the Oil Company or heavily dependent on oil extraction and refining for their continued operation. These service sectors included cooks or domestic workers who had previously worked for the Oil Company and were suddenly left without employment or reassigned to new roles when British and other foreign employees departed:

> According to our correspondent in Abadan, around 200 cooks who had previously been employed by the British staff of the former Oil Company congregated at Telegraph House and initiated a protest, during which they were surrounded. Their sit-in was prompted by the company's decision to reassign them to different positions. Following their demonstration, three of the protesters were subsequently apprehended by the military governor.[39]

The second group of workers comprised those who operated independently but remained dependent on the oil industry, such as workers in ice factories. This category of workers had essentially become unemployed due to the decrease or complete halt in work in specific sectors of the oil industry: A report from Abadan reveals that a group of around 40 individuals who were previously contracted to distribute ice for the Oil Company have become unemployed and are currently occupying the telegraph office. Their joblessness stems from the National Oil Company's choice to allocate their tasks to the company's own employees as a cost-cutting measure.[40]

As labour activism persisted, primarily driven by concerns of unemployment or changes in employment, additional issues such as housing and healthcare gradually gained traction and became part of workers' demands. In May 1953, a significant group of Abadan Refinery workers organised a protest due to the lack of adequate health insurance coverage. They submitted a formal petition addressed to Mosaddeq. The language used in the petition by the workers conveyed loyalty and cooperation with the government, expressing their 'willingness to endure hardship and uphold the government's foundations even during the most challenging periods of the national movement'.[41]

The workers respectfully implored their 'beloved' prime minister to take action by drafting a new insurance law, citing the many deficiencies of the current law, particularly concerning healthcare and hospitalisation. The petition emphasised that 'the harsh living conditions prevailing in Khuzestan and other oil-rich regions disproportionately affected the deprived and working classes, whose welfare should be a priority for the national leader'.[42] Consequently, the workers demanded a 'comprehensive revision of the law to ensure greater protection and support for the marginalized class'.[43]

The labour movement was not confined solely to advocating for their trade union demands. Depending on the dynamic and radical political conditions of the country, the movement also assumed a political character. For instance, during the political crisis of 21 July 1952 (known as 30 Tir 1331 in the Iranian calendar), which resulted in a major upheaval in the governance structure of the country, significant protests erupted in Khuzestan.

Anvar Khameh'i, a prominent political activist who, along with Khalil Maleki, played a leading role in the split from the Tudeh Party, highlights two pivotal events during the Mosaddeq era. According to Khameh'i, the first event, which he considers the national uprising and the zenith of Iran's national movement, took place on 21 July 1952. The second event, which he views as the turning point of the national movement, was the coup d'état of 19 August 1953.

The July uprising can be seen as a consequence of Mohammad Mosaddeq's efforts to strengthen his government's position within the Iranian political landscape. He claimed that his policies aimed to overhaul Iran's financial, economic, and judicial systems. On 22 July 1952, Mosaddeq requested extraordinary powers from the Parliament for a duration of six months as part of his efforts. However, this request faced resistance from the majority of deputies in the Parliament. Ironically, beyond the parliamentary sphere, the pro-court, and Tudeh Party network, although operating underground, remained active and expressed unanimous opposition to Mosaddeq's request. They characterised it as a step toward declaring dictatorship and tyranny.

In response to this opposition, Mosaddeq sought the support of the King for his proposal and visited the court three days later. While the Shah agreed to grant Mosaddeq all the extraordinary powers he had requested, he did not concede to Mosaddeq's request for control over the Ministry of War, which the Shah considered a traditionally royal domain.

After the Shah's refusal to grant Mosaddeq control over the Ministry of War, Mosaddeq tendered his resignation to the Shah. The Shah accepted his resignation, and in the days that followed, he appointed Qavam, a seasoned politician who had played a crucial role in resolving the Azerbaijan crisis in Iran's favour in 1945–46, as the new prime minister. Qavam portrayed himself as the 'capable captain of Iran's ship in the stormy sea of internal and external crisis-causing policies'.

Qavam's appointment triggered a popular uprising in Tehran on 21 July, leading both the Shah and the Parliament to backtrack from their initial positions. This enabled Mosaddeq to return to power the following day. Tehran

Figure 6.1 'We will no longer allow foreigners to plunder our sources of wealth. From Mossadegh's speech in The Hague'. Demonstration in support of Mosaddeq, Tehran, July 1952

commemorated Mosaddeq's restoration to power on the following day. Interestingly, the Tudeh Party celebrated the defeat of the court and

Parliament, rather than Mosaddeq's reinstatement, in a rally held at Toupkhaneh (Sepah) Square. During this event, a young girl from Abadan also took to the stage to convey the message of the Khuzestan oil workers.[44]

Khuzestan responded to the thrilling news that occurred in Tehran in July with a mixture of excitement and apprehension. The Tudeh Party, in accordance with its national policy, alongside the CCFTU, declined to endorse Mosaddeq and condemned both Qavam and Mosaddeq as emanating from the same 'bourgeois lineage', representing mere facets of the same political establishment whose sole aim was to 'serve foreign interests, be they British or American'. Nonetheless, as recounted by Rahmat Jazani, the party's adherents in the province, despite disregarding the call from the party leadership, rallied behind Mosaddeq's National Front or Khalil Maleki's *Niru-ye Sevvom* Party. Both demonstrated remarkable fervour and dedication as they took to the streets.[45]

> This morning at five o'clock, all refinery workers commenced a strike, amassing nearly forty thousand individuals in front of the Telegraph Office. Included among these workers are those who oversee electricity, water, and ice provision in the city, thereby causing the shutdown of Abadan's electricity, water, and ice production sectors since this morning. Police officers have contacted the strike committee representatives, urging them to at least permit the utilisation of the ice, electricity, and water segments. However, the strikers remain unwavering in their demand, declaring that they are unwilling to resume work until Mosaddeq returns to office.[46]

The strike and sit-in at the Telegraph Office attracted substantial participation from Arab tribes residing around Abadan. Moreover, all shops, including bakers and butchers, ceased operations in solidarity with the strike. Several reports emerged in the evening of clashes between governor officers and the strikers across various parts of the city, resulting in injuries sustained by several individuals, including one officer and several soldiers.[47]

Upon learning of Mosaddeq's reinstatement, the strike in Khuzestan came to an end, prompting strikers to resume their work. However, the military governor's office continued to detain several strikers known for their support of the Tudeh party.[48]

The final documented activities of organised labour in the Khuzestan oil industry before the coup d'état of 1953 were meetings held in various oil towns in July 1953. These were convened and organised by the semi-clandestine CCFTU, The CCFTU's call to action urged its members to openly engage in the electoral process to nominate candidates representing oil workers for the third Congress of the World Federation of Trade Unions (WFTU), scheduled for July 1954 in Vienna.

Navid-e Azadi, a newspaper affiliated with the CCFTU, reported that from mid-August, numerous preparatory meetings occurred in Abadan and other oil towns. 'These meetings were characterized by the active involvement of working men and women of varied ages, who openly discussed the challenges encountered in their professions'. Key issues raised included the demand for 'the abolition of the punitive fine system', a remnant of the defunct Anglo-Iranian Oil Company (but still implemented by the Iranian Oil Company, and the call for 'improved healthcare policies'. Female worker representatives specifically advocated for 'equal pay and rights comparable to their male colleagues', along with 'enhanced nursery and maternity hospital facilities'. These demands by female workers received 'unequivocal support from male workers present at these meetings'.[49]

The report from *Navid-e Azadi* further states that while preparations for a Provincial Conference to appoint a delegation for the WFTU were underway, the arrest of oil workers in Aghajari and Ahvaz cast a pall over the campaign. The newspaper interpreted these arrests as an 'ominous sign, indicating imminent challenges for the labour movement in the oil industry'.[50] This apprehension was validated on 19 August 1953, just three days later, when a military coup d'état occurred in Tehran.

The Coup d'état of August 1953

Understanding the 1953 coup d'état merely in the framework of the British attempt to confront the nationalisation of the Iranian oil industry and return to the golden age of the Anglo-Iranian Oil Company is indeed a limited perspective. It's important to recognise that the Cold War context and the United States' anti-communist agenda played a significant role in shaping the events of that time. The global geopolitical landscape, with its ideological and power struggles, added complexity to the situation in Iran and influenced the actions of both Western powers and local actors. A more comprehensive understanding of history takes into account these broader factors that contributed to the 1953 coup d'état and its consequences.[51]

Indeed, there were clear links between the nationalisation of the Iranian oil industry and the coup d'état staged in August 1953. After the nationalisation of the oil industry, the British government focused on ousting Prime Minister Mohammad Mosaddeq through a coup d'état. They sought active support from the United States to achieve this goal and convinced the U.S. to join in opposing the Iranian government.

The change in leadership in the United Kingdom, with the Conservatives coming to power, played a role in shaping British policy towards Iran. Prime Minister Winston Churchill's visit to the United States in March 1952 and his 'Iron Curtain' speech at Westminster College in Fulton were aimed at bridging British oil interests in Iran with the U.S. concern about the spread of communism in the Middle East.

The decisive factor that led the United States to support the coup d'état was the British policy of linking the Iranian nationalisation of the oil industry to American fears of communism. British officials began trying to gain U.S. approval for Mosaddeq's removal in October 1952, and in November 1952, the Central Intelligence Agency collaborated with the British Secret Intelligence Service (MI6) to overthrow Mosaddeq. This collaboration resulted in Operation Ajax, which led to the overthrow of Mosaddeq and the reinstatement of the Shah as the ruler of Iran in August 1953.[52]

The August 1953 coup d'état in Iran cannot be fully understood by solely focusing on British attempts to counter the nationalisation of the Iranian oil industry. It is crucial to consider the broader geopolitical context of the Cold War and the United States' anti-communist policies.

The Cold War was a defining feature of the post-Second World War world order, characterised by the rivalry between the United States and the Soviet Union. During this period, both superpowers were deeply concerned about the spread of communism and sought to influence and control countries and regions that were strategically important.

In the case of Iran, the United States was increasingly worried about the potential for communist influence in the region, especially given Iran's proximity to the Soviet Union and its significant oil resources. This anti-communist obsession played a significant role in shaping U.S. policy towards Iran.

The British, too, were motivated by their interests in Iranian oil, but the alignment of their goals with U.S. anti-communist concerns was a critical factor in gaining U.S. support for the coup d'état against Mosaddeq.[53]

Therefore, a comprehensive understanding of the 1953 coup d'état in Iran must take into account not only the economic interests of Western powers but also the larger global context of the Cold War and the strategic imperatives of the United States in containing communism. These factors converged to shape the events of that period, with far-reaching consequences for Iran and the region.

The coup d'état of 1953 has been the subject of extensive scholarly research, with numerous studies providing intricate and sometimes contradictory accounts and analyses of the event.[54] Nonetheless, the objective of this work is not to delve into the intricate political details of the coup d'état. Instead, the focus will be on exploring the practical implications of the coup d'état in the Khuzestan region, particularly on the employees of the oil industry and the lives of those who were reliant on it. The study examines the consequences that followed the coup d'état and how they impacted the individuals and communities that were most affected.

The news of the military coup d'état in Tehran, as recounted by Najaf Daryabandari, who was then in charge of foreign news of the Oil Company's daily news bulletin *Khabar-ha-ye Ruz*, was transmitted to Abadan via radio.[55] For much of the day, the city remained relatively calm, with no discernible

Figure 6.2 Midday scene in Tehran, 19 August 1953

sense of agitation. However, as the evening hours approached, a palpable sense of disorder began to take hold, as a faction of court and Kashani-Bagha'i supporters, chiefly members of Zahmatkeshan Party (Toilers Party)[56], initiated a series of demonstrations throughout the city.[57]

There was a conspicuous absence of protest by Mosaddeq's supporters within the city. In the months leading up to the coup d'état, the alliance among Mosaddeq's supporters had disintegrated. This alliance, which had reached its zenith during the announcement of the nationalisation of the oil industry, had begun to fracture along the fault lines between Mosaddeq's secular allies and the Ayatollah Kashani Islamists supports.

During this period, Hossein Makki, who had gained prominence during his visit to Abadan as the head of the Provincial Board of Directors of the National Iranian Oil Company with the aim of conquering the oil stronghold, gravitated closer to the Islamist supporters of the court following the crisis of July 1952. The fear of the communist Tudeh Party possibly gaining power had given rise to a new front that distanced a faction of Mosaddeq's supporters from him and drew them nearer to the royal court. This faction included figures such as Hossein Makki, Ayatollah Kashani, and Mozaffar Bagha'i.

The Shah's return three days after the coup d'état elicited a sense of relief, even among the Islamists who harboured deep apprehensions about the spread of communism. Ayatollah Boroujerdi, in a message, extended his congratulations to the Shah upon his return, underscoring the broader sentiment prevailing at the time.[58]

According to Daryabandari, in the days and weeks that followed, although the spectre of the coup d'état continued to loom large over Khuzestan, nevertheless, the daily rhythms of life and work persisted largely uninterrupted, with the exception of sporadic detentions of individuals known to be affiliated with Tudeh or CCFTU. However, matters took a turn for the worse when the government uncovered the Military Organisation of the Tudeh Party in August 1954, leading to a marked escalation in the severity of the situation.

The coup d'état of August 1953 unfolded in Abadan against the backdrop of sweltering summer heat that had melted the asphalt streets. This city, which had been the epicentre of violent and blood-soaked street protests in both 1946 and 1951, now experienced the coup d'état in a tranquil and seemingly disengaged manner.

As recounted by Daryabandari, in the days and weeks that ensued, while the shadow of the coup d'état continued to cast a long pall over Khuzestan, the everyday routines of life and work remained largely undisturbed. There were occasional detentions of individuals with known affiliations to Tudeh or CCFTU.[59] However, a significant shift occurred when the government uncovered the Military Organisation of the Tudeh Party in August 1954, resulting in a pronounced escalation in the severity of the situation.[60]

7

From Disparity to Planned Development: 1954–1962

The denouement of the year 1953 witnessed a series of momentous occurrences, most notably the culmination of Mosaddeq's trial in November. In the aftermath of Mosaddeq's ousting from power in August coup d'état, General Zahedi ascended to the position of prime minister, assuming the mantle of leadership for the nascent government. Under Zahedi's stewardship, the administration undertook two pivotal endeavours: firstly, the prosecution of Mosaddeq and the vigorous suppression of dissident voices, and secondly, the resuscitation of the oil industry through negotiations with a novel Oil Consortium entrusted with the responsibilities of exploration, extraction, refining, and sale of petroleum. Remarkably, the trial of Mosaddeq unfolded concurrently with the intricate deliberations surrounding the Consortium's prospective involvement.

Mosaddeq concluded his final defence in the military court with eloquent expressions, stating:

> The sole transgression of mine, the grave and exceedingly grave transgression, is that I have nationalized Iran's oil industry, dismantling the stronghold of colonisation and the imposition of colossal political and economic influence by the world's mightiest empires from this nation. I have defied the clutches of the most dreadful colonial and international espionage organisations, at the cost of my own and my family's disappearance, at the cost of my life, dignity, and possessions… I am fully aware that my destiny should serve as a lesson to the people who may endeavour, in the future, to break the chains of servitude and colonisation, perhaps in the heart of the Middle East.[1]

The verdict of the military court did not result in a death sentence as the prosecutor had desired. Rather, Mosaddeq was sentenced to three years in prison, followed by exile and a ban from politics. He remained in exile until his death in 1967.

The two architects of the coup, the United States and Britain, each had distinct motivations to find contentment in the consequences of their endeavours to topple Mosaddeq's government. For the United States, the installation of a military regime in Iran offered a sense of assurance, at least in the foreseeable future, in preventing Iran from falling into the Soviet sphere of influence.

Furthermore, this arrangement provided the United States with the lucrative benefit of capitalising on the orchestration of the coup d'état, as American oil companies gained access to exploit Iran's oil resources, resulting in substantial financial gains.

For Britain, the demise of Mosaddeq marked the culmination of a distressing and protracted two years ordeal, which bore significant ramifications for the rapid decline of the once formidable British Empire. While the Empire's decline had commenced with the conclusion of the Second World War and reached its zenith with the independence of India, it was the nationalisation of Iran's oil industry that assumed a global magnitude of greater significance. Nevertheless, the repercussions of ending this ordeal proved to be highly unpalatable for Britain. It entailed severing ties with the longstanding Anglo-Iranian Oil Company (AIOC), relinquishing their monopoly in Iran's oil industry, and reluctantly agreeing to join the nascent Oil Consortium comprising other international oil companies, prominently those from the United States. For Britain, this outcome was undeniably necessary, yet fraught with significant challenges and complexities.

Following the demise of Mosaddeq, the reinstatement of the AIOC in Iran emerged as the favoured course of action for the British authorities. However, the United States government promptly conveyed to their British counterparts, including AIOC chairman Sir William Fraser, that a return to the status quo was unattainable. Instead, a proposition was put forth to establish an Oil Consortium, wherein the AIOC, albeit under a different name, would coexist alongside other companies. In October 1953, a covert meeting orchestrated by the CIA took place in Amsterdam, bringing together Herbert Hoover, a seasoned oil businessman representing the United States government en route to Tehran, with Neville Gass and Basil Jackson from the AIOC. During this encounter, assurances were given to Gass and Jackson that, acknowledging the Iranian public's resistance to the AIOC's comeback, the interests of the AIOC would not be disregarded upon Hoover's arrival in Iran.[2]

Expressing disillusionment with their return to Iran, the management of the AIOC encountered significant obstacles in their endeavour to secure a share exceeding 50 per cent in the nascent Consortium. The United States vehemently opposed this ambition, emphasising its pivotal role in the ousting of Mosaddeq. Subsequently, in mid-December 1953, at the invitation of William Fraser, a pivotal meeting was convened in London. The gathering brought together six internationally renowned oil companies: Standard Oil of California, Standard Oil of New Jersey, Texaco, Gulf, Socony-Vacuum, Compagnie Française des Pétroles (CFP), and Shell, who convened at the AIOC's headquarters.

Following three months of negotiations, the formal establishment of a Consortium holding company known as Iranian Oil Participants Ltd. (IOP) was announced. The distribution of shares among the Consortium's stakeholders was as follows: The AIOC (later in November changed its name to British

Petroleum – BP) agreed to accept a 40 per cent share, five U.S. oil companies, Gulf Oil, Aramco partners – Standard Oil of California (SoCal, later Chevron), Standard Oil of New Jersey (later Exxon), Standard Oil Company of New York (later Mobil, then Exxon Mobile), and Texaco – each held an 8 per cent. The remaining 20 per cent was divided between Royal Dutch Shell (14 per cent), and Compagnie Française des Pétroles (later Total S.A., 6 per cent). The conclusive rendition of the Oil Consortium agreement, executed in September 1954 and subsequently ratified by both the Iranian Parliament and the Senate a month later.

The IOP assumed the role of the parent entity with the task of extracting, refining, and exporting the Iranian oil, overseeing two fully owned operating companies incorporated under Dutch jurisdiction, responsible for managing the oil industry in the southern region of Iran. These entities were named the Iranian Oil Exploration and Producing Company, entrusted with the task of conducting exploration and production activities, and the Iranian Oil Refining Company, tasked with refining operations. Both subordinate companies were granted full authority by the National Iranian Oil Company to supervise operations within the oil industry.

Regarding the geographical scope of the Consortium, it encompassed the area covered earlier by the AIOC, except the management of the Naft-e Shah Oilfield, the Kermanshah Refinery, and internal distribution facilities, aimed at supplying Iran's domestic market, which remained under the purview of the National Iranian Oil Company. The new agreement imposed a limit on Iran's share of income derived from oil sales, capping it at 50 per cent of the customary net profit sharing prevalent in the Middle East. In terms of duration, the agreement was designed to span a period of twenty-five years, extending until 1979, a duration that differed from the expiration of the 1933 Agreement by a mere one year.

In addition to the two operating companies, a separate Consortium entity known as Iranian Oil Services Ltd. was to be established, incorporated in England, and headquartered in London. This company's primary role was to furnish the operating companies with necessary supplies, engineering services, and non-Iranian personnel.[3] Furthermore, the National Iranian Oil Company undertook the task of overseeing auxiliary facilities and infrastructure, encompassing essential services such as water and electricity supply, industrial training and oil technical education, public transportation, road upkeep, housing, medical care, and social amenities.

To accomplish this aim, a designated entity known as the 'non-basic' or Organisation of Non-Industrial Tasks (ONIT) was instituted, with its management falling under the purview of the National Iranian Oil Company. In reference to the name of the newly established organisation, Alinaghi Alikhani, who joined in 1958, contends that the initial selection of a non-basic appellation was ill-suited, lacking in aesthetic appeal for purposes of promotion and failing to align with the fervour of the Iranian populace, who had experienced an unfortunate setback in their endeavour to nationalise the oil industry. Consequently, an alternative name, 'Non-Industrial Tasks', was opted. The ONIT operated from two offices situated in Khuzestan, namely Masjed-Soleyman and Abadan.[4]

By transferring the responsibility for non-industrial operations to the National Iranian Oil Company, the Consortium effectively absolved itself of the obligation to develop public infrastructure, particularly housing, which had garnered widespread attention during the nationalisation campaign. The dire living conditions in makeshift settlements such as *Kaghzabad* underscored the urgency for addressing housing issues. Consequently, in 1959, the Consortium handed over the administration of housing in Abadan to the NIOC, in accordance with the agreement to relinquish all 'non-basic' functions. Subsequently, the responsibility for construction was also transferred to the NIOC, albeit with certain challenges as the availability of capital to sustain the outlined construction program for the forthcoming years was uncertain.

During 1959, the Consortium made significant progress with its plans for establishing a resettlement community in Ahvaz, where houses were to be constructed by the company and offered on favourable terms to retiring workers from Abadan. Additionally, a home-ownership scheme was initiated in Ahwaz, envisioning the construction of over 500 houses to be sold to active employees with low down payments and a twenty-year amortisation period. These initiatives represented the final endeavours undertaken by the Consortium in this regard.[5]

Starting from 1960, a substantial shift in power dynamics occurred with the operational management of non-industrial activities in Abadan and the oil fields, granting the NIOC overarching authority over the day-to-day affairs of the oil industry. Reza Fallah was appointed as the inaugural director of the non-industrial operation organisation, marking a significant milestone in the organisational restructuring process.

The Socio-economic Disparities

After the initial two years period subsequent to the 1953 coup d'état, a time fraught with apprehension and the relentless suppression of former political activists affiliated with both the Tudeh Party and the Mosaddeq National Front, the monarchy orchestrated a momentous political overhaul replacing the pre-coup d'état order. In 1955, a momentous shift unfolded as Fazlullah Zahedi, the orchestrator of the coup d'état, was replaced by Hossein ʿAla, a trusted confidant of the Shah. Concurrently, the establishment of two political parties, namely *Mardom* and *Melliyoun*, emerged as loyalist factions aligned with the royal court.

Further transforming the political landscape, a pivotal development materialised in 1957 with the aid of the CIA, culminating in the formation of the *Sazeman-e Ettelaʿat va Amniyat-e Keshvar* (Organisation of National Intelligence and Security), colloquially referred to as SAVAK. This intelligence and security agency emerged as a substitute for the military governorship, which had wielded active control over the political realm for the four years period following the coup d'état. However, SAVAK's mission extended beyond the mere surveillance and suppression of the government's political adversaries. It embraced a far-reaching purpose that transcended the boundaries of monitoring dissident elements. SAVAK assumed a comprehensive role of monitoring civil society and shaping the public sphere within the national frontiers and exerting influence beyond its confines.

In the 1950s, Iran bore witness to a tumultuous era characterised by severe economic downturn and political oppression. The immediate aftermath of the August 1953 coup d'état resulted in a far-reaching wave of repression that permeated every facet of Iran's political landscape. The reinstatement of autocratic governance effectively quashed the twelve years (1941–53) endeavour of engaging in participatory politics. Subsequently, the period spanning from 1953 to 1960 was marked by desolation, with the labour movement reaching its nadir. In contrast to the extensive nationwide labour movement observed during the 1940s, the post-1953 coup d'état era witnessed the emergence of fragmented labour activities confined to select labour-intensive complexes and industries at the provincial level.

Surprisingly, in contrast to the 1940s, there emerged a notable absence of collaboration between the labour movement and other guilds or political factions. Each of these movements charted its own course, operating independently and exhibiting a disinterest towards one another. The political movement, driven by the objective of challenging the government that had assumed power in the aftermath of the coup d'état, aimed to denounce the ensuing repression. Their aspiration was to create a small opening, allowing a glimmer of hope to penetrate, granting respite to supporters of the anti-government cause, and enabling them to conduct their activities unhindered. In stark contrast, the labour movement displayed indifference towards the tumultuous political climate, directing its attention towards matters directly linked to securing the means for workers to sustain themselves economically.

The precipitous decline of Iranian oil revenue by 55 per cent towards the close of the 1950s served as a catalyst for an unabated economic crisis, which in turn ignited social discontent among industrial workers and the impoverished labouring poor. Furthermore, the subsequent 13 per cent drop in Iranian oil prices in 1960 pushed the nation perilously close to the brink of complete economic collapse. As the Iranian government cautiously navigated negotiations with the Consortium of Oil Companies, their primary objective was to secure an augmentation, or at the very least, the preservation of the country's oil revenue.

Although one of the immediate ramifications of the 1953 coup d'état, next to reaching agreement with Consortium, was the limited restoration of Iran's ability to engage in oil sales within the international market, neither the revenue generated from oil exports, nor the substantial assistance provided by the Eisenhower administration could sufficiently offset Iran's persistent budget deficit. The imperative for sustainable economic growth, capable of securing the government's legitimacy post-coup d'état, was a shared concern for both the government itself and its international backers. Numerous scholars specialising in applied development theories viewed Iran in the 1950s, with its substantial oil income, as an ideal case study to test their proposed strategies, primarily focused on economic rather than political development. For the United States, this endeavour represented a concerted effort to connect Iran's globally acquired oil wealth with its internal economic development, all in alignment with the United States' Cold War strategic objectives.

During the latter part of the 1950s, the government's reliance on loans to address the nation's deficit gave rise to a rapid escalation in both inflation rates and the cost of living index. In the year 1959, it became evident that Iran's foreign exchange reserves were undergoing an extravagant depletion, amounting to an annual loss of approximately fifty million dollars. This alarming situation necessitated the implementation of corrective measures to address the issue of dwindling reserves. Consequently, import restrictions were put into effect, primarily achieved through a rigorous tightening of importers' credits. Furthermore, some steps were taken as a measure to curb the outflow of foreign currency and to safeguard the country's economic stability. By imposing stricter controls on import financing, the authorities aimed to regulate the influx of foreign goods and mitigate the adverse impact of the foreign exchange drain on the national economy. Such prudent actions sought to address the economic challenges and ensure a more sustainable economic trajectory for Iran during that period.

In the annals of 1959, the erstwhile prevailing era of economic euphoria, commonly referred to as the 'honeymoon', reached its culmination, an epoch characterised by burgeoning prosperity since the Consortium oil settlement in late 1954. Over the span of four years, an unabated boom permeated most sectors of the economy, liberating it from the shackles of foreign exchange constraints. This newfound affluence led to a deluge of diverse consumer goods inundating Iran, coinciding with successive years of bountiful agricultural yields.

The affluence of early 1959 surpassed all previous manifestations of plenty, and the overall increments for the year significantly exceeded those of the immediately preceding years. According to the National Bank (*Bank Melli*) composite index for seven cities (with a base of 1936–37), the average stood at 1456 during 1959, indicating an impressive 10.1 per cent surge over the 1958 average figure. By comparison, the corresponding increase in 1958 over 1957 had been a mere 0.2 per cent.[6]

A glimpse into the perspective of the U.S. Embassy's unskilled workers' basket for Tehran during 1959 revealed a noteworthy 9.4 per cent escalation over the 1958 average, signifying the extent of prosperity. Furthermore, the average for Isfahan registered a remarkable 22.3 per cent surge compared to the previous year's figures, providing a glimpse into the broader economic landscape of that time.[7]

In 1961, the Iranian Ministry of Labour conducted a comprehensive survey in Tehran to assess the prices of essential commodities comprising the workers' market basket. The findings were deeply troubling, exposing the stark reality that 'a worker with a wife and two children needed to earn a minimum of 178 rials (2.37 dollars) per day to provide their family with the bare necessities and maintain a minimum standard of decency and well-being'. This stood in stark contrast to the minimum wage of fifty rials (0.66 dollars) per day in Tehran. For the rest of the country, the minimum wage remained unchanged since 1947, at thirty-five rials (0.46 dollars) per day.[8]

In Khuzestan, according to a report compiled by the U.S. Embassy, one of the most pressing long-term challenges confronting the oil industry in Iran was the escalating issue of unemployment affecting a substantial community of workers and their families who maintained a paternalistic relationship with the Consortium companies. In 1957, the population of Abadan was estimated to be around 283,000 inhabitants, of which approximately 160,000 were reported to be directly reliant on the oil companies for their livelihoods. However, the number of wage earners within this group was relatively low, with just over 30,000 individuals, out of which 29,000 were employed by the oil companies themselves. This created a notable disparity between the population dependent on the companies and those actively engaged in wage-earning activities. The report highlighted that Abadan was primarily a mono-industrial region, devoid of prospects for the establishment of additional industries. As a result, the outlook for economic diversification and employment opportunities beyond the oil sector was bleak. The report further projected that by 1960, in addition to the estimated 50,000 unemployed individuals in the bazaar area of Abadan, another 50,000 adults, many of them well-educated and comprising children or other dependents of oil workers, would reside in or near company-provided housing and be partially dependent on the oil companies for their future sustenance.

With the passage of time, this particular group of dependents could potentially become susceptible to exploitation by demagogues and subversive elements if appropriate measures were not taken. However, the report noted that the Consortium did not anticipate the Iranian government being prepared to assume a fair share of responsibility in addressing this matter. As a result, there seemed to be no immediate solution to this escalating problem, which continued to grow more severe with each passing month and year.[9]

The narrative provided by the Bamshad newspaper reporter from Abadan presents a stark contrast in living conditions and privileges among the city's inhabitants:

> Life appears to be exceedingly comfortable and easy for certain individuals associated with the company, particularly office employees and specialists. Residential neighbourhoods like Braim and Bovardeh, constructed in the style of European cities, provide a high standard of living, making life notably comfortable for these privileged individuals. Moreover, exclusive amenities such as the Taj Cinema, reserved for senior employees, and various oil and Iran clubs, serve as prime sources of entertainment. The company bestows special benefits upon its employees, including access to company cars, telephones, and other conveniences, fostering an environment of relative luxury and ease for this specific group. However, the opposite end of the spectrum presents a contrasting reality for the majority of ordinary people in Abadan, who endure harsh conditions, particularly under the relentless heat. These individuals reside in subpar living conditions with dirty and hot houses, uncomfortable transportation, and costly and deteriorated necessities. Additionally, there is a lack of access to adequate healthcare, medicine, and recreational opportunities, leading to a sense of deprivation among this segment of the population.[10]

The reporter's observations of the Hasirabad and Chadorabad neighbourhoods reveal a stark demonstration of class distinction and its unsightly consequences. Abadan appears to be a city divided into two distinct and opposing groups: the corporate employees, living in relatively privileged conditions in neighbourhoods such as Braim and Bovardeh, and the less fortunate residents in areas such as Chadorabad and Hasirabad, grappling with challenging living conditions, including poor housing and limited access to basic necessities.

> The transportation situation is emblematic of the social divide, with two distinct categories of vehicles catering to different socio-economic groups. Neat and tidy individuals enjoy the luxury of two Koran buses, while the less fortunate are forced to travel in covered truck trailers, at the price of one Koran, highlighting the clear disparity in access to basic amenities.
>
> The presence of well-equipped clubs, swimming pools, tennis courts, and other recreational facilities exclusively accessible to a specific group accentuates the divide between the privileged and the marginalized in Abadan. The former group enjoys comfort and respite from the scorching heat under fans and air conditioners, while the latter grapples with the heat in tin and straw houses, alongside livestock, and amid unsanitary conditions.
>
> Overall, what one can see is a divided society, where the lives of oil senior and office employees are replete with comfort and luxury, while a significant portion of the population struggles under dire living conditions, experiencing inequality in access to basic necessities and recreational opportunities.[11]

The economic recession yielded immediate consequences in the form of social and political instability, characterised by widespread social grievances and protests at the grassroots level, as well as political turmoil among the ruling elites at the upper echelons of power. The nation found itself enveloped.

Amid concerns within the Iranian political establishment regarding the nation's declining economy and its subsequent social ramifications, the United States, despite its significant role in orchestrating the existing political deadlock and economic recession through its involvement in the 1953 coup d'état, began aligning itself with Iranian reformist political elites. The United States did not hide its profound apprehension regarding the prevailing social and political unrest in Iran, recognising the potential for the emergence of 'communist agitprop' in the midst of the Cold War.

The post-Second World War era witnessed the apex of anti-colonial and national liberation movements worldwide, which were marked by a strong element of anti-imperialism and anti-American sentiment. These movements were entwined with the escalating tensions of the globally reshaped landscape, commonly known as the Cold War. The necessity for implementing authoritarian reforms, primarily focused on economic and social development, can be traced back to the Four Points Program initiated by Democratic President Harry Truman in 1949. This concern persisted even before the Democrats regained power in the United States in 1961, as they pursued economic and liberal reforms in Iran.[12] The Democrats were apprehensive about the stagnation of their earlier proposals, prompting the United States administration during the presidency of JF Kennedy (1961–63) to issue a clear directive to their allies in the global south: either embrace top-down reforms or risk facing bottom-up revolts that would dismantle their rule.

Life and Work under Non-Industrial Task Management

Nine months following the wage increase and its subsequent repercussions, the ONIT commenced its operations on the 1st of January 1956, under the patronage of the Iranian National Oil Company, in alignment with the implementation of the seventeenth article of the Iranian Oil Participants Agreement. The initial focus of the transfer process was directed towards the healthcare network within the oil industry.[13]

The Department of Public Health, operating within the framework of the ONIT, launched a comprehensive campaign against malaria in Abadan and Khorramshahr. Additionally, the department assumed the responsibility of manufacturing vaccines for diseases such as smallpox, typhoid, diphtheria, pertussis, and tetanus. Vaccination against diphtheria was successfully administered to over 10,000 school students.[14] Furthermore, with the allocation of funds from the Abadan Municipal and the provision of essential equipment by the National Oil Company, the construction of a thirty-bed hospital building in Abadan was completed, marking a significant milestone in the development of healthcare facilities within the region.[15]

The provision of housing for oil industry employees constituted another significant aspect within the ONIT's responsibilities. In early 1955, plans were set forth to construct 500 houses in Abadan. However, by early October, the number had increased to 800, all of which were made available to the workers within a span of two years. Furthermore, a housing program was initiated in the oil fields, resulting in the completion of 450 houses within a year, with 200 of them situated in Aghajari. The era of rudimentary dwellings made of bamboo branches or makeshift cement structures had almost become a relic of the past, as improved housing facilities were now being provided to the workers.[16]

Over the subsequent years, the housing policy of the ONIT underwent gradual transformations. Concurrently with the expansion of various development projects in Khuzestan Province, as will be elaborated upon in the forthcoming pages, the ONIT aligned its housing policies more closely with these development projects, resulting in a comprehensive provision of housing that extended beyond the confines of the oil industry alone. Instead, it encompassed all employees engaged in industrial and development projects within the regional context.[17]

The outsourcing of housing project gradually emerged as a key consideration. Housing construction projects were entrusted to contractors selected through competitive tenders, who were then responsible for directly providing housing to the oil industry employees, either through ownership or rental arrangements. In this new approach, the ONIT's restricted itself to granting housing allowances, relinquishing the responsibility for housing maintenance and repair. This paradigm gradually encompassed all construction initiatives within the oil industry, encompassing not only oil industry guest houses but also other non-industrial buildings under the purview of the National Iranian Oil Company.[18]

In general, discernible indications of amelioration in both labour and living conditions for employees, particularly the oil workers, could be observed. However, these advancements remained insufficient in eradicating the underlying grievances prompting protests among oil industry workers. The protest extended beyond the exorbitant costs associated with securing basic necessities. It encompassed a wider denunciation of the infringement upon the workers' inherent human dignity. Notably, the prohibition imposed upon workers, barring their access to certain entertaining establishments exclusively reserved for the privileged echelons of the employees, was perceived by the workers as a betrayal of the progress achieved during the nationalisation of the oil industry – an era that purportedly dismantled hierarchies governing access to comforts, educational opportunities, and recreational amenities.

The conduct exhibited by certain foreign managers, particularly those of Dutch or British origin, towards Iranian employees constituted an additional source of discontentment. As recounted by numerous Iranian employees within the oil industry, American managers were perceived as displaying a greater willingness to engage with their Iranian counterparts, while simultaneously ridiculing the colonial attitudes demonstrated by their British and, at times, Dutch counterparts. A report highlights an occurrence wherein select foreign technical experts, specifically those of Dutch nationality, engaged in a contentious altercation with certain Iranian employees, subjecting them to derogatory remarks. In response to this deplorable behaviour, the Iranian employees have devised a collective plan to stage a strike in order to bring an end to such offensive treatment perpetuated by foreign specialists. In light of this development, several senior officials from the Consortium journeyed from London to Tehran and Abadan to offer solace and reassurance to the Iranian employees.[19]

In another report featured in the periodic publication *Khwandaniha*, the ill-conduct exhibited by specific foreign technicians or managers towards Iranian employees is documented as follows:

> The Consortium has gradually reinstated regulations that had been lost since the nationalisation of the oil industry. One such regulation entails the prohibition of workers from accessing the Taj Cinema. Although seemingly trivial and inconsequential, this restriction has ignited anger and concern among the workers. It has sparked worries regarding potential future decisions, prompting some to question the intentions behind such actions. These recent events compelled the workers to take drastic measures in order to convey their sentiments to government officials, a course of action that was met with disapproval by the majority. This reaction stemmed from the fact that none of the workers participated in the festivities at the beginning of the week. Additionally, the workers' club refrained from adorning its entrance as it had done in previous years, and no ceremony was held within its premises.
>
> The decision made by the workers in Abadan garnered attention and discussion. Recognizing the immense collective power wielded by the workers in Abadan, both governmental and military circles took note of the matter. Meetings were convened to address the situation, with Dr. Amini, the minister of justice, assuming responsibility for handling the issue and traveling to Khuzestan to partake in the proceedings. Following the meeting, he embarked on a tour of the city and visited the workers' club, where he inquired about the workers' absence from the celebration. Some of the workers' leaders provided explanations, which caught the minister's attention. He urged the workers to set aside their grievances and actively participate in the celebration. Later that evening, a gathering took place with the presence of several high-ranking officials from the Oil Company, including the head of the Abadan Refinery, as well as the governor of Abadan.

> During the assembly, the governor delivered a speech acknowledging that the workers in Abadan had become accustomed to a particular situation over the three years since the nationalisation of the oil industry. He emphasized that the heads of the Oil Company could not carry out their duties in a peaceful environment devoid of suspicion.
>
> In general, the information obtained indicates that Dr. Amini elucidated the morale of Iranian workers during the meetings he held with the managers of the Oil Company and the oil refining company. He underscored the unique circumstances in Iran resulting from the nationalisation of the oil industry, which differ from those in other oil-rich regions of the Persian Gulf. He stressed the need for an approach that avoids arousing suspicion, discomfort, and anger among the workers. Furthermore, in his interactions with the workers, he reminded them that problems can be better resolved within an environment of mutual understanding. Other reports suggest that Dr. Amini's impactful speeches in Abadan partially quelled unrest. Upon his return to Tehran, he submitted a comprehensive report on the situation in Abadan to the government. The aim was to initiate negotiations with the Consortium's leaders in Tehran, with the objective of alleviating anxiety in Abadan.[20]

During the Nowruz 1955 Shah and his wife, Soraya, made a journey to Khuzestan, where they embarked to visit the oil installations. In a speech to the oil workers, the Shah conscientiously acknowledged the prevailing economic challenges confronted by the oil industry, all according to him that arose as a consequence of the nationalisation of the oil and demonstrated his earnest commitment to enhancing the welfare of the oil workers. He solemnly pledged to increase their wages, improve working conditions, and accord paramount importance to the amelioration of their health and overall well-being.[21]

Three weeks later, on 26 March 1955, the General Manager of the Oil Exploration and Producing Company, the Iranian Oil Refining Company by publishing a memorandum, reached between the representative of oil workers,

Table 7.1 *Workers' wage increase (rials per day), 1955*

Grade	Old wage	New wage
Unskilled	40	82
3	48	98.5
2	56	115
1	68	139
Foreman (*Ostadkar*)	84	164

Source: Documentation Centre of the Iran Ministry of Petroleum.

the Management of both oilfields and refinery, announced the increase of the wages of the unskilled, grades rage of 1–3 by 105 per cent and the foreman (*Ostadkar*) by 100 per cent. Astonishingly, the wage increase scheme did not extend to other employees, primarily comprising office employees and engineers.[22]

Moreover, according to the memorandum, the increase included the seven rials per day Temporary Ration Allowance, previously paid to all workers and two rials per day Rental Allowance previously paid to workers not occupying company housing. The two rials per day Transport Allowance previously paid to all 'regular workers' continued to be paid for each day.[23] Nonetheless, in light of the wage increase, it was agreed that the food ration of 480 rials per month to be cut.[24] Furthermore, As stipulated in the memorandum, the food items available for purchase at the Company Food Shops would continue to be sold at the existing price for an additional month. However, it was duly announced that subsequent to this period, the new price structure will be implemented accordingly.[25]

Despite the initial reception of the wage increase with appreciation among the workers, murmurs of dissatisfaction soon emerged. The cause of this discontent stemmed from the subsequent rise in food prices that accompanied the wage hike. According to a report published in the periodical *Khwandaniha*:

> The reports received by the Iranian National Oil Company and the government indicate a significant discontentment among the workers due to a sudden and substantial increase in the prices of essential commodities, such as rice, ice, and housing rent. This increase, ranging from three to five times the previous prices, has generated a strong reaction among the workers. Despite the recent doubling of wages by the Consortium, the subsequent surge in food prices at the Company's Food Shops has led many workers to believe that their previous income, in combination with the prices of three months ago, provided a better standard of living. The unexpected escalation in prices, preceding the salary hike, has greatly unsettled the workers. The exorbitant prices of the Company's food items have also had a ripple effect on the overall market in Abadan, causing a sudden surge in prices of other goods. Consequently, not only the thirty thousand oil workers, but also tens of thousands of residents in Abadan, have experienced discomfort and attribute their dissatisfaction to the actions of the Consortium.[26]

Two-and-half years later, in September 1957, the National Iranian Oil Company's Contractual Department by issuing a circular, announced that as a result of the negotiations conducted by the Minimum Wage Commission, the wages and benefits of all National Iranian Oil Company contractual formal workers, would be implemented as follows:

1. Wages:

Table 7.2 *Legal grades and legal wages, 1957*

Legal grades	Legal wages – rials per day
Unskilled worker	99
Grade 1	11,880
Grade 2	13,860
Grade 3	16,830
Forman	198

Source: The National Iranian Oil Company's Contractual Department, Circular no. 43, 21 September 1957.

2. Assistance in Kind:

A portion of the new wages, equivalent to 417 rials per month, would be provided to workers by the company's grocery stores, and the consumption cost of the following items, as outlined in the Minimum Wage Table, would be covered:

  a. Fifty kilograms of flour per month
  b. Two kilograms of sugar per month

During each wage payment period, an amount equivalent to 192 rials will be deducted from the workers' wages for the aforementioned 417 rials.

3. Provision of Other Grocery Items:

The prices of additional grocery items, as listed in the Minimum Wage Table, would be communicated to the workers by the grocery department based on the agreed-upon prices in the Minimum Wage Commission and through separate circulars.

4. Special Assistance:

In addition to the aforementioned provisions, it was agreed to allocate a one-time special assistance amount for workers to purchase fuel oil. The amount of 480 rials (equivalent to sixty rials per month from the first day of Mordad until the end of Esfand (July–February) would be deposited in a separate account in the name of each worker. These funds would be used to purchase shares from the cooperative company that would be established.

5. Home Keep-Maintenance Expenses:

Starting from the first day of July 1957, the home care expenses of the company's residences will be adjusted as follows:

Table 7.3 *Home care expenses in refinery and oilfields 1959*

Number of rooms	Home care expenses in Abadan Refinery, rials per day	Home care expenses in the oilfields rials per day
One room	10	8
Two rooms	14	14
Three rooms	18	18
Four rooms	22	22

Sources: U.S. Embassy in Tehran, First Secretary Annual Labour Report 1959, U.S. National Archive, 888.06/6-460.

6. Calculation of Differences:

An itemised statement of account would be provided to each worker, as following:

a. The wage difference based on the number of hours worked during this period and the corresponding amount to be received according to the new wage rate.
b. An amount of 179 rials for Abadan and 204 rials for oilfields areas will be deducted accordingly.
c. The price of flour and sugar, as per the new Minimum Wage Table (417 rials), would be paid by the workers each month, resulting in a deduction of 179 rials for Abadan and 204 rials for oilfields areas.
d. The difference in the new and old rates of home care expenses will be deducted from the accounts of workers residing in company residences.

An additional instance of the Consortium's wage negotiations ended with almost same conclusion took place in early April 1959, culminating in the acceptance of a Consortium counteroffer that had undergone multiple revisions. This counteroffer entailed the following provisions: (1) a 10 per cent across-the-board increase in wages; (2) a new allowance of five rials per day for labourers not occupying company-provided housing; (3) a commitment by the Consortium to raise the wages of the most productive 10 per cent of the workforce; and (4) participation in a tripartite committee comprising Government, management, and labour representatives, tasked with evaluating the workers' standard of living over several months, using the workers' current basket of goods as the basis for determining the minimum wage standard.

In response to the ten rials wage increase, the bazaar shopkeepers in the oil communities reacted as one might expect. Upon learning of the wage hike, they promptly raised their prices, effectively nullifying any additional income gained by the oil workers. Consequently, the oil workers found themselves without any substantial increase in disposable income. However, the repercussions

Figure 7.1 Abadan Refinery Fire Department, 1956

extended beyond the oil industry, as labourers in other sectors, who had not received comparable wage increases, were now burdened with the prospect of paying higher prices for goods purchased in the same bazaar shops.

This situation had a definite inflationary impact, leading to a growing realisation that the oil workers' wages had been elevated to a level significantly divergent from the prevailing wage rates in other industries. The disparity in wage levels between oil workers and workers in other sectors became increasingly apparent, sparking concerns about equitable compensation within the broader labour force.[27]

Consortium Scheme: Path for Redeeming 'Surplus Workers'

The Consortium's contemplation of labour force reorganisation and the potential downsizing of the oil workforce, classified as 'surplus labour', was a recurring theme since its inception in the Iranian oil industry in 1954.[28] At that juncture, a comprehensive tally of 46,391 workers was documented. Among this cohort, a contingent of 24,278 workers secured employment at the Abadan Refinery, whereas the oil fields boasted an enlistment of 16,113 workers. As for the residual cohort of 6,000 individuals, they primarily comprised unskilled labourers, officially referred to as contract workers.[29] Amid the deliberations conducted in the realm of workforce downsizing, as exemplified by the Abadan Refinery, a contemplated course of action involved a reduction in the labour force to a count of 12,000 workers.[30]

According to a report compiled by the British Embassy in Tehran in 1955, 'the Consortium of the Oil Companies are probably employing some 11,000 more workers than they need, or likely to need during the next two or three years'.[31] Four years later, in 1959, the U.S. Embassy in Tehran had compiled a report that shed light on the labour situation at the Consortium's refinery operation in Abadan. The report highlighted still a notable surplus of labour at the refinery, as 'it currently employed nearly 20,000 workers'. Interestingly, 'there were observations that the refinery could function efficiently with a labour force half that size, but the immediate objective of the Consortium was not geared towards achieving such reductions at once. Instead, they initially aimed to identify essential positions that could potentially lead to a rationalisation down to approximately 17,000 workers. However, it was hinted that if such a reduction were implemented, there could be subsequent steps taken to further reduce the workforce'. Report continues with further steps taken by the National Iranian Oil Company to address this surplus labour situation by 'enlisting the expertise of Mr. John Alexander-Sinclair, a United Nations resettlement and refugee expert. He was engaged for a trial period of three months to survey the redundant labour situation at the Consortium. At the conclusion of this period, Mr. Alexander-Sinclair presented recommendations centred around the creation of small agricultural communities throughout the country, comprising retiring or terminated oil workers. The intent behind this proposal was to resettle the surplus labour in more sustainable and productive settings. However, the Consortium did not view this scheme as highly practical, and it lacked appeal primarily due to the substantial costs associated with its implementation, which the Consortium would have had to bear'.[32]

The Consortium persisted in its adherence to a predefined criterion for workforce reduction, even in the year 1961, when Iran was grappling with widespread unemployment. Despite the prevailing economic circumstances, the Consortium proceeded to terminate the employment of 4,000 workers. This action elicited a concerned response from the U.S. Embassy's Labour Attaché, who articulated that the true ramifications of this downsizing would not be immediately apparent due to the fact that the industry was providing legally mandated severance pay (equivalent to as much as three years' salary), in addition to a bonus and transportation assistance for laid-off workers relocating to any part of Iran. However, the Attaché lamented the absence of a comprehensive job counselling and relocation program tailored to accommodate the highly skilled oil workers in vacant positions elsewhere in the country, expressing regret over the lack of such an initiative.[33]

It is worth noting that throughout this process of manpower reduction, the Consortium remained wary of the potential for labour protests and sought to devise measures to address this concern. Consequently, a compensation plan was devised, comprising of two primary measures, ostensibly aimed at mitigating the likelihood of protests. Firstly, employees were afforded the opportunity of a voluntary buyout, wherein they could opt for early retirement by providing compensation equivalent to two months' salary for each year of service in the oil industry. Subsequently, workers who fulfilled any of the following conditions were designated as redundant: those aged forty or older, individuals with over twenty years of work experience, or those with less than six years of formal education.

While the Oil Consortium perceived the reduction of manpower as an administrative decision that could be resolved through financial compensation, often surpassing the customary amounts in Iran's employment practices, the Iranian government and the National Iranian Oil Company assigned great significance to the subsequent process of the workers' buyouts. This gave rise to crucial inquiries concerning how the unemployed workforce would utilise the redemption funds and reintegrate into the social fabric of the nation. Matters such as seeking new employment opportunities, embarking on entrepreneurial ventures, or pursuing further education became pivotal considerations for both the government and the National Iranian Oil Company.[34] They recognised the importance of facilitating the transition and successful reintegration of the workforce into various aspects of social life, understanding that it would contribute to the overall stability and welfare of the region.

Among the multitude of employment options available to the redeemed workers, the development projects in the region, such as the Dez Dam Hydroelectric Project and the Haft Tapeh Sugar Cane Project, stood out as highly coveted and advantageous choices.[35] Many skilled workers eagerly joined these ventures, recognising them as opportunities for professional growth and stability. However, a significant number of unskilled workers found themselves at a loss regarding how to effectively utilise the funds received upon their redemption.

In this context, certain prevalent practices emerged, capturing the attention and concern of the ONIT. Among them, undertaking pilgrimages to revered Shiite destinations such as Karbala or engaging in polygamy were commonplace. Reports of these activities reached the ONIT, causing them great apprehension.

To address this issue, the ONIT devised a strategy, as recounted by two eyewitnesses directly involved in the matter: Alinaghi Alikhani, the deputy director of the ONIT, and Manouchehr Mohandes, a young engineer employed by the ONIT. They both describe how the ONIT actively encouraged the redeemed workers, during meetings with the workers and their representatives, to establish small-scale industrial or service projects. Examples of such ventures included small horticultural or cleaning units, as well as blacksmithing or carpentry workshops for those skilled in such techniques. Subsequently, the aim was to establish a link between these small units and the oil industry, enabling oil companies to entrust them with relevant tasks and assignments.[36]

> My endeavours in non-industrial tasks primarily revolved around incorporating the fundamental logistical operations of the Oil Company into Khuzestan's integrated economy, thereby mitigating the region's reliance on oil. For instance, I explored potential employment opportunities for retired or redeemed employees, offering avenues of occupation beyond the realm of the oil industry. During my sojourns in Khuzestan, I often travelled to the elevated terrains of the Zagros mountains in the eastern and north-eastern reaches of Khuzestan, including Masjed-Soleyman, I frequently encountered settlements or towns that the Americans refer to as 'ghost towns' – constructed habitats devoid of human habitation. Contemplation ensued on how to effectively harness the dormant potential of these facilities for alternative ventures. It is important to note that during that time, monumental undertakings were being carried out in Khuzestan. Fortunately, under the aegis of a comprehensive regional program overseen by the Plan Organisation and propelled by the indomitable perseverance of the late Abolhassan Ebtehaj, the economy of Khuzestan underwent a profound transformation.[37]

Labour Activism: Advancing Workers' Welfare Collectively

The haunting spectre of apprehension, stemming from past occurrences of occasionally violent labour protests within the oil industry throughout the preceding decade, persisted and cast its ominous shade over the 1950s. In response to these lingering concerns, the Iranian government implemented internal security measures, possibly driven by the significant economic importance of oil for the nation. As a consequence, the workforce in the oil industry bore the brunt of these security measures more acutely compared to employees in other sectors.

Remarkably, indications of a limited presence of independent trade union activities, which were somewhat discernible in other regions of Iran, were scarcely evident within the Khuzestan oil industry. The lack of notable trade union activity in Khuzestan, further accentuated the distinct vulnerability of oil industry workers in the south to the prevailing security measures and contributed to the unique atmosphere surrounding labour relations in this vital sector.

In the annals of organised labour movements within the oil industry, certain periods or events stand out, where a notable contrast exists between the presence of workers' organisations in different regions. An illustrative example of this occurred in 1961 when workers in Tehran had established a union led by Haider Rahmani, while no such organisation was apparent in the southern oil-rich area. The presence of the oil workers' union in Tehran was a significant development, as it marked a departure from the prevailing circumstances where labour unions were often suppressed. It is worth mentioning that during the same year, the International Federation of Petroleum Workers (IFPW), headquartered in Denver, Colorado, had its regional representative, Curtis Hogan (with assistance from the U.S. AID Labour Division), conduct a three-day seminar for the board of directors of the oil workers' syndicate in Tehran. This seminar proved instrumental, leading the oil workers to seek and receive affiliation with the IFPW, which granted them international recognition and solidarity.

Furthermore, in 1961, the Consortium engaged in negotiations with representatives of the oil workers' syndicate to establish a higher minimum wage for oil workers. This significant milestone resulted in an increase in the minimum wage for Tehran oil workers by 22 rials per day, raising it from 76 to 98 rials. Interestingly enough, oil workers in the Abadan oil fields also secured an increase in the minimum wage by 26 rials per day, raising it from 99 to 125 rials per day. However, it is important to note that in the absence of a syndicate in the south, the role of workers' representatives in Tehran, mandated by law, became crucial in advocating for the rights and welfare of all workers. These representatives played a pivotal role in voicing the concerns and demands of the workers in the absence of a formal labour union in the southern oil region.[38]

To combat the left and nationalist organised workers movement, in March 1953, an agreement was formalised between the Ministers of Labour of Iran, and the Director of the U.S. Technical Co-operation Administration for Iran, known as the U.S. Operations Mission in Iran (USOMI), This agreement aimed to facilitate the provision of American experts to assist the Ministry of Labour in various capacities. It entailed the development of several activities within the Ministry of Labour, with both parties contributing funds to cover expenses related to infrastructure, materials, equipment, salaries, subsistence, travel, and other necessary resources to achieve the project's objectives. Subsequently, in January 1954, a 'first extension' was added to the agreement, which essentially restated the project's objectives and revised the financial contributions. However, due to significant challenges in recruiting and assigning experts for the provincial aspects of the project, combined with slow progress in the preceding eighteen months, a 'second extension' was implemented. This extension involved the Ministry of Labour, the Iran-American Joint Fund for Labour (an entity established jointly by the Government of Iran and USOMI to oversee the project's financial aspects), and the U.S. Foreign Operations Administration. As a result of this additional extension, the project evolved into one focused on 'labour training and services', which comprised two distinct sub-projects: (1) labour training and (2) labour services.[39] Meanwhile,

> the long-planned [Truman] Point IV Workers Education Program was instituted [in 1957], with the first group of worker representatives attending classes in which the labour laws, the organisation and responsibilities of trade unions, and similar subjects are discussed. The classes make use of films on union activities in the United States which were reviewed and approved by the Ministry of Labour (one film which showed an actual picket line was not approved for exhibit despite the fact that its message clearly brought out the idea that the industrial strike is the last resort in union bargaining).[40]

However, the challenging economic conditions experienced during the 1950s created a hostile environment that hindered the implementation of top-down labour rights reforms. In response, workers diligently pursued every available avenue to advocate for their welfare. It is important to note that these approaches were not inherently radical or confrontational; instead, they primarily manifested as organised movements aimed at asserting their rights and pressing for improvements in their working conditions.

The fear of job termination and subsequent unemployment, coupled with the potential for professional or geographical displacement, played a crucial role in driving labour protests within the oil industry during the 1950s. These concerns arose from the ambitious efforts of the Consortium to significantly reduce the workforce, thereby exacerbating the gravity of the situation. For instance, in September 1956, female employees from the clerical department expressed their grievances through a detailed petition. They lamented that despite enduring years of sweltering heat in Khuzestan, they had been dismissed by the Consortium, while 'foreign typists with exorbitant salaries' continued to be employed.[41] Similar petitions from laid-off or redeemed workers of the Consortium were commonplace during this period and often found their way to the National Iranian Oil Company.

Instances of labour protests in 1957 and 1958 serve as examples of the workers' frustration with the Oil Company's disregard for their complaints. These strikes, however, did not endure for more than a few days, and the Consortium eventually yielded to the workers' demands. For instance, in February 1958, 'on Khark (Kharg) Island in the Persian Gulf, where the Consortium was constructing a deep-water tanker loading station, … approximately 100 workers staged a three-day strike, …of many possible causes of the Khark Island trouble one factor stood out – the Consortium surplus labour problem… The operating hire new labour plus stands out – a position to Consortium have not been in expansion projects because of the huge surplus already on hand and have been forced into a policy of utilising extra hands from the refinery and fields. It is obvious that any effort to select the extra hands from an already existing operation will result in a selection of the superannuated, inefficient, or troublesome, and in general terms this describes the Khark Island labour force. Other factors in the situation include delays in construction schedules which make the Khark force too large for present workloads, thereby creating idleness, and the almost forcible transfer of workers to Khark who would much prefer to remain in Abadan with friends and family. At present the workforce is relatively small (about 400 workers) and dissatisfaction on Khark is therefore not one of the Consortium's most pressing labour problems. But this workforce there is constantly being expanded and, in a year, according to present planning, will reach a figure of about 1600 labourers. Dissatisfaction in a group this large can assume great importance, particularly in view of the fact that Khark workers are drawn chiefly from the refinery operation in Abadan, are in constant touch with Abadan, and can spread their dissatisfaction to the Abadan area. The Consortium's approach to this situation has so far consisted largely of granting as many concessions to the workers as possible'.[42]

Another, and indeed a more significant, example of a labour walkout culminating in a conciliatory resolution is evident in the strike of the oil fields workers during the summer of 1958. In June 1958, the workers in Aghajari initiated the strike, and their cause found resonance as 1,500 workers at Masjed-Soleyman, the nerve centre of the Fields' operations, joined the movement in early July. While rumours suggesting external instigation circulated during that time, the officially stated reason for the strike was the workers' profound discontent with their wage rates.

The work stoppage endured for a mere forty-eight hours before measures were undertaken by a special committee of inquiry, which had been convened to investigate the wages predicament in the aftermath of the Aghajari strike. As a result of this inquiry, a committee was established in accordance with the Minimum Wages Regulations. Negotiations for a revision of the minimum wage ensued throughout August and early September, but the prolonged nature of these discussions resulted in growing dissatisfaction among the workers at Masjed-Soleyman, leading to another strike in mid-September. In a ripple effect, a few days later, the Aghajari labourers also resumed their protest.

However, a turning point emerged with the subsequent announcement of an impending wages agreement, prompting a resumption of work at both Aghajari and Masjed-Soleyman. Despite the technically illicit nature of these strikes, the Ministry of Labour refrained from declaring them as such, thereby compelling the Consortium to remunerate the workers for the days they had participated in the strikes.

This episode serves as a compelling testament to the potency of collective action and the efficacy of labour mobilisation in addressing wage disparities and advocating for improved working conditions. The formation of a committee to address concerns about minimum wages exemplifies the recourse to institutional channels for redress, while the Ministry's abstention from deeming the strikes unlawful underscores its reluctance to engage in a confrontational stance.[43]

Khuzestan in the Second Development Plan 1955–1962

Upon the establishment of the Consortium, the commencement of oil production heralded the opportunity for the lucrative sale of oil, consequently enabling a notable influx of financial resources to support the implementation of what was left from the First Development Plan (1948–55). However, despite 80 per cent of the projects launched by the First Development Plan remaining unfinished, the government faced mounting pressure to launch new planning endeavours.[44] Compounding the urgency of these pressures were the exceptionally dire economic conditions prevailing at the time. The substantial and pervasive economic decline witnessed throughout Iran in the mid-1950s engendered profound apprehension among Iran's political observers and activists, who foresaw the imminent spectre of heightened political turmoil. Abolhassan Ebtehaj, encountered repeated criticism from both the media and the Parliament due to perceived delays in the execution of the proposed developmental initiatives.[45]

It was not until September 1955, following a painstaking nine-month period of meticulous study and analysis, that the Second Development Plan was ultimately budgeted at 930 million dollars (later raised to 1.1 billion dollars) and duly sanctioned by the Parliament and the Senate House. In the Second Development Plan, a decision was made to allocate 60 per cent of oil revenues to the Plan Organisation, with an annual increase of 5 per cent until it reached 80 per cent. However, the intended increase from 60 per cent to 80 per cent was never realised. Throughout the years of the Second Development Plan, both the public and private sectors witnessed a notable surge in investment. Correspondingly, the gross national income experienced a growth from 229 billion rials in 1955 to 307 billion rials in 1962, signifying an average economic growth rate of approximately 4 per cent.

A prominent aspect of this development plan was its explicit focus on regional development. The Second Development Plan actively pursued regional investment and development in areas susceptible to underdevelopment, with the aim of establishing development hubs that harnessed natural resources. The construction of large-scale multipurpose dams, designed to bolster agricultural production, held a significant position on the agenda of the Second Development Plan. To this end, the Plan Organisation engaged the expertise of the New York Construction and Resources Company, tasking them with conducting a comprehensive assessment of Khuzestan's water resources and presenting comprehensive plans for their development. The success of the American Tennessee Valley Authority (TVA)[46] in utilising water resources to accelerate the economic growth of a region in the United States resonated with advocates of this approach in various countries, including Iran. The initial contract in this field was concluded in March 1956.

In his memoir, Ebtehaj recollects a poignant encounter with two American developmentalists, David E. Lilienthal and Gordon R. Clapp, founder and manager of the Development and Resources Cooperation, emphasising the imperative nature of implementing reforms. He articulated that the salvation of Iran lay solely in undertaking ambitious endeavours through the execution of a comprehensive and far-reaching program, intended to eradicate the prevailing state of backwardness. He conveyed that the present juncture was opportune for addressing this backwardness, questioning when and how Iran could bridge the gap and ascend to the echelons of developed nations if not now. Drawing an analogy, he likened Iran's predicament to that of a critically ill patient, emphasising that failure to proceed with the necessary operation would lead to certain demise. He addressed the counterargument that operating on the patient would result in post-operative complications, including the risk of fever and other potential consequences, contending that such deterrents should not dissuade them from adhering to a fundamental principle: the patient's survival hinged solely upon the intervention of surgery.[47]

One of the affiliated endeavours associated with the Second Development Plan was the Khuzestan Development Service (KDS). The formulation of the KDS drew inspiration from the TVA, which served as its conceptual framework. At its essence, this blueprint advanced the proposition that within a region such as Khuzestan, graced with copious water resources, extensive stretches of land, abundant sunshine, and a considerable labour, remarkable amelioration of the populace's well-being could be attained through substantial investment, scrupulous planning, comprehensive education, and systematic organisation. The endorsed scheme devised by the Plan Organisation of Iran, encompassed the erection of a multipurpose dam along the Dez River, in a narrow canyon 25 kilometres northeast of Dezful, facilitating the generation of 520,000 kilowatts of electricity. Moreover, the plan entailed the cultivation of 125,000 hectares of fertile land below the dam, the establishment and nurturing of sugarcane plantations, along with the construction of a sugarcane refinery spanning an area of 2,500 hectares. The KDS project was allocated 10 per cent of the total Second Development Plan, or more than 100 million dollars.[48]

On the 14th of March 1963, a multitude of components pertaining to the Dez Dam and the corresponding electricity distribution network were prepared for active deployment. These components encompassed the meticulous construction of numerous water-guiding tunnels, the installation of colossal electricity-generating turbines positioned below the lake's surface, the establishment of a grandiose hall carved into the western rock of the dam, and the construction of extensive electricity transmission infrastructure spanning a distance of 400 kilometres from the dam site to the city of Khorramshahr. Furthermore, the distribution network was expanded to accommodate the urban areas of Andimeshk, Dezful, Ahvaz, and Khorramshahr, necessitating the construction of vital roadways to facilitate the operation and maintenance of the Dez Dam and the electricity distribution network.[49]

Initially, a pair of turbines and generators were meticulously installed at the base of the dam, yielding a total electricity output of 130,000 kilowatts. This substantial amount of electrical power was then efficiently distributed to various cities including Dezful, Andimeshk, Shush, Ahvaz, Khorramshahr, and Abadan, as well as 30 surrounding villages, via a complex network of 400 kilometres of high voltage transmission lines and 17 power stations.

Over a span of four years, an incremental process ensued, leading to the gradual installation of four additional turbines and generators. This methodical expansion culminated in the attainment of the projected maximum capacity of 520,000 kilowatts of electricity generation. Consequently, the surplus electricity generated not only catered to the energy demands of the villages, cities, and industries, including oil, in the Khuzestan region, but also facilitated the provision of a portion of Tehran's electricity requirements through interconnection with the national power grid.

During the year 1963, the Khuzestan Water and Electricity Organisation registered a count of 34,784 electricity subscribers (excluding the Oil Company), resulting in a total power consumption of 610,744,830 kilowatts. Subsequently, in 1964, the number of electricity subscribers rose to 54,465, with a corresponding surge in electricity consumption reaching a total of 860,116,142 kilowatts.

Upon recognising the reliable and cost-effective electricity supply provided by the Dez Dam, the officials within the oil industry swiftly became patrons of the provider. This development proved influential, leading to the establishment of additional industries, including rolling mills, pipe manufacturing, and petrochemical facilities in the Khuzestan region. Consequently, the demand for electricity surged exponentially.

In response to this escalating need, authorities promptly formulated plans for the construction of a new dam along the Karun River. Subsequently, the construction project commenced, ultimately culminating in the successful completion of the dam. This new venture allowed for electricity generation from the Karun River to reach an impressive milestone of one million kilowatts.[50]

The Khuzestan development plan, originating in the mid-1950s, fostered a gradual integration of development initiatives across the Khuzestan region with the Iranian oil industry. Initially, there was a competitive dynamic between the National Iranian Oil Company and, to a lesser extent, the Iranian Oil Services Ltd. with the KDS. However, over time, this connection transformed into a collaborative partnership that encompassed various spheres. Joint planning, resource allocation, technological advancements, logistical infrastructure, such as transportation networks, and storage facilities, ensuring the smooth flow of oil-related activities in Khuzestan.

Furthermore, the collaboration aimed to promote communal well-being. This involved initiatives to enhance the quality of life for the local population.

The entities involved in the partnership provided healthcare facilities, housing options, and other amenities to ensure the well-being of the workforce. Additionally, the collaboration extended to the recruitment of a wide spectrum of human resources, both skilled and unskilled workers included.

Overall, the Khuzestan development plan played a significant role in transforming the relationship between the National Iranian Oil Company and the KDS from a competitive dynamic to a collaborative partnership. This shift had a profound impact on various aspects of development in the region over the course of a decade.

Accentuating these accomplishments is essential; however, it is imperative to acknowledge the shortcomings inherent in the Second Development Plan. As per the analysis of Khodadad Farmanfarmaian, who was one of the major executors of the plan and served as the director of the Economic Office and the Vice President of Economic Affairs of the Plan Organisation from 1958 to 1961, the Second Development Plan encountered a profound deficit in terms of its comprehensibility. Notably, the absence of a long-term vision, unavailability of essential data, and a dearth of proficient experts to execute the outlined strategies constituted major hindrances. Additionally, the matter of financing posed a significant challenge in the plan's implementation.[51] The planning process was hastily executed, driven by political pressures that permeated the nation's public sphere. The overarching intention was to catalyse economic transformation while restoring and consolidating the political legitimacy of the monarchy, or in Farmanfarmaian words 'the government adamantly advocated for expeditious implementation of measures aimed at utilising the oil revenues for the betterment of the populace, exemplifying the government's commitment to allocating oil revenues towards fostering social welfare'.[52]

Throughout the implementation of the Second Development Plan, the incurred costs far exceeded initial estimates, consequently resulting in a significant government budget deficit. The Plan Organisation's access to oil revenue, coupled with Ebtehaj's prioritisation of the plan's execution, set the stage for his confrontation with the Shah. Ebtehaj advocated for channelling oil revenue exclusively towards development planning, a sentiment he explicitly expressed during his discussion with the Shah. Conversely, the Shah adamantly opposed any reduction in the military budget allocation. The blood shedding coup d'état led by Abdul Karim Qasim in July 1958, which marked the downfall of the Hashemite dynasty in Iraq, posed a grave threat to the Shah. Five months prior, in February 1958, SAVAK uncovered a plot to overthrow the Iranian monarchy orchestrated by the youthful Iranian army under the leadership of Lieutenant General Qarni. These events collectively prompted the Shah to perceive economic development planning through the lens of military capability, consequently diverting his attention from the admonitions of Ebtehaj, who had once been his most trusted agent. Ebtehaj's statement, 'Iran lacks the capacity to implement a consequential development plan that tangibly improves the lives of its people while simultaneously shouldering the burdensome expenses of the armed forces', encapsulated his core assertion to the Shah.[53] Within three days, Ebtehaj paid the price for his candid remark by tendering his resignation. Unbeknownst at the time, this marked the inauspicious commencement of the Second Development Plan's descent towards an unfavourable denouement.

In summary, the Second Development Plan encompassed two primary features. First, the Plan Organisation underwent a gradual transformation, becoming a hub for highly educated technocrats who had received their education from prestigious universities in the United States and Europe. A considerable number of these individuals held left and liberal political leanings, recognising the importance of public participation in the advancement of a developing society. Second, it placed significant emphasis on prioritising regional development initiatives, with Khuzestan reaping the greatest benefits from this prioritisation.

8

Oil, Workforce, and the Developmental State: 1960s–1970s

The world emerging from the Second World War marked the advent of a novel global order, known as the Cold War, accompanied by new political alliances, economic restructuring, and social reconstruction, facilitated by the developmental states in the global south. The concept of a 'developmental state' refers to a model of economic development that is characterised by significant intervention by the government in the economy to foster industrial growth and economic development. This model contrasts with the laissez-faire approach of minimal state intervention.[1] Historians such as Fredrick Cooper, regard the developmental ideas of the Cold War and the decolonisation period as an interconnected continuum that can be traced back to the latter stages of colonial rule, particularly during the 1930s.[2]

In this context, the late 1950s and early 1960s marked a pivotal moment as scholars from institutions such as Harvard University and the Massachusetts Institute of Technology sought to address the economic stagnation in Third World countries. These scholars' endeavour led to the formation of Modernisation Theory,[3] with significant contributions from Daniel Lerner and Walt Whitman Rostow.[4] Their works aimed to define development models that aligned with United States Cold War strategies, promoting development programs in the global south, including Iran, and articulating paths for economic progress and political stability within Western capitalist discourse.

However, the prominence of Modernisation Theory soon met with critical opposition from the emerging Dependency Theory, led by figures such as Argentine economist Raúl Prebisch.[5] This critique highlighted the unequal economic relationships and adverse effects of modernisation policies, arguing that underdevelopment resulted from a global hierarchy favouring developed nations. This scholarly discourse, enriched by contributions from Fernando Henrique Cardoso, Samir Amin, Immanuel Wallerstein, Andre Gunder Frank, and Arghiri Emmanuel, called for a re-evaluation of global economic relations and the pursuit of equitable development strategies.[6]

In the aftermath of the Iranian Revolution of 1979, a substantial body of scholarly work has emerged, critically examining the developmental state model's application and the intricacies of its implementation, shedding light on both its successes and limitations globally and within Iran. Two pivotal themes in these analyses are 'uneven development', which underscores the disparate outcomes of socio-economic and political policies and exemplifies the complex nature of development as it varies across different societal, economic, and political dimensions.

Another critical concept is the 'rentier state', as originally proposed by Hossein Mahdavi in 1970.[7] This concept, referring to states that derive a significant portion of their national revenues from the extraction and sale of indigenous resources, such as oil, is particularly relevant to the political economy of Middle Eastern countries, including Iran. These frameworks have been instrumental in dissecting the nuances of Iran's political and economic development during the fifteen years leading up to the 1978–79 revolution, highlighting the interplay between Iran's abundant natural resources and the broader sociopolitical dynamics at play.[8]

In my study, applying Mahdavi's rentier state theory to Iran reveals how the country's economic dependency on oil exports has significantly contributed to uneven development within the country. This perspective provides a critical lens through which to view the socio-economic and political conditions leading up to the revolution.

Resurgence of Discontent

In the late 1950s, Iran faced a challenging economic situation marked by a negative balance of payments. This predicament was primarily a result of the escalating imports and foreign direct investments that the country had been experiencing. To address this issue, Iranian elites sought a solution and shifted their focus towards Import Substitution Industrialisation as a viable economic policy. Embracing the principles of the Modernisation Theory in various economic aspects, Iran embarked on a path that aimed to bolster its industrial capabilities over the subsequent years.

The strategy of Import Substitution Industrialisation involved promoting domestic production of goods that were previously imported, with the intention of reducing reliance on foreign imports and enhancing self-sufficiency in essential industries. By fostering the growth of domestic industries, the Iranian government sought to curb the negative impact of imports on the country's balance of payments. Over time, this approach allowed Iran to expand its industrial capacities, stimulating economic development and fostering a sense of independence in its economic pursuits. The adoption of Import Substitution Industrialisation proved instrumental in transforming Iran's economic landscape, allowing it to establish a stronger industrial base and mitigate some of the adverse effects of its previous economic challenges.[9]

During the 1960s and 1970s, a complex interplay of factors emerged, driven by the geopolitical landscape of the Cold War, the strategic alliance between the United States and the Iranian government, the unprecedented influx of oil revenues, and a profound transformation within the Iranian state. Notably, the state apparatus embarked on a trajectory of self-reproduction and modernisation, all the while neglecting the imperative of political participation from the grassroots.

The unwavering support provided by the United States to the Iranian monarchy following the Second World War experienced a noteworthy shift in the early 1960s under the Kennedy administration. This shift was largely driven by concerns sparked by the Cuban Revolution (1953–59), perceived as a direct consequence of Cuba's oppressive regime and profound social inequities. Additionally, the Iraqi military coup d'état of 1958, known as the 14 July Revolution, which led to the downfall of the Hashemite monarchy, heightened the United States administration's apprehension regarding the socio-economic landscape in Iran.

In response to the pervasive poverty and social unrest in Latin America, perceived as fertile grounds for the spread of communism amid the Cold War and following the Cuban Revolution, President Kennedy promptly initiated the 'Alliance for Progress' in 1961. This extensive economic development program aimed to foster economic cooperation between the United States and Latin American countries. Through this initiative, the Kennedy administration sought to address the underlying issues contributing to regional instability by promoting social and economic development. The broader objective was to deter the influence of communism by improving living standards and reinforcing democratic governance.

Similarly, in Iran, advocating for the government to implement social and economic reforms became a critical aspect of the United States' strategy. However, it quickly became apparent that neither the Iranian monarchy nor the opposition had a comprehensive strategy or a unified plan for advancing socio-economic reforms that would also include a reformation of the country's political framework. Neither the National Front nor the Tudeh Party demonstrated a clear analysis of the situation. Concurrently, the Shah increasingly believed that his reforms would enable him to outmanoeuvre both the resurgent National Front and the remnants of the Tudeh Party.

The economic downturn that gripped the late 1950s and early 1960s served as a catalyst for rejuvenating previously disorganised clandestine political non-movements. Primarily, a number of political organisations, which had been silenced following the 1953 coup d'état, emerged from the shadows and re-established their presence. The immediate imposition of Martial Law during the coup d'état had led to extensive repression, stifling their activities at the time. However, in the wake of the economic recession, these organisations found new avenues for organising and resurfaced prominently. Notably, the formation of the Second National Front (*Jebheh-ye Melli-ye Dovvom*) was a hallmark of this period, characterised by a deepening political crisis. The repercussions of this crisis were evident in the successive changes within the ruling cabinets.

In May 1961, a nationwide strike was organised by teachers, demanding a pay raise in response to the economic challenges. During the protests held in front of the parliament building in Tehran, a tragic incident occurred when a teacher named Esmaʿil Khanʿali was fatally shot by a policeman. This incident led to the resignation of the then-Prime Minister, Jaʿfar Sharif-Emami. Subsequently, the teacher's protest was followed by a rally organised by the National Front in Jalaliyyeh, north of Tehran, demanding an end to political exclusion and repression. Nine months later, on 21 January 1962, students at the University of Tehran, with the support of the National Front, went on strike, further galvanising the opposition movement. After a decade of absence, the streets once again bore witness to the presence of protesters expressing opposition to the government and its policies. The resurgence of political opponents and opposition forces marked a significant shift in the political landscape. These protesters, through their presence on the streets, not only voiced their dissatisfaction with the dismal economic conditions but also sought to claim their rightful share in political participation. Their demonstrations served as a powerful statement, indicating their desire to have a meaningful voice in the governance and decision-making processes of the nation.

Conversely, the government exhibited no inclination to cede the political stage to the opposition or entertain the notion of sharing governance with them. The king maintained his stance of ruling rather than merely reigning. In August 1961, the Shah orchestrated a rally in Dushan-Tappeh, located east of Tehran, during which he declared his intention to introduce a comprehensive set of economic reforms in the country. This march set the stage for a series of extensive socio-economic plans, which subsequently gained prominence as the *White Revolution*.

Approximately a year and a half later, on 26 January 1963, a pivotal moment arrived when a referendum was held to ascertain public support for the Shah's initial reform plan. This referendum marked a significant juncture in the nation's trajectory as it ushered in the era of the White Revolution – a transformative period characterised by a range of ambitious socio-economic initiatives.

The White Revolution, also known at times as the Shah and People's Revolution, was initially introduced through the Six Principles and put to the vote of the people. These principles encompassed:

1) Land reforms and the abolishment of the landlord-tenant system.
2) Nationalisation of forests and pastures.
3) Selling shares of government-owned factories to support land reforms.
4) Providing workers with a share of factory profits.
5) Electoral reforms granting women the right to vote and ensuring political equality with men.
6) Establishing the '*Sepah-e Danesh*' (literally Literacy Corps), aimed at promoting literacy and education.

Later, these principles were expanded to nineteen principles.

At the core of the White Revolution laid the pivotal element of land reform. Its purpose was to change the prevailing pre-capitalist social relations within rural regions, thereby paving the way for a rapid surge in capitalist economic growth. Furthermore, the aspiration was to circumvent the pre-industrial stages of societal advancement, propelling a predominantly agrarian-based society into a capitalist one, fully equipped to partake in the global economic arena. Central to this transformative endeavour was the industrialisation of the economy, serving as a fundamental pillar for the said process.

The Third Development Plan (1962–67) served as the blueprint for the aforementioned process. However, to claim credit for the White Revolution, the Shah insisted on dissociating the outcomes of his reforms from the Third Development Plan. Despite this divergence, the plan yielded noteworthy results, propelling the national GDP growth to a remarkable 8.8 per cent during its implementation. Notably, the industrial and mining sectors played a crucial role, contributing an average annual growth rate of 7.7 per cent.[10]

During this period, a notable phenomenon emerged with the migration of the workforce from rural to urban areas, leading to a decline in the agricultural labour force and a concurrent rise in the urban industrial labour force. This exodus from rural regions resulted in a substantial influx of hundreds of thousands of villagers into the cities. Remarkably, between 1956 and 1966, out of the total of 950,000 newly generated jobs, a significant majority of 623,000 positions were created within the industrial and mining sectors. The individuals employed in these sectors were predominantly drawn from the surplus labour pool in rural areas.

Over the span of 1962 to 1968, in terms of the overall active labour force in the country (6.6 million in 1962 and 7.8 million in 1968), the share of the agricultural sector underwent a substantial reduction of 6.1 per cent. In stark contrast, the number of people employed in industrial sectors experienced a notable growth of 4.2 per cent, reaching a figure of over two million people.[11]

In the context of gender diversity within the workforce, a range of positive social transformations emerged, characterised by a significant and enduring presence of women across all professional sectors. This period witnessed an appreciable augmentation in the female labour force, extensive literacy initiatives, expanded access to higher education, advancements in healthcare provision, and the enhancement of communication infrastructures, among other developments. These direct outcomes of the development-oriented policies contributed to population mobility as citizens sought to seize new opportunities. The Shah, employing left-leaning rhetoric, enigmatically referred to them as 'liberated men' and 'liberated women' (*Azad-mardan va Azad-zanan*). The enforced top-down reforms, coupled with the growing influence of social forces from the grassroots level, culminated in the demand for rights from the populace. As these developments unfolded, they became impossible for political activists of the era to ignore.

Amid the backdrop of economic growth and noteworthy social transformations, visible dynamic change between urban and rural communities, political development remained conspicuously absent. The prevailing political landscape remained characterised by exclusive and coercive practices, mirroring the situation before the transformative period. While the social sphere experienced notable shifts in the urban and rural dynamics, the political arena continued to bear the scars of repression stemming from the post-1953 coup d'état.

Upon the inception of governmental reforms, considerable bewilderment befell the various political parties and organisations that stood in opposition to the ruling regime. They found themselves grappling with uncertainty regarding their response to these reformative measures, torn between endorsing, opposing, or adopting a nuanced stance. Emanating from the University of Tehran's students during that period, the protest rallying cry 'yes to reforms, no to dictatorship' resonated widely, gaining traction among several political entities, most notably the National Front.

The Tudeh Party's reaction to the governmental reforms, on the other hand, underwent a metamorphosis, which was significantly influenced by the diplomatic relations existing between the Soviet Union and Iran.[12] Initially marked by rejection in the early months of 1962, their stance evolved to a more receptive disposition by the year's end. Throughout the ensuing years, the Tudeh Party remained steadfast in its adherence to the doctrine of a 'Non-Capitalist Path of Development' seeking to reconcile its alignment with the Soviet Union's support for the Iranian monarchy and its concurrent implementation of reforms.[13] Concurrently, they endeavoured to reorganise their clandestine network within Iran, with a particular focus on cultivating support among the labourers of the oil industry in Khuzestan. Unforeseen, however, was the emergence of an Islamist opposition during the tumultuous events of June 1963.

Some clerics were of the belief that the White Revolution's plans, particularly the land reforms and the recognition of women's rights for political participation, contradicted the foundations of Islamic law. One prominent opposing cleric was Ruhollah Khomeini, who deemed the referendum 'illegitimate' and declared it forbidden (*haraam*), thus imposing a boycott on it. In a letter dated 1 March 1963, Khomeini considered the acceptance of women's rights to vote and be elected as contrary to the principles of the Quran and Islam. Certain objectionable proclamations from some clerics, notably the speeches of Ruhollah Khomeini, led to street protests in certain cities, including Qom and Mashhad. The peak of these protests occurred on 5 June 1963. On 4 November 1964, Khomeini was exiled to Turkey and later went to Najaf until his return to Iran on 1 February 1979.

The clerics' opposition to the White Revolution stemmed not solely from their religious motivations. It was also driven by the revolutionary changes it brought about, as it undermined the hierarchical structure of the clergy, depriving them of the special rights and privileges they had enjoyed for centuries.

The June 1963 riot was the last street manifestation of opposition against the government in Iran. From that date until late 1977, the streets remained devoid of any significant anti-government protests. In the dearth of any viable political avenue that could overtly demonstrate its resistance against the Pahlavi autocracy within the confines of the constitution, the political landscape in Iran became interwoven with radical rhetoric, and armed struggle became the sole recourse for the opposition's political engagement against the prevailing system.[14]

Iran in the 1960s and 1970s: Rise of a Developmental State

As previously mentioned, the crux of the White Revolution was centred around the crucial aspect of land reform. Prior to the referendum for the White Revolution, it was the implementation of the Third Development Plan (1962–67) that laid out the roadmap for comprehensive land reforms and other far-reaching changes. This plan came after two consecutive seven years development plans that yielded relatively unsatisfactory outcomes.

The First Development Plan (1948–55) coincided with the nationalisation of Iranian oil in 1951 and the 1953 coup d'état. Despite its limited tangible achievements, this plan marked the initiation of development planning in Iran, which was overseen by a newly established institution called the Plan Organisation, founded in 1948.[15] The Second Development Plan (1955–62) was launched with the allocation of 60 per cent of the oil revenue to support development initiatives, particularly regional planning, all under the coordination of the Plan Organisation.[16] Additionally, the plan aimed to increase the share of oil revenue in the development efforts by five per cent annually, reaching a maximum contribution of 80 per cent.[17] However, the Second Development Plan faced significant challenges, including a poor harvest in 1959–60 and a deficit in financing due to a 26 per cent decline in the posted price of Persian Gulf oil from 2.04 dollars per barrel to 1.78 dollars per barrel between 1957 and 1960.[18] Consequently, the cost of living surged by over 35 per cent, leading to heightened social grievances among the working class and labouring poor.[19]

Since the early 1960s, Iran initiated a transformative period marked by the implementation of the Third Development Plan, concurrent with the White Revolution. This era, notable for its ambitious land reforms, witnessed the rapid industrialisation of the country. The White Revolution, often characterised as an authoritarian modernisation effort, played a pivotal role, particularly in conjunction with the Third Development Plan, in the comprehensive overhaul and modernisation of Iran's infrastructure, public healthcare system, education, family law, and the status of women within the public sphere. The Third Five-Year Development Plan achieved a notable Gross National Product (GNP) growth rate of 8.8 per cent. Notably, the industrial and mining sectors played a significant role in this progress, experiencing an average annual growth rate of 7.12 per cent during the same period.[20]

The government actively supported the private sector by means of public investments, import regulations, and the provision of low-interest credit. This support was facilitated by the considerable expansion of oil revenues. Consequently, Iran enjoyed a remarkable annual real growth rate of nearly 9.6 per cent for nearly fifteen years following the White Revolution, ranking among the highest growth rates globally during this period.[21]

However, this economic advancement was not without its challenges. As the labour force migrated from rural to urban areas, the agricultural sector faced a decrease in its workforce, while the labour force in urban industries grew. Consequently, urban unemployment rates escalated as hundreds of thousands of villagers flocked to the cities seeking employment opportunities. Out of the 950,000 newly created jobs between 1956 and 1966, a substantial portion, 623,000 positions, emerged in the industrial and mining sectors. These roles were predominantly filled by surplus labour from rural regions.

Between 1962 and 1967, the agricultural sector's share of the total active labour force experienced a decline of 6.1 per cent. Simultaneously, the number of white-collar employees in the industrial sectors grew by 4.2 per cent, reaching a workforce of more than two million. While some large industries saw an improvement in real wages, with the purchasing power of workers increasing by 40 per cent between 1962 and 1967, it is essential to note that this progress was uneven and varied across industries. The government's wage policy played a role in shaping these disparities in development.[22]

Overall, the Third Development Plan brought significant economic growth, especially in the industrial and mining sectors. Nevertheless, the mass migration from rural to urban areas and the subsequent rise in urban unemployment raised socio-economic concerns and highlighted the need for balanced and equitable development strategies.

Undoubtedly, Iran's oil revenue played a pivotal role in the success of the Third Development Plan, contributing significantly to the country's economic reconstruction. As estimated, the oil revenue witnessed a substantial increase of 13.6 per cent, serving as a primary driver of economic growth during this period. As astutely argued by Fesharaki, the fiscal impact of oil revenues on the Iranian economy had a twofold effect. First, it provided the government with a vital source of income, enabling it to supplement its budgetary expenditures. Second, the oil revenues were channelled through the Plan Organisation to fund various development projects.[23]

According to Alinaghi Alikhani, the Iranian Minister of Economy from 1963 to 1969, in the 1960s, the oil revenue accounted for an average of 81.5 per cent of Iran's development plans' funding.[24] Within the Third Development Plan, the annual increase of 13.6 per cent in oil revenue led to a remarkable boost in its share, surging from 38 to 71.7 billion rials. This substantial escalation not only doubled the value added by oil revenue but also significantly increased the oil sector's contribution to the country's GNP, rising from 11.6 per cent in 1962 to 14.5 per cent in 1967.[25]

The mutual and interdependent interaction among the institutions embedded within Iran's economic framework conferred a distinct and commendable impact upon the Fourth Development Plan. Spanning the five years period from March 1968 to March 1973, this plan played a pivotal role in shaping Iran's economic topography. The triumph of its predecessor, the Third Development Plan, served as a catalyst for the meticulous formulation and regulation of the ensuing fourth developmental scheme, which was distinguished by its heightened precision in terms of principles and directives.

The Fourth Development Plan yielded remarkable outcomes; a result facilitated by its adept harmonisation. The central objective of the plan was to attain a notable growth rate, marked by a targeted average annual increase of 9 per cent in the real GNP. Furthermore, the plan delineated several secondary objectives encompassing areas such as employment, income distribution, balance of payments, and general price levels.

The initial projected scale of the Fourth Plan was set at 810 billion rials (10.8 billion dollars), with a substantial 92 per cent of this funding slated for domestic sourcing, primarily through oil revenues. Impressively, the Iranian economy experienced substantial expansion during this timeframe. Over the course of the plan, the value added contributions of the oil, industry, and services sectors grew at an average annual rate of 14–15 per cent. This initiative was launched during a phase of heightened momentum in Iran's developmental trajectory, as the country's evolution had gathered impetus and coalesced into cohesive programs, structures, and contextual frameworks.

Employment saw a notable upswing during the Fourth Development Plan, resulting in an increase of 1.2 million individuals in the workforce. In the wake of the Third Development Plan, the paradigm of regional planning underwent a transformative evolution during the Fourth Development Plan's tenure. Within Iran, regional planning embarked upon a new trajectory, characterised by the formulation of comprehensive regional development blueprints in collaboration with consultancy engineering firms. This endeavour, while aligning with the strategic outlook of the Fourth Development Plan, witnessed the resurgence of the practice of engaging foreign consultancy engineers as seen in the context of the preceding Third Development Plan. Anchored in this approach, the regional civil engineering division of the Plan Organisation harnessed the expertise of eminent Iranian and international consultancy engineering entities.

However, despite these commendable achievements, the abrupt escalation in oil prices during the closing year of this period precipitated changes in the trajectory of macroeconomic policies. These modifications engendered significant disruptions across various domains, including economic growth, inflation, and employment, particularly during the subsequent years that encapsulated the Fifth Development Plan (1973–78).[26]

The impressive achievements of the Fourth Development Plan served as an inspiration to the planning authorities, propelling them with greater determination to advance the objectives of the Fifth Development Plan. Within the Fifth Development Plan, emphasis was placed on prioritising social welfare programs, more equitable income distribution, and overall enhancement of economic quality. However, the sudden and intense surge in oil prices, coupled with the monarch ambitious and visionary aspirations for achieving rapid development and progress using the abundant oil revenues, left little room for economic calculations. The economic path that had been set to nurture even and steady growth, suffered repercussions that continue to afflict Iran's economy as an incurable ailment.

With an unprecedented annual average growth rate of 16.7 per cent, the share of income derived from oil sales in the Fifth Development Plan approached three times that of a similar figure in the Fourth Development Plan. This extraordinary increase during the years 1973–74 brought Iran's projected oil revenues for the entire plan period from 25 billion dollars to 100 billion dollars, defying prior estimates. Oil revenues, accompanied by significant financial and currency resources, created considerable potential for exceptional growth in Iran. The country's Gross Domestic Product experienced an almost 10 per cent annual average real growth rate, and per capita income surged from around 175 dollars to over 1,500 dollars.

Conversely, the reliance on oil revenues undermined the necessity for a balanced growth strategy. Government investments, whether direct or indirect, in establishing industrial units such as steel and automotive manufacturing did not prioritise support for small and medium-sized industries.

The hegemonic authority of the monarch and his direct involvement in economic planning, particularly his direct management of the oil industry, created a divergence in economic planners' perspectives from that of the Shah's. This, along with monarch's lack of confidence in economic planning agencies, led to a lack of trust in economic program designers. The seeds of this distrust and competition could be traced back to the Third Development Plan. The Third Plan, which the Plan Organisation had invested significant effort in formulating, focused on rural development and social participation. However, Shah's announcement of the Six-Point White Revolution effectively stripped it of its autonomy in evaluating its performance. In the Fifth Plan as well, under the direct decree of the monarch, the government decided to allocate a substantial portion of the increased revenues without considering the various non-capital constraints that were central to the design of the Fifth Development Plan. The distribution of national income and wealth was not equitably spread among households and geographical regions, as well as between rural and urban areas.[27] These issues, coupled with a relative recession in the agricultural sector that led to widespread rural-to-urban migration, could potentially culminate in socio-economic discontent.[28]

Throughout these phases of development planning, the heightened significance of oil not only emphasised its pivotal role in Iran's developmental trajectory but also drew intensified focus towards the production sector within this industry. Workers and white-collar employees within this sector assumed a prominent mantle in propelling Iran's economic and societal progress, a status that undoubtedly surpassed that of workers and white-collar employees in other sectors. Moreover, it is readily apparent that the substantial surge in oil revenue exerted a profound influence on Iran's economic topography throughout the Third, Fourth, and Fifth development plans. This surge bolstered the country's economic prospects, catalysing advancements across diverse sectors.

The establishment of the Organisation of Petroleum Exporting Countries (OPEC) presented a significant opportunity for Iran, as it provided a platform to negotiate with the Oil Consortium. This development infused a sense of optimism, as it was believed that the subsequent increase in oil revenues would serve as a catalyst for rapid economic and social development. With OPEC's formation, Iran gained leverage in its dealings with the Oil Consortium, allowing for more favourable terms and conditions regarding its oil exports. The newfound ability to collectively negotiate with other oil-producing nations empowered Iran to assert its interests and secure a fair share of the oil revenues.

The prevailing optimism was rooted in the belief that the augmented oil revenues would fuel economic growth and social progress within the country. The expected increase in funds was anticipated to be directed towards funding vital developmental projects, infrastructure, and social welfare initiatives, thereby uplifting the standard of living for the population.

Fuelling Development: Oil and Economic Planning

The inception of the OPEC in 1960 marked a significant turning point, clearing the path for enhanced oil revenues and consequently fostering burgeoning prosperity for oil-producing nations.

Concerning the contribution of oil to economic growth and development, and the underlying objectives that led to the establishment of OPEC, Fuad Rohani, the First Secretary-General of the organisation, alluded to the preamble of the Resolutions of the First OPEC Conference with these words:

> The desperate need for accelerated economic development amongst the so-called underdeveloped countries of the world is self-evident. Mankind has at its disposal today technical knowledge sufficient to ensure for all of us the material comfort and security which we need. We must put this knowledge to work, and employ all our resources, both human and material, in order to combat the evils of hunger, sickness and lack of adequate shelter which still plague the majority of countries throughout the world. As a nation, we have the will power to do so. What we need now is to create a larger body of people familiar with already known techniques

> in agriculture, industry, and commerce and to make the enormous investment required in each sector. The formation of these professional bodies and the investment of the huge sums required, will tax our financial resources to the utmost.
>
> ...In the face of these difficulties, the responsibility for channelling the resources of a nation towards economic development must lie with the government. Nowhere is this truer than in the great oil exporting nations, most of whom are members of OPEC, and earn almost all of their foreign exchange from payments by the oil companies exports of the nation's production of crude oil and refined petroleum products.[29]

On 29 May 1963, Fuad Rohani, serving concurrently as the First Secretary-General of OPEC and Deputy Chairman of the Board of the National Iranian Oil Company (NIOC), delivered a lecture at the Society for the Advancement of Management in Tehran. The lecture was titled 'OPEC and Economic Development of its Member Countries'.[30] During the lecture, Rohani discussed the primary objectives that led to the establishment of OPEC, referencing the preamble to the Resolutions of the First OPEC Conference:

> The desperate need for accelerated economic development among the so-called underdeveloped countries of the world is self-evident. Mankind has at its disposal today technical knowledge sufficient to ensure for all of us the material comfort and security which we need. We must put this knowledge to work, and employ all our resources, both human and material, in order to combat the evils of hunger, sickness and lack of adequate shelter which still plague the majority of countries throughout the world. As a nation, we have the willpower to do so. What we need now is to create a larger body of people familiar with already known techniques in agriculture, industry, and commerce and to make the enormous investment required in each sector. The formation of these professional bodies and the investment of the huge sums required, will tax our financial resources to the utmost.
>
> ...In the face of these difficulties, the responsibility for channelling the resources of a nation towards economic development must lie with the government. Nowhere is this more true than in the great oil exporting nations, most of whom are members of OPEC, and earn almost all of their foreign exchange from payments by the oil companies exports of the nation's production of crude oil and refined petroleum products.[31]

The establishment of OPEC marked a significant milestone, laying the foundation for the burgeoning prosperity of oil-producing countries. This collective effort brought about increased oil revenues and offered a promising path towards the smoother industrialisation of their economies. By forming OPEC, oil-producing countries found strength in unity, enabling them to collectively address the challenges and opportunities presented by the global oil market. Through coordinated action and negotiations, OPEC members were able to assert their interests and secure more favourable terms for their oil exports.

Table 8.1 *Iran oil production in the world, Middle East, OPEC production 1,000 barrel per day, 1955–1970*

					Iran share percentage		
Year	World	Middle East	OPEC	Iran	World	Middle East	OPEC
1955	16,190	3,220	–	329	2	10.2	–
1960	21,046	5,269	7,876	1,052	5	20	3.3
1965	30,530	8,333	13,172	1,885	6.2	22.6	14.3
1967	35,580	9,970	15,624	2,596	7.3	26	16.6
1968	38,835	11,170	17,652	2,848	7.3	25.5	16.1
1970	46,130	13,725	21,131	3,829	8.3	27.9	18.1

Source: Compiled from NIOC Publications, OPEC Annual Statistical Bulletin, and Fereidun Fesharaki, *Development of the Iranian Oil Industry. International and Domestic Aspects* (New York: Praeger Publishers, 1976), 203.

The result was a notable surge in oil revenues, injecting a much-needed economic boost into these countries. These increased revenues, in turn, fuelled economic growth and development (Table 8.1). Countries found themselves better equipped to invest in crucial infrastructure projects, social welfare initiatives, and the diversification of their economies beyond oil, leading to a more sustainable and robust industrialisation process.

In Iran, the country's engagement, and effectiveness in negotiations with both the Consortium and OPEC were largely guided by the annual directives prepared by the Assembly of Shareholders of the National Iranian Oil Company (ASNIOC). This assembly brought together key figures such as the Iranian Prime Minister, Minister of Finance, Minister of Economy, Minister of Energy, Director of the Central Bank of Iran, Chairman of the Board of NIOC, and the Head of the Plan Organisation.[32] The establishment of ASNIOC dates back to the nationalisation of the Iranian oil in 1951, but it gained more prominence and functionality during the late 1950s when it began coordinating the nation's short- and long-term oil policies.[33]

ASNIOC convened biannually, holding meetings in March and December. During the March meeting, which coincided with the Persian New Year, the assembly outlined the country's annual policy, including projections for expected oil revenues. The December meeting primarily focused on assessing the accomplishments and setbacks of the year. Between the biannual meetings of ASNIOC, a committee known as the Directorial of Oil, operating under the Ministry of Finance, assumed responsibility for implementing all decrees issued by ASNIOC. This committee comprised representatives from NIOC, the Plan Organisation, and the Ministry of Finance.

Iran's Position in OPEC: Evolution and Engagement

With the establishment of OPEC, Iran's involvement and performance in the organisation became an additional responsibility for both ASNIOC and the Directorial of Oil. Later, in 1974, the Office of OPEC was founded within NIOC as a part of the International Department to oversee Iran's engagements and interactions with OPEC.[34]

These institutional structures and mechanisms played a crucial role in guiding Iran's participation in the global oil industry, allowing the country to navigate negotiations with the Consortium and OPEC effectively and strategically. While the significance of institutions such as ASNIOC, the Directorial of Oil, and the Office of OPEC in Iran's dealings with the Consortium and OPEC is well documented through newly disclosed documents and witness accounts, it is essential not to overlook the crucial role played by the Shah in shaping the country's relations and negotiations with both entities. His intervention and leadership in these matters were instrumental.[35]

According to Fuad Rohani during the early days of OPEC, there existed some degree of apprehension within the NIOC towards potential cooperation with other oil-producing countries. This mistrust stemmed from the events that followed the nationalisation of Iranian oil in 1951 when major oil companies worldwide imposed a blockade on the country's oil exports. In response, Arab oil-producing countries adopted a non-cooperative stance towards Iran and increased their own oil production, compensating for Iran's share in the global oil market.[36]

The period of 1965–69 is indeed recognised as a time of consolidation for OPEC.[37] However, during this period, the Arab–Israeli conflict, specifically the eruption of the Six Days War in 1967, introduced a series of disturbances, primarily of a political nature, that affected the total unity and harmony within OPEC. In March 1967, the Fifth Arab Petroleum Congress commenced in Cairo, and it differed from OPEC's assemblies by adopting a more radical stance against the international oil companies and those countries perceived as undermining Arab interests. During the congress, the Saudi Red Sheikh, Abdullah Tariki, not only advocated for the nationalisation of oil in Arab countries but also declared that 'oil prices are a political matter, entirely unrelated to supply and demand'.[38]

It is essential to note that Iran did not endorse these radical stances, as Fuad Rohani pointed out in his account of OPEC's history.[39] The country maintained a more measured approach during the proceedings. Following the Six Days War in June 1967, an alliance between some OPEC member states expanded. Algeria, Kuwait, Iraq, and Libya implemented an oil embargo to varying degrees against countries supporting Israel. However, Iran remained impartial during the conflict, continuing its oil exports, and even increasing its production rate from 2,603,000 barrels per day in 1967 to 2,840,000 barrels per day in 1968.[40]

Iran's measured stance during the Six Days War allowed it to navigate through the political complexities of the time while continuing to contribute to the global oil market. This approach stood in contrast to the more radical actions taken by some other OPEC member states, showcasing the diverse perspectives and challenges that the organisation faced during this critical period of its history. Indeed, the bitter memory of the events in 1951, when Arab oil-producing countries adopted a non-cooperative policy towards Iran and increased their oil production in response to the sanctions on Iran's oil exports, had a significant impact on the Iranian government's stance within OPEC in 1967. The recollection of this experience justified Iran's cautious and uncommitted approach during that period.

However, Iran's reservations were not limited solely to its neighbouring Arab oil producers. There were also concerns about Venezuela, the other non-Arab member of OPEC, and its actions within the organisation. The executive of NIOC and its Chairman of the Board, Abdollah Entezam, believed that Venezuela was pursuing its own profit by obstructing the flow of Middle Eastern oil to the world market through an egalitarian policy within OPEC.[41] This perception likely contributed to Iran's careful and pragmatic stance during that time. The country sought to protect its interests and ensure that any decisions made within OPEC were not detrimental to its own economic goals and global market presence. The complexities and diverging interests among OPEC members during this period highlight the challenging dynamics within the organisation as it sought to navigate a rapidly changing global oil landscape.

Indeed, within the Iranian political establishment, there were differing opinions and factions regarding the alignment with OPEC during that period. Some officials, including figures such as Asadollah Alam, who served as the prime minister and later as the minister of court, or Manouchehr Eghbal, who succeeded Abdollah Entezam as the Chairman of the Board of NIOC, were sceptical about Iran's involvement with OPEC. They viewed OPEC as nothing more than a 'radical club' that could potentially jeopardise Iran's relations with the Consortium.

During the period of 1960–63, the anti-OPEC bloc attempted to persuade the Shah to adopt a more cautious and sceptical approach towards the organisation. However, despite these efforts, the Shah remained eager to explore any opportunity or platform that could increase Iran's oil revenue. As a result, Iran chose to remain actively engaged within OPEC, although not necessarily in a leadership role. The Shah's primary concern was to maximise Iran's benefits from its oil resources and enhance the country's economic standing. While some officials within the Iranian government were hesitant about OPEC's radical stance, the Shah's strong inclination was to actively participate in the organisation to safeguard Iran's interests and capitalise on opportunities for revenue growth.

This divergence of opinions and strategies within the Iranian political establishment during the 1960s reflects the complexities and challenges faced by the country in navigating its position within OPEC and the global oil market. The Shah's determination to seize opportunities for increased oil revenue ultimately influenced Iran's stance in remaining an active member of OPEC.[42] On the eve of the Baghdad Conference in September 1960, Manuchehr Farmanfarmaian, a prominent figure and leading director in NIOC, was scheduled to represent the Iranian government at the Conference. Two days before departing for Baghdad, he had an urgent meeting with the Shah.

In his diary entry recounting the meeting, Farmanfarmaian has expressed his concerns and sought the Shah's guidance regarding Iran's participation in the upcoming conference. The meeting was likely crucial in discussing Iran's approach and strategy during the conference, as well as its overall stance towards OPEC. Given the significance of the Baghdad Conference, where OPEC was formally established, it was understandable that high-level discussions and considerations were held between key government officials and the Shah. The decisions made during this period would shape Iran's engagement within OPEC and its position in the evolving global oil market.

Manuchehr Farmanfarmaian's diary entry provides valuable insights into the internal dynamics and debates within the Iranian government regarding OPEC's formation and Iran's role in the organisation. Such historical records offer a glimpse into the complexities and considerations that influenced Iran's approach to this critical juncture in the history of OPEC:

> Shah was standing on the stairs of the Saʿdabad Palace when I arrived. He told me: 'you will be representing Iran in Baghdad. I want you to put asides all past disputes and find a common stand with the Arab states. Oil is the soil revenue for us, and we need money to feed our growing population'. Then he added 'the shameless oil companies are stealing our poor people's wealth and keeping us at their mercy. I want to cooperate with the Arab states to end this.[43]

Manuchehr Farmanfarmaian's surprise at not being appointed as the head of the Iranian delegation to the Baghdad Conference was overshadowed by the decision to appoint Fuad Rohani instead. This choice by NIOC demonstrated a shift in the leadership's attitude towards cooperation with oil producers in the region and beyond. Fuad Rohani, a seasoned jurist with extensive experience in the Iranian oil industry and a track record of effectively promoting Iran's interests in negotiations with the Consortium, proved to be a strategic and suitable candidate for the role.

Rohani's appointment was not merely a matter of representation; it signified a change in approach and a willingness to engage with other oil-producing nations on a more substantive level. As someone who was already deeply involved in negotiating Iran's share of oil with the Consortium, Rohani brought valuable expertise to the table. His understanding of the intricacies of the oil industry and prior experience in promoting Iran's interests in international negotiations made him an ideal candidate to lead the Iranian delegation. Moreover, the decision to appoint Fuad Rohani showcased NIOC's commitment to securing Iran's position in the evolving global oil landscape. It signalled a proactive approach to cooperation with other oil producers and a strategic shift towards strengthening Iran's position within OPEC. Rohani's appointment as the head of the delegation foreshadowed the critical role he would play in Iran's involvement with OPEC and its efforts to assert itself on the international oil stage.

Fuad Rohani's diary provides insights into the pressures the Consortium, particularly represented by British Petroleum (BP), exerted on the Iranian government to distance itself from OPEC. In one notable meeting between Abdollah Entezam, the General Director of NIOC, and Bridgeman, the representative of BP, which took place in Tehran in October 1962, BP offered a loan to Iran on the condition that it leaves OPEC.[44] The Consortium's intention was likely to weaken OPEC's influence and maintain its own dominance over Iran's oil resources.

The rejection of the British Petroleum's offer by NIOC and the Iranian government demonstrates their commitment to remaining in OPEC and maintaining their engagement with other oil-producing countries. However, the radical stances occasionally adopted by some OPEC members, such as Venezuela or Iraq, did create challenges for the Iranian government in OPEC. To navigate these complexities and ensure its interests were safeguarded, the Iranian government adopted a more moderate approach within OPEC. This balanced stance allowed Iran to be an active participant in the organisation while also taking into account its unique geopolitical and economic considerations.[45]

According to Parviz Mina, the Iranian performance in OPEC during the early years of the organisation was characterised by unevenness. While many oil experts and historians often attribute this inconsistency solely to the uninterrupted pressure exerted by the Consortium, Mina argues that there were other significant factors at play.

One of the major obstacles that the Iranian government faced in adopting a more consistent and homogeneous policy towards OPEC was its commitment to ambitious development plans initiated and restructured since the early 1960s. These development plans aimed to drive economic growth, modernisation, and social welfare initiatives in Iran. As a result, the government had to carefully balance its involvement in OPEC to secure a better share of oil revenues while also ensuring sufficient funds for these development projects. This balancing act put Iran in a position where it had to fluctuate its stance within OPEC. The government sought to assert its interests and negotiate favourable terms for its oil exports, while simultaneously managing its commitments to development initiatives. This fluctuation in policy was a response to the complex and competing demands placed on the Iranian government both domestically and internationally.

By considering the broader context of Iran's development plans and its economic ambitions, Mina highlights that the Iranian government's approach to OPEC was not solely driven by external pressure from the Consortium. Instead, it was a result of the intricate web of interests, goals, and challenges that the country faced during that period.[46] Indeed, the high dependency of Iran's economy on oil revenue played a pivotal role in shaping the country's approach to both the Consortium and OPEC. As a major oil-producing country, Iran sought to maximise its oil revenue through increased production and also to adopt a more competitive stance within OPEC to secure a larger share of oil revenues.

During the 1960s, Iran's oil production ranked fourth among OPEC members, providing about 13 per cent of the total OPEC production. Venezuela, Kuwait, and Saudi Arabia were the top three oil-exporting nations during this period, and their outputs were relatively close to each other. This competitive environment within OPEC, where leading Middle Eastern oil producers had nearly equal outputs, further underscored the importance for Iran to strategically position itself to optimise its oil revenue. As a result, the Iranian government's approach to both the Consortium and OPEC was shaped by the economic imperatives of securing sufficient funds for its ambitious development plans and mitigating the country's high dependency on oil revenue.

Asadollah Alam, noted in his diary the critical importance of oil revenue for Iran in 1966, particularly in the context of ongoing development plans that faced serious jeopardy.[47] Alam's diary highlights a meeting where the Shah expressed his frustration with the Consortium for not meeting Iran's development needs. The Shah's frustration was evident, and he went as far as suggesting that the Directorial of Oil issue an ultimatum to the Consortium. The ultimatum proposed by the Shah aimed to pressure the Consortium to reach an agreement within a month; otherwise, Iran would take unilateral action against the Consortium. This strong reaction from the Shah reflected the country's urgent need for sufficient oil revenue to support its ambitious development plans.

The Shah's passionate response and call for an ultimatum demonstrate the level of concern and urgency within the Iranian government to secure adequate oil revenue. This situation further highlights the complex dynamics and negotiations between Iran and the Consortium during the 1960s, as both parties sought to safeguard their respective interests and ensure a fair distribution of oil revenue.[48]

In 1967, the NIOC sponsored the publication of a book authored by David Missen, a British financial consultant. In this book, Missen compared Iran's population, per capita revenues from oil, and share of total Middle East oil

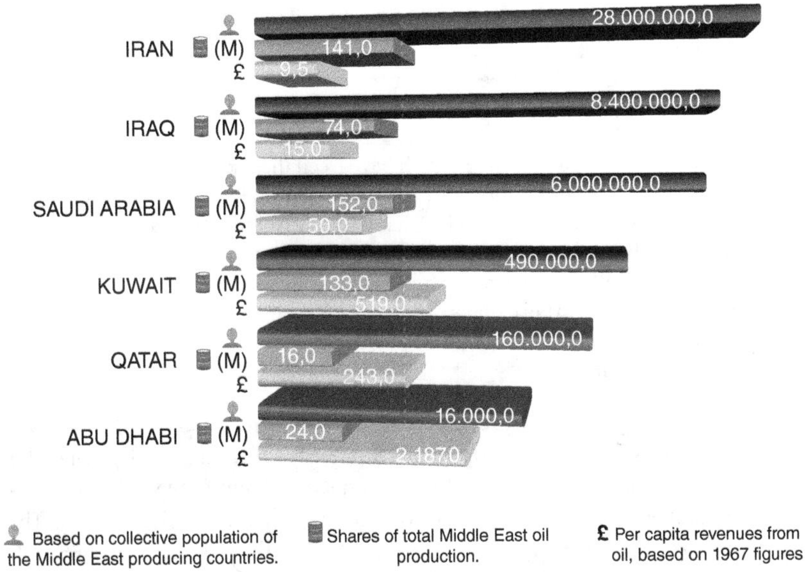

Figure 8.1 Population and income in relation to oil production in the Middle East, 1968[49]

production to those of its neighbouring oil-exporting countries, including Kuwait, Abu Dhabi, Qatar, Saudi Arabia, and Iraq. Missen's argument was chiefly centred on Iran's substantial population, totalling more than twenty-eight million, which was approximately twice the combined population of the other Middle East oil-exporting countries (Figure 8.1). Despite being a significant producer and exporter of oil, Iran's current level of output was characterised as modest when considering its large population. This resulted in a per capita revenue from oil that amounted to less than ten British Pounds per person annually, which was considerably lower compared to the considerably higher revenues per capita attained by Kuwait and Abu Dhabi.

The book explicitly presented Iran's oil demands, emphasising the necessity of increasing oil revenues to support the country's impressive economic and social development planning. Missen argued that Iran had managed to free itself from dependence on foreign aid, but in doing so, the country's reliance on increasing earnings from the export of its own produce, particularly oil, had intensified. He pointed out that internationally accepted justifications for economic development, particularly through trade rather than aid, strongly underscored Iran's essential need for export opportunities. Given the stage of Iran's economic development at that time, increased opportunities for exporting Iranian oil became crucial for the country's economic growth. The revenue generated from oil exports could support the implementation of Iran's ambitious development plans and foster sustained progress in various sectors of the economy.

By presenting a case for Iran's increased oil export opportunities, the Missen reinforced the country's position in international negotiations with the Consortium and underscored the importance of oil revenue for Iran's economic and social development plans:

> Iran is one of the few countries which have freed themselves from dependence on aid. But in the process Iran's dependence on increasing earnings from the export of her own produce has been enhanced. The internationally accepted case for justified economic development, and where possible for development through trade rather than aid, strongly emphasise Iran's essential need for export opportunities. Inevitably at the present stage of Iran's economic development this means increased opportunities for export of Iranian oil.[50]

David Missen's argument for the increase in oil incomes aligns with the inauguration of Iran's Fourth Development Plan. According to this plan, in order to achieve the ambitious goals outlined, Iran's oil revenue needed to experience a substantial increase, with an average growth rate of 17 per cent. The target was for the oil revenue to climb from 865 million dollars to 1,555 million dollars in 1972, contributing 80 per cent of the planned development expenditure.

To attain such a significant inflow of foreign exchange for the country's economic development, Iran aimed to increase its share of the Middle East oil production from 25 to 35 per cent. This growth in Iran's oil output was in contrast to the output of other major Middle Eastern oil producers at that time, including Iraq, Saudi Arabia, Kuwait, Qatar, and Abu Dhabi.

In his survey, Missen examined the geostrategic status of these major Middle Eastern oil producers compared to Iran. The increased share of Middle East oil production that Iran sought to achieve was part of its broader economic development strategy. By enhancing its oil production and securing a larger portion of the regional market, Iran aimed to bolster its financial resources for the implementation of the Fourth and Five-Year Development Plan.

Missen's analysis likely emphasised the importance of oil revenue for Iran's development plans and the country's positioning within the competitive landscape of Middle Eastern oil producers. Iran's drive to increase its oil output and revenue was a reflection of its determination to achieve economic self-sufficiency and fulfil its developmental objectives during this period of significant growth and modernisation efforts. The book likely served as a lobbying tool to garner support for Iran's push for higher oil production. It underscored the economic advantages of increasing output and argued that doing so would result in a substantial boost to Iran's per capita income from oil exports. By making a case for increased production, the NIOC aimed to promote Iran's economic interests and position the country as a more competitive player within the Middle Eastern oil market.

In 1968, Iran's efforts to increase its oil revenue targeted both OPEC and the Consortium. The country insisted that its oil production rate within OPEC should be associated with its relatively high population compared to other OPEC member nations. Additionally, Iran emphasised its need to pursue its development plans, as outlined in the Fourth Development Plan. In March 1968, Prime Minster Amir-Abbas Hoveyda, in a speech to the Iranian Parliament, announced his government's intention to align oil output with Iran's development program:

> The oil income figures contained in the 1968 budget reflect neither Iran's true needs nor its demands. They merely represent the bare minimum required by Iran during the five years period of the Fourth Development Plan. We cannot stand by idly while our own oil resources are kept unexploited underground and not utilized for the country's development.[51]

The Iranian government's focus on connecting its oil production to its population size and development requirements was an attempt to make a compelling case within OPEC for a more favourable allocation of oil revenues. This ongoing promotion by Iran for increased oil revenue demonstrated the country's commitment to economic growth and self-sufficiency. It also reflected Iran's assertive approach in international negotiations with both OPEC and the Consortium, as it sought to ensure its fair share of oil revenue to fuel its development plans and drive progress in various sectors of the economy.

During the Fourth Development Plan, Iran's Directorial of Oil, which operated under the Ministry of Finance, presented a comprehensive list of the country's development expenditure to the Consortium.[52] This list included the planned allocation of funds for various development projects and initiatives envisioned in the development plan. Notably, over 63 per cent of the total development expenditure was expected to come from oil revenue. This highlights the significant reliance of Iran's economy on oil income during this period. The country aimed to utilise a substantial portion of its oil revenue to finance its ambitious development goals, which encompassed projects across different sectors of the economy.

The Fourth Development Plan aimed to boost Iran's annual national Gross Domestic Product by 9 per cent.[53] This ambitious target reflected Iran's determination to achieve rapid economic growth and modernisation during the specified period. By presenting the comprehensive list of development expenditure to the Consortium, Iran sought to ensure that its projected oil revenue would be sufficient to fund the planned development initiatives. It demonstrated the country's proactive approach in seeking financial support and favourable terms from the Consortium to support its economic growth and development aspirations. The country's focus on using oil income to drive economic growth underscored the crucial role of the oil sector in financing the nation's developmental initiatives and boosting its GDP during this period.

Life and Work in Oil Industry: Navigating Change

In a study, Hassan Hakimian proffers a meticulous chronicle concerning the process of industrialisation and the corresponding living standards experienced by the working class within Iran's societal tapestry during the temporal span extending from 1960 to 1979.[54] According to Hakimian, the economic recession that transpired in the waning years of the 1950s, coupled with the nascent years of the 1960s, gradually relinquished its hold to a phase of moderate recuperation commencing post-1964.

In relation to the working class stratum engaged in industrial vocations, their purchasing power underwent a relatively swift restoration; indeed, by the year 1967, their real wages exhibited an ascension by approximately 17 per cent, when contrasted against the benchmarks of 1962. This upward trajectory is emblematic of the overarching expansion that pervaded the industrial milieu, an expansion incited under the aegis of protective policy frameworks intrinsic to the stabilisation program. This developmental thrust persisted harmoniously within the broader edifice of successive Five-Year development plans, characterising the ensuing years.

> The introduction, in particular, of the Fourth Development Plan in 1968 gave a new impetus to this recovery. Under this plan, the government placed particular emphasis on the construction of heavy industries. As a result, these years saw the initiation of some of Iran's most important basic industries. A steel mill complexes in Isfahan, two machine-tool plants in Arak and Tabriz and petrochemicals complex in Shahpur were some of the most outstanding.[55]

In reference to the working class within the industrial sector, data compiled for specific industries during the years 1969–74, as well as for major manufacturing firms from 1974 to 1979, both attest to a notably enhanced advancement in authentic purchasing capacities. In the year 1975 alone, these capacities experienced a substantial surge of up to 22 per cent, and within a mere span of two years starting from 1974, they escalated by a full one-third. By 1976, real wages had reached a twofold increase compared to their level in 1969, and come 1978, the purchasing potency of labourers within the expansive manufacturing establishments had soared by 50 per cent in comparison to the figures of 1974.[56]

For the industrial workforce, a recovery process initiated by the expansion of heavy industries in the latter part of the 1960s was further propelled by the oil boom. In actuality, their purchasing power exhibited an estimated augmentation of 40–50 per cent between the years 1962 and 1973, and a remarkable surge of as much as 100 per cent between 1969 and 1978.

In 1963 and 1964, the NIOC disseminated two pamphlets titled Oil and Abadan (*Naft va Abadan*) and Activities of the NIOC (*Faʿaliyat-ha-ye Sherkat-e Melli-ye Naft-e Iran*), that commenced with a succinct exposition concerning the historical trajectory of the oil industry within Iran, followed by an examination of the operations conducted at the in both oilfield and the Abadan Refinery. Subsequently, these pamphlets provided a comprehensive report delineating the labour conditions and lifestyles of the workforce engaged in the oil industry at large, with a particular focus on the municipality of Abadan.

In accordance with the pamphlets, from the years 1963–64, it is revealed that among the overall workforce of 56,000 individuals employed within the oil industry during that period, a notable contingent of 18,000 personnel was engaged in labour primarily centred at the Abadan facility, particularly in the refinery sector, while the remaining 38,250 individuals were deployed within the oilfields. By taking into account the conventional family unit comprising an average of four members, it can be inferred that the collective populace affiliated with the NIOC amounted to a total of 225,000 individuals. These individuals were distributed across a network encompassing forty distinct urban centres and rural settlements.

As delineated in Chapter 7, commencing with the inception of the Consortium's operations in 1954, the Consortium undertook various non-industrial responsibilities on behalf of the NIOC. Over time, the management of these non-industrial responsibilities was progressively transferred to the NIOC. A substantial portion of these non-industrial functions was officially transitioned to the NIOC's purview in the year 1961. These responsibilities encompassed a wide range of activities, including those related to engineering and residential construction, water and electricity provisioning, road maintenance, healthcare services, technical and educational initiatives, industrial training programs, dining establishments, social welfare undertakings, and recreational provisions.

According to data provided by the NIOC for the period spanning from 1961 to 1964, a cumulative total of 2,650 new residences were erected to accommodate workers and other personnel employed within the oil industry (Table 8.2). When incorporating this figure into the existing housing stock allocated for oil industry employees, the total number of residential units available as of the conclusion of the year 1964 stood as follows.

Based on the data presented in the table, it can be deduced that in the year 1964, approximately 80 per cent of the oil industry employees based in Abadan

Table 8.2 *The number of houses of the NIOC by the end of 1964*

Location	Workers	Other personals	Total
Abadan	10,176	4,355	14,531
Oil fields	9,440	2,514	11,964
Along pipelines	528	217	745

Source: Activities of the NIOC (Tehran: NIOC, 1964).

were residing in company-provided housing. Conversely, for employees stationed in the oilfields, this proportion was notably lower, with approximately 31 per cent of them residing in company-provided accommodations.

The pamphlets published by the NIOC offer concise accounts of the healthcare infrastructure within the oil industry. According to the NIOC's records, Abadan, boasting two 570-bed hospitals, 10 urban clinics, and 20 mobile clinics dedicated primarily to addressing the prevalent trachoma ailment within the city, stands out as the primary provider of healthcare services within the oil industry. In the year 1964, Abadan had a total medical workforce of 101 physicians, 6 dentists, 5 pharmacists, and 430 nurses diligently serving the community.

Besides Abadan, hospitals and clinics were also established within the extensive oil infrastructure network of Khuzestan, encompassing oil fields and oil transfer routes. Cities such as Masjed-Soleyman, which stands as the oldest epicentre of Iran's oil industry, boasted the highest concentration of healthcare facilities. Among these were a 165-bed hospital and ten clinics. Aghajari followed closely, featuring three hospitals with a combined total of 157 beds and seven clinics. Similarly, in urban centres such as Ahvaz, Gachsaran, Khark, Haftgel, and Tehran, the NIOC operated dedicated hospitals and clinics catering to its workforce.

Health education, the drive against communicable diseases, public vaccination campaigns, and the establishment of sanatoriums, including the tuberculosis sanatorium in Kut-ʿAbdullah neighbourhood of Ahvaz, were integral components of the health initiatives spearheaded by the Oil Company. In 1941, the Abadan Higher School of Nursing was founded, and its scope gradually expanded starting in 1958. Housed in a building adjoining the Abadan Central Hospital, this institution assumed the vital responsibility of training nurses to serve in various hospitals and clinics associated with the oil industry.

Reshaping the Fabric of Everyday Life

The enduring legacy of the Anglo-Iranian Oil Company era within the oil industry persisted in the form of pervasive discrimination at all levels. This discrimination permeated every aspect of life, encompassing disparities in access to housing, education, healthcare, and recreational opportunities. Such discrimination, emblematic of a highly rigid hierarchical structure, manifested not solely among Iranian employees of the Oil Company but also extended to foreign personnel engaged in the oil industry. In the context of segregation, it is pertinent to observe that although workers and office employees were afforded equal access to healthcare facilities in emergency cases, a pronounced disparity existed within the realm of the Oil Company's housing, healthcare commercial outlets, recreational venues, and cinematic establishments.

The city of Abadan was broadly categorised into four distinct neighbourhoods: (1) Working-Class Areas: This sector includes neighbourhoods such as

Ahmedabad, Kofeysheh, Chadorabad, Jamshidabad, and Bahmanshir. These areas primarily housed the working class population. (2) City Centre: The central area of Abadan, characterised by the presence of shops, cinemas, and various government buildings. This part of the city served as a bustling commercial and administrative hub. (3) Foreign and Iranian Oil Company Residential Zone: This section was reserved for foreign employees and Iranian staff of the Oil Company. It accommodated both local and international employees associated with the oil industry. (4) Braim neighbourhood: The Brim region was reserved for high-ranking foreign employees, military commanders, and police high personnel. It was a prestigious and exclusive area within the city, catering to individuals in positions of authority. These distinct neighbourhoods reflected the social and occupational stratification within Abadan during the era of the Anglo-Iranian Oil Company.

The Oil Company Hospital in Abadan was comprised of two distinct departments, referred to as 'number one' and 'number two'. Hospital number one primarily catered to the needs of the workers and provided services through general practitioners. In contrast, hospital number two was exclusively reserved for the company's employees. This department not only had general practitioners but also specialised doctors on staff. In cases where a patient from hospital number one was needed specialised medical attention, they would grant permission for that individual to be transferred to hospital number two. This transfer typically occurred when the medical condition warranted the expertise available at the second hospital.

Within the domains of entertainment, a clear-cut segregation policy was rigorously enforced. As a case in point, the retail establishments and recreational clubs designated for office employees and engineers were distinct from those allocated for the labouring workforce. By way of illustration, during the mid-1960s, the city of Abadan boasted seven retail stores designated exclusively for office employees, while the workers enjoyed access to ten such establishments for their own.

Entertainment and sports clubs in Abadan were organised to cater to different segments of the population, each with varying levels of exclusivity and amenities: (1) Naft Club (formerly Gymkana Club): This club, situated in Braim, was exclusively designated for the highest-ranking oil managers. It provided a wide range of entertainment and sports facilities for this elite group. (2) Golestan and Bovardeh Clubs: These clubs were established to serve engineers and high-ranking clerks. Golestan was located in Braim, while Bovardeh was situated in the Bovardeh neighbourhood. These clubs offered a range of leisure and recreational activities for their members. (3) Iran Club: The Iran Club was designed to accommodate lower-ranking oil employees and was located in Sikh-Lane. It provided entertainment and sports facilities suitable for this demographic. (4) Abadan Workers Club: In the city of Abadan, there existed two distinct workers' clubs. The first, situated in Bahmanshir, was the older and larger of the two clubs, specifically designed to cater exclusively to the requirements and inclinations of oil industry workers. The second club, known as the Piruz Club, was situated in Piruzabad. In general, these clubs reflected the social hierarchy and different categories of employees within the oil industry in Abadan during that period.

In addition to sports clubs, in Abadan, there were distinct cinemas catering to different groups of workers and office employees, each with its own set of rules and ambience: (1) Taj Cinema was designated for the employees of the Oil Consortium. To gain entry, employees were required to be dressed in formal attire, including a tie and suit. Taj Cinema provided a more upscale and formal cinematic experience. (2) Bahmanshir Cinema was intended for the workers and their families. It was an open-air cinema without a roof, featuring low and flat walls. Seating was limited, and many attendees would bring twenty-liter boxes of beer to use as makeshift seats. The atmosphere at Bahmanshir Cinema was more casual and open. (3) Annex Cub and Cinema, exclusively reserved for the high-ranking employees. Workers were not granted access to this club, which suggests a clear distinction in social and recreational spaces based on employment status. These examples reflect the social stratification and distinct leisure facilities provided to different categories of individuals within the oil industry in Abadan.

In the 1960s, a rigid hierarchy and ethnic segregation permeated every facet of daily existence, both among Iranians and non-Iranians. Willie Nijman, at that time a young woman from the Netherlands, reflects on her experiences living in Khuzestan during that period and her employment within the oil sector. She shares her story, giving us a glimpse into the challenges and experiences of working in the oil industry amid the backdrop of a divided society:

> In the year 1963, at the tender age of twenty-one, I married to Masoud Akhbari. The journey of life led me to Iran, where we took up residence in the heart of Masjed-Soleyman. Masoud, gainfully employed in the Oil Consortium as a junior surveyor in the Department of Drawing of Aerial Photography, toiled to support our livelihood. Our abode was a modest two-room dwelling for junior employees, a world apart from the grandeur of the senior executives' residences. Amidst the humble abode of Masjed-Soleyman, I embraced the role of a typist and later ascended to the esteemed position of secretary within the Consortium of Oil Company. Yet, what tugged at my heartstrings incessantly was the absence of interaction with fellow Dutch nationals.
>
> One fateful day, as Masoud returned from a spirited game of cricket, he relayed the news of an encounter with a Dutch lady, one who might alleviate my sense of isolation. Eagerly, I accepted his offer to introduce us. The prospect of meeting a fellow Dutchwoman named Ms. Flokman, though older than myself, was a ray of hope. However, our initial exchange transpired in a manner that shook me to my core. With bluntness that could have felled me like a boulder, she declared, 'I must be frank; you will never be embraced by the Dutch community due to your marriage to an Iranian.' Stunned, I was left reeling by her words. As time passed, I

> begrudgingly acknowledged that there was some truth to her statement. For instance, when the Dutch Ambassador graced Khuzestan with his presence, I received an invitation to the ladies' morning coffee, alongside other Dutch women. Yet, the moment I entered, conversations ceased, and a palpable sense of exclusion enveloped me. Subsequently, at the evening cocktail party attended by the ambassador and his spouse, my husband and I found ourselves conspicuously omitted from the dinner guest list. When I inquired with the Head of Public Relations, Mr. Afshari, as to the rationale behind this oversight, he attributed it to the ambassador's preference for conversing exclusively in Dutch, insinuating that my husband's lack of Dutch fluency was the impediment. This explanation, however, rang hollow, for there was another Dutch lady serving as a secretary, whose husband hailed from the United States and was wholly unversed in the Dutch language, yet they had secured a place at the dinner table.
>
> On yet another occasion, a St. Nicholas celebration for children was organised in Masjed-Soleyman, featuring the arrival of St. Nicholas via helicopter instead of the traditional boat. Ms. Flokman, enlisting my assistance to prepare the program for the festivity, casually inquired whether I had children of my own. My response was affirmative, and I proudly divulged that I had two sons from my husband's previous marriage, both well-versed in the customs and songs of St. Nicholas. To my astonishment, Ms. Flokman promptly conveyed her reluctance to have these children participate, asserting, 'I regret to inform you that we do not wish to include those children in our event.' I swiftly retorted that I would not be complicit in such exclusionary sentiments and declined to draft the program on her behalf.[57]

Masoud Akhbari, while acknowledging the pronounced segregation prevalent throughout all echelons of the oil industry, resonant with the historical practices of the Anglo Iranian Oil Company in this sector, posits that this segregation gradually abated as the 1960s drew to a close:

> By the culmination of the 1960s, an era of transformation was ushered in with the proliferation of welfare amenities tailored for the workers and those occupying lower strata within the oil industry. The once conspicuous disparities began to recede into the annals of history. In the early 1970s, a remarkable upsurge in the strength of labour and employee unions, accompanied by resolute grassroots advocacy, impelled the management of the oil industry to adopt a more accommodating stance, acquiescing to the collective demands. This shift heralded a substantial metamorphosis in both the living and working milieu. Moreover, this transformation exerted a profound influence on the interplay between Iranian and non-Iranian employees within the oil industry.[58]

The veracity of this assertion will be subject to further scrutiny in the following chapter.

9

Shop Floor Labour Activism: From the White to the Islamic Revolution

In the period leading up to the revolution, an intricate array of narratives emerged concerning the state of the Iranian working class, reflecting diverse and sometimes conflicting viewpoints. On one hand, a segment of the academic community firmly rejected any claims of enhancements in the living and working conditions of workers during the era of state-led development. This view interpreted the absence of confrontational labour activism as clear evidence of the state's suppression of the labour movement. In stark contrast, another group of scholars highlighted the social welfare policies enacted by the government in the 1960s and 1970s, arguing that these measures made any form of labour movement, whether radical or moderate, unnecessary during that period. According to this viewpoint, it was the government's interventions that were instrumental in elevating the quality of life and work for the labour force.

In her study, Maral Jefroudi review and criticise the perspectives of certain Marxist scholars, including Fred Halliday, who dismiss labour activism in Iran during the 1960s, as the period of 'long night of the 1960s' for working people.[1] In contrast, Jefroudi contends that the absence of 'transformative or antagonistic' labour activism during the 1960s should not be equated with a lack of labour activism altogether. She accurately argues that 'as a study of collective actions of Iranian oil workers during the 1960s demonstrate, action can have short life span and be co-opted in discursive ways they are articulated, but the does not mean they did not occur or were not successful'.[2] Moreover, following a comprehensive examination that includes a critical assessment of a July 1970 report from the United States State Department,[3] coupled with a comparative analysis of various other narratives, Jefroudi articulates her conclusions regarding the activism of oil workers during the 1960s in the following terms:

> Most of these strikes were short and nonviolent and appeared to be spontaneous and focused on one demand. They were mostly successful. The 1965, 1969, and 1970 strikes in Abadan were quickly settled, with the longest one lasting two weeks, and the workers' demands were met to a large extent. Furthermore, despite the 'illegality' of strikes in the post-coup d'état regime, none of the strikes, except that of the bus drivers of Tehran, were recorded as illegal, and the participants were paid in full for the time they spent on strike. The labour affairs report of the Department of State

> points out that most of the work stoppages were settled quickly and, most of the time, informally through the intervention of the Ministry of Labour and generally on more favourable terms than the labour laws required.[4]

In discussing the essentialist perspective adopted by certain Marxist scholars and activists, including Fred Halliday, it is important to recognise that Halliday was not the only prominent figure within Marxist academia to explore the complex development of Iran in the decades leading up to the revolution. The situation of the Iranian working class during the 1960s and 1970s presented a complex and contentious issue, sparking confusion not only among scholars but also among many Marxist revolutionary activists. Bijan Jazani, a scholarly and fervent Marxist revolutionary, known for his theoretical contributions as well as his activism within the Iranian New Left, was similarly committed to analysing the intricate socio-economic changes in Iran at the time.

In the autumn of 1967, when the Third Development Plan had ended, Bijan Jazani and his comrades published a study of Iranian society and the living standards of the different strata of workers and peasants.[5] The main argument of this thesis was that:

> Following the coup d'état of 19 August [1953], militarisation and the rule of a police state over socio-political milieus has become the regime's main underlying policy. This policy even at the peak of the regime's reform manoeuvres remained constantly in force.... The reform manoeuvres which the regime began since 1962 were not comparable to any previous reforms in terms of their form or content. When we use the word manoeuvre for the regime's reforms it does not mean that steps were not taken towards reforms.... Every manoeuvre leads to its own impact, depending on its depth and range and this impact in turn leads to change. A closer observation of the regime's current reform manoeuvres is important since some erroneously believe that the nadir of the political movement and silence of the people is due to these manoeuvres, and this has hindered any progress the [political] movement might have made. However, in our opinion, although we do not refute some of the impacts of these manoeuvres, the main reason for the silence of Iranian society is indeed the unprecedented suppression and dictatorship which silences any opposition with bullets.[6]

Masoud Ahmadzadeh, another guerrilla warfare pioneer, in his book *Mobarezeh-e Mosallahaneh, ham Esteratezhi, ham Taktik* (Armed Struggle, Both Strategy and Tactic), which carries the date of publication, summer 1970, discusses the outcome of the White Revolution and land reform and addresses the different stages of its implementation. According to Ahmadzadeh the goal of the White Revolution was to extend the influence of imperialism in urban and rural areas. When the feudal economy conflicted with the interests of imperialism, without facing a serious problem or needing the help of people for the suppression of feudalism, the regime buried feudalism which was already in demise. Moreover, he claims that the lack of widespread spontaneous movements which is inextricably linked with the harsh police state has practically distanced workers from any political views or actions. Thus, in this respect the workers are not ready to accept political leadership and develop the class consciousness. Accordingly, in the absence of any notable spontaneous mass movements, it is not possible to witness the formation of widespread labour movement.[7]

The reassessment of literature and analysis of the labour movement during the 1960s by two eminent theorists in guerrilla warfare, Jazani and Ahmadzadeh, underscores their divergent yet similarly constrained, prejudiced, and ideologically tinted comprehension of the reforms implemented in the 1960s by the developmental state. Nevertheless, despite these differences, it is noteworthy that both theorists concurred on the notion that the labour movement acts as a revolutionary apparatus for the acquisition of political power. Within this paradigm, they posited that there is no allowance for the accommodation of trade union demands or for the non-radical articulation of such demands within the labour movement.

Considering the old left, Siavush Randjbar-Daemi, in his comprehensive analysis of the historical perspective on the Tudeh Party's position regarding the Shah's White Revolution, concludes that although the Tudeh Party, in alignment with other opposition groups, abstained from participating in the White Revolution's referendum. They cited concerns that the Shah intended to exploit the referendum as a means to further 'enhance his absolute authority, consolidate it, and legitimize his unlawful authoritarian rule'. It is important to note, however, that their decision to abstain from the referendum should not be interpreted as opposition to key components of the White Revolution. These included land redistribution among farmers, the elimination of the peasant-landlord (*arbab-raʿiyat*) system, improvements in workers' conditions, eradication of widespread illiteracy, and the nationalisation of forest resources.[8]

The analysis of labour activities throughout Iran, with a specific focus on the oil industry, during the fifteen years leading up to the extensive political strike by oil workers that began in the months prior to the Islamic Revolution, provides strong evidence supporting the claim that the sequence of union-driven efforts by workers to secure trade union demands did not lead to a passivity within the labour movement. These endeavours predominantly concluded with the triumph of the workers in securing their demands. The majority of these trade union endeavours were orchestrated under the auspices of unions established by the workers over this fifteen years period, aligning themselves within the contours of the prevailing political order. Yadollah Khosrowshahi, a prominent activist within the realm of oil workers, recounts the genesis of these unions in his published memoirs:

> Commencing in 1961, the question of workers' representation gained prominence, and by 1962, workers within various sectors, such as refinery repair workers and distribution personnel, began selecting representatives. Following the election of these representatives, workers articulated their grievances and concerns. Over time, these individual demands coalesced into collective expressions, yet they did not evolve into the establishment of a formal syndicate or union. Notably, in 1964, the inaugural assembly for Collective Agreements among oil workers transpired. Concurrently, a delegation of representatives journeyed to Tehran to finalize the contract, thereby instigating speculations about the potential formation of a union within the oil industry upon their return.[9]

Corroborating Khosrowshahi's first-hand narrative, Robert Livernash and Kamal Argheyd assert in their study that the dynamics of labour relations in Iran, particularly within the industrial sector, underwent a gradual transformation starting from 1964:

> In the early 1960s, the political situation in the country had stabilized. The government also had adopted a positive labour relations posture encouraging the organisation of syndicates and requiring the election of employee representatives in industrial establishments with more than ten employees. Gradually over these years, led by the sponsorship of a powerful Ministry of Labour, a limited but increasingly significant industrial relations system was created. An important milestone in this development was the comprehensive revision of the Labour Act with the assistance of experts from the International Labour Organisation. This was begun in 1958 and passed by Parliament in 1965. A key provision of this act was that neither the workers nor syndicate representatives nor officers could be discharged or have their jobs changed in a manner hindering the execution of their duties without prior approval of the Ministry of Labour.[10]

As a result, the count of syndicates or industry-based labour unions increased from 16 in 1964 to a total of 519 by 1972. Notably, the oil industry constituted a share of twenty-eight syndicates within this overall figure.[11] According to Khosrowshahi, the syndicates of oil workers played a significantly more proactive role. Formal collective bargaining within this sector extended to a more comprehensive spectrum of issues, encompassing considerations such as wages, various allowances for housing and travel, health benefits, annual leaves, as well as pensions and retirement plans. Noteworthy is the fact that collective bargaining within the oil industry operated on a regional basis.[12]

In the presence of these syndicates within the oil industry, a pressing concern among detractors of Iran's political system during that period revolved around the assessment of these syndicates' functions. Particularly within the revolutionary political spectrum, for many adversaries, any endeavour lacking a revolutionary spirit, despite advocating for specific demands and endeavouring to realise them through various means, was not perceived as a genuine struggle.

Instead, it was deemed as contributing to the entrenchment of the political system and its authoritarian reforms. Such a perspective rigidly viewed the established system as immutable. One must acknowledge that the labour movement of that decade was reformist in nature rather than revolutionary, driven by demands articulated within the framework of the law.

Nevertheless, the workers ardently pursued their objectives through the employment of distinct methodologies. Principally, these strategies were intricately interwoven with the references incorporated by the Shah in his addresses to the working class, a facet integral to the promotion of his White Revolution. These references were directed towards cultivating more propitious conditions for labour and life, encompassing advancements in the working milieu, amplified purchasing power, enhanced healthcare, and more adequate housing – all of which, as asserted by the Shah, constituted inherent entitlements of the working class. Afshin Matin-asgari posits that the official discourse of the White Revolution bore substantial indebtedness to a Marxist interpretation of modern history. The Shah contended that his revolution had effectively eradicated feudalism, liberated the workers, peasants, and women, instituted an exemplary welfare system, and championed the global struggle against imperialist oil cartels.[13] In a 1973 interview with Oriana Fallaci, the Shah, identifying himself as socialist, asserted that, 'My White Revolution is an incentive to work. It is a new original kind of socialism'.[14]

In the early 1970s, as articulated by Habib Ladjevardi, the injection of oil revenues into the national economy precipitated a surge in prices, notably in the realm of housing costs. In response, a concerted effort was initiated to construct company housing for workers. Following a televised proclamation by the Shah mandating that all industrial proprietors' erect residences for their workforce, the workers of one of the oil industry's plants initiated a strike, demanding immediate adherence to the Shah's directive. Facing an impasse, the plant's personnel office sought assistance from the Ministry of Labour. However, attempts by Ministry officials to pacify the workers proved futile. In a somewhat naive move, 'worker deputies in the Majles' were summoned to elucidate that the implementation of His Majesty's orders necessitated time. This stratagem, too, fell short of assuaging the workers, who, attuned to government tactics, were in the process of devising their own strategies. Accusing the visiting deputies of deceit and betrayal of the White Revolution, the strikers insisted that the Shah himself make another television appearance to elucidate his authentic intentions. The workers astutely realised that by professing loyalty to the Shah, they could critique the policies implemented by Ministry officials. Earlier reports had conveyed an incident in Abadan where oil workers obstructed their managers from leaving the refinery. This was accomplished by affixing pictures of the Shah onto the managers' automobile doors, accompanied by chants of 'Javid Shah' (long live the king). To open their car doors, the managers would have had to deface His Majesty's photograph.[15]

In 1960s and 1970s the aspirations tied to the initiatives of 'His Royal Majesty' consistently materialised seamlessly in the fulfilment of the oil workers' desires. Yadollah Khosrowshahi contends that throughout this period, in 1970, 1971 and 1972, a series of strikes emerged within the oil industry, predominantly enduring for periods ranging from one to five days.[16] Mohammad Safavi, an esteemed activist among the Abadani oil workers, corroborates that these strikes were orchestrated in collaboration with the oil workers' syndicates, yielding significant accomplishments and tangible outcomes. These encompassed crucial provisions such as adequate housing, access to mortgages, the availability of cold and potable water, equitable remuneration, inclusive benefits, the establishment of a structured job classification system, the prioritisation of safety and health measures, advancements in public healthcare, the initiation of savings and pension funds, and the establishment of a specialised clinic catering to the needs of the workers. However, it remains vital to recognise that notwithstanding these concerted endeavours led by labour activists, challenges persisted. Specifically, certain oil workers encountered arrest and prolonged incarceration by SAVAK due to their involvement in labour-related activities during this period.[17]

The paramount strike of this period was the notably triumphant 1974 strike, a subject extensively chronicled in Khosrowshahi's memoir. The strike aimed to address various pivotal issues:

- The disparity in benefits between non-workers employees and workers, wherein employees received additional perks such as refinery allowances, transportation subsidies, housing provisions, compensation for exposure to toxic gases, car purchase loans, housing repair loans, among others.
- Non-disbursement of rations and burdens.
- Housing predicaments and inadequate mortgage allowances.
- Non-payment of annual bonuses, Nowruz bonuses, and travel expenses, which were provided to workers in other industries as special benefits.

The Collective Agreement meetings, slated for January 1974, were anticipated to address these concerns. However, as most demands were unmet during the 1972 Collective Agreement, the decision was made to initiate the strike before these meetings, leveraging pressure on the Oil Company. Recognising the optimal timing during the general repairs of the refinery in May 1974, workers commenced the strike, understanding that such action would impede the entire refinery's production. Abadan and Shiraz refineries' workers mobilised during this period, working tirelessly from dawn to dusk, often through mealtimes.[18]

Approximately four or five days into the strike, representatives from the Ministry of Labour and the Oil Company attempted to address the workers but were disregarded. Subsequently, the local SAVAK chief intervened, urging Khosrowshahi to inform the workers about the labour law's provisions on strikes. Khosrowshahi, through a public address, 'highlighted the disparity between the law's provisions and its actual application, leading to a loss of dignity for the SAVAK head'.[19]

After protracted negotiations through the union with the Ministry of Labour, the workers' proposals were eventually acknowledged. Following these discussions, the workers agreed to terminate their strike. Manouchehr Eghbal, the Chairman of the National Iranian Oil Company, convened a meeting with representatives from oil workers nationwide, engaging in extensive deliberations that persisted from morning until evening, ultimately conceding to the workers' demands. Therefore, the twelve-day strike culminated in a resounding victory.

However, despite the triumph for the workers, Khosrowshahi faced arrest by SAVAK. During interrogation, he endured torture, including flogging on the soles of his feet. Pressured to confess in front of oil workers to connections with a communist network and the distribution of communist literature in the refinery, Khosrowshahi, at the end of his 'confession' in front of the workers collapsed due to severe injuries. Subsequently he hospitalised and upon recovery, he received a ten year prison sentence from a military court.[20]

Indeed, the 1974 oil workers' strike stood as the final notable strike preceding the pivotal 1978 oil strike, which played a substantial role in the downfall of the Pahlavi monarchy and the subsequent establishment of the Islamic republic in Iran. The 1978 strike was a watershed moment, significantly influencing the sociopolitical landscape and contributing significantly to the transformative events that reshaped Iran's governance structure.

On the Brink of Change

The study of the agency and position of workers and employees in the oil industry during the 1978–79 revolution in Iran cannot be undertaken without reference to its economic, and indeed political, antecedents.[21]

The roots of the Iranian Revolution can be traced to several complex factors, particularly the economic crisis that cast its shadow over Iran in a short period. While the oil price hike in 1973 and the subsequent inflation in 1975–76 played a significant role, this economic factor was part of a larger context. These backgrounds included the sharp increase in oil prices in 1973 due to the Arab countries oil embargo and OPEC-led price hikes. During the 1973 Arab Israeli War, Arab members of the OPEC imposed oil embargo against the United States in retaliation for the United States support of Israel and resupply the Israeli military. This surge in oil prices brought considerable export foreign revenues for oil-producing countries such as Iran. When developmental states including Iran, injected these oil export revenues into their national economies, liquidity inevitably surged, seeking an outlet in increased wages and the expansion of state social services, ultimately taking an unbalanced form. One of the governments most distinguished initiatives amid this context was the launch of a nationwide school-based nutrition intervention program. This program, alongside free feeding for infants up to two years of age and their mothers, mandated educational institutions to supply school children with complimentary milk and confectionery items each morning.

The minimum wage rate, which had remained stable in 1972, increased by 23.1 per cent in 1973, and the inflation rate rose from 6.3 to 11.4 per cent. The rising cost of living led to a 63.8 per cent increase in the minimum wage rate in 1974. In the short period following 1973, wage increases exceeded the consumer price index for goods and services. Between 1972 and 1974, inflation accelerated, but it was less than the growth of the nominal minimum wage. In March 1974, the Supreme Labour Council announced a new minimum wage, raising the daily industrial wage from 100 to 204 rials.[22]

The substantial increase in wages significantly propelled the migration of rural inhabitants to urban areas. In 1976, the country's urban population reached to 46.7 per cent of the total population. Living in cities, despite all its problems, became preferable to remaining in villages. In the case of Khuzestan province, this trend was markedly evident, as the population expanded by 43.28 per cent growing from 883,057 to 1,265,291. Concurrently, the urban populations of Ahvaz, Khorramshahr, and Aghajari experienced significant growth. Ahvaz saw a 59.42 per cent increase, reaching 229,006 inhabitants; Khorramshahr witnessed a 65.70 per cent rise, culminating in a population of 146.709; and Aghajari grew by 21.93 per cent, arriving at a total of 30,117 residents. During this period the population of Abadan with an increase of 8.46 per cent reached to 296.081. This demographic shift underscores the transformative impact of economic changes on population distribution within the region.[23]

Following the increase in oil revenues, people benefited from unprecedented financial wealth. Public expectations deliberately increased, bringing costs to the government that it was neither prepared for nor had a strategy to implement. As a result, the government's policy of injecting new wealth into the economy through increased public spending led to an unprecedented increase in per capita income, which in practice widened the gap between aggregate supply and demand in the macroeconomy. National income increased by an average of 35 per cent annually, and per capita income tripled in two years. Higher incomes and subsidised prices led to increased consumption. While the population grew at a rate of 3 per cent, the demand for consumer goods increased by 12 per cent annually. The value of food imports increased more than fourfold from 1973 to 1976. Consequently, due to increased imports and government current expenses, there was a deficit of 117 billion rials in 1974, which reached nearly 194 billion in 1975. Increased demand led to severe inflation. From 1973, prices increased sharply. According to official figures, the compounded inflation rate between 1973 and 1977 was 93.8 per cent, or an average annual rate of 18 per cent. In 1976, the inflation rate reached 16.5 compared to a negative 7.2 increase in the minimum wage. From the end of the same year, we witnessed several strikes. Strikes for wage increases and implementation of a law involving workers in factory profits, although this did not include the oil industry. In 1977, strikes became more widespread, although primarily cantered around trade demands, until in 1978 they increasingly took on a political hue.

The fifteen years period that began with the inauguration of the Third Development Plan in 1962 and laid the groundwork for new developmental status and rapid economic growth until 1976, ended with an intensified economic crisis in 1977. Unlike common and prevalent models of revolutions, the Iranian Revolution was the result of more than a decade of rapid economic growth followed by a short-term phase of economic recession or decline.[24]

However, it is an essentialist view to attribute the revolution solely to the prominent role of the economic crisis and ignore other factors that played a role in setting the stage for the revolution. One such factor was the political deadlock resulting from neglecting political development alongside economic development. In the authoritarian modernisation model, political agency was confined to the Shah and his political elites. There was no recourse for the people to hold anyone accountable for the widespread misconduct of coercive institutions and economic mismanagement. Political parties, unions, and other independent institutions were virtually non-existent. Repression of dissenters, corruption, inequality, and misallocation of financial resources led to either protest or passive acceptance of authoritarian modernisation. The government's inability to address economic inequalities and maintain economic stability fuelled dissatisfaction.

Internationally, the Iranian Revolution was also influenced by broader geopolitical factors, including the dynamics of the Cold War, Iran's relationship with the United States, and regional power conflicts. The United States' support for the Iranian government during the Cold War and Western intervention in Iran's affairs were so significant that any major shift in American policies quickly impacted Iran's political stability or instability. This entangled relationship with the West fuelled anti-government sentiments and brought forth demands for independence alongside freedom.

In the initial stages of protest, the rallying cries centred on the pursuit of freedom and independence, with no references to Islam or the establishment of an Islamic Republic. From the letter penned by three prominent leaders of the National Front to the Shah, Chapour Bakhtiar, Karim Sanjabi and Dariush Forouhar, on 12 June 1977, which called for the cessation of autocracy, adherence to constitutional monarchy principles, the Universal Declaration of Human Rights, freedom of press and assembly, the release of political prisoners and exiles, and governance without autocratic rule, to the Tabriz protests on 18 February 1978, there was no advocacy for an Islamic Republic. This eight-month period highlighted the secular opposition's failure to present a new political vision and to establish effective organizational and social networks crucial for revolutionary momentum. The slogan 'The Shah should reign, not rule' lacked a novelty vision. Fundamentally, a vision serves as a comprehensive, motivational, and creative declaration that encapsulates a movement's fundamental principles and values. It not only provides direction but also outlines the long-term objectives and aspirations, envisioning the anticipated state of social change that the movement aims to realise.

Against this backdrop, marked by an absence of a new political vision and the scarcity of secular parties and organizations with substantial, organised support bases, Ayatollah Khomeini recognised and seized the opportunity to assert his influence over the political landscape. The organised secular opposition was sparse, apart from a few underground armed groups remaining, which had had faced significant suppression less than two years earlier, leaving a scattered supporter base. Consequently, the secular opposition in Iran was predominantly fragmented, consisting merely of a small contingent of followers of Mosaddeq within the National Front. Ayatollah Khomeini, leveraging the role of Shiʿa Islam in Iranian society and the semi-political-social networks enabled through the unrestricted activities of mosques and Hosseiniyehs, effectively unified opponents of the Pahlavi regime with the rallying cry 'The Shah must go' and the call for the establishment of an Islamic Government.

The explicit concept of an Islamic Republic would only be articulated later. Ayatollah Khomeini's vision for change, albeit reactionary in contrast to the constitutionalist vision from seventy years prior – which targeted the confrontation of political tyranny and a privileged clerical hierarchy – presented a novel perspective for many Iranians disenchanted with both the monarchy and the inefficacy of the secular opposition. Khomeini's alternative approach to change resonated with those in search of a different future, capturing their imagination and hopes for a new direction.

In summary, the oil price surge in 1973 and subsequent economic challenges were important catalysts for the Iranian Revolution, as they contributed to economic inequalities and dissatisfaction among the people. However, these factors were intertwined with political repression, religious ideals, and a broader context of social and political unrest, all culminating in the overthrow of the Pahlavi monarchy in 1979.

The Agency of Oil Employees in the 1978–1979

Eric Hobsbawm characterised the Russian Revolution of October 1917 as the paramount event of the Twentieth Century, asserting its practical ramifications on a global scale to surpass even those of the French Revolution. In a similar vein, Hobsbawm positioned the Iranian Revolution of 1978–79 as one of the major social revolutions of the Twentieth Century.[25] While the Twentieth Century bore witness to other social revolutions, such as the Chinese and Cuban revolutions, which Hobsbawm grouped within the same paradigm as the Russian Revolution concerning their revolutionary agenda and agency, questions arise regarding the Iranian Revolution's comparability. Do the Russian and Iranian Revolutions share common attributes? Was the agency of the working class similar in both upheavals, particularly concerning their revolutionary agency?[26]

The utilisation of Eric Hobsbawm's insights regarding the Russian and Iranian Revolutions serves the purpose of evaluating the significant role undertaken by the Iranian working class, particularly highlighting the participation of oil workers during the Iranian Revolution. While the comparison concerning the decisive role of the working class in both revolutions remains contentious, similarities persist between the Russian and Iranian uprisings. Notably, both revolutions emanated from the paradigm of authoritarian modernisation. They both defied predictability, with external pressures exerting influential roles in determining their outcomes. Furthermore, both revolutions conveyed messages of global significance that transcended their regional boundaries. Ultimately, in their progression, each culminated in the establishment of a totalitarian regime. Despite their distinct limitations, their aims converged in endeavouring to inaugurate a novel archetype of humanity: the *New* Soviet *Person (novy sovetsky chelovek)*, envisioned by Lenin for the Soviet Union, and the monotheist, believer, and adherent of Shiite Islam, in alignment with religious convictions (*Ensan-e movahhed-e moslman-e Shiʿeh-ye taraz-e din*), who adheres to Ayatollah Khomeini's interpretation of Islam.

When examining the agency of the Iranian working class during the 1978–79 Iranian Revolution, there are differing perspectives among historians when it comes to evaluating the agency and timing of the working class's involvement in the revolution. While a cohort of historians highlights the agency and influential impact of the workers in large industries within the revolution, assigning them a distinct level of significance during the period yet preceding February 1979, another faction highlights the late integration of industrial workers, particularly those in relatively prosperous conditions, into the revolutionary movement.

The late involvement of oil industry workers, in particular, is seen as noteworthy by this second group of scholars. For the latter group, the industrial workers, including those in large industries such as textiles, steel, and oil, were not initially at the forefront of the revolutionary movement. Instead, they suggest that these workers joined the protests and strikes later in the course of the revolution, after other segments of society had already initiated the anti-Shah demonstrations. The reason of such late involvement of industrial workers is often pointed to the relatively favourable economic conditions that some of these workers enjoyed. For example, oil industry workers were often better paid and had more stable employment compared to workers in other sectors. This relative prosperity may have initially made them less inclined to join the early protests. Some scholars even argue that these workers were cautious about participating in the revolution because they were aware of the potential consequences of disrupting oil production and exports, which were vital for Iran's revenue.

Another facet pondered by these erudite scholars delves into the role of political and organisational elements in the belated engagement of laborers. They posit that the absence of efficacious labour unions among the industrial workforce might have hindered their timely immersion in the tumultuous currents of revolution. These academics assert that the revolutionary fervour swelled as disparate strata of society, comprising students, intellectuals, and denizens of the urban bourgeoisie, spearheaded the inaugural protests. As the movement burgeoned, an increasing number of labourers, including those employed in the oil sector, gradually cast their lot with the cause.

However, if one accords credence to the narratives chronicling the final act of the oil workers, the rationale for their late participation appears less compelling. Indeed, by the mid-1970s, there existed twenty-eight syndicates within the oil industry, each sufficiently active to foment the watershed strike of 1974.[27]

Ahmad Ashraf and Ali Banuazizi stand out as pioneers in revisiting the 1978–79 revolution through their exceptional and groundbreaking research. They rigorously examine the widespread narratives of the revolution, providing precise statistics on protests, strikes, and the acts of setting fire to and destroying public places, cafes, and restaurants in the months preceding the revolution. Their work notably includes exact figures for casualties during the revolution, challenging the dominant narratives found in Islamic historiography.[28] According to their analysis, the revolution unfolded in tumultuous stages, each more intense than the last, ultimately overthrowing the established system on 11 February 1979. By analysing the year and a half leading up to the revolution's climax, they identify five distinct phases. Each phase is marked by its own mobilisation methods, the emergence of specific opposition coalitions, and the adoption of unique strategies in confrontational tactics.[29]

This progression evolves from nonviolent mobilisation stage (June–December 1977) in the initial phase, progressing to cyclical urban riots (January–August 1978) in the second phase, subsequently transforming into large-scale demonstration (August–September 1978) in the third phase. Thereafter, it veers towards disruptive and expansive strikes (October–November 1978) in the fourth phase, ultimately culminating in the establishment of dual sovereignty (December 1978–February 1979), during the conclusive phase.[30]

Following the 1978–79 revolution, scholarly discourse has delved into the myriad factors that were pivotal to the revolution's success and the circumstances under which these factors became influential. Within this scholarly discourse, one interpretation highlighted the essential and influential role of the working class, particularly those employed in the oil sector.[31] This interpretation posits that the workers' engagement was underpinned by a heightened class consciousness advocating for change. This consciousness, according to the interpretation, emerged from the workers' prolonged struggles, if not spanning decades, then certainly in the fifteen years preceding the revolution. Prior discussions have addressed the occupational and living conditions of workers in this sector, alongside a review of labour activism within the same timeframe. In the subsequent sections, prior to discussing the timeline regarding the delayed engagement of oil industry workers with the vessel of agency, we shall examine the critical currents that not only drew these workers towards the vessel of revolution but also propelled it towards an Islamic destination.

Hoisting the Green Flag over Khuzestan

The historiographical discourse surrounding the 1978–79 revolution in Khuzestan and its intertwined relationship with the oil industry is characterised by two overarching essentialist perspectives. On one hand, there exists a viewpoint that emphasises the distinctive and paramount role played by Islamic militant activists, predominantly interpreted through the prism of radical Islam. Conversely, there is a counter-narrative that accentuates the involvement of non-religious activists, particularly leftist elements, and advocates for a secular interpretation of the sociopolitical dynamics prevailing in the geographical landscape of Khuzestan, particularly within its oil industry sector.

What ensues is an endeavour to present a more multifaceted and nuanced account of the onset of the revolution in Abadan, a city that stood as a potent symbol of the nation's oil industry, marked prominently by its sprawling refinery. All eyes were fixated upon this city, as it assumed a pivotal role in the unfolding events of this transformative period.

Subsequent to the publication of an article in *Ettelaʿat* on 6 January 1978, marked by its unreserved and acerbic critique that branded Ayatollah Khomeini as the instigator of a reactionary movement, one that vehemently opposed the White Revolution while distorting its accomplishments, the repercussions were swift and significant. On 9 January 1978, seminaries and fervent supporters of Ayatollah Khomeini took to the streets of Qom, expressing their dissent in a manner that was both dramatic and fraught with violence. These demonstrations in Qom resulted in a grim toll, with nine lives lost and forty-five individuals sustaining injuries.

The profound gravity of the situation in Qom resonated far beyond its borders, serving as a catalyst for the people of Tabriz to congregate on 18 February 1978, the 40th day following the tragic events in Qom, adhering to the Shiite tradition. The resolute demonstrations by the citizens of Tabriz, in response to the prevailing turmoil, stand as a testament to the pervasive discontent and marked a poignant juncture in the burgeoning nationwide upheaval. It was this momentous gathering in Tabriz that ultimately set the wheels of the revolution's second phase into relentless motion.

While a pervasive sense of disorder gripped various cities throughout Iran, the province of Khuzestan remained relatively insulated from the tumultuous events that were unfolding. Apart from sporadic local protests and isolated incidents loosely connected to the broader demonstrations in other Iranian cities, Khuzestan remained largely unaffected by the uprisings.

However, the winds of revolution finally reached Khuzestan, ushered in by the sombre and distressing event of the Cinema Rex being set ablaze on 20 August 1978. This tragic incident prompted various urban groups to voice their discontent through protests. Subsequently, four months later, on the morning of 23 December, the assassination of two employees within the oil industry further exacerbated the situation. This event served as the catalyst that led to a widespread strike among all echelons of the oil industry's workforce, from workers to engineers, managers, and administrative staff alike.

Prior to these pivotal events, the Islamic revolutionaries harboured a sense of disappointment and apprehension concerning the inhabitants of Khuzestan, who seemed to be somewhat detached from the surging tides of the revolution. Of particular concern was the perceived apathy of the oil industry workers towards the strike appeals made by both Islamic militants and communist groups, urging them to join the ranks of the revolutionary movement.

In an effort to kindle revolutionary fervour within Khuzestan, particularly within the emblematic Abadan Refinery, an incident occurred that underscored the determination of the Islamic revolutionaries. As recounted by one of the Islamic militants from Abadan, during a period when news of protests was emerging from various parts of Iran, the Islamic revolutionary youth of Bushehr resorted to an extreme and provocative gesture. They dispatched a suitcase containing multiple pieces of women's undergarments to the youths of Abadan, accompanied by a message that conveyed, rather crudely, that if the men of Abadan were unwilling to engage in the struggle, they should perhaps consider donning women's attire as an alternative.

Subsequent investigations disclosed that the arson attacks on public venues, including cinemas and cafes in Abadan, were strategically coordinated with Islamic groups based in Isfahan. These deliberate actions were directed by leading figures loyal to Ayatollah Seyyed Hossein Khademi, himself a protégé of Ayatollah Khomeini.[32] It became apparent, however, that the practice of setting public spaces aflame was not a tactic exclusive to Abadan. Instead, it had become a widespread method of protest utilised by Islamic revolutionaries throughout Iran, commencing in early August of 1978. This orchestrated pattern of incendiary attacks was evident in several cities, including Mashhad, Isfahan, Shiraz, Ardabil, and Tehran, signifying a unified strategy to challenge the existing regime by targeting symbols of Western influence and places of leisure.[33] Despite the widespread nature of these actions, the tragedy in Abadan stood out for its sheer scale. Later, Mousavi Tabrizi, the presiding judge of the Cinema Rex Revolutionary Tribunal, characterised the cinema's burning as an act of protest, asserting that it had been executed 'in accordance with all relevant considerations, not as it was carried out in Abadan'.[34]

On the evening of 19 August 1978, as the residents of Abadan sought refuge from the sweltering summer heat within the comfort of their homes, observing the sacred month of Ramadan – a time of fasting and special prayer for Muslims – nearly 400 individuals disregarded the religious obligations of the moment. Instead, they sought solace in the cool confines of the Cinema Rex, where they gathered to watch the film *Gavazn-ha* (The Deers), a production written and directed by Masoud Kimiai. The Deers was a cinematic work renowned for its profound exploration of societal disparities and injustices.

It was on this fateful night that at 20:20 four Islamic militants, prompted by the summons of religious clerics in Isfahan, resolved not to lag behind their counterparts in other Iranian cities. In a decisive and shocking move, they barred the doors of the cinema and doused it with petrol from a can. The fire started outside three entrance doors to the main hall, after the attackers allegedly dropped a match into the petrol. Situated in the heart of the city, Cinema Rex was an established venue with a seating capacity of 680, of which 600 seats had been occupied on that ill-fated night.

In the wake of the conflagration's eruption, a wave of panic gripped the assembled throng, prompting a frenzied rush towards the exit doors. However,

Figure 9.1 The poster of the screened film *Gavazn-ha*. Remnants of the Cinema Rex, Abadan, August 1978[35]

their frantic efforts were met with the grim and harrowing realisation that the doors had been securely bolted, sealing their tragic and fateful demise. Adding to this dire situation, none of the three fire department tankers dispatched to the scene were equipped with water, and despite the police department's close proximity, located just 100 meters away, their response was lamentably delayed and ineffective.

Speculation abounds regarding the precise count of casualties resulting from the fire. Various sources have put forth different figures, including 377, 410, 430, and 422. Terisa Turner recorded the total number of people burned in the fire of Islamic militants as 800 people, without naming the source of this estimate.[36] The official account, as documented, acknowledges the profound toll exacted by this catastrophe, officially reporting a death toll of 377 individuals.[37]

In the aftermath of the devastating cinema fire, the city of Abadan bore witness to a remarkable transformation. For the first time in its history, thousands of people spilled into its streets, their voices raised in unison, expressing their fervent support for the burgeoning revolution. With resounding cheers, they vehemently accused the Pahlavi regime of being the culprits behind this heinous crime. This narrative, which casts the Pahlavi regime as the orchestrator of the cinema tragedy, remains enshrined in the official historiography of the Islamic Republic's account of the revolution. On one of the perpetrators of the fire, Takbaʿalizdeh, throughout the last four, the Islamic Republic historiography has progressively presented various narratives, ranging from accusing him of having ties with Savak, attributing his behaviour to the use of drugs, to ultimately labelling him as a fool.[38]

However, it is crucial to acknowledge that a multitude of documents, originating from both within and outside of Iran, have emerged, casting doubt upon this narrative. While a significant account did surface from one of the four arsonists who survived the incident, Takbʿalizadeh, who delivered a comprehensive and detailed narrative of the circumstances during his court appearance three years after the revolution, it appears that the Islamic Republic has chosen to selectively dismiss these accounts.[39] This selective dismissal perpetuates a form of historical amnesia that aligns with the regime's ideological interests.

According to the account provided by Mohammad Safavi, a notable socialist labour activist during that period, a significant response followed the tragic incident of the Cinema Rex fire. In the wake of this calamity, a clandestine committee was formed by labour activists within the oil industry, consisting of project workers and seasonal laborers from Abadan. It was on the seventh day after the cinema fire that this committee convened.[40]

To commemorate the seventh day since the Cinema Rex tragedy, the victims' families organised a substantial demonstration that commenced at the Abadan cemetery and proceeded towards the heart of the city. This historic gathering drew the participation of well known labour activists, some of whom had previously endured imprisonment in the years leading up to these events. These figures held immense popularity among the residents of Abadan and played a pivotal role in leading thousands of demonstrators.

A distinctive feature of this gathering was the prominent display of red and black flags, symbolising the labour and socialist movements. As the demonstrators marched, they passionately played local instruments known as Sanj and Damam, evoking a strong sense of unity and determination. Remarkably, this event marked the first and most extensive demonstration witnessed in Abadan for decades.

As the demonstration approached the city's gate, police resorted to the use of force, opening fire on the protestors. This resulted in injuries to several individuals, including one of the prominent labour and socialist leaders, Ebrahim Gharibzadeh. Gharibzadeh, a skilled welder, had previously been incarcerated for his involvement in labour-related activities during the reign of the Shah, and during this incident, he sustained an injury to his hand.

Subsequent to this significant display of civil unrest, the oil workers themselves initiated a series of actions. This included the formation of underground strike committees and secret coordination bodies aimed at advancing labour strikes within the oil industry. These activities were indicative of the escalating labour movement and the growing momentum of the revolution.[41]

Four months later, on the sombre morning of 23 December 1978, another violent incident unfolded. On this fateful day, Paul E. Grimm and Malek Boroujerdi, both holding senior managerial positions within the Iran Oil Services Company located in Ahvaz, met a tragic end. Despite the prevailing strike calls, these individuals had opted to continue working and had reported to their workplaces. As they made their way to work, both Paul E. Grimm and Malek Boroujerdi were assassinated near their respective homes in the neighbourhoods of Kurosh and Kian Pars in Ahvaz.[42]

The assassinations on 23 December were perpetrated by two distinct yet interconnected militant Islamic factions, namely the Movahhedin and Mansurun[43] groups. These factions can be traced back as distant offshoots of the People's Mojahedin Organisation of Iran,[44] with their emergence significantly influenced by the backdrop of religious and political schisms in Abadan following the nationalisation of the oil industry.

As delineated in the Chapter 6, subsequent to the proclamation of the nationalisation of the oil industry, the conspicuous solidarity that had hitherto characterised the supporters of Mohammad Mosaddeq gradually dissipated, yielding to the emergence of schisms primarily cantered around Mosaddeq's intricate affiliations or disassociations with the royal court and the Tudeh Party. Subsequent to the coup d'état of 1953 and the subsequent contract with the Oil Consortium, this factionalism assumed a more pronounced character. A faction comprised of erstwhile associates of Mosaddeq aligned themselves with the court, positioning themselves in opposition to the Mosaddeq National Front.

Within the ranks of the clergy, Ayatollah Abdolrasoul Qa'emi emerged as the preeminent figure among those who had once been aligned with Mosaddeq. During the 1950s, Qa'emi directed the bulk of his efforts towards contesting the Baha'i faith. However, the tide of political engagement would sweep him back into its current during the 1963 rebellion, as he became an adherent of Ayatollah Khomeini, subsequently assuming the mantle of his representative. In this capacity, he voiced vehement opposition to the underpinnings of the Shah's White Revolution. Responding affirmatively to the summons issued by Ayatollah Seyyed Mohammad-Hadi Milani to convene in Tehran in support of Khomeini, Qa'imi journeyed to the Iranian capital as the envoy of the clerical community in Abadan. Following Khomeini's exile to Najaf, Qa'imi continued to maintain his ties with the latter, persistently soliciting financial support on his behalf. Through Qa'imi's intermediary role, a cadre of devout youth in Abadan accustomed themselves with the social and political grievances against the Pahlavi monarchy, thus brushing against the fringes of disseminating the doctrines of militant Islam, particularly in the region of Khuzestan, with Abadan, Ahvaz, and Dezful serving as focal points for this burgeoning ideological dissemination.

In 1967, Ayatollah Qa'imi aided by Abadani traditional merchants (*bazaris*), established Hosseiniyeh-ye Isfahaniha, a Shiite institution in Abadan that deviated from traditionalist norms. The Hosseiniyeh served as Abadan's counterpart to similar institutions such as the Hosseiniyeh-ye Ershad in Tehran, functioning as a focal point for the assembly of fervent religious adherents of Ali Shariati and Ayatollah Khomeini alike.

Hosseiniyeh-ye Isfahaniha maintained a close affiliation with the religious circles of Isfahan, and this connection became more pronounced during the 1970s. In 1977, Hosseiniyeh-ye Isfahaniha assumed a pivotal role as the primary centre of dissent for religious groups in Abadan opposing the monarchy. During this period, the most fervent endeavour of revolutionary youth was to foment a revolutionary atmosphere in Abadan. Initiatives such as arson attacks on cinemas, the destruction of liquor shops, and confrontations with non-religious political factions opposed to the Pahlavi regime, including socialists, communists, and supporters of Mosaddeq, were among the principal objectives pursued by the youth who found their way to the clergy in Isfahan through their association with Hosseiniyeh-ye Isfahaniha.[45]

The incendiary incident at the Cinema Rex and the targeted assassinations of individuals such as Paul E. Grimm and Malek Boroujerdi stood out as notable actions undertaken by these Islamist militants in their efforts to catalyse Abadan's involvement in the revolution and to enlist the oil industry workers into the ranks of the striking workforce.[46]

In the statements released by the Mansurun group following the assassination, they articulated their objectives while elucidating the reasons behind these acts of violence. They cited, 'In response to the heightened protests of

Muslim employees within the oil industry and in accordance with the directives of Ayatollah Khomeini concerning the oil strike, certain individuals with vested interests persistently opposed the strike's objectives. Among them was Boroujerdi, who played a significant role in overseeing large-scale oil installations that directly facilitated oil exports to Israel. Consequently, he was subjected to trial within the Islamic court system and subsequently sentenced to death … concurrently, Paul E. Grimm, a prominent figure in American politics with a controversial reputation in Iran, met his demise at the hands of a different faction of Mujahidans in Ahvaz. This incident served as a stark warning to any traitors who align themselves against the will of both God and the people'. Furthermore, the group cautioned, 'we admonish all those who, for whatever reason, have not aligned themselves with the revolutionary cause to promptly join its ranks. Failure to do so may lead to the divine retribution manifesting itself through the barrels of the people's machine guns'.[47]

The Movahhedin group also explicitly conveyed, 'with the demise of Paul E. Grimm, the Oil Company strike assumed a nationwide character'. Furthermore, in a formal declaration, they justified Grim's assassination within the context of the oil strike, asserting that 'those who betrayed the strike had not resorted to any peaceful means to thwart its progress'. They condemned Paul E. Grimm, who 'served as the chief operations manager of the oil service company, for allegedly advancing the colonial interests of American imperialism within the Oil Company and for fostering discord among the striking employees'.[48]

These measures were instrumental in the broader campaign to expand and solidify the influence of Ayatollah Khomeini's supporters within the Khuzestan province and the city of Abadan, as asserted by 'Elam: 'As a consequence, these assassination, as anticipated, galvanised the strike, transforming it into a nationwide and coordinated movement. It had a more profound impact on undermining the stability of the Shah's regime than any other actions undertaken during his rule, bringing it perilously close to the brink of collapse.'[49]

Chronicle of a Pivotal Strike: Abadan, Sep–Dec 1978

The historiography sanctioned by the Islamic Republic of Iran regarding the 1978–79 revolution, particularly in its depiction of the role of oil workers, epitomises the active employment of historical revisionism. This approach, designed to recast the historical narrative, actively aims to shape both contemporary and future interpretations of historical events. In this milieu, historical revisionism is deliberately utilised to construct a narrative that bolsters the incumbent regime, thereby imbuing it with an appearance of legitimacy. Such revisionism, a hallmark of the Islamic Republic's approach to history, involves the deliberate reinterpretation or manipulation of historical occurrences to align with and reinforce the regime's ideological and political aspirations. This often results in a curated depiction of past events and personalities, prioritising the advancement of the state's ideological aims over factual accuracy. The process typically involves the glorification of historical facets favourable to the regime, coupled with the diminution or outright exclusion of elements that are perceived as inconvenient or antithetical to the established narrative.[50]

Being close to the date of the oil industry workers' strike in September–December 1978 does not imply that the narration and analysis of this strike are straightforward. There are several key challenges to consider:

- Limited access to archives: It is important to acknowledge that numerous documents from the archives of the Islamic Republic, especially those related to the Islamic Revolution, remain unavailable. The materials made accessible by the Islamic Revolution Documents Centre are highly selective, further complicating comprehensive research.
- Diverse and contradictory eyewitness: The strike's historical accounts are characterised by a wide range of eyewitness testimonies, some of which are contradictory. Even the periodisation of the oil industry workers' strike, which began sporadically in the third decade of September 1978 and concluded on 31 December 1978, when workers and other industry employees returned to work to address domestic needs, varies depending on the political inclinations of the eyewitnesses or researchers involved.
- Influence of political orientation: The periodisation of the strike is heavily influenced by the political leanings of the academics. Those aligned with the victorious Islamists tend to emphasize the role of religious leaders in this periodisation, particularly those in positions of power. Conversely, the counter-Islamic narrative seeks to downplay the contribution of Islamic activists to the strike's outcomes.

In the following sections, we base the periodisation of the strike on the shifting political landscape and the often-unpredictable stances taken by workers, whether they were driven by religious or non-religious motivations. In other words, the periodisation is crafted from the bottom up, influenced by the agency and actions of workers in their daily struggles. By considering these complexities, our objective is to offer a more nuanced and comprehensive analysis of the oil industry workers' strike.

The research draws upon various sources, including newspapers from the period, documents published by the Islamic Revolution Documents Centre (comprising secret reports from SAVAK operatives documenting the fluctuations in protests and strikes), and narratives provided by religious workers who were supporters of Ayatollah Khomeini. Additionally, the research incorporates the narratives of non-religious workers and employees. These perspectives are gleaned from both written sources, whether published within or outside Iran, as well as oral accounts obtained through conversations with the author, serving as key reference points for the study.[51]

In this research, Abadan Refinery, along with its oil workers, has been deliberately chosen as a prominent symbol of the oil industry. This decision is predicated on the fact that it serves as the primary workplace for the majority of oil industry employees in Khuzestan, where they collaborate closely and maintain direct connections. This selection, which emphasises labour concentration, does not, however, entail a dismissal of worker agency in dispersed fields, such as oil fields.

Furthermore, it is imperative to clarify that the examination of the refinery should not be misconstrued as a neglect of the broader urban context, which encompasses neighbourhoods inhabited by both workers and non-workers and non-residential districts. As elucidated in previous chapters, conducting a comprehensive analysis of everyday life within the oil industry necessitates an understanding that extends beyond the geographic confines of the refinery walls. Surely, if one were to undertake the task of documenting the history of Abadan during the 1978–79 revolution, it is undeniably essential to consider all relevant agencies and entities in a thorough manner. Nevertheless, due to the specific focus on labour activism within this section, deliberate attention has been exclusively directed towards the refinery.

To gain deeper insights into the events, we have examined the organisational structure of the oil industry within Abadan Refinery during the strike. We have closely followed developments in nine units of the refinery:

1. Oil Processing and Refining
2. Laboratory
3. Central Workshop and Repair
4. Material
5. Transport (inside and outside the refinery)
6. Work Health and Safety
7. Education and Training
8. Administration and Recruitment
9. Refinery Protection Guards

While the oil industry workers had conspicuously remained on the periphery of the protest-revolutionary movement until the conclusion of the summer in 1978, the onset of the autumn that year witnessed a significant shift. Not only did the role of the oil workers and employees within the movement become more conspicuous, but it also assumed increasingly Islamic hues. The span of four months, spanning from September to December in 1978, marked a pivotal phase during which the oil industry played a determinative role in the unfolding revolutionary developments, ultimately culminating in its Islamic denouement on 10–11 February 1979 insurrection.

It is pertinent to discuss the evolving demands of the oil industry workers engaged in the strike. These demands, shaped significantly over the four-month duration of the strike, were influenced by the rapid political developments occurring nationwide. The variation in these demands was not only observable between the oil workers in Tehran and Khuzestan, but also within different locales of Khuzestan. This divergence was particularly noticeable during the peak of the strike in November 1978.

In the context of historiography concerning the oil industry workers' strike in the months preceding the revolution, it appears that certain narratives put forth by some scholars tend to conform more to specific historical interpretations rather than offering an authentic representation of the workers' socio-political agency during the autumn and winter of 1978. Their focus seems to be more on framing a narrative that aligns with a particular historical perspective rather than on exploring the roots and dynamics of the strike's efficacy. An example can be seen in Terisa Turner's article, where she lists the workers' demands in an organised, structured manner, as supposedly presented at the height of the strike, yet without providing source citations.[52] Unfortunately, her article has become a reference for many researchers studying the oil industry workers' strike during that period.

In terms of the demands themselves, the available evidence suggests that the oil workers and staff employees' movement, initially driven by professional slogans, gradually incorporated political demands as well. This shift occurred without forsaking their original professional requests, which included demands for increased wages, housing rights, improved job classifications, and the dismissal of managers implicated in financial corruption.

In response to the intensifying revolutionary conditions within the country and the government's oppressive actions in the oil industry, the workers and staff employees sustained their professional slogans while incrementally adopting political demands. These included the expulsion of foreign managers in the oil industry, the release of detained workers and employees, the withdrawal of security forces from oil sites, the repeal of Martial Law, the dissolution of SAVAK and its related security organisations in the oil industry, and the punishment of those responsible for the killings of protesters. However, as highlighted, these political demands did not emerge simultaneously or uniformly. Yadollah Khosrowshahi, a leader in the strike, later identified 'a significant weakness of the movement during the revolution as being the lack of a clear future-oriented vision and pre-emptive planning. The movement was reactive to the unfolding revolutionary events, lacking a strategic plan for future action'.[53]

Approximately three months had elapsed since the inception of revolutionary waves in Iran, waves that surged to greater heights with each passing moment, when their swell also reached Abadan. This impact was felt not within the oil fields or refineries but rather at the Abadan Oil College. In mid-May 1978, the students initiated a boycott, opting not to partake in their scheduled classes. They disseminated pamphlets, declaring their strike as an act of solidarity with university students across the nation who had also embarked on strikes.

The *Ettelaʿat* newspaper reported that when a group of Iranian, Pakistani, and Indian students attempted to attend classes, their peers intervened, effectively preventing them from participating in the academic sessions.[54] However, it was during the latter part of September 1978 that the initial signs of workers' dissent began to emerge more distinctly. Demonstrating a burgeoning sense of agency, the workers initiated scattered acts of dissent, which, though not yet coalescing into a full-fledged strike, signalled a significant shift towards collective action within the workforce.

This early protest involved several groups of employees and workers affiliated with companies associated with the oil industry. The majority of protestors were contract workers, and their primary demand cantered around trade union rights. They sought the elimination of discriminatory practices and the equalisation of their economic status and benefits with those of permanent employees within the Oil Company. These protests were temporarily halted following assurances that the welfare demands of the employees and workers would be addressed.[55]

The initial phase of the strike within the oil industry commenced on first October, coinciding with the spread of strikes across the nation. On this day, the workers, and employees of the Material Unit, primarily composed of young individuals, staged a two-hour sit-down strike. They submitted a written list of demands to the director of the Material Unit, which included requests for wage increases, a job classification plan, as well as housing and food allowances. The following day, Majid Diba, the Deputy Director of the National Iranian Oil Company, during a meeting with the workers, officially announced the concessions granted included:

- A 10 per cent salary increase.
- Raising the housing allowance for singles from 3,000 rials to 6,000 rials per month, and for married individuals from 4,000 rials to 9,000 rials.
- Elevating the daily food allowance from 50 rials to 100 rials.

Following this agreement there was a period of approximately two weeks during which no reports or indications of protests or strikes were recorded.

The second phase of the strike commenced on 16 October, coinciding with a nationwide strike marking the fortieth day since the tragic incident in Zhaleh Square. This nationwide strike was initiated in response to an invitation from four prominent Ayatollahs: Khomeini, Shariʿatmadari, Golpaygani, and Marʿashi Najafi. On that day, all workers, and employees, excluding those employed in the two units dedicated to Oil Processing and Refining, as well as Transport units, gathered and converged at the Central Workshop, where they formally initiated the strike. In response to this collective action, the refinery's military guard entered the premises and forcibly removed seventy employees, leaving them stranded in the outskirts of Abadan. Additionally, they detained eight of the protesters until nightfall.

The following day, refinery workers initiated a strike in protest of these actions. Employees of the Non-Industrial Operations Organisation rallied in front of the Central Office of the National Oil Company to show their support for the striking workers, swelling the number of protesters to 3,000. The units participating in the strike included the Engineering Department, Laboratory Department, Material Unit, Audit Department, Budget Department, Administrative Management of Warehouses, Central Workshop and Repair. Notably, the strike had not yet extended to other units of the oil refinery. On 18 October, the workers of the Transport Unit also joined the strike, further increasing the number of strikers to 5,000.[56]

During this period, a significant incident unfolded, drawing public attention to the critical role of oil flow in the nation's economy and the daily lives of its citizens. On 21 October 1978, the workers at the Tehran Oil Depot embarked on a strike that lasted several hours, primarily to press for their welfare demands. Subsequently, they returned to work once their demands were met. However, this brief interruption in gasoline delivery to tankers had a profound impact on the situation in Tehran. For the first time in history, the capital of oil-rich Iran, following the discovery of oil, experienced chaos due to the shortage of gasoline. Approximately 200 petrol stations faced a shortage, leading to widespread disruptions.[57]

The strike extended to encompass all the oil-rich regions of Khuzestan. In response to this extensive strike, the military governor at that time, General Esfandiari, found it necessary to release all the strike leaders with the intention of preventing, suppressing, and bringing the strike to a halt. However, the workers did not accept this resolution. Following the release of the detained strike leaders, they raised a pertinent question regarding the authority under which General Kia'i, the Commander of the Abadan Oil Refinery Guard, had allowed military forces to enter the refinery. Consequently, in addition to their existing demands, the strikers insisted on obtaining a written apology from the commander of the refinery guard and the withdrawal of military forces from key oil industry locations.

The four demands put forth by the striking workers were as follows:

- The payment of a 12.5 per cent additional salary retroactively from the 1st of October.
- A payment of 7,500 rials for job assistance.
- The provision of food rations for employees and their families.
- The removal of General Kia'i, the head of the Abadan Refinery Guard, and a thorough investigation into the circumstances surrounding the incident of security agents entering the refinery and insulting the employees.

The strike and the daily gatherings in front of the Central Office persisted, with the workers' demands evolving each day. According to the *Ettela'at* newspaper on 22 October, 'the strike involving 5,000 oil industry employees continued, and the strikers convened in front of the Central Office every day at 7:30 in the morning'. Over time, the number of female employees participating in these gatherings increased.[58]

On 22 October, Houshang Ansari, the Director of the National Iranian Oil Company, visited the striking workers and employees in Abadan. He addressed them by mentioning the intention to raise the salaries of the workers and employees and agreeing to meet all the demands of the strikers, excluding political demands. The political demands of the strikers encompassed the following:

- The repeal of Martial Law throughout the country.
- The release of all political prisoners.
- The repatriation of all political exiles.
- The dismissal of the head of the Abadan Oil Refinery Guard.

Ahmad Ashraf, as noted, suggests that the resolve of the striking workers during their discussions with Houshang Ansari was instigated by the events of several hours on 21 October in Tehran. This event had emboldened the workers, making them feel empowered. Consequently, when they engaged in discussions with Ansari, they expressed their demands from a position of strength and assertiveness. It was during this period that their political demands began to take shape.[59]

Houshang Ansari departed from Abadan after assuring the workers that he would address their demands. Meanwhile, the representatives of the striking workers declared their commitment to continue the strike until all four of their demands were met. On this particular day, not only did the workers from Crude Oil Processing and Refining Unit join the strike, but also employees from the Health Department, the Oil Company's hospital, and the Water and Electricity Department of the Oil Company joined the strikers. It's worth noting that the hospital continued its operations despite the strike.[60]

Subsequent to the Abadan strike, workers from various oil industry locations including Ahvaz, Khark Island, Gachsaran, Aghajari, Masjed-Soleyman, Maron, and Bibi-Hakimeh also joined the strike. The Ahvaz strike, in particular, possessed distinctive characteristics. Firstly, it had a close and direct connection with the oil production wells, making it strategically significant. Additionally, it had a stronger connection with religious activists, especially the supporters of Ayatollah Khomeini.

In contrast to the Abadan strikers, whose leadership was primarily composed of non-religious and left-wing elements, in Ahvaz, religious leadership played a more prominent role. Over time, Ahvaz assumed a pivotal role in advancing the political demands of oil industry workers, contributing to the deepening of their political activism.

Such development gradually imbued with Islamic coercion and violence cast its pall over the oil industry, coinciding with the widespread propagation of a movement advocating fundamental social change across Iran. Beyond the pervasive climate of intimidation, Islamist factions sought to assert their exclusive dominance over the labour and employee protests within the oil industry, vehemently rejecting secular ideologies, particularly those aligned with leftist orientations.[61]

As time went by, the strike's influence grew more intricate and seemingly unresolvable, as neither side showed willingness to yield or seek a compromise. Concurrently, the oil industry began to draw the attention of religious leaders, who encouraged the workers to sustain the strike by disseminating official notices and messages.

Following Ansari's unsuccessful visit to Abadan, where he requested ten days to discuss the workers' demands with security authorities in Tehran, a group of oil workers decided to return to work. However, as the ten-day deadline passed with no word from Ansari regarding the resolution of the workers' demands, on 31 October, in coordination with the joint committee consisting of representatives from the Oil Industry Employees Union and workers from other southern oil regions, which comprised thirteen members, most of the Abadan oil industry workers resumed their strike.

During the inaugural meeting of this committee, attended by sixty representatives from staff employees and workers of the oil industry, the political demands of the oil workers were comprehensively articulated as follows:

- Release of detained workers and employees and all political prisoners,
- Withdrawal of security forces from oil sites.
- Repeal of Martial Law throughout the country.
- Dismissal of the head of the Abadan Oil Refinery Guard.
- Dissolution of SAVAK and its related security organisations in the oil industry.
- Punishment of those responsible for the killings of protesters.[62]

On 1 November 1978, the military occupied the oil facilities. Reports from 4 November stated: 'At 8:00 am today, two army jeeps armed with machine guns stationed themselves in front of the entrance to the Central Office of the Oil Company in Abadan, which served as the gathering point for striking employees. Upon noticing this development, other striking employees from various locations hurried to the Central Office. In a short span of time, the gathering swelled from 300 striking employees to a crowd of 2,000 people'.[63]

In the subsequent days, a marked division emerged among two distinct groups: seasoned workers and permanent staff, as well as between younger workers and staff employees, concerning their perspectives on the ongoing strike's legitimacy. The seasoned workers predominantly leaned towards restricting the workers' demands to those that align with union objectives. Conversely, the permanent workforce showed a stronger inclination to prolong the strike, advocating for the inclusion of political demands in their collective actions.

Yadollah Khosrowshahi recalls that:

> One of the challenges faced during the revolution was the initial lack of unity between workers and staff employees. These two groups held distinct job positions and had differing responsibilities. Staff employees were regarded as the representatives of the employer within the workshop and were mandated to safeguard the interests of the Oil Company. Importantly, in the oil industry, staff employees were not permitted to establish trade unions. Under the Shah's regime, the formation of trade unions was exclusively reserved for those subject to labour laws, while individuals, like oil industry employees, governed by civil or military laws were prohibited from organizing.
>
> Furthermore, a multitude of disparities existed between staff employees and workers, contributing to their divergence. In particular, staff employees exhibited lower levels of activity and a reduced overall capacity for collective action compared to the workers. Additionally, the workers held negative perceptions of the employees due to these discriminatory practices. These divisions led to a fragmented nature in the initial movements of oil workers.
>
> For instance, in Khuzestan, during the early days of October 1978, the workers at the Central Workshop of the Abadan Refinery embarked on a strike that lasted several days, with staff employees abstaining from participation. Subsequently, Ahvaz's staff employees initiated a strike of their own, prompting the workers to contemplate retaliation and initially refrain from supporting the employees' strike. However, after deliberations among key workers, it was determined that responding to the initial misstep of the employees with another error was unwarranted. Consequently, after three days, the workers initiated a strike in solidarity with their counterparts in Ahvaz.[64]

On 15 November, the military government assumed control, with General Azhari serving as Prime Minister. The new administration promptly issued a directive stating that any worker or employee failing to fulfil their work duties would face termination, and those who resisted this decree would be subject to arrest. In the city of Abadan, approximately 200 leaders of the striking workers were apprehended by the authorities.

As time progressed, employees within the oil industry, along with workers in various government and private institutions and organisations, gradually returned to their respective posts in response to mounting pressure from the military government. Consequently, the oil production, which had dwindled to a mere one million barrels per day during the strike, witnessed a resurgence, reaching approximately six million barrels per day.

In the wake of the military deployment to oil facilities on 1 November 1978, a month elapsed characterised by a relative absence of significant unrest. During this period, religious leaders, with Ayatollah Khomeini at the forefront, made efforts to sustain the momentum of the strike, although their attempts were met with limited success. On 12 November, Hojjatoleslam Musavi Tabrizi, Ayatollah Khomeini's representative, travelled to Abadan to lead the Eid-e Qorban (Eid al-Adha) prayers. In his sermon, he conveyed Khomeini's support for the strikes throughout Khuzestan, particularly in the oil industry. He further quoted Khomeini's fatwa declaring that continuing work in this industry was religiously forbidden (haram). Additionally, on 15 November, Ayatollah Khomeini issued a statement urging the employees of the Oil Company to persist in their strike, framing it as a noble act in the service of God and Islam. He characterised those who chose to return to work as traitors to the nation and collaborators with foreign interests:

> Greetings from me and the people of Iran, to the workers and employees of the National Iranian Oil Company! May the mercy of the Almighty God be upon you, the conscious individuals who, through your valuable strike, have whitened the face of the nation! Your strike, every day, and every hour of it, is both valuable and impactful; it holds great worth for the plundered nation of Iran, which for years has suffered from the treachery of those who have looted from the flow of this black gold and the rich reservoir of the country. You have prevented them from squandering the wealth of the impoverished nation to the best of your abilities, and your strike has been a powerful blow against those traitors who view the proceeds of their auctions as support for their tyrannical regime and their devilish, shaky throne.
>
> Each hour of your strike is a service to the Almighty God and to the Islamic country. Those who seek to forcibly break this sacred strike are criminals and servants of foreign interests, traitors to the nation and the country.
>
> It is incumbent upon the noble people of Iran, in times when the workers and employees of the National Oil Company and other government institutions and agencies go on strike, to support them with the utmost respect and compensate for their losses in the best possible manner. They should encourage and commend them in their sacred strikes, which serve as expressions of resentment against the treacherous Shah and his corrupt dynasty, and as support for the collective struggles of the people.[65]

Furthermore, in another communication, Ayatollah Khomeini deemed the escalation of strikes a religious duty according to Islamic *Sharia* and instructed the public to assist the oil workers in their cause, advocating the utilisation of obligatory *Sharia* financial resources for this purpose.[66]

Nevertheless, these messages failed to galvanise the strike into a widespread and pandemic phenomenon within the oil industry. The protests predominantly took the form of presenteeism, with many workers attending their workplaces but refraining from active participation in their duties. It is important to note that even this form of presenteeism did not encompass the entirety of the oil industry in Khuzestan. Some employees and workers opted not to join the strike, either out of apprehension regarding potential arrest or termination, or because they held the view that shutting down the machinery of the oil industry and halting the oil export process was an inappropriate course of action.

Simultaneously, the looming threat of arresting strike leaders or terminating the employment of those participating in the strike persisted. In Ahvaz, there was even a menacing ultimatum to reclaim company-provided residences from the striking workers. It was communicated that the striking oil workers were offered a 22 per cent salary increase and reparations for the losses sustained during the strike, with the condition that they resume their duties. Alternatively, they were warned that failure to return to work would result in their dismissal, accompanied by the confiscation of their residences.[67]

The revolution seemed to require a more assertive and, at times, even violent approach. As a result, certain religious activists who aligned themselves with Ayatollah Khomeini's cause, recognising the challenges in securing widespread support for the strike and the halting of oil exports through peaceful means, began to consider the use of force against those who either actively promoted workers' continued labour or passively opposed the strike. This sombre strategy became a subject of deliberation within specific factions.

Consequently, as previously mentioned, on the morning of 23 December 1978, Paul E. Grimm and Malek Boroujerdi, executives at the Iran Oil Services Company dedicated to sustaining the operation of the oil industry, were fatally attacked by two militant Islamic groups, supporters of Ayatollah Khomeini. In the wake of this targeted act of violence, a significant exodus of foreign employees from Iran's oil regions ensued, lasting until 28 December. Consequently, oil production dwindled dramatically, plummeting from 6,000,000 barrels per day to a mere 340,000 barrels per day.

According to one of the Islamic narrators of the revolution, 'Immediately following these assassinations, the predicted short-term and long-term consequences began to materialize. In the short term, it became immediately apparent that the evacuation of foreign oil personnel, which had been ongoing in a gradual and discreet manner for some time, escalated dramatically. Numerous flights were swiftly arranged to transport foreign oil employees, particularly Americans, out of Iran. Additionally, the interruption of oil exports, stemming from these assassinations, sent shockwaves through global oil markets, resulting in significant disruptions. Moreover, these assassinations conveyed a clear message: they reinforced the acceptance of Imam Khomeini's call that the movement's fate hinged on the outcome of the strike. This underscored the readiness of Islamic revolutionaries, revealing their cohesive and deeply rooted organisations capable of making decisive moves during critical junctures. These actions had profound consequences, yielding favourable outcomes for their cause while inflicting harm upon the regime and its supporters, including the United States'.[68]

As the strikes continued to spread, the export of oil came to a complete halt, creating a significant challenge for the populace in obtaining the necessary fuel.

Lengthy queues of people at petrol stations, waiting for meagre fuel allocations, grew longer with each passing day. This situation had the potential to fuel dissatisfaction among the public, posing a challenge to the revolution's support.

During this critical juncture, the Islamic Revolutionary Council, established by Ayatollah Khomeini's decree to oversee the transition to the Islamic Republic, sought a solution. On 28 December, the council formed the Domestic Fuel Supply Board and appointed Mehdi Bazargan, who would later become the first Prime Minister of the Islamic Republic, as its chairperson. In a message addressed to this delegation, Ayatollah Khomeini delineated specific conditions for oil production to meet domestic needs. These conditions included the withdrawal of the military from oil-producing regions with no interference in their affairs, the restriction of oil production to domestic consumption levels, the prohibition of oil exports until the government's complete downfall, and the prevention of oil material hoarding by the military. Furthermore, Ayatollah Khomeini issued instructions to this delegation to express their gratitude to the workers and employees of the Oil Company and to issue a directive for them to promptly resume their work duties. The delegation's visit to Khuzestan from 6 to 20 January 1979, marked the culmination of the most protracted strike in the annals of the Iranian oil industry. The Joint Syndicate of the Iranian Oil Industry Employees displayed unwavering support for the revolution, actively preparing for the provision of domestic fuel.

Following the return of employees to work, oil production, which was chiefly allocated for domestic use, witnessed a significant increase, achieving a level of 220,000 barrels. As a result, this administrative entity effectively assumed control over the oil sector, thus reinforcing Ayatollah Khomeini's control over one of the country's pivotal resources. This period signified the beginning of an era characterised by dual sovereignty, a development with far-reaching implications. Nonetheless, this phase of bifurcated governance proved ephemeral, concluding with the uprising on 10–11 February 1979. Subsequently, a new chapter unfolded in the history of the oil workers' movement, a chapter that, upon reflection, quickly proved to be neither fortunate nor illuminating.

Epilogue

Oil transcends its status as a mere commodity; it constitutes capital. Yet, this capital is not entwined exclusively with economic and financial relations; it is intricately woven into the fabric of social relations as well. This argument, which I initially put forward a decade ago in a proposal that garnered support from the Dutch Research Council (NWO), emphasises the profound connection between the oil industry and the social, geographical, and environmental stratifications. It posits that these interconnections have played a pivotal role in shaping the course of Iran's history over the Twentieth Century, highlighting the multifaceted influence of the oil industry on the nation's development, societal dynamics, and its interaction with natural and built environments.

The role of oil in Iran's political and social history rivals the importance of the Constitutional Revolution. Its influence has been pervasive for over a century, casting a significant shadow across the lives of Iranians. Despite its contributions, oil has occasionally been disparagingly described in Iranian culture as the 'black calamity', 'scourge', or 'curse of the earth'. Such descriptions suggest that, in its absence, Iranians might have enjoyed a more prosperous era. This negative perception largely arises from the belief that oil's presence has facilitated colonial interests and exacerbated issues due to the inadequately regulated interaction between the state and society, thereby shaping the country's challenges.

The colonial entanglement of oil in Iran is incontrovertible. The Anglo-Persian/Iranian Oil Company, acting in sync with the strategic interests of the British Empire, arrogated exclusive rights within Khuzestan. This strategic move was underscored by the discovery of oil in Masjed-Soleyman, a seminal event that predated the bombardment of the Iranian National Constitution Assembly and the onset of the Minor Tyranny by merely a month. The subsequent reopening of the Assembly a year later, after the constitutionalists' capture of Tehran, elicited a dismissive response from the Anglo-Persian Oil Company's manager in Khuzestan: 'Here is Khuzestan, and we have nothing to do with the events in Tehran.' During the First World War, as articulated in Chapter 2, the company's adamant stance that Khuzestan should be considered an integral part of the British Empire's dominions, and the Persian Gulf a 'British Lake' governed by imperial laws, was notably assertive. It was not until the coup d'état of February 1921, which heralded the establishment of a modern state structure in Iran, that the oil company formally acknowledged Khuzestan as an inseparable part of Iran's territorial sovereignty.

The historiography of Iran's oil industry is primarily shaped by political and economic discussions, often resorting to conventional references concerning colonialism's influence. This restricted viewpoint chronicles the industry's history from the Nationalisation Movement to the workers' participation in the 1979 Revolution, while overlooking the era before nationalisation. Notably, the discourse rarely extends beyond a legalistic examination of oil, starting from the establishment of the D'Arcy Concession to the critical 1933 agreement that augmented the British government's involvement in the Iranian oil sector. Such accounts diminish oil's significance to merely a source of revenue for Iran, eclipsing its pivotal role in fostering substantial geographical and social shifts. The founding of the oil industry spurred Khuzestan's transformation into Iran's leading industrial hub, and the formation of alliances among the Bakhtiari khans, Arab sheikhs, and the National Oil Company significantly altered the traditional tribal and regional frameworks of southern Iran. This era marked the rise of major urban centres such as Abadan and Masjed-Soleyman and promoted the growth of a cash-based economy. These changes highlight the necessity for a historiographical methodology that surpasses the traditional emphasis on legal and economic aspects to fully acknowledge the oil industry's deep-seated influence on Iran's socio-economic fabric.

In the latter part of the Twentieth Century, the historiography of Iran's oil sector is overwhelmingly concentrated on the nationalisation of the oil industry and the ensuing August 1953 coup d'état. References to Mosaddeq and these seminal events underscore their fundamental relevance to the oil narrative. Yet, there is a discernible shortfall in academic inquiry into oil's role in Iran's industrial advancement and the patterns of demographic shifts. The narrative appears to halt, implying a historical void beyond these significant occurrences. Additionally, a deep-rooted culture of xenophobia and hostility towards foreigners, stemming from Iran's lengthy encounters with colonialism, has side-lined alternative narratives and the contributions of Iranians within the oil story. The prevailing themes in the political historiography of oil thus focus on dependency and colonial exploitation, presenting a somewhat narrow perspective of its comprehensive impact.

> In my own abode did I see last night,
> A Water burning like Fire bright.
> 'Who art thou,' I asked, 'and whence dost thou come,
> O Water that a fire thou canst ignite?'
> With tongues of flames did the fire to me reveal,
> His secret and brought it in clear sight:
> 'I'm Oil,' he blazed, 'and how can I not burn,
> When my kin sells me to strangers? Such be my plight.'[1]

In the scholarly narratives prevalent during the two decades leading up to the revolution of 1979, the conceptualisation of oil transcended social and political interpretations, firmly anchoring itself within an economic and industrial paradigm. Within this framework, oil was exclusively considered a segment of the economic infrastructure, managed by the state, and was perceived as an industry completely detached from any form of social engagement or influence. It was in this period, particularly marked by a substantial escalation in oil revenues, that a novel discourse concerning oil materialised. This discourse, known as the 'rentier discourse' and discussed in Chapter 8, was prominently introduced by Hossein Mahdavi during this period. Mahdavi posited that oil should not be viewed merely as an industrial category but rather as a pivotal source of financial income. Furthermore, he suggested that the essence of the state's structure and its operational dynamics could be comprehensively understood only through an analysis of this income and its allocation strategies. This theory inherently suggests that the interaction between the state and society in Iran is intrinsically linked to the nature of oil revenue and the methods employed in its distribution.

In addition to the political and economic historiography of oil, it is imperative to acknowledge the company historiography as well. The term 'company historiography' or 'factory historiography' within the broader discipline of historiography denotes the systematic study and chronicling of the historical evolution, operational dynamics, and influence of distinct companies or manufacturing establishments. This particular area of study intersects with both business and industrial history, highlighting the development and impact of specific corporations on economic, managerial, technological, and at times political changes over historical periods. The company historiography of the Anglo-Persian/Iranian Oil Company by Ronald Ferrier and James Bamberg, published by the Cambridge University Press, is an example of this lineage.

Acknowledging the significance of social history does not imply the disregard of other historiographical domains concerning oil, including those focusing on economic, political, and company narratives. The scholarly contributions of historians such as Ronald Ferrier and James Bamberg present in-depth analyses of the operations, strategies, and impacts of the Anglo-Persian/Iranian Oil Company. Their work illuminates the ways in which corporate decisions and actions, aligned with political developments, have not only driven the evolution of the oil sector but also moulded the broader socio-economic landscape of Iran and regions beyond. This body of research is critical for unravelling the complex interrelations among British interests, company strategies, and international politics within the oil domain.

Additionally, the detailed political accounts provided by Fuad Rohani and Mohammad-Ali Movahhed on the process of oil nationalisation in Iran from inception to conclusion, as shown in Chapters 5 and 6, significantly deepen our understanding of the Iranian political framework. Their perspectives, coming from within, offer valuable insights into the interaction between Iran's political framework and the global stage.

Despite the breadth of historiographical work on oil, a conspicuous void remains in the social historiography of this narrative. There is a critical demand for academic focus on the individuals who tirelessly mined oil from beneath the earth's surface and enabled its delivery to our everyday lives. In the grand narratives of modernisation and development, oil and its labourers are paradoxically absent; while every element and actor is seemingly included and considered expert, the workers, and employees – whose efforts have significantly contributed to modernisation and the enactment of modernity – remain overshadowed and forgotten. The history of oil discovery is missing. The emergence of the working class within this industry is absent. The efforts of the industry's workers to build a civil society are not documented. The history of urbanisation and city life associated with this industry is also absent.

Beyond the lens of colonialism, oil has often been overlooked as a form of capital possessing profound and far-reaching social implications – a phenomenon that has engendered novel political, social, and geographical dynamics. These dynamics are rooted in the rise and empowerment of new social groups and classes, crafting an innovative framework for the interaction and contention between the state and society. Although oil indeed represents a form of capital, it is crucial to recognise that capital, in essence, is a social relation, capable of reflecting either democratic or non-democratic social structures. The non-democratic and opaque nature of oil's role within the Iranian social fabric is not an attribute of the oil itself but stems from the characteristics of oil-related institutions and the nature of state interactions concerning oil. This perspective underscores the need to critically evaluate the sociopolitical infrastructures surrounding oil, emphasising the impact of governance and institutional practices on the social consequences of oil as a capital form.

In a structuralist analysis concerning the influence of oil on social dynamics within Iran, the state is frequently depicted as a homogeneous entity, with the society cast in a role of passivity and acquiescence, essentially acting as a mere recipient. However, a careful scrutiny of the historical trajectory of oil in Iran unveils the significant contributions of the society to substantial social transformations. The endeavours of individuals employed in the oil sector, striving for more humane working, and living conditions – manifesting through a spectrum of actions from negotiations to both radical and non-radical protests – unequivocally affirm the notion that society was, in reality, far from passive.

The extensive history of oil over the past century, and the behaviours exhibited by participants in this industry – from unskilled labourers to skilled workers, engineers, staff, and management – illustrate a distinctive social behavioural model. This model, arguably, became a blueprint for other sectors of Iranian society, who emulated this pattern of social conduct. Their efforts towards modernity, modernisation, and the establishment of a civil society are commendable.

For instance, the earliest record of labour protests can be traced back to fifteen years after the discovery of oil, wherein workers voiced their demands for citizenship rights, a systematic and lawful work environment, and their place within the social fabric. As portrayed in Chapter 3, these demands, ultimately acknowledged by both the Anglo-Persian Oil Company and the Iranian government of the time, set precedents for the formulation of labour laws. This narrative challenges the perception of a passive society, highlighting the active and transformative role played by various social actors within the context of oil's history in Iran, thereby contributing significantly to the discourse on modernisation and civil rights.

The establishment and growth of oil cities and towns, envisioned as modern and developed enclaves distinct from the local milieu, were fundamentally predicated on the creation and preservation of social hierarchies and the observance of ethnic-class divisions. As delineated in Chapters 3 and 5, the living arrangements within the context examined were characterised by segregation based on nationality and occupation. Europeans, Indians, and Iranians were distinctly separated, with managers, engineers, skilled workers, and unskilled labourers each allocated to specific living quarters. The unskilled labourers, in particular, were frequently housed in makeshift settlements, highlighting the structured social divisions. However, this ethnic displacement and the gathering of diverse peoples within oil cities catalysed the emergence of new social identities that were previously non-existent, such as 'Abadani' or 'Masjed-Soleymani'. Thus, the affiliation with the oil industry transcended mere employment and evolved into a potent social identity, influencing how individuals and communities perceived themselves and interacted with others. This phenomenon underscores the profound impact of the oil industry on the fabric of society, not only reshaping physical landscapes but also moulding new cultural and social identities amid the complex interplay of ethnicity, class, and occupation.

Acknowledging the advantages of oil and its influence on social relations does not preclude recognising its adverse impacts on the environment. The advent of oil ushers in a landscape replete with industrial complexes, refineries, pipelines, thoroughfares, and urban centres. Simultaneously, it undermines the pre-existing natural environment that served as the cornerstone of livelihood for local communities, including agriculture, animal husbandry, small-scale maritime commerce, and the vitality of fishing ports. The initial years post-oil discovery saw an amplification of such adverse effects, coinciding with the identification of new oil reserves. This era was marked by the obliteration of villages and the displacement of their inhabitants, a testament to the profound alteration of the landscape and social fabric.

The anticipated job creation within this nascent industry often proved elusive, compelling numerous individuals to embark on migrations in quest of employment opportunities. Concurrent with the sprawl of oil fields has been the pervasive issue of soil and water contamination – a legacy of pollution with far-reaching implications on the health and well-being of both industry workers and local populations.

From the onset of oil discovery, the recruitment of a workforce emerged as a critical challenge for the Anglo-Persian Oil Company and a matter of concern for the Iranian government. The scarcity of both skilled and unskilled settled labour underscored the necessity for migrant workers within the oil sector. These migrant labourers, predominantly congregating in Khuzestan, played a pivotal role in mediating the distinct social hierarchy existing between Europeans and Iranians. Notably, the oil company exhibited a preference for employing Indian migrant workers, who were not only conversant in English but also well-acquainted with the colonial culture of Britain in India. Chapters 1 and 2 provide a detailed examination of the difficulties encountered by the Oil Company in recruiting its workforce, tracing the recruitment journey from major Indian cities such as Calcutta, Mumbai, and Delhi, to Iranian locales including Shiraz, and Isfahan.

A significant shift occurred a quarter-century after oil's discovery, during the reign of Reza Shah when the strategy of Iranianisation of the workforce was embedded in the 1934 Agreement. As discussed in Chapter 3, this initiative aimed at progressively favouring local and national labour, effectively altering the workforce composition from 68 per cent to 94 per cent comprised of local and national workers. Remarkably, in the aftermath of this agreement, the oil company initiated the employment of women in administrative roles for the first time, marking a significant milestone in the industry's employment practices. This transition not only reflected a broader strategy of workforce nationalisation but also underscored the evolving dynamics of labour and employment within the context of Iran's burgeoning oil industry.

As part of the initiative to broaden educational opportunities for unskilled and skilled Iranian workers, aimed at substituting the predominantly Indian foreign workforce, the Oil Company pledged to set up elementary and technical high schools, or vocational schools, along with an oil college dedicated to the training of Iranian engineers. This educational expansion coincided with the onset of war in Europe, leading to the inauguration of the Abadan Oil College in September 1939.

At the end of the First World War, Henri Bérenger, the French Minister of Energy, insightfully noted that control over an empire hinged on the possession of oil. In the ensuing context, Iranian oil emerged as a highly sought after asset among empires, which found themselves entangled in conflict once more. Chapter 4 delves into the significance of Iranian oil during the Second World War.

Merely two years following the commencement of hostilities in Europe, the conflagration extended to Iran, culminating in the occupation of the country by the armies of the Soviet Union and Britain. In Chapter 4, the discussion centres on the work and life of Iranians involved in the oil industry during the Second World War. By the early 1940s, the landscape of the Iranian oil industry, along with its cadre of skilled and unskilled Iranian labourers, had undergone a significant transformation from its state at the conclusion of the First World War in the early 1920s. The erstwhile labourers had evolved into workers endowed with a pronounced sense of worker identity. This period marked the emergence of the modern labour movement within the industry, a phenomenon that was unique in the Middle East and witnessed some of the most tumultuous events in the region's labour history. However, the lasting impact of this movement was mitigated by its lack of independence and its entanglement with political parties, factors that ultimately precluded it from becoming a sustaining force in the fight for the nationalisation of the Iranian oil industry.

The discourse surrounding the nationalisation of the oil industry, which began with discussions on its feasibility in the fourteenth Iranian Parliament in 1944 as a countermeasure to Soviet demands for oil concessions in the north, reached its culmination in less than seven years. Following its ratification, the Iranian oil industry was nationalised, leading to the departure of British employees and their associates from Iranian territory. The nationalisation of the oil industry, however, rather than ameliorating the working and living conditions of oil workers, paradoxically exacerbated their predicaments. The imposition of an embargo on Iranian oil, leading to the cessation of refinery operations, significantly impaired the livelihoods of numerous individuals employed within this sector, particularly those engaged on a contractual basis.

The British departure did not equate to a withdrawal from Iran's political landscape. Merely two years subsequent to the coup d'état in August 1953, these former stakeholders made a return to Iran, this time accompanied by other European and American partners. Together, they reintroduced the oil industry to the oversight of an international Consortium, effectively reshaping its management and control dynamics.

The active participation of the United States, alongside Britain, in the coup d'état and the ensuing governance of Iran's oil reserves underscored the global strategic importance of Iran's oil sector. It also illustrated the intricate nexus between national interests and the broader dynamics of international politics, spotlighting the geopolitical stakes associated with control over vital energy resources.

In the wake of the Second World War and against the backdrop of the burgeoning Cold War, the coup d'état of 1953 marked a seminal event in the annals of American foreign policy, representing the first instance of US-backed intervention to orchestrate a coup d'état, setting a precedent for the United States engagement in the internal affairs of other countries. This engagement bestowed upon the United States a distinct role in both the national and international policymaking realms of Iran during the Cold War period. The ramifications of this event profoundly influenced Iran's political landscape, precipitating a significant shift in the direction of its oil industry, and moulding its foreign relations and domestic politics for subsequent decades.

The concluding Chapters 8 and 9, scrutinise the pivotal epoch commencing in the early 1960s, marked by profound economic and social transformations instigated by the White Revolution of 1963, and culminating in the revolution of 1978–79. This period witnessed remarkable shifts in the working and living conditions of oil industry employees, attributable to a substantial augmentation in oil revenues and the execution of expansive development projects by the government.

This significant transformation within the oil sector crucially influenced the disposition of its workers towards the revolutionary movement in late 1970s, leading to their delayed and occasionally reluctant participation in the revolution. Despite the initial reluctance, the eventual alignment of the oil industry workforce with the revolutionary cause marked a decisive point in the revolution's momentum, underscoring the critical role of this sector's employees in the broader revolutionary movement. Once the oil industry's workforce firmly backed the revolution, there was a definitive shift in the revolution's dynamics, illustrating the strategic importance of this group within the context of Iran's transformative social and political landscape.

Reflecting on the social history of oil throughout the last 100 years prompts a re-evaluation of its significance as a key resource with extensive social repercussions. As referred to, it's crucial to move beyond labels of oil as a 'black calamity', 'scourge', or 'curse of the earth'. Equally, it should not be viewed as the sole reason for a government's avoidance of responsibility and accountability to its populace. It is vital to eschew essentialist interpretations of Iran's history at large and the specific narrative of Iran's oil industry. Acknowledging the complex impact of oil, encompassing both its benefits and drawbacks, facilitates a deeper insight into its influence on societal structures, economic growth, and both domestic and global political landscapes. This comprehensive perspective underscores the significance of oil as a dynamic force capable of driving profound changes across various dimensions of human endeavour and geopolitical relations.

Revisiting the history of oil and meticulously chronicling it, while recognising the efforts of all individuals who have carried the substantial weight of this industry's operations – not solely concentrating on select pivotal historical moments – can elucidate oil's integral role in Iran's social fabric. Such a comprehensive approach may lay the groundwork for more equitable and effective exploitation of this 'black gold', ensuring that its benefits are more broadly shared among Iranians. This re-evaluation could foster a more informed and inclusive strategy for managing oil resources, aligning them more closely with the national interest and the well-being of the entire population.

NOTES

Introduction

1. Karl Polányi, *The Great Transformation. The Political and Economic Origins of Our Time* (Boston: Beacon Press, 2001), 5. The adjective 'European' needs to be appended to Polányi's 'hundred years' peace', otherwise the notion would be Eurocentric. During this 'hundred years', the world witnessed many colonial wars outside Europe.
2. For a study of Iranian nationalist historiography see Touraj Atabaki, 'Agency and Subjectivity in Iranian National Historiography', in Touraj Atabaki (ed.), *Historiography and Political Culture in Twentieth Century Iran* (London & New York: I.B. Tauris, 2009).
3. Ranajit Guha, 'On Some Aspect of the Historiography of Colonial India', in *Subaltern Studies I. Writing on South Asian History and Society* (Delhi: Oxford University Press, 1982), 4–5.
4. Touraj Atabaki, 'Constitutionalists Sans Frontières: Iranian Constitutionalism and Its Asian Connections', in Houchang Esfandiar Chehabi & Vanessa Martin (eds.), *Constitutional Revolution: Popular Politics, Cultural Transformations and Transnational Connections* (London: I.B. Tauris, 2010), 341–56.
5. Touraj Atabaki, 'Missing Labour in the Metanarratives of Practicing Modernity in Iran: Labour Agency in Refashioning the Discourse of Social Development', in David Mayer and Jürgen Mittag (eds.), *Interventions: The Impact of Labour Movement on Social Development* (Leipzig: Akademische Verlagsanstalt, 2013), 171–95.
6. Eric Hobsbawm, *The Age of Extremes: A History of the World, 1914–1991* (London: Michael Joseph, 1994), 29–30.
7. James C. Davis, 'Towards a Theory of Revolution', *American Sociological Review*, 27 (February, 1962), 1–19; Hossein Bashiriyeh, *The State and Revolution in Iran, 1962–1982* (London: Palgrave Macmillan, 1984).
8. Abu-Afzl-Mohammad Beyhaqi, *Tarikh-e Beyhaqi* [History of Beyhaqi], Ali-Akbar Fayyaz (ed.) (Mashhad: Entesharat-e Daneshgah-e Mashhad, 1970), 221–22.

1 Oil Discovery and the Formation of a New Iranian Society

1. At the turn of the century, Iranian industries employing 23,500 workers comprised 0.7 per cent of the total workforce in the country. See Touraj Atabaki, Willem Floor, and Nazanin Sadeghi *Global Collaboratory on the History of Labour Relations, 1500–2000*, https://iisg.amsterdam/en/research/projects/global-collaboratory-on-the-history-of-labour-relations-1500-2000 (Accessed May 2015).

2. The unrestricted exploitation of oil deposits in the Absheron Peninsula, located along the Caspian coast, initiated in 1872, rapidly transformed the region into the source of approximately 95 per cent of Russia's domestic oil supply. Prior to its occupation and annexation, this territory was primarily valued for its geopolitical and military significance. However, Russian state authorities soon recognised the potential to capitalised on its rich subterranean resources. The late nineteenth century in Russia was marked by a state-centric approach to industrialisation. This policy facilitated a dramatic growth in domestic industries, the initiation of extensive mining endeavours, and the remarkable expansion of railway networks extending into the southern territories of the Tsarist Empire. See M. E. Falkus, *The Industrialisation of Russia, 1700–1914* (London: Palgrave, 1972), 44–46 and 64–66. The 'oil rush' had a profound impact on Baku's demographics, with the city's population escalating from 13,000 in 1859 to 112,000 in 1879, and further swelling to 300,000 by 1917. Similarly, the workforce employed in the Baku oilfields experienced a significant increase, growing from 1,800 in 1872 to 30,000 by 1907.
3. J. C. Hurewitz, *Diplomacy in the Near East, and Middle East: A Documentary Record* (London: Literary Licensing, 2011), 251.
4. R. W. Ferrier, *The History of the British Petroleum. Volume 1, The Developing Years, 1901–1932* (London: Cambridge University Press, 1982), 114.
5. BP Archive, ARC 78726, March 19 and 22, 1907.
6. Arnold T. Wilson, *S.W. Persia. Letters and Diary of a Young Political Officer, 1907–1914* (London: Oxford University Press, 1942), 28.
7. Ferrier, *The History of the British Petroleum*, 124.
8. Arash Khazeni, *Tribes and Empire on the Margins of Nineteenth Century Iran* (Seattle: University of Washington Press, 2009), 112–58.
9. Interview with Houshang Keshavarz Sadr, Paris, 21 January 2009. See also Javad Safinezhad, *ʿAshayer-e Markazi-ye Iran* [Tribes of Central Iran] (Tehran: Amir-Kabir, 1989), 461–71 and 525–48. For more study on Bakhtiaris and other tribes in modern Iran, see Khazeni, *Tribes and Empire on the Margins of Nineteenth Century Iran*; Gene R. Garthwaite, *Khans and Shah: A History of the Bakhtiyari Tribe in Iran* (London: I.B. Tauris 2009); Stephanie Cronin, *Tribal Politics in Iran: Rural Conflicts and the New State, 1921–1941* (New York: Routledge, 2007).
10. BP Archive, ARC 141294, January 1938, Laurence Lockhart, *Unpublished Record of the Anglo-Iranian Oil Company, Volume 1, 1901–1918*, 68.
11. British National Archive, FO 248/894, British Chargé d'Affaires, Evelyn Grant Duff to Sir Edward Grey, Secretary of State for Foreign Affairs, Tehran, 18 May 1906.
12. Ibid. 90.
13. Ferrier, *The History of the British Petroleum*, 128.
14. Ibid. 123.
15. Hurewitz, *Diplomacy in the Near East, and Middle East*, 249.
16. Iran National Archives, 240014788, Sadiq al-Saltaneh to the Iranian Chargé d'Affaires in London, 11 December 1910.
17. BP Archive, ARC 141294, January 1938, Laurence Lockhart, *Unpublished Record of the Anglo-Iranian Oil Company*, 146.
18. J. W. Williamson, *In a Persian Oil Field: A Study in Scientific and Industrial Development* (London: Ernest Benn, 1927), 120.
19. Ibid.
20. Ibid.

21. Kenneth. L. Gillion, *Fiji's Indian Migrants: A History to the End of Indenture in 1920* (London: Oxford University Press, 1962); Hugh Tinker, *New System of Slavery 1830–1929* (London: Oxford University Press, 1974); Brij V. Lal, 'Girmitiyas: The Origins of the Fiji Indians', *Journal of Pacific History* (1983); P. C. Emmer (ed.), *Colonialism and Migration: Indentured Labour before and after Slavery* (Dordrecht: M. Nijhoff, 1986); Marina Carter, *Servants, Sirdars and Settlers: Indians in Mauritius, 1834–1874* (London: Oxford University Press: 1995); Prabhu Mohapatra, 'Following Custom? Representations of Community among Indian Immigrant Labour in the West Indies 1880–1920', in P. Behal, P. Rana, and Masrcel van der Linden (eds.), *India's Labouring Poor: Historical Studies, c. 1600-c. 2000* (Cambridge: Cambridge University Press, 2007), 173–202.
22. Radhika Singha, 'Finding Labour from India for the War in Iraq: The Jail Porter and Labour Corps, 1916–1920', *Comparative Studies in Society and History*, 49 (2007): 412–45. Stefan Tetzlaff, 'The Turn of the Gulf Tide: Empire, Nationalism, and South Asian Labour Migration to Iraq, c. 1900–1935', *International Labour and Working-Class History*, 79 (Spring 2011): 7–27.
23. Wilson, *S. W. Persia*, 22.
24. The name of the Oil Company changed from 'Anglo Persian Oil Company' to 'Anglo Iranian Oil Company' after the government in Tehran decided on 21 March 1935 to change the name of the country from Persia to Iran.
25. George Thomson, 'Abadan in its Early Days', *Naft*, 4 (July 1931): 15.
26. I. J. Seccombe and R. I. Lawless, 'Foreign Worker Dependence in the Gulf, and the International Oil Companies: 1910–50,' 549.
27. J. B. Backhouse, 'Oil-1904–1928', in Harry Townsend (ed.), *A History of Shaw Wallace & Co. and Shaw Wallace & Co. Ltd.* (Calcutta: n.p., 1965), 46.
28. Ferrier, *The History of the British Petroleum*, 12; J. H. Bamberg, *The History of the British Petroleum, Volume 2, The Anglo-Iranian Years, 1928–1954* (London: Cambridge University Press, 1994), 11.
29. Willem van Schendel, 'Spatial Moments: Chittagong in Four Scenes', in Helen Siu and Eric Tagliacozzo (eds.), *Asia Inside Out: Connected Places* (Cambridge, MA: Harvard University Press, 2014). I am grateful to Willem van Schendel for providing me with valuable information on the categorisation of the Chittagonian workforce.
30. BP Archive, ARC 68877.
31. Ibid.
32. During the war the average salary of Indian workers was between 80 and 100 rupees per month. In the same period, the salary of Iranian workers was on average about one-third of the salary of Indian workers. Ibid.
33. Ibid.
34. Nicholas A. Lambert, *Sir John Fisher's Naval Revolution* (Columbia: University of South Carolina Press, 2002), 274–304.
35. Marian (Kent) Jack, 'The Purchase of the British Government's Shares in the British Petroleum Company 1912–1914', *Past and Present*, 39 (April 1968): 139–168.
36. Agreement with the Anglo-Persian Oil Company, Limited: Navy. Presented to Parliament by Command of His Majesty. London: His Majesty's Stationery Office, 1914, Cd. 7419.
37. Ferrier, *The History of the British Petroleum*, 151.
38. Ibid. 128.
39. Ibid.
40. Wilson, *S. W. Persia*, 97.

41. Ibid.
42. Ferrier, *The History of the British Petroleum*, 276.
43. The figure presented here as the population of Masjed-Soleyman around 1920 is based on the estimation derived from differed data collecting from the BP Archive and the Iran National Archive.
44. For the making of Masjed-Soleyman and Abadan as company towns, see Kaveh Ehsani, 'Social Engineering and the Contradictions of Modernisation in Khuzestan's Company Towns: A Look at Abadan and Masjed-Soleyman', *International Review of Social History* 3 (2003): 361–399.
45. Williamson, *In a Persian Oil Field*, 142.
46. C. E. Capito, 'Early Days in Masjed-Soleyman', *Naft*, 4 (1940): 5–11.
47. Kamal Athari, 'Masjed-Soleyman; Shahrak-e Shahri-ye Madaniyyat-yafteh', *Ettelaʿat-e Siyasi-Eqtesadi* 47–48 (1991): 65–69.
48. Iran National Archives, 240004338.
49. BP Archive, ARC 70335, July 24, 1911.
50. Ibid.
51. Carlo M. Cipolla, *Clocks & Culture 1300–1700* (London: W. W. Norton & Company; Reissue edition, 1967), 88.
52. For a comparative study of time and labour discipline in Iran and Turkey, see Touraj Atabaki, 'Time, Labour Discipline and Modernisation in Turkey and Iran', in Touraj Atabaki (ed.), *The State and the Subaltern: Society and Politics in Turkey and Iran* (London, I.B. Tauris, 2007), 1–16.
53. Ardeshir Avanesian, *Safahati chand az Jonbesh-e Kargari va Komunisti dar Dowran-e Avval-e Saltanat-e Reza Shah (1922–1933)* [Some pages of Worker and Communist Movement in the First Period of Reza Shah's Reign (1922–1933)] (Leipzig: Hezb-e Tudeh-e Iran, 1979), 75–83.
54. For a detailed study of labour activities aiming to reduce the working day in Iran, see Touraj Atabaki, 'The Comintern, the Soviet Union and Labour Militancy in Interwar Iran', in Stephanie Cronin (ed.), *Iranian-Russian Encounters. Empires and Revolutions since 1800* (London, Routledge, 2012), 298–323.
55. See, for example, Ali Ashtiyani, 'Formation of the Working Class in Iran', *Nazm-e Novin* 5 (1984).
56. Zachary Lockman, 'Reflections on Labour and Working-Class History in the Middle East and North Africa', in Jan Lucassen (ed.), *Global Labour History: A State of the Art* (Bern: Peter Lang AG, 2008), 136.
57. Zachary Lockman, 'Imagining the Working Class: Culture, Nationalism, and Class Formation in Egypt, 1899–1914', *Poetics Today* 5 (1994): 158–159.
58. Marcel van der Linden, 'Labour History: The Old, the New and the Global', *African Studies*, 2–3 (2007): 169–180.
59. Raymond Williams, *Marxism and Literature* (Oxford: Oxford University Press, 1977), 131.
60. For a detailed study of petitions in Persia and beyond, see Lex Heerma van Vos (ed.), *Petitions in Social History* (Supplement of *International Review of Social History Supplement* 9, 2002); Irene Schneider, *The Petitioning System in Iran: State, Society and Power Relations in the Late 19th Century* (Wiesbaden: Harrassowitz Verlag, 2006); Mansoureh Ettehadieh Nezam-Mafi, 'The Council for the Investigation of Grievances: A Case Study of Nineteenth Century Iranian Social History', *Iranian Studies*, 22 (1989): 51–61; John Chalcraft 'Engaging the State: Peasants and Petitions in Egypt on the Eve of Colonial Rule', *International Journal of Middle East Studies*, 37 (2005): 303–325.

61. Iran National Archives, 240014788, 11 December 1910.
62. Iran National Archives, 293005892, 27 August 1921. In south and southeast Asia, the term *tandil* was often used to name the overseer or foreman. See Russell Jones, (ed.), *Loan-words in Indonesian, and Malay* (Jakarta: n.p., 2008), 312 and David, 'Workers, Trust Us!' Labour Middlemen and the Rise of the Lower Castes in Andhra Pradesh', *post-print* hal-03239988, HAL, 2009.
63. Iran National Parliament Archives, Documents of the Fifth Parliament, 5 June 1924.
64. Ibid.

2 Oil and Labour in the First World War

1. Stuart Cohen, 'Mesopotamia in British Strategy, 1903–1914', *International Journal of Middle East Studies*, 2 (May 1978); Lev Ivanovich Miroshnikov, 'Iran in the World War I, Lecture Read at Harvard University in November 1962' (Persian translation by A. Dokhaniyati), *Iran dar Jang-e Jahani-ye Avval* (Tehran: Simorgh, 1965).
2. Ahmad-ʿAli Sepher (Movarrekh al-Dowleh), *Iran dar Jang-e Bozorg 1914–1918* [Iran in the Great War 1914–1918] (Tehran: Adib, 1983), 102.
3. Ibid. 15.
4. *Kaveh*, 29 and 30, July 1918.
5. Sepher (Movarrekh al-Dowleh), *Iran dar Jang-e Bozorg 1914–1918*, 239.
6. For the Provincial National Government see Mansoureh Ettehadieh Nezam-Mafi, 'The Iranian Provincial Government', in Touraj Atabaki (ed.), *Iran and the First World War, A Battleground of the Great Powers* (London, I.B. Tauris, 2006), 9–27; ʿAli-Reza Malaiʾi Tavani, ʿAli-Reza. *Iran va Dowlat-e Melli dar Jang-e Jahani-ye Avval* [Iran and the National Government in the First World War] (Tehran, 1999); Hossein Samiʿi and Amanollah Ardalan, *Avvalin Qiyam-e Moqadas-e Melli dar Jang-e Beinolmelel-e Avval* [The First National Holly War in the First World War] (Tehran: Ebn-e Sina, 1953); ʿAbdolhossein Sheibani (Vahid al-Molk), *Khaterat-e Mohajerat. Az Dowlat-e Movaqqat-e Kermanshah ta Komiteh-ye Meliyyun-e Berlan* [The Memoire of Migration: From Resistance Government in Kermanshah to Nationalist Committee in Berlin] (Tehran: Shirazeh, 1999).
7. For a British account of the impact of the Russian Revolution on the eastern front in the First World War, see Arnold T. Wilson, *Loyalties Mesopotamia* (London: Wipf & Stock Publishers, 1931).
8. Touraj Atabaki, *Azerbaijan. Ethnicity and the Struggle for Power in Iran* (London: I.B. Tauris, Second Edition 2000), 39–51.
9. For a study of the migrant Iranian labourers in the Caucasus see Touraj Atabaki, 'Disgruntled Guests: Iranian Subaltern on the Margins of the Tsarist Empire', *International Review of Social History*, 3 (2003), 401–26.
10. Iran National Archive, 240–3920, 293–3828, 240–1493, 240–6246, 240–5161.
11. Iran Ministry of Foreign Affairs, Archive of Documents and Diplomatic History, GH-133-58-4-91, GH-1333-58-4-68.
12. Iran National Archive, 293-003828.
13. Iran National Archive, 240-18279.
14. Willem Floor, *Labour Unions, Law and Conditions in Iran (1900–1941)* (Durham: Durham University, 1985), 12.
15. For an eyewitness account of the famine and epidemics spreading across Iran during the First World War, see Qahreman Mirza Salur, *Ruznameh-ye Khaterat-e ʿAyn al-Saltaneh [The Diary ʿAyn al-Saltaneh], Volume 7* (Tehran: Asatir, 1999), 5275–77.

16. Iran National Archive, 360–1569.
17. ʿAbdollah Mostowfi, *Sharh-e Zendegi-ye Man, [My Life], Volume 2* (Tehran: Zavvar, 1964); T. H. Vail Motter, *The Persian Corridor and Aid to Russia* (Washington: Office of the Chief of Military History, Department of Army, 1952), 513.
18. Report from the US Legation in Tehran, 1 November 1918, U.S. National Archive 891.00/1072.
19. Majid Foroutan, *Owzaʿ-e Siyasi va Ejtemaʿi-ye Hamedan dar Jang-e Jahangir-e Avval* [The Political and Social Conditions in Hamedan in the First World War] (Tehran: Farzaneh, 2011); L. C. Dunsterville, *The Adventure of Dunsterforce* (London: E. Arnold, 1920).
20. Cohen, 'Mesopotamia in British Strategy, 1903–1914', 171–81.
21. Ferrier, *History of the British Petroleum*, 288–90.
22. Between 1914 and 1918, British troops in Near East and Middle East numbered nearly Three million. At maximum strength, there were 1.3 million. They suffered 303,000 casualties during this period, that is, one out of every ten men. See Roger Adelson, *London and the Invention of the Middle East, Money, Power, and War, 1902–1922* (New Haven: Yale University Press, 1995), 171.
23. For the presence of the Indian workers in the Persian oil industry and Persian Gulf in wartime period see Touraj Atabaki, 'Far from Home, But at Home: Indian Migrant Workers in the Iranian Oil Industry', *Studies in History*, 1 (2015): 85–114. Radhika Singha, 'Finding Labour from India for the War in Iraq: The Jail Porter and Labour Corps, 1916–1920', *Comparative Studies in Society and History*, 49 (2007): 412–45; Stefan Tetzlaff, 'The Turn of the Gulf Tide: Empire, Nationalism, and South Asian Labour Migration to Iraq, c. 1900–1935', *International Migration Review*, 20 (1986): 548–74.
24. Adelson, *London and the Invention of the Middle East, Money, Power, and War*, 171.
25. BP Archive, ARC 141294, 265.
26. ʿAbbas Mirza Farmanfarmian-Salar Lashkar, *Jang-e Engelis va ʿOsmani dar Bein al-Nahrein va ʿAvaqeb-e An dar Iran* [The British-Ottoman War in Mesopotamia and Its Consequence for Iran], Mansoureh Ettehadieh Nezam-Mafi and Bahman Farman (eds.) (Tehran: Nashr-e Tarikh-e Iran, 2007), 27–28.
27. Christopher Sykes, *Wassmuss: 'The German Lawrence'* (London: Bernhard Tauchnitz, 1936), 51.
28. BP Archive, ARC 141294, January 1938. Lockhart, *Record of the Anglo-Iranian Oil Company, Volume I, 1901–1918*, 262.
29. George Thomson, 'Abadan during the World War', *Naft*, 8 (September 1932); Lev Ivanovich Miroshnikov, *Iran dar Jang-e Jahani-e Avval*, 37.
30. Ferrier, *The History of the British Petroleum*, 276.
31. Ulrich Gehrke, *Persien in der deutschen Orientpolitik während des Ersten Weltkrieges, Darstellungen zur Auswärtigen Politik, Volumes 1 & 2* (Stuttgart: W. Kohlhammer, 1960). Persian translation *Pish beh Su-ye Sharq. Iran dar Siyasat-e Sharqi-ye Alman dar Jang-e Jahani-ye Avval*, translated Sadri, Parviz (Tehran: Siamak, 1998), 133–36. For more narratives on Wassmuss activities see Dagobert von Mikusch, *Wassmuss, der deutsche Lawrence* (Berlin: Metropol Verlag, 1938); translated into Persian by Kaikavus Jahandari, *Wasmus* (Qom: Hamsayeh, 1998), 77–84. Oliver Bast, *Almani-ha dar Iran: Negahi beh Thavvolat-e Iran dar Jang-e Jahani-ye Avval bar Asas-e Manabeʿ-e Diplomatik-e Faranseh* [Germans in Iran: A Look at the Development in Iran during the First World War Based on the French Diplomatic Sources] (Tehran: Shirazeh, 1998), 35–43. See also: Sykes, *Wassmuss*.

32. Ulrich Gehrke, *Pish beh Su-ye Sharq. Iran dar Siyasat-e Sharqi-ye Alman dar Jang-e Jahani-ye Avval*, 133–36.
33. Ibid. 97.
34. BP Archive, ARC 141294, January 1938. Lockhart, *Record of the Anglo-Iranian Oil Company, Volume I, 1901–1918*, 269. Ferrier, *History of the British Petroleum*, 280; Gehrke, *Pish beh Su-ye Sharq*, 163.
35. BP Archive, ARC 141294, January 1938. Lockhart, *Record of the Anglo-Iranian Oil Company, Volume I, 1901–1918*, 265.
36. Iran Ministry of Foreign Affairs, Archive of Documents and Diplomatic History, GH-132-66-35-014.
37. BP Archive, ARC 141294, January 1938. Lockhart, *Record of the Anglo-Iranian Oil Company, Volume I, 1901–1918*, 270.
38. Iran Ministry of Foreign Affairs, Archive of Documents and Diplomatic History, GH-132-66-35-075.
39. BP Archive, ARC 70297, 24 April 1915. See also: ʿAli-Reza Abtahi, *Naft va Bakhtiari-ha* [Oil and Bakhtiaris] (Tehran: Tarikh-e Moʿaser, 2005), 39.
40. BP Archive, ARC 141294, 272. See also Lashkar, *Jang-e Engelis va 'Osmani dar Beyn al-Nahrain va ʿAvaqeb-e An dar Iran*, 64.
41. Ferrier, *The History of the British Petroleum*, 282.
42. For a study of *Taşkilat-i Mahsusa* in Iran, see Touraj Atabaki, 'Going East, The Ottomans' Secret Service Activities in Iran', in Touraj Atabaki (ed.), *Iran and the First World War. Battleground of the Great Powers* (London: IB Tauris, 2006), 29–42.
43. For the political geography of the region during the First World War, see Seyyed Qasem Yahosseini, 'Parkandegi-ye Qodrat dar Jonub-e Iran dar Astaneh-ye Jang-e Jahani-ye Avval' [the Diversity of Powers in Iran on the eve of the First World War] Safa Akhavan (ed.), *Iran dar jahani Avval* [Iran in the First World War] (Tehran: Verzarat-e Omur-e Kharejeh, 2005), 311–17. If the landing of British troops in Bushehr in 1909 was as result of the 1907 treaty between Britain and Russia, dividing Iran into their zone of interest, the landing in 1915 was mainly linked with APOC's interests in the region.
44. Iran Ministry of Foreign Affairs, Archive of Documents and Diplomatic History, GH-1302-27-19-19; GH-1320-27-19-20. For a comprehensive study about the South Persia Rifles unit, see Florida Safiri, *Polis-e Jonub Iran* (Tehran: Nashr-e Tarikh-e Iran, 1985). For more on South Persia Rifles's activities, see F. J. Moberly, *Operations in Persia, 1914–1919*, Reprint (London: Unipup, 1987). The history of the popular resistance against the British in the region has been the subject of series of studies. See, for example, Seyyed Qasem Yahosseini, *Reis ʿAli Delvari. Tajavoz-e Nezami-ye Britania va Moqavemat-e Jonub* (Tehran: Pardis-e Danesh, 1997).
45. Iran Ministry of Foreign Affairs, Archive of Documents and Diplomatic History, GH-1336-48-14-89.
46. BP Archive, ARC 141294, 273.
47. Lashkar (Mansoureh Ettehadieh Nezam-Mafi and Bahman Farman eds.), *Jang-e Engelis va 'Osmani dar Beyn al-Nahrain va ʿAvaqeb-e An dar Iran*, 90.
48. Mehdi-Qoli Hedayat, *Khaterat va Khatarat* [Memoires and Dangers] (Tehran: Zavvar, 1996).
49. BP Archive, ARC 141294, 270.
50. Thomson, 'Abadan during the World War', *Naft*, 8 (September 1932).

51. BP Archive, ARC 141294, January 1938. Lockhart, *Record of the Anglo-Iranian Oil Company 1901–1918,* 264. BP Archive, ARC 176338.
52. India National Archives, General Department 1915, 689. Department of Commerce and Industry 1915, 332.
53. Indian Emigrations Act of 1883, in *Royal Commission on Labour. Foreign Reports, Volume II.* The Colonies and the Indian Empire. House of Commons Parliamentary Papers, C. 6795-XI, 1892, 234; Stefan Tetzlaff, *Entangled Boundaries: British India and the Persian Gulf Region during the Transition from Empires to Nation States, c. 1880–1935,* 30, https://fid4sa-repository.ub.uni-heidelberg.de/3202/ (Accessed March 2013).
54. India National Archives, ARC 332-12, 1915. Tetzlaff, *Entangled Boundaries,* 68–70.
55. India National Archives, ARC 332-12, 1915.
56. For the Anglo-Russian 1907 Convention see Firuz Kazemzadeh, *Russia, and Britain in Persia, 1864–1914* (New Haven: Yale University Press, 1968). For a detailed study of this convention, and the reaction of the Iranians, see Mahmoud Mahmoud, *Traikh-e Ravabet-e Siyasi-ye Iran va Engelis dar Qarn-e Nuzdahom Miladi, [History of Political Relation between Iran and Britain in Nineteenth Century], Volume 8* (Tehran: Eqbal, 1954), 2228–2266.
57. India National Archives, ARC 332-12, 1915.
58. Ibid.
59. Tetzlaff, *Entangled Boundaries,* 72.
60. BP Archive, ARC 71754; Works Manager, Abadan to Strick, Scott & Co., 12 May 1916.
61. Thomson, 'Abadan during the World War', *Naft,* 8 (September 1932).
62. For an eyewitness account of the famine and epidemic spreading over Iran during the First World War see Sepehr (Movarrekh al-Dowleh), *Iran dar Jang-e Bozorg 1914–1918.*
63. BP Archive, ARC 68779. Strick, Scott & Co. to Wilson, 7 October 1916.
64. Thomson, 'Abadan during the World War', *Naft,* 8 (September 1932).
65. BP Archive, ARC 68799. Strick, Scott & Co. to Civil Commissioner, Basra, 24 Oct 1917.
66. Michael Edward Dobe, *A Long Slow Tutelage in Western Ways of Work: Industrial Education and the Containment of nationalism in Anglo-Iranian and ARAMCO, 1923–1963,* PhD thesis (Graduate School-New Brunswick, Rutgers, the State University of New Jersey, 2008), 62; Rasmus Christian Elling, 'On Lines and Fences: Labour, Community and Violence in an Oil City', in Ulrike Freitag, Nelida Fuccaro, Cludia Ghrawi, and Nora Lafi (eds.), *Urban Violence in the Middle East: Changing Cityscapes in the Transition from Empire to Nation State* (New York: Berghahn Books, 2015), 197–221; Henry Longhurst, *Adventure in Oil* (London: Sidgwick & Jackson, 1959), 72–73.
67. Tetzlaff, *Entangled Boundaries,* 68–70.
68. Ferrier, *History of the British Petroleum,* 276.
69. The figure for the population of Masjed-Soleyman around 1920 is based on an estimate derived from data in the BP Archive and the Iran National Archive.
70. Iran Ministry of Foreign Affairs, Archive of Documents and Diplomatic History, GH-1337-2-14-2.
71. The figure for the population of Abadan in the early 1920s is based on an estimate derived from data in the BP Archive and the Iran National Archive.
72. BP Archive, ARC 71879.

73. For the city planning of Abadan, see Mark Crinson, 'Abadan, Planning and Architecture under the Anglo-Persian Oil Company', *Planning Perspectives*, 3 (1997), 341–60; Kaveh Ehsani, 'Social Engineering and the Contradiction of Modernisation in Khuzestan's Company Towns, a Look at Abadan and Masjed-Soleyman', 361–90.

3 Oil and Authoritarian Modernisation During Interwar Period

1. Cyrus Ghani, *Iran and the Rise of Reza Shah. From Qajar Collapse to Pahlavi Power* (London: I.B. Tauris, 1998), 21–39.
2. Homa Katouzian, *State and Society in Iran. The Eclipse of the Qajars and the Emergence of the Pahlavis* (London: IB Tauris, 2006), 88–116.
3. Willem Floor, *Industrialisation in Iran 1900–1941, Working Paper at the Centre for the Middle Eastern and Islamic Studies* (Durham: University of Durham, 1984), 3.
4. Manuchehr Zia'i, *Majmuʿeh-ye Qavanin-e Vezarat* Kar [Collection of Amendments Ratified by the Ministry of Labour] (Tehran: Vezart-e Kar, 1976).
5. Vezarat-e Kar, *Amar Sanayeʿ-e Iran* [Industrial Statistic of Iran] (Tehran: Vezarat-e Kar, 1948).
6. Habib Ladjevardi, *Labor Unions and Autocracy in Iran* (New York: Syracuse University Press, 1984), 7; Willem Floor, *Labour Unions, Law, and Conditions in Iran 1900–1941*, 12.
7. Seyyed Mohammad Dehgan, 'Report to the International Red Labour Union (Profintern)', in Cosroe Chaqueri (ed.), *The Historical Documents: The Workers, Social Democrats, and the Communist Movement in Iran (1903–1963), Volume 6* (Florence: Mazdak, 1976), 106. The data presented in this report lacks corroboration from other sources and, therefore, should be approached with a degree of caution.
8. Abdolhossein Agahi, '60 Sal Az Tarikh-e Ta'sis-e Hezb-e Komonist-e Iran Gozasht' [Sixty Years Passed since the Foundation of the Communist Party of Iran], *Donya*, 3 (1980): 30–63.
9. Dehgan, 'Report to the International Red Labour Union (Profintern)', 106.
10. Shokrollah Mani, *Tarikhcheh-ye Nehzaht-e Kargari dar Iran* [A Concise History of the Labour Movement in Iran] (Tehran: n.p., 1946), 14.
11. Dehgan, 'Report to the International Red Labour Union (Profintern)', 106.
12. 'Maramnameh-ye Ferqeh-ye Siyasi-ye Demokrat-e Iran' [The Program of Democrat Political Party of Iran], in *Maramnameh va Nezamnameh-ha-ye Ahzab-e Siyasi-ye Iran dar Dovomin Dowreh-ye Majles-e Shora-ye Melli* [The Programmes and Bylaws of Iranian Political Parties in the Iranian Second National Parliament], Mansoureh Ettehadiyyeh Nezam-Mafi (ed.) (Tehran: Nashr-e Tarikh-e Iran, 1982), 6.
13. 'Qavaʿed va Nezamnameh-e Ferqeh-ye Dmokrat-e Iran' [The Bylaw and the Regulation of the Democrat Party of Iran], in *Maramnameh va Nezamnameh-ha-ye Ahzab-e Siyasi-ye Iran dar Dovomin Dowreh-ye Majles-e Shora-ye Melli* [The Programmes and Bylaws of Iranian Political Parties in the Iranian Second National Parliament], Mansoureh Etehadiyyeh Nezam-Mafi (ed.) (Tehran: Nashr-e Tarikh-e Iran, 1982), 12.
14. Fereydun Adamiyat, *Fekr-e Demokrasi-ye Ejtemaʿi dar Nehzat-e Mashrutiyat-e Iran* [The Idea of Social Democracy in the Iranian Constitution Movement] (Tehran: Payam, 1976), 96–97.

15. Edward G. Browne, The Press and Poetry of Modern Persia. Partly based on the manuscript work of Mirza Muhammad ʿAli Khan Tarbiyat of Tabriz (Los Angeles: Bahai Pub Trust, Reprint 1983), 52. See also Janet Afary, *The Iranian Constitutional Revolution, 1906–1911. Grassroots Democracy, Social Democracy, and Origin of Feminism* (New York: Columbia University Press, 1996), 273.
16. *Iran-e Nowww*, 7, 29 October 1910.
17. For an abridged history of the Socialist Party of Iran, see Mohammad-Taqi Bahar (Malek al-Shoʿara), *Tarikh-e Mokhtasr-e Ahzab-e Siyasi-ye Iran* [A Short History of Political Parties in Iran] (Tehran: Amir-Kabir, Third edition, 1957), 130–35.
18. Ibid. 130.
19. *Haqiqat*, as some have argued, never was the official organ of the Communist Party of Iran (CPI). Despite the contribution of a prominent member of the CPI, Pishevari, whose involvement in the publication is often misinterpreted as a proof that *Haqiqat* was the official organ of the Communist Party of Iran. For such argument see *Salnameh-ye Hezb-e Tudeh-e* Iran [Tudeh Party of Iran's Yearbook] (Leipzig: Hezb- Tudeh-e Iran, 1970), 176–77.
20. *Haqiqat*, 1, 30 December 1921.
21. *Haqiqat*, 58, 12 April 1922.
22. *Haqiqat*, 49, 29 March 1922.
23. *Haqiqat*, 70, 1 May 1922.
24. *Sur-e Esrafil*, 12, 5 September 1907.
25. *Haqiqat*, 60, 16 April 1922.
26. Ibid.
27. *Haqiqat*, 86, 29 May 1922.
28. *Haqiqat*, 68, 28 April 1922.
29. *Haqiqat*, 72, 5 May 1922.
30. Ibid.
31. Ibid.
32. Ibid.
33. Ibid.
34. Ferrier, *The History of the British Petroleum*, 432.
35. For example, see Floor, *Labour Unions*, 28.
36. Iran National Archive, File no. 240025870.
37. British National Archive, F.O. 371/7836. Intelligence Summary Persian Gulf, 23 March 1922.
38. Dr Ghore, 'Indian Workers in Persia. Miserable Condition', *Bombay Chronicle*, 10 January 1922. British National Archive, F.O. 371/781. Floor, *Labour Unions*, 29.
39. *Bombay Chronicle*, 10 January 1922.
40. Ibid.
41. Ibid.
42. Ardeshir Avanesian, *Safahati chand az Jonbesh Karigari va Komonisti da Dowran Avval Saltanat Reza Shah (1922–1933)*, 75–83; L. P. Elwell Sutton, *Persian Oil: A Study in Power Politics* (New York: Westport, 1975), 68–69. For More on the workers strike of oil industry in 1929, see Kaveh Bayat, 'With or Without Workers in Reza Shah's Iran', in Touraj Atabaki, *The State and the Subaltern. Modernisation, Society and the State in Turkey and Iran* (London: IB Tauris, 2007), 111–22; Stephanie Cronin, 'Popular Politics, the New State and the Birth of the Iranian Working Class: The 1929 Abadan Oil Refinery Strike', *Middle East Studies*, 46 5 (September 2010), 669–732.

43. BP Archive, ARC 59010. Abadan to London, Telegram 6 May 1929.
44. BP Archive, ARC 59010. Abadan to London, Telegram 4 May 1929.
45. Ibid.
46. BP Archive, ARC 59010. Abadan to Tehran, Telegram 12 May 1929.
47. BP Archive, ARC 59010. Secret Report, 8 May 1929. Yousuf Efekhari, *Khatirat Dowran Separi-shodeh, 1299–1329* [Memoires of the Passed Period], eds. Kaveh Bayat and Majid Tafreshi (Tehran: Ferdows, 1991), 39.
48. Yusef Eftekhari, *Khaterat-e Dowran-e Separi-shodeh, 1299–1329* [Memoires of the Passed Period, 1920–1950], Kaveh Bayat and Majid Tafreshi (eds.) (Tehran: Ferdows, 1991), 60–62; Touraj Atabaki, 'The Comintern, the Soviet Union and Working-Class Militancy in Interwar Iran', 298–323.
49. BP Archive, ARC 59010. Secret Report, 17 May 1929.
50. Ibid.
51. BP Archive, ARC 59010. Abadan to London, Telegram 16 May 1929.
52. Ibid.
53. Russian State Archive of Social-Political History (RGASPI) r. 10291 tom 1, Delo 16930 str. 31. This was not the first mission of Sultanzadeh to Iran. Following his earlier visit in 1920, on more than one occasion Sultanzadeh illegally visited Iran, always with forged identity papers.
54. Ibid.
55. Ibid.
56. Floor, *Labour Unions*, 54.
57. Fredrick Cooper, 'The Dialectics of Decolonisation: Nationalism and Labour Movements in Post-war Africa', *CSST Working Paper 884*, May 1992. http://deepblue.lib.umich.edu/bitstream/handle/2027.42/51246/480.pdf?sequence=1
58. Touraj Atabaki, 'Disgruntled Guests: Iranian Subalterns on the Margin of the Tsarist Empire', in Touraj Atabaki (ed.), *The State and the Subaltern. Society and Politics in Turkey and Iran* (London: I.B. Tauris, 2007), 31–52.
59. BP Archive, ARC 59010. Abadan to London, Telegram 6 May 1929; Avanesian, *Safahati chand,* 75–83; Sutton, *Persian Oil,* 68–69. For a detailed study of labour activities aiming to reduce the working day in Iran, see Atabaki, 'The Comintern'. For recent studies of the workers' strike in the oil industry in 1929, see Kaveh Bayat, 'With or Without Workers in Reza Shah's Iran', in Atabaki, *The State and the Subaltern,* 111–122; Cronin, 'Popular Politics and the Birth of Iranian Working Class', 699–732.
60. Iran President Office Archives, no. 117, Report by the Head of Khorramshahr Office of Post and Telegraph on Abadan strike (6 May 1929). *Naft dar doreh Reza Shah* (Tehran: Vezarat Farhang va Ershad Eslami, 1999), 101–102.
61. BP Archive, ARC 59010. Abadan to London, Telegram of 6 May 1929.
62. *Habl al Matin* 21, 4 June 1929. BP Archive, ARC 59010.
63. Iran National Parliament Archives, Documents of the Fifth Session, Ref. 5/146/35/13, the Petition Commission, 1924, 1–4.
64. Ibid. 6.
65. BP Archive, ARC 54499, October 8, 1925.
66. *Shafaq-e Sorkh,* 3 December 1929.
67. Iran President Office Archives, 930, Letter from the Consulate of the Imperial Iran in Basreh to Tehran, 11 March 1928. *Naft dar doreh Reza Shah* (Tehran: Vezarat Farhang va Ershad Eslami, 1999), 35–38.
68. BP Archive, ARC 59010, Labour Affairs, 15 June 1929.

69. J. H. Bamberg, *The History of the British Petroleum, Volume 2, The Anglo-Iranian Years, 1928–1954* (London: Cambridge University Press, 1994), 78.
70. Julian Bahrier, *Economic Development in Iran 1900–1970* (London: Oxford University, Press), 172–76.
71. BP Archive, ARC H16/23 and 4308.
72. Ibid. Bamberg, *The History of the British Petroleum*, 69.
73. The National Archives, 297037647. Report of the Education Department of Khuzestan, 6 September 1931.
74. For a detailed study of this agreement see Abolfazl Lesani, *Tala-ye Siyah ya Bala-ye Iran* [Black Gold or the Affliction of Iran] (Tehran: Mehr, 1950).
75. Bamberg, *The History of the British Petroleum*, 37.
76. Ibid.
77. British National Archives, FO 371/17909.
78. *Shafaq-e Sorkh*, 25 October, 1933.
79. *The Times*, 28 November 1933.
80. BP Archive, ARC 85909.
81. Bamberg, *The History of the British Petroleum*, 55.
82. Ibid. 232.
83. British National Archives, FO 371/24572.
84. The date of this interview is 2 March 1940. Mohammad Torkaman, *Asnad-e Naqz-e Bitarafi-ye Iran dar Shahrivar-e 1320* [Documents Regarding the Violation of Iran's Neutrality in August 1941] (Tehran: Kavir, 1991), 14.
85. BP Archive, ARC 54506. Letter Book ARC 9, H.E. Nichols to R.I. Watson, 9 May 1921.
86. BP Archive, ARC 54499. Letter nos. 209–210, H.E. Nicolas to Shaw Wallace & Co, 3 December 1925.
87. BP Archive, ARC 54499. November 5, 1925.
88. Iran National Archive, ARC 297/34982. Ministry of Finance to the Ministry Endowment and Education, 9 August 1927.
89. Michael Edward Dobe, *A Long Slow Tutelage in Western Ways of Work: Industrial Education and the Containment of Nationalism in Anglo-Iranian and ARAMCO, 1923–1963*, 52; J. W. Williamson, *In a Persian Oil Field. A Study in Scientific and Industrial Development*, 156; Stefan Tetzlaff, *Entangled Boundaries: British India and the Persian Gulf Region during the Transition from Empires to Nation States, c. 1880–1935*, 75–87.
90. Ibid. 34.
91. BP Archive, ARC 133277. January 1938. Laurence Lockhart, *Unpublished Record of the Anglo-Iranian Oil Company, Relations between Persian (Iranian) Government 1918–1946*, 77–78.
92. Figure drawn based on the data provided by Ferrier, *The History of the British Petroleum, The Developing Years 1901–1932* and Bamberg, *The History of the British Petroleum*.
93. Ibid. 77–78.
94. Ibid. 81.
95. BP Archive, ARC 72614. 4 December 1932.
96. BP Archive, ARC 54374, ARC 54375.
97. BP Archive, ARC 78/63/1-205; Bamberg, *The History of the British Petroleum*, 69.
98. BP Archive, ARC 96659.
99. BP Archive, ARC 85909.

100. Bamberg, *The History of the British Petroleum*, 103.
101. BP Archive, ARC 85908.
102. Janet Abu-Lughod, *Rabat, Urban Apartheid in Morocco* (Princeton: Princeton University Press, 1981), 374. For more study on colonial urban development see Anthony D. King, *Colonial Urban Development: Culture, Social Power, and Environment* (London: Routledge, 2007); Mariam Dossal, *Imperial Designs and Indian Realities: The Planning of Bombay City, 1845–1875* (London: Oxford University Press, 1991).
103. Nezar Alsayyad and Mrinalini Rajagopalan, 'Colonial City' in *Encyclopaedia of Urban Studies* (Thousand Oaks: SAGE Publications, 2010), 166–71. See also Eva T. van Kempen, 'The Dual City and the Poor: Social Polarisation, Social Segregation and Life Chances', *Urban Studies*, 7 (1994): 99–105.
104. H.A., 'Anglopersian Oil Kompany va Joziyat an' [The Anglo-Persian Oil Company and its details], *Setareh-e Sorkh*, 7–8, April 1930, 87.
105. BP Archive, ARC 71879.
106. Ibid.
107. Williamson, *In a Persian Oil Field*, 14.
108. Abdolali Lahsaeizadeh, *Jamehshenasi Abadan* [Sociology of Abadan] (Tehran: Kiyan-Mehr, 2006), 289.
109. For the city planning of Abadan, see Mark Crinson, 'Abadan: Architecture and Planning under the Anglo-Persian Oil Company', *Planning Perspectives*, 12, 3 (1997): 341–60. See also Kaveh Ehsani, 'Social Engineering and the Contradiction of Modernisation in Khuzestan's Company Towns: A Look at Abadan and Masjed-Soleyman', 361–90.
110. APOC Magazine, Volume 4, 2, March 1928.
111. Reidar Visser, *The Gibraltar That Never Was* (www.historiae.org), 9 (Accessed March 2014).
112. BP Archive, ARC 71183. 'Item 21; Social Activities', 18 March 1926; 'Item 5; Conference at Fields Manager's Office', 2 April 1926; 'Dossier 12; Social Services Department- Fields', 2 April 1926. Also: *Naft* (1926). BP Archive, ARC 71183, 1926.
113. BP Archive, ARC 68723. M.Y. Young to Strick & Co., 3 March 1921.
114. BP Archive, ARC 71183. 'Social Services Department Fields', 2 April 1926. Michael Edward Dobe, *A Long Slow Tutelage in Western Ways of Work: Industrial Education and the Containment of Nationalism in Anglo-Iranian and ARAMCO, 1923–1963*, 45.

4 The Second World War: The Great Powers' Rivalry for Oil

1. Geoffrey Jones, *The State, and the British Oil Industry* (London: Macmillan, 1981).
2. Among notable Persian language works are the following: Baqer 'Aqeli, *Khaterat-e yek Nakhostvazir: Ahmad Matin Daftari* [A Prime Minister's Memoir: Ahmad Matin Daftari] (Tehran: 'Elmi, 1991); Mohammad Torkaman, *Asnad-e Naqz-e Bitarafi-ye Iran dar Shahrivar-e 1320*; Reza Azari Shahreza'i, *Dowlat-e Iran va Motekhassesan-e Mohajer-e Almani* [Iran and German Expert Immigrants] (Tehran: Sazman-e Asnad-e Melli-ye Iran, 1995); Mohammad Movahhed, *Khab-e Ashofteh-e Naft: Az Qarardad-e D'Arcy ta Soqut-e Reza Shah* [The Turbulent Dream of Oil: from D'Arcy Concession to the Fall of Reza Shah] (Tehran: Karnameh, 2014); Aliasghar Zargar, *Tarikh-e Ravabet-e Siyasi-e Iran va Englis dar Dowreh-e*

Reza Shah [The History of Diplomacy between Iran and Britain during the Reza Shah Period] (Tehran: Parvin, 1993). Among English works see Reader Bullard, *Letters from Tehran: A British Ambassador in World War II Persia* (London: I.B. Tauris, 1991); Reader Bullard, *The Camels Must Go: An Autobiography* (London: Faber, 1961); Richard A. Stewart, *Sunrise at Abadan: The British and Soviet Invasion of Iran, 1941* (New York: Prager, 1988).

3. *The Illustrated Weekly of India*, 4 June 1941 cited in Torkaman, *Asnad-e Naqz-e*, 88.
4. On the eve of the Second World War, *Ettela'at* detailed the number of foreigners who were living in Iran as follows: 'The majority of the foreign subjects are working in the major industrial institutions such as the Anglo-Iranian Oil Company, The Railways, The Iranian Fish Company, the governmental and national factories of which 2,590 are British subjects [which of course includes the labour force coming from the British colonies including India], 390 from the Soviet Union, 690 Germans, 310 Italians, 180 from Czechoslovakia, 70 Swiss, 260 Greeks, 140 Yugoslavians. There are also a small number of other foreign subjects who are working in industrial and business institutions among others'. *Ettela'at*, 4588, 8 July 1941.
5. L.P. Elwell Sutton, *Persian Oil: A Study in Power Politics*, 104–105.
6. Abdalreza Houshang Mahdavi, *Tarikh-e Ravabet-e Khareji-ye Iran* [The History of Iran's Foreign Affairs] (Tehran: Simorq, 1976), 378–88.
7. Indeed, it is important to acknowledge that, following the coup d'état orchestrated by Rashid 'Ali Gilani in Iraq and the pro-German stance of those behind the coup d'état, the British Minister engaged in discussions with the Iranian Foreign Minister. During these conversations, the British Minister underscored the acute sensitivity of the oil fields, particularly those located in Iran, to the British government. Furthermore, he emphasised the critical nature of neutralising Germany's subversive interference in the affairs of countries within that region. Rashid 'Ali Gilani, a prominent Iraqi politician, instigated an anti-British coup d'état in Iraq in April 1941. His government's tenure lasted no more than two months, and it was ultimately brought to an end through British intervention. This episode underscores the intricate geopolitical dynamics of the era and the pivotal role that oil resources played in the strategies and concerns of major powers during the Second World War. Torkaman, *Asnad-e Naqz-e*, 86–7.
8. *Ettela'at*, 3941, 1 September 1939.
9. *Ettela'at*, 3942, 2 September 1939.
10. Qahreman Mirza Salour, *Ruznameh-e Khaterat-e 'Ain al-Saltaneh, Volume 10*, 7857.
11. James Bamberg, *The History of the British Petroleum Company*, 48, 68.
12. 'For over a month, German and Soviet Diplomacy has been bending every effort to undermine Iran's morale and weaken her will to resist blandishments and threats from Berlin and Moscow. The partition of Poland and the virtual loss of the independence of the Baltic States have created fear that the Soviets will next turn their attention to the Black Sea and Caspian Sea and that crucial days lie ahead for Iran.' Stewart, *Sunrise at Abadan*, 15.
13. 'Aqeli, *Khaterat-e yek Nakhostvazir*, 159.
14. Torkaman, *Asnad-e Naqz-e*, 13.
15. Ibid.
16. 'Aqeli, *Khaterat-e yek Nakhostvazir*, 159.
17. Bamberg, *The History of the British Petroleum Company*, 230.

18. Bamberg, *The History of the British Petroleum Company*, 232–33.
19. Mostafa Fateh, *Tarikh-e Panjah Sal Naft-e Iran* [History of Fifty Years of the Iranian Oil] (Tehran: Payam, 1979), 314.
20. 'Aqeli, *Khaterat-e yek Nakhostvazir*, 159.
21. Bamberg, *The History of the British Petroleum Company*, 234.
22. Bullard, *Letters from Tehran*, 51.
23. Mohammad Sajjadi (Tamadon al- Molk), *Iran va Engelstan* [Iran and England] (Calcutta: Art Press, 1942), 21. This treaty comprises a collection of essays initially published in issues 10 to 15 of the second year of his publication *Nameh-e Azad* (Letter of Liberty). During the onset of the Second World War, Mohammad Sajjadi assumed the role of a Persian-language radio announcer broadcasting from India. His radio broadcasts conveyed news supporting the British war effort. Following the Allied occupation of Iran, Sajjadi returned to Iran. In his memoirs, Abolhassan Ebtehaj refers to him as 'the representative of the British Embassy in Tehran'. Abolhassan Ebtehaj, *Khaterat* [Memoir] (London: Peka, 1991), 360.
24. For the text of the Tripartite Treaty, signed by Britain, USSR, and Iran, see Hurewitz, J.C., *Diplomacy in the Middle East, 1914–1956, Volume 2*, 233–34.
25. Vail Motter, T.H., *The Persian Corridor and Aid to Russia* (Washington: Office of the Chief of Military History, Department of Army, 1952), 281–83. For the United States account of the Allied Military withdrawal from Iran, see Robert Ghobad Irani, *American Diplomacy: An Option Analysis of the Azerbaijan Crisis, 1945–1946* (Hyattsville, MD: Institute of Middle Eastern and North African Affairs, 1978), 25–34.
26. For a detailed account of the 'Azerbaijan Crisis' see Touraj Atabaki, *Azerbaijan: Ethnicity and the Struggle for Power in Iran*.
27. Bamberg, *The History of the British Petroleum Company*, 216.
28. Chris Paine and Erica Schoenberger, 'Iranian Nationalism and the Great Powers: 1872–1954', *MERIP Reports*, 37 (1975): 18.
29. Bamberg, *The History of the British Petroleum Company*, 240.
30. Ibid. 242.
31. Figure drawn based on the data provided by Bamberg, *The History of the British Petroleum Company*.
32. Sutton, *Persian Oil*, 138.
33. There are numerous reports from provinces reaching the capital on agricultural labour leaving the villages for urban employment. An example can be found in Iran National Archive, DocNo. 240-993.
34. BP Archive, ArcRef. 118823. Donald McNeil, *The Lesson of 1946: An Essay on the Personnel Problems of the Oil Industry in South Iran*.
35. Fateh, *Tarikh-e Panjah Sal Naft-e* Iran, 434.
36. Ibid. 434.
37. BP Archive, ArcRef. 16249. Some Impressions in Iran, March 1946.
38. Fateh, *Tarikh-e Panjah Sal Naft-e* Iran, 435.
39. For the Second World War history of labour in the Iranian oil industry see Touraj Atabaki and Kaveh Ehsani, 'Oil and Beyond Expanding British Imperial Aspirations, Emerging Oil Capitalism, and the Challenge of Social Questions in the First World War', in Helmut Bley and Anorthe Kremers (eds.), *The World during the First World War* (Essen: Klartext Verlag, 2014), 261–87.
40. International Labour Office (ILO), *Labour Conditions in the Oil Industry in Iran: Report of International Labour Office (January-February 1950)* (Geneva: International Labour Office, 1950), 27–30.

41. Ibid.
42. Ibid.
43. For a detailed study of this incident, see Rasmus Christian Elling 'On Lines and Fences: Labour, Community and Violence in an Oil City', in *Urban Violence in the Middle East: Changing Cityscapes in the Transition from Empire to Nation State*, eds. Ulrike Freitag, Nelida Fuccaro, Claudia Ghrawi and Nora Lafi (New York: 2015), 197–221.
44. Iran National Archive, DocNo. 240-993.
45. BP Archive, ArcRef. 118823. Donald McNeil, *The Lesson of 1946: An Essay on the Personnel Problems of the Oil Industry in South Iran.*
46. Iran National Archive, DocNo. 240-1132 and DocNo. 240-24733.
47. Stephen L. McFarland, 'Anatomy of an Iranian Political Crowd: The Tehran Bread Riot of December 1942', *International Journal of Middle East Studies*, 1 (1985): 51–65.
48. Iran National Archive, DocNo. 240-8362.
49. Iran National Archive, DocNo. 240-993.
50. BP Archive, ArcRef. 118823.
51. BP Archive, ArcRef. 16249. Some Impressions in Iran, March 1946.
52. BP Archive, ArcRef. 118823. See also Sutton, *Persian Oil*, 140. The official rates of exchange then were 1 Rials = 0.011 British Pounds = 0,031 US Dollars.
53. Out of 783 women employed in Abadan and fields in 1949 there were 63 non-Iranian salaried employees in the medical services and 449 Iranian salaried employees in the medical services and for commercial work. There were also 271 Iranian women wage earners, of whom about half were trainee clerks and the remainder chiefly sanitary and laundry workers. International Labour Office (ILO), *Labour Conditions in the Oil Industry in Iran.*
54. BP Archive, ArcRef. 16249. Discussion on Labour Condition, 1, March 1946.
55. BP Archive, ArcRef. 16249. Jones to Elkington, 7 March 1946.
56. Ibid.
57. Fateh, *Tarikh-e Panjah Sal Naft-e* Iran, 435.
58. Manuchehr Farmanfarmaian, *Blood and Oil* (New York: Modern Library, 1997), 184–85.
59. BP Archive, ArcRef. 43762. Report of British M.Ps. visit to Persia, 19 June 1946. See also BP Archive, ArcRef. 16249, Jones to Elkington, 7 March 1946.
60. Morteza Dehqan-Nezhad and Elham Lotfi, 'Bimari-ye Tifus, Peyamad-e Voquʿ va Gostaresh-e Jang-e Dovvom-e Jahani dar Iran' [The Typhus and its Expansion in Iran during the Second World War], *Faslnameh-ye Ravabet-e Khareji* (2010): 49.
61. BP Archive, ArcRef. 16249, Discussion on Labour Conditions, 1st March 1946.
62. Ibid.
63. Ibid.
64. Ibid.
65. BP Archive, ArcRef. 43762. Report of British M.Ps. visit to Persia, 19 June 1946.
66. For a detailed account of life and political career of individuals in the Second World War labour movement in Iran see Touraj Atabaki, 'L'Organisation Syndicate Ouvriere en Iran, de 1941 a 1946', *Soual*, 8 (1988): 35–60.
67. Abdolsamad Kambakhsh, 'Tashkil-e Hezb-e Tudeh-ye Iran' [Foundation of Tudeh Party of Iran] *Donya*, 7 (3) (1966): 30–31.
68. British National Archives, F.O. 371/45450. 'The Visit of the Soviet Trade Union Delegation to Persia',
69. British National Archives, F.O. 371/61993.

70. BP Archive, ArcRef. 118823. Donald McNeil, *The Lesson of 1946: An Essay on the Personnel Problems of the Oil Industry in South Iran.*
71. Ibid.
72. Vezarat-e Kar va Tablighat. *Showra-ye Mottaheddeh-ye Iyalati-ye Khuzestan. Tashkilat, Eqdamat-e Gheir-e Qanuni, Khiyanat va Su'-e estefadeh* [The Provincial Council of Unified Trade Unions of Khuzestan. Organisation, Illegal Performance, Betrayal and Manipulation] (Tehran: Khodkar, 1947), 10.
73. *Zafar*, 264, 24 May 1325.
74. British National Archives, FO. 371/52714. British Council in Khorramshahr, Report on Tudeh activities in the oil industry, 1946.
75. Indian Office, L/PS/12/3490A. British Consulate, Khorramshahr, 1 July 1946. *Zafar*, 248, 6 May 1946.
76. British National Archives, FO. 371/52718. Tehran to Foreign Office, 7 May 1946.
77. *Zafar*, 262, 22 May 1946.
78. Bamberg, *The History of the British Petroleum Company*, 352.
79. BP Archive, ArcRef. 118823. Donald McNeil, *The Lesson of 1946: An Essay on the Personnel Problems of the Oil Industry in South Iran.*
80. British National Archives, FO. 371/52718. Tehran to Foreign Office, 13 May 1946.
81. BP Archive, ArcRef. 43762. Report on Delegation to Persia, June 1946.
82. Fateh, *Panjah Sal Naft-e Iran*, 438.
83. *Zafar*, nos. 257 and 258, 16 and 17 May 1946.
84. British National Archives, FO. 371/52718. Tehran to Foreign Office, 13 May 1946.
85. British National Archives, FO. 371/52718. Note of latest information from Anglo-Iranian Oil Company, 14 May 1946.
86. *Zafar*, 256, 15 May 1946.
87. Fateh, *Panjah Sal Naft-e Iran*, 437.
88. *Zafar*, 258, 17 May 1946. BP Archive, ArcRef. 118823. Donald McNeil, *The Lesson of 1946: An Essay on the Personnel Problems of the Oil Industry in South Iran.*
89. In the new Labour Law, the question of minimum wage and Friday pay was addressed, although with some degree of ambiguity: The minimum wages of a workman shall be determined, in accordance with the condition in each different part of the country, in such manner as to meet the expenses of living of himself and his family. If the employer does not pay his workman wages for Friday, he is bound to fix their weekly wages in such a manner that the wages paid him for six days shall be equivalent to wages for seven days. For a review of the new Labour Law, see Habib Ladjevardi, *Labour Unions and Autocracy in Iran*, 61–64.
90. British National Archives, FO. 371/52718. Tehran to Foreign Office, 23 May 1946.
91. *Zafar*, 256 and 266, 26 and 27 May 1946.
92. British National Archives, FO. 371/52718. *Shahbaz*, 26 May 46.
93. BP Archive, ArcRef. 118823. Donald McNeil, *The Lesson of 1946: An Essay on the Personnel Problems of the Oil Industry in South Iran.*
94. *Zafar*, 301, 9 July 1946.
95. British National Archives, WO. 208/1570. Tribal and Political Weekly Intelligence Summery, 31 December 1945.
96. Indian Office, L/PS/12/3490A. British Consulate, Khorramshahr, 21 July 1946.
97. Ibid.
98. The Proceedings of the Military Tribunal on 24 July 1946 Abadan Incident, in F. M. Javanshir, *Hemaseh-ye 23 Tir: Gushe-ha-'i az Mobarezat-e Kargaran-e Naft-e Khuzestan* [The Saga of 23 Tir: An account of the Struggle of the Khuzestan Oil

Workers] (Tehran: Hezb-e Tudeh-e Iran, 1980), 47. This Military Tribunal for the trial of the Tudeh Party leaders and activists was inaugurated in March 1949 and lasted for three months. Although the mission of the Tribunal was to examine the attempt to assassinate the Shah on 4 February 1949, there were detailed discussions of the entire modus operandi of the Tudeh party and the CCFTU since they were founded. Some sessions of the Tribunal were devoted to the July 1946 strike in the oil industry and the fatal episode of Abadan.

99. Ibid. With the consent of the Iranian government, the Arab Union later was renamed as the *Ettehadieh-ye ʿAshayer-e Khuzestan* (Union of Tribes of Khuzestan) see Vezarat Kar va Tablighat, *Shora-ye Motahedh-ye Iyalati-ye Khuzestan. Tashkilat, Eqdamat-e Gheyr-e Qanuni, Khiyanat va Sou'estefadeh*, 30.
100. British National Archives, FO. 248/1468. Underwood to General Manager AIOC, 11 July 1946.
101. For the study of Iranian Arab activities in Khuzestan in early 1940s see Brian Maan, 'The Khuzestan Arab Movement, 1941–1946: A Case of Nationalism?' in *Rethinking Iranian Nationalism and Modernity*, Kamran Scot Aghaie and Afshin Marashi (eds.) (Austin: University of Texas Press, 2014), 113–136.
102. Indian Office, L/PS/12/3490A. British Consulate, Khorramshahr, 21 July 1946.
103. BP Archive, ArcRef. 43762. Report by Elkington, Tudeh Party Activities Amongst Anglo-Iranian Oil Company Labour, 25 July 1946. For more on formation of the Tudeh Party see Ervand Abrahamian, *Iran between Two Revolutions* (Princeton: Princeton University Press, 1982), 326–418.
104. Indian Office, L/PS/12/3490A. British Consulate, Khorramshahr, 21 July 1946.
105. British National Archives, FO. 371/52718. TUC Report on Iranian Visit, 1946.
106. BP Archive, ArcRef. 16249. Ivor Jones to Edward Elkington, 12 May 1946.
107. BP Archive, ArcRef. 43762. Report by Elkington, Tudeh Party Activities Amongst Anglo-Iranian Oil Company Labour, 25 July 1946.
108. Indian Office, L/PS/12/3490A. British Consulate, Khorramshahr, 26 June 1946. Mohammad Ahmad Farooqi's previous career was in the British Air Force, but he was dismissed from that position due to his communist beliefs. When the AIOC terminated Farooqi's employment, they had two proposed options for handling the situation: either transferring him to Baghdad and then dismissing him there or requesting the Governor of Abadan to issue an order for his internment. The Oil Company ultimately chose the latter option.
109. Indian Office, L/PS/12/3490A. Additional Consul for Indian Affairs, British Embassy Tehran, 17 July 1946.
110. Ibid.
111. Ibid.
112. Indian Office, L/PS/12/3490A. British Consulate, Khorramshahr, 21 July 1946.
113. BP Archive, ArcRef. 130264. Summary of Abadan General strike, 19 July 1946.
114. Indian Office, L/PS/12/3490A. British Consulate, Khorramshahr, 21 July 1946. Vezarat Kar va Tablighat, *Shora-ye Motahedh-ye Iyalati-ye Khuzestan. Tashkilat, Eqdamat-e Gheyr-e Qanuni, Khiyanat va Sou'estefadeh*, 41.
115. Ibid. 31.
116. Ibid. 35. *Zafar*, 306, 15 July 1946.
117. Indian Office, L/PS/12/3490A. British Consulate, Khorramshahr, 21 July 1946.
118. Ibid.
119. U.S. National Archives, RG. 84/2256. Williams, 3 September 1946, cited in *Labour Unions and Autocracy in Iran*, Habib Ladjevardi, 134.

120. Reza Allamehzadeh's interview with Nasser Khaksar, Utrecht, July 2010. Javanshir, *Hemaseh-ye 23 Tir*, 57.
121. Indian Office, L/PS/12/3490A. British Consulate, Khorramshahr, 21 July 1946. The anti-Arab wording in the Company's intelligence report should indeed be viewed with caution. The report might have been influenced by the context of the time and the tensions between different groups, including Arab and Persian contractors.
122. Javanshir, *Hemaseh-ye 23 Tir*, 60. Tablighat, *Shora-ye Motahedh-ye Iyalati Khuzestan*, 36.
123. U.S. National Archives. RG. 84/2256, 134.
124. *Zafar*, 310, 22 July 1946.
125. BP Archive, ArcRef. 130264, Summery of Abadan General strike, 19 July 1946.
126. British Nation Archives, FO 371/52718. Report of three members of the Parliament visiting south Iran. 19 June 1946.
127. British Nation Archives, FO 371/52715. Records of the meeting held by Sir O. Sargent. 18 June 1946.
128. British Nation Archives, FO 371/52715. 'Persian Situation', Sargent to Bevin. 20 June 1946.
129. BP Archive, ArcRef. 130264, Summary of Abadan General Strike, 19 July 1946.
130. *Zafar*, 314, 26 July 1946.
131. Sutton, *Persian Oil*, 146–47.
132. British Nation Archives, FO 248/1471, Military Intelligence Report, 19 July 1946.
133. British Nation Archives, FO 371/52715. Bevin to Sargent, 23 June 1946.
134. Frederick Cooper, *Decolonisation and African Society. The Labour Question in French and British Africa* (Cambridge: Cambridge University, 1996), 202.
135. Ibid. 205.

5 Poised to Leap: Towards Oil Nationalisation

1. On 4 February 1949, an unsuccessful assassination attempt targeted Mohammad-Reza Shah Pahlavi while he was visiting Tehran University. The would-be assassin, Nasser Fakhraii, was killed on the spot during the attempt. Notably, among the items found in Fakhraii's possession were a press card associated with an Islamic journal and a note indicating his probationary membership in the Tudeh Party. Following this assassination attempt and in response to the heightened security situation, military governorship was declared in Iran. As a result, the Tudeh Party of Iran was officially outlawed, and all its activities, along with those of its affiliated organisations, including the Central Council of Unified Trade Unions of Iran (CCFTU); were deemed illegal. *Dad*, 1439, 28 January 1949; *Keyhan*, 1748, 30 January 1949.
2. For the archetypal of such studies see Fakhreddin Azimi, *The Crisis of Democracy* (London: I.B. Tauris, 2009); Darioush Bayandor, *Iran and the CIA: The Fall of Mosaddeq Revisited* (New York: Palgrave, 2010); Christopher de Bellaigue, *Patriot of Persia: Muhammad Mossadegh and a Tragic Anglo-American Coup* (New York: Harper Collins, 2012); James Bill and Wm. R. Louis, *Mussadiq, Iranian Nationalism, and Oil* (London: Tauris, 1988); Andrew Cooper, *The Oil Kings* (New York: Simon & Schuster, 2011); Andrew Cooper, *The Fall of Heaven* (New York: Henry Holt, 2016); Mostafa Elm, *Oil, Power and Principle: Iran's Oil Nationalisation and Its Aftermath* (Syracuse: Syracuse University Press, 1992);

L. P. Elwell Sutton, *Persian Oil: A Study in Power Politics*; Mustafa Fateh, *Panjah Sal Naft*; Mark Gasiorowski and Byrne Malcolm (ed.), *Mohammad Mosaddeq and the 1953 Coup in Iran* (Syracuse: Syracuse University Press, 2004); Mohammad Movahhed, *Khab-e Ashofteh-e Naft: Az Qarardad-e D'Arcy ta Soqut-e Reza Shah*; Ali Rahnema, *Behind the 1953 Coup in Iran* (Cambridge: Cambridge University Press, 2015).

3. Khalil Maleki, *Khaterat-e Siyasi* [Political Memoirs] (Tehran: Ravaq, 1978), 250.
4. For a detailed study of 1947 crisis in the Tudeh party see Ervand Abrahamian, *Iran between Two Revolutions*, 307–31.
5. Khalil Maleki, *Majmuʿeh-ye Maqalat* [Collected Articles], Reza Azari Shahrezaʾi, (ed.) (Tehran: Akhtaran, 2017), 917–66.
6. Anvar Khamehʾi, *Az Ensheʿab ta Kudeta* [From Split to Coup d'état] (Tehran: Hafteh, 1984), 36–68.
7. Ibid. 169.
8. U.S. National Archives, RG 84/148, U.S. Government 'MLR', 1 June 1948. Cited in Habib Ladjevardi, *Labour Unions and Autocracy in Iran*, 173.
9. U.S. National Archives, RG 84/148, U.S. Government 'Annual Labour report, 1947–48', 1 October 1948. Cited in *Labour Unions and Autocracy in Iran*, Habib Ladjevardi, 177.
10. Ibid. 179.
11. Ibid. 191.
12. Vezarat-e Kar va Tablighat, *Eqdamat-e Gheir-e Qanuni-ye Showara-ye Mottaheddeh-ye Markazi* [Illegal Activities of the Central Council of Federated Trade Unions] (Tehran: Vezarat-e Kar va Tablighat, 1947), 55.
13. British National Archives, FO 248/1468. 10 December 1946.
14. ʿEsmat Yazdanpanah-Daʾi, *Diary* (Unpublished). Received 11 May 2016, Author's private collection.
15. British National Archives, FO 371/61933, 27 January 1947.
16. British National Archives, FO 248/1475, 26 February 1947.
17. Chapour Bakhtiar, *Yekrangi* [Veracity], translated by Mahshid Amirshahi (Paris: Khavaran, 1982). For a detailed account of Bakhtiar's life and time see Hamid Shokat, *Flight into Darkness. A Political Biography of Shapour Bakhtiar*, translated by M. R. Ghanoonparvar (Bethesda: Ibex Publishers, 2019).
18. Sutton, *Persian Oil*, 152–53.
19. British National Archives, FO 371-62008-E5512, 25 June 1947.
20. Interview with Chapour Bakhtiar, *Iranian Oral History Project*, Harvard University, 6 March 1984. https://nrs.harvard.edu/urn-3:FHCL:1091327.
21. British National Archives, FO 248/1475, 30 July 1947.
22. Ibid.
23. Ibid.
24. British National Archives, FO 248/1475, 21 May 1947.
25. Habib Ladjevardi, *Labdour Union and Autocracy in Iran*, 147.
26. British National Archives, FO 248/1475, 2 September 1947.
27. British National Archives, FO 248/1475, 27 August 1947. Ladjevardi, *Labor Unions and Autocracy in Iran*, 146.
28. British National Archives, FO 14058, 19 October 1948.
29. Marcel van der Linden and Lex Heerma van Voss (eds.), *Class and Other Identities: Gender, Religion and Ethnicity in the Writing of European Labor History* (New York and Oxford: Berghahn Books, 2002).

30. NLAI 310-061506. 8 October 1948.
31. NLAI 310-061506.
32. Bakhtiar, *Yekrangi*, 60–61.
33. Manuchehr Behzadi (1927–1988)
34. Interview with Rahmat Jazani, Paris, June 2015.
35. British National Archives, FO 248/1475, 27 August 1947.
36. Interview with Rahmat Jazani, Paris, 14 June 2015.
37. *Ettelaʿat-e Haftegi*, 507, 27 April 1951.
38. *Tehran Mosavvar*, 142, 8 February 1946.
39. *Tehran Mosavvar*, 140, 25 January 1946.
40. Ibid.
41. *Tehran Mosavvar*, 141, 1 February 1946.
42. Ibid.
43. *Tehran Mosavvar*, 144, 22 February 1946.
44. *Tehran Mosavvar*, 143, 15 February 1946.
45. *Asiya-ye Javan*, 37, 2 May 1951.
46. For an in-depth and thorough exploration of the company towns in Khuzestan, see Kaveh Ehsani. 'Social Engineering and the Contradictions of Modernisation in Khuzestan's Company Towns: A Look at Abadan and Masjed-Soleyman', 361–99.
47. *Javan*, 37.
48. Norman Kemp, *Abadan. A first-hand Account of the Persian Oil Crisis* (London: Allan Wingate, 1953), 74.
49. Siamak Lotfollahi, *Khaterat-e Siamak Lotfollahi* [Siamak Lotfollahi's Memoire], Mohammad-Hossein Khosrowpanah (ed.) (Tehran: Khojasteh, 2015), 21–22.
50. For the location of the Abadan Refinery within the social engineering of Abadan, see Ehsani, 'Social Engineering and the Contradictions of Modernisation in Khuzestan's Company Towns', 361–99. See also M. Crinson, 'Abadan: Planning and Architecture under the Anglo-Iranian Oil Company', *Planning Perspectives*, 3: 341–59.
51. The Sikh Temple was destroyed during the Iran-Iraq War (1980–1988).
52. Kemp, *Abadan*, 75.
53. International Labour Office (ILO), *Labour Conditions in the Oil Industry in Iran*, 33.
54. *Javan*, 37.
55. Ehsani, 'Social Engineering and the Contradictions of Modernisation in Khuzestan's Company Towns: A Look at Abadan and Masjed-Soleyman', 393.
56. *Ettelaʿat-e Haftegi*, 515, 22 June 1951.
57. Interview with Hassan Kamshad, London, 8 May 2014.
58. International Labour Office (ILO), *Labour Conditions in the Oil Industry in Iran*, 40.
59. Ibid.
60. Iranian Government, *Some Documents on the Conditions of the Iranian Workers under the Ex-Anglo Iranian Oil Co.* (Tehran, Iranian Government Publishing House, 1951), 18.
61. International Labour Office (ILO), *Labour Conditions in the Oil Industry in Iran*, 28–29.
62. Lotfollahi, *Khaterat-e Siamak Lotfollahi*, 39–41.
63. Following the nationalisation of oil in 1951, the name of the Gymkana club was changed to *Naft Club*.
64. Abdolali Lahsaeizadeh, *Jamehshenasi Abadan*, 353.
65. Najaf Daryabandari, *Sal-ha-ye Javani va Siyast: Khaterat-e Najaf Daryabandari dar Goftogu ba Hossein Mirzaʾi* [The Years of Youth and Politics: The Memoirs of Najaf

Daryabandari from Abadan in Interview with Hossein Mirza'i] (Abadan: Abadan-Nameh, 2015), 72–73. Lotfollahi, *Khaterat-e Siamak* Lotfollahi, 26.

66. Mustafa Fateh, *Panjah Sal Naft*, 455–56.
67. Lotfollahi, *Khaterat-e Siamak* Lotfollahi, 26.
68. Ibid. 27–28.
69. Interview with Nasim Khaksar, Utrecht, 2 December 2016.
70. *Asiya-ye Javan*, 38, 9 May 1951.
71. Rasmus C. Elling, 'On Lines and Fences. Labour, Community and Violence in an Oil City', 209.
72. Nasim Khaksar, *Qafas-e Tuti-ye Jahan Khanom* (The Parrot's Cage of Mrs Jahan) (London: H&S Media, Second Edition 2011), 35. Shatt bank is a reference to the bank of Aravadroud (Shatt al-Arab).
73. Yazdanpanah-Da'i, *Diary*.
74. *Javan*, 38.
75. Khaksar, *Qafas-e Touti-ye Jahan Khanom*, 126.
76. The establishment of the State of Israel in May 1948 played a significant role in the expulsion of Jews from Iraq. The Zionist movement had been active in promoting Jewish immigration to Palestine, and the declaration of Israel's independence intensified the Arab Israeli conflict. This led to increased tensions and hostilities between Jewish and Arab communities in various Middle Eastern countries, including Iraq.
77. *Javan*, 38.
78. Ibid. 37.
79. Ehsani, 'Social Engineering and the Contradictions of Modernisation in Khuzestan's Company Towns', 393.
80. BP Archive, ArcRef. 118823. Donald McNeil, *The Lesson of 1946: An Essay on the Personnel Problems of the Oil Industry in South Iran.*
81. Iran National Archives, DocNo. 1947, 293-1424. International Labour Office, 31.
82. Iran National Archives, DocNo. 1947, 293-1424.
83. The AIOC public relation policy has been discussed in detail in E. H. O. Elkington, 'Public Relations and Publicity: The Information Branch', January–March 1947, BP Archive, ARC 16255. Mona Damluji in her studies examines the AIOC's propaganda policies in a larger context: Mona Damluji, 'The Image World of Middle Eastern Oil', in Hannah Appel, Arthur Mason, Michael Watts (eds.), *Subterranean Estates: Life Worlds of Oil and Gas* (Ithaca: Cornell University Press, 2015), 147–64; Mona Damluji, 'The Oil City in Focus: The Cinematic Spaces of Abadan in the Anglo-Iranian Oil Company's Persian Story', *Comparative Studies of South Asia, Africa, and the Middle East*, 1 (2013): 75–88. References to the oil companies' propaganda campaigns in the global contexts could be found in Daniel Yergin, *The Prize: The Epic Quest for Oil, Money, and Power* (New York: Simon & Schuster, 1991) and Daniel Yergin, *The Quest: Energy, Security, and the Remaking of the Modern World* (New York: Penguin Press, 2011).
84. Mostafa Fateh, *Panjah Sal Naft-e* Iran, 440.
85. R. W. Ferrier, *The History of the British Petroleum Company* and James Bamberg, *The History of the British Petroleum Company*. For a detailed biography of Laurence Lockhart, see *Encyclopaedia Iranica*, https://iranicaonline.org/articles/lockhart-laurence
86. BP Archive, ARC 176930/00 and ARC 72131/001. For life and Archive of Geoffrey Keating see https://rimakeating.co.uk/Geoffrey.J.Keating%2CMC%2CPHOTO%20ARCHIVE

87. *Dad*, 3 April 1947.
88. *Nameh-e Mardom*, 70, 13 April 1947.
89. *Piruzi*, 22 April 1947. BP Archive, ArcRef 66101.
90. *Saba*, 3, 16 April 1947.
91. *Kasra*, 22 April 1947. BP Archive, ArcRef 66101.
92. *Mardom*, 70.
93. *Kasra*, 22 April 1947.
94. *Mardom*, 70. Khalil Maleki was incarcerated as a political prisoner in Tehran's Qasr Prison for a duration of four years, from 1937 to 1941.
95. *Nameh-e Mardom*, 74, April 1947.
96. *Nameh-e Mardom*, 71, 14 April 1947.
97. *Nameh-e Mardom*, 73, 16 April 1947.
98. James Bamberg, *The History of the British Petroleum Company*, 378.
99. *Nameh-e Mardom*, 75, 18 April 1947.
100. BP Archive, ARC 72131/001.
101. The periodicals published by the Information Department in Abadan were: *Naft* (English) *Daily News Bulletin* (English), *Abadan Daily* (English), *Iran Digest* (English), *Indian Weekly News* (English), *Akhbar-e Ruz* (Persian), *Akhbar-e Hafteh* (Persian), *Nameh-ye Varzeshi* (Persian), *Kholaseh-ye Nashriyat-e Tehran* (Persian), *Servis Khabari Abadan* (Persian).
102. Hossein Mirza'i, *Khastgah-e Ravabet-e ʿOmumi dar Iran. Daramadi be Tarikh-e Ravabet-e ʿOmumi-ye Sherkat-e Palayesh-e Naft-e Abadan* [The Origin of Public Relations in Iran. An Introduction to the History of Public Relations in the Oil Refinery of Abadan] (Abadan: Ravabet-e ʿOmumi-ye Sherkat-e Palayesh-e Naft-e Abadan, 2016), 102.
103. *Tehran Mosavvar*, 409, 15 June 1951.
104. Kemp, *Abadan*, 63.
105. Interview with Ebrahim Golestan, Bolney, West Sussex, 9 May 2014.
106. *Javan*, 38.
107. Iranian Government, *Some Documents on the Conditions of the Iranian Workers under the Ex-Anglo Iranian Oil Co*, 3.
108. International Labour Office (ILO), *Labour Conditions in the Oil Industry in Iran.*
109. Iranian Government, *Some Documents on the Conditions of the Iranian Workers under the Ex-Anglo Iranian Oil Co*, 4.
110. Ibid. 5.
111. Ibid. 7.
112. International Labour Office (ILO), *Labour Conditions in the Oil Industry in Iran*, 28.
113. Iranian Government, *Some Documents on the Conditions of the Iranian Workers under the Ex-Anglo Iranian Oil Co*, 8.
114. International Labour Office (ILO), *Labour Conditions in the Oil Industry in Iran*, 28–29.
115. Ibid. 31.
116. Ibid. 32.
117. *Bazarian*, 5, 11 April 1951.
118. International Labour Office (ILO), *Labour Conditions in the Oil Industry in Iran*. 34.
119. Ibid. 32.
120. Ibid. 76.
121. Iranian Government, *Some Documents on the Conditions of the Iranian Workers under the Ex-Anglo Iranian Oil Co.*, 15.

122. *Dad*, 1561, 4 May 1949.
123. James Bamberg, *The History of the British Petroleum Company*, 419.
124. British National Archives, F.O. 371/91524, 29 March 1951.
125. *Ettela'at*, 7484, 4 April 1951. *Ettela'at-e Haftegi*, 505, 13 April 1951.
126. BP Archive, 33732, 68908, 71148.
127. Iran National Archives, 293-5875, 5 April 1951.
128. *Ettela'at*, 7488, 9 April 1951.
129. British National Archives, F.O. 371/91456-1951, F.O. 248/1524-1951.
130. I benefitted enormously from the interviews I had with Manouchehr Mohandes on the education and training scheme at the 1940s AIOC.
131. *Ettela'at-e Haftegi*, 56, 20 April 1951.
132. *Ettela'at*, 7488.
133. British National Archives, F.O. 248/1524-195.
134. British National Archives, F.O. 371/91456-1951, F.O. 248/1524-195.
135. *Ettela'at*, 7481, 31 March 1951.
136. *Tehran Mosavvar*, 403, 4 May 1951.
137. Iran National Archives, Petition sent to Tehran from Bandar Shahpur, 293-4670, 13 April 1951.
138. Sutton, *Persian Oil*, 211.
139. *Haftegi*, 56, 20 April 1951.
140. Iran National Archives, Petition sent to Tehran from Ahvaz, 293-5875, 14 April 1951.
141. *Ettela'at*, 7492, 14 April 1951; Sutton, *Persian Oil*, 211.
142. Iran National Archives, Petition sent to Tehran from Ahvaz, 293-5875, 15 April 1951.
143. *Ettela'at*, 7488.
144. *Haftegi*, 56, 20 April 1951.
145. *Haftegi*, 56, 20 April 1951.
146. BP Archive, ARC 211627, Relation with The Iranian Government 1947–1952. British National Archives, F.O. 248/1524-1951.
147. Yazdanpanah-Da'i, *Diary*.
148. *Ettela'at*, 7496, 18 April.
149. *Asiya-ye Javan*, 36, 25 April 1951.
150. Kemp, *Abadan*, 66.
151. *Javan*, 36; *Mosavvar*, 403, 4 May 1951; *Ettela'at*, 7492. For a British detailed account see Kemp, *Abadans*, 66–69.
152. *Haftegi*, 56, 20 April 1951. The British diplomatic account confirms the eye-witness account of the *Ettela'at-e Haftegi*. See British National Archivess, F.O. 248/1524-195.
153. *Ettela'at*, 7492 *Asiya-ye Javan*, 36.
154. F.O. 248/1524 21 British Consulate Khorramshahr, 21 May 1951.
155. Kemp, *Abadan*, 77.
156. Rohan Butler, *British Policy in the Relinquishment of Abadan*, British National Archives, F.O., Secret, 1962, 97–104; *Haftegi*, 56, 20 April 1951.
157. Kemp, *Abadan*, 77.
158. Interview with Nasim Khaksar.
159. Sutton, *Persian Oil*, 211.
160. Ibid. 211–212.
161. *Ettela'at-e Haftegi*, 508, 4 May 1951.

162. Iran National Archives, 293-46/70/47.
163. BP Archive, ARC 71148, 23 April 1951. ARC 211627, Relation with the Iranian Government 1947–1952.
164. Interview with Nasim Khaksar.
165. *Javan*, 38.
166. *Ettela'at*, 7493, 15 April 1951.
167. Kemp, *Abadan*, 229.
168. BP Archive, ARC 211627, Relation with The Iranian Government 1947–1952.
169. Interview with Rahmat Jazani, Paris, 14 June 2015.
170. *Haftegi*, 507, 27 April 1951.
171. British National Archives, F.O. 248/1524 21 British Consulate Khorramshahr, 21 May 1951.
172. BP Archive, ARC 211627, Relation with The Iranian Government 1947–1952.
173. *Asiya-ye Javan*, 35, 18 April 1951.
174. F. M. Javanshir, *Tajrobeh-ye 28 Mordad: Nazari beh Tarikh-e Jonbesh-e Melli Shodan-e Naft-e Iran* [The Experience of 28 Mordad: A Look at the History of the Movement of the Nationalisation of Oil in Iran] (Tehran: Hezb-e Tudeh-e Iran, 1980), 120.
175. Interview with Rahmat Jazani, Paris, 14 June 2015.
176. British National Archives, F.O. 248/1524 21 British Consulate Khorramshahr, 21 May 1951.
177. *Bakhtar-e Emruz*, 14 April 1951.
178. Interview with Rahmat Jazani, Paris, 14 June 2015.
179. British National Archives, F.O. 248/1524 21 British Consulate Khorramshahr, 21 May 1951.
180. Butler, *British Policy in the Relinquishment of Abadan*, 79–106.
181. *Tarraqi*, 428, 26 March 1951; *Kushesh*, 7473, 26 March 1951.
182. Sutton, *Persian Oil*, 212.
183. *Haftegi*, 515.
184. Bamberg, *History of the British Petroleum Company*, 425.
185. Ibid.
186. Kemp, *Abadan*, 141. See also Bamberg, *History of the British Petroleum Company*, 425.
187. Butler, *British Policy in the Relinquishment of Abadan*, 146–72. BP Archive ARC 100171.
188. BP Archive ARC 100171. Rahmat Jazani recalls that there were workers associated with the Tudeh Party who pushed Bazargan to take the chair of Derek. Interview with Rahmat Jazani, Paris, 14 June 2015. See also Kemp, *Abadan*, 162.
189. BP Archive, ARC 43859.
190. BP Archive, ARC 100652.
191. Kemp, *Abadan*, 183.
192. Ibid. 235.
193. BP Archive, ARC 100572. Kemp, *Abadan*, 239.
194. Ibid.
195. Iran National Parliament Archives, Documents of Sixteenth Session 164, 5 July 1951.
196. Yazdanpanah-Da'i, *Diary*.
197. Nasser Najmi, *Havades-e Tarikhi-ye Iran az Shahrivar-e 20 ta 28 Mordad-e 1332* [The Historical Events in Iran from August 1941 to 19 August 1953] (Tehran: Koleini, 1991), 267.

6 Sovereignty's Interlude: Iran's Oil in 1951–1954

1. *Ettelaʿat* (Monthly), 525, 19 September 1951, 27.
2. Ibid.
3. See for example, Mohammad-Ali Movahhed, *Khab-e Ashofteh-e Naft: Az Qarardad-e D'Arcy ta Soqut-e Reza Shah*, and Ervand Abrahamian, *The Coup: 1953, the CIA, and the Roots of Modern U.S.-Iranian Relations* (The New Press, 2013).
4. For the foundation of the Consortium see: Mary Ann Heiss, 'The United States, Great Britain, and the Creation of the Iranian Oil Consortium, 1953–1954', *The International History Review*, 3 (August 1994): 511–35.
5. Exceptional in previous studies is Maral Jefroudi PhD thesis: *'If I Deserve It, It Should Be Paid to Me'. A Social History of Labour in the Iranian Oil Industry 1951–1973*, PhD thesis, Leiden University, October 2017.
6. Iran National Archives, 24000820.
7. Iran National Archives, 290084370.
8. Hossein Makki, *Khalʿ-e Yadd: Ketab-e Siyah* [Eviction: The Black Book] (Tehran: Bongah-e Tarjomeh va Nashr-e Ketab, 1981), 830–31.
9. *Asiya-ye Javan*, 2 May 1951.
10. *Javan*, 2 May 1951.
11. *Niru-ye Sevvom*, 103, 15 February 1953.
12. *Shahed-e Iran*, 11, 8 May 1952.
13. *Bakhtar-e Emruz*, 1110, 27 May 1953.
14. Mostafa Fateh, *Panjah Sal Naft-e Iran*, 643.
15. *Bakhtar-e Emruz*, 1139 and 1145, 4 July and 12 July 1953.
16. *Navid-e Azadi*, 159, 1 August 1953.
17. Parviz Mina joined the Iranian oil industry in 1947. Following the nationalisation of Iranian oil, he worked at the NIOC Department of Exploration and Production and later in 1974 he became the Director of the International Department of National Iranian Oil Company.
18. Gholam-Reza Afkhami (ed.), *Tahavvolat-e Sanʿat-e Naft-e Iran, Negahi az Darun: Mosahebeh ba Parviz Mina* [The Evolution of Iran's Oil Industry, an Insider's Account: An Interview with Parviz Mina] (Washington: Foundation of Iranian Studies, 1998), 9.
19. Ibid. c and Byrne Malcolm (ed.), *Mohammad Mosaddeq and the 1953 Coup in Iran*, 185.
20. Mary Ann Heiss, 'The International Boycott of Iranian Oil and the Anti-Mosaddeq Coup of 1953' in Mark Gasiorowski and Malcolm Byrne (ed.), *Mohammad Mosaddeq and the 1953 Coup in Iran*, 182.
21. Mostafa Elm, *Oil, Power, and Principle*, 267–70.
22. Heiss, 'The International Boycott of Iranian Oil and the Anti-Mosaddeq Coup of 1953', 190.
23. Iran National Archives, 240-35805.
24. Jefroudi, PhD thesis: *'If I deserve it, it should be paid to me'*, 88.
25. *Bakhtar-e Emruz*, 860, 13 July 1952.
26. Makki, *Khal'-e Yad*, 861–68.
27. Ibid.
28. *Ettelaʿat*, 7505, 29 April 1951.
29. Ibid.
30. Ibid.

31. Ibid.
32. *Emruz*, 860, 13 July 1952.
33. *Emruz*, 1110, 27 May 1953.
34. Habib Ladjevardi, *Labor Unions and Autocracy in Iran*, 189–90.
35. Ibid.
36. *Pravda*, 288, 15 October 1951.
37. *Pravda*, 295, 22 October 1951.
38. Author's Interview with 'Esmat Yazdanpanah-Da'i, Vienna, 11 May 2016.
39. *Bakhtar-e Emruz*, 805, 5 May 1952.
40. *Bakhtar-e Emruz*, 803, 3 May 1952.
41. *Emruz*, 803, 27 May 1953.
42. Ibid.
43. Ibid.
44. The girl who had graced the stage at Toupkhaneh Square was Farideh, an Abadani girl and then member of the Youth Organisation of the Tudeh Party recounted being subjected to military administration surveillance upon her return to Abadan, which ultimately compelled her to depart from the city. Author's interview with G. Farideh, Washington (online). 14 April 2020.
45. Interview with Rahmat Jazani, Paris, 14 June 2015.
46. *Bakhtar-e Emruz*, 866, 28 July 1952.
47. Ibid.
48. *Bakhtar-e Emruz*, 874, 30 July 1952.
49. *Navid Azadi*, 159, 13 August 1953.
50. Ibid.
51. Rohan Butler, *British Policy in the Relinquishment of Abadan*, 82–97.
52. NARA, RG 59, General Records of the Department of State, 1950–1954 Central Decimal File, File: 788.00/11-2652. https://nsarchive.gwu.edu/briefing-book/iran/2017-08-08/1953-iran-coup-new-us-documents-confirm-british-approached-us-late (Accessed December 1918).
53. Butler, *British Policy*, 79–106.
54. For recent publication on coup d'état 1953 in Iran See: Ali Rahnema, *Behind the 1953 Coup in Iran: Thugs, Turncoats, Soldiers, and Spooks*; Ervand Abrahamian, *The Coup: 1953, the CIA, and the Roots of Modern U.S.-Iranian Relations;* Darioush Bayandor, *Iran and the CIA: The Fall of Mosaddeq Revisited* (Palgrave Macmillan, 2010); Christopher de Bellaigue, *Patriot of Persia: Muhammad Mossadegh and a Tragic Anglo-American Coup* (New York: Harper Perennial, 2013); Stephen Kinzer, *All the Shah's Men: An American Coup and the Roots of Middle East Terror* (John Wiley & Sons, 2008); Mark Gasiorowski and Malcolm Byrne (eds.), *Mohammad Mosaddeq and the 1953 Coup in Iran* (Syracuse: Syracuse University Press, 2004).
55. Najaf Daryabandari, *Salha-ye Javani van Siyasat. Khaterat-e Najaf Daryabandari az Abadan dar Goftogou ba Hossein Mirza'i*, 113–15.
56. Hezb-e Zahmatkeshan Mellat-e Iran (Toilers Party of Iranian Nation) was founded by Mozaffar Bagha'i and Khalil Maleki in 1951 and affiliated to Mosaddeq's National Front policy of nationalisation of the oil. In 1952 the party split, and while Khalil Maleki continued supporting Mosaddeq and left the party, Bagha'i formed an alliance with Ayatollah Kashani's *Society of Mujahed Muslims* and opposed Mosaddeq and later actively participated in the 1953 coup d'état.

57. Daryabandari, *Sal-ha-ye Javani va Siyast*, 113–14. ʿEsmat Yazdanpanah in her interview with the author confirms the Najaf Daryabandari's account. Interview with ʿEsmat Yazdanpanah-Daʾi.
58. Rasul Jafarian, *Jariyan-ha va Sazeman-ha-ye Mazhabi-Siyasi Iran* (1320–1357) [Religio-Political Currents and Organisations in Iran – 1941–1979] (Tehran: Mo'alef, 2006), 173.
59. Najaf Daryabandari was arrested for the second time and faced legal proceedings following his dismissal from the Oil Company. Initially, he was handed a death sentence, which was subsequently changed to life imprisonment and later to four years.
60. Daryabandari, *Sal-ha-ye Javani va Siyast*, 114. For the Military Organisation of the Tudeh Party (1944–1954) see Mohammad-Hossein Khosrowpanah, *Sazeman-e Afsaran-e Hezb-e Tudeh-e Iran* [The Organisation of Military Officers of the Tudeh Party of Iran] (Tehran: Shirazeh, 1998).

7 From Disparity to Planned Development: 1954–1962

1. Jalil Bozorgmehr, *Mosaddeq dar Mahkameh-ye Nezami* [Mosaddeq in the Military Tribunal] (Paris: Nehzat-e Moqavemat-e Melli-ye Iran, n.d.), 778–79.
2. Mostaf Elm, *Oil, Power, and Principle. Iran Oil Nationalisation and Its Aftermath*, 311–14.
3. Parviz Mina, 'Oil Agreements In Iran', *Encyclopaedia Iranica*, Published: 20 July 2004.
4. The author's interview with Alinaghi Alikhani, Washington, 21 November 2016; Gholam-Reza Afkhami (ed.), *Siyasat va Siyasatgozari-ye Eqtesadi dar Iran 1340–1350: Mosahebeh ba Alinaghi Alikhani* [Politics and Economic Planning in Iran, 1961–1971: An Interview with Alinaghi Alikhani] (Washington: Foundation for Iranian Studies, 2001), 14.
5. 'U.S. Embassy in Tehran, First Secretary Annual Labour Report 1959, U.S. National Archives, 888.06/6-460', 'Annual Labour Report 1959', in *The Condition of the Working Class in Iran*, 156.
6. U.S. Embassy in Tehran, First Secretary Annual Labour Report 1959, U.S. National Archives, 888.06/6-460. 'Annual Labour Report 1959', in Cosroe Chaqueri (ed.), *The Condition of the Working Class in Iran, Volume 4* (Florence: Mazdak, 1976), 154.
7. Ibid.
8. U.S. Government Records, report about labour, 1960, 4 July 1963, in Habib Ladjevardi, *Labor Unions and Autocracy in Iran*, 205.
9. 'Notes for Information of ICFTU Mission to Iran', in Cosroe Chaqueri (ed.), *The Condition of the Working Class in Iran*, 154, 117.
10. *Bamshad*, 40, 10 June 1957.
11. Ibid.
12. Abbas Amanat, *Iran. A Modern History* (New Haven: Yale University Press, 2017), 584.
13. *Atash*, 1546, 31 December 1955.
14. Ibid.
15. *Khwandaniha*, 58, 13 April 1955.
16. *Atash*, 1489, 24 October 1955. The author's interview with Alinaghi Alikhani, Washington, 21 November 2016.

17. The author's interview with Alikhani.
18. Afkhami (ed.), *Siyasat va Siyasatgozari Eqtesadi dar Iran 1340–1350*, 15; Alinaghi Alikhani, *Eqtesad va Amniyat: Khaterat-e Doktor Alinaghi Alikhani* [Economy and Security: The Memoirs of Dr Alinaghi Alikhani], Hossein Dehbashi (ed.) (Tehran: Sazeman-e Asnad va Ketabkhaneh-ye Melli-ye Iran, 2014), 93. The author's interview with Alikhani, Washington, 21 November 2016.
19. *Khwandaniha*, 72, 31 May 1955.
20. *Khwandaniha*, 98, 30 August 1955.
21. *Kushesh*, 8940, 30 March 1955.
22. British National Archives, British Embassy Tehran, July 1955, FO 371/114871. See also *Atash*, 1603, 7 March 1956.
23. Iran Ministry of Petroleum Documentation Centre, 46005/11, 27 March 1955. D. L. Hussey, General Refinery Manager.
24. Ibid.
25. Ibid.
26. *Khwandaniha*, 98, 30 August 1955.
27. 'U.S. Embassy in Tehran, First Secretary Annual Labour Report 1959', U.S. National Archives, 888.06/6-460, 'Annual Labour Report 1959', in Cosroe Chaqueri (ed.), *The Condition of the Working Class in Iran*, 155.
28. Gholam-Reza Afkhami (ed.), *San'at Petroshimi-ye Iran Az Aghaz ta Astaneh-ye Enqelab, Mosahebeh ba Baqer Mostowfi* [The Evolution of Iran's Petrochemical Industry from the Beginning to the Eve of the Revolution: An Interview with Baqer Mostowfi] (Washington: Foundation for Iranian Studies, 2001), 152.
29. BP Archive, ArcRef: 195723.
30. 'U.S. Embassy in Tehran, First Secretary Annual Labour Report 1961', U.S. National Archives, 888.06/6-460, 'Annual Labour Report 1959', in Cosroe Chaqueri (ed.), *The Condition of the Working Class in Iran*, 171.
31. British National Archives, British Embassy Tehran, July 1955, F.O. 371/114871.
32. 'U.S. Embassy in Tehran, First Secretary Annual Labour Report 1959', U.S. National Archives, 888.06/6-460, 'Annual Labour Report 1959', in Cosroe Chaqueri (ed.), *The Condition of the Working Class in Iran*, 153–56.
33. 'U.S. Embassy in Tehran, First Secretary Annual Labour Report 1959', U.S. National Archives, 888.06/6-460, 'Annual Labour Report 1959', in Cosroe Chaqueri (ed.), *The Condition of the Working Class in Iran*, 171.
34. *Tehran Mosavvar*, 682, 28 September 1956.
35. Ibid.
36. The author's interviews with Manouchehr Mohandes, Brighton, 22 January 2015 and Alikhani, Washington, 21 November 2016.
37. Afkhami (ed.), *Siyasat va Siyasatgozari Eqtesadi dar Iran 1340–1350*, 15–16.
38. 'U.S. Embassy in Iran: Labour Affairs in Iran. September-January 1957', U.S. National Archives, 888.06/1-3157, in Cosroe Chaqueri (ed.), *The Condition of the Working Class in Iran*, 117.
39. British National Archive, British Embassy Tehran, July 1955, FO 371/114871. 'U.S. Embassy in Tehran, First Secretary Annual Labour Report 1961', U.S, National Archives, 888.06/6-460. 'Annual Labour Report 1959', in Cosroe Chaqueri (ed.), *The Condition of the Working Class in Iran*, 171.
40. 'Quarterly Economic Summary: Labour', U.S. National Archives, 888-06/101957, in Cosroe Chaqueri (ed.), *The Condition of the Working Class in Iran*, 131.
41. *Mosavvar*, 682.

42. 'Labour Unrest in Iran, May 1958', U.S. National Archives, 888.06/5-858, in Cosroe Chaqueri (ed.), *The Condition of the Working Class in Iran*, 137.
43. British National Archives, F.O. Lab., 13/1092, in Cosroe Chaqueri (ed.), *The Condition of the Working Class in Iran*, 143–44.
44. Firuz Towfiq, 'Barnameh-ye Avval: Fekr-e Barnamehrizi dar Iran' [First Plan: The Idea of Planning in Iran], in Hoda Saber (ed.), *Panjah Sal Barnamehrizi* [Fifty Years Planning] (Tehran, Parseh, 2018), 87–97.
45. *Ashofteh*, 19, 19 May 1955. Abolhassan Ebtehaj, *Khatera-e Abolassan Ebtehaj*, 361.
46. On 18 May 1933, the United States President Franklin Roosevelt signed the Tennessee Valley Authority Act, creating the TVA as a federal corporation. The mission of TVA was setup as to oversee the construction of dams to control flooding, improve navigation, and create cheap electric power in the Tennessee Valley basin. See www.archives.gov/milestone-documents/tennessee-valley-authority-act (Accessed December 2018).
47. Ebtehaj, *Khatera-e Abolhassan Ebtehaj*, 366.
48. Abdolreza Ansari, Hassan Shahmirzadi, Ahmad-Ali Ahmadi, *Omran-e Khuzestan* [Khuzestan Development], Electronic Book, Afkhami, Gholam-Reza (ed.) (Washington: Foundation for Iranian Studies, 1994).
49. Ibid.
50. Ibid.
51. Khodadad Farmanfarmaian, *Barnameh-e Dovvom* [Second Plan], *Panjah Sal Barnamehrizi*, Hoda Saber (ed.), *Panjah Sal Barnamehrizi* [Fifty Years Planning] (Tehran, Parseh, 2018), 87–97.
52. Farmanfarmaian, *Barnameh-e Dovvom*, 91.
53. Ebtehaj, *Khatera-e Abolhassan Ebtehaj*, 445.

8 Oil, Workforce, and the Developmental State: 1960s–1970s

1. For a historical review of the formation and practices of the developmental states see David Ludden, 'Development Regimes in South Asia: History and the Governance Conundrum', *Economic and Political Weekly*, 40 (2005): 4042–51.
2. Frederick Cooper, *Decolonisation and African Society: The Labor Question in French and British Africa* (Cambridge: Cambridge University Press, 1996).
3. Daniel Lerner, *The Passing of Traditional Society: Modernizing the Middle East* (London: Macmillan, 1958).
4. Walt Whitman Rostow, *The Stages of Economic Growth: A Non-Communist Manifesto* (Cambridge: Cambridge University Press, 1960).
5. Raúl Prebisch, *The Economic Development of Latin America and Its Principal Problems* (New York: United Nations, 1950).
6. Fernando Henrique Cardoso and Faletto Enzo, *Dependency and Development in Latin America* (New York: University of California Press, 1979); Samir Amin, *Accumulation on a World Scale: A Critique of the Theory of Underdevelopment* (New York: Monthly Review Press, 1974); Andre Gunder Frank, *Dependent Accumulation* (New York: Monthly Review Press, 1979); Emmanuel Arghiri, *La Dynamique des inégalités* (Paris: Economica, 1999); Giorgio Secondi, *The Development Economics Reader* (London: Routledge, 2008).
7. Hossein Mahdavi, 'The Patterns and Problems of Economic Development in Rentier States: The Case of Iran', in M. A. Cook (ed.), *Studies in the Economic History of the Middle East* (Oxford: Oxford University Press, 1970), 428–67.

8. For a more study and argument on 'rentier state' see Giacomo Luciani, 'Allocation vs. Production States: A Theoretical Framework', in H. Beblawi and G. Luciani (ed.), *The Rentier-state* (London: Croom Helm, 1987), 63–82; L. M. Ross, 'Does oil hinder democracy?', *World Politics*, 3 (2001): 325–61.
9. Gregory Brew, *Petroleum and Progress in Iran. Oil, Development, and the Cold War* (London: Cambridge University Press, 2022), 159; Ramin Nassehi, 'Domesticating Cold War Economic Ideas: The Rise of Iranian Developmentalism in the 1950s and 1960s', in Roham Alvandi (ed.), *The Age of Aryamehr* (London: Gingko Library, 2018), 35–69.
10. *Gozaresh-e ʿAmalkard-e Barnameh-e 'Omrani-ye Sevvom 1341–1346* [Report of the Results of the Third Development Plan 1962–1967] (Tehran: Organisation of Planning, 1968).
11. Ibid.
12. In order to refashion its relationship with the Soviet Union, in July 1962, the Iranian government announced that Iran never let nay country to install any military base for long range missiles. A stand, welcomed by the Soviet Union and opened a new chapter in diplomatic relation between two countries.
13. Ehsan Tabari, 'Rah-e Eqtesadi-ye Ma az Kodam Sust?' [What is the Road Map of our Economic Development?], *Donya*, 1–2 (1963): 3–8; Gh. Saqaʾi, 'Rah-e Roshd-e Gheyr-e Sarmayehdari va Dowlat-e Demokrasi-ye Melli' [Non-Capitalist Road to Socialism and National-Democratic State], *Donya*, 4 (1963): 72–83; N. Ghaziyani, 'Az do Rah-e Takamol-e Eqtesadi, Kodamyek ra Bayad Bargozid?' [Of Two Paths of Economic Development, Which One Should be Adopted?], *Donya*, 3 (1964): 71–85; Nuralddin Kiyanuri, 'Nazari Ejmali beh Tahavvollat-e Siyasi va Eqtesadi-ye Iran' [A Reflection on Political and Economic Development in Iran], *Donya*, 4 (1964): 37–80.
14. For a comprehensive examination of the challenges and stances adopted by political armed groups in response to the economic policies implemented by the state during the 1960s, see Touraj Atabaki, 'The Perplexity of the Iranian Marxist Intellectuals in the 1960s', in Ramin Jahanbegloo (ed.), *Mapping the Role of Intellectuals in Modern and Contemporary History* (London: Lexington Books, 2021), 175–89.
15. For the history of development planning in Iran see Manuchehr Gudarzi, Khodadad Farmanfarmaian and Abdolmajid Majidi, *Barnamehrizi-ye 'Omrani va Tasmimgiri-ye Siyasi* [Development Planning and Political Decision Making] (Washington: Foundation for Iranian Studies, 1999).
16. Along with the mega-national planning, the Second Development Plan introduced the regional development schemes, by implementing new hydroelectric and irrigation projects in the north-west, south-west and south-east Iran. See the memoire of Abolhassan Ebtehaj: *Khaterat-e Abolhassan Ebtehaj*, 353–452.
17. Gudarzi, Farmanfarmaian and Majidi, 219–20.
18. Fereidoun Fesharaki, *Development of the Iranian Oil Industry. International and Domestic Aspects* (New York: Praeger Publishers, 1976), 97.
19. The author's interviews with Manouchehr Mohandes, Brighton, 22 January 2015 and Alinaghi Alikhani, Washington, 21 November 2016. According to Ervand Abrahamian, 'The number of major strikes, which had totalled no more than three in 1955–1957, jumped to over twenty in 1957–1961'. Ervand Abrahamian, *Iran between Two Revolutions*, 422.
20. *Gozaresh-e ʿAmalkard-e Barnameh-ye ʿOmrani-ye Sevvom 1341–1346* (Report of the Results of the Third Development Plan 1962–1967) (Tehran: Plan Organisation, 1968).

21. Jahangir Amuzegar, *Dynamics of the Iranian Revolution: The Pahlavis' Triumph and Tragedy* (New York: State University of New York Press, 1991), 414.
22. *Gozaresh-e 'Amalkard-e Barnameh-ye 'Omrani-ye Sevvom 1341–1346.*
23. Fereidun Fesharaki, 130.
24. The author's interview with Alinaghi Alikhani, Washington, 21 November 2016.
25. Ibid.
26. Farhad Daftari, 'Development Planning in Iran: A Historical Survey', *Iranian Studies*, 4 (Autumn 1973): 205–28.
27. Farhad Kazemi, *Poverty and Revolution in Iran: The Migrant Poor, Urban Marginality and Politics* (New York: New York University Press, 1850), 52.
28. Farhad Daftari, 'BARNĀMA-RĪZĪ', *Encyclopaedia Iranica*, December 1988.
29. National Iranian Oil Company (NIOC), *Newsletter*, 60, 1963.
30. National Iranian Oil Company, *Newsletter*, 60, July 1963.
31. Ibid.
32. Contrary to most of the oil-producing countries, prior to the revolution of 1978–79, Iran never had a ministry of oil. The Ministry of Petroleum of Islamic Republic of Iran (*Vezarat-e Naft*) was established in September 1979.
33. The author's interview with Parviz Mina, Paris, 24 March 2017.
34. Ibid.
35. The author's interview with Alinaghi Alikhani, Washington, 21 November 2016.
36. Golam-Reza Tadjbakhsh and Farrokh Najmabadi (eds.), *Yad-dasht-ha-ye Fuad Rohani. Nakhostin Dabir Koll-e Sazeman-e Keshvar-ha-ye Sader Konandeh Naft (OPEC)* [Diaries of Fuad Rohani: First Secretary General of the Oil Producing Countries (OPEC)] (Bethesda, MD: Foundation for Iranian Studies: 2012), 35–37.
37. Ian Skeet, *OPEC. Twenty-Five Years of Price and Politics* (Cambridge: Cambridge University Press, 1988), 35–57.
38. Skeet, *OPEC*, 43.
39. Fuad Rohani, *Tarikh-e Opek* (A History of OPEC) (Tehran: Sherkat-e Sahami-ye Ketab-ha-ye Jibi, 1974), 216–22.
40. *OPEC Annual Statistical Bulletin 1968* (Vienna: OPEC, 1969).
41. Rohani, *Yaddasht-ha-ye Fuad Rohani*, 171.
42. The author's interview with Alinaghi Alikhani, Washington, 21 November 2016 and Parviz Mina, Paris, 24 March 2017.
43. Manuchehr Farmanfarmaian, *Az Tehran ta Karkas: Naft va Siyasat dar Iran* [From Tehran to Caracas: Oil and Politics in Iran] (Tehran: Nashr-e Tarikh-e Iran, 1999), 632.
44. Rohani, *Yaddasht-ha-ye Fuad Rohani*, 318.
45. Ibid.
46. The author interview with Parviz Mina. Paris, 24 March 2017.
47. Alinaghi Alikhani (ed.), *Yaddasht-ha-ye Alam [Diaries of Alam], Volume 1* (Washington: Ibex Publisher, 1992), 164–65.
48. Alikhani (ed.), *Yaddasht-ha-ye Alam*, 83–84, 279. Overall, Alam's diary entry provides valuable insights into the high stakes involved in Iran's reliance on Oil revenue to sustain its ambitious development plans and underscores the intensity of negotiations with the Consortium to meet the country's economic needs.
49. David Missen, *Iran: Oil at the Service of the Nation* (London: Transorient, 1969), 6. I would like to extend my sincere appreciation to Pourya Motaghedi for his invaluable support in creating this diagram.
50. Missen, *Iran*, 12–13.

51. *Middle East Economic Survey*, 8 March, 1968.
52. Fesharaki, *Development of the Iranian Oil Industry. International and Domestic Aspects*, 105.
53. *Osul va Hadaf-ha-ye Barnameh-ye ʿOmrani-ye Chaharom-e Keshvar* [The Essence and Targets of the Fourth Development Plan] (Tehran: Majles-e Showra-ye Melli, 1968), 3.
54. Hassan Hakimian, 'Industrialisation and the Standard of Living of the Working Class in Iran, 1960–79' *Development and Change*, 19 (1988): 3–32.
55. Ibid. 11.
56. Ibid. 13.
57. Interview with Willie Akhbari (Nijman), Barendrecht, 25 February 2015.
58. Interview with Masoud Akhbari, Barendrecht, 25 February 2015.

9 Shop Floor Labour Activism: From the White to the Islamic Revolution

1. Fred Halliday, *Iran: Dictatorship and Development* (New York: Penguin 1978), 202.
2. Maral Jefroudi, 'Revisiting 'the Long Night' of Iranian Workers: Labor Activism in the Iranian Oil Industry in the 1960s', in Touraj Atabaki (ed.), 'Social History of Iranian Oil Workers', *International Labor and Working-Class History*, 84 (Fall 2013), 177.
3. U.S. Washington National Records Center, U.S. National Archives, Records of Foreign Service Posts of the Department of State, Airgram to Department of State, Labor in Iran, 1st July 1970.
4. Jefroudi, 'Revisiting 'The Long Night' of Iranian Workers', 189.
5. Bizhan Jazani, *Masaʾel-e Jonbesh-e zedd-e Esteʿmari va Azadibaksh-e Khalq-e Iran va ʿOmdeh-tarin Vazayef-e Komunist-ha-ye Iran* [The Problem of Anti-Colonial and Libation Movement of the People of Iran and the Main Tasks of the Iranian Communists] (Reprinted in Paris: Sazeman-e Ettehad-e Fadaiyan-e Khalq-e Iran, 2003).
6. Ibid. 4–9.
7. Masʿud Ahmadzadeh, *Mobarezeh Mosalahaneh, ham Esteratezhi, ham Taktik* [Armed Struggle, Both Strategy and Tactic] (Tehran: Sazeman-e Cherik-ha-ye Fadʾi Khalq Iran, 1971), 2–4.
8. Siavush Randjbar-Daemi, 'The Tudeh Party of Iran and the Land Reform Initiatives of the Pahlavi State, 1958–1964', *Middle Eastern Studies*, 4 (2022): 625.
9. Yadollah Khosrowshahi, *Bakhshi az Tarikh-e Jonbesh-e Kargaran Sanʿat Naft-e Iran [A Part of History of Workers Movement in the Oil Industry of Iran], Volume 1* (London: Houshang Ansari, 2019), 34.
10. Albert A. Blum (ed.), *International Industrial Relations. Contemporary Developments and Research* (London: Aldwych Press, 1981), 266–67.
11. Ibid. 268–69.
12. Khosrowshahi, *Bakhshi az Tarikh-e Jonbesh-e Kargaran Sanʿat Naft Iran*, 38–73. See also Blum (ed.), *International Industrial Relations*, 269.
13. Afshin Matin-Asgari, 'Marxism, Historiography and Historical Consciousness in Modern Iran: A Preliminary Study', in Touraj Atabaki (ed.), *Twentieth Century Iran: Historiography and Political Culture* (London: IB Tauris, 2009), 220.
14. Ibid. 219.

15. Habib Ladjevardi, *Labor Unions and Autocracy in Iran*, 240.
16. Khosrowshahi, *Bakhshi az Tarikh-e Jonbesh-e Kargaran Sanʿat Naft Iran*, 52.
17. Mohammad Safavi, 'Rag-ha-ye Zamin, Rag-ha-ye Ma: Sad Sal Mobarezeh-ye Kargaran-e Naft Baraye 'Edalat-e Ejtemaʿi-Eqtesadi' [Earth's Veins, our Veins: One Hundred Years of Oil Workers Fighting for Socio-Economic Justice], *Naqd-e Eqtesda-e Siyasi*, 4 January 2021.
18. U.S. Washington National Records Center, U.S. Archive, Records of Foreign Service Posts of the Department of State, Airgram to Department of State, Labor in Iran, 11 September 1975.
19. Khosrowshahi, *Bakhshi az Tarikh-e Jonbesh-e Kargaran Sanʿat Naft Iran*, 53.
20. Ibid. 52–54, 75–81.
21. The roots of the Islamic Revolution in Iran has been the subject of numerus study. Hossein Bashiriyeh's study is one the most significant contribution. Hossein Bashiriyeh, *The State and Revolution in Iran, 1962–1982* (London: Palgrave Macmillan, 1984).
22. U.S. Washington National Records Center, U.S. Archives, Records of Foreign Service Posts of the Department of State, Airgram to Department of State, Labor in Iran, 11 September 1975. *Sal-nameh Amari* [Calendar Statistic] (Tehran: Markaz-e Amar-e Iran, diverse years) cited in Farshid Yazdani, 'Hadeaql Dastmozd dar Iran' [Minimum Wage in Iran], *Goftogou*, 55 (March 2010): 155–69.
23. *Amar-Nameh-ye Ostan-e Khuzestan* [Statistical Records of the Khuzestan Province], Nos. 738 and 785 (Tehran: Sazman-e Barnameh va Budjeh, Markaz-e Amar-e Iran, 1977, 1979).
24. James C. Davis, 'Towards a Theory of Revolution', *American Sociological Review*, 27 (February 1962): 1–19; Hossein Bashiriyeh, *The State and Revolution in Iran, 1962–1982.*
25. Eric Hobsbawm, *The Age of Extremes* (New York: Pantheon Books, 1994), 453.
26. Timothy Mitchell, *Carbon Democracy: Political Power in the Age of Oil* (London: Verso, 2011).
27. Blum (ed.), *International Industrial Relations*, 267–68.
28. Ahmad Ashraf and Ali Banuazizi, 'The State, Class and Mode of Mobilisation in the Iranian Revolution', *State, Culture and Society*, 6 (Spring 1985): 3–40.
29. Ibid. 33–40.
30. Ibid.
31. See for example, Terisa Turner, 'Iranian Oil Workers in 1978–79 Revolution', in Petter Nore and Terisa Turner (eds.), *Oil and Class Struggle* (London: Zed Book, 1980). 272–292. Asef Bayat, *Workers and Revolution in Iran: A Third World Experience of Workers' Control* (London: Zed Book, 1987). Peyman Jafari's study on oil workers' strike in 1978 is the most meticulous and comprehensive analysis of the oil industry's role in the Iranian Revolution of 1978–1979: Peyman Jafari, *Fluid History: Oil Workers and the Iranian Revolution*, University of Amsterdam (Digital Academic Repository). DOI 10.1007/978-3-319-56445-6_4, 2018.
32. Karim Nikunazar, *Sinama Jahanam* [Hell Cinema] (Tehran: Cheshmeh, 2019), 173. For life and activities of Ayatollah Khademi see Markaz-e Barresi-ye Asnad-e Tarikh, *Yaran-e Emam be Revayat-e Asnad-e Savak* [Imam Associates According to Savak Documents] (Tehran: Markaz-e Barresi-ye Asnad-e Tarikh, 2001).
33. *Ayandegan*, 3196, 19 August 1978, 3198, 21 August 1978, 3199, 22 August 1978.
34. Karim Nikunazar, *Sinama Jahanam*, 127–28.
35. Photograph Cinema Rex, courtesy of Manoochehr Deghati.

36. Terisa Turner, 'Iranian Oil Workers in 1978–1979 Revolution', 273. Unfortunately, her article has many of these inaccuracies.
37. Karim Nikunazar, *Sinama Jahanam*, 19–20.
38. Masʿud Foruzandeh, *Tarikh-e Sanʿat Naft-e Iran 1280–1357* [History of the Iranian Oil Industry 1901–1978] (Tehran: Vezarat-e Naft, 2009), 563.
39. Mohammad-Reza ʿElm, *Enqelab-e Eslami dar Ahvaz* [Islamic Revolution in Ahvaz] (Tehran: Markaz-e Asnad-e Enqelab-e Eslami, 2007), 163–64.
40. Interview with Mohmad Safavi, 15 August 2023.
41. Ibid.
42. For details of the assignations see Mohammad-Reza ʿElm, *Enqelab-e Eslami dar Ahvaz*, 679–80, 714–16.
43. To delve into the origins and founders of the Movahhedin and Mansouroun groups, whose leaders subsequently ascended to prominent positions within the Islamic Revolutionary Guard Corps, one should consult the following sources: Mohammad-Reza ʿElm, *Enqelab-e Eslami dar Ahvaz*, 651–729; Rasul Jafarian, *Jariyan-ha va Sazeman-ha-ye Mazhabi-Siyasi-ye Iran* (1320–1357), 520.
44. Rasul Jafarian, *Jariyan-ha va Sazeman-ha-ye Mazhabi-Siyasi-ye Iran* (1320–1357), 376–456.
45. Karim Nikunazar, *Sinama Jahanam*, 167–176. Interview with Mehrzad Boroujerdi, 19 August 2023.
46. For the impact of Cinema Rex see Yadollah Khosrowshahi interview with Mohammad Fattahi, *Tarikh-e Shafahi-ye Showra-ye Kargaran-e Naft* [Oral History of the Oil Workers' Council], Archive of Iranian Opposition Documents, 2013, 30–31.
47. Mohammad-Reza ʿElm, *Enqelab-e Eslami dar Ahvaz*, 683–88.
48. Ibid. 626–27.
49. Ibid. 716.
50. For an exemplary illustration of the Islamic Republic of Iran's practice of historical revisionism, one can refer to Saeed Ta'eb, *Az Eʿtesab-e Karkonan-e Sanʿat-e Naft ta Piruzi-ye Enqelab-e Eslami* [From the Oil Industry Employees' Strike to the Victory of the Islamic Revolution] (Tehran: Islamic Revolution Document Centre, 2003). Ta'eb's book provides a clear instance of how historical events are reinterpreted within the framework of the state's ideological agenda. This text serves as a notable case study in understanding the methods and implications of the state-sponsored revision of history, particularly in the context of the 1978–1979 Iranian Revolution and the pivotal role of the oil industry employees.
51. The written sources will be detailed as the study progresses. The individuals mentioned have played a crucial role in providing diverse accounts that deviate from the official historiography of the Islamic Republic. Their contributions have significantly enhanced the study's comprehension of the atmosphere during those revolutionary days.
52. Terisa Turner, 'Iranian Oil Workers in 1978–79 Revolution', 282.
53. Khosrowshahi, *Bakhshi az Tarikh-e Jonbesh-e Kargaran Sanʿat Naft Iran*, 99.
54. *Ettelaʿat*, 15612, 17 May 1978.
55. Mohammad Safavi, 'Baz-khani-ye Mobarezat-e Gozashteh-ye Kargaran-e Prozheh'-Fasli' [Revisiting the Historical Struggles of Seasonal and Contract Workers], *Naqd-e Eqtesad-e Siyasi*, 2 October 2021.
56. *Ettelaʿat*, 15737, 19 October 1978.

57. *Ettela'at*, 15739, 21 October 1978. Ahmad Ashraf, 'Kalbodshekafi-ye Eqelab: Naqsh-e Kargaran-e San'ati dar Enqelab-e Iran' [Autopsy of the Revolution: The Role of Industrial Workers in the Iranian Revolution], *Iran-Nameh*, 3–4 (2011): 4–53.
58. *Ettela'at*, 15740, 22 October 1978.
59. Ahmad Ashraf, 'Kalbodshekafi Eqelab: Naqsh-e Kargaran-e San'ati dar Enqelab-e Iran', 4–53.
60. *Ettela'at*, 15740, 22 October 1978.
61. Interview with Mohmad Safavi, 15 August 2023 and Mehrzad Boroujerdi.
62. Interview with Yadollah Khosrowshahi, London, 14 June 2009. Safavi, 'Rag-ha-ye Zamin, Rag-ha-ye Ma', *Ettela'at* 15751, 1 November 1978.
63. *Ettela'at*, 15754, 4 November 1978.
64. Khosrowshahi, *Bakhshi az Tarikh-e Jonbesh-e Kargaran San'at Naft Iran*, 110–11.
65. Imam Khomeini, Rouhollah, *Sahifeh-ye Imam [Imam's Folder], Volume 4* (Tehran: Mo'asseseh-ye Tanzim va Nashr-e Asar-e Imam Khomeini, 1989), 498.
66. Imam Khomeini, Rouhollah, *Sahifeh Imam*, 251.
67. Mohammad Mazra'ehkar, *Khaterat* [Memoire] (n.p., Markaz-e Farhang va Ketab-e Gutenberg, n.d.). http://andishegbg.blogspot.com/2020/02/blog-post_16.html; Mohammad-Reza 'Elm, *Enqelab-e Eslami dar Ahvaz*, 210.
68. Mohammad-Reza 'Elm, *Enqelab-e Eslami dar Ahvaz*, 211.

Epilogue

1. The poem attributed to Mostafa Sarkhosh, one of the nationalist activists and a supporter of Mosaddeq. Credits to the translation by my friend, Saeed Yousef.

دوشینه به چشم خویش، در خانه خویش،
آبی دیدم، به سان آتش می‌سوخت.
گفتم که که‌ای و از کجا آمده ای؟
ای آب که می‌توانی آتش افروخت.
با چند زبان زبانه آتش گفت،
رازی که مرا زبان پندار بدوخت.
من نفتم و چون نسوزم از غیرت خویش؟
جایی که مرا خودی به بیگانه فروخت.

BIBLIOGRAPHY

Archives

British National Archive, London
British Petroleum (BP) Archive, University of Warwick, in the notes: BP Archive
Indian National Archive, Delhi, Mumbai
Iran Ministry of Foreign Affairs, Archive of Documents and Diplomatic History, Tehran
Iran National Archive, Tehran
Foreign Ministry Records.
Interior Ministry Records.
Ministry of Treasury Records.
Ministry of Finance Records
Iran National Parliament Archives, Tehran
Iran President Office Archives, Tehran
Russian State Archive of Social-Political History (RGASPI), Moscow
United State National Archive, Washington

Online Collection

- Touraj Atabaki, Willem Floor and Nazanin Sadeghi. *Global Collaboratory on the History of Labour Relations, 1500–2000*, https://iisg.amsterdam/en/research/projects/global-collaboratory-on-the-history-of-labour-relations-1500-2000
- *Iranian Oral History Project*, Harvard University. 6 March 1984. https://nrs.harvard.edu/urn-3:FHCL:1091327
- Laurence Lockhart, *Encyclopaedia Iranica*, https://iranicaonline.org/articles/lockhart-laurence
- Geoffrey Keating see: https://rimakeating.co.uk/Geoffrey.J.Keating%2CMC%2CPHOTO%20ARCHIVE
- NARA, RG 59, General Records of the Department of State, 1950–54 Central Decimal File, File: 788.00/11-2652. https://nsarchive.gwu.edu/briefing-book/iran/2017-08-08/1953-iran-coup-new-us-documents-confirm-british-approached-us-late (Accessed December 1918).
- Tennessee Valley Authority Act, www.archives.gov/milestone-documents/tennessee-valley-authority-act

Periodicals

Anglo Persian Oil Company Magazine
Ashofteh
Asiya-ye Javan
Atash
Ayandegan
Bakhtar-e Emruz
Bamshad
Bazarian
Mumbai Chronicle
Donya
Ettela'at (Monthly)
Ettela'at-e Haftegi
Ettela'at
Faslnameh-ye Ravabet-e Khareji
Habl al-Matin
Haqiqat
Illustrated Weekly of India
International Journal of Middle East Studies
Iran-e Now
Kaveh
Keyhan
Khwandaniha
Kushesh
MERIP Reports
Middle East Economic Survey
Naft
Nameh-ye Mardom
Navid-e Azadi
Nazm-e Novin
Newsletter (National Iranian Oil Company)
Niru-ye Sevvom
OPEC Annual Statistical Bulletin
Pravda
Shafaq-e Sorkh
Shahed-e Iran
Sur-e Esrafil
Tarraqi,
Tehran Mosavvar
Times
Zafar

Interviews

Akhbari, Masoud (1931–).
He was born in Masjed-Soleyman in 1949. He joined the Anglo-Persian Oil Company assuming the function of a cartographic draughtsman within the Geological and Palaeontology Division. The subsequent nationalisation of the Iranian oil industry in 1951 led to Masoud's transition to the National Iranian Oil Company. His career trajectory took a notable turn in 1954 when, upon the establishment of the Oil Consortium, Masoud was appointed as the Head of Drafting and Reproduction Services. In 1969; following the Consortium's strategy of outsourcing, he established his own business entity and entered into a contractual agreement with the Iranian Oil Exploration and Producing Company, providing drafting and reproduction services. The 1979 Iranian revolution prompted Masoud to depart from Iran.

Interviewed: Barendrecht, February 2015.

Alikhani, Alinaghi (1929–2019).
Graduated from Tehran University in 1949, Alikhani continued his study at the Paris University when he got his PhD in Economics. He joined the National Iranian Oil Company and became the head of the Department of Non-Industrial (Non-Basic) Operations in 1960. Three years later he was appointed as and first Iran's Minister of Economy (1963–1969). Alikhani's next post was the Chancellor of Tehran University to which he was appointed in 1969 and held the post until 1971.

Alinaghi Alikhani died in exile in Washington in 2019.

Interview: Washington, November 2016.

Boroujerdi, Mehrzad (1962–).
Originated from a family associated with the oil industry. His educational journey encompassed studies in Aghajari, Ahvaz, and Gachsaran. In 1978, he ventured to the United States for advanced studies. It was during his tenure there that the news of his father's assassination compelled his immediate return to Iran.

Currently, Boroujerdi holds the position of Vice Provost and Dean of the College of Arts, Sciences, and Education at the Missouri University of Science and Technology.

Interview: Rolla, Missouri (online), August 2023.

Farideh G., adhering to her preference for privacy by omitting her surname.
Born in Abadan, Farideh was an active member of the Tudeh Party Youth Organisation in Abadan during the 1920s to early 1930s.

Interview: Washington (online), 2020.

Golestan, Ebrahim (1922–2023).
Film maker and novelist, Golestan became affiliated with the Tudeh Party in the early 1940s, initiating his contributions as a writer for the party's publications, Mardom and Rahbar, eventually ascending to the position of chief editor for the latter. During his tenure with the Tudeh Party, he notably served as the leader of

the party's Mazandaran Provincial Committee for a period. In 1949, Golestan transitioned to Abadan, where he was employed in the Publishing Department of the Anglo-Iranian Oil Company. It was also in 1949 that he decided to dissociate from the Tudeh Party. By the mid-1950s, he had begun producing documentary films for the Oil Consortium, marking another significant phase in his career. Ebrahim Golestan died in Bolney, West Sussex in 2923.

Interview: Bolney, West Sussex, May 2014.

Jazani, Rahmat (1924–2017).
Born in Kashan, Rahmat Jazani served as the head of the Tudeh Party's Khuzestan Provincial Committee commencing in 1950. During his leadership, he covertly resided in Ahvaz, and for a time, sought refuge in the residence of Hassan Kamshad. In the aftermath of the 1953 coup d'état, Jazani was incarcerated, yet he received a pardon from the Shah during Nowruz in 1956. Rahmat Jazani married with Monireh Mehran (Asfiya), a distinguished translator renowned for her contributions to the Persian translations of literary works. Monireh, a sibling of Safi Asfiya, the director of the Plan Organisation (1962–1968), facilitated Rahmat Jazani joining the Plan Organisation. Additionally, Rahmat Jazani was the paternal uncle of Bijan Jazani, a distinguished advocate for guerrilla warfare in the reign of Mohammad Reza Shah Pahlavi. Rahmat Jazani died in exile in Paris in 2017.

Interview: Paris, June 2015.

Kamshad, Hassan (1925–).
Upon completing his studies at Tehran University, Kamshad was employed by the Anglo-Iranian Oil Company in 1948 and subsequently relocated to Abadan. He resided in Abadan for a year and a half before moving to Ahvaz for a brief period. During his tenure at the Oil Company, Kamshad was tasked with overseeing labour affairs and facilitating communication between the labour department and the company. Later, he was transferred to Masjed-Soleyman, where he assumed the role of an English language instructor for newly recruited Iranian interns and a Persian language educator for newly appointed English nurses. In the same year, Kamshad affiliated himself with the Tudeh Party, initially engaging in activities in Masjed-Soleyman before being dispatched to Ahvaz to lead the party's labour initiatives there. He dissociated from the Tudeh Party in 1954. Following his studies in Britain, which commenced in 1949, Kamshad ascended to the role of chief editor within the public relations department of the Consortium. His concluding position was that of a representative for the National Iranian Oil Company in London.

Interview: London, May 2014.

Keshavarz Sadr, Houshang (1933–2013).
Born into the family of a distinguished individual in Tehran, he was introduced early to a world where prominence and political engagement were part of his heritage. His inclination towards politics was further evidenced by his youthful membership in the Tudeh Party of Iran. His academic journey commenced at Tehran University with an initial focus on philosophy. However, under the mentorship of Gholam-Hossein Sadighi, for whom Houshang harboured a special admiration throughout his life, he pivoted towards the social sciences. In 1943, he found

himself imprisoned for several months. Despite this setback, his academic and research career flourished. He secured a position in the Department of Nomadic and Rural Research at the University of Tehran. In 1981, he left Iran and began his life of exile in Paris. This displacement, however, did not deter his commitment to academic and political endeavours. Through his initiatives, the Foundation of Dr. Sadighi was established at the International Institute of Social History in Amsterdam, aimed at fostering research in social sciences within Iran.

Interview: Paris: January 2009

Khaksar, Nasim (1944–).

Born into a family of oil workers in Abadan, Nasim Khaksar pursued his education at a Teaching Training Institute and subsequently embarked on a career as a teacher in Abadan. Khaksar is a novelist whose literary journey commenced in 1965. His engagement in political activism resulted in periods of incarceration in both Tehran and Abadan prisons. Over the course of his career, thirty-five volumes of his work have been published, encompassing a diverse array of genres including short stories, novels, plays, poems, translations of travelogues, and literary criticism.

Interview: Utrecht, December 2016.

Khaksar, Nasser (1935–2020).

Nasser Khaksar, the brother of Nasim Khaksar, was born in Abadan. Following the completion of his primary education, he entered the workforce, acquiring expertise as a plumber and welder. His career took him to various locales across Iran, especially within the Khuzestan province, including Abadan, Ahvaz, and the cities of Masjed-Soleyman and Aghajari. Leading up to the revolution of 1979, alongside his professional pursuits, he was fervently engaged in the labour union movement. After the conclusion of the Iran-Iraq War (1980–1988), he moved to the Isfahan province, and it was there, in Shaheen Shahr, that he died in 2020.

Interview: Utrecht, July 2010.

Khosrowshahi, Yadollah (1942–2019).

Originating from an oil worker's family in Abadan, Yadollah Khosrowshahi commenced his employment at the Abadan Refinery at the age of sixteen. In 1969, he was reassigned to the Tehran Refinery, and after a period of two years, ascended to the role of the workers' representative within their union, subsequently attaining the position of secretary for the Tehran Refinery Workers Union. In 1974, Khosrowshahi was incarcerated, enduring imprisonment until the advent of the 1979 Revolution. Yadollah Khosrowshahi died in exile in London in 2019.

Interview: London, June 2009.

Mina, Parviz (1927–).

Born in Tehran, Mina pursued and obtained his academic degree in chemical engineering from the University of Birmingham. His professional career spanned three decades within the Iranian oil industry, culminating in his pre-1979 Revolution roles as a Member of the Board of Directors and the Managing Director of International Affairs at the National Iranian Oil Company. Mina held several positions, including Chairman of the Iranian Italian Oil Company, Director of the Iranian Oil Tanker Company, and Chairman of the Iranian Oil Company in Britain. He was also a Member of the OPEC Long Term Strategy Committee and served as the Secretary of the Iranian Petroleum Institute for a decade.

Interview: Paris, March 2017.

Mohandes, Manouchehr (1929–2022).

Joined Anglo-Iranian Oil Company (1948). Following studying Geology at Birmingham University (1950–1954), return to Iran and joined National Iranian Oil Company and later the Consortium Iranian Oil Exploration and Producing Company -Oil Service Company of Iran as Manager Field Operations. Manouchehr Mohandes died in Brighton in 2022.

Interview: Brighton, January 2015.

Nijman-Akhbari, Willie (1943–).

Wille Nijman was born in Rotterdam in 1942. She encountered Masoud Akhabari in 1963 during Masoud tenure at the International Training Centre in the Netherlands. Following this meeting, Willie relocated to Masjed-Soleyman to marry Masoud. She subsequently embarked on a career with the National Iranian Oil Company, initially joining the Department of Method and System, and later assuming the role of Secretary to the General Manager of the Department of Non-Industrial Operations. Willie continued her life in Iran until the revolution of 1979.

Interviewed: Barendrecht, February 2015.

Safavi, Mohmmad (1957–).

Born in Abadan, Mohammad Safavi embarked on a professional journey in 1975 by joining the Petro-Chemical complex as a project worker. He distinguished himself as an active member of the Seasonal and Project Worker Union of Abadan.

Interview: Vancouver (online), August 2023.

Yazdanpanah-Da'i, 'Esmat (1932–).

Member of the Tudeh Party Youth Organisation in Abadan (1946–1954).

Interview: Vienna, May 2016.

Zehtab-Fard, Qader (1935–)

Joined the Iranian Oil Exploration and Producing Company in 1963 as mechanical engineer in Ahvaz. He worked in different location of oil company in Khuzestan. His last position before the 1979 revolution was the Area Manager Field Operations of Aghajari at Oil Service Company of Iran.

Interview: Stockholm, April 2021.

Published Primary and Secondary Sources

Abrahamian, Ervand. *Iran between Two Revolutions* (Princeton: Princeton University Press, 1982).

Abrahamian, Ervand. *The Coup: 1953, the CIA, and the Roots of Modern U.S.-Iranian Relations* (New York: The New Press, 2013).

Abrahamian, Ervand. *Oil Crisis in Iran: From Nationalism to Coup D'Etat* (Cambridge and New York: Cambridge University Press, 2021).

Abtahi, ʿAli-Reza. *Naft va Bakhtiari-ha* [Oil and Bakhtiaris] (Tehran: Tarikh-e Moʿaser, 2005).

Abu-Lughod, Janet. *Rabat, Urban Apartheid in Morocco* (Princeton: Princeton University Press, 1981).

Adamiyat, Fereydun. *Fekr-e Demokrasi-ye Ejtemaʿi dar Nehzat-e Mashrutiyat-e Iran* [The Idea of Social Democracy in the Iranian Constitution Movement] (Tehran: Payam, 1976).

Adelson, Roger. *London and the Invention of the Middle East: Money, Power, and War, 1902–1922* (New Haven: Yale University Press, 1995).

Adib-Moghaddam, Arshin. *The International Politics of the Persian Gulf: A Cultural Genealogy* (London: Routledge, 2006).

Afary, Janet. *The Iranian Constitutional Revolution, 1906–1911: Grassroots Democracy, Social Democracy, and Origin of Feminism* (New York: Columbia University Press, 1996).

Afkhami, Gholam-Reza (ed.). *Tahavvol-e Sanʿat-e Naft-e Iran, Negahi az Darun: Mosahebeh ba Parviz Mina* [The Evolution of Iran's Oil Industry, an Insider's Account: An Interview with Parviz Mina] (Washington, DC: Foundation of Iranian Studies, 1998).

Afkhami, Gholam-Reza (ed.). *Sanʿat Petroshimi-ye Iran Az Aghaz ta Astaneh-ye Enqelab, Mosahebeh ba Baqer Mostowfi* [The Evolution of Iran's Petrochemical Industry from the Beginning to the Eve of the Revolution: An Interview with Baqer Mostowfi] (Washington, DC: Foundation for Iranian Studies, 2001).

Afkhami, Gholam-Reza (ed.). *Siyasat va Siyasatgozari-ye Eqtesadi dar Iran, 1340–1350: Mosahebeh ba Alinaghi Alikhani* [Politics and Economic Planning in Iran, 1961–1971: An Interview with Alinaghi Alikhani] (Washington, DC: Foundation for Iranian Studies, 2001).

Agahi, Abdolhossein. '60 Sal Az Tarikh-e Ta'sis-e Hezb-e Komonist-e Iran Gozasht' [Sixty Years Passed since the Foundation of the Communist Party of Iran], *Donya*, 3 (1980).

Ahmadzadeh, Masʿud. *Mobarezeh-ye Mosallahaneh, ham Esteratezhi, ham Taktik* [Armed Struggle, Both Strategy and Tactic] (Tehran: Sazeman-e Cherik-ha-ye Fada'i-ye Khalq-e Iran, 1971).

Alikhani, Alinaghi (ed.). *Yaddasht-ha-ye Alam* [Diaries of Alam], Vols. 2–3 (Washington, DC: Ibex Publisher, 1992–1993).

Alikhani, Alinaghi. *Eqtesad va Amniyat: Khaterat-e Doktor Alinaghi Alikhani* [Economy and Security: The Memoirs of Dr Alinaghi Alikhani], Hossein Dehbashi (ed.). (Tehran: Sazeman-e Asnad va Ketabkhaneh-ye Melli-ye Iran, 2014).

Alsayyad, Nezar and Mrinalini Rajagopalan. *'Colonial City' Encyclopaedia of Urban Studies* (Thousand Oaks: SAGE Publications, 2010).
Alvandi, Roham (ed.). *The Age of Aryamehr* (London: Gingko Library, 2018).
Amanat, Abbas. *Iran: A Modern History* (New Haven: Yale university Press, 2017).
Amar-Nameh-ye Ostan-e Khuzestan [Statistical Records of the Khuzestan Province], Nos. 738 and 785 (Tehran: Sazman-e Barnameh va Budjeh, Markaz-e Amar-e Iran, 1977, 1979).
Amin, Samir. *Accumulation on a World Scale: A Critique of the Theory of Underdevelopment* (New York: Monthly Review Press, 1974).
Amuzegar, Jahangir. *Dynamics of the Iranian Revolution: The Pahlavis' Triumph and Tragedy* (New York: State University of New York Press, 1991).
Anderson, Terry H. *The United States, Great Britain, and the Cold War, 1944–1947* (Columbia: University of Missouri Press, 1981).
Ansari, Ali M. *Confronting Iran: The Failure of American Foreign Policy and the Next Great Crisis in the Middle East* (New York: Basic Books, 2006).
Ansari, Ali M. (ed.). *The Politics of Nationalism in Modern Iran* (Cambridge: Cambridge University Press, 2012).
Ansari, Abdolreza, Hassan Shahmirzadi and Ahmad-Ali Ahmadi. *Omran-e Khuzestan* [Khuzestan Development], Electronic Book, Afkhami, Gholam-Reza (ed.). (Washington, DC: Foundation for Iranian Studies, 1994).
Aqeli, Baqer. *Khaterat-e yek Nakhost Vazir: Ahmad Matin Daftari* [A Prime Minister's Memoir: Ahmad Matin Daftari] (Tehran: 'Elmi, 1991).
Arghiri, Emmanuel. *La Dynamique des inégalités* (Paris: Economica, 1999).
Ashraf, Ahmad. 'Kalbodshekafi-ye Eqelab: Naqsh-e Kargaran-e Sanʿati dar Enqelab-e Iran' [Autopsy of the Revolution: The Role of Industrial Workers in the Iranian Revolution], *Iran-Nameh*, 3–4 (2011).
Ashraf, Ahmad and Ali Banuazizi. 'The State, Class and Mode of Mobilisation in the Iranian Revolution', *State, Culture and Society*, 6 (Spring 1985).
Ashtiani, Ali. 'Formation of the Working Class in Iran', *Nazm-e Novin*, 5 (1984).
Atabaki, Touraj. 'L'Organisation Syndicate Ouvriere en Iran, de 1941 a 1946', *Soual*, 8 (1988).
Atabaki, Touraj. *Azerbaijan. Ethnicity and the Struggle for Power in Iran* (London: I.B. Tauris, Second Edition, 2000).
Atabaki, Touraj. 'Disgruntled Guests: Iranian Subaltern on the Margins of the Tsarist Empire', *International Review of Social History*, 3 (2003).
Atabaki, Touraj. 'Going East, The Ottomans' Secret Service Activities in Iran', in Touraj Atabaki (ed.). *Iran and the First World War: Battleground of the Great Powers* (London: I.B. Tauris, 2006).
Atabaki, Touraj. 'Time, Labour Discipline and Modernisation in Turkey and Iran', in Touraj Atabaki (ed.). *The State and the Subaltern: Society and Politics in Turkey and Iran* (London: I.B. Tauris, 2007).
Atabaki, Touraj. 'Agency and Subjectivity in Iranian National Historiography', in Touraj Atabaki (ed.). *Historiography and Political Culture in Twentieth Century Iran* (London & New York: I.B. Tauris, 2009).
Atabaki, Touraj (ed.). *Historiography and Political Culture in Twentieth Century Iran* (London: I.B. Tauris, 2009).

Atabaki, Touraj. 'Constitutionalists Sans Frontières: Iranian Constitutionalism and Its Asian Connections', in Houchang Esfandiar Chehabi and Vanessa Martin (eds.). *Constitutional Revolution: Popular Politics, Cultural Transformations and Transnational Connections* (London – New York: I.B. Tauris, 2010).

Atabaki, Touraj. 'The Comintern, the Soviet Union and Labour Militancy in Interwar Iran', in Stephanie Cronin (ed.). *Iranian-Russian Encounters: Empires and Revolutions since 1800* (London: Routledge, 2012).

Atabaki, Touraj. 'Missing Labour in the Metanarratives of Practicing Modernity in Iran: Labour Agency in Refashioning the Discourse of Social Development', in David Mayer and Jürgen Mittag (eds.). *Interventions: The Impact of Labour Movement on Social Development* (Leipzig: Akademische Verlagsanstalt, 2013).

Atabaki, Touraj. 'Far from Home, But at Home: Indian Migrant Workers in the Iranian Oil Industry', *Studies in History*, 1 (2015).

Atabaki, Touraj. 'Persia/Iran', in Ute Daniel, Peter Gatrell and Oliver Janz et al. (eds.). *1914–1918 Online: International Encyclopaedia of the First World War* (Berlin: Free University Berlin, 2016). https://encyclopedia.1914-1918-online.net/article/persiairan/2016-05-02.

Atabaki, Touraj. 'The Perplexity of the Iranian Marxist Intellectuals in the 1960s', in Ramin Jahanbegloo (ed.). *Mapping the Role of Intellectuals in Modern and Contemporary History* (London: Lexington Books, 2021).

Atabaki, Touraj and Ehsani, Kaveh. 'Oil and Beyond Expanding British Imperial Aspirations, Emerging Oil Capitalism, and the Challenge of Social Questions in the First World War', in Helmut Bley and Anorthe Kremers (eds.). *The World during the First World War* (Essen: Klartext Verlag, 2014).

Avanesian, Ardeshir. *Safahati chand az Jonbesh-e Kargari va Komunisti dar Dowran-e Avval-e Saltanat-e Reza Shah (1922–1933)* [Some pages of Worker and Communist Movement in the First Period of Reza Shah's Reign (1922–1933)] (Leipzig: Hezb-e Tudeh-e Iran, 1979).

Avery, Peter. *Modern Iran* (London: E. Benn, 1965).

Azari Shahreza'i, Reza. *Dowlat-e Iran va Motekhassesan-e Mohajer-e Almani* [Iran and German Expert Immigrants] (Tehran: Sazman-e Asnad-e Melli-ye Iran, 1995).

Azimi, Fakhreddin. *The Crisis of Democracy* (London: I.B. Tauris, 2009).

Backhouse, J. B. 'Oil-1904–1928', in Harry Townsend (ed.). *A History of Shaw Wallace & Co. and Shaw Wallace & Co. Ltd.* (Calcutta: n.p., 1965).

Bahar, Mohammad-Taqi (Malek al-Sho'ara). *Tarikh-e Mokhtasr-e Ahzab-e Siyasi-ye Iran* [A Short History of Political Parties in Iran] (Tehran: Amir-Kabir, Third Edition, 1957).

Bahrier, Julian. *Economic Development in Iran 1900–1970* (London: Oxford University, Press).

Bakhtiar, Chapour. *Yekrangi* [Veracity], translated by Mahshid Amirshahi (Paris: Khavaran, 1982).

Bamberg, J. H. *The History of the British Petroleum, The Anglo-Iranian Years, 1928–1954* (London: Cambridge University Press, 1994).

Bashiriyeh, Hossein. *The State and Revolution in Iran, 1962–1982* (London: Palgrave Macmillan, 1984).

Bast, Oliver. *Almani-ha dar Iran: Negahi beh Thavvolat-e Iran dar Jang-e Jahani-ye Avval bar Asas-e Manabe'-e Diplomatik-e Faranseh* [Germans in Iran: A Look at the Development in Iran during the First World War based on the French Diplomatic Sources] (Tehran: Shirazeh, 1998).
Bast, Oliver. *La Perse et la grande guerre* (Tehran: Institut fran.ais de recherche en Iran, 2002).
Bayandor, Darioush. *Iran and the CIA: The Fall of Mosaddeq Revisited* (New York: Palgrave, 2010).
Bayat, Asef. *Workers and Revolution in Iran: A Third World Experience of Workers' Control* (London: Zed Book, 1987).
Bayat, Kaveh. 'With or Without Workers in Reza Shah's Iran', in Touraj Atabaki (ed.). *The State and the Subaltern: Modernisation, Society and the State in Turkey and Iran* (London: I.B. Tauris, 2007).
Bayat, Mangol. *Iran's Experiment with Parliamentary Governance: The Second Majles, 1909–1911* (Syracuse: Syracuse University Press, 2020).
Beblawi, H. and Giacomo Luciani (eds.). *The Rentier State* (London: Croom Helm, 1987).
Bellaigue de, Christopher. *Patriot of Persia: Muhammad Mossadegh and a Tragic Anglo-American Coup* (New York: Harper Perennial, 2013).
Beyhaqi, Abu al-Fazl-Mohammad. *Tarikh-e Beyhaqi* [History of Beyhaqi]. 'Ali-Akbar Fayyaz (ed.). (Mashhad: Entesharat-e Daneshgah-e Mashhad, 1970).
Bharier, Julian. *Economic Development in Iran 1900–1970* (New York: Oxford University Press, 1971).
Bill, James and Wm. Roger Louis. *Musaddiq, Iranian Nationalism, and Oil* (London: I.B. Tauris, 1988).
Blum, Albert A. (ed.). *International Industrial Relations: Contemporary Developments and Research* (London: Aldwych Press, 1981).
Bonakdarian, Mansour. *Britain and the Iranian Constitutional Revolution of 1906–1911: Foreign Policy, Imperialism, and Dissent* (Syracuse: Syracuse University Press, 2006).
Bozorgmehr, Jalil. *Mosaddeq dar Mahkameh-ye Nezami* [Mosaddeq in the Military Tribunal] (Paris: Nehzat-e Moqavemat-e Melli-ye Iran, n.d.).
Brew, Gregory. *Petroleum and Progress in Iran: Oil, Development, and the Cold War* (London: Cambridge University Press, 2022).
Browne, Edward G. *The Press and Poetry of Modern Persia*. Partly based on the manuscript work of Mirza Muhammad 'Ali Khan Tarbiyat of Tabriz (Los Angeles: Bahai Pub Trust, Reprint 1983).
Bullard, Reader. *The Camels Must Go: An Autobiography* (London: Faber & Faber, 1961).
Bullard, Reader. *Letters from Tehran: A British Ambassador in World War II Persia* (London: I.B. Tauris, 1991).
Burrell, Robert Michael and Robert L. Jarman (eds.). *Iran Political Diaries 1881–1965*. Vol. 5, 7–9, 11. 14 vols (Slough: Archive Editions, 1997).
Butler, Rohan. *British Policy in the Relinquishment of Abadan*, British National Archives. 1962.
Capito, C. E. 'Early Days in Masjed-Soleyman', *Naft*, 4 (1940).

Cardoso, Fernando Henrique and Enzo Faletto. *Dependency and Development in Latin America* (New York: University of California Press, 1979).

Carter, Marina. *Servants, Sirdars and Settlers: Indians in Mauritius, 1834–1874* (London: Oxford University Press: 1995).

Chalcraft, John. 'Engaging the State: Peasants and Petitions in Egypt on the Eve of Colonial Rule', *International Journal of Middle East Studies*, 37 (2005).

Chaqueri, Cosroe (ed.). *The Condition of the Working Class in Iran*, Vol. 4 (Florence: Mazdak, 1976).

Chaqueri, Cosroe (ed.). *The Historical Documents: The Workers, Social Democrats, and the Communist Movement in Iran (1903–1963)*. Vol. 6 (Florence: Mazdak, 1976).

Chaqueri, Cosroe. *The Soviet Socialist Republic of Iran, 1920–1921: Birth of the Trauma* (Pittsburgh: University of Pittsburgh Press, 1995).

Chehabi, Houchang Esfandiar and Vanessa Martin (eds.). *Iran's Constitutional Revolution. Popular Politics, Cultural Transformations and Transnational Connections* (London: I.B. Tauris, 2010).

Chubin, Shahram and Sepehr Zabih. *The Foreign Relations of Iran: A Developing State in a Zone of Great Power Conflict* (Berkeley: University of California Press, 1974).

Cohen, Stuart. 'Mesopotamia in British Strategy, 1903–1914', *International Journal of Middle East Studies*, 2 (May 1978).

Cooper, Andrew. *The Oil Kings* (New York: Simon & Schuster, 2011).

Cooper, Andrew. *The Fall of Heaven* (New York: Henry Holt, 2016).

Cooper, Frederick. 'The Dialectics of Decolonisation: Nationalism and Labour Movements in Post-war Africa', *CSST Working Paper 884*, May 1992.

Cooper, Frederick. *Decolonisation and African Society: The Labour Question in French and British Africa* (Cambridge: Cambridge University Press, 1996).

Cottam, Richard W. *Iran and the United States: A Cold War Case Study* (Pittsburgh: University of Pittsburgh Press, 1988).

Crinson, Mark. 'Abadan, Planning and Architecture under the Anglo-Persian Oil Company', *Planning Perspectives*, 3 (1997).

Cronin, Stephanie. *The Army and the Creation of the Pahlavi State in Iran, 1910–1926* (London: Tauris Academic Studies, 1997).

Cronin, Stephanie. *Tribal Politics in Iran: Rural Conflicts and the New State, 1921–1941* (New York: Routledge, 2007).

Cronin, Stephanie. 'Popular Politics, the New State and the Birth of the Iranian Working Class: The 1929 Abadan Oil Refinery Strike', *Middle East Studies*, 46(5), (September 2010).

Cronin, Stephanie. *Social Histories of Iran: Modernism and Marginality in the Middle East* (Cambridge: Cambridge University Press, 2021).

Daftari, Farhad. 'Development Planning in Iran: A Historical Survey', *Iranian Studies*, 4 (1973).

Daftary, Frahad. 'BARNĀMA-RĪZĪ', *Encyclopaedia Iranica*, December 1988.

Damluji, Mona. 'The Oil City in Focus: The Cinematic Spaces of Abadan in the Anglo-Iranian Oil Company's Persian Story', *Comparative Studies of South Asia, Africa, and the Middle East*, 1 (2013).

Damluji, Mona. 'The Image World of Middle Eastern Oil', in Hannah Appel, Arthur Mason and Michael Watts (eds.). *Subterranean Estates: Life Worlds of Oil and Gas*, (Ithaca: Cornell University Press, 2015).

Daryabandari, Najaf. *Sal-ha-ye Javani va Siyast: Khaterat-e Najaf Daryabandari dar Goftogu ba Hossein Mirza'i* [The Years of Youth and Politics: The Memoirs of Najaf Daryabandari from Abadan in Interview with Hossein Mirza'i] (Abadan: Abadan-Nameh, 2015).

Davenport, Ernest Harold and Sidney Russell Cooke. *The Oil Trusts and Anglo-American Relations* (New York: The Macmillan Company, 1924).

Davis, James C. 'Towards a Theory of Revolution', *American Sociological Review*, 27 (February 1962).

Davis, Simon. 'The Persian Gulf in the 1940s and the Question of an Anglo-American Middle East', *History*, 1 (January 2010).

Degras, Jane Tabrisky. *Soviet Documents on Foreign Policy* (London: Oxford University Press, 1951).

Dehgan, Seyyed Mohammad. 'Report to the International Red labour Union (Profintern)', in Cosroe Chaqueri (ed.). *The Historical Documents: The Workers, Social Democrats, and the Communist Movement in Iran (1903–1963)*, Vol. 6 (Florence: Mazdak, 1976).

Dehqan-Nezhad, Morteza and Elham Lotfi. 'Bimari-ye Tifus, Peyamad-e Voquʿ va Gostaresh-e Jang-e Dovvom-e Jahani dar Iran' [The Typhus and its Expansion in Iran during the Second World War], *Faslnameh-ye Ravabet-e Khareji* (2010).

DeNovo, John Augustus. *American Interests and Policies in the Middle East, 1900–1939* (Minneapolis: University of Minnesota Press, 1963).

Diba, Farhad. *Mohammad Mossadegh: A Political Biography* (London: Croom Helm, 1986).

Dobe, Michael Edward. *A Long Slow Tutelage in Western Ways of Work: Industrial Education and the Containment of nationalism in Anglo-Iranian and ARAMCO, 1923–1963*, PhD thesis (Gradate School-New Brunswick, Rutgers, the State University of New Jersey, 2008).

Dossal, Mariam. *Imperial Designs, and Indian Realities: The Planning of Bombay City, 1845–1875* (London: Oxford University Press, 1991).

Dunsterville, L. C. *The Adventure of Dunsterforce* (London: E. Arnold, 1920).

Ebtehaj, Abolhassan. *Khaterat* [Memoir] (London: Peka, 1991).

Eftekhari, Yusof. *Khaterat-e Dowran-e Separi-shodeh, 1299–1329* [Memoires of the Passed Period, 1920–1950]. Kaveh Bayat and Majid Tafreshi (eds.). (Tehran: Ferdows, 1991).

Ehsani, Kaveh. 'Social Engineering and the Contradictions of Modernisation in Khuzestan's Company Towns: A Look at Abadan and Masjed-Soleyman', *International Review of Social History* 3 (2003).

Ehsani, Kaveh. 'Oil, State, and Society in Iran in the Aftermath of the First World War', in T. G. Fraser (ed.). *The First World War and Its Aftermath: The Shaping of the Middle East* (London: Ginko Library, 2015).

Elling, Rasmus Christian. 'On Lines and Fences: Labour, Community and Violence in an Oil City', in Ulrike Freitag, Nelida Fuccaro, Cludia Ghrawi and Nora Lafi (eds.). *Urban Violence in the Middle East: Changing Cityscapes in the Transition from Empire to Nation State* (New York: Berghahn Books, 2015).

Elm, Mostafa. *Oil, Power and Principle: Iran's Oil Nationalisation and Its Aftermath* (Syracuse: Syracuse University Press, 1992).

'Elm, Mohammad-Reza. *Enqelab-e Eslami dar Ahvaz* [Islamic Revolution in Ahvaz] (Tehran: Markaz-e Asnad-e Enqelab-e Eslami, 2007).

Elwell-Sutton, Laurence Paul. *Modern Iran* (London: George Routledge & Sons, 1941).

Elwell-Sutton, Laurence Paul. *Persian Oil: A Study in Power Politics* (New York: Westport, 1975).

Emmer, P. C. (ed.). *Colonialism and Migration: Indentured Labour before and after Slavery* (Dordrecht: M. Nijhoff, 1986).

Ettehadieh Nezam-Mafi, Mansoureh. *Maramnameh va Nezamnameh-ha-ye Ahzab-e Siyasi-ye Iran dar Dovomin Dowreh-ye Majles-e Shora-ye Melli* [The Programmes and Bylaws of Iranian Political Parties in the Iranian Second National Parliament] Tehran: Nashr-e Tarikh-e Iran, 1982).

Ettehadieh Nezam-Mafi, Mansoureh. 'The Council for the Investigation of Grievances: A Case Study of Nineteenth Century Iranian Social History', *Iranian Studies*, 22 (1989).

Ettehadieh Nezam-Mafi, Mansoureh. 'The Iranian Provincial Government', in Touraj Atabaki (ed.). *Iran and the First World War, A Battleground of the Great Powers* (London: I.B. Tauris, 2006).

Fakhimi, Qobad. *Si Sal Naft-e Iran* [Thirty Years of Iran's Oil] (Tehran: Mehrandish, 2008).

Falkus, M. E. *The Industrialisation of Russia, 1700–1914* (London: Palgrave, 1972).

Farmanfarmian-Salar Lashkar, 'Abbas Mirza. *Jang-e Engelis va 'Osmani dar Bein al-Nahrein va 'Avaqeb-e An dar Iran* [The British-Ottoman War in Mesopotamia and Its Consequence for Iran]. Mansoureh Ettehadieh Nezam-Mafi and Bahman Farman (eds.). (Tehran: Nashr-e Tarikh-e Iran, 2007).

Farmanfarmaian, Khodadad. *Barnameh-e Dovvom* [Second Plan]. *Panjah Sal Barnamehrizi*, Hoda Saber (ed.). *Panjah Sal Barnamehrizi* [Fifty Years Planning] (Tehran: Parseh, 2018).

Farmanfarmaian, Manuchehr. *Blood and Oil* (New York: Modern Library, 1997).

Farmanfarmaian, Manuchehr. *Az Tehran ta Karkas: Naft va Siyasat dar Iran* [From Tehran to Caracas: Oil and Politics in Iran] (Tehran: Nashr-e Tarikh-e Iran, 1999).

Fateh, Mostafa. *Tarikh-e Panjah Sal Naft-e Iran* [History of Fifty Years of the Iranian Oil] (Tehran: Payam, 1979).

Fatemi, Nasrollah Saifpour. *Diplomatic History of Persia, 1917–1923: Anglo-Russian Power Politics in Iran* (New York: Russell F. Moore, 1952).

Fattahi, Mohammad. *Tarikh-e Shafahi-ye Showra-ye Kargaran-e Naft* [Oral History of the Oil Workers' Council]. Archive of Iranian Opposition Documents, 2013.

Fawcett, Louise L'Estrange. *Iran and the Cold War: The Azerbaijan Crisis of 1946* (Cambridge: Cambridge University Press, 1992).

Ferrier, Ronald W. *The History of the British Petroleum. The Developing Years, 1901–1932* (London: Cambridge University Press, 1982).

Ferrier, Ronald W. 'The Iranian Oil Industry', in Peter Avery, Gavin R. G. Hambly and Charles Melville (eds.). *The Cambridge History of Iran*, Vol. 7 (Cambridge: Cambridge University Press, 1991).

Fesharaki, Fereydoun. *Development of the Iranian Oil Industry: International and Domestic Aspects* (New York: Praeger Publishers, 1976).

Floor, Willem. *Industrialisation in Iran, 1900–1941* Working Paper at the Centre for the Middle Eastern and Islamic Studies (Durham: University of Durham, 1984).

Floor, Willem. *Labour Unions, Law and Conditions in Iran (1900–1941)* (Durham: Durham University, 1985).

Floreeda, Safiri. 'South Persia Rifles'. *Encyclopaedia Iranica online*. https://referenceworks.brillonline.com/entries/encyclopaedia-iranica-online/south-persia-rifles-COM_432?s.num=0&s.f.

Ford, Alan Wayne. *The Anglo-Iranian Oil Dispute of 1951–1952: A Study of the Role of Law in the Relations of States* (Berkeley: University of California, 1954).

Forutan, Majid. *Owza'-e Siyasi va Ejtema'i-ye Hamedan dar Jang-e Jahangir-e Avval* [The Political and Social Conditions in Hamedan in the First World War] (Tehran: Farzaneh, 2011).

Foruzandeh, Mas'ud. *Tarikh-e San'at Naft-e Iran 1280–1357* [History of the Iranian Oil Industry 1901–1978] (Tehran: Vezarat-e Naft, 2009).

Fuad Rohani. *Tarikh-e Opek* [A History of OPEC] (Tehran: Sherkat-e Sahami-ye Ketab-ha-ye Jibi, 1974).

Garavini, Giuliano. *The Rise and Fall of OPEC in the Twentieth Century* (New York: Oxford University Press, 2019).

Garthwaite, Gene R. *Khans and Shah: A History of the Bakhtiyari Tribe in Iran* (London: I.B. Tauris, 2009).

Gasiorowski, Mark J. *U.S. Foreign Policy and the Shah: Building a Client State in Iran* (Ithaca: Cornell University Press, 1991).

Gasiorowski, Mark and Malcolm Byrne (eds.). *Mohammad Mosaddeq and the 1953 Coup in Iran* (Syracuse: Syracuse University Press, 2004).

Gehrke, Ulrich. *Persien in der deutschen Orientpolitik während des Ersten Weltkrieges*, Darstellungen zur Auswärtigen Politik, Vols. 1 & 2. (Stuttgart: W. Kohlhammer, 1960). Persian translation *Pish beh Su-ye Sharq. Iran dar Siyasat-e Sharqi-ye Alman dar Jang-e Jahani-ye Avval*, translated Sadri, Parviz (Tehran: Siamak, 1998).

Ghani, Cyrus. *Iran and the Rise of Reza Shah: From Qajar Collapse to Pahlavi Power* (London: I.B. Tauris, 1998).

Ghaziyani, Nasser. 'Az do Rah-e Takamol-e Eqtesadi, Kodamyek ra Bayad Bargozid?' [Of Two Paths of Economic Development, which one should be Adopted?], *Donya*, 3 (1964).

Gillion, Kenneth. L. *Fiji's Indian Migrants: A History to the End of Indenture in 1920* (London: Oxford University Press, 1962).

Glazunova, E. N. 'K Voprosy o Sootnoshenii Vnutrennikh i Vneshnikh Faktorov v Gosudarstvennom Perevorote v Irane 1953 g' [On the Balance of Internal and External Factors in the 1953 Iranian Coup D'état], *Bulletin of Moscow University*, 3 (2015).

Golestan, Ebrahim. *Barkhord dar Zamaneh-ye Barkhord-ha* [Clashes in the Era of Clash] (Tehran: Baztab Negar, 2021).

Goode, James F. *The United States and Iran: In the Shadow of Musaddiq* (New York: Palgrave Macmillan, 1997).

Gozaresh-e 'Amalkard-e Barnameh-ye 'Omrani-ye Sevvom 1341–1346 (Report of the Results of the Third Development Plan 1962–1967) (Tehran: Plan Organisation, 1968).

Gudarzi, Manuchehr, Khodadad Farmanfarmaian, Abdolmajid Majidi and Gholam-Reza Afkhami, Gholam-Reza (eds.). *Barnamehrizi-ye 'Omrani va Tasmimgiri-ye Siyasi* [Development Planning and Political Decision Making] (Washington, DC: Foundation for Iranian Studies, 1999).

Guha, Ranajit. 'On Some Aspect of the Historiography of Colonial India', in *Subaltern Studies I: Writing on South Asian History and Society* (Delhi: Oxford University Press, 1982).

Gunder Frank, Andre. *Dependent Accumulation* (New York: Monthly Review Press, 1979).

Hakimian, Hassan. 'Industrialisation and the Standard of Living of the Working Class in Iran, 1960–79', *Development and Change*, 19 (1988).

Halliday, Fred. *Iran: Dictatorship and Development* (New York: Penguin 1978).

Hasanli, Jamil. *At the Dawn of the Cold War: The Soviet-American Crisis over Iranian Azerbaijan, 1941–1946* (Lanham: Rowman & Littlefield, 2006).

Hedayat, Mehdi-Qoli. *Khaterat va Khatarat* [Memoires and Dangers] (Tehran: Zavvar, 1996).

Heiss, Mary Ann. 'The United States, Great Britain, and the Creation of the Iranian Oil Consortium, 1953–1954', *The International History Review*, 3 (August 1994).

Heiss, Mary Ann. *Empire and Nationhood: The United States, Great Britain, and Iranian Oil, 1950–1954* (New York: Columbia University Press, 1997).

Heiss, Mary Ann. 'The International Boycott of Iranian Oil and the Anti-Mosaddeq Coup of 1953', in Mark Gasiorowski and Malcom Byrne (eds.). *Mohammad Mosaddeq and the 1953 Coup in Iran* (Syracuse: Syracuse University Press, 2004).

Hobsbawm, Eric. *The Age of Extremes: A History of the World, 1914–1991* (London: Michael Joseph, 1994).

Hurewitz, J. C. *Diplomacy in the Near East, and Middle East: A Documentary Record* (London: Literary Licensing, 2011).

Hushang Mahdavi. Abdolreza. *Tarikh-e Ravabet-e Khareji-ye Iran* [The History of Iran's Foreign Affairs] (Tehran: Simorq, 1976).

International Labour Office (ILO). *Labour Conditions in the Oil Industry in Iran: Report of International Labour Office (January-February 1950)* (Geneva: International Labour Office, 1950).

'Iran: Whose Oil? Britain's Stake Murder and Threats'. *The New York Times*, 18 March 1951.

'Iran's House Votes to Nationalise Oil'. *The New York Times*, 16 March 1951.

Irani, Robert Ghobad. *American Diplomacy: An Option Analysis of the Azerbaijan Crisis, 1945–1946* (Hyattsville, MD: Institute of Middle Eastern and North African Affairs, 1978).

Iranian Government. *Some Documents on the Conditions of the Iranian Workers under the Ex-Anglo Iranian Oil Co* (Tehran: Iranian Government Publishing House, 1951).

Jackson, Ashley. *Persian Gulf Command: A History of the Second World War in Iran and Iraq* (New Haven: Yale University Press, 2018).

Jack, Marian (Kent). 'The Purchase of the British Government's Shares in the British Petroleum Company 1912–1914', *Past and Present*, 39 (April 1968).

Jafari, Peyman. *Fluid History: Oil Workers and the Iranian Revolution*, University of Amsterdam (Digital Academic Repository). DOI 10.1007/978-3-319-56445-6_4, 2018.

Jafarian, Rasul. *Jariyan-ha va Sazeman-ha-ye Mazhabi-Siyasi-ye Iran (1320–1357)* [Religio-Political Currents and Organisations in Iran – 1941–1979] (Tehran: Mo'allef, 2006).

Javanshir, F. M. *Hemaseh-ye 23 Tir: Gushe-ha-'i az Mobarezat-e Kargaran-e Naft-e Khuzestan* [The Saga of 23 Tir: An account of the Struggle of the Khuzestan Oil Workers] (Tehran: Hezb-e Tudeh-e Iran, 1980).

Javanshir, F. M. *Tajrobeh-ye 28 Mordad: Nazari beh Tarikh-e Jonbesh-e Melli Shodan-e Naft-e Iran* [The Experience of 28 Mordad: A Look at the History of the Movement of the Nationalisation of Oil in Iran] (Tehran: Hezb-e Tudeh-e Iran, 1980).

Jazani, Bizhan. *Masa'el-e Jonbesh-e zedd-e Este'mari va Azadibaksh-e Khalq-e Iran va 'Omdeh-tarin Vazayef-e Komunist-ha-ye Iran* [The Problem of Anti-Colonial and Libation Movement of the People of Iran and the Main Tasks of the Iranian Communists] (Reprinted in Paris: Sazeman-e Ettehad-e Fadaian-e Khalq-e Iran, 2003).

Jefroudi, Maral. 'Revisiting "the Long Night" of Iranian Workers: Labor Activism in the Iranian Oil Industry in the 1960s', *International Labor and Working-Class History*, 84 (Fall 2013).

Jefroudi, Maral. '*"If I deserve it, it should be paid to me:" A Social History of Labour in the Iranian Oil Industry 1951–1973*', PhD thesis, Leiden University, October 2017.

Jones, Geoffrey. *The State, and the British Oil Industry* (London: Macmillan, 1981).

Jones, Russell (ed.). *Loan-words in Indonesian, and Malay* (Jakarta: n.p., 2008).

Kalinovsky, Artemy M. 'The Soviet Union and Mosaddeq: A Research Note', *Iranian Studies*, 3 (2014).

Kambakhsh, 'Abdolsamad. 'Tashkil Hezb-e Tudeh-e Iran' [Foundation of Tudeh Party of Iran], *Donya*, 7(3) (1966).

Kamshad, Hassan. *Hadis-e Nafs* [Internal discourse], 2 Vols., (Tehran: Ney, 2008).

Kashani-Sabet, Firoozeh. *Frontier Fictions: Shaping the Iranian Nation, 1804–1946* (Princeton, NJ: Princeton University Press, 1999).

Katouzian, Homa. *State and Society in Iran: The Eclipse of the Qajars and the Emergence of the Pahlavis* (London: I.B. Tauris, 2006).

Katouzian, Homa. *Musaddiq and the Struggle for Power in Iran* (New York: I.B. Tauris, 2009).

Kazemi, Farhad. *Poverty and Revolution in Iran: The Migrant Poor, Urban Marginality and Politics* (New York: New York University Press, 1980).

Kazemzadeh, Firuz. *Russia, and Britain in Persia, 1864–1914* (New Haven: Yale University Press, 1968).

Keddie, Nikki R. *Modern Iran: Roots and Results of Revolution* (New Haven: Yale University Press, 2006).

Kemp, Norman. *Abadan: A first-hand Account of the Persian Oil Crisis* (London: Allan Wingate, 1953).

Kempen, Eva T. van. 'The Dual City and the Poor: Social Polarisation, Social Segregation and Life Chances', *Urban Studies*, 7 (1994).

Keshavarzian, Arang and Ali Mirsepassi (eds.). *Global 1979: Geographies and Histories of the Iranian Revolution* (Cambridge: Cambridge University Press, 2021).

Khaksar, Nasim. *Qafas-e Tuti-ye Jahan Khanom* (The Parrot's Cage of Mrs Jahan) (London: H&S Media, Second Edition, 2011).

Khameh'i, Anvar. *Az Enshe'ab ta Kudeta* [From Split to Coup d'état] (Tehran: Hafteh, 1984).

Khatib Shahidi, Rashid Armin. *German Foreign Policy towards Iran before World War II: Political Relations, Economic Influence and the National Bank of Persia* (New York: I.B. Tauris, 2013).

Khazeni, Arash. *Tribes and Empire on the Margins of Nineteenth Century Iran* (Seattle: University of Washington Press, 2009).

Khomeini Imam, Ruhollah. *Sahifeh-ye Imam* [Imam's Folder], Vol. 4 (Tehran: Mo'asseseh-ye Tanzim va Nashr-e Asar-e Imam Khomeini, 1989).

Khosrowshahi, Yadollah. *Bakhshi az Tarikh-e Jonbesh-e Kargaran San'at Naft-e Iran* [A Part of History of Workers Movement in the Oil Industry of Iran], Vol. 1 (London: Houshang Ansari, 2019).

Khosrowpanah, Mohammad-Hossein. *Sazeman-e Afsaran-e Hezb-e Tudeh-e Iran* [The Organisation of Military Officers of the Tudeh Party of Iran] (Tehran: Shirazeh, 1998).

Kianuri, Nuralddin. 'Nazari Ejmali beh Tahavvollat-e Siyasi va Eqtesadi-ye Iran' [A Reflection on Political and Economic Development in Iran], *Donya*, 4 (1964).

King, Anthony D. *Colonial Urban Development: Culture, Social Power, and Environment* (London: Routledge, 2007).

Kinzer, Stephen. *All the Shah's Men: An American Coup and the Roots of Middle East Terror* (Hoboken, NJ: John Wiley & Sons, 2008).

Kocheshkov, A. A. 'Neft i Okhlazhdenie Sovetsko-Iranskikh Otnosheniy na Rannem Etape «Kholodnoy Voyny» 40–50 gg. XX v' [Oil and the Deterioration of Soviet-Iranian Relations in the Early Phases of the 'Cold War' 40s–50s of the 20th Century], Department of the History of Near and Middle Eastern Countries, Institute of Asian and African Countries at Lomonosov Moscow

State University. *Rudn Journal of World History*, 3 (2009). Online version: https://journals.rudn.ru/world-history/article/view/1284 (Accessed December 2010).

Koyagi, Mikiya. *Iran in Motion: Mobility, Space, and the Trans-Iranian Railway* (Stanford: Stanford University Press, 2021).

Kozhanov, Nikolay A. 'The Pretexts and Reasons for the Allied Invasion of Iran in 1941'. *Iranian Studies*, 4 (July 2012).

Kuniholm, Bruce Robellet. *The Origins of the Cold War in the Near East: Great Power Conflict and Diplomacy in Iran, Turkey and Greece* (Princeton, NJ: Princeton University Press, 1980).

Kurzman, Charles. *The Unthinkable Revolution in Iran* (Cambridge: Harvard University Press, 2004).

Ladjevardi, Habib. *Labor Unions and Autocracy in Iran* (New York: Syracuse University Press, 1984).

Lahsaeizadeh, Abdolali. *Jamehshenasi-ye Abadan* [Sociology of Abadan] (Tehran: Kian-Mehr, 2006).

Lal, Brij V. 'Girmitiyas: The Origins of the Fiji Indians', *Journal of Pacific History* (1983).

Lambert, Nicholas A. *Sir John Fisher's Naval Revolution* (Columbia: University of South Carolina Press, 2002).

Lenczowski, George. *Russia and the West in Iran, 1918–1948: A Study in Big-Power Rivalry* (Ithaca: Cornell University Press, 1949. Carolina Press, 2002).

Lerner, Daniel. *The Passing of Traditional Society: Modernizing the Middle East* (London: Macmillan, 1958).

Lesani, Abolfazl. *Tala-ye Siyah ya Bala-ye Iran* [Black Gold or the Affliction of Iran] (Tehran: Mehr, 1950).

Linden, Marcel van der. 'Labour History: The Old, the New and the Global', *African Studies*, 2–3 (2007).

Linden, Marcel van der. *Workers of the World.* Essays towards a Global Labor History (Leiden: Brill, 2008).

Linden, Marcel van der and Lex Heerma van Voss (eds.). *Class and Other Identities: Gender, Religion and Ethnicity in the Writing of European Labor History* (New York and Oxford: Berghahn Books, 2002).

Lockman, Zachary. 'Imagining the Working Class: Culture, Nationalism, and Class Formation in Egypt, 1899–1914', *Poetics Today*, 5 (1994).

Lockman, Zachary. 'Reflections on Labour and Working-Class History in the Middle East and North Africa', in Jan Lucassen (ed.). *Global Labour History: A State of the Art*, (Bern: Peter Lang AG, 2008).

Longhurst, Henry. *Adventure in Oil* (London: Sidgwick & Jackson, 1959).

Lotfollahi, Siamak. *Khaterat-e Siamak Lotfollahi* [Siamak Lotfollahi's Memoire] Mohammad-Hossein Khosrowpanah (ed.). (Tehran: Khojasteh, 2015).

Louis, William Roger. *Imperialism at Bay, 1941–1945: The United States and the Decolonization of the British Empire* (Oxford: Clarendon Press, 1977).

Lucassen, Jan (ed.). *Global Labour History: A State of the Art* (Bern: Peter Lang AG, 2008).

Ludden, David. 'Development Regimes in South Asia: History and the Governance Conundrum', *Economic and Political Weekly*, 40 (2005).

Maan, Brian. 'The Khuzestan Arab Movement, 1941–1946: A Case of Nationalism?' in Kamran Scot Aghaie and Afshin Marashi (eds.). *Rethinking Iranian Nationalism and Modernity* (Austin: University of Texas Press, 2014).

Mahdavi, Hossein. 'The Patterns and Problems of Economic Development in Rentier States: The Case of Iran', in M. A. Cook (ed.). *Studies in the Economic History of the Middle East* (Oxford: Oxford University Press, 1970).

Mahmud, Mahmud. *Traikh-e Ravabet-e Siyasi-ye Iran va Engelis dar Qarn-e Nuzdahom-e Miladi* [History of Political Relation between Iran and Britain in the Nineteenth Century], Vol. 8 (Tehran: Eqbal, 1954).

Majd, Mohammad Gholi. *Oil and the Killing of the American Consul in Tehran* (Lanham: University Press of America, 2006).

Majd, Mohammad Gholi. *Iran under Allied Occupation in World War II: The Bridge to Victory & a Land of Famine* (Lanham: University Press of America, 2016).

Makki, Hossein. *Khalʿ-e Yadd: Ketab-e Siyah* [Eviction: The Black Book] (Tehran: Bongah-e Tarjomeh va Nashr-e Ketab, 1981).

Malaiʾi Tavani, ʿAli-Reza. *Iran va Dowlat-e Melli dar Jang-e Jahani-ye Avval* [Iran and the National Government in the First World War] (Tehran, 1999).

Maleki, Khalil. *Khaterat-e Siyasi* [Political Memoirs] (Tehran: Ravaq, 1978).

Maleki, Khalil. *Majmuʿeh-ye Maqalat* [Collected Articles], Reza Azari Shahrezaʾi, (ed.). (Tehran: Akhtaran, 2017).

Mani, Shokrollah. *Tarikhcheh-ye Nehzaht-e Kargari dar Iran* [A Concise History of the Labour Movement in Iran] (Tehran: n.p., 1946).

Mann, Brian. 'The Khuzistani Arabs: The Khuzistani Arab Movement, 1941–1946: A Case of Nationalism?' in Kamran Scot Aghaie and Afshin Marashi (eds.). *Rethinking Iranian Nationalism and Modernity* (Austin: University of Texas Press, 2014).

Marashi, Afshin. *Nationalizing Iran: Culture, Power and the State, 1870–1940* (Seattle: University of Washington Press, 2008).

Markaz-e Barresi-ye Asnad-e Tarikh. *Yaran-e Emam be Revayat-e Asnad-e Savak* [Imam Associates According to Savak Documents] (Tehran: Markaz-e Barresi-ye Asnad-e Tarikh, 2001).

Matin-Asgari, Afshin. 'Marxism, Historiography and Historical Consciousness in Modern Iran: A Preliminary Study', in Touraj Atabaki (ed.). *Twentieth Century Iran: Historiography and Political Culture* (London: I.B. Tauris, 2009).

Matin-Asgari, Afshin. *Both Eastern and Western: An Intellectual History of Iranian Modernity* (Cambridge: Cambridge University Press, 2018).

Mazraʿehkar, Mohammad. *Khaterat* [Memoire] (n.p.: Markaz-e Farhang va Ketab-e Gutenberg, n.d).

McFarland, Stephen L. 'Anatomy of an Iranian Political Crowd: The Tehran Bread Riot of December 1942', *International Journal of Middle East Studies*, 1 (1985).

Mikusch, Dagobert von. *Wassmuss, der deutsche Lawrence* (Berlin: Metropol Verlag, 1938); translated into Persian by Kaikavus Jahandari, *Wasmus* (Qom: Hamsayeh, 1998).

Milani, Abbas. *The Persian Sphinx: Amir Abbas Hoveyda and the Riddle of the Iranian Revolution* (Washington, DC: Mage, 2000).

Milani, Abbas. *The Shah* (New York: Palgrave, 2011).

Millspaugh, Arthur Chester. *Americans in Persia* (Washington, DC: The Brookings Institute, 1946).

Mina, Parviz. 'OIL AGREEMENTS IN IRAN', *Encyclopaedia Iranica*, Published: 20 July 2004.

Miroshnikov, Lev Ivanovich. 'Iran in the World War I, Lecture read at Harvard University in November 1962' (Persian translation by A. Dokhaniyati), *Iran dar Jang-e Jahani-ye Avval* (Tehran: Simorgh, 1965).

Mirza'i, Hossein. *Khastgah-e Ravabet-e 'Omumi dar Iran. Daramadi be Tarikh-e Ravabet-e 'Omumi-ye Sherkat-e Palayesh-e Naft-e Abadan* [The Origin of Public Relations in Iran. An Introduction to the History of Public Relations in the Oil Refinery of Abadan] (Abadan: Ravabet-e 'Omumi-ye Sherkat-e Palayesh-e Naft-e Abadan, 2016).

Missen, David. *Iran. Oil at the Service of the Nation* (London: Transorient, 1969).

Mitchell, Timothy. *Carbon Democracy: Political Power in the Age of Oil* (London: Verso, 2011).

Moberly, F. J. *Operations in Persia, 1914–1919*, Reprint (London: Unipup, 1987).

Mohapatra, Prabhu. 'Following Custom? Representations of Community among Indian Immigrant Labour in the West Indies 1880–1920', in P. Behal, P. Rana and Masrcel van der Linden (eds.). *India's Labouring Poor: Historical Studies, c. 1600–c.2000*, (Cambridge: Cambridge University Press, 2007).

Mostowfi, 'Abdollah. *Sharh-e Zendegi-ye Man* [My Life]. Vol. 2 (Tehran: Zavvar, 1964).

Motter, T. H. Vail. *The Persian Corridor and Aid to Russia* (Washington, DC: Office of the Chief of Military History, Department of Army, 1952).

Movahhed, Mohammad. *Khab-e Ashofteh-e Naft: Az Qarardad-e D'Arcy ta Soqut-e Reza Shah* [The Turbulent Dream of Oil: from D'Arcy Concession to the Fall of Reza Shah] (Tehran: Karnameh, 2014).

Nabavi, Negin. *Intellectuals and the State in Iran: Politics, Discourse and the Dilemma of Authencity* (Gainesville: University Press of Florida, 2003).

Najmi, Nasser. *Havades-e Tarikhi-ye Iran az Shahrivar-e 20 ta 28 Mordad-e 1332* [The Historical Events in Iran from August 1941 to 19 August 1953] (Tehran: Koleini, 1991).

Nassehi, Ramin. 'Domesticating Cold War Economic Ideas: The Rise of Iranian Developmentalism in the 1950s and 1960s', in Roham Alvandi (ed.). *The Age of Aryamehr* (London: Gingko Library, 2018).

Nikunazar, Karim. *Sinama Jahanam* [Hell Cinema] (Tehran: Cheshmeh, 2019).

Osul va Hadaf-ha-ye Barnameh-ye 'Omrani-ye Chaharom-e Keshvar [The Essence and Targets of the Fourth Development Plan] (Tehran: Majles-e Showra-ye Melli, 1968).

O'Sullivan, Adrian. *Nazi Secret Warfare in Occupied Persia (Iran): The Failure of the German Intelligence Services, 1939–45* (New York: Palgrave Macmillan, 2014).

Ovendale, Ritchie. *Anglo-American Relations in the Twentieth Century* (New York: St. Martin's Press, 1998).

Pahlavi, Mohammad Reza. *Mission for My Country* (New York: McGraw-Hill, 1960).

Paine, Chris and Erica Schoenberger. 'Iranian Nationalism and the Great Powers: 1872–1954', *MERIP Reports*, 37 (1975).

Painter, David S. 'Oil and the American Century', *The Journal of American History*, 1 (2012).

Parsa, Misagh. *Social Origins of the Iranian Revolution* (New Brunswick: Rutgers University Press, 1989).

Picherit, David. 'Workers, Trust Us!': Labour Middlemen and the Rise of the Lower Castes in Pradesh, Andhra'. post-print hal-03239988, HAL, 2009.

Polányi, Karl. *The Great Transformation. The Political and Economic Origins of Our Time* (Boston: Beacon Press, 2001).

Prebisch, Raúl. *The Economic Development of Latin America and Its Principal Problems* (New York: United Nations, 1950).

Rahnema, Ali. *Behind the 1953 Coup in Iran* (Cambridge: Cambridge University Press, 2015).

Ramazani, Rouhollah K. *The Foreign Policy of Iran: A Developing Nation in World Affairs, 1500–1941* (Charlottesville: University Press of Virginia, 1966).

Ramazani, Rouhollah K. *Iran's Foreign Policy, 1941–1973: A Study of Foreign Policy in Modernizing Nations* (Charlottesville: University of Virginia Press, 1975).

Randjbar-Daemi, Siavush. 'The Tudeh Party of Iran and the Land Reform Initiatives of the Pahlavi State, 1958–1964', *Middle Eastern Studies*, 4 (2022).

Razavi, Hossein and Firouz Vakil. *The Political Environment of Economic Planning in Iran, 1971–1983: From Monarchy to Islamic Republic* (Boulder: Westview Press, 1984).

Roosevelt, Kermit. *Countercoup, the Struggle for the Control of Iran* (New York: McGraw-Hill, 1979.

Ross, L. M. 'Does Oil Hinder Democracy?' *World Politics*, 3 (2001).

Rostow, Walt Whitman. *The Stages of Economic Growth: A Non-Communist Manifesto* (Cambridge: Cambridge University Press, 1960).

Safavi, Mohammad. 'Baz-khani-ye Mobarezat-e Gozashteh-ye Kargaran-e Prozheh'-Fasli' [Revisiting the Historical Struggles of Seasonal and Contract Workers]. *Naqd-e Eqtesad-e Siyasi*, 2 October 2021.

Safavi, Mohammad. 'Rag-ha-ye Zamin, Rag-ha-ye Ma: Sad Sal Mobarezeh-ye Kargaran-e Naft Baraye 'Edalat-e Ejtema'i-Eqtesadi' [Earth's Veins, our Veins: One Hundred Years of Oil Workers Fighting for Socio-Economic Justice]. *Naqd-e Eqtesda-e Siyasi*. 4 (January 2021).

Safinezhad, Javad. *'Ashayer-e Markazi-ye Iran* [Tribes of Central Iran] (Tehran: Amir-Kabir, 1989).

Safiri, Florida. *Polis-e Jonub-e Iran* (Tehran: Nashr-e Tarikh-e Iran, 1985).

Sajjadi (Tamaddon al- Molk), Mohammad. *Iran va Engelstan* [Iran and England] (Calcutta: Art Press, 1942).

Salnameh-ye Hezb-e Tudeh-e Iran [Tudeh Party of Iran's Yearbook] (Leipzig: Hezb- Tudeh-e Iran, 1970).

Salur, Qahreman Mirza. *Ruznameh-ye Khaterat-e ʿAyn al-Saltaneh* [The Diary ʿAyn al-Saltaneh]. Vol. 7 (Tehran: Asatir, 1999).

Samiʿi, Hossein and Amanollah Ardalan. *Avvalin Qiyam-e Moqadas-e Melli dar Jang-e Beinolmelel-e Avval* [The First National Holly War in the First World War] (Tehran: Ebn-e Sina, 1953).

Saqa'i, Gh. 'Rah-e Roshd-e Gheyr-e Sarmayehdari va Dowlat-e Demokrasi-ye Melli' [Non-Capitalist Road to Socialism and National-Democratic State], *Donya*, 4 (1963).

Schendel, Willem van. 'Spatial Moments: Chittagong in Four Scenes', in Helen Siu and Eric Tagliacozzo (eds.). *Asia Inside Out: Connected Places* (Cambridge, MA: Harvard University Press, 2014).

Schneider, Irene. *The Petitioning System in Iran: State, Society and Power Relations in the Late 19th Century* (Wiesbaden: Harrassowitz Verlag, 2006).

Seccombe, I. J. and R. I. Lawless. 'Foreign Worker Dependence in the Gulf, and the International Oil Companies: 1910–50', *International Migration Review*, 20 (1986).

Secondi, Giorgio. *The Development Economics Reader* (London: Routledge, 2008).

Sepher (Movarrekh al-Dowleh), Ahmad-ʿAli. *Iran dar Jang-e Bozorg 1914–1918* [Iran in the Great War 1914–1918] (Tehran: Adib, 1983).

Shannon, Matthew K. *American-Iranian Dialogues: From Constitution to White Revolution, c. 1890s–1960s* (London: Bloomsbury Academic, 2021).

Sheibani (Vahid al-Molk), ʿAbdolhossein. *Khaterat-e Mohajerat. Az Dowlat-e Movaqqat-e Kermanshah ta Komiteh-ye Meliyyun-e Berlan* [The Memoire of Migration: From Resistance Government in Kermanshah to Nationalist Committee in Berlin] (Tehran: Shirazeh, 1999).

Shokat, Hamid. *Flight into Darkness. A Political Biography of Shapour Bakhtiar*, translated by M. R. Ghanoonparvar (Bethesda: Ibex Publishers, 2019).

Siavoshi, Sussan. *Liberal Nationalism in Iran: The Failure of a Movement* (Boulder: Westview Press, 1990).

Singha, Radhika. 'Finding Labour from India for the War in Iraq: The Jail Porter and Labour Corps, 1916–1920', *Comparative Studies in Society and History*, 49 (2007).

Skeet, Ian. *OPEC: Twenty-Five Years of Price and Politics* (Cambridge: Cambridge University Press, 1988).

Sreberny, Annabelle and Massoumeh Torfeh. *Persian Service: The BBC and British Interests in Iran* (London: I.B. Tauris, 2014).

Stewart, Richard A. *Sunrise at Abadan: The British and Soviet Invasion of Iran, 1941* (New York: Prager, 1988).

Sykes, Christopher. *Wassmuss: 'the German Lawrence'* (London: Bernhard Tauchnitz, 1936).

Ta'eb, Saeed. *Az Eʿtesab-e Karkonan-e Sanʿat-e Naft ta Piruzi-ye Enqelab-e Eslami* [From the Oil Industry Employees' Strike to the Victory of the Islamic Revolution] (Tehran: Islamic Revolution Document Centre, 2003).

Tabari, Ehsan. 'Rah-e Eqtesadi-ye Ma az Kodam Sust?' [What is the Road Map of our Economic Development?], *Donya*, 1–2 (1963).

Tadjbakhsh, Golam-Reza and Farrokh Najmabadi (eds.). *Yad-dasht-ha-ye Fuad Rohani. Nakhostin Dabir Koll-e Sazeman-e Keshvar-ha-ye Sader Konandeh Naft (OPEC)* [Diaries of Fuad Rohani: First Secretary General of the Oil Producing Countries (OPEC)] (Bethesda, MD: Foundation for Iranian Studies, 2012).

Tetzlaff, Stefan. 'The Turn of the Gulf Tide: Empire, Nationalism, and South Asian Labour Migration to Iraq, c. 1900–1935', *International Labour and Working-Class History*, 79, Spring 2011.

Tetzlaff, Stefan. *Entangled Boundaries: British India and the Persian Gulf Region during the Transition from Empires to Nation States, c. 1880–1935*, 30. https://fid4sa-repository.ub.uni-heidelberg.de/3202/ (Accessed March 2013).

Thomson, George. 'Abadan in Its Early Days', *Naft*, 4 (July 1931).

Thomson, George. 'Abadan during the World War', *Naft*, 8 (September 1932).

Tinker, Hugh. *New System of Slavery 1830–1929* (London: Oxford University Press, 1974).

Torkaman, Mohammad. *Asnad-e Naqz-e Bitarafi-ye Iran dar Shahrivar-e 1320* [Documents Regarding the Violation of Iran's Neutrality in August 1941] (Tehran: Kavir, 1991).

Towfiq, Firuz. 'Barnameh-ye Avval: Fekr-e Barnamehrizi dar Iran' [First Plan: The Idea of Planning in Iran], *Panjah Sal Barnamehrizi* [Fifty Years Planning]. Hoda Saber, (ed.). (Tehran: Parseh, 2018).

Turner, Terisa. 'Iranian Oil Workers in 1978–79 Revolution', in Petter Nore and Terisa Turner (eds.). *Oil and Class Struggle* (London: Zed Book, 1980).

Vahabzadeh, Peyman. *A Guerrilla Odyssey: Modernization, Secularism, Democracy, and the Fadai Period of National Liberation in Iran, 1971–1979* (Syracuse: Syracuse University Press, 2010).

Vezarat-e Farhang va Ershad-e Eslami. *Naft dar dowreh-ye Reza Shah* (Tehran: Vezarat-e Farhang va Ershad-e Eslami, 1999).

Vezarat-e Kar. *Amar Sanaye'-e Iran* [Industrial Statistic of Iran] (Tehran: Vezarat-e Kar, 1948).

Vezarat-e Kar va Tablighat. *Showra-ye Mottaheddeh-ye Iyalati-ye Khuzestan. Tashkilat, Eqdamat-e Gheir-e Qanuni, Khianat va Su'-e estefadeh* [The Provincial Council of Unified Trade Unions of Khuzestan. Organisation, Illegal Performance, Betrayal and Manipulation] (Tehran: Khodkar, 1947).

Vezarat-e Kar va Tablighat. *Eqdamat-e Gheir-e Qanuni-ye Showara-ye Mottaheddeh-ye Markazi* [Illegal Activities of the Central Council of Federated Trade Unions] (Tehran: Vezarat-e Kar va Tablighat, 1947).

Visser, Reidar. *The Gibraltar That Never Was* (www.historiae.org). (Accessed March 2014).

Vitalis, Robert. *America's Kingdom: Mythmaking on the Saudi Oil Frontier* (Stanford: Stanford University Press, 2006).

Voss, Lex Heerma van (ed.). *Petitions in Social History* (Supplement of *International Review of Social History Supplement* 9, 2002).

Watt, Donald Cameron, Kenneth Bourne, Robin Leonard Bidwell, and Great Britain Foreign Office. *British Documents on Foreign Affairs-Reports and Papers from the Foreign Office Confidential Print* (Frederick: University Publications of America, 1985).

Williams, Raymond. *Marxism and Literature* (Oxford: Oxford university Press, 1977).

Williamson, J. W. *In a Persian Oil Field. A Study in Scientific and Industrial Development* (London: Ernest Benn, 1927).

Wilson, Arnold. 'Persia and the Oil Concessions', *The Listener*, 205 (14 December 1932).

Wilson, Arnold. 'Tapping Persia's Oilfields', *The Listener*, 302 (24 October 1934).

Wilson, Arnold T. *S.W. Persia: Letters and Diary of a Young Political Officer, 1907–1914* (London: Oxford University Press, 1942).

Wilson, Arnold T. *Loyalties Mesopotamia* (London: Wipf & Stock Publishers, 1931).

Yahosseini, Seyyed Qasem. 'Parkandegi-ye Qodrat dar Jonub-e Iran dar Astaneh-ye Jang Jahani-ye Avval', [the Diversity of Powers in Iran on the eve of the First World war] in Safa Akhavan (ed.). *Iran dar jahani-ye Avval* [Iran in the First World War] (Tehran: Verzarat-e Omur-e Kharejeh, 2005).

Yazdanpanah-Da'i, 'Esmat. *Diary* (Unpublished). Received 11 May 2016, Author's private collection.

Yergin, Daniel. *The Prize: The Epic Quest for Oil, Money, and Power* (New York: Simon & Schuster, 1991).

Yergin, Daniel. *The Quest: Energy, Security, and the Remaking of the Modern World* (New York: Penguin Press, 2011).

Zabih, Sepehr. *The Communist Movement in Iran* (Berkeley: University of California Press, 1966).

Zabih, Sepehr. *The Mossadegh Era: Roots of the Iranian Revolution* (Chicago: Lake View Press, 1982).

Zargar, Ali-Asghar. *Tarikh-e Ravabet-e Siyasi-e Iran va Englis dar Dowreh-e Reza Shah* [The History of Diplomacy between Iran and Britain during the Reza Shah Period] (Tehran: Parvin, 1993).

Zia'i, Manuchehr. *Majmu'eh-ye Qavanin-e Vezarat Kar* [Collection of Amendments Ratified by the Ministry of Labour] (Tehran: Vezart-e Kar, 1976).

INDEX

For EU product safety concerns, contact us at Calle de José Abascal, 56–1°, 28003 Madrid, Spain or eugpsr@cambridge.org.

www.ingramcontent.com/pod-product-compliance
Lightning Source LLC
LaVergne TN
LVHW011700200926
848484LV00004B/1015
* 9 7 8 1 1 0 8 8 4 5 8 7 8 *